# POISONING THE MINDS OF
# THE LOWER ORDERS

# POISONING
# THE MINDS OF THE
# LOWER ORDERS

—∞∞∞—

*DON HERZOG*

PRINCETON UNIVERSITY PRESS

PRINCETON, NEW JERSEY

Copyright © 1998 by Princeton University Press
Published by Princeton University Press, 41 William Street,
Princeton, New Jersey 08540
In the United Kingdom: Princeton University Press,
Chichester, West Sussex

*Library of Congress Cataloging-in-Publication Data*

Herzog, Don, 1956–
Poisoning the minds of the lower orders / Don Herzog.
p.  cm.
Includes bibliographical references and index.
ISBN 0-691-04831-2 (alk. paper)
1. Conservatism—Great Britain—History.  2. Democracy—
Great Britain—History.  3. Great Britain—Politics and
government—1789–1820.  4. Great Britain—Politics and
government—19th century.  5. Great Britain—Social
conditions—18th century.  6. Great Britain—
Social conditions—19th century.  I. Title.
JC573.2.G7H47  1998
320.52′0941′09034—dc21      98-5126

This book has been composed in Baskerville

Princeton University Press books are printed
on acid-free paper and meet the guidelines
for permanence and durability of the Committee
on Production Guidelines for Book Longevity
of the Council on Library Resources

http://pup.princeton.edu

Printed in the United States of America

1  3  5  7  9  10  8  6  4  2

*For Jenny*

# CONTENTS

# PREFACE

I SET OUT meaning to write a book on conservatism. I was bemused by the recent complaint that the academy has fallen into the clutches of rabid leftists and right-wing ideas are ignored: this seems to me horribly wrong. But I also was troubled by what I describe below as balkanization, a world in which conservatives write on conservatism for conservative readers, liberals on liberalism for liberals, Marxists on Marxism for Marxists, and so on. An unreconstructed liberal myself, I hoped to strike a modest blow for the rationality of free speech by scrutinizing conservative ideas.

There is in fact much here on conservatism, much of it sharply critical, all of it I hope relentlessly fair. But along the way I found myself working on a book on conservatism and democracy. Conservatism, I discovered, was locked in combat with democracy, was best understood as a fundamental assault on the possibility and desirability of democratic politics. Since I've long worried that democratic theory tends toward the pious and flabby, this struck me as a promising discovery. It enabled me, or so I hoped, to bring democratic theory into sharper focus by subjecting it to withering critique.

I focus on Britain between 1789, the year of the French Revolution, and 1834, the year of the new poor law. (Though the dates are porous in both directions: I sometimes reach back as far as Tudor England, occasionally into the 1840s.) I've rounded up the usual suspects: Austen, Bentham, Blake, Burke, Burney, Byron, Cobbett, Coleridge, Godwin, Hazlitt, Keats, Malthus, More, Paine, Peacock, Price, Priestley, Ricardo, Scott, Mary Shelley, Percy Shelley, Southey, Wollstonecraft, Wordsworth, and more. I've also drawn on newspapers, pamphlets, cartoons, sermons, letters, diaries, trashy novels, trashier poems, periodicals, parliamentary proceedings, and more. Crucially, I've incorporated social and political history. I want to reconstruct and explore a social world, terribly familiar in part, bewitchingly strange in part (sometimes these are the same parts); I don't simply want to explore "texts" or "discourses," though naturally such entities, odd on their own, figure prominently in the social world.

To put it bluntly, I don't trust the distinction between intellectual and social history. So I've ignored it. In these pages, Burkean appeals to tradition rub shoulders with workers plotting in alehouses; paeans to enlightenment jostle against contemptible hairdressers. Not for bleakly comic relief, but to advance a more incisive account of what finally is at stake in all of them, to provide accounts of conservatism and democracy with more nuance than shopworn formulations. Put differently, the "theory" on offer comes with a generous dollop of "facts."

I haven't burdened the account with any sort of methodological defense. Briefly, I've come to fret that political theory all too often resembles a conceptual shell game, where various lofty abstractions are whirled around in dazzling ways that reveal more about the dexterity of the author than about the subject matter at hand. To be curmudgeonly about it: sometimes political theorists mock social scientists for being barefoot positivists wedded to a bankrupt distinction between fact and value—but then go on to defend their own resolute indifference to mastering empirical contingencies by reminding us that their work is normative. Surely something here has to give. My strategy is to situate the abstractions, to work up a genealogical account of how some familiar views were developed by painting a detailed portrait.

We have long associated conservatism with the reaction to the French Revolution. The association isn't arbitrary or mistaken. Nor is it to be written off as a merely contingent point about the context of discovery of certain ideas. It bears on their justification: as a pragmatist, I conceive of political theories not as explorations of a timeless and abstract realm of fundamental questions, but as efforts to solve problems thrown up by contingent social change. It bears too on their content: I hold that the meaning of these theories is fixed in part by reference to the social world, both because particular terms refer directly to contingent social arrangements and because the social world provides background conditions of intelligibility, making it clear what one might be talking about in talking this way.

So mine is a detailed portrait, sometimes cantankerously so, some of the details quirky, others nauseating: it might help, then, to have a stark outline of the structure of the argument. In deference to tradition, I begin by puzzling through Burke. Less deferentially, I wonder what *tradition* means, anyway. Sometimes it means self-conscious allegiance to inherited practices or narrative continuity with the past, which Burke wants to exhibit as a kind of political rationality. But sometimes it means prejudice or illusion, the refusal to engage in critical argument, the opposite of rationality. These two understandings of tradition are tailored for different audiences, respectively for the tiny political nation and for the vast mass of subjects. I explore the instinctively staunch loyalty of Burkean subjects, manifest in different ways: scrubbing themselves for communal celebrations, sobbing for poor mad George III, burning down the houses of radicals.

Burke's opponents liked to gloat that the dawning sun of enlightenment was destroying the illusions he so prized, was turning deferential subjects into saucy citizens. The metaphor is opaque: what was this sun? I prowl through coffeehouses, alehouses, debating societies, circulating libraries, the explosion of journalistic outlets, mechanics' institutes, Sunday schools, and more. These, I argue, were the bearers or vehicles of reason and enlightenment. They represented alarming new developments that left Burke and his allies reeling in dismay.

Burke died in 1797 before seeing the worst of it. His allies had no such luck. Their conservatism took the shape of a vehement rejection of the desirability, even the possibility, of democratic politics. As the bizarre and bloody news from across the Channel was making terribly clear, the consequences of vigorous political debate among the lower orders might not be all that enchanting. But conservatives weren't the least bit surprised by the French experience. It was precisely what longstanding arguments against educating the lower orders led them to expect. They developed powerful objections to the view that democratic debate answered to even minimal demands of rationality. Instead, as they saw it, that debate was poisoning the minds of the lower orders. So they sprang into action with a wide range of strategies designed to provide antidotes.

Patrons of democratic debate were sometimes smug in dismissing conservative indictments. They invoked what I call an irreversibility thesis: once subjects had been roused from the dogmatic slumbers of tradition, there was no putting them back to sleep. And they imagined democratic debate as a realm in which equals offered arguments and the best argument won. Was—is—this realm somehow prior to politics? I argue that there's something deeply misconceived in the image of bringing political conflicts to the bar of reason. Instead, there are crucial political disputes internal to the practice of democratic debate. What is more (or worse, if you like), I argue that it is anything but obvious that we should think of democratic debate as reason, Burkean tradition as prejudice. With all his pungent irony, Burke thought the world of popular political debate less rational than the world of loyal subjects. Who or what earns the mantle of reason? Or, as I put it, who or what ought to enjoy epistemic authority? That itself is a crucial political debate.

Having fought my way to this uplifting conclusion, I abruptly change the subject to a more dispiriting one: in the second part, I launch an investigation of contempt. We shouldn't see the emotions as private or not of political interest. I distinguish condescension, insolence, impudence, and contempt. All depend on background practices of social hierarchy. (All also reinforce or even help constitute that hierarchy.) Political disputes about the cogency and attractiveness of that hierarchy, background changes in what counts as high and low, transform the emotional landscape. They change condescension from a virtue into a vice, insolence and impudence from antonyms into synonyms. I ask what was at stake in the Duke of Devonshire's flared nostrils, Robert Peel's distinctive gait, and Byron's kindness to dogs.

Next I dwell on contempt. A warning: these chapters sometimes make for grisly reading. There is nothing charming about exploring the vicissitudes of contempt for women, workers, blacks, and Jews. We shouldn't discreetly brush this material under the rug as if it were beneath our dignity—or that of the people who produced and consumed it so industriously. Nor should we seize on it as the secret key to Western civilization. Instead we should consider it dispassionately; at least that is what I do, and I do it relentlessly. Not out of misanthropy—I find no glee and take no solace in showing how extraordinarily ugly people can be—but out of interest in politics. Contempt for pariah groups is the ground of unholy community between conservatives and democrats. Both traffic in it shamelessly. Here we meet one famous poet thunderstruck by a pair of large breasts; a churchman arguing that the poor are actually better off than the rich, even in this world; another famous poet attempting to secure the objectivity of aesthetic judgments by musing on blacks' preference for the color white; and a traveller, disgusted by all the Jews, fleeing a fashionable resort. Here too I explore the logic of race, also what was at stake in contemporaries' classifying Jews as a race, nation, tribe, religious persuasion, or political artifact.

The untoward fact of unholy community invites challenges to conservatives and democrats alike. I don't pursue these challenges below but might as well state them here. Thanks to their affection for tradition, conservatives today—I mean the real ones, the ones with the infamous social agenda, not those patrons of free markets and limited government who, despite their liberal-bashing, are just old-fashioned liberals—face a dilemma. Their own tradition is rabidly antidemocratic, both in disdaining the possibility that vulgar workers and the like might be up to the elevated business of citizenship and in a more freewheeling rejection of equality and dignity, a willingness publicly to express vehement contempt for most people. Do they want to embrace this tradition, to affirm it as their own? If not, what's so great about tradition?

Democrats shouldn't snicker: their own—our own—political ancestors are every bit as implicated, and I see no reason to be sanguine about the current scene. At least conservatives who traffic in contempt can claim to be acting on principle: they can argue that what I style emotional investment in social hierarchy is required to maintain social order. Are democrats trafficking in contempt base hypocrites? Or is the presence of lowly inferiors required to give substance to democratic equality? Generations of readers have embraced William Cobbett as the very model of a modern minor radical. Cobbett, I show, was a misogynist, a racist, and arguably the most flagrant anti-Semite of his day. Perhaps the category *populist* covers the case of those whose affection for (native male) workers depends on demonizing others. But perhaps the category *democrat* does. Surely it has.

After charting the contours of contempt for women, workers, blacks, and Jews, I turn to the perplexing uses of contempt. A world full of such pariahs as stupid and smelly blacks, Christ-killing and penny-pinching Jews, offers the socially high the reassuring possibility of securing their own status by trampling on their inferiors—also of gratifying themselves by caring for their inferiors, for that too is a form of contempt. But the grammar of high and low is contested. Worse, there are plenty of different dimensions along which one might qualify as high: aristocrats, the wealthy, the beautiful, the virtuous all press their claims. So too, thanks to the celebrated inversions offered by Christianity, do the meek and humble.

That means that the battlefield of contempt is strewn with surprising land mines. None of these actors could ever be fully secure in holding others in contempt. Admiring black and Jewish boxers, fretting about man-milliners and the effeminacy of English workers, they knew that dispensing contempt was risky business. More perversely, the very same people holding the pariahs in contempt sometimes admired them enormously, credited them with superhuman virtues, felt morose in confronting their own patent inferiorities. However crazy or contradictory, theirs was also a world where Jews turned out to be secretly generous and blacks heroically grateful; where parliamentary leaders Pitt and Fox were branded as loathsome Jews; where it was excruciatingly difficult to tell the difference between an English worker and a Jamaican slave; where a series of distinguished poets resignedly described themselves as blacks and Jews. Throughout these chapters, I pay much less attention to change: my best assessment is that on the questions that concern me, change in this period was glacial.

How is this dizzying barrage of contempt tied to my discussion of enlightenment in the first part? In the third part, I explore what I call public standing. What is the plight of those routinely held in contempt who wish to participate in democratic politics? What can they do if others sneer at them, dismiss them out of hand, refuse to take them seriously as conversational partners and political equals? What resources did women, consigned to the domestic sphere, command in justifying their appearances in public and in print? And with what sort of redoubled contempt did their foes greet them?

Here I devote a chapter to what seems to have been a curious obsession: hairdressers. Perhaps this material has some weird entertainment value of its own; it surely isn't so ugly as the earlier material on contempt. But reconstructing contempt for hairdressers isn't just a matter of cultural voyeurism. Our own literature on equality is chock full of increasingly bizarre and invidiously abstract arguments. The anxiety about hairdressers turns out to have been mainly an anxiety about equality, in various socially concrete meanings. So it offers a useful corrective to our own arcane arguments.

I close this circuitous tour by returning, finally, to Edmund Burke and one of his most celebrated phrases, *a swinish multitude*. The phrase was potently dismissive in consigning the lower orders to the political sidelines, embarrassingly transparent in revealing the contempt in which they were held. Those vulgar subjects were eavesdropping on the conversations of their betters and some of them didn't much like what they heard. I trace the broader circulation of Burke's phrase and show how Burke became contemptible by holding others in contempt, how the conservative views once proudly brandished became publicly unmentionable.

Those seeking a guiding thread through the labyrinth might wish to focus on the transformation of subjects into citizens. Or—to restate the point—on how it became possible to credit the lower orders with dignity and political agency, to deny that they were the lower orders in the first place, and to do so without being cranky or going into mourning.

I'M DELIGHTED to have friends willing to wrestle with an unruly manuscript and offer advice on how to discipline it: thanks to Nancy Burns, Shelley Burtt, Doug Dion, Phoebe Ellsworth, Larry Kramer, Danielle LaVaque-Manty, Kirstie McClure, Jim Oakes, Adela Pinch, Andy Stark, Jackie Stevens, Dror Wahrman, Ann Himmelberger Wald, and Bernie Yack. Thanks to Liz Anderson for many years of pleasant and profitable conversation, to Liz Wingrove for such conversation and intensive comments. I've long thought of Bill Miller as an unindicted co-conspirator, so I'm glad to indict him: thanks to Bill for comments, conversation, and encouragement to pursue the emotions. I owe more than I can say to the late Jack Pressman; here I fondly recall an afternoon tramping around San Francisco and dinner at the Greens, all peppered by Jack's incisive and witty questions about the manuscript.

My grateful acknowledgments also go to a series of institutions and audiences. I presented papers along the way at Boston University, Cornell, Harvard, Northwestern, New York University, St. Louis University, Stanford, the University of California at Berkeley, the University of California at San Diego, the University of Chicago, the University of Michigan, the University of Toronto, the University of Wisconsin at Madison, and Yale. I was a Fellow at the Center for Advanced Study in the Behavioral Sciences in 1990–91; thanks to the Andrew W. Mellon Foundation for funding. While there, I worked extensively in the rare books room of Stanford University's Green

Library, gifted with a terrific staff. So too I am grateful to the terrific staffs at the University of Michigan's Hatcher Graduate Library rare books room and William Clements Library. I wrote a draft as the Hunting Family Faculty Fellow at the University of Michigan's Institute for Humanities in 1995–96.

Thanks, finally, to my colleagues at the University of Michigan Law School for adopting a wayward political theorist and offering magnificent institutional support and collegiality. A notable part of that support is a cheerful and tireless library staff second to none: my thanks to them for tracking down one rare text after another.

I draw on material that appeared as "Puzzling through Burke," *Political Theory* (August 1991) 19(3):336–63; a brief version of Chapter 11 appeared as "The Trouble with Hairdressers," *Representations* no. 53 (Winter 1996), pp. 21–43. Thanks to Sage Publications and the University of California Press for permitting me to use my words again.

# ENLIGHTENMENT

I T'S A CURIOUS broadside, a work of austere graphics and polite prose far removed from the mischievous engravings and bawdy ballads usually appearing on such sheets. Drawn from an address that 345 printers had signed and 138 had presented to the queen, the original text was committed to parchment "and accompanied by a Copy superbly printed on white Satin, edged with white Silk Fringe, backed with Purple Satin, and mounted on an Ivory Roller with appropriate Devices." Even in the published version, the arch is full of intricately detailed work. The printers took pride in their craftsmanship: "This Specimen of the Typographic Art," they bragged, "was surrounded by the Border and Ornaments on this Sheet, which alone contain upwards of Twenty-six Thousand moveable Pieces of Metal." The quantitatively inclined will want to know that it measures 21 ⅝ by 15 ¼ inches.

On the top, an arch marked LORDS on one end, COMMONS on the other, supports a crown. So much is unremarkable, a casual reference to very old theories of mixed government: English politics was a balance of monarchy, aristocracy, and democracy. But on the bottom, an equally impressive display of filigree work surrounds, of all things, a printing press.

The published version reproduces the printers' address to the queen, presented on 14 October 1820, and adds her response. (Well, not precisely her response. The queen's English wasn't very good; she couldn't have turned out the impeccably clipped cadences of the published response, and through the tawdry events of 1820 her advisers produced one text after another published in her name.) The printers congratulate the queen on her safe arrival in England and accession to the throne. They describe themselves as "the humble instruments of that mighty power," the press, "which, in advocating your MAJESTY's cause, so energetically sustains the declining liberties of England"; they advert ominously to a conspiracy against her; they close with a bravado flourish:

In future times, should the page of History record the present era as one in which overwhelming Power combined with Senatorial Venality to crush an unprotected Female, we trust it will also preserve the gratifying remembrance, that the base Conspiracy was defeated by the irresistible force of Public Opinion, directed and displayed through the powerful medium of a FREE, UNCORRUPTED, and INCORRUPTIBLE BRITISH PRESS.

Posterity, even history's page, has no particularly sharp memory of the matter, gratifying or otherwise. As far as it has survived, though, it usually hasn't been framed quite this way.

Whatever her own beliefs about posterity, the queen exhibits a doughty courage in responding. She too embraces public opinion: "It is Public Opinion which has supported me in the otherwise unequal conflict with numerous adversaries, who not only possess unbounded resources, but who have never scrupled any means by which their vengeance could be gratified. This Public Opinion is the concentrated force of many enlightened minds, operating through the medium of THE PRESS." Not all the press, concedes the queen, serve as the medium of enlightenment. Thanks to the vicious tactics of her nameless adversaries, their tireless efforts to intimidate and corrupt the press, some are "busily employed in fabricating the most atrocious slanders against myself. . . ." But the queen is sanguine, pleasantly surprised that in the face of such tactics, so much of the press has remained honest, smugly confident that "The force of truth is ultimately irresistible;—but truth, without some adventitious aid, moves with a slow pace, and sometimes its motion is so slow as to be imperceptible—THE PRESS is its accelerating power—THE PRESS gives it wings—THE PRESS does more for truth in a day, than mere oral teaching could in a century."[1]

But why the lionization of the press? Who was the queen? Who her nefarious enemies? I don't mean to be coy. The queen was Caroline.[2] Her husband was George IV, finally about to take the throne in 1820 after a painfully long tenure in that trying role of Prince of Wales. As prince, George had a nasty habit of running up fabulous gambling debts and turning to Parliament to pay them off. Hundreds of thousands of pounds later, George faced an arranged marriage with Caroline of Brunswick in an attempt to make him properly settled.

---

[1] *BMC* no. 13947 [October–November 1820].

[2] There's now an expert biography: Flora Fraser, *The Unruly Queen: The Life of Queen Caroline* (New York: Alfred A. Knopf, 1996).

George already was secretly married to a Catholic widow, Mrs. Maria Fitzherbert. Or sort of secretly: rumors had swirled through London.[3] But Charles James Fox, the great Whig leader, assured Parliament that there was nothing to the rumors; and George married Caroline in April 1795.

They didn't live happily ever after; apparently, one night together was enough to disgust the groom. Unluckily enough, though, George managed to get Caroline pregnant. "I shudder at the very thoughts of sitting at the same table with her," George confided in one friend about a year later, "or even of being under the same roof with her."[4] Watching her dance, one observer was appalled: "Such an over-dressed, bare-bosomed, painted eye-browed figure one never saw!"[5] Though the prince's father, George III, was her staunch ally, Caroline departed in 1814 for a career of continental travel—and, or so it seemed to many, of carousing and sexual escapades. She befriended and rapidly promoted one Bartolomeo Bergami to ever more prestigious and intimate positions in her household. Their relationship scandalized observers.

George III died on 29 January 1820; Caroline landed in England on 5 June, with every intention of asserting her place as crowned queen. Eyebrows were raised, curiosity provoked, appetites for gossip inflamed: indefatigable diarist Charles Greville moaned on 25 June that the affair was "an intolerable nuisance," monopolizing conversation in polite society.[6] What was George to do?

Years before Bergami's appearance on the scene, George already was charging Caroline with sexual infidelities, trying in vain to rid himself of her. A "delicate investigation" in 1806, pursued behind the

[3] Note, for instance, *BMC* no. 6924 [13 March 1786].

[4] Prince of Wales to Earl of Moira, 11 June 1796, *The Correspondence of George, Prince of Wales 1770–1812*, ed. A. Aspinall, 8 vols. (London: Cassell, 1963–1971), 3:220.

[5] Mary Berry's journal, 31 May 1809, *The Berry Papers*, ed. Lewis Melville (London: John Lane, The Bodley Head, 1914), p. 291. Note too Lady Charlotte Bury, *Diary Illustrative of the Times of George the Fourth*, new ed., 4 vols. (London, 1838–1839), 2:85–86 [1814]; Lady Bessborough to Granville Leveson Gower, 12 May 1815, *Lord Granville Leveson Gower (First Earl Granville): Private Correspondence 1781 to 1821*, ed. Castalia Countess Granville, 2 vols. (London: John Murray, 1916), 2:535; *Memoirs of the Lady Hester Stanhope, as Related by Herself in Conversations with Her Physician*, 3 vols. (London, 1845), 1:308.

[6] *The Greville Memoirs 1814–1860*, ed. Lytton Strachey and Roger Fulford, 8 vols. (London: Macmillan, 1938), 1:99.

scenes and kept fairly quiet, cleared her.[7] Quiet, but not quiet
enough: Caroline and her advisers got as far as printing, but not publishing, *The Book,* a collection of confidential negotiations and accusations. Writers learning about the proceedings approached George for
hush money.[8] 1813 saw a flurry of activity—shades of the seven-year
itch—and the appearance of *The Book!* for public delectation.[9] Now
George was ready to move more decisively. A green bag, the ordinary
parliamentary device for conveying documents but soon to become
infamous in radical circles as a dread symbol of secrecy and corruption, revealed to Parliament the case against Caroline. Soon the
House of Lords considered a special Bill of Pains and Penalties designed to abrogate the marriage. So ensued what amounted to a trial,
beginning 17 August, with lawyers for both sides introducing evidence and interviewing witnesses. Monarchy was on display in all its
tattered and seedy glory. Legal proceedings on adultery ("crim.
con.," short for criminal conversation, in the thinly veiled parlance of
the day) had long made for popular reading; so too had stories about
sexual antics at court.[10] The intersection of these two genres was
sizzling, even explosive. Perhaps the dignity of the House of Lords was
threatened by the endless days of testimony on the particular positions of hands, postures in carriages, bodies gliding silently through
dark chambers, stains on bed sheets, and the like, testimony that
came for the most part from an apparently disreputable band of foreign servants. But the nation found the spectacle enticing, even rivet-
ing. These were issues of momentous constitutional import. They

[7] See the "Report of Lords Grenville, Spencer, Ellenborough, and Erskine, on the
Charges Brought by the Prince of Wales against the Princess His Wife," 14 July 1806,
*Correspondence of George, Prince of Wales,* 5:401–5.

[8] Earl Temple to Prince of Wales, 28 April 1807, *Correspondence of George, Prince of
Wales,* 6:165–66; J. Glynn to Colonel McMahon, 16 February 1809, *Correspondence of
George, Prince of Wales,* 6:362.

[9] *"The Book!" or, The Proceedings and Correspondence upon the Subject of the Inquiry into the
Conduct of Her Royal Highness the Princess of Wales,* Edwards's genuine ed. (London, 1813).

[10] On adultery, for instance, *Select and Curious Cases of Polygamy, Concubinage, Adul-
tery, Divorce, &c. Seriously and Learnedly Discussed* (London, 1736); A Civilian, *Trials for
Adultery: or, The History of Divorces: Being Select Trials at Doctors Commons, for Adultery,
Fornication, Cruelty, Impotence, &c. from the Year 1760, to the Present Time,* 7 vols. (London,
1779–1780; reprint ed. New York: Garland, 1985); A Civilian of Doctors' Commons, *A
New Collection of Trials for Adultery: or, General History of Modern Gallantry and Divorces*
(London, 1799); *Crim. Con.: The Trial between Lieut. Trelawney, Plaintiff, and Captain
Coleman, Defendant* (London, 1817). On sexual misdeeds at court, for instance, Charles
Pigott, *The Jockey Club* (London, 1792).

were inescapably also issues of titillating folly. The gossip, already bubbling up before Caroline's return to England, comes fast and furious in contemporary sources. Caroline dressed like a man![11] Bergami was a woman![12] Caroline was actually crazy![13]

George, who didn't appear himself,[14] had a hard time posing as the innocent and injured husband, and not only because he was a bigamist. Portly, even bloated, providing an easy target for hostile cartoonists and pamphleteers, "the dandy of sixty"[15] remained inordinately fond of pretty women and had one intimate affair after another. This notorious fact gave Whig lawyer Henry Brougham, the queen's chief advocate during the proceedings, an opportunity that he exploited to excruciating effect. Calmly instructing the Lords that he was happy to draw a veil over what had transpired between Caroline's initial arrival in 1795 and her departure for the continent in 1814, Brougham declared airily that the queen's cause "does not require recrimination at present," but he added that later he might need to explore those years. A legal advocate, he continued, must be relentless in pursuing his client's interest: "He must go on reckless of the consequences, if his fate it should unhappily be, to involve his country in confusion for his client's protection!"[16] Insinuated, retracted, and finally pressed forcibly home, the threat was palpable. Should the king approach victory, his own inglorious sexual history would be explored.

---

[11] *The Diary of Joseph Farington,* ed. Kenneth Garlick, Angus Macintyre, and Kathryn Cave, 16 vols. (New Haven: Published for the Paul Mellon Centre for Studies in British Art by Yale University Press), 16:5469 [29 February 1820], 16:5519 [9 June 1820].

[12] *Diary of Farington,* 16:5553 [28 August 1820]; Hobhouse to Byron, 14 July 1820, *Byron's Bulldog: The Letters of John Cam Hobhouse to Lord Byron,* ed. Peter W. Graham (Columbus, OH: Ohio State University Press, 1984), p. 296.

[13] Lady Jerningham to Lady Bedingfield, 7 July 1820, *The Jerningham Letters (1780–1843),* ed. Castle Egerton, 2 vols. (London, 1896), 2:172; *Diaries of a Lady of Quality from 1797 to 1844,* ed. A. Hayward, 2d ed. (London, 1864), pp. 198–200; more tentatively, Henry Richard, Lord Holland, *Memoirs of the Whig Party during My Time,* ed. Henry Edward, Lord Holland, 2 vols. (London, 1852–1854), 2:121.

[14] But see the *Letter from the King to His People,* 12th ed. (London, 1820).

[15] William Hone, *The Political House that Jack Built,* 30th ed. (London, 1819), as paginated in *Radical Squibs & Loyal Ripostes: Satirical Pamphlets of the Regency Period, 1819–1821,* ed. Edgell Rickword (New York: Barnes & Noble, 1971), p. 45, capitals removed. Besides the pamphlets conveniently collected in this volume, see for instance *A Groan from the Throne,* 2d ed. (London, 1820).

[16] *Speeches of Henry Lord Brougham,* 4 vols. (Edinburgh, 1838), 1:104–5 [3 October 1820].

George was laboring under burdens besides those of dalliance and girth. Memories of his spendthrift days stood in poignant contrast to the burdens of taxation and poverty created by war with France. (I wonder how many knew of his fetching proposal that an £8 million budget surplus be transferred "to my private coffer, in consideration of my exertions & all I have done for the country as well as for the whole world. Such are my deserts, at least such I feel them to be."[17]) Some, too, thought George's apparent eagerness to assume the regency in the days of his father's madness unseemly. So George's enemies found Caroline a convenient weapon; much of the apparently warm affection for her is nothing but poorly disguised hostility to him. "Poor woman," wrote Jane Austen, "I shall support her as long as I can, because she *is* a Woman, & because I hate her Husband. . . ."[18] Protagonists be damned, thought some radicals, relishing the stakes in public discussion of these matters. Leigh Hunt told the poet Shelley that the proceedings would help topple belief in monarchy and provoke discussion of "questions of justice respecting the intercourse of the sexes."[19]

Others were irritated or appalled by the transparency of the sexual double standard. David Ricardo complained, "The question of her innocence or guilt is not the important one,—she has been abominably treated, and no grounds have been, or can be stated, to prove this disgusting enquiry either just, or necessary for the public good."[20] Similarly, Samuel Taylor Coleridge, a decidedly dyspeptic Tory by then, conceded years later, "The People were too manly to consider whether the Queen was guilty. 'What right had the King to complain!' was their just argument."[21] Caroline starred as darling of the radical

[17] Prince Regent to the Marchioness of Hertford, 16 October 1815, *Correspondence of George, Prince of Wales,* 8:424.

[18] Austen to Martha Lloyd, 16 February 1813, *Jane Austen's Letters to Her Sister Cassandra and Others,* ed. R. W. Chapman, 2d ed. (Oxford: Oxford University Press, 1979), p. 504. See too Bury, *Diary,* 1:268 [August 1813], 4:39 [1 September 1820].

[19] Hunt to Percy Bysshe Shelley, 23 August 1820, in *The Correspondence of Leigh Hunt,* ed. Thornton Hunt, 2 vols. (London, 1862), 1:156. See too Cobbett to Dr. Taylor, 2 July 1822, in Lewis Melville, *The Life and Letters of William Cobbett in England & America,* 2 vols. (London: John Lane, The Bodley Head, 1913), 2:202.

[20] Ricardo to John Ramsay McCulloch, 15 September 1820, *The Works and Correspondence of David Ricardo,* ed. Piero Sraffa with M. H. Dobb, 11 vols. (Cambridge: Cambridge University Press, 1951–1973), 8:240.

[21] *Table Talk,* in *The Collected Works of Samuel Taylor Coleridge,* ed. Kathleen Coburn, Bart Winer, and others, in progress (Princeton, NJ: Princeton University Press, 1969–), 14(1):134 [12 May 1830].

press, some of the mainstream press too, in maudlin celebrations: "History has no example," gushed one writer, "of a spirit so noble in unmerited suffering, a fortitude so meek and so immoveable."[22] Whatever the impact of public opinion, the proceedings didn't go well for George. Witnesses faltered: "Non mi ricordo," one Italian witness's favorite dodge, became proverbial in English as a way of avoiding saying something embarrassing. On 10 November 1820, a scant majority of nine votes on the bill's third reading forced the government to withdraw the bill.

A joke limped its way among the nobility: "If anybody asks you why the Queen is like the Bill of Pains and Penalties, you must say because they are both abandoned."[23] In the streets, the crowds were jubilant. In time-honored fashion, all over England, they demanded illumination: home owners could display candles in their windows at night, joining the celebration, or risk having their windows broken. Robert Southey, poet laureate and sidekick of Wordsworth and Coleridge, sullenly refused to join one such celebration and was grudgingly relieved to find his windows intact.[24] "Lord, what a stupid monster John Bull is," scoffed Walter Scott.[25]

A dour George withdrew from the public eye for a couple of months, stewing over what to do with a detested wife neither con-

---

[22] William Carey, *The Queen: The Conspiracies of 1806 and 1813, against the Princess of Wales, Linked with the Atrocious Conspiracy of 1820, against the Queen of England* (London, 1820), p. iii; see too the rapturous closing paragraphs of J. Nightingale, *The Last Days of Queen Caroline* (London, 1822), pp. 547–48. For the radical periodicals, see for instance Richard Carlile's *Republican* (25 February 1820) 2(6):189–93, (16 June 1820) 3(8):253–60, (23 June 1820) 3(9):289–91, (30 June 1820) 3(10):325–36, (7 July 1820) 3(11):361–66, (14 July 1820) 3(12):397–403, (21 July 1820) 3(13):433–37, (4 August 1820) 3(15):519–22, (25 August 1820) 3(18):513–20, (1 September 1820) 4(1):1–6, (8 September 1820) 4(2):47–49, (15 September 1820) 4(3):81–85, (13 October 1820) 4(7):221–27, (20 October 1820) 4(8):353–56, (27 October 1820) 4(9):289–92, (3 November 1820) 4(10):325–33, (10 November 1820) 4(11):362–74, 384–88, (17 November 1820) 4(12):397–412, (24 November 1820 [mismarked 1822]) 4(13):433–50, (8 December 1820) 4(15):505–20, (15 December 1820) 4(16):541–47.

[23] Countess Granville to Lady Harroway, 14 December 1820, *Letters of Harriet Countess Granville 1810–1845*, ed. F. Leveson Gower, 2 vols. (London, 1894), 1:196.

[24] Southey to C. W. Williams Wynn, 13 November 1820, *Selections from the Letters of Robert Southey*, ed. John Wood Warter, 4 vols. (London, 1856), 3:219; Southey to Wade Browne, 28 December 1820, *New Letters of Robert Southey*, ed. Kenneth Curry, 2 vols. (New York: Columbia University Press, 1965), 2:220.

[25] Walter Scott to Lady Louisa Stuart, 14 December 1820, *The Letters of Sir Walter Scott*, ed. H. J. C. Grierson, 12 vols. (London: Constable & Co., 1932–1937), 6:310; note too *The Journal of Sir Walter Scott*, ed. W. E. K. Anderson (Oxford: Clarendon, 1972), p. 218 [20 October 1826].

victed nor cleared by the parliamentary proceedings. Others had to face the question: Was she going to be crowned queen? Fumbling over what title to assign Caroline, the *Anti-Jacobin Review* retailed some of the salacious details:

> But not contented with travelling in Europe, the princess hired a vessel to take her to Asia; and among her suite was Bergami. On board the Polacco many acts of gross indecency are sworn to have taken place. Bergami accompanied her when she was bathing; he was seen kissing her on a gun; a tent was erected on the deck of this vessel, which was on various occasions closed during the day . . . the Queen and Bergami remaining under it; and finally under this tent Bergami and the Princess slept for thirty-five nights!
>
> Such are a few, and only a few, of the FACTS of this case; do they not speak for themselves? Is such a woman fit to be Queen of England?[26]

Guided by the broadside, one presumes that the *Review* was part of the dishonest press, intimidated and bribed by George and his under-lings. So too, perhaps, was *John Bull,* a caustic Sunday newspaper launched precisely to combat public affection for Caroline: "I have not the slightest respect for your Majesty," sneered the paper in one of its many blistering editorials.[27] Readers were aghast: "There is the most infamous newspaper just set up that was ever seen in the world—by name *John Bull,*" wrote one observer the day after this edi-torial. "Its personal scurrility exceeds by miles anything ever written before."[28] But the paper had one notable fan. A year or so later, George would expatiate on *John Bull's* literary and political virtues— it had done more for the country, he insisted, than he and his minis-ters and Parliament and the courts—and would add that he had been obliged to recall a judge, in part for finding the editors guilty of libel.[29]

[26] *Anti-Jacobin Review* (December 1820) 59:368.

[27] *John Bull* (14 January 1821) no. 5, p. 36.

[28] Thomas Creevey to Elizabeth Ord, 15 January 1821, *The Creevey Papers,* ed. Her-bert Maxwell (New York: E. P. Dutton, 1904), pp. 343–44.

[29] John Wilson Croker's diary, 11 January 1822, *The Croker Papers,* ed. Louis J. Jen-nings, 2d ed. rev., 3 vols. (London, 1885; reprint ed. New York: AMS Press, 1972), 1:246. Two years after that, the paper's editor, in debt and in jail, would seek George's helpful intercession: Theodore Edward Hook to Sir William Knighton, 15 February 1824, *The Letters of King George IV 1812–1830,* ed. A. Aspinall, 3 vols. (Cambridge: Cam-bridge University Press, 1938), 3:64–66.

Caroline did her best to join George at his coronation on 19 July 1821. But the guards had been ordered to refuse her entry. Besides, she hadn't a ticket. Riding around Westminster Abbey, Caroline tried persistently to get in, but in vain. Suddenly, public opinion turned against her. She died less than a month later. (One must relish the delicious accidents of timing: word of Napoleon's death wound its way to England about the same time. Someone hustled to bring George the news: "'Sir, your bitterest enemy is dead.' 'Is she, by God!' said the tender husband."[30]) This disorderly woman wasn't the enemy of social order as such; she was the champion or figurehead of a new order against an old one.[31]

Unattractive as George was, duplicitous as his efforts against her, it's hard to believe in Caroline's pristine purity. The exigencies of political debate might seem to require that we pretend that our side, whatever it is, has no vices, the other side no virtues. If historical distance is good for anything, though, it's good for overcoming such Manichaean fantasies. So the handbill's easy dichotomies—the incorruptible press against base conspiracy, the honest press against the hireling press—are glib, moralized, unhelpful. The printers offer them to flatter Caroline and demonize George, but they're as plausibly available to her opponents. *Blackwood's*, in fact, charged that "the radical newspapers were bribed into daring activity."[32] Caroline is at best an ironic badge of enlightenment, the press's frenetic attention to the debacle at best an uneasy sign of the march of truth.

Afflicted by a bit of a misanthropic streak, I relish the irony, but I also want it for theoretical purposes. Everyone knows the tiresome off-the-shelf tropes of enlightenment: the age of reason, the assault on priestcraft and statecraft, *écrasez l'infâme*, and all the rest. No doubt they could be rehabilitated. Still, they're lifeless. Enlightenment-bashing may not be all the rage, but it's a perfectly well-respected academic activity. The enlightenment has come to stand for a commitment to "reason," whatever that is, or to "foundationalism" or "universalism" or "human nature" or some such naive category that

---

[30] *The Journal of the Hon. Henry Edward Fox (Afterwards Fourth and Last Lord Holland) 1818–1830*, ed. Earl of Ilchester (London: Thornton Butterworth, 1923), p. 81 [25 August 1821].

[31] Contrast Carole Pateman, *The Disorder of Women: Democracy, Feminism and Political Theory* (Stanford, CA: Stanford University Press, 1989), chap. 1.

[32] *Blackwood's Edinburgh Magazine* (November 1820) 8(44):217.

we (enlightened ones?) have outgrown in the name of some comfortable if vague communitarian relativism and some fashionable if equally vague set of views about social construction. All too soon we are back in the land of ghostly and puerile abstractions, moths drawn to noxious theoretical flame. I'm never sure what the political stakes of such debates are.

I am, though, confident that launching an investigation by pondering this tacky affair doesn't load the dice in favor of—or against—a scarecrow named enlightenment. And I'm pretty sure I know what's at stake in the printers' missive to Caroline. Or at least I know how to start thinking about a text that in the midst of a vulgar scandal makes a printing press an almost sacred icon and burbles on about the redemptive power of public opinion.

*ONE*

# A CONSERVATIVE
# INHERITANCE

I F CONSERVATISM has a master text, that text is Edmund Burke's *Reflections on the Revolution in France,* published on 1 November 1790. The Revolution is in its early days. The Bastille has fallen, feudalism and the nobility have been abolished, and church property has been nationalized. Still, Louis XVI nominally reigns; he and Marie Antoinette enjoy the flow of blood through their carotid arteries; and Robespierre and Napoleon are not yet on the scene, so the reign of terror and wars from Europe to Egypt and Russia are still in the future. Yet Burke has seen plenty; he's furious. By turns garrulous and telegraphic, lachrymose and acidulous, haunted and haunting, the *Reflections* are brilliant. They're also frustrating, at least for readers inclined to reconstruct a theory, to articulate a text's implicit presuppositions and trace the inferences supposed to generate its conclusions. In its inception a letter to a young French correspondent, Burke's text sprawls for hundreds of pages. He's exercised by Dissenting minister Richard Price's sermon, *Of the Love of Our Country,* and he wants to urge that Price's reading of the English constitution as an elective monarchy is deeply misconceived. But he casts his net far more widely, opportunistically or even capriciously jabbing at the likes of moneygrubbing Jews and third-rate lawyers. Chock full of feverish metaphors and gorgeous wording, this is a deeply literary text, no more amenable to logic chopping than an epic poem or a first-rate novel.

I won't attempt a thorough account of the *Reflections,* nor for that matter a sustained portrait of Burke. In deference to convention, though, I do want to use Burke's texts to commence my investigation. We can think of the *Reflections* not as a master text or blueprint, but as a quirky crystallization of a disparate ensemble of practices and views, a window onto the rich and bizarre tapestry of Britain.

### Tradition as Narrative Continuity

"I put my foot in the tracks of our forefathers, where I can neither wander nor stumble."[1] The slogan, already Burke's cherished sentiment in 1775, came to contrast his own approach to political life with those of the intoxicated Jacobins and innovators he so cordially detested. Many have enlisted this stance, coupled with Burke's notorious antipathy to metaphysics, as a way of chastening the arrogance of theorists and revolutionaries, those who would make over society from scratch in accordance with some putatively rational argument.[2]

Tradition here isn't the enemy of change or progress. Still less is it a reactionary nostalgia for past glories. So critics can score no points with jeers about the impossibility of turning back the clock or the pathetic psychology of those clinging fearfully to the present, afraid of what might lie around the corner. Burke himself insists that all states require endless tinkering, continual reform: "A state without the means of some change is without the means of its conservation."[3] Nor is this vision of tradition wrapped up with any mystified reverence for authority. Indeed, Burke charges the powers that be with a complacent refusal to shoulder the burdens of responsible reform: "We

---

[1] "Speech on Conciliation with America" [22 March 1775], in *The Works of the Right Honorable Edmund Burke*, 9th ed., 12 vols. (Boston: Little, Brown, 1889), 2:156.

[2] To take just one recent case, Conor Cruise O'Brien, *The Great Melody: A Thematic Biography and Commented Anthology of Edmund Burke* (Chicago: University of Chicago Press, 1992), pp. 596–602 enlists Burke as a prophet who already understood the disasters of twentieth-century totalitarianism. The distinction between lofty metaphysics and hardheaded empiricism crosscuts the distinction between conservatism and radicalism. See David Bromwich, *Hazlitt: The Mind of a Critic* (New York: Oxford University Press, 1983), pp. 245–51, contrasting the empirical conservatism of Burke with the metaphysical conservatism of Coleridge. For empirically oriented radicalism, long on facts about political corruption and conspicuously short on arguments about natural rights, consider T. H. B. Oldfield, *An Entire and Complete History, Political and Personal, of the Boroughs of Great Britain*, 3 vols. (London, 1792); Oldfield, *The Representative History of Great Britain and Ireland*, 6 vols. (London, 1816); Oldfield, *A Key to the House of Commons: Being a History of the Last General Election, in 1818; and a Correct State of the Virtual Representation of England and Wales* (London, 1820); John Wade, *The Black Book; or, Corruption Unmasked!*, 2 vols. (London, 1820–1823); Wade, *The Extraordinary Black Book: An Exposition of Abuses in Church and State, Courts of Law, Representation, Municipal and Corporate Bodies; with a Précis of the House of Commons, Past, Present, and to Come*, new ed. (London, 1832). For skepticism on Wade's accuracy, see Philip Harling, "Rethinking 'Old Corruption,'" *Past & Present* (May 1995) no. 147, pp. 133–44.

[3] *Reflections on the Revolution in France* [1790], in *Works*, 3:259.

all know that those who loll at their ease in high dignities, whether of the Church or of the State, are commonly averse to all reformation."[4]

At bottom, this conception of tradition requires narrative continuity with the past. Burke is suspicious of those who would attempt an apocalyptic break with the past. Such wholesale efforts at change he consistently brands *innovation*, not the gentle *reform* that he endorses.[5] What makes such innovation so perilous? Burke argues that individuals aren't very bright and, what matters more, that individuals aren't as wise as existing institutions. "We are afraid to put men to live and trade each on his own private stock of reason; because we suspect that the stock in each man is small, and that the individuals would do better to avail themselves of the general bank and capital of nations and of ages."[6] Things work reasonably well right now; people have been ironing out problems for centuries; striking off into the political wilderness is horribly chancy business. Here's a Socratic version of political skepticism. Burke is bright enough to know that he's not all that bright, so he can adopt "a perfect distrust of my own abilities" right alongside "a profound reverence for the wisdom of our ancestors," where the thought is not that the ancestors weren't dullards, but that they acted collectively over the long run.[7]

It's deceptively easy to imagine that a society has a single tradition. But surely societies have many traditions jostling uneasily together. So something needs to be said about how we choose a particular tradition to guide us, else we may well surmise that politically crucial work is being done offstage. The problem is already manifest in the *Reflections*. There Burke wants to labor over the contrast between the ghastly events of 1789 and the inspiring events of 1688, between grotesque French gyrations and phlegmatic English plodding. In England's Glorious Revolution, after all, no crazed mobs marched through the streets with bishops' heads on pikes. The English rou-

---

[4] "Speech on the Acts of Uniformity" [6 February 1772], in *Works*, 7:5.

[5] See, for instance, "A Letter to William Elliot, Esq." [1795], in *Works*, 5:123; *A Letter to a Noble Lord* [1796], in *Works*, 5:187; *Letters on a Regicide Peace* [1796–1797], in *Works*, 5:422–23. For one example of the use of this language as cant, see J. Symmons, *Reform without Innovation: Or, Cursory Thoughts on the Only Practicable Reform of Parliament, Consistent with the Existing Laws, and the Spirit of the Constitution* (London, 1810), in *Pamphleteer* (1810) 9(18):401–13.

[6] *Reflections*, in *Works*, 3:346. See too "Speech on Reform of Representation of the Commons in Parliament" [7 May 1782], in *Works*, 7:94.

[7] "Speech on Conciliation with America" [22 March 1775], in *Works*, 2:145.

tinely congratulated themselves on 1688, when—or so the story
went—they vindicated their time-honored constitution against the
depredations of the villainous Stuarts. But Burke is conspicuously silent about the gory events of 1649, when Cromwell and his Puritan
minions put Charles I to death; later they would declare England a
republic.

Burke can't resist taunting Price: "Dr. Price, when he talks as if he
had made a discovery, only follows a precedent. . . ."[8] His precedent,
Burke divulges, was the infamous Hugh Peter, chaplain of Cromwell's
New Model Army, another lupine champion of human rights in ovine
religious garb. So Price is unoriginal. But the blow is artless, because
it enables Price to pose as a traditionalist, adhering to what English
radicals long referred to as the good old cause. (Decades after
Charles's execution, members of the Calves' Head Club in London
were still meeting to commemorate the great event.[9]) Plunging
deeper into English history, Burke indignantly dredges up John Ball,
"that reverend patriarch of sedition, and prototype of our modern
preachers," and hurls him accusingly at those sympathetic to the
French revolution.[10] But this charge merely furnishes Price a more
ancient and distinguished lineage.

Burke is confident that "the people of England will not ape the
fashions they have never tried, nor go back to those which they have
found mischievous on trial."[11] The comment is a terse allusion to the
days of Puritan regicide. Its abrupt dismissiveness is a sign that a significant dilemma is being evaded. For here Burke admits that English
history has this other tradition, itself an unfolding story that perhaps
hasn't yet reached its end. Later on, we may be able to look back and
decide the tradition was or soon became defunct. Yet if we place ourselves in Burke's present and construe tradition as a matter of narrative
continuity with the past, Price's appeal can't be ruled out. Again, the
political choice is never a matter of (our single) tradition against radical innovation. It's always in part a matter of which tradition to choose.

Now suppose that we agree on which tradition we want to take as
authoritative, which ancestral footprints we want to follow. We may

---

[8] *Reflections*, in *Works*, 3:318.

[9] Edward Ward, *The Secret History of the Calves-Head Club, Compleat: or, The Republican Unmask'd* (London, 1707).

[10] *Appeal from the New to the Old Whigs*, 2d ed. [1791], in *Works*, 4:177–78.

[11] *Reflections*, in *Works*, 3:264.

well reach an interpretive fork in the road, an anomalous event or problem where it suddenly becomes unclear what our tradition's guiding principles dictate. Then the injunction to turn to tradition isn't helpful.

For the Whigs, the French Revolution was such an anomaly. Burke, himself a Whig (though even before the French Revolution, Boswell was convinced that Burke was a Tory at heart[12]), was dismayed that Fox kept saying nice things about the Revolution. So Burke bitterly renounced Fox on the floor of Parliament, leaving his old friend in tears. Bemoaning the "new, republican, frenchified Whiggism . . . gaining ground in this Country,"[13] Burke wrote the *Appeal from the New to the Old Whigs,* a truculent attempt to show that he was the true inheritor of 1688, of what the English ironically called revolution principles, that the right reading of those principles would lead to a condemnation of French innovation.[14]

The problem was that Burke's former Whig allies had competing accounts of such central categories as the liberty of the subject. They saw Burke as the renegade, Fox as the great champion of long-settled Whig orthodoxy. They too had a reasonably unified account of Whig tradition, of the revolution principles of 1688. It just happened not to point in the same direction as Burke's account.

Burke's impatience with his failure to persuade his fellow Whigs led to a revealing expostulation:

> Whether [my principles] are allowed to be Whigg principles, or not, is a very small part of my concern. I think them exactly such as the sober, honourable, and intelligent in that party, have always professed. I think, I have shewn, beyond a possibility of debate, that they are exactly the same. But if any person or any number of persons, choose to think oth-

---

[12] *Boswell: The Applause of the Jury 1782–1785,* ed. Irma S. Lustig and Frederick A. Pottle (New York: McGraw-Hill, 1981), p. 87 [27 March 1783]; Boswell to John Johnston, 22 April 1783, *The Correspondence of James Boswell and John Johnston of Grange,* ed. Ralph S. Walker (New York: McGraw-Hill, 1966), pp. 297–98. See too *Boswell: The Great Biographer 1789–1795,* ed. Marlies K. Danziger and Frank Brady (New York: McGraw-Hill, 1989), pp. 36–37 [23 January 1790].

[13] Burke to William Weddell, 31 January 1792, *The Correspondence of Edmund Burke,* ed. Thomas W. Copeland, 10 vols. (Chicago: University of Chicago Press, 1958–1978), 7:52.

[14] For an account of early grappling with the legacy of 1688, see J. P. Kenyon, *Revolution Principles: The Politics of Party 1689–1720* (Cambridge: Cambridge University Press, 1977).

erwise, and conceive that they are contrary to the Doctrines of their Whigg party,—be it so. I am certain, that they are principles of which no reasonable man or good citizen need be ashamed of. If they are Tory principles, I shall always wish to be thought a Tory, If the contrary of these principles be Whigg principles, I beg, that you, my Dear Friend will never consider me as belonging to that description: For I look upon them to be wicked and absurd in the highest degree; and that wherever they shall become the ruling maxims, they must produce exactly the same Effects, which they do, in the miserable, depraved, and contemptible Nation in which they now predominate. So far for the Whiggs, who do not consider me as a Whigg.[15]

What's in a word? What matter, perhaps, are the substantive merits of the position, not any verbal quibbles about its label. More is at stake, though, than the mere meaning of a word, more even than Burke's membership in the community of Whigs. Here Burke unequivocally scraps the strategy of guiding himself by tradition. He turns to that tired and decrepit workhorse, the reasonable man, the last refuge of a theoretical scoundrel.

The mistake here is thinking that only one way of extending a narrative is faithful to what's come before, that there's only one proper way to continue writing a novel or composing a sonata or living a life or respecting a precedent or crusading for long-standing political principles. The mildly paradoxical correction is remembering that only the continuation commits us to any particular account of what in fact did come before and commits us only temporarily, that the shape of the existing pages of the novel or passages of the sonata or years of the life or doctrines of the law or principles of the crusade is made and remade as its narrative continues to unfold, that even apparently surprising lurches can be integrated seamlessly. Think of what counts as jazz, what one's sense of that tradition is, after the arrival of bebop, then after Ornette Coleman, then after the Art Ensemble of Chicago, then after Anthony Braxton or Henry Threadgill.

Now consider the case of the rude innovation as time passes. After being reviled by those clinging to older traditions, it gradually becomes part of the settled landscape. Its noxious origins, now faintly embarrassing, are discreetly swept under the rug. Finally it emerges as tradition. The process may be speedy. So tradition is a mode of inter-

---

[15] Burke to Dr. Richard Brocklesby, n.d., *Correspondence*, 9:446.

pretation, not a category thrust upon us by the brute fact of elapsed time. Anyway, what are the angry opponents' descendants to say once the innovation is transformed into tradition?

Burke himself faces the quandary in addressing the Reformation, once a sudden innovation. Burke writes some twenty-five decades after the fact. In the *Reflections,* recall, Burke wants to insist on the gradual nature of English reform. Distressed, too, by French anticlericalism, convinced of the merits of an established church, he also wants to describe the English as faithful to a prescriptive religion. "So tenacious are we of the old ecclesiastical modes and fashions of institution, that very little alteration has been made in them since the fourteenth or fifteenth century: adhering in this particular, as in all things else, to our old settled maxim, never entirely nor at once to depart from antiquity."[16]

It's an odd claim. The Reformation involved intense upheavals, and even if we construe *institution* narrowly, as a reference to education, the dissolution of the monasteries meant sweeping changes there, too.[17] A couple of dozen pages later, Burke abruptly corrects himself. He christens Henry VIII "one of the most decided tyrants in the rolls of history" for the dissolution of the monasteries.[18] The choice of words is significant, for Burke already has announced that the name *tyrant* is "expressive of everything which can vitiate and degrade human nature."[19] Warming to his theme, Burke revels in likening the Reformation to the French Revolution. What did Henry lack that the audacious leaders in Paris have? Only a newly fashionable vocabulary, only "one short form of incantation:—'*Philosophy, Light, Liberality, the Rights of Men.*' "[20] In his *Thoughts on French Affairs,* Burke would take fiendish pleasure in pursuing the analogy. Both the Reformation and the Revolution, he would argue, established an international and vividly ideological politics.[21] Nor was Burke alone on the

---

[16] *Reflections,* in *Works,* 3:363.

[17] For evidence on just how sweeping a change the English Reformation was and just how hard to accomplish, see G. R. Elton, *Policy and Police: The Enforcement of the Reformation in the Age of Thomas Cromwell* (Cambridge: Cambridge University Press, 1972) and Christopher Haigh, *Reformation and Resistance in Tudor Lancashire* (Cambridge: Cambridge University Press, 1975).

[18] *Reflections,* in *Works,* 3:385.

[19] *Reflections,* in *Works,* 3:371.

[20] *Reflections,* in *Works,* 3:385.

[21] *Thoughts on French Affairs* [1791], in *Works,* 4:318–20.

right. One pamphleteer described Henry as "that monster"; Coleridge denounced "that detestable tyrant, Henry the Eighth"; Robert Southey branded the dissolution of the monasteries an "abominable robbery."[22] The frequency of such complaints counts against the ready identification of English conservatism with support of the Anglican church.[23]

Burke stumbles again when insisting on the autonomy of the English church, declaring blithely that "she claims, and has always exercised, a right of reforming whatever appeared amiss in her doctrine, her discipline, or her rites. She did so, when she shook off the Papal supremacy in the reign of Henry the Eighth, which was an act of the body of the English Church, as well as of the State (I don't inquire how obtained)."[24] The offhand addition of the state undercuts the view that the church is autonomous; the parenthetical aside aggravates the confusion. Burke was capable of writing better history: "I admit, however, that the established religion of this country has been three or four times altered by act of Parliament. . . ."[25] The obvious candidates are the Reformation, Mary's reversion to Catholicism, and Elizabeth's return to Protestantism.

Burke is lost here in a terribly tricky maze. Routinely accused of being a crypto-Catholic, of being educated by Jesuits, long startling onlookers with his passionate sympathies with the plight of Irish Catholics, he finds himself an Irish outsider, always suspect, daring to assault what any loyal English Protestant would have saluted as the great event liberating England from the chains of popery, indeed from the Antichrist and the whore of Babylon. Whatever his religious sympathies finally amounted to, he is acutely aware that his audience prizes the Reformation as the inception of a most valuable tradition. So he must be aware, too, that if Price is victorious, future generations might well end up prizing Jacobin politics. There could be bicenten-

---

[22] Thomas Green, *Slight Observations upon Paine's Pamphlet, Principally Respecting His Comparison of the French and English Constitutions* (London, 1791), in *Political Writings of the 1790s*, ed. Gregory Claeys, 8 vols. (London: William Pickering, 1995), 5:231; *Morning Post* (28 January 1800), in *The Collected Works of Samuel Taylor Coleridge*, ed. Kathleen Coburn, Bart Winer, and others, in progress (Princeton, NJ: Princeton University Press, 1969–), 3(1):136; Robert Southey, *The Life of Wesley; and the Rise and Progress of Methodism*, 2 vols. (London, 1820), 1:313.

[23] This is the central thesis of James J. Sack, *From Jacobite to Conservative: Reaction and Orthodoxy in Britain, c. 1760–1832* (Cambridge: Cambridge University Press, 1993).

[24] "Speech on the Acts of Uniformity," in *Works*, 7:7.

[25] "Letter to the Sheriffs of Bristol" [1777], in *Works*, 2:225.

nial celebrations of the French Revolution. Comments about the rights of man and the consent of the governed might lose their explosively radical force and become the worn coin of the realm. The royal family might become mere titular heads of state. They might be attacked publicly for their sexual misdeeds and failure to pay taxes, or worse yet, defended publicly as a tourist attraction.

Next: sometimes tradition becomes obsolete, even pernicious. Social change can mean that a gently reformed tweaking of our policies and practices won't suffice. Nothing but radical departure will do. Those fond of tinkering will be not prudent but timid, oblivious to politically pressing demands. Their lugubrious dispositions will now qualify as diffidence, even cowardice, not merely a character flaw but a politically debilitating threat to the realm.

Though conventional wisdom forgets it, Burke brandishes this point in one political crisis after another. Tradition would provide no guide to relations with America, with its tricky mix of colonial government, commerce, and the bold spirits of the population:

> Whoever goes about to reason on any part of the policy of this country with regard to America, upon the mere abstract principles of government, or even upon those of our own ancient constitution, will be often misled. Those who resort for arguments to the most respectable authorities, ancient or modern, or rest upon the clearest maxims, drawn from the experience of other states and empires, will be liable to the greatest errors imaginable. The object is wholly new in the world. It is singular; it is grown up to this magnitude and importance within the memory of man; nothing in history is parallel to it. All the reasons about it, that are likely to be at all solid, must be drawn from its actual circumstances.[26]

Tradition would provide no guide to reforming the finances of the royal household, based as they were on obsolete feudal principles:

> But when the reason of old establishments is gone, it is absurd to preserve nothing but the burden of them. This is superstitiously to embalm a carcass not worth an ounce of the gums that are used to preserve it. It is to burn precious oils in the tomb; it is to offer meat and drink to the

[26] *Observations on a Late Publication on the Present State of the Nation* [1769], in *Works*, 1:395.

dead: not so much an honour to the deceased as a disgrace to the survivors.[27]

Both these passages precede the French Revolution. Perhaps the central point is that there's a chronological shift: before 1789, Burke is a child of the Scottish enlightenment, devoted to free trade, a quaintly mechanistic psychologist devoted to unpacking the principles generating our judgments of the sublime and the beautiful; after 1789, he discards such lines of argument, worried about their corrosive impact. True, the earlier Burke writes otherwise odd passages: "Too little dependence cannot be had, at this time of day, on names and prejudices. The eyes of mankind are opened, and communities must be held together by an evident and solid interest."[28] So it would be rash to suggest that chronology makes no difference.

Still, Burke continues to develop this same line in historicist criticism after the Revolution. Tradition would provide no guide to foreign policy relations with that horrid new regicide republic of France, whose ideologically fervent militarism made mincemeat of the balance of power:

> I cannot persuade myself, that this War bears any the least resemblance (other than that it is a War) to any that has ever existed in the world—I cannot persuade myself, that any examples or any reasonings drawn from other Wars and other politicks are at all applicable to it—and I truly and sincerely think, that all other wars and all other politicks have been the games of Children in comparison to it.[29]

No foot dutifully planted in forefathers' tracks for this Burke. His battle cry is, "New things in a new world! I see no hopes in the common tracks."[30]

Like any other political view, the appeal to tradition, to moderate reform and narrative continuity with the past, has its quiet empirical presuppositions, background beliefs required to make the view attractive, even to make it fully intelligible. The traditionalist has to believe that the pace of social change is restrained, so that we have time to

[27] "Speech on the Plan for Economical Reform" [11 February 1780], in *Works*, 2:305.

[28] "Two Letters to Gentlemen in Bristol" [1778], in *Works*, 2:251.

[29] Burke to Captain Emperor John Alexander Woodford, 13 January 1794, *Correspondence*, 7:521–22.

[30] "Letter to William Elliot," in *Works*, 5:128.

tinker with our policies and that tinkering is good enough. Ironically, the French Revolution comes to be exemplary of the (in)famously rapid pace of social change in modernity. That looks like an irreversible fact, something that has happened to us, not any kind of mistaken choice we could regret and renounce. For crassly empirical reasons, then, "new things in a new world!" must increasingly be our slogan and these paeans to tradition must be sadly misguided.

I don't imagine that these hasty objections dispose of the appeal of tradition. Notice, though, that this conception of tradition furnishes a depressingly second-order or depoliticized account of conservatism. One could be equally conservative in upholding and reforming England's ancient constitution or the Soviet gulag: in this view, we called the hard-liners in the closing years of the Soviet empire *conservative* because they didn't want any radical breaks from the sordid and dreary arrangements bequeathed by the likes of Brezhnev.

Sometimes we use the predicate *conservative* in this sense. But we also have stubborn if murky intuitions that conservatism names a position, or anyway a loose-knit family of positions, with more specifically political content. I want now to begin to clarify those intuitions. I suggest that the Soviet hard-liners earned the label *conservative* by embracing the same hatred of democratic politics, of vigorous public debate, that other conservatives did. Conveniently, I turn again to Burke, whose capacious sleeves conceal another account of tradition.

### Tradition as Prejudice and Illusion

Consider again Burke's contrast between reforming the institutions bequeathed by the past and starting from scratch on the basis of a rational theory: "I feel an insuperable reluctance in giving my hand to destroy any established institution of government, upon a theory, however plausible it may be."[31] This contrast leads Burke, as we've seen, to think of narrative continuity as a kind of political rationality, of tradition as the opposite of innovation. But it also leads him to worry about rationality itself, to conceive of tradition as the opposite of reason.

In this latter mood, Burke embraces prejudice. "You see, Sir," he instructs the recipient of the *Reflections*, the prose dripping sardonic

---

[31] "Speech on Mr. Fox's East India Bill" [1 December 1783], in *Works*, 2:442.

scorn, "that in this enlightened age I am bold enough to confess that we are generally men of untaught feelings: that, instead of casting away all our old prejudices, we cherish them to a very considerable degree. . . ."[32] When Burke hails "the cold sluggishness of our national character,"[33] he means that it's hard to get the English excited about the latest gimmicky rational argument. The English are stolid, grave, sleepy, maybe even a bit dim-witted. These traits, too, though it may pain intellectuals to admit it, are political virtues. They are the stuff of staunch English patriotism, a love of country far deeper and more reliable than that any logical demonstration might fuel.

From prejudice, Burke drifts easily to ignorance. "What a firm dependence is to be had upon ignorance and prejudices! A party which depended upon rational principles must perish the moment reason is withdrawn from it."[34] If people aren't going to engage in argument, they might as well not know anything about difficult and contested questions. Reason is an acid corroding the cement of society. "It is always to be lamented, when men are driven to search into the foundations of the commonwealth."[35] Embracing reason, the French will find themselves forced to safeguard social order with the gallows, a threat addressed to calculating citizens.[36] Here a social practice stripped down to rational choice is taken, aptly enough, as social pathology, not hardheaded empiricism.

From ignorance, finally, it's an easy step to illusion. Consider Burke's comment on the *gabelle*, the French tax on salt assailed so bitterly in the run-up to the Revolution: "The sophisters and declaimers, as soon as the Assembly met, began with decrying the ancient constitution of the revenue in many of its most essential branches, such as the public monopoly of salt. They charged it, as truly as unwisely, with being ill-contrived, oppressive, and partial."[37] Worse, adds Burke, they publicized the charge throughout the nation. As truly as unwisely: the point is emphatically not that the Jac-

---

[32] *Reflections*, in *Works*, 3:346.

[33] *Reflections*, in *Works*, 3:344.

[34] Burke to Richard Champion, 13 August 1779, *Correspondence*, 4:115.

[35] "Speech on the Duration of Parliaments" [8 May 1780], in *Works*, 7:71; and see "Speech on the Petition of the Unitarians" [11 May 1792], in *Works*, 7:49. See too the prosecution's argument in *The Trial of Wm. Winterbotham*, 2d ed. (London, 1794), pp. 68–69.

[36] *Reflections*, in *Works*, 3:333.

[37] *Reflections*, in *Works*, 3:537.

obins are relying on their insufficient individual rationality, that they should try instead to discover what superior rationality is embedded in French practices; for what they say is true. But they shouldn't say it. Or consider Burke's commending the Parliament of 1689 for throwing "a politic, well-wrought veil"[38] over the difficult constitutional negotiations and legal settlement surrounding James II's stylized abdication. (Already in 1779, a Mr. Smelt had appreciated that Parliament's regard for the politics of "reverence": "The hand of Legislature did not then rashly draw aside the veil, and authorize the subject to invade and scan the secret recesses of majesty."[39]) Or consider his grumbling that "all the pleasing illusions which made power gentle and obedience liberal . . . are to be dissolved by this new conquering empire of light and reason. All the decent drapery of life is to be rudely torn off."[40]

Or consider a curiously elliptical passage in the *Reflections:* "The men of England, the men, I mean, of light and leading in England, whose wisdom (if they have any) is open and direct, would be ashamed, as of a silly, deceitful trick, to profess any religion in name, which by their proceedings they appear to contemn."[41] The stammering hesitation might distract the reader's attention from what I take to be a deliberate omission. Burke never says that these leading men are in fact religious. In fact, the utter lack of religiosity of the great Tory leader, William Pitt, discomfited his parliamentary allies. Other leading political figures were lax about attending church, too.[42] But none of these men publicly paraded their ragged religious credentials. It's not that Pitt and the others cheerfully admitted to being atheists rather than be known as hypocrites. Knowing that religion mattered politically, they kept quiet about their own lackadaisical sentiments. Here's another well-wrought veil that it would be imprudent to rip aside.

Prejudice and ignorance, veils and illusions: these are the ingredients of tradition. Tradition isn't exhumed by innocent empiricist

[38] *Reflections,* in *Works,* 3:255. See the response of James Mackintosh, *Vindiciae Gallicae* (London, 1791; reprint ed. Oxford: Woodstock Books, 1989), pp. 315–23.

[39] Debate at York, 30 December 1779, in Christopher Wyvill, *Political Papers,* 6 vols. (York, 1794–1805), 1:18.

[40] *Reflections,* in *Works,* 3:332–33.

[41] *Reflections,* in *Works,* 3:365.

[42] Sack, *From Jacobite to Conservative,* pp. 84–85, 256. John Cam Hobhouse, *A Letter to Lord Viscount Castlereagh,* 2d ed. (London, 1819), pp. 21–22, 37, seizes on this point in his searing attack on the authorities for their repressive response to Peterloo.

sleuths, out to furnish as accurate a description as they can; it's constructed by cunning poets ever attentive to the political exigencies of the day. Is the Reformation an untoward blot on the record? Downplay or deny it. Are the trial and execution of Charles I unfortunate precedents? Brush them aside. Tradition here isn't the site of rational argument; it's the site of unthinking compliance. Patrons of enlightenment will deride this vision of tradition as mindless, robotic, a way of sleepwalking; they will long for a cold, bracing slap of reason, truth, or vigorous argument as a political tonic.

Burke himself was sometimes willing to administer such bracing slaps. Spurning friendly advice and hostile guffawing, he devoted thankless years to investigating the outrages perpetrated by the East India Company. Pursuing the impeachment of Warren Hastings in 1794, trying in vain to persuade the House of Lords that Hastings's rule in India was shot through with matchless corruption, Burke is at pains to emphasize that Hastings's misdeeds couldn't be described as mistakes, that he'd deliberately kept phony accounts and the like. In a typically florid moment, Burke then invites his audience to ponder the elaborate administrative machinery of evil he has unveiled:

> Now, my Lords, was there ever such a discovery made of the arcana of any public theatre? You see here, behind the ostensible scenery, all the crooked working of the machinery developed and laid open to the world. You now see by what secret movement the master of the mechanism has conducted the great Indian opera,—an opera of fraud, deceptions, and harlequin tricks. You have it all laid open before you. The ostensible scene is drawn aside; it has vanished from your sight. All the strutting signors, and all the soft signoras are gone; and instead of a brilliant spectacle of descending chariots, gods, goddesses, sun, moon, and stars, you have nothing to gaze on but sticks, wire, ropes, and machinery. You find the appearance all false and fraudulent; and you see the whole trick at once.[43]

In this context, Burke is willing to generalize the point, instructing his noble audience that "whenever in any matter of policy there is a mystery, you must presume a fraud. . . ."[44]

[43] "Speech in General Reply" [5 June 1794], in *Works,* 11:413. On another occasion, Burke's ornate language enabled Pitt to suggest drily that the commons return "to sobriety and seriousness," that they "break the magician's wand" and "dispel the cloud" in order to face facts: *The Speeches of the Right Honourable William Pitt, in the House of Commons,* 3d ed., 3 vols. (London, 1817), 1:18 [6 December 1782].

[44] "Speech in General Reply" [11 June 1794], in *Works,* 12:79.

No politic, well-wrought veil for Hastings. He is rudely unmasked. Why? Consider Burke's audiences, first in some straightforward cases of divergence between Burke's published works and his private correspondence. For public consumption, Burke eulogizes Marie Antoinette as "the late glorious queen, who on all accounts was formed to produce general love and admiration, and whose life was as mild and beneficent as her death was beyond example great and heroic"; for private consumption, exasperated by her failure to take the lofty and unyielding position he recommended in the name of safeguarding monarchy, he spits out, "It is not to be expected, that she should elevate her Mind" and bemoans her "foolish dread of the influence of Calonne. . . ."[45] For public consumption, he eulogizes "the unhappy Louis the Sixteenth [as] a man of the best intentions that probably ever reigned"; for private consumption, Louis is "a figure as ridiculous as pitiable."[46] In these cases, the public assessments are politically convenient, the private assessments unflinchingly frank. It's easier to motivate a crusade against the French Revolution if the king and queen are taken to be paragons of virtue, even if actually they're petty and risible.

Take next a more complex case. Addressing the reading public in the *Reflections,* Burke coos admiringly, "Nobility is a graceful ornament to the civil order. It is the Corinthian capital of polished society."[47] In a letter to the Duke of Richmond, Burke fawns, casting aristocrats as "the great Oaks that shade a Country"—but it isn't only fawning, because Burke is sternly instructing the duke that this is what the aristocracy are or ought to be.[48] Speaking in the House of Commons, he snarls, asserting that "many of the nobility are as perfectly willing to act the part of flatterers, tale-bearers, parasites, pimps, and buffoons, as any of the lowest and vilest of mankind can possibly be."[49] This is the speech on economical reform from 1780, and here I would enlist chronology as a supporting point: I don't

---

[45] *Regicide Peace,* in *Works,* 5:370; Burke to Richard Burke, Jr., 16 August 1791, *Correspondence,* 6:340; Burke to Richard Burke, Jr., 17 August 1791, *Correspondence,* 6:348.

[46] *Regicide Peace,* in *Works,* 5:378; Burke to Richard Burke, Jr., *circa* 10 October 1789, *Correspondence,* 6:30.

[47] *Reflections,* in *Works,* 3:416. Mary Wollstonecraft Shelley, *The Last Man,* 3 vols. (London, 1826), 2:126–27 quotes this passage in imagining a debate in England on eradicating noble titles—in 2092.

[48] Burke to the Duke of Richmond, between 15 and 25 November 1772, *Correspondence,* 2:377.

[49] "Speech on Economical Reform," in *Works,* 2:337.

think that Burke, knowing that his speeches were published, would have addressed Parliament on this acutely sensitive topic in such strident language after 1789. Nor would he have been as eager to pursue such wholesale reform, from which he might recoil as innovation. Still, a concern for audience courses through these comments. Like the Lords in Hastings's trial, the Commons here are ushered into the chamber of acerbic truths unmentionable in more public settings. Their political role requires that they face grimly unpleasant facts.

The last case is perhaps the most intricate. Toward the end of his life, Burke was attacked by the Duke of Bedford for receiving money from the Crown. Enraged, he penned the *Letter to a Noble Lord,* a fiercely proud exercise in self-justification. It is a celebration of "the mediocrity of humble and laborious individuals,"[50] contrasting Burke the hardworking patriot, the self-made man, and Bedford, born to a colossal fortune. The *Letter* makes it possible to enlist Burke as a bourgeois radical, if you like that sort of thing.[51]

The *Letter* is also an expertly orchestrated and debunking use of history in political argument. Burke growls menacingly, "Let us turn our eyes to history, in which great men have always a pleasure in contemplating the heroic origin of their house."[52] The first Bedford, we learn, attained the peerage for being "a minion of Henry the Eighth."[53] The family gained its fabulous wealth from other newly expropriated nobles and from Henry's "plunder of the Church."[54] So the current Duke of Bedford is bloated in obscene wealth, his holdings "a downright insult upon the rights of man."[55] Stupidly, though, the duke is a champion of those very rights, a Jacobin sympathizer. Burke chortles with disdain at the incongruity. The "*sans-culotte* carcass-butchers" are preparing to carve the duke "into rumps, and sirloins, and briskets, and into all sorts of pieces for roasting, boiling, and stewing," while the duke, "poor innocent!", oblivious to his exposed flank, is assaulting pathetic Edmund Burke, a powerless old

---

[50] *Letter to a Noble Lord,* in *Works,* 5:200.

[51] Isaac Kramnick, *The Rage of Edmund Burke: Portrait of an Ambivalent Conservative* (New York: Basic Books, 1977).

[52] *Letter to a Noble Lord,* in *Works,* 5:201.

[53] *Letter to a Noble Lord,* in *Works,* 5:201.

[54] *Letter to a Noble Lord,* in *Works,* 5:202.

[55] *Letter to a Noble Lord,* in *Works,* 5:217.

man.[56] The duke may owe his fortune to unjust innovation, but now he ought to be a patron of tradition.[57]

This is a published work, not a private letter, and it's written after the French Revolution. So why is Burke willing to vent such unflattering sentiments about the Corinthian capital of polished society? Even in the *Reflections,* again, Burke's fury about the Reformation isn't tightly controlled. Nor can he have been pleased to see a singularly powerful aristocrat embracing Jacobin politics, further evidence of the rot setting in. But the decisive consideration is Burke's need to defend himself from a public attack. Nor is this freewheeling psychological speculation. With studied hostility, Burke tells us that he would have been happy to leave the duke to the "gentle historians" of the herald's college, their pens dipped "in nothing but the milk of human kindness"; he would have been happy, that is, had not Bedford seen fit to attack him.[58] Public flattery, the exceedingly decent drapery supplied by the herald's college and rhapsodic intellectuals, is another rightful inheritance of aristocrats. Yet they can forfeit their inheritance if they misbehave egregiously.

## SUBJECTS AND CITIZENS

Tradition, construed as veils and illusion, isn't for everyone. It's for the lower orders. But members of the tiny political nation, surely members of Parliament, are fit for more cognitively demanding tasks. They must make careful assessments of what reforms of ongoing practices are needed. So it's narrative continuity for the elite, prejudice and illusion for the masses. This is a way of drawing a distinction of class or social status, but it's drawn in terms of political psychology or epistemology, not wealth or power. That is, it's not a matter of the privileged classes bamboozling the yokels in order to safeguard their illicit assets. Or, if it happens to work out that way, that's not the content and force of the distinction.

Let's begin to explore the world outside Burke's texts. His distinction between audiences might be put as that between subjects and

---

[56] *Letter to a Noble Lord,* in *Works,* 5:221.

[57] Compare William Augustus Miles, *A Letter to the Duke of Grafton, with Notes* (London, 1794), pp. 11–12; Christianus Laicus, *A Letter, Addressed to the Hon. Charles James Fox, in Consequence of a Publication, Entitled, "A Sketch of the Character of the Most Noble Francis Duke of Bedford"* (Bath, 1802).

[58] *Letter to a Noble Lord,* in *Works,* 5:200.

citizens. Contemporaries sometimes used *citizen* in one sense given by Johnson's *Dictionary:* "a townsman; a man of trade; not a gentleman."[59] Yet this sense isn't centrally relevant here. Instead take Johnson's imagined scolding of those who would fan the smoldering flames of popular political resentment: "it is the duty of men like you, who have leisure for enquiry, to lead back the people to their honest labour; to tell them, that submission is the duty of the ignorant, and content the virtue of the poor; that they have no skill in the art of government. . . ."[60] As a matter of public law, a subject isn't entitled to vote and a citizen is. Subjects aren't powerless. They may offer petitions complaining of their grievances. Riots, too, were sometimes deemed constitutional. Nor are subjects to be exploited. In exchange for deference, they're owed paternal care.

The narrowly legal reading of these categories is impoverished. Citizenship is a matter of equality, dignity, full membership in the polity. Even if the franchise is taken to be its crucial marker, its content can't be so simply exhausted. Though consistent in its opposition to a universal franchise, the *Edinburgh Review* conceded that "the humbler classes" gained a "grave independence, and calm pride" by holding the franchise—and by watching their social superiors bend the knee in seeking their votes.[61] So arise the familiar political struggles of citizens to gain substantive legal equality, education, housing, health care, and so on, struggles pursued in the name of making citizenship real, not a mere name. Such struggles make plausible the view that citizenship is a sprawling and ever-expanding set of rights.[62]

*Citoyen* and *citoyenne* became more or less obligatory titles for greeting people in revolutionary France, a pregnant cultural gesture intended to flesh out the legal abolition of feudalism and aristocracy.

[59] Samuel Johnson, *A Dictionary of the English Language,* 2d ed., 2 vols. (London, 1755–1756), s.v. *citizen.* The etymology here, like that of *bourgeois,* mixes the legal status of city dwellers with their occupations as merchants and the like. For later instances of the usage Johnson has in mind, see Fanny Burney, *Cecilia, or Memoirs of an Heiress* [1782], ed. Peter Sabor and Margaret Anne Doody (Oxford: Oxford University Press, 1988), p. 362; *Journals of Dorothy Wordsworth,* ed. E. de Selincourt, 2 vols. (New York: Macmillan, 1941), 1:238 [23 August 1803]; Benjamin Disraeli, *Vivian Grey* [1826–1827], ed. Herbert van Thal (London: Cassell, 1968), p. 157.

[60] *The False Alarm* [1770], in *The Yale Edition of the Works of Samuel Johnson,* ed. Herman W. Liebert and others, in progress (New Haven, CT: Yale University Press, 1958–), 10:338–39.

[61] *Edinburgh Review* (December 1818) 31(61):179–80.

[62] The classic if schematic statement is T. H. Marshall, *Class, Citizenship, and Social Development* (Chicago: University of Chicago Press, 1977), chap. 4.

That was enough to make some observers across the Channel skittish. At the trial of Thomas Hardy (the radical shoemaker, not the later novelist) for high treason in October and November 1794, the Solicitor General cautioned against the use of the radical distinction between subjects and citizens.[63] Not that he believed all Englishmen were on equal political footing; still less that he imagined Englishwomen were. But the distinction made explicit just the sort of political information that the lower orders ought not to have at their disposal. Its biting accuracy had to remain surreptitious.[64]

Circulate the distinction did, though, in radical circles of the 1790s, among men who might not have enjoyed the franchise but took that as an outrageous deprivation. "Britons!—Fellow Citizens!" was the salutation of one 1792 address,[65] "Fellow Citizens" the repeated salutation of a 1793 pamphlet imploring the people to exercise their sovereignty and forge a new constitution.[66] At his January 1794 trial for sedition, Maurice Margarot addressed the jury: "Fellow citizens, and I fear not to call you by that name—we are fellow citizens of one society. By the word Citizen I mean a free man; a man enjoying all the rights and all the privileges, and paying his quota towards all the expence of Society."[67] A *Political Dictionary* of 1795, an often vitriolic exercise in unmasking, defined *citizen* as "the most honorable of titles," *subjects* as "a body of people who submit to the tyranny of one man; and yet they complain!"[68] "In this neighbourhood Citizens abound," a Cornwall informant reported to the London Corresponding Society in 1796.[69] Decades later, scolded for launching a new journal not only with prophecies of imminent revolution and republican-

[63] *The Trial of Thomas Hardy for High Treason,* rep. Joseph Gurney, 4 vols. (London, 1794–1795), 4:229–30.

[64] See the January 1770 Westminster petition and reaction in John Almon, *Memoirs of a Late Eminent Bookseller* (London, 1790), pp. 56–59 n.

[65] *Holborn Society, of the Friends of the People; Instituted 22d November, 1792, for the Purpose of Political Investigation* (London, 1792), p. 2.

[66] Joseph Gerrald, *A Convention the Only Means of Saving Us from Ruin* (London, 1793).

[67] *The Trial of Maurice Margarot, before the High Court of Justiciary, at Edinburgh, on the 13th and 14th of January, 1794, on an Indictment for Seditious Practices,* rep. Mr. Ramsey (New York, 1794), p. 20. Cecil Thelwall, *The Life of John Thelwall* (London, 1837), pp. 152–53 reports a 1794 conversation with "Citizen" used as a title.

[68] Charles Pigott, *A Political Dictionary: Explaining the True Meaning of Words* (London, 1795), pp. 9, 138.

[69] John Rule, *Albion's People: English Society, 1714–1815* (London: Longman, 1992), p. 224.

ism but with the same old greeting, one radical asserted that *citizen* was "the most honourable appellation by which a man can be designated."[70]

That only citizens are really free is a profoundly controversial view. "I love a manly, moral, regulated liberty,"[71] declared Burke, and there is no reason to impeach his sincerity. That freedom, in all its pointedly gendered splendor, was available to English subjects. It was far removed from the repulsive spectacle of angry working-class women on the rampage in the streets of Paris, a spectacle motivating Burke's sputtering about the "obscene harpies" of the French Revolution who "flutter over our heads, and souse down upon our tables, and leave nothing unrent, unrifled, unravaged, or unpolluted with the slime of their filthy offal."[72] France had perverted the very meaning of freedom. But radicals bristled at the traditional political rights of subjects. Insisted Thomas Wooler in his sizzling *Black Dwarf,* "the right of petition is only the privilege of slaves. Freemen would blush to hear it boasted of, in its modern acceptation."[73] The article got Wooler arrested.[74]

Proud citizens: the image was alluring for some, disgusting for others. Loyal subjects: the image beckoned some, piqued others. "Still the idea of *every* man voting, has something *noble,* and *constitutional* in it," whines Will in one dialogue. "It has something *levelling* in it, and very *democratical,*" fires back Thomas.[75] William Pitt conceded that the people had a right to petition Parliament with their grievances. Still, he urged, "he did not consider those to be the best friends of the constitution, or of the lower ranks of the people, who were always goading them to bring forward petitions, and encouraging the agitation and discussion of public affairs. . . ."[76] Samuel Horsley, bishop of the Church of England, became notorious for instructing the House of Lords that "he did not know what the mass of the people in any country had to do with the laws but to obey them,"

---

[70] J. R. Dinwiddy, *Radicalism and Reform in Britain, 1780–1850* (London: Hambledon Press, 1992), pp. 215–16: this is Lorymer's *Republican,* scolded by the *Morning Chronicle* in 1831.

[71] *Reflections,* in *Works,* 3:240.

[72] *Letter to a Noble Lord,* in *Works,* 5:187.

[73] *Black Dwarf* (12 February 1817) 1(3):41. See too *Black Dwarf* (7 May 1823) 10(19):645.

[74] *Black Dwarf* (7 May 1817) 1(15):225–30.

[75] *The Street Politicians, or A Debate about the Times* (Manchester, 1817), p. 12.

[76] *Speeches of Pitt,* 2:112 [17 November 1795].

though Horsley offered the routine exception for petitioning for grievances.[77] The accidents of publishing history kept Dr. Johnson from becoming notorious for his injunction in one sermon: "It is indeed very hazardous for a private man to criticise the laws of any country. . . ."[78]

## SOCIAL ORDER AS HIERARCHY AND SUBORDINATION

But Johnson did become notorious for a vivid account of social order: "Subordination is very necessary for society," he insisted; or again, "Order cannot be had but by subordination."[79] Johnson twitted republican Catherine Macaulay by urging that in the name of equality she invite her footman to sit and dine with them: "I thus, Sir, shewed her the absurdity of the levelling doctrine," he gloated. "She has never liked me since."[80] Such passages from the *Life* were dutifully reproduced in the *Bristol Job Nott,* a folksy newspaper of the early 1830s dispensing soothing conservative wisdom to local workers.[81] When not serving literally as copy-text, Johnson's wisdom on social order recurred constantly. So one should expect: it had been readily available in England for centuries.

One striking exposition, the *Homily on Obedience,* was preached across England at the behest of the government for decades beginning in 1547.[82] Full of pope-bashing, it seems to have dropped out of circu-

[77] *Parliamentary History* (11 November 1795) 32:258. Note Horsley's not particularly apologetic apology of 30 November in *The Speeches in Parliament of Samuel Horsley* (Dundee, 1813), pp. 168–83. For ripostes, *The Plot Discovered* [1795], in *Works of Coleridge,* 1:285–86; *The Speeches of the Right Honourable Charles James Fox, in the House of Commons,* 6 vols. (London, 1815), 6:23–24 [27 November 1795]; *Speeches of the Late Right Honourable Richard Brinsley Sheridan (Several Corrected by Himself),* ed. A Constitutional Friend, 5 vols. (London, 1816), 4:153 [24 November 1795], 4:391 [4 April 1797]; *Agrarian Justice* [1797], in *The Life and Works of Thomas Paine,* 10 vols. (New Rochelle, NY: Thomas Paine National Historical Association, 1925), 10:33.

[78] Sermon no. 26, in *Works of Johnson,* 14:279 [first published in 1978; for the history of the manuscript, see 14:xxxv–xxxix].

[79] *Boswell's Life of Johnson: Together with Boswell's Journal of a Tour to the Hebrides and Johnson's Diary of a Journey into North Wales,* ed. George Birkbeck Hill, rev. L. F. Powell, 6 vols. (Oxford: Clarendon, 1934–1950), 1:442 [20 July 1763], 3:383 [8 April 1779]. Boswell put the view in his own voice: see *The Hypochondriack,* ed. Margery Bailey, 2 vols. (Stanford, CA: Stanford University Press, 1928), 1:245–46 [April 1779].

[80] *Life of Johnson,* 1:447–48 [21 July 1763].

[81] *Bristol Job Nott* (20 December 1832) no. 54, p. 216.

[82] The text is readily available in *"Certain Sermons or Homilies" (1547) and "A Homily against Disobedience and Wilful Rebellion" (1570),* ed. Ronald B. Bond (Toronto: University of Toronto Press, 1987), pp. 161–73.

lation briefly in the 1550s after Mary prevailed on Parliament to reim-
pose Catholicism. But the *Homily* returned with Protestantism under
Elizabeth. The *Homily* emphasizes that hierarchy and subordination
are divinely mandated guiding principles of the entire universe. It
portrays the great chain of being, a cosmos in which divine command
keeps the planets in orbit and rebellious subjects trigger strange disturbances of the weather. In 1793, prolific pamphleteer John Bowles still
inhabited that cosmos—or at least wished his readers to: "The order of
civil society (partaking of the invariable principle of nature itself)
requires a progressive gradation. . . ."[83] In an uncharacteristically lyrical moment, Henry Dundas, renowned for his harsh policies, informed the House of Commons that it was "a gross calumny" to suggest
that the higher orders wished to detach their interests from those of
the lower. "If ever there was a country in which these classes were
united; in which, from the humblest cottager to the monarch on the
throne, all ranks of society were cemented and connected by one
continued chain, each giving assistance to the other, it was the country
in which we lived."[84] How many political theories have remained so
intact through the ravaging centuries of historical change?

Order is no merely human arrangement. In 1790, the poet Cowper
derided the new French affectations of social equality, which left
"gentles reduced to a level with their own lacqueys": "Difference of
rank and subordination, are, I believe of God's appointment, and
consequently essential to the well being of society. . . ."[85] Burke's *Reflections* brusquely spurns Lockean social contract theory in the name
of "the great primeval contract of eternal society, linking the lower
with the higher natures, connecting the visible and invisible world,
according to a fixed compact sanctioned by the inviolable oath which
holds all physical and all moral natures each in their appointed
place." Authority and subject alike "move with the order of the universe," an order finally depending on the divine "Institutor and Author and Protector of civil society."[86]

[83] Bowles, *A Protest against T. Paine's "Rights of Man" Addressed to the Members of a Book
Society* (London, 1793), p. 16. See too James Mackintosh, *A Discourse on the Study of the
Law of Nature and Nations* (London, 1799), p. 67.

[84] *Parliamentary History* (17 November 1795) 32:338.

[85] Cowper to Lady Hesketh, 7 July 1790, *The Letters and Prose Writings of William
Cowper,* ed. James King and Charles Ryskamp, 5 vols. (Oxford: Clarendon, 1979–1986),
3:396. See too Richard Munn, *The Loyal Subject, or Monarchy Defended; and Republican
Principles Exploded by the Word of God,* 2d ed. (London, 1793).

[86] *Reflections,* in *Works,* 3:359–61.

The great chain of being routinely was coupled with a principle of plenitude, according to which the hierarchy was smoothly continuous from top to bottom, with no tiers left uninhabited. So Hannah More patiently explained that it was fine that women, the young, the elderly, the poorly educated, and the just plain poor were excluded from the pursuit of arts and letters: "The wisdom of God is wonderfully manifested in this happy and well-ordered diversity . . . the whole scheme of human affairs is carried on with the most agreeing and consistent economy, and no chasm is left for want of an object to fill it, exactly suited to its nature."[87] "Money confounds subordination," Johnson already had reported in analyzing the feudal vestiges of the Hebrides, "by overpowering the distinctions of rank and birth";[88] in 1833 the ultra-Tory *Fraser's* would embrace feudalism itself as "a perfect chain of subordination."[89]

The structure of the *Homily*'s view also lent itself to the antique imagery of the body politic, imagery not lovingly burnished as a museum piece, but constantly put to political work. John Reeves's Association for Preserving Liberty and Property against Republicans and Levellers (a mouthful, I suppose, but a tasty one) seized on the view to show that Tom Paine's views were "not more pernicious than absurd," an

> attempt to persuade the Feet, that, considering their importance and utility, they ought not to submit to those offices which are assigned them—that it is a hardship and an injustice for them to be obliged to wade through the dirt, and to bear the weight of the whole body—that they are entitled to some nobler capacity, some more elevated station— that having nerves as well as the Head (the pretended seat of intelligence), their opinions ought to be taken, their will consulted, and themselves admitted into the council; and that they ought, in maintenance of their rights, to rebel against the subsisting inequality of arrangement, and refuse to perform their accustomed works of drudgery.[90]

[87] "Importance of Religion to the Female Character" [1777], in *The Works of Hannah More*, 9 vols. (London, 1840–1843), 6:333. See too Robert Southey, *Letters from England* [1807], ed. Jack Simmons (London: Cresset Press, 1951), p. 368.

[88] *A Journey to the Western Islands of Scotland* [1775], in *Works of Johnson*, 9:113.

[89] *Fraser's* (June 1833) 7(42):633.

[90] *Association Papers* (London, 1793), pt. 1, no. 3, pp. 8–9. See too *On the Constitution of the Church and State* [1830], in *Works of Coleridge*, 10:84–85. For Burke's skepticism about the body politic, see "Letter to William Elliot," in *Works*, 5:124.

The feet are the lower orders. Their democratic claims will turn the body politic topsy-turvy. "Civil bodies used to be composed of head, feet, hands, and other subordinate and correspondent members," fumed another writer; "but here is a community that wishes to be *all head!!!*"[91] These passages are eerily reminiscent of Sir Richard Morison's *Remedy for Sedition* of 1536.[92] They have an even more distinguished lineage: they echo Scripture.[93]

It was also traditional to take paternal and political authority as mirror images. "In all large communities," the *Guardian of Education* explained, "subordination of rank is necessary to preserve harmony; and so it is in the smaller circles of domestic life. . . ."[94] Society was a patriarchal family, the king the father of his people. Lamented one diarist,

> How preferable is patriarchal government . . . to the cold theories pedantic sophists would establish, and which, should success attend their selfish atheistical ravings, bid fair to undermine the best and surest props of society! When parents cease to be honoured by their children, and the feelings of grateful subordination in those of helpless age or condition are unknown, kings will soon cease to reign, and republics to be governed by the councils of experience; anarchy, rapine, and massacre will walk the earth, and the abode of daemons be transferred from hell to our unfortunate planet.[95]

Whether great chain of being, body politic, or patriarchal family, social order required hierarchy and subordination. The view doesn't require any exploitation of the lower orders. In its rosier incarnations, crucially, their interests too are served by inequality. Dr. Johnson routinely emphasized this last element of the view: "Subordination tends greatly to human happiness. Were we all upon an equality,"

[91] William Hamilton Reid, *The Rise and Dissolution of the Infidel Societies in This Metropolis* (London, 1800), p. 74.

[92] *Humanist Scholarship and Public Order: Two Tracts against the Pilgrimage of Grace,* ed. David Sandler Berkowitz (Washington: Folger Shakespeare Library, 1984), pp. 117–18.

[93] 1 *Corinthians* 12.

[94] *Guardian of Education* (October 1802) 1(6):367.

[95] *The Travel-Diaries of William Beckford of Fonthill,* ed. Guy Chapman, 2 vols. (Cambridge: Constable & Company; Houghton Mifflin, 1928), 2:33 [3 June 1787]. Note too Charles Burney to Hannah More, April 1799, in William Roberts, *Memoirs of the Life and Correspondence of Mrs. Hannah More,* 2d ed., 4 vols. (London, 1834), 3:73.

he warned, "we should have no other enjoyment than mere animal pleasure."[96] The cryptic conclusion depends on the belief that civilization itself depends on inequality, so the pursuit of equality would drive people back to some grisly state of nature. Social class and inequality were, "when well considered, the chief blessing we enjoy," agreed an anonymous publication.[97]

That social order is a matter of hierarchy and subordination seemed not an elaborate inference but a straightforward matter of fact. As the 1790s progressed and the news from France grew ever more surreal and bloodcurdling, conservatives triumphantly appealed to the evidence. "We know that English practice is good—we know that French theory is bad," held Arthur Young in *The Example of France a Warning to Britain,* appealing to "what all France experiences to be mischievous."[98] "What then must we think of that man, who wishes to destroy all kind of subordination, and to put each individual on one and the same level?" indignantly demanded An Oxford Graduate. "Ought he not to be treated with scorn and contempt, as an enemy to the happiness of mankind?"[99]

Those sympathetic to revolutionary aspirations, then, confronted cogent arguments. Didn't they believe the evidence of their senses? France had announced the rights of man and abolished aristocracy. Any fool could see what had ensued. Could the English Jacobins explain how social order might cohere with freedom and equality? Or were they just whistling in the dark, imprudently trying to topple long-established and successful practices in the name of a mere theory, of seductive principles "most pernicious to the tranquillity of society"?[100]

---

[96] Boswell, *Life,* 1:442 [20 July 1763]. See too *Life,* 2:219 [13 April 1773]; and compare *Boswell's London Journal 1762–1763,* ed. Frederick A. Pottle (New York: McGraw-Hill, 1950), p. 284 [25 June 1763].

[97] *Notes upon Paine's Rights of Man* (London, 1791), no. 5, pp. 14–15. See too *An Address to the Inhabitants of Great Britain and Ireland; in Reply to the Principles of the Author of the Rights of Man* (London, 1793), pp. 40–42.

[98] Arthur Young, *The Example of France a Warning to Britain,* 2d ed. (Bury St. Edmund's, 1793), pp. 69–70.

[99] An Oxford Graduate, *A Rod in Brine, or A Tickler for Tom Paine* (Canterbury, 1792), p. 2; see too p. 80.

[100] Daniel Mitford Peacock, *Considerations on the Structure of the House of Commons; and on the Plans of Parliamentary Reform Agitated at the Present Day* (London, 1794), p. 83.

## PRACTICES OF SUBJECTION

What sustained a culture of loyal deference? Not that deference is unnatural, whatever that might mean, or that special and opprobrious efforts are required to prevent people from lapsing into the preferred (by whom? and why?) state of skeptical cynicism or democratic agitation. Glib invocations of false consciousness paper over pressing explanatory problems: as though left-wing workers just got it right, but we need special theories explaining how right-wing workers were deceived; or as though radicals' thought is autonomous and rational, conservatives' thought manipulated and delusory. Similarly, we must beware thinking that Burke's prejudice, illusion, and veils summon up a nightmarish anti-utopia with cynical elites manipulating the beliefs of wide-eyed victims.[101]

James Oakes, a banker in Bury Saint Edmunds, was steeped in the proud traditions of staunch English loyalism. His diary records the anniversaries of Charles I's execution (or, as he calls it, his "Martyrdom"), the restoration of Charles II, and the gunpowder plot, a 1604–1605 Catholic scheme to blow up the Parliament building while Parliament was convened.[102] The government didn't require that these dates be privately noted. (Though, for the record, intermittently during George III's reign Parliament didn't meet on the anniversary of Charles's death; they did sometimes hear special sermons on that day.[103])

Nor did the government require that George III's birthday be celebrated. But in 1798, Oakes noted the elaborate proceedings: a parade of the city notables, his majesty's health toasted, local troops firing "3 excellent volleys," and three large dinners. "The Day passd off very pleasantly in all Company many loyal Tosts & constitutional Songs."[104] Some participants might have noticed that such celebrations would help instill loyalty in the broader population and would have chalked that up as an advantage. But is there any reason to think

[101] Helpful on these matters is Linda Colley, "The Apotheosis of George III," *Past & Present* (February 1984) no. 102, pp. 94–129.

[102] *The Oakes Diaries: Business, Politics and the Family in Bury St Edmunds 1778–1827*, ed. Jane Fiske, 2 vols. (Suffolk: Boydell Press, 1990), 1:341 [30 January 1797], 2:117 [29 May 1809], 2:244 [5 November 1819].

[103] *The Correspondence of George, Prince of Wales 1770–1812*, ed. A. Aspinall, 8 vols. (London: Cassell, 1963–1971), 7:191, 8:350; Sack, *From Jacobite to Conservative*, p. 127.

[104] *Oakes Diaries*, 1:364–65 [4 June 1798].

they understood the advantage as securing them a dutifully steady flow of rent payments and peaceful compliance? or that they understood their own loyalty in crassly instrumental terms, as a price worth paying or pretending to pay for a political establishment that had accorded them wealth and power? Couldn't Oakes and the other diners themselves have been genuinely loyal and have thought loyalty the right stance for everyone else, too? Weren't they? True, we inherit an interpretive tradition comically named "realism" that instructs us to unmask lofty principle and sentiment as a mask for base self-interest. But that seems contrived, even zany, in these contexts.

Now let's jump forward sixteen years to June 1814. Oakes noticed that it was time for the "Festival for the Poor" and that it happened to coincide with peace with France. Napoleon was off to Elba, the Bourbons back on the throne, and no one was expecting Napoleon to escape the next year, regain control of France, and reignite war. So there was a public dinner, funded by subscription of aristocrats and local notables. The bells started pealing early in the morning; by ten o'clock the town was "completely throngd." Oxen and roast and boiled beef were prepared a day or two ahead to be served cold. But plum puddings were served hot and there was good beer, too. In attendance were a whopping four thousand locals, some from the countryside as far as twenty miles away. The town alderman, sitting on an elevated platform, presided over the proceedings. There was another parade, with Napoleon in effigy. "The whole of the dinner," Oakes noted proudly, was "conducted with the greatest order & good management &, what was particularly to be remarkd, *the very lowest & poorest order of the people attended dressd neat & clean.*"[105]

I don't doubt that some came merely for free food and drink, that they scowled at the alderman, that they grumbled about the obscene and unjust wealth that enabled the notables to front such a lavish feast, that they found paternalism offensive, that any relief they felt at the end of the war had only to do with anxieties about taxes, poverty, and the impending loss of loved ones. But surely others were rejoicing at a national triumph, happy too for the experience of communal solidarity, flattered by the festival, dressed in their Sunday best and

[105] *Oakes Diaries,* 2:180–81 [17 June 1814]. See *The Diary of Joseph Farington,* ed. Kenneth Garlick, Angus Macintyre, and Kathryn Cave, 16 vols. (New Haven: Published for the Paul Mellon Centre for Studies in British Art by Yale University Press), 13:4534 for another well-dressed and orderly crowd at a 9 June 1814 celebration of peace.

scrubbed clean to express their respect for the occasion. And I do doubt the instinct to frame the first group as authentic or autonomous, the second as stupid victims. It's as easy—and as unhelpful—to cast grumbling radicals as impotent stooges of left-wing propaganda, grinning loyalists as clear-sighted political observers.

There are profound political stakes in the very staging of the event, let alone its reception. Like any other social ritual, it's vulnerable to disruption. Imagine the alderman's platform unceremoniously collapsing, an aristocrat's getting raucously drunk, or hundreds of people contracting food poisoning from the meat left out in the summer sun. (Or, to take an actual case: in 1821, Manchester celebrated the coronation of George IV. Tens of thousands of children marched; bands played music; hundreds of barrels of ale and the meat from twenty oxen and sixty sheep were handed out to the crowd. Then the festivities degenerated into drunken brawling; three died.[106]) But the difference between the day's successful performance and the imagined flop is not the difference between getting away with a con job and getting foiled.

Such celebrations were commonplace. In 1791, a poor baker recounted a celebration in the town of Sidmouth for the recovery of George III from one of his bouts of madness: the loaves (she baked 110 of them herself), the bullock, the sermon, the parade, everyone singing "God Save the King," a mass subscription for an illumination. She insisted on personal attachment to George, not just reverence for his office: "all because not so much for a being he was a King, but because they said as a was such a worthy Gentleman, & that the like of un was never known in this nation before. . . ." She recalled the tears of joy shed on the occasion—and she broke down crying again.[107] Are these crocodile tears? Are they signs of neurotic confusion? Or are they spontaneous signs of sincere emotion to be taken, despite all our jaded sophistication, very much at face value?

### A BIRMINGHAM MOB IN ACTION

What about popular political action in less sniffling, more alarming modes? Two days' rioting by a bellicose church-and-king mob in 1791

---

[106] *The Diaries of Absalom Watkin: A Manchester Man 1787–1861,* ed. Magdalen Goffin (Phoenix Mill: Alan Sutton, 1993), p. 51 [19 July 1821].

[107] *The Journals and Letters of Fanny Burney (Madame D'Arblay),* ed. Joyce Hemlow and others, 12 vols. (Oxford: Clarendon, 1972–1984), 1:27 [9 August 1791].

led to the emigration of Joseph Priestley, distinguished scientist, Unitarian minister and theologian, and radical. Burke would later complain in Parliament that Priestley was out to destroy the established church.[108] But Priestley was already infamous. Boswell eagerly repelled the horrible accusation that Dr. Johnson might have been interested even in talking to Priestley.[109] A week before the riots, one Anglican parson labelled Priestley an apostate.[110]

Priestley and some of his Dissenting friends planned to meet privately on 14 July, the anniversary of the taking of the Bastille, and celebrate the glorious event. In some accounts, "the Dissenters began drinking Treasonable Toasts—as Confusion to the present Government &c. . . ."[111] Priestley would later demur that he had little to do with the meeting.[112] Be that as it may, he was cast as the ringleader. A crowd of some five thousand assembled.[113] They burned the meeting house Priestley preached in, another meeting house, and moved on to burn Priestley's home. All his papers and scientific equipment were destroyed. Many others in Birmingham suffered, too. In the end, hundreds of thousands of pounds of property damage were done. His life in danger, Priestley fled to fight another day as any other intellectual would: in a couple of smarmy pamphlets.[114]

Radicals and Dissenters howled. William Hazlitt fired off a letter to a newspaper, wondering what had become of Christian charity and compassion.[115] One pamphleteer asserted that Priestley was "as peaceable a citizen as any in the community," including Burke.[116]

[108] "Speech on the Petition of the Unitarians," in *Works*, 7:49.

[109] Boswell, *Life of Johnson*, 4:238 n. 1.

[110] James Woodforde, *The Diary of a Country Parson*, ed. John Beresford, 5 vols. (London: Oxford University Press, 1926–1931), 3:283 [7 July 1791].

[111] *Thraliana: The Diary of Mrs. Hester Lynch Thrale (Later Mrs. Piozzi) 1776–1809*, ed. Katharine C. Balderston, 2d ed., 2 vols. (Oxford: Clarendon, 1951), 2:813 [16 July 1791].

[112] *Memoirs of Dr. Joseph Priestley, to the Year 1795, Written by Himself: with A Continuation, to the Time of His Decease, by His Son, Joseph Priestley: and Observations on His Writings, by Thomas Cooper . . . and the Rev. William Christie*, 2 vols. (London, 1806–1807), 1:118.

[113] *Letters on the Present State of England and America* (London, 1794), p. 92 [15 July 1791].

[114] Priestley, *An Appeal to the Public, on the Subject of the Riots in Birmingham*, 2d ed. (Birmingham, 1792); Priestley, *An Appeal to the Public, on the Subject of the Riots in Birmingham, Part II* (London, 1792).

[115] Hazlitt to the editor of the *Shrewbury Chronicle*, summer 1791, *The Letters of William Hazlitt*, ed. Herschel Moreland Sikes, assisted by Willard Hallam Bonner and Gerald Lahey (New York: New York University Press, 1978), pp. 57–59.

[116] A Welsh Freeholder, *Strictures on a Pamphlet, Entitled, Thoughts on the Late Riot at Birmingham* (London, 1791), p. 14.

Even apparently more impartial representatives of public opinion lined up behind Priestley. A London debating society decided overwhelmingly that the riots were the fault of Burke's *Reflections,* not any misbehavior by Priestley and his colleagues.[117]

Not all the establishment was amused, either. The Bishop of London regretted being reminded of the mobs of revolutionary France.[118] George III himself approved the order to call out troops to restore the peace.[119] Legal proceedings were launched against some of the principals in the mob.[120] Similarly, some loyalist commentators condemned the mob's actions. "What a horrid zeal for the church, and what a horrid Loyalty to Government have manifested themselves there!" protested Cowper.[121]

Then again, some loyalists thought that the rioters gave Priestley and his fellows just what was coming to them. Hester Piozzi, once a close friend of Dr. Johnson, exulted: "Their Zeal was flaming hot sure enough, & perverse in its Effects; but tis a good Spirit, & will cure the Taste these Madmen have gained for Revolutions better than any thing that could have happened."[122] Burke himself, Priestley would charge years later, was beside himself with joy: Priestley marvelled at the "peculiar malignity" of this display.[123] Still others suspected that the authorities were skulking in the background, happy to unloose this particular mob. "That this infuriated mob was originally instigated by somebody does not admit of a doubt," insisted one woman from a leading Dissenting family of the city.[124]

The authorities did in fact sometimes condone such mobs. (Such unsavory cooperation between state officials and local ruffians, endemic in modern politics, should refine Weber's dictum that the

---

[117] *London Debating Societies, 1776–1799,* comp. Donna T. Andrew (Great Britain: London Record Society, 1994), p. 310 [22 August 1791].

[118] Bishop Porteus to Hannah More, 1791, in Roberts, *Memoirs of Hannah More,* 2:294.

[119] George III to Henry Dundas, 17 July 1791, *The Later Correspondence of George III,* ed. A. Aspinall, 5 vols. (Cambridge: Cambridge University Press, 1962–1970), 1:551.

[120] *A Full and Accurate Report of the Trials of the Birmingham Rioters* (London, 1791).

[121] Cowper to John Newton, 22 July 1791, *Letters and Writings of Cowper,* 3:547.

[122] *Thraliana,* 2:813 [16 July 1791].

[123] Priestley to editor of *Monthly Magazine,* 1 February 1804, *Memoirs of Priestley,* 1:462.

[124] Catherine Hutton to Mrs. André, 25 August 1791, in *Reminiscences of a Gentlewoman of the Last Century: Letters of Catherine Hutton,* ed. Catherine Hutton Beale (Birmingham, 1891), p. 89.

modern state claims a monopoly on the legitimate use of force.) In December 1792, riots against parliamentary reform broke out in Manchester.[125] "Where were the friends of 'social order' during this destruction of property?" demanded one journalist. "They were there encouraging the drunken mob."[126] A modern historian agrees that this mob was managed by the authorities.[127] Or again, a June 1794 riot in Nottingham against those opposed to war with France met with the cheerful cooperation of the magistrates. The mayor was even spotted encouraging the rioters to break into others' homes.[128]

I don't know if the Birmingham rioters had reason to believe that the authorities would wink at their arson, let alone if they had official marching orders.[129] Even if they did, though, we should beware invoking such categories as marionettes and pawns, of thinking that the obliging mob was putty in the hands of the villainous elite. For this again is to dodge some pressing questions about agency: as if the mob were so pliable that they would do whatever the authorities wanted; as if there were no genuine resentment of Priestley, of Unitarianism, of affection for the French Revolution; as if leaders weren't routinely constrained by their putative followers. Even if the mob were marionettes, of course, even if they were casual enough to relish a summer day's brawl without worrying about the stakes, they could be culpable for allowing themselves to be used.

One Birmingham rioter landed in court for burning down a house. The indictment against him charged that he forgot the fear of God and was "seduced by the instigation of the devil"; the prosecution charged that "he committed this excess without the smallest provocation, without the smallest reason,—being actuated by frenzy,—I mean the frenzy of delusion."[130] Yet none of this language suggested to the government that he wasn't fully responsible for what he did

[125] For a contemporary account, see Thomas Walker, *A Review of Some of the Political Events Which Have Occurred in Manchester, during the Last Five Years* (London, 1794).

[126] Archibald Prentice, *Historic Sketches and Personal Recollections of Manchester* (London, 1851), p. 9.

[127] John Bohstedt, *Riots and Community Politics in England and Wales 1790–1810* (Cambridge, MA: Harvard University Press, 1983), chap. 5.

[128] Malcolm I. Thomis, *Politics and Society in Nottingham 1785–1835* (Oxford: Basil Blackwell, 1969), pp. 175–76.

[129] Consider the evidence adduced in R. B. Rose, "The Priestley Riots of 1791," *Past & Present* (November 1960) no. 18, pp. 78–82.

[130] *Full and Accurate Report of the Trials*, pp. 5, 7.

that day. In contemplating the political psychology of prejudice and illusion, we ought to remember the government's position.

Like the tearful celebrant of George III's recovery, then, like the prim diners at the Bury Saint Edmunds festival, the unruly mob out in the streets of Birmingham was expressing a kind of loyalism. So were the inhabitants of Sheffield who celebrated good news from the battlefields by firing their pistols into the windows of the town's democrats.[131] So we should treat loyalism with gingerly care.

### A Landscape Observed

One summer, a traveller set out to explore western England. Not quite forty, not yet a viscount, he made his way to Great Malvern. Later he would regret not exploring the area more intensively. It was home to the ruins of an abbey, "like other old grand, and religious houses, abandoned of comfort and peace, and affording shelter only to a wretched family,"[132] the kind of thing he found captivating through his travels. This time, contemplating the scene, he jotted down these verses:

> A tyrant monarch with rapacious hand
> Of greedy pow'r, usurped the Churches land;
> Rebellion follow'd next in spacious shew
> To give religion an o'erwhelming blow,
> With fiery zeal a Puritanic flood
> Deluged the state, and bathed the throne in blood.
> By glare and pomps the vulgar are confined,
> 'Tis those that gratify the human mind;
> 'Tis holy robes that swell the prelate great,
> And with his wig the judge would quit his state;
> For if the mystic veil be once withdrawn,
> The reverence were lost for sacred lawn,
> The law itself wou'd quickly be o'erthrown,
> And all its blunders, all its quibbles known.
> 'Twas awful mystery that link'd the band
> Of order, regulation, thro' the land;

---

[131] *Trial of Thomas Hardy,* 3:411.

[132] John Byng, *The Torrington Diaries,* ed. C. Bruyn Andrews, 4 vols. (London: Eyre & Spottiswoode, 1934–1938), 1:40 [29 June 1781].

That once dissolv'd, fair freedom went astray,
Lost and bewilder'd in the thorny way,
    From prudery, an harlot she became,
Of frantic liberty she took the name;
And like this ruin, with destructive haste,
Must sink (too soon!) a venerated waste.[133]

The crumbling landscape mirrors the crumbling political order. It's not just a contrived poetic device, but also another nod in the direction of that centuries-old model of social order. And here are Burke's stirring refrains, set to not entirely amateurish verse: the tyrant Henry VIII, the gruesome expropriation of church lands, the "mystic veil" and "awful mystery" safeguarding social order ripped and punctured, freedom itself perverted. But the young poet didn't have to read Burke's *Reflections* to produce this verse: he was travelling in 1781.

John Byng (to accord our traveller a name) didn't much like the great public celebrations that so appealed to James Oakes. He thought them a proud display of contempt for the poor. Better, he insisted, to give the poor more land or to donate warm clothes at Christmas than to squander wealth in a "Blaze of Riot ending in Drunkenness and Prostitution" and to create a desperate appetite for luxury.[134] Nor did he have much patience for Priestley, whose party he blamed for provoking the mob.[135] A stern paternalist, Byng was equally suspicious of aristocrats' profligate public displays and subjects' insurrectionary private talk.

But back to Great Malvern, where the abbey's ruins provoke a richly bitter line of thought. Once again misgivings surface about the Reformation, about the repulsive innovation giving birth to England's proud tradition of Protestantism. Not that Byng was any kind of crypto-Catholic. In the same verse he grants that "stern bigotry did long preside" in the once vibrant abbey.[136] Yet there's another pressing irony here. A stock contrast between free Protestant England and slavish Catholic Europe relied upon the right of Protestants to read Scripture themselves, in translation, and make up their own minds about its meaning.

[133] Byng, *Torrington Diaries*, 1:41 [29 June 1781]. In the tenth line, *with* must bear the sense of *without.*
[134] Byng, *Torrington Diaries*, 4:101–2 [30 May 1789].
[135] Byng, *Torrington Diaries*, 2:411 [19 July 1791].
[136] Byng, *Torrington Diaries*, 1:40 [29 June 1781].

So Burke's hatred of Henry, his nostalgia for the church of the fourteenth and fifteenth centuries, coalesces into his fondness of illusion and hatred of light. (I deliberately sidestep the question of how intentional the linkage is.) Burke's opponents gleefully exploited the point. *The Pernicious Effects of the Art of Printing upon Society, Exposed; A Short Essay, Addressed to the Friends of Social Order* was one of the many pamphlets cascading out of Daniel Isaac Eaton's radical shop in the 1790s. This one, mischievously signed by Antitype, is a mournful tirade on the course of history, pretending that printing and literacy have brought destruction in their wake. Contemporary readers recognizing Eaton's imprint immediately would have recognized the pamphlet as heavy-handed satire. Others eventually would have picked up on its mordant tone as a sign of irony. Even the slowest readers would have been jolted by this blow: "But for Printing, those two disturbers of the repose of society, and rascally innovators, Calvin and Luther, would never have been able to propagate their doctrines of Reform, as they audaciously called them—"[137]

Quite so. But that drives a threatening wedge into the structure of any loyally Protestant conservative position. When it comes to politics, subjects are to be docile, unthinking, automatically loyal. They are fit for no more. But when it comes to religion, subjects are to assume the heavy burdens of the priesthood of all believers. They are fit for no less. At least officially: but Anglican churchmen routinely worried about that and took it for granted that they should guide their parishioners, enabling Dissenting critics of the church to continue their time-honored gibes about its disturbing resemblance to the Roman Catholic Church. Here Protestant theology is tempered by political sensibilities.

## PANDORA'S BOX?

I want to juxtapose two passages I've already quoted. Recall the 1778 comment from Burke that I dismissed as an oddity, the sort of early enlightenment sentiment that he ruthlessly squelched after 1789: "Too little dependence cannot be had, at this time of day, on names and prejudices. The eyes of mankind are opened, and communities must be held together by an evident and solid interest." The later Burke sometimes sounds impassively assured that the cold sluggish-

---

[137] Antitype, *The Pernicious Effects of the Art of Printing upon Society, Exposed: A Short Essay Addressed to the Friends of Social Order* (London, 1793), p. 12.

ness and prejudices of his peers will preserve them from the jaundiced fever afflicting France. Already in 1779, in fact, he inverts his 1778 judgment: "A firm dependence is to be had upon ignorance and prejudice," he avers.

Those inclined to score points can chalk this up as a contradiction if they like. But we might also take it as a sign that Burke is wrestling with a dilemma. Sometimes he's edgy. Jacobinism, he frets, is "an attempt (hitherto but too successful) to eradicate prejudice out of the minds of men," and "there is no Rank or class, into which the Evil of Jacobinism has not penetrated. . . ."[138] Worse, the damage threatens to be irreversible: "If anything is . . . out of the power of man, it is to *create* a prejudice."[139] Here Burke's grand project threatens to collapse. The tranquilizing invocation of prejudice, of veils and illusion, itself may turn out to be a dangerous piece of obsolete wisdom, another carcass we idiotically embalm. Those adhering to it may need that stern injunction, "new things in a new world!"

Pandora's box was open, agreed a series of commentators. Their chorus had varied inflections, some anxious, some defiant, some ecstatic, some sarcastic. "When men have begun to think for themselves," cautioned Sir Brooke Boothby, "when they have carried their temerity of free-thinking perhaps so far as to suspect that nations may exist without monks or tyrants, it is already too late to burn libraries or philosophers."[140] "The mysterious art of state juggling is discovered," announced one pamphleteer smugly; "and however unwilling Mr. Burke may be to believe it, the French never will be ridden by kings or priests again."[141] "Those persons, if there be any such," agreed Southey, "who would keep the people ignorant because they rely upon their ignorance as a preservative, are not more lamentably erroneous in judgement than ignorant themselves of the state of society in which they live."[142] One Whig M.P. lampooned the sentiment:

[138] "Letter to William Smith, Esq., on Catholic Emancipation" [29 January 1795], in *Works*, 6:367; Burke to William Windham, 17 November 1795, *Correspondence*, 8:343.

[139] "Letter on Catholic Emancipation," in *Works*, 6:368.

[140] Sir Brooke Boothby, *Observations on the Appeal from the New to the Old Whigs, and on Mr Paine's Rights of Man* (London, 1792), p. 86 n.

[141] William Williams, *Rights of the People; or, Reasons for a Regicide Peace* (London, 1796), p. 28. See too Thomas James Mathias, *The Pursuits of Literature: A Satirical Poem in Four Dialogues*, 12th ed. (London, 1803), p. 244 [1797].

[142] Robert Southey, *Essays, Moral and Political*, 2 vols. (London, 1832), 1:120 [1812]. See too Southey to John Rickman, March 1813, *The Life and Correspondence of Robert Southey*, ed. Charles Cuthbert Southey, 6 vols. (London, 1849–1850), 4:28.

the vulgar "were happy and content when they looked up to the great ones of the earth, as beings of a superior order; but the pleasing delusion from whence they enjoyed so much felicity will quickly vanish. . . ."[143]

Other observers exuded a more easygoing confidence. The Birmingham Society for Constitutional Information asked ingenuously, "Now, if we have a good constitution, why fear a wise, cool, and deliberate investigation?"[144] Burke nonchalantly relegated such radical groups to the political sidelines as no more significant than half a dozen noisy grasshoppers.[145] But he wasn't always so serene in dismissing them.

Priestley, for instance, struck him as more of a threat. Never mentioned by name in the *Reflections,* he is very much on Burke's mind, bubbling up in metaphors about "the wild gas, the fixed air"[146] thanks to his work on oxygen and phlogiston, himself like Price a radical divine. In his own response to Burke, Priestley sounded calm tones about the developments plunging Burke into anguish. Imperturbably, maybe recklessly, he singled out the execution of Charles I, which Burke had tried desperately to obscure, for praise: it was "a *proud day* for England," just as the overthrow of the Bastille was a proud day for France.[147] (A couple of pamphleteers shrank in horror from this claim.[148]) Placidly, maybe mockingly, he offered his own ornate metaphors:

[143] John Courtenay, *Philosophical Reflections on the Late Revolution in France, and the Conduct of the Dissenters in England, in a Letter to the Rev. Dr. Priestley,* 2d ed. with additions (London, 1790), p. 46. For Courtenay's literary reputation as "a man of wit and satire," see *Diary & Letters of Madame D'Arblay,* ed. Charlotte Barrett, 6 vols. (London: Macmillan, 1904–1905), 4:404 [June 1790]; also Anna Seward to Courtenay, 17 May 1790, *Letters of Anna Seward,* 6 vols. (Edinburgh, 1811), 3:20–21; John Wolcot, *The Works of Peter Pindar, Esq.,* 4 vols. (London, 1797–1806), 1:250; David Rivers, *Literary Memoirs of Living Authors of Great Britain,* 2 vols. (London, 1798), 1:118–19.

[144] Birmingham Society for Constitutional Information, *Address* (Birmingham, 1792), p. 4.

[145] *Reflections,* in *Works,* 3:344; for a contemptuous dismissal of the Society for Constitutional Information, *Reflections,* in *Works,* 3:236–37.

[146] *Reflections,* in *Works,* 3:241.

[147] Joseph Priestley, *Letters to the Right Honourable Edmund Burke, Occasioned by His Reflections on the Revolution in France, &c.* (Birmingham, 1791), p. 48.

[148] *Considerations on Mr. Paine's Pamphlet on the Rights of Man* (Edinburgh, 1791), p. 47 n; Thomas Gould, *A Vindication of the Right Honorable Edmund Burke's Reflections on the Revolution in France, in Answer to All His Opponents* (London, 1791), in *Political Writings,* ed. Claeys, 7:106.

Prejudice and error is only a *mist*, which the sun, which has now risen, will effectually disperse. Keep them about you as tight as the country-man in the fable did his cloak; the same sun, without any more violence than the warmth of his beams, will compel you to throw it aside, unless you chuse to sweat under it, and bear the ridicule of all your cooler and less encumbered companions. The spirit of free and rational enquiry is now abroad, and without any aid from the powers of this world, will not fail to overturn all error and false religion, wherever it is found, and neither the church of Rome, nor the church of England, will be able to stand before it.[149]

Calm indeed: but is it magnificent poise? or dreadful irresponsibility? The passage might well seem to vindicate Burke's charge that Priestley was out to destroy the Church of England. That aside, wasn't he play-ing with fire? How did he and others remain resolute in the face of gory news from France? What did they imagine might maintain social order? What does this talk about the sun and free and rational enquiry amount to? What did Priestley and others imagine was replacing the rule of prejudice and illusion? If Pandora's box was open, what had slipped out?

[149] Priestley, *Letters to Burke,* pp. 111–12.

*TWO*

# OF COFFEEHOUSES AND
# SCHOOLMASTERS

———⁂———

Eighty years before the French Revolution, the *Tatler* touched on the widespread passion for politics. Perhaps the public-spirited could open a madhouse, suggested one of the perennially popular essays, and "apprehend forthwith any Politician whom they shall catch raving in a Coffee-house"; *politician* here means not a state official, but one interested in politics.[1] British subjects had contracted a "Touch in the Brain" by reading newspapers, another essay drily noted, just as Don Quixote had gone mad by reading works of chivalry.[2] The spectacle triggered perplexed drollery. Men and women were quarreling over abstruse issues of political theory; even "the very silliest of the Women" divided themselves into Whig and Tory.[3]

"Coffee-house Politicians," announced the *Spectator*, successor to the *Tatler*, suffered an "Eternal Thirst" because newspapers were so lamentably thin; they'd be better off reading full books.[4] Encountering "a Circle of Inferior Politicians" in one coffeehouse, the *Spectator* eavesdropped for a while on an arcane debate, but "with little Edification; for all I could learn at last from these honest Gentlemen was, that the Matter in Debate was of too high a Nature for such Heads as theirs, or mine, to Comprehend."[5]

[1] *Tatler* (24–26 January 1710) no. 125.
[2] *Tatler* (27–30 May 1710) no. 178. For the quixotic upholsterer and his passion for politics, *Tatler* (4–6 April 1710) no. 155, (15–18 April 1710) no. 160, (27–30 May 1710) no. 178, (30 September–3 October 1710) no. 232.
[3] *Tatler* (30 September–3 October 1710) no. 232.
[4] *Spectator* (8 August 1712) no. 452, in *The Spectator*, ed. Donald F. Bond, 5 vols. (Oxford: Clarendon, 1965), 4:91.
[5] *Spectator* (11 September 1712) no. 481, ed. Bond, 4:206.

A few decades later, Henry Fielding joined the refrain. Launching the *True Patriot*, he explained that because his sage bookseller had informed him that "no Body at present reads any thing but News-Papers, I have determined to conform myself to the reigning Taste."[6] He later printed a letter wondering at the shamelessness of those refusing to recognize the claims of political expertise: "in Politics," protested the writer (presumably Fielding himself), "every Man is an Adept; and the lowest Mechanic delivers his Opinion, at his Club, upon the deepest Public Measures, with as much Dignity and Sufficiency as the highest Member of the Commonwealth."[7]

Samuel Johnson kept it up in the next decade in an early *Idler.* "To us," writer here generously describing reader as polite and literate, "who are regaled every morning and evening with intelligence, and are supplied from day to day with materials for conversation, it is difficult to conceive how man can subsist without a news-paper" or what served to amuse people inhabiting "those wide regions of the earth" without newspapers.[8] Pretending to observe England through the eyes of a foreigner a few years later, Oliver Goldsmith reported that "every man here pretends to be a politician," the "universal passion for politics" depending on the highly unreliable information collected from coffee-house gossip.[9] (*Pretends* is a matter not of playacting but of adopting a pretension, with pretentiousness never far in the background.) That same year, Smollett assailed the disreputable malcontents—"desperate gamblers, tradesmen thrice bankrupt, prentices to journeymen, understrappers to porters, hungry pettifoggers"—who "publicly declaim upon politics, in coffee-houses," and dare to call themselves freeborn Englishmen.[10]

The next year, Chesterfield told his son that if he really wanted to know why the conference between King and the older Pitt had broken off, he would have to "ask the newsmongers, and the coffee-

[6] *True Patriot* (5 November 1745) no. 1, in Henry Fielding, *The True Patriot and Related Writings*, ed. W. B. Coley (Middletown, CT: Wesleyan University Press, 1987), p. 106.

[7] *True Patriot* (4–11 March 1746) no. 19, ed. Coley, p. 235.

[8] *Idler* (27 May 1758) no. 7, in *The Yale Edition of the Works of Samuel Johnson*, ed. Herman W. Liebert and others, in progress (New Haven, CT: Yale University Press, 1958–), 2:23.

[9] *The Citizen of the World* [1762], in Oliver Goldsmith, *Collected Works*, ed. Arthur Friedman, 5 vols. (Oxford: Clarendon, 1966), 2:29–30.

[10] *The Briton* (11 September 1762) no. 16, in Tobias Smollett, *Poems, Plays, and The Briton*, ed. O. M. Brack, Jr. (Athens, GA: University of Georgia Press, 1993), pp. 319–20.

houses," never hesitant to invent a story in the embarrassing absence of genuine knowledge.[11] In 1762, Boswell sat in Child's Coffee House and enjoyed the "society of citizens and physicians who talk politics very fully and are very sagacious and sometimes jocular."[12] In 1778, in one of his more dyspeptic moods, Boswell sat in a coffeehouse and read so many newspapers that he felt jaded.[13]

Walpole, wry about the foibles of newspapers, insisted that a future historian who depended on them would "write as fabulous a romance as Gargantua" or perhaps the *Arabian Nights*.[14] "Everybody knows they are stuffed with lies or blunders."[15] Wry too about parliamentary politics, in 1757 he thought "the House of Commons little better than a coffee-house."[16] By 1792 he had amended the view. Lords and Commons alike were "but the first coffee-houses of the day," their chatter giving the others stuff to chatter about.[17]

Coffeehouses, newspapers, people crazy about politics: these provide grist for the literary mill straight through the eighteenth century. In fact, London already had a lively coffeehouse scene in the seventeenth century.[18] Prominent too is a dour skepticism about mechanics who dare to frame and voice political views with aplomb. If we want to decipher fetching but mysterious claims about enlightenment, about sun clearing away mist and the like, we should direct our attention here. To put it polemically, a reconstruction of coffeehouse life offers far more of theoretical interest than a philosophical account of reason or ruminations on optimism about human nature.

---

[11] Chesterfield to his son, 1 September 1763, *The Letters of Philip Dormer Stanhope, 4th Earl of Chesterfield*, ed. Bonamy Dobrée, 6 vols. (London: Eyre and Spottiswoode, 1932), 6:2533.

[12] *Boswell's London Journal 1762–1763*, ed. Frederick A. Pottle (New York: McGraw-Hill, 1950), p. 74 [11 December 1762]. For Child's, see Bryant Lillywhite, *London Coffee Houses* (London: George Allen and Unwin, 1963), pp. 156–58.

[13] *Boswell in Extremes 1776–1778*, ed. Charles McC. Weis and Frederick A. Pottle (New York: McGraw-Hill, 1970), p. 220 [17 March 1778].

[14] Walpole to Horace Mann, 17 September 1788, *The Yale Edition of Horace Walpole's Correspondence*, ed. W. S. Lewis, 48 vols. (New Haven, CT: Yale University Press, 1937–1983), 24:412; Walpole to Lady Ossory, 4 November 1786, *Correspondence*, 33:536.

[15] Walpole to Hannah More, 4 July 1788, *Correspondence*, 31:267.

[16] Walpole to Horace Mann, 30 January 1757, *Corespondence*, 21:52.

[17] Walpole to Lady Ossory, 4 February 1792, *Corespondence*, 34:138.

[18] See, without footnotes, Aytoun Ellis, *The Penny Universities: A History of the Coffee-Houses* (London: Secker & Warburg, 1956); with footnotes, Steve Pincus, "'Coffee Politicians Does Create': Coffeehouses and Restoration Political Culture," *Journal of Modern History* (December 1995) 67:807–34.

That aside, there's a puzzle. If observers already had been noting these developments for some eighty years, why focus on the English reaction to the French Revolution? What's so special about the years 1789 to 1834? Two things, worth keeping in mind for understanding the sort of explanations I'm offering here. First, there were real changes in these years, changes of decisive political importance. Second, the Revolution heightened anxieties, threw things in bold relief, posed worrisome choices that preceding generations managed more easily to evade. The *Tatler*'s decorous ironies depended on the belief that those coffeehouse discussions were merely laughable, that nothing could come of them. But after the Revolution, it was harder to believe that. Heated political discussions, it became painfully (or exhilaratingly) clear, might well issue in hated revolutionary politics.

Goldsmith's line, routinely echoed, became a platitude: "Almost every man has become a politician," complained one 1794 volume, worried about newspapers fanning the flames of popular passion and rage replacing civility.[19] "All who read newspapers are politicians," agreed Southey in 1807.[20] Concerned in 1819 that even rural dwellers were afflicted with a "morbid appetite for politics," Evangelical M.P. and staunch Tory William Wilberforce deemed newspapers a terrible evil and confronted a body politic oozing "sour, morbid secretions, instead of the sweet and whole chyle of a healthful constitution."[21] It's not just that these writers themselves seem more uneasy about these longstanding facts than their predecessors, though that's true too. It's rather that regardless of their own degrees of equanimity or hysteria, their readers are more prone to sense that something dangerous is afoot. That sense is a key prerequisite of conservative politics.

The word *conservative*, for what it's worth, goes back as far as Chaucer.[22] Its specifically political meaning is traditionally assigned

---

[19] *Letters on the Present State of England and America* (London, 1794), p. 96 [1 August 1791]. See too *The Political Crisis: or, A Dissertation on the Rights of Man* (London, 1791), p. 72; "Public Political Meetings," in *The Universal Songster; or, Museum of Mirth,* 3 vols. (London, 1825–1826), 3:39.

[20] Robert Southey, *Letters from England* [1807], ed. Jack Simmons (London: Cresset Press, 1951), p. 347.

[21] William Wilberforce to Henry Bankes, 1819, in Robert Isaac Wilberforce and Samuel Wilberforce, *The Life of William Wilberforce*, 5 vols. (London, 1838), 5:47–48.

[22] *OED* s.v. *conservative*, adj. Throughout I have used the second edition of the *OED* on CD-ROM.

to an article by Tory politician John Wilson Croker in the January 1830 *Quarterly Review:* "We are, as we always have been, decidedly and conscientiously attached to what is called the Tory, and which might with more propriety be called the Conservative, party"; perhaps some party members resisted all change, but most thought a "prudent and practicable amelioration of the state" desirable.[23] In fact, in summoning up the struggle that would accompany a necessary reform of the poor laws, the *Quarterly* already had referred in 1818 to "the destructive and conservative principles in society, the evil and the good, the profligate against the respectable,"[24] and I've encountered other earlier usages. In 1799, Coleridge reported on the new "Conservative Senate" of France.[25] In 1800, John Bowles wistfully recalled "that conservative pride of character" that once had led women to spurn fallen women.[26] In 1816, the *Anti-Jacobin Review* thought that admirers of Burke should realize that Pitt's principles were "those conservative principles which all good men ought not passively to foster and cherish," but actively to promote.[27] In an 1818 speech, George Canning, future prime minister, referred affectionately to property as "the conservative principle of society" in explaining why he would never provoke the nation with complaints about "incurable imperfections" or tantalize them with visions of "imaginary and unattainable excellencies. . . ."[28] A couple of months later, Southey found his faith in "the conservative principles of society" strengthened by reading Claren-

[23] *Quarterly Review* (January 1830) 42:276.

[24] *Quarterly Review* (January 1818) 18:304. This article was by Southey: Hill Shine and Helen Chadwick Shine, *The Quarterly Review under Gifford: Identification of Contributors 1809–1824* (Chapel Hill, NC: University of North Carolina Press, 1949), p. 59. See too John Weyland, *The Principles of Population and Production* (London, 1816; reprint ed. London: Routledge/Thoemmes Press, 1994), p. 232.

[25] *Essays on His Times*, in *The Collected Works of Samuel Taylor Coleridge*, ed. Kathleen Coburn, Bart Winer, and others, in progress (Princeton, NJ: Princeton University Press, 1969–), 3(1):52 [27 December 1799]. In 1813, thanks to the indefatigable efforts of the constitution-mongering Sieyès, William Cobbett reported on the new "conservative Senate" of France: *Political Register* (24 April 1813) 23(17):638.

[26] John Bowles, *Reflections at the Conclusion of the War* (London, 1800), in *Political Writings of the 1790s*, ed. Gregory Claeys, 8 vols. (London: William Pickering, 1995), 8:405.

[27] *Anti-Jacobin Review* (June 1816) 50:553.

[28] *The Speeches of the Right Honourable George Canning*, ed. R. Therry, 6 vols. (London, 1828), 6:365 [29 June 1818]. The radical *Gorgon* (18 July 1818) no. 9, p. 68 seized on this claim.

don, adviser to Charles I.[29] One can quibble about the meaning of some of these early instances—I don't know what the exotically radical Society of Spencean Philanthropists meant in establishing a "Conservative Committee" in 1816[30]—but it matters that these are the years in which the word gains its now familiar political sense.

Then again, the word isn't anywhere in Burke either (or at least I haven't noticed it). That doesn't mean that we should refuse in the name of historical fidelity to call him a conservative. More generally, people may have a concept without having a word for it; or a concept may correctly apply to them even if it's not at their disposal. So we may ask if Hume was a conservative or for that matter if Aristophanes was: recall that democratic merchant hawking laws in the marketplace, the nostalgia for the days when Athenian men loved dignified Aeschylus and not decadent Euripides, when they exercised, when homosexual relationships were more modest. I have no objections to such enquiries. But they depend on our commanding a reasonably clear account of conservatism. And surely examining the political struggles in which people self-consciously forged the word is a prudent strategy for advancing our command of the concept.

But back to those coffeehouses.

### The Case of the Silent Coffeehouses

Sure you all must agree, that the world's epitome
  May be found in the London newspapers;
Why, from parts far and wide, we have news, ev'ry tide,
  Of all the grand fetes and rum capers.
In the coffee-room met, what a queer looking set,
  With their spectacles placed on their noses;
Politicians a score, o'er the pages how they pore,
  And devour the strange news it discloses—
    Electioneering, privateering—
    Auctioneering, volunteering—

---

[29] Southey to John Rickman, 1 September 1818, *Selections from the Letters of Robert Southey*, ed. John Wood Warter, 4 vols. (London, 1856), 3:95. Compare Southey, *The Book of the Church*, 2 vols. (London, 1824), 1:98.

[30] Malcolm Chase, *The People's Farm: English Radical Agrarianism 1775–1840* (Oxford: Clarendon, 1988), pp. 93–94.

Revolution, execution—
Hanging, dying, wedding, trying—
Haut-ton, crim. con.—
In business who wins and who loses.[31]

So opened one rollicking popular song. In 1791, a German resident
of London published a travel guide for those on the continent. He
estimated that London alone then had three thousand coffeehouses,
compared to a mere six or seven hundred in Paris. (An 1817 observer
thought London had just five hundred coffeehouses.[32] I doubt the
market was collapsing, though perhaps there had been some tempor-
ary consolidation: a parliamentary committee was informed in 1840
that there were eighteen hundred London coffeehouses where an
artisan could grab a good breakfast.[33]) He warned his readers that
they would find the locals hunched over newspapers, diligently reading. "Turbulent noise and loud talking are not to be heard": so wasn't
it tedious? Well, he conceded, he had thought so himself, but once he
mastered the details of English politics he gained the knack of
tirelessly reading long newspapers.[34]

Foreign observers found the quiet remarkable. "Quietness is the
rule," reported one, so much so that a clergyman could stop by to
prepare his sermon on the way to church.[35] Another was reminded
unpleasantly of attending a Quaker meeting.[36] "No voice rises above a
low whisper," reported a third.[37] Similarly, when the English artist
Joseph Farington made a foray to Ireland in 1795, he was struck by
the "boisterous, noisy & unceremonious" coffeehouses of Dublin.[38]

[31] "The London Newspapers," *Universal Songster,* 3:230.

[32] David Hughson, *Walks through London* (London, 1817), p. 2.

[33] Charles Knight, *Passages of a Working Life during Half a Century: with A Prelude of
Early Reminiscences,* 3 vols. (London, 1864–1865), 2:272.

[34] Fred. Aug. Wendeborn, *A View of England towards the Close of the Eighteenth Century,*
trans. the author, 2 vols. (London, 1791), 1:305–7.

[35] Carl Philip Moritz, *Journeys of a German in England in 1782,* trans. and ed. Reginald
Nettel (New York: Holt, Rinehart and Winston, 1965), p. 72 [17 June 1782].

[36] C. A. G. Goede, *The Stranger in England; or, Travels in Great Britain,* 3 vols. (London,
1807), 1:75; see too 2:89.

[37] Erik Gustaf Geijer, *Impressions of England 1809–1810,* trans. Elizabeth Sprigge and
Claude Napier (London: Jonathan Cape, 1932), p. 119 [1809].

[38] *The Diary of Joseph Farington,* ed. Kenneth Garlick, Angus Macintyre, and Kathryn
Cave, 16 vols. (New Haven, CT: Published for the Paul Mellon Centre for Studies in
British Art by Yale University Press, 1978–1984), 2:396 [1 November 1795].

In Paris in 1802, he encountered a coffeehouse for foreigners marked, *"without noise."*[39]

The coffeehouses remained silent in later decades. Hoping to relax over newspapers and tea, whimsical Doctor Syntax was rudely surprised when he entered one coffeehouse: "So far from finding social quiet, / The room itself was in a riot. . . ."[40] When William Lovett opened a coffeehouse in 1834, he paid his respects to tradition by using two separate rooms, "to separate the talkers from the readers." The conversation room hosted debates, classes, and public readings. The coffee and reading room featured many radical periodicals and several hundred books to boot.[41] Lovett later gained fame as one of the leaders of the Chartist movement; he was already on the left and advertised his coffeehouse in the scrupulously radical *Poor Man's Guardian*. Even radical workers, then, expected their coffeehouses to provide a tranquil site for reading.

The demand for newspapers turned coffeehouses into libraries. Eager to check on newspaper coverage of the Royal Academy in 1805, a concerned Farington headed over to Peck's Coffee House and ransacked the files, where he found an offending paragraph in four daily papers but no evening paper.[42] By 1824, Peel's and the Chapter Coffee House featured extensive collections of London and provincial newspapers going back some years along with monthly and quarterly reviews.[43] The next year, poet Thomas Moore was working on his biography of Richard Brinsley Sheridan. In need of a nine-year-old article from the *Morning Post,* he dutifully trooped over to Peel's.[44] The practice seems not to have been the specialty of a couple of London coffeehouses, but fairly common for some time. By the later years

[39] *Diary of Farington,* 5:1864 [20 September 1802].

[40] William Combe, *The Second Tour of Doctor Syntax, in Search of Consolation* (London, 1820), pp. 179–80.

[41] William Lovett, *Life & Struggles of William Lovett in His Pursuit of Bread, Knowledge, and Freedom* [1876], intro. R. H. Tawney (London: G. Bell and Sons, 1920), pp. 89–90; *Poor Man's Guardian* (25 January 1834) 2(138):452, (1 February 1834) 2(139):460.

[42] *Diary of Farington,* 7:2575 [17 June 1805], 7:2583 [1 July 1805].

[43] *Real Life in London; or, The Rambles and Adventures of Bob Tallyho, Esq. and His Cousin, the Hon. Tom. Dashall, through the Metropolis,* 2 vols. (London, 1824), 1:387. Despite ripping off Pierce Egan's characters and his breezy writing style, this book isn't by Egan: see J. C. Reid, *Bucks and Bruisers: Pierce Egan and Regency England* (London: Routledge & Kegan Paul, 1971), p. 74.

[44] *The Journal of Thomas Moore,* ed. Wilfred S. Dowden and others, 6 vols. (Newark: University of Delaware Press, 1983–1991), 2:830–31 [7 September 1825].

of the eighteenth century, in fact, coffeehouses bulging with
newspapers were to be found outside London, catering to—and
inflaming—the passion for politics. In 1777, one Birmingham coffeehouse advertised that an express messenger from London enabled it
to provide eleven London newspapers by two o'clock the day after
they were published, along with a variety of rural and Irish newspapers, a foreign paper, parliamentary and legal proceedings, and
more.[45] One Manchester coffeehouse in 1833 offered ninety-six different newspapers.[46]

This evidence suggests, contrary to legend, that coffeehouses were
quiet, even funereal. I don't want to overstate the point. No doubt the
foreigners in England, just like Farington abroad, were groping for a
way to express their sense of cultural dislocation and seizing on hyperbole. One wonders, too, about the clergyman who would dare to be
seen sitting in a coffeehouse on Sunday morning, let alone jauntily
composing his sermon right before delivering it. Similarly, there's evidence that people still talked in coffeehouses, just as the *Tatler,* the
*Spectator,* Smollett, and the rest had reported in the preceding decades. Describing the convenience of life in London, one essayist
wrote, "Provided a man has a clean shirt and three pence in his
pocket, he may talk as loud in the coffee-house as the 'squire of ten
thousand pounds a year."[47] In 1831, Francis Place was delighted to
learn the details of Lord John Russell's plan for parliamentary reform. Eager to circulate the information, he turned to the local coffeehouses. "It spread like wild fire, to great distances," he recorded
happily; within an hour of the close of Russell's speech, the whole city
knew the news.[48]

[45] John Money, *Experience and Identity: Birmingham and the West Midlands 1760–1800*
(Montreal: McGill—Queen's University Press, 1977), pp. 102, 118 n. 24. I presume this
is the same coffeehouse (it's on the same street, anyway) that William Hutton, *An
History of Birmingham,* 2d ed. (Birmingham, 1783; reprint ed. Wakefield: EP Publishing,
1976), p. 129 notes: "Drawing into its vortex the transactions of Europe, [it] finds
employment for the politician." Oddly, Thomas Newte, *Prospects and Observations; on a
Tour in England and Scotland* (London, 1791), p. 10, claims that people in Birmingham
have been unable to establish a coffeehouse. See too *The Trial of Thomas Hardy for High
Treason,* rep. Joseph Gurney, 4 vols. (London, 1794–1795), 3:226.

[46] E. P. Thompson, *The Making of the English Working Class* (New York: Vintage Books,
1966), p. 718.

[47] Francis Grose, *The Olio* (London, 1792), p. 207. See too Elizabeth Hamilton,
*Translation of the Letters of a Hindoo Rajah; Written Previous to, and during the Period of His
Residence in England,* 2 vols. (London, 1796), 2:70–71.

[48] *London Radicalism 1830–1843: A Selection from the Papers of Francis Place,* ed. D. J.
Rowe (London: London Record Society, 1970), p. 13 [1 March 1831]. Consider too *Mr.*

Still, the evidence on quiet shouldn't be dismissed. So perhaps we could learn to recall that there were plenty of places for people to talk politics besides those notorious coffeehouses, to relax the relentless hold that the coffeehouse has exercised on our historiographical and sociological imaginations. For now, consider alehouses and debating societies.

### "MEETINGS OF HALF-DRUNK MECHANICKS . . . CONVENED TO PASS JUDGMENT"[49]

The tongues of alehouse politicians were loosened by alcohol, not quickened by caffeine. Alehouses, too, were the preserve of male workers: genial affection for their saucy vulgarity is one thing; frightened resentment at their donning the mantle of citizenship is another.[50] Southey cast a baleful eye at these alehouse proceedings. "The journalist poisons the minds of the populace with his weekly dose of sedition, while the distiller is poisoning their livers with ardent spirits. . . ." Picture the setting, he implored: the crackling fire, a day's hard labor done, camaraderie, and the harmful brew furnish a tantalizing opportunity "to the weekly epistles of the apostles of sedition": the workers' "pores are open, and the whole infection is taken in."[51] "Every pot-house also is supplied with the Sunday papers,— doses of weekly poison," Southey wrote to his brother in anguish; "one reader serves for a tap-room full of open-mouthed listeners, and the consequence is, that at this moment the army is the single plank between us and destruction."[52] Southey wrote this letter the day after the prime minister, Spencer Perceval, was assassinated. Perhaps his assassin was insane or was pursuing some obscure private grievance;

---

*Joseph Southcott, the Brother of Joanna Southcott, Will Now Come Forward as Dinah's Brethren Did* (London, 1804), pp. 10–11.

[49] Cuthbert Collingwood to Walter Spencer-Stanhope, 10 July 1805, in A. M. W. Stirling, *The Letter-Bag of Lady Elizabeth Spencer-Stanhope,* 2 vols. (London: John Lane, The Bodley Head, 1913), 1:60–61.

[50] For an assault on alehouses that is sympathetic to the problems they created for wives, see *A New and Diverting Dialogue, Both Serious and Comical, That Passed the Other Day between a Noted Shoemaker and His Wife* (London, 1770).

[51] Southey, *Essays, Moral and Political,* 2 vols. (London, 1832), 1:186–87 [1816]; note too 1:303–4 [1816].

[52] Southey to Capt. Southey, 12 May 1812, *Letters,* ed. Warter, 2:272. Note too the assessment of the Sunday papers in James Savage, *An Account of the London Daily Newspapers, and the Manner in Which They Are Conducted* (London, 1811), p. 21.

still, there was the disturbing matter of outbursts of popular ap-
proval.[53] Others too worried in the ensuing weeks.[54] It's easy enough
in hindsight to say they overreacted: I leave their apparently extravagant views aside so that I can continue tracing "the intoxicating poisons of the revolutionary press."[55]

Workers banded together in clubs, some more formal than others,
and met in alehouses to talk about politics. One churchman catalogued
the rise of "Revolution Clubs," figuring they meant the onset of riots
and worse.[56] Other conservatives were unhappy, too, pondering the
malignant example of France's Jacobin Clubs.[57] In 1802, the *Leeds
Mercury* printed a letter musing over such nightly meetings: "Almost
every street in a large town has a little senate of this description; and the
priviledges of sitting in council over the affairs of the nation, and a pot
of porter has long been claimed by free Britons. . . ."[58] Free Britons,
not lowly subjects: here again, there's an assumption of the cultural
baggage of citizenship without the legal trappings of the franchise.

I don't want too much to hang on the word *citizenship*. In 1833, the
*Bristol Job Nott,* that folksy newspaper dispensing soothing conservative
bromides, ecstatically saluted a petition signed by ten thousand males
"for the better observance of the Sabbath": "Then what will become
of the *beer houses,* with all their demoralizing apparatus of infidel and
seditious publications, &c.? There are ten thousand good citizens
who have declared open war against them," holding, the paper de-

[53] Geoffrey Carnall, *Robert Southey and His Age: The Development of a Conservative Mind*
(Oxford: Clarendon, 1960), pp. 141–47.

[54] Thomas Moore to James Power, 23 May 1812, *The Letters of Thomas Moore,* ed.
Wilfred S. Dowden, 2 vols. (Oxford: Clarendon, 1964), 1:189; Walter Scott to Robert
Southey, 4 June 1812, *The Letters of Sir Walter Scott,* ed. H. J. C. Grierson, 12 vols. (Lon-
don: Constable & Co., 1932–1937), 3:125–26.

[55] *Quarterly Review* (December 1832) 48:548 n.

[56] James Woodforde, *The Diary of a Country Parson,* ed. John Beresford, 5 vols. (London: Oxford University Press, 1926–1931), 3:389 [24 November 1792], 3:390 [28 November 1792]; more cheerfully, 3:400 [29 December 1792].

[57] *The Friend* [1818], in *Works of Coleridge,* 4(1):447; William Playfair, *The History of
Jacobinism, Its Crimes Cruelties and Perfidies,* 2 vols. (Philadelphia, 1796), 1:150–60; *Buck
Whaley's Memoirs,* ed. Edward Sullivan (London: Alexander Moring Ltd, 1906),
pp. 279–80. For a recent treatment of France's Jacobin Clubs, see Michael L. Kennedy,
*The Jacobin Clubs in the French Revolution: The First Years* (Princeton, NJ: Princeton Uni-
versity Press, 1982), and Kennedy, *The Jacobin Clubs in the French Revolution: The Middle
Years* (Princeton, NJ: Princeton University Press, 1988).

[58] Quoted in Roger Wells, *Insurrection: The British Experience 1795–1803* (Gloucester:
Alan Sutton, 1983), p. 52.

clared approvingly, that they ruined families, principles, even souls.[59] Possibly the word *citizen* is accidentally invoked here. More likely it's subversively deployed: a real citizen, the paper suggests, or, better, a citizen of the sort worth approving, crusades for the Sabbath and spurns intoxicated political discussion.

Richard Carlile wished that workers would stay at home with intellectually cultivated wives instead of heading off to alehouses. "These ale-house politics and politicians are never good for anything," he insisted. "The multiplicity of ale-houses in this Island sadly deteriorates the national character." The lament sounds suspiciously like that of the *Bristol Job Nott*. But Carlile had no particular regard for the Sabbath. A republican radical and spirited atheist, an admirer of Tom Paine, he was all for citizenship.[60] He doubted only that vigorous public debate would produce more rational political views. So he continued his tirade against alehouses by explaining that "in public boisterous assemblies there is no mental deliberation, no calm discussion; and it would be well if every question was previously stated, and privately deliberated upon, and that the men should assemble in public but to give their voice."[61]

Compare the young and quirky Coleridge's scornful address to a "Good Citizen." This citizen, we learn, is a would-be radical, fond of Godwin's *Enquiry Concerning Political Justice,* that pudgy handbook of philosophical anarchism. He's hypocritical enough to rail against the slave trade but consume sugar, thus supporting the slaveholders of Jamaica; to blame economic scarcity on war but wear powder in his hair, thus wasting valuable flour and fattening the tax coffers. Coleridge is scathing, denying this citizen's claims to be any sort of patriot. "You talk loudly and rapidly," he jeers; "you like victory in an argument; you are the tongue-major of every company; therefore you love a Tavern better than your own fire-side." No real patriot would "get drunk on claret, and . . . frequent public dinners"; any real patriot would spurn Godwin's licentious philosophy and turn to a bracing Christianity.[62] Here *citizen* is handled ironically, even abusively, and the focus is a contest over what it means to be a patriot: that is, not

---

[59] *Bristol Job Nott* (7 March 1833) no. 65, pp. 257–58.

[60] Note Carlile's reverential *Life of Thomas Paine, Written Purposely to Bind with His Writings* (London, 1820).

[61] *Republican* (8 February 1822) 5(6):177–78.

[62] *The Watchman* (17 March 1796) no. 3, in *Works of Coleridge,* 2:98–100.

over the best dictionary entry for the meaning of the word, but over
how best to realize the abstract ideal of love of country. That ideal,
holds Coleridge, is travestied by getting sloshed in an alehouse and
railing against the authorities.

So the political disagreements here run very deep. Why were
workers devoted to alehouses turning their attention to politics? What
did it mean? One writer blamed the endless political complaints of
"every cobler or tinker, as he quaffs his can of beer at the ale-house"
on the overheated political contest between Pitt and Fox. Those two
were no better than baboons seizing fruit wherever it could found, no
better than prostitutes embracing whoever would pay them, opportunistically adopting and discarding lofty principles. This shameless
lack of integrity made them laughable candidates for deference and
so emboldened or even excused the alehouse critics.[63]

In 1819, the magistrates of Dudley issued a warning, or, better, a
threat. They had learned that at the local alehouses, "SEDITIOUS PA-
PERS are taken in, for the purpose of poisoning the minds of the
ignorant and unwary," so they reminded the publicans that their
business could be closed down "*at any time*" and would be unless they
stopped taking in such publications.[64] 1830 changes in the licensing
procedures for alehouses meant that publicans no longer needed to
fear the disapproving glare of local officials: once the Excise granted
the right to sell alcoholic beverages, they were in business.[65] Still,
whatever the supply of newspapers and pamphlets, whatever the controversies over citizenship and patriotism, the alehouses provided a
lively, even rowdy, setting for working-class political debate. "Every
alehouse resounded with the brawls of contending politicians,"
wrote Walter Scott in portraying the early eighteenth-century setting
of *Rob Roy*.[66] Some contemporary readers would have cheered,
some would have shuddered, but they all would have nodded in
recognition.

[63] Donald Campbell, *A Letter to the Marquis of Lorn, on the Present Times* (London,
1798), pp. 18–19. More sympathetically, see Robert W. Malcolmson, *Popular Recreations
in English Society 1700–1850* (Cambridge: Cambridge University Press, 1973), p. 72.

[64] A. Aspinall, *Politics and the Press c. 1780–1850* (London: Home & Van Thal, 1949),
p. 44 n. 2.

[65] Patricia Hollis, *The Pauper Press: A Study in Working-Class Radicalism of the 1830s*
(London: Oxford University Press, 1970), p. 38.

[66] Walter Scott, *Rob Roy* [1818], in *Waverley Novels*, 48 vols. (Edinburgh, 1829–1833),
7:56.

## DEBATING SOCIETIES

We've already met the London debating society that decided that Burke, not Priestley, was to blame for the Birmingham riots. London boasted as many as thirty-five different debating societies in 1780. By the 1790s, though, there were only a handful.[67] By 1830, one observer could dismiss them as an obsolete fashion.[68] But in fact at least radicals in the city were still running debating societies.[69]

These societies offered public discussion on set controversial topics. After paid speakers did their best to argue either side of the topic, the audience participated in discussion. Then they would vote. Some of the topics, even the fact of public discussion itself, struck observers as inflammatory. A jittery Southey, once again monitoring the nation's fevered pulse, erupted at the "apostles of anarchy and atheism at debating clubs."[70] More judiciously, one overview of London worried that the debating society had become "a theatre of licentious discussion" instead of a useful and amusing institution.[71] Other observers were more facetious. One described the British Forum as a place to train "mercers, men-milliners, and managing clerks . . . for the bar, the pulpit, and the senate." Any garrulous man could be a speaker, but the requirements for being chair were more daunting: not just clean clothes, but especially desirable was a huge pair of beetling eyebrows with which to scorn those speaking too long.[72]

Consider some of the topics discussed. In 1789, the audience at City Debates listened to discussion on whether Britain's interests permitted the abolition of the slave trade and on whether Dissenters sought relief from their legal disabilities out of patriotism or ambition.[73] Birmingham's Society for Free Debate proposed a discussion

[67] *London Debating Societies, 1776–1799,* comp. Donna T. Andrew (Great Britain: London Record Society, 1994), p. x n. 9.

[68] *Reminiscences of Henry Angelo,* 2 vols. (London, 1830), 2:112.

[69] Iain McCalman, *Radical Underworld: Prophets, Revolutionaries and Pornographers in London, 1795–1840* (Cambridge: Cambridge University Press, 1988), pp. 89–90, 139–41, and generally chap. 6.

[70] Robert Southey, *The Life of Wesley; and The Rise and Progress of Methodism,* 2 vols. (London, 1820), 1:401.

[71] William Henry Pyne and William Combe, *The Microcosm of London,* 3 vols. (London, 1808–1811), 1:224.

[72] Pindar Minimus, *Little Odes to Great Folks* (London, 1808), pp. 35–36 n. The notes are by one Sextus Scriblerus.

[73] *London Debating Societies,* p. 259 [18 May 1789].

of whether Brutus should have killed Caesar. The date, October 1792, was just about three months before Louis XVI headed off to the guillotine, and magistrates squelched further discussion.[74] In 1810, the British Forum wondered if John Gale Jones deserved his prison sentence for vigorously criticizing powerful M.P. Castlereagh (who would later slit his own throat).[75] In 1819, at the Hopkins Street Chapel, Robert Wedderburn, radical mulatto son of a Jamaica planter, urged the affirmative in a debate on whether slaves had the right to kill their masters. The handbill advertising this event promised further debates two nights every week. A churchman spying on the proceedings informed the government that contemptible as the likes of Wedderburn were, they still were corrupting the lower orders.[76]

Religion, too, was discussed. In 1794, the Westminster Forum scrutinized the claims of millenarian prophet Richard Brothers.[77] In 1796, the London Forum mulled over the vexing image of the whore of Babylon in the book of Revelations: did it refer to the church of Rome? or "the Mahometan Church"? or infidelity? or Tom Paine himself?[78] These topics might seem quaint, even cute, and entirely reassuring. But religious disputes could be more menacing. In 1819, the Hopkins Street Chapel witnessed a debate on whether the Bible was the word of God.[79] In 1831, the Philadelphian Chapel was regularly reserving Thursday evenings for "Theological Debate, and especially for examining the claims of a certain Book to infallibility," so offering support for those fearing the unholy nexus between political discussion and atheism.[80]

Unsavory workers may have haunted Wedderburn's Hopkins Street Chapel, but the debating societies attracted audiences more diverse than alehouse patrons. Doctors attended discussions of vaccination, the world of "elegance, beauty and fashion" turned out for more nar-

[74] Robert K. Dent, *Old and New Birmingham: A History of the Town and Its People*, 3 vols. (Birmingham, 1879; reprint ed. Yorkshire: EP Publishing, 1972–1973), 2:315.

[75] J. Ann Hone, *For the Cause of Truth: Radicalism in London 1796–1821* (Oxford: Clarendon, 1982), p. 198.

[76] Robert Wedderburn, *The Horrors of Slavery and Other Writings*, ed. Iain McCalman (Edinburgh: Edinburgh University Press, 1991), pp. 113, 117.

[77] *London Debating Societies*, p. 329 [28 October 1794].

[78] *London Debating Societies*, p. 350 [28 November 1796].

[79] David Worrall, *Radical Culture: Discourse, Resistance and Surveillance, 1790–1820* (New York: Harvester Wheatsheaf, 1992), p. 166; more generally on the Hopkins Street Chapel in 1819, see pp. 165–86.

[80] *Poor Man's Guardian* (3 September 1831) 1(9):72.

rowly political topics, and men and women alike considered the old claim from poet Alexander Pope that every woman is at heart a rake.[81] More vocal than the coffeehouse, less boisterous than the alehouse, the debating society might seem a civil or even exquisitely chaste locale for democratic discussion. But again, some observers recoiled. Take the *Anti-Jacobin Review:* "The debating societies, which, to the eternal shame of the police be it spoken, have been suffered to propagate the most seditious and mischievous notions among the lower classes of people in the metropolis, and its vicinity, without let or molestation, have dared to propose some discussions of a most dangerous and inflammatory nature."[82]

Political talk had the untoward habit of bursting out in the unlikeliest places. Even Friendly Societies, voluntary community organizations devoted to aiding the needy, found themselves in the grips of political debate.[83] Perhaps those vicious Jacobins deliberately were infiltrating charitable groups to foment discord.[84] I want now to shift my attention to readers and reading, to resurrect the shadowy world of newspapers, pamphlets, and the rest. Where did people read? Who could read? What did they read?

## CIRCULATING LIBRARIES

In Sheridan's *The Rivals,* crusty Sir Anthony Absolute seethes that women have been taught to read. He admonishes hapless Mrs. Malaprop: "I observed your niece's maid coming forth from a circulating library!—She had a book in each hand—they were half-bound volumes, with marble covers!—From that moment I guess'd how full of duty I should see her mistress!" Managing for once not to stumble over her tongue, Mrs. Malaprop agrees: "Those are vile places, indeed!" This tidbit of encouragement provokes a jeremiad linking female literacy to illicit sexuality: "Madam, a circulating library in a town is, as an ever-green tree, of diabolic knowledge!—It

---

[81] *Microcosm of London*, 2:4–5.

[82] *Anti-Jacobin Review* (May 1810) 36:106.

[83] Frederic Morton Eden, *The State of the Poor,* 3 vols. (London, 1797; reprint ed. Bristol: Thoemmes Press, 1994), 1:631, 3:889. On the societies, see Eden, *Observations on Friendly Societies, for the Maintenance of the Industrious Classes, during Sickness, Infirmity, Old Age, and Other Exigencies* (London, 1801).

[84] W. Massey, *Hints, Relative to Mr. Owen Jones's Charity, or Serious Reflections, in Consequence of a Letter from J. Bramwell* (Chester, 1801), pp. 22–23.

blossoms through the year!—And depend on it, Mrs. Malaprop, that they who are so fond of handling the leaves, will long for the fruit at last."[85]

If the link seems mysterious or contrived, remember that those marble-covered books are probably novels, many of them wonderfully implausible and extravagantly emotional romances. Instructing women on their duties, Thomas Gisborne trembled at the thought of those circulating library texts, "devoured with indiscriminate and insatiable avidity. Hence the mind is secretly corrupted."[86] The *Quarterly Review* defended its decision to begin reviewing novels. Even inferior novels were widely read: "The customers of the circulating library are so numerous, and so easily imposed upon, that it is of the utmost importance to the public, that its weights and measures should be subject to the inspection of a strict literary police, and the standard of its morality and sentiment kept as pure as the nature of things will admit."[87] But recalling his bedridden adolescence, Walter Scott fondly conjured up Edinburgh's circulating library, "especially rich in works of fiction." It might have been misguided, he conceded, but he was left to his own devices in selecting what to read.[88]

One guide to the city of London had no hesitations. Circulating libraries, strewn across the city, were "a blessing to mankind" because they diffused knowledge among the population.[89] Wilberforce, by no means enamored of aspirations for citizenship, embraced the

---

[85] *The Rivals* [1775], in *The Dramatic Works of Richard Brinsley Sheridan*, ed. Cecil Price, 2 vols. (Oxford: Clarendon, 1973), 1:85.

[86] Thomas Gisborne, *An Enquiry into the Duties of the Female Sex*, 5th ed. corrected (London, 1801), p. 229. For more worry about women reading novels, see *Vindication of the Rights of Woman* [1792], in *The Works of Mary Wollstonecraft*, ed. Janet Todd and Marilyn Butler, assistant ed. Emma Rees-Mogg, 7 vols. (London: William Pickering, 1989), 5:255–58; *The Journal of the Rev. William Bagshaw Stevens*, ed. Georgina Galbraith (Oxford: Clarendon, 1965), p. 284 [21 August 1795]; *Essays by a Society of Gentlemen, at Exeter* (Exeter, 1796), pp. 330–31; Emily Middleton to Harriet Middleton, 24 August 1804, *The Jerningham Letters (1780–1843)*, ed. Egerton Castle, 2 vols. (London, 1896), 1:248; William Playfair, *An Inquiry into the Permanent Causes of the Decline and Fall of Powerful and Wealthy Nations* (London, 1805), pp. 227–28; *Guardian of Education* (September 1806) 5(28):426; *Quarterly Journal of Education* (October–January 1832) 3(5):137.

[87] *Quarterly Review* (August 1809) 2:146.

[88] *Waverley Novels*, 1:v–vi [1829].

[89] *Modern London; Being the History and Present State of the British Metropolis* (London, 1804), p. 441. For more unequivocal enthusiasm, see *The Penny Magazine of the Society for the Diffusion of Useful Knowledge* (28 September 1833) 2(95):373–75.

libraries: he thought that they would encourage domesticity and keep the poor out of alehouses.[90]

Circulating libraries mushroomed far away from London. One Birmingham library, reorganized by Priestley, featured learned works in science and theology. A mere twelve shillings a quarter entitled patrons of another Birmingham library in 1790 to draw on some 2,400 books. Nearby small towns had libraries, too, or their rough equivalents: in 1805, tiny Thaxted gained a book society whose members met periodically to swap books they bought themselves.[91] Rochester's circulating library in 1796 procured London's newspapers by three o'clock the day after publication.[92] Liverpool in 1808 offered six different reading establishments, including a circulating library of 10,000 volumes whose members paid under eleven shillings a year.[93] Haddington gained a library in 1817; twenty years later it too had some 2,400 volumes.[94] A town with a library gained a bit of prestige. Jane Austen confessed to her sister that she had charged out a volume from the Chawton Reading Society. With her usual asperity, she sniffed that efforts to the east to emulate the Society only demonstrated Chawton's superiority.[95] By 1821, contemporaries estimated, London had at least one hundred circulating libraries, the rest of the country another nine hundred.[96]

The commercial aspect of the libraries was straightforward. Members paid a small annual fee entitling them to borrow books. Others could leave a deposit covering a book's value.[97] The same fees paid for the acquisition of books.[98] So-called reading rooms charged for access to publications, usually periodicals, but didn't circulate them.

[90] William Wilberforce to Samuel Wilberforce, 3 April 1829, *Private Papers of William Wilberforce*, ed. A. M. Wilberforce (London, 1897), p. 250.

[91] Leonore Davidoff and Catherine Hall, *Family Fortunes: Men and Women of the English Middle Class, 1780–1850* (London: Hutchinson, 1987), pp. 156–57.

[92] John Gale Jones, *Sketch of a Political Tour through Rochester, Chatham, Maidstone, Gravesend, &c.: Part the First* (London, 1796), p. 26.

[93] *Diary of Farington*, 9:3351–52 [22 September 1808].

[94] Richard D. Altick, *The English Common Reader: A Social History of the Mass Reading Public 1800–1900* (Chicago: University of Chicago Press, 1957), p. 221.

[95] Jane Austen to Cassandra Austen, 24 January 1813, *Jane Austen's Letters to Her Sister Cassandra and Others*, ed. R. W. Chapman, 2d ed. (Oxford: Oxford University Press, 1979), p. 292.

[96] *Quarterly Review* (March 1827) 35:567.

[97] Southey, *Letters from England*, p. 28.

[98] For the rules of Cornwall's library in 1792, see Richard Polwhele, *The History of*

Circulating libraries represent real change, not just anxieties heightened by the Revolution. In 1770, London could claim only four such libraries.[99] One French observer travelling through Norfolk in 1810 was struck by the ready availability of all kinds of printed material. Politics and science, anecdotes and fashions penetrated the entire realm; those who couldn't afford to subscribe could always head off to the local circulating library or reading room or book club.[100]

## "WAGGON-LOADS OF POLITICAL TRASH"[101]

In the 1780s, the debating societies investigated whether newspapers were socially helpful or harmful.[102] Take just two bleak 1809 estimates of the power of the press. A disappointed aristocrat surveyed the glibly optimistic newspaper coverage of the war with France: "The newspapers combine to mislead the public opinion, and to create a foolish and lying vanity, which has changed and vitiated our national character."[103] A pamphleteer, defiantly writing as One Who Dares to Think for Himself, waxed savagely indignant: "A great majority of Englishmen think, speak, and act, just as they are led to think, speak, and act, by the press, and particularly the Newspaper press," but they had the idiocy to pride themselves on escaping the dark ages, as if deferring to priests were any worse than deferring to the press.[104]

Setting aside such morose sentiments for now: it was easy to marvel at the mounting circulation of prose. In 1800, William Blake thought that London had been transformed abruptly from a vulgar commercial city to an elegant city of Grecian refinement, with "as many Booksellers as there are Butchers & as many Printshops as of any other

---

Cornwall, 7 vols. (Falmouth, 1803–1808; reprint ed. Dorking: Kohler and Coombes, 1978), 5:100–103 n.

[99] Quarterly Review (March 1827) 35:567.

[100] Louis Simond, Journal of a Tour and Residence in Great Britain, during the Years 1810 and 1811, by a French Traveller, 2 vols. (Edinburgh, 1815), 1:186 [18 June 1810].

[101] British Critic (January–June 1795) 5:vii.

[102] London Debating Societies, pp. 134 [12 March 1781], 179 [2 March 1786].

[103] Lord Auckland to Lord Grenville, 22 August 1809, Historical Manuscripts Commission, Report on the Manuscripts of J. B. Fortescue, Esq., Preserved at Dropmore, 10 vols. (London, 1892–1927), 9:314.

[104] One Who Dares to Think for Himself, Reason versus Passion; or, An Impartial Review of the Dispute between the Public and the Proprietors of Covent Garden Theatre (London, 1809), pp. 1–2.

trade."[105] By then a radical journalist gifted with a stunning prose style, William Cobbett was reaching some 300,000 readers a week in 1817.[106] Eleven million daily newspapers circulated in London for the year 1821, reported the *Quarterly*, later amending the number to 14 million.[107] Some 24 million papers sold in Great Britain that year.[108] *John Bull*, the Sunday newspaper launched to attack Queen Caroline, had a weekly circulation of some 9,000 that year.[109] In 1824, not counting London, England had some 135 different newspapers, none of them yet daily.[110] In 1829, the kingdom (including Ireland and Scotland) had 308 different newspapers, 55 of them in London.[111] One hundred ten thousand Sunday papers a week were published, 500,000 more papers during the week.[112] True, one publisher complained in 1807 that the increasing sale of newspapers was making it harder to sell political pamphlets and books.[113] Still, this is fundamentally a story of increase. No doubt it was helped along by changes in printing technology, most notably the invention and deployment of the steam-driven printing press in 1814,[114] and a 1774 legal decision that put an end to perpetual copyright, enabling the cheap reprinting of works in the public domain.[115]

The government required that newspapers be printed on specially stamped paper, for which they had to pay a tax. Stamp revenues almost doubled between 1800 and 1830.[116] The figure, already striking, overlooks the alarming numbers of unstamped radical publications that flouted the laws. Nor does it include the likes of Cobbett's *Two-*

[105] William Blake to George Cumberland, 2 July 1800, *The Letters of William Blake: with Related Documents,* ed. Geoffrey Keynes, 3d ed. (Oxford: Clarendon, 1980), p. 17.

[106] J. R. Dinwiddy, *Radicalism and Reform in Britain, 1780–1850* (London: Hambledon Press, 1992), p. 11.

[107] *Quarterly Review* (October 1822) 28:203, (March 1827) 35:567.

[108] *Quarterly Review* (March 1827) 35:567.

[109] *The Journal of Mrs. Harriet Arbuthnot 1820–1832,* ed. Francis Bamford and the Duke of Wellington, 2 vols. (London: Macmillan, 1950), 1:89 [25 April 1821].

[110] *The Periodical Press of Great Britain and Ireland: or An Inquiry into the State of the Public Journals, Chiefly as Regards Their Moral and Political Influence* (London, 1824), p. 149.

[111] *Westminster Review* (January 1829) 10(19):216.

[112] *Westminster Review* (April 1829) 10(20):469, 478.

[113] *Diary of Farington,* 8:3157–58 [5 December 1807].

[114] Marjorie Plant, *The English Book Trade: An Economic History of the Making and Sale of Books,* 3d ed. (London: George Allen & Unwin, 1974), pp. 274–75.

[115] *Donaldson* v. *Beckett,* 1 Eng. Rep. 837 (H.L. 1774).

[116] Altick, *English Common Reader,* p. 330.

*Penny Trash,* priced low to evade the tax legally. And many people could read the same copy of a newspaper: newsmen illegally rented out papers an hour at a time; groups of readers banded together so they could afford a single subscription.[117]

London bookseller James Lackington proudly charted his own success by parading the dazzling numbers in 1792. Faced with excess stock, his fellow booksellers would unload some seventy or eighty thousand volumes in an evening at low rates. The majority of them would be destroyed so that the remaining ones could be sold at full price. A convention, what Lackington describes as "a kind of standing order," dictated that anyone daring to discount books would be excluded from such sales. Lackington decided to defy the convention; he claimed not just that he had originated discount bookselling and remaindering, but that he was "highly instrumental in diffusing that general desire for READING, now so prevalent among the inferior orders of society," pointing to farmers who had volumes by Fielding, Smollett, and Richardson "stuck upon their bacon racks" and read aloud. He gloated too that he sold over 100,000 volumes a year.[118] That sounds impressive enough, but thirty years later another London bookselling firm was selling 5 million volumes a year.[119] As with the circulating libraries, these numbers indicate real change, not just insecurity induced by the Revolution.

This period, too, witnessed the birth and rise of the classic quarterly reviews. The *Edinburgh Review,* organ of the Whigs, first appeared in 1802. Its tones of magisterial complacence and censoriousness soon become familiar: "This will never do," began a prim shellacking of Wordsworth's *Excursion.*[120] The *Edinburgh* was feared, mocked, ex-

[117] Altick, *English Common Reader,* p. 323; William Hone, *The Table Book,* 2 vols. (London, 1827–1828; reprint ed. Detroit: Gale Research Co., 1966), 1:63–64.

[118] *Memoirs of the First Forty-Five Years of the Life of James Lackington,* new ed. (London, 1792), pp. 346–48, 350–51, 386–87, 408. By 1799, Lackington had sold the business and was apologetic about the spirited Methodist-bashing of the *Memoirs,* written when he was an infidel: see *Confessions of J. Lackington, Late Bookseller, at the Temple of the Muses* (London, 1804), pp. vii, 138. Did he get out of the bookselling business because of its unsavory ties to atheism?

[119] *Quarterly Review* (March 1827) 35:567.

[120] *Edinburgh Review* (November 1814) 24(47):1. One of their regular reviewers caught the tone nicely, teasing Francis Jeffrey about what his review of the solar system might sound like: "Damn the solar system! bad light—planets too distant—pestered with comets—feeble contrivance;—could make a better with great ease" (Sydney Smith to Francis Jeffrey, 25 February 1807, *The Letters of Sydney Smith,* ed. Nowell C. Smith, 2 vols. [Oxford: Clarendon, 1953], 1:121).

coriated, but always a force to be reckoned with. The *Quarterly Review,* voice of the Tories, commenced in 1809. It too launched salvoes at those poets it despised: Shelley was convinced that Keats had died "in paroxysms of despair at the contemptuous attack on his book in the *Quarterly Review.*"[121] The *Westminster Review,* headquarters of Benthamite philosophic radicalism, hit the streets in 1824: conservatives were appalled at an outlet for "the opinion of the most blood-thirsty and dangerous crew of political speculators in England."[122] (One wonders how they would have reacted to Bentham's fond memory of himself as a very young man at Oxford, lighting on the greatest-happiness principle in a "little circulating library belonging to a little coffee-house" where he stumbled on a pamphlet by Priestley.[123]) So, too, this period saw the launch of Cobbett's infamous *Political Register* in 1802. In its early years, Cobbett was still conservative, and anyway he was stuffing the pages of the *Register* with parliamentary debates and formal government documents; but later he was recognized as a truculent voice of working-class radicalism and a splendid writer. The *Age,* a conservative Sunday paper and scandal sheet, spoke for many in paying unconscious tribute to Cobbett's stature by branding him "a CONFIRMED LIAR . . . A PITIFUL COWARD . . . a HEARTLESS ASSASSIN . . . an APPARENT FILICIDE . . . in fact a perfect monster."[124]

These leading journals responded to the demand for vividly partisan writing, but they also stoked that demand. To say something that only sounds trivial, there was nothing quite like them before the Revolution.

### "OUR BLESSED SYSTEM OF PRINTING DEBATES"[125]

The newspapers didn't just increase in number. Their content changed, too, in one momentous if boring way: sustained coverage of parliamentary debates became routine. Through the eighteenth century, it was illegal to publish parliamentary debates. The laws were

---

[121] Shelley to Byron, 17 April 1821, *The Letters of Percy Bysshe Shelley,* ed. Frederick L. Jones, 2 vols. (Oxford: Clarendon, 1964), 2:284.

[122] *Blackwood's Edinburgh Magazine* (August 1824) 16(91):224.

[123] "Article on Utilitarianism" [1829], in Jeremy Bentham, *Deontology together with A Table of the Springs of Action and The Article on Utilitarianism,* ed. Amnon Goldworth (Oxford: Clarendon, 1983), pp. 291–92.

[124] *Age* (13 August 1826) 2(66):524.

[125] William Windham to Thomas Amyot, 22 January 1806, *The Windham Papers,* 2 vols. (London: Herbert Jenkins, 1913), 2:282.

evaded: in one typical dodge, Samuel Johnson wrote reports from the senate of Lilliput, complete with speakers' names in transparent disguises. He managed to do so without attending Parliament himself and later dismissed his reporting as pure imagination, though the best assessment is that it was reasonably accurate.[126] Until 1778, the Commons routinely excluded any visitors from the gallery; until 1783, visitors weren't allowed to take notes.[127] Doubts about the merits of publicity lingered. In 1803, the still conservative Cobbett opined "that the publishing of parliamentary debates is a violation of the spirit of the English government," though he'd been publishing them himself.[128] Even in 1819, one newspaper reporter narrowly escaped a prison stay when he perched in the front row of the gallery, conspicuously took notes, and refused to heed the Speaker's order that he refrain.

By the late eighteenth century, though, if they were willing to show up early enough to get a coveted space, to be discreet about their note-taking, to put up with the jostling and noise in the awkwardly placed gallery, to crane their necks and strain their ears to have a chance of following the debates, reporters could publish their accounts. William Woodfall earned the nickname "Memory" by sitting in the gallery, eyes closed, rapt in concentration, and then heading

[126] Benjamin Beard Hoover, *Samuel Johnson's Parliamentary Reporting: Debates in the Senate of Lilliput* (Berkeley: University of California Press, 1953). At the end of his life, Johnson regretted this work: see *Boswell's Life of Johnson: Together with Boswell's Journal of a Tour to the Hebrides and Johnson's Diary of a Journey into North Wales*, ed. George Birkbeck Hill, rev. L. F. Powell, 6 vols. (Oxford: Clarendon, 1934–1950), 4:408 [December 1784]. Alvin Kernan, *Printing Technology, Letters & Samuel Johnson* (Princeton, NJ: Princeton University Press, 1987), p. 163 attributes Johnson's regret to his longstanding concern for distinguishing truth from falsehood. Boswell does report that Johnson worried that he had imposed on others, especially since some of his reported speeches were wholly fabricated. But I suspect that Johnson also tasted the political fruits of his work and found them sour.

[127] A. Aspinall, "The Reporting and Publishing of the House of Commons' Debates 1771–1834," in *Essays Presented to Sir Lewis Namier,* ed. Richard Pares and A. J. P. Taylor (London: Macmillan, 1956), p. 230. For facts in this section not otherwise attributed, I've relied on Aspinall's magisterial account. Useful too is Peter D. G. Thomas, "The Beginning of Parliamentary Reporting in Newspapers, 1768–1774," *English Historical Review* (October 1959) 74:623–36. For a review of early reporting by one of the key players, see John Almon, *Memoirs of a Late Eminent Bookseller* (London, 1790), pp. 118–21. For colorful anecdotes on the history of parliamentary reporting, Michael MacDonagh, *The Reporters' Gallery* (London: Hodder and Stoughton, 1913).

[128] *Political Register* (19 March 1803) 3(11):385.

home and writing up detailed accounts of what he had heard.[129] (Sometimes it would take him a few days to get around to the writing.) By the early 1800s, the reporters were using shorthand. Each newspaper would send a small group of reporters who worked in a relay system, each one in turn slipping out of the gallery to write up his notes and hand them over to the printer.[130] Parliamentary sessions might drag on till four or five o'clock in the morning, but the morning newspapers would contain full accounts of the debates. In the 1820s, one paper was investing between two and three thousand pounds every session to procure these reports.[131]

The published reports were inaccurate. One speaker after another griped that he could barely recognize his words in the next day's newspapers. Some complained that the reports actually inverted the meaning of their speeches.[132] The great Tory Robert Peel stands alone, as far as I know, in expressing complete satisfaction in looking back over twenty years' reporting of his speeches.[133] Then again,

---

[129] John Taylor, *Records of My Life*, 2 vols. (London, 1832), 2:245.

[130] *Modern London*, pp. 432–33; *Periodical Press*, pp. 136–37; *Westminster Review* (July 1824) 2(3):204, 206, (January 1829) 10(19):225–26.

[131] *Edinburgh Review* (February 1823) 38(75):50; Sholto Percy and Reuben Percy, *London: or Interesting Memorials of Its Rise, Progress & Present State*, 3 vols. (London, 1824), 3:222.

[132] For a sampling of complaints, see *The Speeches of the Right Honourable Charles James Fox, in the House of Commons*, 6 vols. (London, 1815), 3:405 [12 December 1788]; Sheridan to his wife, 23 July 1800, *The Letters of Richard Brinsley Sheridan*, ed. Cecil Price, 3 vols. (Oxford: Clarendon, 1966), 2:135; Pitt to Addington, 10 February 1802, in George Pellew, *The Life and Correspondence of . . . Henry Addington, First Viscount Sidmouth*, 3 vols. (London, 1847), 1:489; William Windham to Thomas Amyot, 22 January 1806, *Windham Papers*, 2:282; Bentham to Francis Burdett, late May 1811, *The Correspondence of Jeremy Bentham*, ed. Timothy L. S. Sprigge and others, 10 vols. to date (London: Athlone Press; Oxford: Clarendon, 1968–), 8:147; Earl of Donoughmore to Parr, 13 June 1811, *The Works of Samuel Parr, LL.D.*, ed. John Johnstone, 8 vols. (London, 1828), 7:25; Judge Leycester to Parr, n.d., *Works of Parr*, 7:182–83; Canning to J. S. Sawbridge, 3 June 1825, *Some Official Correspondence of George Canning*, ed. Edward J. Stapleton, 2 vols. (London, 1887), 1:359; Thomas Creevey to Elizabeth Ord, 15 March 1822, *The Creevey Papers*, ed. Herbert Maxwell (New York: E. P. Dutton, 1904), p. 377; *Journal of Thomas Moore*, 2:641 [6 June 1823]; John Cam Hobhouse, Baron Broughton, *Recollections of a Long Life*, ed. Lady Dorchester, 6 vols. (New York: Charles Scribner's Sons, 1909–1911), 3:243 [diary, 15 February 1828]; Macaulay to Selina Macaulay, 13 July 1831, *The Letters of Thomas Babington Macaulay*, ed. Thomas Pinney, 6 vols. (Cambridge: Cambridge University Press, 1974–1981), 2:69.

[133] *The Speeches of the Late Right Honourable Sir Robert Peel, Bart. Delivered in the House of Commons*, 4 vols. (London, 1853; reprint ed. New York: Kraus Reprint Co., 1972), 2:742 [29 July 1833].

other members gained some satisfaction by secretly retailing their own corrected copies of their speeches to the newspapers or publishing them themselves.

We needn't think of the inaccuracies as deliberate, the nefarious attempt of reporters to make their heroes look valiant and their opponents stupid, or the sleazy attempt of newspapers to advance their editorial perspectives in the same way. Some of that may have gone on; contemporaries suspected that it did.[134] That aside, different reporters covering the same speeches might agree in broad outlines on what the gist was, even on the basic arguments. But they would employ strikingly different language.[135] Members would sometimes go back to the newspaper reports years after the fact, when collected volumes of their speeches were being assembled, and correct them. But what counts as correction here? How accurate were their memories, anyway? and how eager were they to represent themselves as having said then what they did not in fact say, but wished that they had? In short, we have to be cautious in deploying the reports as evidence.

Newspaper editors didn't always relish publishing the debates. The editor of the *Morning Chronicle* groaned at "the enormous expense of the disgusting, though necessary, reports of Parliamentary chattering" in 1812.[136] The *Age* was relieved in 1830 that Parliament was taking a break. They explained that they'd often thought of entirely eliminating the reports and were already curtailing their length: "Our space is too valuable to be cumbered with trash void of either wit or reason."[137] Still, the reports were published. So there's genuine consumer demand at work here. Those bespectacled coffeehouse readers poring over the newspapers may have sought the titillation of stories about fashion and adultery, haut-ton and crim. con. But they also sought endless columns of parliamentary speeches. And they argued vehemently about them, if not in their coffeehouses then in alehouses, debating societies, and elsewhere.

---

[134] The charge is most pointed in *Fraser's* (October 1831) 4(21):319–20; see too *Diary of Farington*, 9:3217 [6 February 1808]; *Political Register* (23 May 1835) 88(8): 449–60.

[135] Dror Wahrman, "Virtual Representation: Parliamentary Reporting and the Languages of Class in the 1790s," *Past & Present* (August 1992) no. 136, pp. 83–113.

[136] James Perry to Thomas Moore, 4 December 1812, *Memoirs, Journals, and Correspondence of Thomas Moore*, ed. John Russell, 8 vols. (London, 1856), 8:127.

[137] *Age* (11 April 1830), p. 116.

### POPULAR LITERACY, POPULAR EDUCATION

Addressing the House of Commons in 1828, Henry Brougham, Caroline's former lawyer, conceded that an orthodox constitutionalist might worry about the dangerous accretion of power by the Duke of Wellington, serving as prime minister and commander-in-chief of the army. But he assured the members that soldiers could no longer threaten English liberty. Why not? "The schoolmaster is abroad," Brougham triumphantly revealed. The published report records that the announcement was met with cheers.[138] The phrase was taken up, applauded, ridiculed, subjected to the withering ministrations of cartoonists.

So, too, was another one of his catchphrases, that the age was witnessing "the march of intellect." But this, amusingly, was a catchphrase Brougham never uttered. It was saddled on him after his spectacularly successful 1825 *Practical Observations upon the Education of the People,* a turgid rhapsody on the liberating possibilities offered by cheap publications and popular literacy. Despite Brougham's wooden prose, readers rushed the *Observations* through twenty editions in six months.[139] "Why then may not every topic of politics, party as well as general, be treated of in cheap publications?" demanded the great Whig.[140] Book clubs, reading societies, circulating libraries, places away from alehouses for quiet discussion: all could work their white magic. Provided, that is, they were organized and run by workers themselves. "I really should be disposed to view any advantage in point of knowledge gained by the body of the people, as somewhat equivocal, or at least as much alloyed with evil, if purchased by the increase of their dependence upon their superiors."[141] Happily, "the progress of knowledge"[142] was already well under way. Ever the no-nonsense sort, Brougham took a swipe at the pusillanimous. "To the Upper Classes of society, then, I would say, that the question no longer is whether or not the people shall be instructed—for that has been determined long ago, and the decision is irreversible—but

---

[138] *Parliamentary Debates* (29 January 1828), new series, 18:58.

[139] Robert Stewart, *Henry Brougham 1778–1868: His Public Career* (London: The Bodley Head, 1986), p. 186.

[140] Henry Brougham, *Practical Observations upon the Education of the People, Addressed to the Working Classes and Their Employers* (London, 1825), p. 5.

[141] Brougham, *Practical Observations,* p. 16.

[142] Brougham, *Practical Observations,* p. 32.

whether they shall be well or ill taught—half informed or as thoroughly as their circumstances permit and their wants require."[143]

Brougham himself would organize the Society for the Diffusion of Useful Knowledge in 1826. The *Quarterly Journal of Education,* its official mouthpiece, would call in 1831 for publicly funded elementary schools—so echoing a demand from a 1794 pamphlet from Eaton's shop.[144] But Brougham was right. Educational efforts were already underway, enlarging the reading public, maybe changing the character of subjects or puncturing a political culture of deference and illusion. From 1813 to 1816, the West London Lancasterian Association struggled to offer cheap education to needy children.[145] They weren't alone.

In the 1790s, Burke estimated that England and Scotland had about 400,000 "political citizens," that is, not voters but independent adults with "some means of information" and some leisure for political discussion; 80,000 of these he reckoned were unrepentant Jacobins not open to argument.[146] (The other 320,000 he figured were utterly staunch loyalists. Somehow he doesn't indict them as close-minded. Nor does he envision any readers between these polar extremes: no one eager to learn from public discussion, no one pressing any other agenda, no one genuinely undecided.) It's rash to take this as an estimate of the reading public, though it has been construed that way. It is presumably somewhat smaller than the class of those flocking to coffeehouses, alehouses, circulating libraries, debating societies, and the like to learn more about politics. In 1826, Southey contemplated the aggressive pursuit of discount bookselling: "the largest class of readers is now beginning to be found in a lower stage of life."[147] In 1832, the *Penny Magazine of the Society for the Diffusion of Useful Knowledge*—this was the publication conveyed to the great unwashed—gloated over sales of 200,000 copies of each issue. That

[143] Brougham, *Practical Observations,* p. 32.

[144] *Quarterly Journal of Education* (April 1831) 1(2):213–24; *Revolutions without Bloodshed; or, Reformation Preferable to Revolt* (London, 1794), p. 3.

[145] Alice Prochaska, "The Practice of Radicalism: Educational Reform in Westminster," in *London in the Age of Reform,* ed. John Stevenson (Oxford: Basil Blackwell, 1977); J. Ann Hone, *For the Cause of Truth,* pp. 239–44.

[146] *Letters on a Regicide Peace* [1796–1797], in *The Works of the Right Honorable Edmund Burke,* 9th ed., 12 vols. (Boston: Little, Brown, 1889), 5:284–85. The *Edinburgh Review* (July 1804) 4(8):329 estimates "at least" 80,000 readers for the whole realm.

[147] Southey to John Rickman, 18 January 1826, *Letters,* ed. Warter, 3:523.

meant, they suggested, that they had 1 million readers.[148] Indeed it was routine to look back from the early and mid-1800s and remark upon the vast increase in reading and education.[149] Similarly, one later observer, Charles Knight, could quote and doubt the stirring claims of Lackington, the London bookseller, on just how much reading was going on around 1792, especially in the countryside: what struck Lackington as a lot struck Knight as not a lot at all, compared to what he was seeing.[150] I can redouble the point. Already in 1697, Jonathan Swift was mocking the mindlessly ritual invocation of the explosion of publications.[151] But conservatives a century later were right to look back longingly at Swift's day. They were dealing with much more reading and writing than he could have imagined.

Excepting the economically difficult war years of 1800 to 1805, the percentage of men and women able to sign their names in parish registers was on a bumpy rise. From 1750 to 1840, the rate for men goes from around 60 percent to around 65 percent, for women from around 35 percent to around 50 percent.[152] The figures require a set of hesitations, reservations, and qualifications: there were sharp regional variations, which disappear in aggregate data; while writing may be more difficult than reading, signing one's name is no evidence of full literacy. Then again, one doesn't even have to read to ingest newspapers and pamphlets. Recall Southey: "one reader serves for a tap-room full of open-mouthed listeners," listeners who didn't

---

[148] *Penny Magazine* (18 December 1832) 1:iii; 1:iii–iv goes on to emphasize the importance of new printing technology and cheap transportation.

[149] Prospectus for *Manchester Guardian* (first issued 5 May 1821), in Archibald Prentice, *Historic Sketches and Personal Recollections of Manchester* (London, 1851), p. 205; *New Times* (13 January 1825), in *The Works of Charles and Mary Lamb*, ed. E. V. Lucas, 6 vols. (New York: Macmillan, 1913), 1:320–21; *England and America* [1833], in *The Collected Works of Edward Gibbon Wakefield*, ed. M. F. Lloyd Prichard (Glasgow: Collins, 1968), pp. 387–88; Wordsworth to the editor of the *Kendal Mercury*, 12 April 1838, in *The Prose Works of William Wordsworth*, ed. W. J. B. Owen and Jane Worthington Smyser, 3 vols. (Oxford: Clarendon, 1974), 3:309; *The Life, and Literary Pursuits of Allen Davenport* (London, 1845), pp. 73–76.

[150] Charles Knight, *The Old Printer and the Modern Press* (London, 1854), pp. 226–27; Knight, *Passages of a Working Life*, 1:24–26.

[151] *A Tale of a Tub*, 5th ed. [1710], in *The Prose Works of Jonathan Swift*, ed. Herbert Davis, 14 vols. (Oxford: Basil Blackwell, 1939–1968), 1:27–28 [1697].

[152] R. S. Schofield, "Dimensions of Illiteracy, 1750–1850," *Explorations in Economic History* (Summer 1973) 10:443–46. See too Barry Reay, "The Context and Meaning of Popular Literacy: Some Evidence from Nineteenth-Century Rural England," *Past & Present* (May 1991) no. 131, p. 95.

need to be literate to be curious or politically astute—or unrepentant Jacobins.

One of the *Edinburgh Review*'s stalwarts shrewdly surmised that there were deep connections between the increase of popular literacy, consumer demand, and the shape of British politics.

> There are four or five hundred thousand readers more than there were thirty years ago, among the lower orders. A market is open to the democrat writers, by which they gain money and distinction. Government cannot prevent the commerce. A man, if he know his business as a libeller, can write enough for mischief, without writing enough for the Attorney-General. The attack upon the present order of things will go on; and, unfortunately, the gentlemen of the people have a strong case against the House of Commons and the borough-mongers, as they call them. I think all wise men should begin to turn their faces reform-wards.[153]

Here the brute fact of a popular audience ready to stoke the fires of radical criticism seems to doom Burkean loyalty. Other social developments seemed to doom it, too.

## Sunday Schools

Legend assigns the origins of the Sunday school movement to one Robert Raikes and his work in Gloucester in 1780. Be that as it may, the goals of the movement are nicely stated in a circular prepared in 1785 for the Society for the Support and Encouragement of Sunday Schools:

> To prevent vice—to encourage industry and virtue—to dispel the darkness of ignorance—to diffuse the light of knowledge—to bring men cheerfully to submit to their stations—to obey the laws of God and their country—to make that part of the community, the country poor, happy—to lead them in the pleasant paths of religion here, and to endeavour to prepare them for a glorious eternity.[154]

Here again, we find the language of enlightenment. But now the political agenda is very different. Literacy itself is no bugbear. It inspires no alarm about citizenship. Instead, the light of the Gospel will rein-

---

153 Sydney Smith to Edward Davenport, 3 January 1820, *Letters of Sydney Smith*, 1:343.
154 Quoted in Thomas Walter Laqueur, *Religion and Respectability: Sunday Schools and Working Class Culture 1780–1850* (New Haven, CT: Yale University Press, 1976), p. 34.

force the loyalty of subjects. And that means that they have to learn to read so that they can study the Bible, as good Protestants.

One Cambridge Sunday school was linked to a circulating library with short moral and religious writings. At the end of Sunday school sessions, the woman who founded the library would read a tract aloud and then lead a discussion.[155] So too the Reverend Francis Wrangham set up a parish library in Yorkshire and circulated similarly pious texts for evening reading: "Thus a few visitors are perhaps detained from the ale-house."[156] (Religious books would be good for the poor, Wordsworth wrote to Wrangham, if in fact they wanted to read.[157]) Antitype, remember, had sneered that so-called friends of social order such as Burke must despise Luther and Calvin, who depended on printing and literacy to bring about the Reformation. The Sunday school movement implicitly accepted the legitimacy of the sneer. No unthinking prejudice and illusion here, but still a devout deference.

The movement took off. By 1800, some 200,000 children were in the schools; by 1830, some 1.4 million children.[158] (Some adults were taught, too.) Not all the friends of social order embraced the project. We can distinguish two worries. First, the heavy responsibility of running a Sunday school might end up in the wrong hands. Samuel Horsley, the bishop who thought that the mass of people had nothing to do with the laws but obey them, gnashed his teeth in the House of Lords over "schools of Jacobinical religion, and of Jacobinical politics; that is to say, schools of atheism and disloyalty,—schools in the shape and disguise of charity-schools and Sunday-schools, in which the minds of the children of the very lowest orders are enlightened; that is, taught to despise religion and the laws, and all subordination."[159] He would later instruct the clergy of his diocese that "a misrepresentation I suppose in the public prints" had placed this comment out of context. Only some Sunday schools, he thought, were nurseries of

---

[155] *The Reports of the Society for Bettering the Condition and Increasing the Comforts of the Poor,* 5 vols. (London, 1798–1808), 3:170–73 [18 April 1801].

[156] *Reports of the Society,* 5:223–24 [17 October 1807].

[157] William Wordsworth to Francis Wrangham, 5 June 1808, *The Letters of William and Dorothy Wordsworth,* 2d ed., ed. Ernest de Selincourt, rev. Chester L. Shaver and others, 8 vols. (Oxford: Clarendon, 1967–1993), 2:247.

[158] Linda Colley, *Britons: Forging the Nation 1707–1837* (New Haven, CT: Yale University Press, 1992), p. 226. There is a great deal of quantitative data in Laqueur, *Religion and Respectability,* chap. 2.

[159] *The Speeches in Parliament of Samuel Horsley* (Dundee, 1813), p. 355 [10 July 1800].

Jacobin outrages. But Sunday schools were fine—*if* they were kept under the firm guidance of the Anglican church. "Sunday-Schools, therefore, under your own inspection, I would advise you to encourage. But you must keep a vigilant eye over them. Leave nothing to the discretion of a master or a mistress. Suffer no books to be introduced, but such as have had your previous approbation."[160]

Second, literacy is an ominously flexible tool. Those who learn to read the Bible might eventually pick up a titillating novel or a radical pamphlet. Just before the French Revolution, John Byng archly suggested that "the great voice, that now brawls aloud in favour of Sunday schools" must be right, and he must be mistaken in thinking that "immorality cou'd be taught by books, or that forgery was, ever, the consequence of learning to write."[161] A few years later—here's the anxiety effect again—he was less snide, more wrathful. In Kettering, he exploded:

> There is establish'd here, now most common, a Sunday School: a fine institution? Where all are taught to read; What?—Amours, or Paine's Pamphlets.—Our *ignorant* forefathers,—who could neither read nor write, were instructed in politics, and religion, by their superiors, and the clergy; and believ'd what they heard:—learning was confined to a few.—But in this refined age, we burst from our egg-shells full of information;—we crawl sceptics; we fly philosophers, spinning webs of sophistry to entangle all around us: And, soon, to be freed from religion, and Government,—we shall become *as happy* as the French.[162]

Divines somberly asked what kind of Christians could want to keep others in the shadows of ignorance and illiteracy.[163] Radicals sweetly asked the same question, though in their voices it sounded leering.[164] Journalist Archibald Prentice looked back calmly from the vantage point of 1851 and applauded the Sunday school teachers: "If there is

---

160 *The Charge of Samuel Lord Bishop of Rochester, to the Clergy of His Diocese, Delivered at His Second General Visitation, in the Year 1800* (London, 1800), pp. 25–26. See too *Anti-Jacobin Review* (July 1815) 49:57.

161 John Byng, *The Torrington Diaries*, ed. C. Bruyn Andrews, 4 vols. (London: Eyre & Spottiswoode, 1934–1938), 2:80 [22 June 1789].

162 Byng, *Torrington Diaries*, 3:211 [15 July 1793].

163 John Liddon, *The General Religious Instruction of the Poor, the Surest Means of Promoting Universal National Happiness* (London, 1792), pp. 7–8.

164 James Thomson Callender, *The Political Progress of Britain* (London, 1795), p. 119. Note too "Orson and Ellen," in John Wolcot, *The Works of Peter Pindar, Esq.*, 4 vols. (London, 1797–1806), 4:252.

to be any hero-worship, let it be paid to those patient, unregarded, unrewarded, unknown, often much despised workers in the over-crowded, stifling garret, or the dark under-ground school-room. With the single undeviating purpose of promoting the eternal welfare of their pupils, they were preparing them for the fit discharge of their social and political duties."[165] Richard Guest, chronicler of the cotton industry, thought that workers had made great strides: "From being only a few degrees above their cattle in the scale of intellect, they became Political Citizens." He attributed the dramatic change partly to cotton manufacturing, which threw workers together for conversa-tion and forced them to pay attention to politics and the war with France, if only because of concern about their wages; but also to Sun-day schools, which grabbed workers once "sunk in the depths of igno-rance," "content to believe every thing their superiors told them," and transformed them.[166] The contrast is stylized, but Guest was onto something.

His hyperbole mirrors the frantic edge in Byng's indictment. Neither one believed—nobody could believe—that popular literacy made no political difference or that universal literacy was uncon-troversially good. The political stakes of literacy were huge and I sus-pect that Byng, Prentice, and Guest were right: the Sunday schools inadvertently helped create proud citizens.

### THE SOCIETY FOR THE DIFFUSION OF USEFUL KNOWLEDGE AND MECHANICS' INSTITUTES

Not only the fact of literacy was politically controversial; so too was just what people ought to be reading. The publications of Brougham's Society for the Diffusion of Useful Knowledge were uni-formly refined materials administered to disheveled workers. In 1827, for instance, Brougham sought out Mary Somerville, on her way to becoming a distinguished scientist, and asked her to write a popular but serious account of astronomy for the Society.[167] (Actually, he

---

[165] Prentice, *Historic Sketches*, p. 116.

[166] Richard Guest, *A Compendious History of the Cotton-Manufacture* (Manchester, 1823), pp. 37–38. See too Mary Russell Mitford, *Our Village*, 5 vols. (London, 1824–1832), 4:298.

[167] Brougham to Dr. Somerville, 27 March 1827, in Mary Somerville, *Personal Recol-lections, from Early Life to Old Age* (London, 1874), pp. 161–62. For a glowing review, see *Edinburgh Review* (April 1832) 55(109):1–25.

communicated with Somerville's husband.) The Society's *Penny Magazine* was chock full of bombastic articles on natural science, classical history, linguistics, statistics, political economy, and the like. But was this the sort of thing the lower orders wanted? or needed? That same year, popular novelist Maria Edgeworth brooded over the Society's publications, fearing that they were written over the heads of their intended audience and no one would read them.[168]

Why did the Society want to circulate such terribly earnest materials, to enshrine them as the essence of useful knowledge? It was keen to show that education wasn't political propaganda: and who could quarrel with learned essays on linguistics? The more boring the safer, and the safer the better. It may be, too, that the Society fastened on such intellectually uplifting materials because its vision was blinkered by unthinking commitments—call them prejudices—about class and culture. Educating the workers, in this view, was tantamount to equipping them to perform credibly at polite dinner parties.

Radicals bristled with impatience. They mocked "the Society for the Diffusion of Useful (or rather Useless) Knowledge,"[169] "the Society for the Effusion of Useless Knowledge."[170] The *Westminster Review* condemned the publications as "preposterous": "What, for example, could be expected from a treatise on Dynamics being read by one of the poor labourers of Kent, who clamorously demanded a rise of wages?"[171] It was worse than preposterous, charged the *Poor Man's Guardian*. Purveying "nonsensical tittle tattle about forks and spoons, and smock frocks, bridges, waterfalls, and a thousand other things, no doubt entertaining enough, but to the poor and ignorant, utterly useless" was "concealed villainy." The telltale sign was that insidiously clever Henry Brougham was the manager. His cloven Whig foot revealed an attempt to sedate the poor by distracting their attention from social injustice. The sprinkling of articles in political economy was a covert attempt to persuade them that their sufferings were necessary.[172]

---

[168] Maria Edgeworth to Mr. Bannatyne, 4 December 1827, in Francis Anne Edgeworth, *A Memoir of Maria Edgeworth*, 3 vols. (London: privately printed, 1867), 2:300.

[169] John Stuart Mill to Gustave d'Eichthal, 15 May 1829, *The Earlier Letters of John Stuart Mill 1812–1848*, ed. Francis E. Mineka, 2 vols. (Toronto: University of Toronto Press, 1963), 1:33.

[170] *Tait's Edinburgh Magazine* (September 1832) 1(6):658–60.

[171] *Westminster Review* (April 1831) 14(28):372.

[172] *Poor Man's Guardian* (4 August 1832) 1(60):486. See too *Black Dwarf* (5 July 1820) 5(1):21.

But conservatives found the same publications incendiary. This campaign for popular enlightenment, warned one, was just what had led to the French Revolution.[173] "A FLOOD OF SEDITION AND BLAS-PHEMY is now daily poured upon the town," lamented the *Age*. Aggravating matters, the Society's publications were cheap enough to be printed unstamped.[174] It's not that the *Age* uncovered scurrilous radical essays hidden inside the wrappers of the impeccably polite *Penny Magazine*. Nor is it that they thought that the publication of statistics was itself political dynamite. Rather it's that once the flood gates of literacy are thrown open, chaos will surely follow.

Similar debates surrounded the mechanics' institutes, another forum for educating the lower orders. Mechanics' Institutions were founded in Glasgow, London, and a few other cities in 1823; by 1826 there were over 100 institutes scattered around Britain.[175] The institutes assembled libraries, sponsored regular classes, and held public lectures.[176] *Mechanics* meant skilled workers or artisans, presumptively male, but there were always disputes about who should be attending, and over time the clientele drifted upward in the conventional status hierarchy.[177] (One champion of such institutes interrupted his triumphal history to concede that workers "are very slightly imbued with a taste for mental improvement."[178] Better, he thought, to aim at the middle classes.) Initially the institutes resolutely steered clear of theological and political controversy, but in the later 1830s, popular demand led them to furnish newsrooms with newspapers.[179] As early as 1826, one institute was admitting "the Female friends or relatives of Members" to lectures.[180]

As critics saw it, this was part of a tidal wave of disorder. In the objections to mechanics' institutes, the venerable model of social or-

---

[173] John Philips Potter, *A Letter to John Hughes . . . on the Systems of Education Proposed by the Popular Parties*, 2d ed. (London, 1828), in *Pamphleteer* (1828) 29(57):258.

[174] *Age* (6 May 1832), p. 149.

[175] Thomas Kelly, *George Birkbeck: Pioneer of Adult Education* (Liverpool: Liverpool University Press, 1957), p. 74, chap. 5, p. 148.

[176] Mabel Tylecote, *The Mechanics' Institutes of Lancashire and Yorkshire before 1851* (Manchester: Manchester University Press, 1957), p. 70.

[177] Kelly, *George Birkbeck*, pp. 86, 104, 132–34.

[178] James Williamson, *On the Diffusion of Knowledge amongst the Middle Classes: Introductory Discourse, Delivered at the Opening of the Leeds Literary Institution, May 9th, 1834* (London, 1835), p. 25; see too p. 27.

[179] Tylecote, *Mechanics' Institutes*, pp. 116, 154–56, 234–35, 272–73.

[180] *The First Year's Report of the Hackney Literary and Mechanic Institution, Read August 3rd, 1826: To Which Are Annexed, Catalogues of the Apparatus and Books Belonging to the Institution* (Hackney, 1826), p. 4.

der is always lurking in the margins. Or indeed prominently displayed in the main text: one of Brougham's critics patiently drew a triangle, with the king at its apex and the common people at its base, and for the benefit of the desperately slow elucidated on it. Raise the base by educating the common people and the whole structure would teeter and collapse. "There can be no doubt, that, equally taught, the lower classes will equally contend for superiority, and consequently all subordination, the very key-stone of the government, and character of the country, must be dissolved."[181] Dr. Johnson couldn't have said it better.

*Blackwood's* protested the 1824 repeal of the combination laws, which had made labor unions illegal. Workers needed the salutary authority of their employers, the masters, they insisted, not independence. What about discipline and control? What would keep the lower orders in their place? Could anyone take seriously the thought that mechanics' institutes were going to replace the masters, that education would provide self-control? "If these mechanics' institutions are to be subsidiary to the education given by, and the authority of, the masters, let them prosper; if they are to destroy these, let us at once have an Act of Parliament for their suppression."[182]

*John Bull* wasted no pity on an 1828 advertisement that Robert Owen, busy reforging human nature in New Lanark, would lecture at the London Institute. Bad enough that "Infidels and Atheists" surreptitiously ran Sunday schools, thus "undermining every thing like religion and good order"; more appalling, Owen's blathering was scheduled for the Sabbath, in fact for the very same time as church services.

> We do say, if these prophane and political ravings are allowed to be delivered in the theatre of a mechanics institution (built, as it was *pretended,* for very different purposes) during the hours of divine service on Sundays, that the character of the country, of her Church and her Government, IS GONE. If divine ordinances are to be scoffed at, and civil regulations defied with impunity, who shall be safe? and what Judge, what Government, will dare to punish crimes against the State, if they suffer such outrages, insults and mockeries, against GOD himself?[183]

[181] A Country Gentleman, *The Consequences of a Scientific Education to the Working Classes of This Country Pointed Out; and the Theories of Mr. Brougham on That Subject Confuted; in a Letter to the Marquess of Lansdown* (London, 1826), pp. 10–11, 15.

[182] *Blackwood's Edinburgh Magazine* (July 1825) 18(102):29.

[183] *John Bull* (18 April 1830) 10(488):124. For evidence of what would have struck

"Mr. Owen proclaims Sunday lectures upon things in general," fumed the paper the next week, "'to supersede the useless attendance on divine service, and public worship,'" with the likes of atheist Richard Carlile bolstering his efforts.[184] In fact, years before Carlile had embraced the mechanics' institutes as the best replacement for churches.[185] He'd also suggested that the mechanics' institutes were indebted to Tom Paine's assaults on monarchy and Christianity and that they would finish the job he had started.[186]

## PRINTING PRESSES AND GODS

Coffeehouses and alehouses and libraries and debating societies and Sunday schools and mechanics' institutes: these were the vehicles of reason, the schoolmaster abroad, the march of intellect, the acid bath corroding the prejudice Burke prized. These were fueling the blazing sun that was clearing away the mists of ignorance, as dozens of authors echoed Priestley in maintaining.[187] In the *Rights of Man,* Paine chuckled over Burke's predicament. "Ignorance is of a peculiar nature; once dispelled, it is impossible to re-establish it."[188] Decades later, the *Liberal* held a similar view: "In this age any revival of supersti-

---

*John Bull* as a frightfully cavalier attitude about Christianity, see for instance Robert Owen, *A New View of Society: or, Essays on the Formation of Human Character Preparatory to the Developement of a Plan for Gradually Ameliorating the Condition of Mankind,* 2d ed. (London, 1816; reprint ed. London: Macmillan, 1972), pp. 53–54.

[184] *John Bull* (25 April 1830) 10(489):132.

[185] *Republican* (26 December 1823) 8(25):767–68.

[186] *Republican* (11 November 1825) 12(19):583–84.

[187] A partial list: Catherine Macaulay Graham, *Observations on the Reflections of the Right Hon. Edmund Burke* (Boston, 1791), p. 10; George Rous, *A Letter to the Right Honourable Edmund Burke, in Reply to His Appeal from the New to the Old Whigs* (London, 1791), pp. 11–12; *Letters on the Present State,* pp. 114 [1 September 1791], 136–37 [1 September 1791]; Robert Torrens to Francis Place, 11 September 1817, in Hone, *Cause of Truth,* p. 322; *Life and Opinions of Thomas Preston, Patriot and Shoemaker* (London, 1817), p. 13; *Black Dwarf* (25 March 1818) 2(12):177; John Cartwright, *The English Constitution Produced and Illustrated* (London, 1823), pp. 169, 346; "Declaration of 150 Female Volunteers in Birmingham and Its Vicinity," 8 August 1833, in *Gauntlet* (25 August 1833), in *Political Women 1800–1850,* ed. Ruth and Edmund Frow (London: Pluto Press, 1989), pp. 52–53.

[188] *Rights of Man* [1791], in *The Life and Works of Thomas Paine,* 10 vols. (New Rochelle, NY: Thomas Paine National Historical Association, 1925), 6:162. See too *Dissertation on First Principles of Government* [1795], in *Works of Paine,* 5:226; Birmingham Society for Constitutional Information, *Address* (Birmingham, 1792), pp. 8–9.

tion must be quite hopeless. . . ."[189] So too the *Pioneer:* "The tide of thought is fast flowing into the mind of the operative; to turn it is impossible."[190]

Let's dub this view the irreversibility thesis. Once the mists of Burkean prejudice and illusion clear, there's no scaring them up again. Pandora's box can't be closed. Burke himself, remember, was committed to a version of this thesis: "If anything is . . . out of the power of man, it is to *create* a prejudice." The irreversibility thesis suggests that there is no point in attempting a measured assessment of the merits of illusion and enlightenment, because once enlightenment is on the scene, illusion is no longer a live possibility. So even if coffeehouse reading and political debate were repulsive, we would have to learn to live with them.

Is the irreversibility thesis true? Or how strong a version of it is true? Is reading like riding a bicycle, tough to learn but impossible to forget? That's perhaps true of individuals, but it would be foolhardy to suggest that it must then be true of whole societies. Or once a society embarks on the path of coffeehouse reading and public debate, are mystifications of all kinds doomed? Is reading the kind of prose turned out by Southey's despised "apostles of sedition" an experience guaranteed to jolt subjects out of their deference?[191] In the *Rights of Man,* Paine routinely associates reason with republics, prejudice with monarchy and aristocracy. Does the irreversibility thesis then entail that kings and nobles are doomed?[192]

The irreversibility thesis suggests that conservatism is doomed by a paradox of timing. Before the sun of enlightenment rises, there would be no point rhapsodizing over prejudice. Or, worse, it would be pernicious: some of those sleepy subjects might get suspicious. After reason is eating away at prejudice, there again would be no point: for no amount of magisterial diagnosis, let alone desperate whining, could restore the *ancien régime.* To put the paradox of timing most sharply, it's never the right time to be a conservative. If that conclu-

---

[189] *Liberal* (1823) 1(2):347.

[190] *Pioneer* (9 November 1833) no. 10, p. 73.

[191] Compare Roger Chartier, *The Cultural Origins of the French Revolution,* trans. Lydia G. Cochrane (Durham, NC: Duke University Press, 1991), chap. 4.

[192] So Reinhart Koselleck, *Critique and Crisis: Enlightenment and the Pathogenesis of Modern Society* [1959] (Oxford: Berg, 1988), p. 116: "Criticism spelled the death of kings."

sion seems counterintuitive, even bizarre, we have reason to challenge the credentials of the irreversibility thesis itself.

It is undeniable, though, that the rhetoric of conservatism unhappily tends toward the nostalgic, the melodramatic, the fearful. The conservative imagination is captured by things slipping away, the maelstrom swirling: young Cobbett quivered in horror when contemplating the French Revolution, "that Pandora's box, which opened upon mankind more malignant principles than all the vast regions of hell contain."[193] It's as undeniable—and as unattractive—that the rhetoric of democratic radicalism tends toward the smug, the sanctimonious, the complacent. Both sentiments depend on some sense that something like the irreversibility thesis is right. They diverge only in inferring that history's course is set remorselessly against or for their political agendas.

We're now in a better position to grasp the profound political stakes of that oddity, the printing press engraved so painstakingly on the missive to Queen Caroline. The printing press is the authoritative emblem of the changes I've canvassed here. So we find Paine declaring that "the art of printing . . . gives to man a sort of divine attribute. It gives to him mental omnipresence."[194] So we find the Society of Spencean Philanthropists proclaiming that "gross and contemptible delusions have entirely disappeared at the majestic approach of almighty truth" thanks to the "Inestimable Press! Sacred pillar of science and liberty!"[195]

It is one of brilliant essayist William Hazlitt's great themes. He can sound the theme as crudely as one might wish: "The French Revolution might be described as a remote but inevitable result of the invention of the art of printing."[196] But he can be subtle, too. Take his

[193] *Porcupine's Gazette* (October 1797), in William Cobbett, *Porcupine's Works,* 12 vols. (London, 1801), 7:265.

[194] *Reply to the Bishop of Llandaff* [1810], in *Works of Paine,* 9:77. See too A Lover of Order, *Considerations on Lord Grenville's and Mr. Pitt's Bills, concerning Treasonable and Seditious Practices, and Unlawful Assemblies* (London, 1795), pp. 69–70, in William Godwin, *Uncollected Writings (1785–1822): Articles in Periodicals and Six Pamphlets,* ed. Jack W. Marken and Burton R. Pollin (Gainesville, FL: Scholars' Facsimiles and Reprints, 1968), pp. 263–64.

[195] *Address of the Society of Spencean Philanthropists to All Mankind, on the Means of Promoting Liberty and Happiness* (London, n.d.), p. 2.

[196] *The Life of Napoleon Buonaparte* [1828], in *The Complete Works of William Hazlitt,* ed. P. P. Howe, 21 vols. (London: J. M. Dent and Sons, 1930), 13:38. For similarly crude technological determinism, see *Black Dwarf* (7 February 1821) 6(6):204; Christophilus,

account of his arrival in Sardinia. He presented his two trunks at the customs house. Like any other diligent intellectual on the road, he had one trunk crammed full of reading matter: Bacon, Milton, Destutt de Tracy, an *Edinburgh Review,* some issues of the *Morning Chronicle,* and more.

> When it was unlocked, it was as if the lid of Pandora's box flew open. There could not have been a more sudden start or expression of surprise, had it been filled with cartridge-paper or gun-powder. Books were the corrosive sublimate that eat out despotism and priestcraft—the artillery that battered down castle and dungeon-walls—the ferrets that ferreted out abuses—the lynx-eyed guardians that tore off disguises—the scales that weighed right and wrong—the thumping make-weight thrown into the balance that made force and fraud, the sword and the cowl, kick the beam—the dread of knaves, the scoff of fools—the balm and the consolation of the human mind—the salt of the earth—the future rulers of the world!

The officials soberly seized the trunk and sealed it shut, to be returned to Hazlitt when he left the kingdom.[197]

Conservatives did not, in fact, roll over and play dead when confronted with talismans of printing presses. Even if they had misgivings based on some form of the irreversibility thesis, they fought on bravely. But how?

---

*Vindiciae Britannicae: Christianity Interested in the Dismissal of Ministers: A Vindication of the People from the Charge of Blasphemy, and a Defence of the Freedom of the Press,* 2d ed., in *Pamphleteer* (1828) 19(38):395.

[197] Hazlitt, *Notes of a Journal through France and Italy* [1826], in *Works,* 10:186–87.

# THREE

# POISON AND ANTIDOTE

———∞∞∞———

M Y HEART is sick; my stomach turns; my head grows dizzy; The world seems to me to reel and stagger. The Crimes of Democracy, and the madness and folly of Aristocracy alike frighten and confound me."[1] Toward the end of his life, Burke was bitter and maudlin. The Duke of Bedford attacked him in Parliament; France descended rapidly; the popular press grew ever more strident. Worse, perhaps, in 1794 he faced the death of his son Richard, a son whose promise and talents Burke vehemently insisted on. No wonder he hoped to die while the old order he had championed still survived.[2] He died in July 1797, a couple of months before Napoleon's coup of 18 Fructidor and the cancerous expansion of war.

Those loyal to Burke hadn't the luxury of resting in the grave. They needed to figure out how to deal with the nauseating world of newspaper readers and alehouse debate. Priestley was made an honorary citizen by the French assembly; he turned down election to the assembly in 1792.[3] Facing prosecution for publishing his *Rights of Man,* Paine sailed the Channel and was elected to the assembly. (There he argued, with endearing political innocence, that Louis XVI ought not be executed but should be sent to America to learn the virtues of a simple, sturdy life.[4] At the end of 1793, he was arrested in Paris.)

---

[1] Burke to Mrs. John Crewe, *circa* 23 March 1795, *The Correspondence of Edmund Burke,* ed. Thomas W. Copeland, 10 vols. (Chicago: University of Chicago Press, 1958–1978), 8:216.

[2] *Observations on the Conduct of the Minority* [1793], in *The Works of the Right Honorable Edmund Burke,* 9th ed., 12 vols. (Boston: Little, Brown, 1889), 5:62–63; "A Letter to William Elliot, Esq." [1795], in *Works,* 5:121.

[3] Clarke Garrett, *Respectable Folly: Millenarians and the French Revolution in France and England* (Baltimore: Johns Hopkins University Press, 1975), p. 135.

[4] *Regicide and Revolution: Speeches at the Trial of Louis XVI,* ed. Michael Walzer,

Pamphleteers debated whether British radicals were the unwitting pawns of the French or worse yet in cahoots with them.⁵ "WHETHER those who write in defence of the Religion, Property and Laws of their Country, do it for hire or not, we cannot take upon us to say," drawled the *Anti-Jacobin*. But they were sure the radical press was at the beck and call of their French paymasters.⁶ Insurrection broke out in Ireland in the summer of 1798, complete with French troops landing.⁷

So it won't do to dismiss the concerns of the authorities, to paint them as cardboard villains clutching their power and privileges and crushing noble artisans striving for citizenship. Nor will it do to tighten the grips of the irreversibility thesis by cataloguing the bleary-eyed observers who went on echoing Burke's sentiments of gloom and doom. More poignant, many spied the hand of Providence in the day's events or longed for Providential intervention.⁸ Surely those

---

trans. Marian Rothstein (Cambridge: Cambridge University Press, 1974), pp. 208–14.

⁵ For instance, see James Currie, *A Letter, Commercial and Political, Addressed to . . . William Pitt* (London, 1793), and the response in George Chalmers, *An Estimate of the Comparative Strength of Great-Britain, during the Present and Four Preceding Reigns,* new ed. (London, 1794), pp. lxxix–xciv.

⁶ *Anti-Jacobin* (19 March 1798) no. 19, p. 148. This is the celebrated and glittering weekly edited by William Gifford, later editor of the *Quarterly,* and featuring poetry by George Canning, then Under-Secretary for Foreign Affairs and later prime minister: see *George Canning and His Friends,* ed. Josceline Bagot, 2 vols. (London: John Murray, 1909), 1:135. It is not the later, long-running, and relatively soporific *Anti-Jacobin Review.*

⁷ For an excellent account, see Marianne Elliott, *Partners in Revolution: The United Irishmen and France* (New Haven, CT: Yale University Press, 1982).

⁸ For instance, An Englishman, *A Rejoinder to Mr. Paine's Pamphlet, Entitled, Rights of Man* (London, 1791), p. 78; Mark Wilks, *The Origin & Stability of the French Revolution, a Sermon Preached at St. Paul's Chapel, Norwich, July 14, 1791* (n.p., 1791), pp. 7–8, 34–43; William Jones, *A Small Whole-Length of Dr. Priestley, from His Printed Works* (London, 1792), p. 36; James Bicheno, *The Signs of the Times* (Providence, 1794), pp. i, 9; Joseph Priestley, *The Present State of Europe Compared with Antient Prophecies; A Sermon, Preached at the Gravel Pit Meeting in Hackney, February 28, 1794,* 3d ed. (London, 1794), pp. 25–26, 31; *Thraliana: The Diary of Mrs. Hester Lynch Thrale (Later Mrs. Piozzi) 1776–1809,* ed. Katharine C. Balderston, 2d ed., 2 vols. (Oxford: Clarendon, 1951), 2:913–14 [2 March 1795]; *Some Account of the Life and Writings of Mrs. Trimmer, with Original Letters, and Meditations and Prayers, Selected from Her Journal,* 2 vols. (London, 1814), 2:330–31 [23 July 1797]; *The Speeches of the Right Honourable William Pitt, in the House of Commons,* 3d ed., 3 vols. (London, 1817), 3:92 [3 February 1800]; Samuel Horsley, *The Charge of Samuel Lord Bishop of Rochester, to the Clergy of His Diocese, Delivered at His Second General Visitation, in the Year 1800* (London, 1800), p. 3; George III to Lord Hawkesbury, 30 April 1801, *The Later Correspondence of George III,* ed. A. Aspinall, 5 vols. (Cambridge:

who feared and loathed the ruckus of citizenship did more than sit around and sigh or wait for God to save them. What did they say? What did they do?

## EDUCATION AND INSUBORDINATION

Educating the lower orders was worse than useless, agreed another chorus of eighteenth-century writers. The ever acerbic Mandeville punctured complacency about charity schools by arguing in 1723 "that all hard and dirty Work ought in a well-govern'd Nation to be

---

Cambridge University Press, 1962–1970), 3:642–43; *Hints toward Forming the Character of a Young Princess* [1805], chaps. 28–29, in *The Works of Hannah More*, 9 vols. (London, 1840–1843), 4:362–92; Hannah More to Mr. Knox, 21 January 1806, in William Roberts, *Memoirs of the Life and Correspondence of Mrs. Hannah More*, 2d ed., 4 vols. (London, 1834), 3:238–39; *Christian Morals* [1812], chap. 2, in *Works of Hannah More*, 9:26–39; Thomas Clarkson, *The History of the Rise, Progress, & Accomplishment of the Abolition of the African Slave-Trade, by the British Parliament*, 2 vols. (London, 1808), 1:201–2; *Quarterly Review* (June 1812) 7:437, (July 1832) 47:587; *The Present Revolutions in Europe, and Other Signs of the Times, Compared with Scripture Predictions and History, Shewing, that in 1822 the Regeneration of the European Dynasties Will Be Completed* (Glasgow, 1820); Robert Southey, *History of the Peninsular War*, 3 vols. (London, 1823–1832), 2:25; Southey to Henry Taylor, 5 May 1827, *The Life and Correspondence of Robert Southey*, ed. Charles Cuthbert Southey, 6 vols. (London, 1849–1850), 5:295; Southey to Mrs. Hodson, 10 February 1829, *Life and Correspondence of Southey*, 6:24–25; Southey to Caroline Bowles, 2 May 1831, *The Correspondence of Robert Southey with Caroline Bowles*, ed. Edward Dowden (Dublin, 1881), pp. 224–25; Southey to John May, 20 May 1833, *The Letters of Robert Southey to John May 1797 to 1838* (Austin, TX: Jenkins Publishing Co., The Pemberton Press, 1976), pp. 258–59; Southey to Caroline Bowles, 12 October 1833, *Correspondence of Southey with Bowles*, pp. 284–85; Southey to May, 30 December 1833, *Letters of Southey to May*, p. 263; Southey to C. W. W. Wynn, 26 April 1834, *Selections from the Letters of Robert Southey*, ed. John Wood Warter, 4 vols. (London, 1856), 4:373; James Stephen, *The Slavery of the British West India Colonies Delineated*, 2 vols. (London, 1824–1830), 2:394–95; *John Bull* (11 March 1827) 7(326):76, (20 May 1827) 7(336):156; Mary Berry, *A Comparative View of the Social Life of England and France, from the Restoration of Charles the Second, to the French Revolution* (London, 1828), p. 3; Lord Ellenborough's diary, 2 March 1831, in *Three Early Nineteenth Century Diaries*, ed. A. Aspinall (London: Williams and Norgate, 1952), p. 62; Wellington to Gleig, 11 April 1831, in *Three Early Nineteenth Century Diaries*, p. xxxv; *The Journal of Sir Walter Scott*, ed. W. E. K. Anderson (Oxford: Clarendon, 1972), p. 669 [20 October 1831]; William Ewart Gladstone, *The Gladstone Diaries*, ed. M. R. D. Foot and H. C. G. Matthew, 11 vols. (Oxford: Clarendon, 1968–1990), 1:596 [31 December 1832]; Marquess of Londonderry to Wellington, 1 January 1833, in Historical Manuscripts Commission, *The Prime Ministers' Papers: Wellington Political Correspondence I: 1833–November 1834*, ed. John Brooke and Julia Gandy (London: Her Majesty's Stationery Office, 1975), p. 9; *Table Talk*, in *The Collected Works of Samuel Taylor Coleridge*, ed. Kathleen Coburn, Bart Winer, and others, in progress (Princeton, NJ: Princeton University Press, 1969–), 14(1):369–70 [4 May 1833].

the Lot and Portion of the Poor, and that to divert their Children from useful Labour till they are fourteen or fifteen Years old, is a wrong Method to qualify them for it when they are grown up."[9] Mandeville struck a nerve. *Cato's Letters,* scourge of courtly corruption, laid into the absurd pretensions cultivated by charity schools two months later: "No Education ought to be more discountenanced by a State, than putting Chimera's and airy Notions into the Heads of those who ought to have Pickaxes in their Hands. . . ."[10] In 1757, Soame Jenyns pressed the idea:

> Ignorance, or the want of knowledge and literature, the appointed lot of all born to poverty, and the drudgeries of life, is the only opiate capable of infusing the insensibility which can enable them to endure the miseries of the one, and the fatigues of the other. It is a cordial administered by the gracious hand of providence; of which they ought never to be deprived by an ill-judged and improper education.[11]

Reviewing Jenyns's book, Dr. Johnson offered hedging agreement, worrying about the inhumane business of identifying some as born for poverty and the cruelty of malevolent dominion masquerading as judicious social policy.[12] Lord Kames had no such hesitations: "Knowledge is a dangerous acquisition to the labouring poor: the more of it that is possessed by a shepherd, a ploughman, or any drudge, the less satisfaction he will have in labour."[13] Why educate people to live beyond their appointed station?

Observers kept pressing this query after the French Revolution, but again with a more pointed edge: Sunday schools, mechanics' institutes, and the like meant there was in fact more popular education going on; and the Revolution justifiably made people more troubled about such matters. *John Bull* dourly warmed to the theme: "We overeducate the poor and what do they say?—that they are superior to the

[9] Bernard Mandeville, *The Fable of the Bees; or Private Vices, Publick Benefits,* ed. F. B. Kaye, 2 vols. (Oxford: Clarendon, 1924; reprint ed. Indianapolis, IN: LibertyClassics, 1988), 1:409; see too 1:286–88; for the dating of this part of the text, 1:xxxiv n. 1.

[10] John Trenchard and Thomas Gordon, *Cato's Letters,* 3d ed., 4 vols. (London, 1733; reprint ed. New York: Russell and Russell, 1969), 4:243 [15 June 1723].

[11] *A Free Inquiry into the Nature and Origin of Evil* [1757], in *The Works of Soame Jenyns, Esq.,* 4 vols. (London, 1790), 3:49.

[12] *The Works of Samuel Johnson, LL.D.,* 11 vols. (London, 1787), 10:231–33.

[13] Henry Home, Lord Kames, *Sketches of the History of Man,* 2d ed., 4 vols. (Edinburgh, 1778), 3:90. Compare Joseph Priestley, *Lectures on History, and General Policy,* 2 vols. (Philadelphia, 1803), 1:35–36.

drudgery of cotton-spinning, or digging, or doing menial offices."
Once chimney sweeps and pork butchers pose as philosophers and
read and write for newspapers, "who will sweep the chimnies and kill
the pigs?"[14] "We are to have our pots and pans mended, our clothes
made, our fields ploughed, and our streets macadamized—by philosophers!" jeered A Country Gentleman. "Thrice happy nation, to enjoy blessings such as these!"[15]

Some critics were happy to conclude that the very thought of educating the lower orders was a mistake, or at least that education ought
to be restricted to somber instruction in their station and its duties.
Young Cobbett disparaged "Sunday schools for making scholars of
those whose business it is to delve" as another symptom of British
madness.[16] Twenty years before Brougham founded the Society for
the Diffusion of Useful Knowledge, one social critic qualified his enthusiasm about educating workers:

> It is not, however, proposed . . . that the children of the poor should be
> educated in a manner to elevate their minds above the rank they are
> destined to fill in society. . . . Utopian schemes for an extensive diffu-
> sion of knowledge would be injurious and absurd. A right bias to their
> minds, and a sufficient education to enable them to preserve, and to
> estimate properly, the religious and moral instruction they receive, is all
> that is, or ought ever to be, in contemplation. To go beyond this point
> would be to confound the ranks of society upon which the general hap-
> piness of the lower orders, no less than those that are more elevated,
> depends; since by indiscriminate education those destined for laborious
> occupations would become discontented and unhappy in an inferior
> situation of life. . . .[17]

[14] *John Bull* (30 October 1825) 5(44):348. See too Richard Polwhele, *The History of Devonshire*, 3 vols. (Exeter, 1797), 1:316–17; Priscilla Wakefield, *Reflections on the Present Condition of the Female Sex; with Suggestions for Its Improvement* (London, 1798; reprint ed. New York: Garland, 1974), pp. 156–57; William Playfair, *An Inquiry into the Permanent Causes of the Decline and Fall of Powerful and Wealthy Nations* (London, 1805), pp. 97, 227.

[15] A Country Gentleman, *The Consequences of a Scientific Education to the Working Classes of This Country Pointed Out; and the Theories of Mr. Brougham on That Subject Confuted; in a Letter to the Marquess of Lansdown* (London, 1826), p. 44.

[16] *Political Register* (14 May 1803) 3(19):729.

[17] Patrick Colquhoun, *A New and Appropriate System of Education for the Labouring People* (London, 1806), pp. 12–13; see too Colquhoun, *A Treatise on Indigence* (London, 1806), chap. 5.

Instruction had better be religious and the religion had better be the right sort. Because Joseph Lancaster was a Quaker whose educational agenda deftly sidestepped any commitments to the Anglican church, some denounced his work.[18]

Others went on to design schools that would inculcate social hierarchy instead of democratic equality. Elizabeth Hamilton envisioned students organized into landlords, tenants, and undertenants, their classroom responsibilities mimicking and preparing them for the world outside.[19] Even radical John Wade conceded that "education ought to have a reference to the atmosphere in which we are destined to live and move," that those born to fortune or political power needed different schooling from those born to the plough. A bit feebly, Wade added that anyway no portion of the community ought to be prevented from pursuing any kind of learning.[20]

We need not restrict our attention to class or status, the Weberian categories summoned up by talk of the lower orders. Observers worried, too, about making sure that boys and girls grew up appropriately masculine and feminine; or, to invoke a distinction I'll gnaw at later on, making sure that each sex attained its proper gender identity. Mrs. West—like many other woman writers of the day, she advertised her marital status on the title page, in part to show that she wrote authoritatively—complained that too many writers on education paid no attention to the differences between boys and girls. Unless men and women were to be assigned the same duties, she held, "mothers should early endeavour to give to each sex the proper bias; for, surely, fribbles and viragos are equally contemptible and unnatural." Boys needed to attain "energy, courage, and enterprise"; girls needed to be "docile, contented, prudent and domestic."[21] So some schools molded their young charges for the tasks of both gender and work-

[18] See the comments of Mrs. Trimmer and Andrew Bell in Robert Southey and Charles Cuthbert Southey, *The Life of the Rev. Andrew Bell*, 3 vols. (London, 1844), 2:136, 2:149. For a stirring bit of self-defense, see Joseph Lancaster, *An Appeal for Justice, in the Cause of Ten Thousand Poor Children; and for the Honour of the Holy Scriptures*, 3d ed. with additions (London, 1807).

[19] Elizabeth Hamilton, *The Cottagers of Glenburnie: A Tale for the Farmer's Ingle-Nook* (Edinburgh, 1808; reprint ed. New York: Garland, 1974), pp. 387–89. See too Wakefield, *Reflections*, pp. 61–63.

[20] John Wade, *History of the Middle and Working Classes; with A Popular Exposition of the Economical and Political Principles Which Have Influenced the Past and Present Condition of the Industrious Orders* (London, 1833), p. 497.

[21] Jane West, *Letters to a Young Lady*, 3d ed., 3 vols. (London, 1806), 3:218–19.

place by giving boys and girls separate curricula. In 1791, a Hampshire churchman opened one school for girls, another for boys. Both learned to read. But the girls learned to "knit, spin, sew, and mend their own clothes, so as to fit them to be useful daughters, and good wives"; the boys learned neat handwriting and arithmetic.[22]

The challenge put squarely to the proponents of popular education, then, was that it would leave the lower orders disaffected. The hierarchical model of social order suggested that children be groomed for their places, that further education would make them restless. Intergenerational mobility is gracefully finessed here on purpose. Social mobility, equal opportunity, the career open to talents: these noisome categories belong to disreputable Jacobins. In an orderly world, we can be confident that the son of a farmer will take his place behind the plow. And we ought not disturb his stolid assurance in his work by cramming his cranium, lest he notice that the manure stinks. How did the champions of education respond to this challenge?

It was sometimes disposed of by an appeal to the logic of positional goods. Literacy or education, in this view, permitted the upper crust to sniff disdainfully at manual labor because it was a certificate of high status. But if everyone were literate or educated, the upper crust couldn't preen themselves and the lower orders couldn't be malcontent—not on those grounds, anyway. "It is said that the poor, proud of their attainments in learning, will no longer submit to the drudgery to which they have been accustomed in their state of ignorance." But, responded the *Edinburgh Review,* if everyone could read, no one would be proud of reading.[23] The National Society for the Education of the Children throughout England and Wales in the Principles of the Established Church, whose masthead boasted a list of establishment luminaries as imposing as its name, adopted the same line. "If the whole body is elevated, none of its component parts will be displaced."[24]

---

[22] *The Reports of the Society for Bettering the Condition and Increasing the Comforts of the Poor,* 5 vols. (London, 1798–1808), 1:273, 275 [5 April 1798]. Note the description of Kendal's schools of industry: *Reports,* 3:244–64 [10 August 1801]; the Kendal curriculum is reproduced in *Reports,* vol. 3, app., pp. 16–20. Note too *Rules and Orders for Governing the Mile-End, New-Town, Stepney Charity-School, for Educating and Cloathing Sixty Poor Children* (London, 1801), p. 4.

[23] *Edinburgh Review* (October 1807) 11(21):70. See too *Quarterly Review* (October 1813) 10:33–34.

[24] Paidophilos, "A Letter to the Editor of the *National Adviser,* on the Subject of

In this light, consider the frustrations of one Somerset rector. John Skinner was pompous and patronizing, blessed with an irascible and finely discriminating sensitivity and a capacity to nurse grudges for years on end. He seems to have experienced life as a series of outrageous assaults on his dignity, assaults from all quarters, even from his children. And he was perceptive enough to link these petty everyday slights not with his own idiosyncratic personality, but with the politics of the day; honest enough to sculpt a diary in which he doesn't appear as a hero.

One day, some of his servants announced that their beds and accommodations were inadequate, what one might find in a rustic farmhouse instead of a gentleman's abode, and notified Skinner that they would be quitting that same day. Skinner suspected that another of his servants was stirring up trouble again. "This is the march of intellect with a vengeance," he wrote. "I wish Mr. Brougham had only a tythe of what I am obliged to submit to from the lower orders. He would not then shew himself so strenuous an advocate for the liberty of their doing what they please, which in fact is anarchy and insubordination."[25] In Whig-infested parliamentary corridors and energetically reforming parlors of London, in Brougham's stilted prose and bustling organizational enterprise, the march of intellect looked ennobling. On the ground in Somerset, it made the servants uppity. So too in a bit of deathless poetry the *Age* mocked "Cockney Students," linen drapers' assistants out to pursue an education, as pathetic social climbers.[26] Decades later, a writer remembered a Belfast landlord in 1816: "We were greatly surprised one day to see him reading, or pretending to read, the newspapers. He had the wrong end turned towards him, and it afterwards appeared he could not read."[27]

---

National Education," in *National Education; or A Short Account of the Efforts Which Have Been Made to Educate the Children of the Poor, According to the New System Invented by the Rev. Dr. Bell* (London, 1811?), p. 20; the group's masthead is on p. 4. Compare Jeremy Bentham, *Chrestomathia* [1817], ed. M. J. Smith and W. H. Burston (Oxford: Clarendon, 1983), pp. 44–47.

[25] John Skinner, *Journal of a Somerset Rector 1803–1834*, ed. Howard and Peter Coombs (Bath: Kingsmead, 1971), p. 346 [5 July 1828]. Contrast Francis Edward Witts's calm admiration of "the march of intellect" in scientific experiments in *The Diary of a Cotswold Parson*, ed. David Verey (Dursley, Gloucestershire: Alan Sutton, 1978), p. 67 [29 September 1826].

[26] *Age* (18 September 1825) no. 19, pp. 148–49.

[27] James Paterson, *Autobiographical Reminiscences* (Glasgow, 1871), p. 50. I'm not sure what to make of Samuel Bamford's recollection in his *Early Days* (London, 1849), p. 280 of reading "Hume's decline and fall of the Roman Empire."

Francis Place, the radical tailor, ruefully revealed the consequences of putting on airs. Upstairs from his shop, he had a library of some 1,000 volumes, a collection he always tried to keep secret from his clients. But Place's foreman happened to take one customer upstairs when he came to try on some pantaloons. Surprised, the customer turned sarcastic; a few days later, he taunted Place for some "trifling omission," suggesting that he was paying too much attention to his books, not enough to his business. The customer didn't just take his business elsewhere. "His pride was hurt," so he persuaded some others to desert Place as well.

> Had these persons been told that I had never read a book, that I was ignorant of every thing but my business, that I sotted in a public house, they would not have made the least objection to me. I should have been a "fellow" beneath them, and they would have patronized me; but,—to accumulate books and to be supposed to know something of their contents, to seek for friends, too, among literary and scientific men, was putting myself on an equality with themselves, if not indeed assuming a superiority; was an abominable offence in a tailor, if not a crime, which deserved punishment. . . .[28]

Notice the appropriate play here on *patronizing* a tailor, which means both giving him one's business and looking down on him. This isn't an accidental homonym. In this world the tailor loses the subservient status that qualifies him for business if he reads and talks to intellectuals. According to the *Oxford English Dictionary*, both meanings first emerge right around 1800.[29]

## CONTAGION, POISON, AND AGENCY

The sun streaming in, clearing the mists of prejudice away, the march of intellect, the schoolmaster abroad: these are the catchphrases of those sanguine about enlightenment. Their opponents are at no loss for imagery. Theirs is a litany of contagion, plague, disease, intoxication, pollution, poison, venom, conflagration.

In his enthusiastic campaigns to promote war with France, Burke hammered away at the theme of contagion. So he applauded

---

[28] *The Autobiography of Francis Place (1771–1854)*, ed. Mary Thale (Cambridge: Cambridge University Press, 1972), pp. 222–23; see too p. 16. Place is recalling events from 1812.

[29] *OED* s.v. *patronize*, v., senses 3 and 4.

the most clearly just and necessary war that this or any other nation ever carried on, in order to save my country from the iron yoke of [France's] power, and from the more dreadful contagion of its principles,—to preserve, while they can be preserved, pure and untainted, the ancient, inbred integrity, piety, good-nature, and good-humor of the people of England, from the dreadful pestilence which, beginning in France, threatens to lay waste the whole moral and in a great degree the whole physical world. . . .[30]

So too he felt "great dread and apprehension from the contagious nature of these abominable principles," principles which would take on a life of their own, the parlous monster summoned up by a hapless sorcerer's apprentice, and "blast all the health and vigour of that happy constitution which we enjoy. . . ."[31] Indeed, all Europe was contracting "some new and grievous malady, from the contagion of which I am far from thinking that this Country is likely to be exempted."[32] The great chain of being allows Burke to slide effortlessly from moral to physical waste, just as the body politic allows him to think of England's constitution as healthy but threatened.

William Windham, Burke's avid disciple, echoed the master's language. Rejecting innovation, parliamentary reform, "the strange mixture of metaphysics with politics," and the advice of theorists, a seductive package of pernicious nonsense, he urged the House of Commons, "Let us, in good time, avoid the infection."[33] The "whole Jacobin tribe," novelist Fanny Burney reported in explaining everyone's alarm, was "spreading contagion over the whole surface of the Earth."[34] Describing Scotland in 1795, the sturdy narrator of one novel invoked a "seditious infection which fevered the minds of the sedentary weavers and, working like flatulence in the stomachs of the

[30] *Letter to a Noble Lord* [1796], in *Works,* 5:204–5.

[31] Burke to the Comtesse de Montrond, 25 January 1791, *Correspondence,* 6:211.

[32] Burke to Earl Fitzwilliam, 17 August 1792, *Correspondence,* 7:170.

[33] William Windham, *Speeches in Parliament,* 3 vols. (London, 1812), 1:193 [4 March 1790]. See too Walpole to Henry Seymour Conway, 31 August 1792, *The Yale Edition of Horace Walpole's Correspondence,* ed. W. S. Lewis, 48 vols. (New Haven, CT: Yale University Press, 1937–1983), 39:491–92; *Thraliana,* 2:848–49 [October to December 1792]; *Thoughts on the Present Critical Situation of These Kingdoms: Addressed to the Serious Consideration of Every Friend to His Country* (London, 1796), p. 32.

[34] Fanny Burney to Mrs. Locke, 20 December 1792, *The Journals and Letters of Fanny Burney (Madame D'Arblay),* ed. Joyce Hemlow and others, 12 vols. (Oxford: Clarendon, 1972–1984), 2:5.

cotton-spinners, sent up into their heads a vain and diseased fume of infidel philosophy."[35] Cobbett feared being suffocated "with the infected and pestilential air of a democratic club room."[36] George III himself described the spread of Jacobinism in terms of "disease," "infection," and "contagion."[37]

George saw it too as a smoldering fire that would blaze out again.[38] Others feared an inferno of revolutionary enthusiasm. "The triumph of philosophy is the universal conflagration of Europe," thought Burke.[39] Mixing his metaphors, the Marquis of Buckingham advised Lord Grenville that "the infection is gaining ground in every quarter; and . . . there is not in this country a military force which can effectually check the first burst of the fire, if it should catch here with the same rapidity with which it spreads in other parts of Europe."[40] Mixing his own metaphors a bit more nimbly, Southey managed to accommodate "the plague of diseased opinions" and "a conflagration or a flood" in just one sentence.[41] Desolate after the passage of the Reform Bill of 1832, a bombastic Tory intoned, "We have been for half a century the ark which preserved in the great democratic deluge the principles of social order and Monarchical Government. We are now become a fire-ship, which will spread the conflagration."[42]

The spread of Jacobin opinions could also be cast as venom coursing through the body politic. One intellectual was warily confident in Britain's legislators, but still she feared that radicals "were beginning

[35] *Annals of the Parish* [1821], in *The Works of John Galt*, ed. D. S. Meldrum and William Roughead, 10 vols. (Edinburgh: John Grant, 1936), 1:215.

[36] *The Life and Adventures of Peter Porcupine*, 2d ed. (Philadelphia, 1796), p. 22, reprinted in William Cobbett, *Porcupine's Works*, 12 vols. (London, 1801), 4:42.

[37] Dr. Burney's journal, 1805, in Fanny Burney, *Memoirs of Doctor Burney*, 3 vols. (London, 1832), 3:361–62.

[38] *Diaries and Correspondence of James Harris, First Earl of Malmesbury*, ed. his grandson, 4 vols. (London, 1844), 4:63 [26–28 November 1801].

[39] "Preface to Brissot's Address to His Constituents" [1794], in *Works*, 5:89.

[40] Marquis of Buckingham to Lord Grenville, 8 November 1792, Historical Manuscripts Commission, *Report on the Manuscripts of J. B. Fortescue, Esq., Preserved at Dropmore*, 10 vols. (London, 1892–1927), 2:327.

[41] Robert Southey, *Sir Thomas More: Or, Colloquies on Progress and Prospects of Society*, 2 vols. (London, 1829), 1:31. See too Southey, *The Life of Wesley; and the Rise and Progress of Methodism*, 2 vols. (London, 1820), 1:329; Southey, *Essays, Moral and Political*, 2 vols. (London, 1832), 1:330 [1816]; Southey, *Journal of a Tour in the Netherlands in the Autumn of 1815* (Boston: Houghton, Mifflin and Company, 1902), pp. 68–69.

[42] Croker to a friend, 29 May 1832, *The Croker Papers*, ed. Louis J. Jennings, 2d ed. rev., 3 vols. (London, 1885; reprint ed. New York: AMS Press, 1972), 2:182.

to diffuse, with alarming success, the venom of ungrateful and rebellious sedition amongst the easily-dazzled vulgar."[43] The same language became the careening stuff of burlesque and spoof in Eaton's
publications.[44]

So I should sharpen my too casual suggestion that the venom is
coursing through the body politic: for it's especially the lower orders
that these political toxicologists inspect and find wanting. The image
dovetails elegantly with the schism Burke finds—or installs—between
the lower orders and the political nation, between those who should
rely on prejudice and illusion and those who need to face bracing gusts
of political argument. The venom in question is the noxious substance
that dissolves prejudice or unthinking loyalty, that leaves the minds of
the people "sore and ulcerated,"[45] that irritates the stout bellies of
English subjects. Not that it's impossible to fear for the health and
purity of one's own mind. One devout Christian refused to read a piece
by Carlile, on one of his crusades to promote atheism: "Oh! no Mr.
Carlile, I cannot, I cannot indeed, I am afraid it will poison my mind."[46]
Nor is it impossible to fear the poisoning of a singularly elite mind. One
cartoonist exhibited hapless George, Prince of Wales, with a naked
Lady Douglas, chief witness against Caroline, sprawled in his lap over
the caption, "A Venomous Viper Poisoning The R—l Mind."[47] Usually,
though, those liable to poisoning are lowly others whose cognitive
capacities the lofty speaker doubts. Poisoning the minds of the lower
orders: this is not just a favorite verbal formula of the conservatives; it's
also their most macabre nightmare.

One of Paine's opponents tossed and turned with this nightmare:
"A pamphlet called the RIGHTS of MAN has intoxicated the irreflec-
tive part of the British community, and poisoned the minds of the
plebean inhabitants of great cities. . . ."[48] An anonymous writer, dis-

---

[43] Anna Seward to Helen Williams, 17 January 1793, *Letters of Anna Seward,* 6 vols.
(Edinburgh, 1811), 3:208–9.

[44] A Gentleman, *The Pernicious Principles of Tom Paine, Exposed, in an Address to Labourers and Mechanics,* 2d ed. (London, 1794), pp. 3–5; also in *Politics for the People,* vol. 1,
pt. 2(1):4–7 [1794].

[45] *Appeal from the New to the Old Whigs,* 2d ed. [1791], in *Works,* 4:201.

[46] *Lion* (26 December 1828) 2(26):808.

[47] *BMC* no. 12029 [1 April 1813].

[48] John Stewart, *Good Sense: Addressed to the British Nation, as Their Pre-Eminent and
Peculiar Characteristic, in the Present Awful Crisis, or War of Social Existence* (London, 1794),
p. 10.

tressed by the lackadaisical efforts of the government, sweated through it: "Secret associations of a seditious complexion are continued, and infamous libels are still circulated to poison the patriotism and loyalty of the lower classes—"[49] Sir Richard Hill had the chills over it: he warned the prime minister of "the inconceivable mischief done, through the channel of inflammatory newspapers poisoning the public mind. . . ."[50]

The *Anti-Jacobin Review* suffered through harrowing versions of the nightmare, recurrent ones too:

> The man who should leave arsenic on his kitchen dresser would be considered a madman; yet the worst consequence that could follow such an act, would be harmless, would be insignificant, compared with the eradication of all religious and moral principles from the minds of his family. But *this* effect *might* ensue from his introduction of the Edinburgh Review into his house. Yet, alas! numbers who would shudder at the *least* evil, would not hesitate to encourage the *greatest*. Such is the thoughtlessness, such the inconsistency, of man. Tremblingly alive to personal inflictions; but perfectly insensible to mental poison.[51]

*Blackwood's* sat bolt upright, eyes bulging: "The mania of reform is raging far and wide, and the people have taken the radical infection in the *natural way*,—the necessary consequence of inhaling the pestiferous miasmata which spring from the publications of the Cobbetts and Carliles of the day. . . ."[52]

I could go on quoting in this vein for many lachrymose pages. The language suggests that when workers turn radical, they haven't done anything. Instead, something (awful) has happened to them. They haven't adopted a new political view; it has adopted them. What philosophers term the intentional stance is sometimes justified as a matter of predictive efficacy.[53] But it's also a matter of expressing respect for others. To think of the workers as buffeted about by causal forces beyond their control, as mere objects in the world, is to deny them

---

[49] *A Concise Sketch of the Intended Revolution in England; with a Few Hints on the Obvious Methods to Avert It* (London, 1794), p. 13.

[50] Sir Richard Hill to Addington, August 1802, in George Pellew, *The Life and Correspondence of . . . Henry Addington, First Viscount Sidmouth*, 3 vols. (London, 1847), 2:157.

[51] *Anti-Jacobin Review* (February 1811) 38:138. See too AntiJacobin in *Anti-Jacobin Review* (February 1817) 51:643; *Anti-Jacobin Review* (December 1819) 57:322–24.

[52] *Blackwood's Edinburgh Magazine* (February 1821) 8(47):493.

[53] Daniel C. Dennett, *The Intentional Stance* (Cambridge, MA: MIT Press, 1987).

dignity and responsibility. The basic intuition is that agency depends on rationality, that if one hasn't acted rationally, one hasn't *acted*, strictly speaking, at all. (So far the category of rationality is left empty, a promissory note of whopping dimensions.) True, we can say "I acted impulsively." But we can also discard that as mere behavior or at least think that it's barely action at all.

Not that this is the only viable conception of agency around. The legal view of criminal responsibility, with its focus on *mens rea,* is structurally different. Jeremiah Brandreth ran afoul of the difference after leading an abortive insurrection in 1817. He marched toward London, collecting arms and men, threatening those he met that they could join or be killed. The evidence against him and his followers was imposing. Imaginatively, coyly, desperately, Brandreth's lawyer reminded the jury that Cobbett's writings, "the most malignant and diabolical that had ever issued from the English press . . . were hawked up and down the country poisoning the minds of the poor and ignorant," and pleaded that Brandreth was just their innocent victim.[54] Unsurprisingly, this novel argument failed. Brandreth and two others were executed, eleven more transported for life, three more transported for fourteen years, and six imprisoned.[55]

To return briefly to the church-and-king mobs, the sort that cheerfully burned down Priestley's home: our vexed and vexing debates about their putative false consciousness are in part debates about the rationality or reasonableness of what they do, not simple descriptive debates. The facts of the matter are, as always, relevant: in assessing their good works, we want to know how significant a range of options they faced, what range of viewpoints they could consider, and so on. But the facts aren't finally dispositive. Deciding on their false consciousness, their agency, their responsibility, is in part making a political judgment.[56]

[54] Pellew, *Life and Correspondence of Addington,* 3:177 n. A somewhat different transcript is offered in *The Trials of Jeremiah Brandreth, William Turner, Isaac Ludlam, George Weightman, and Others, for High Treason,* rep. William Brodie Gurney, 2 vols. (London, 1817), 1:198–200. See too Robert Adams's cross-examination in George Theodore Wilkinson, *An Authentic History of the Cato-Street Conspiracy* (London, 1820; reprint ed. New York: Arno Press, 1972), p. 292.

[55] *Trials of Brandreth and Others,* 2:501–2.

[56] See Marion Smiley, *Moral Responsibility and the Boundaries of Community: Power and Accountability from a Pragmatic Point of View* (Chicago: University of Chicago Press, 1992).

Anyway, these conservatives with nightmares don't credit those ale-house patrons, greedily drinking in radical prose from the apostles of sedition along with their beer, with reflecting on the arguments and rationally criticizing their previous views. Instead the lethal effects occur behind their backs, in ways they're unaware of. They're not in control. They're not agents. Or at least the scope of their agency is radically diminished.

Why take that view? Imagine first a substantive account. Jacobin views are on their face absurd. We don't have to investigate what is supposed to justify them or what process gave rise to them, because we know already that no sound justification or reliable process could yield such crazy doctrines. Indeed—and I conjecture that this line of argument motivated much conservative criticism—we're justified in concluding that there must be something deeply wrong with whatever the process was, however superficially attractive it was. If alehouse debate brews enthusiasm for the rights of man, so much the worse for debate.

Perhaps this substantive account seems question-begging. How do we know that Jacobin views are so crazy? So imagine instead a pro-cedural account. Regardless of the substance of Jacobin views, the ways in which they're ingested by workers are not conducive to critical thinking. Workers aren't used to political theory, so they're innocent to begin with, easily deceived. Nothing needs to be said about the native stupidity of the lower orders, but any such view would fill out the account nicely. And sometimes such things were said. For some conservatives, deliberative ability, that delicate combination of intel-ligence and caution, mapped perfectly onto social class. One of those ubiquitous government spies at meetings of the London Correspond-ing Society (LCS) distinguished "some of decent tradesmen-like ap-pearance" who were "cautious"; "others of an apparent lower Order," "resolute and determined"; and "the very lowest order of Society," "wretched looking blackguards," "very violent," "ready to adopt every thing tending [to] Confusion & Anarchy."[57]

Then again, the rhetoric of Jacobin arguments plays on base pas-sions, on resentment of social superiors and the like, not on judicious considerations of justice or social order. Worse, the settings in which

---

[57] *Selections from the Papers of the London Corresponding Society 1792–1799*, ed. Mary Thale (Cambridge: Cambridge University Press, 1983), p. 184 [1794].

the lower orders encounter these arguments disrupt any attempts at careful consideration. Even some radicals granted this much. Recall Carlile's facile dismissal of "public boisterous assemblies" and his desire that workers deliberate in the peace and quiet of their own homes. Or consider William Godwin's disgust with loud assemblies and heated partisanship, his devotion to placid chats between just two speakers and "the patient lucubrations of the philosopher, and the labour of the midnight oil."[58] So when a worker exposed to Tom Paine in an alehouse gets excited about democracy, it's reasonable to cast him as an unwitting victim. It's not that he's changed his mind; it's rather that his mind has been changed, by the inexorable operation of some cognitive process he neither understands nor endorses.

This is a quick pass over a knotty terrain; I want briefly to indicate some of the complications. It is not obvious that it begs the question to decide *a priori* that Jacobinism or any other view is unacceptable. It seems plausible to evaluate belief-generating procedures not just by the mechanisms they rely on but also by the products they crank out. So, too, we might decide that an apparently eccentric view deserves more respect because it emerged from a procedure we have independent reason to endorse.

Or again: it might be rational to submit to a process even if it operated by irrational means and even if you knew that. Consider the epistemic plight of someone who begins to think that his unflagging loyalty to George III is itself not particularly rational. A calculated series of political rituals gave rise to it, say, not any process of careful intellectual investigation; and on reflection it seems hard to endorse. Still, the thought of venturing into the local alehouse is repugnant: he shrinks back instinctively at the thought of the rascals in there cheerfully toasting the King's speedy death. Probably they're blaspheming Christianity, too. Suppose such a worker followed the advice of Carlile and Godwin and read radical pamphlets at home. Suppose he came to think that they were right, or at least more attractive politically than his prior loyalism. But suppose he found himself unable actually to adopt them. He might rationally submit to the dubious

---

[58] William Godwin, *Enquiry Concerning Political Justice and Its Influence on Morals and Happiness,* ed. F. E. L. Priestley, 3 vols. (Toronto: University of Toronto Press, 1946), 1:285–300, 2:368 [1798]. See too Godwin to Percy Bysshe Shelley, 4 March 1812, *The Letters of Percy Bysshe Shelley,* ed. Frederick L. Jones, 2 vols. (Oxford: Clarendon, 1964), 1:261.

tactics of the alehouse, to the alcohol and the boisterous good fellow-
ship, in order to overcome his instinctive disgust.

Complications aside, conservatives were inclined to doubt the
agency of radical workers. They flirted instead with assigning a black
magical agency to revolutionary plague and poison itself. The French
Revolution, according to Southey, "threatened to propagate itself
throughout the whole civilised world."[59] Or, more picturesquely,
"Dogmatical Atheism struts and crows upon its dunghills," laying
eggs, hatching "hissing, wriggling, and venomous" cockatrices.[60] Conservative worries scaled wondrous heights of schematic splendor in
*Waldorf; or, The Dangers of Philosophy,* a dreadful novel. There listening
to philosophical argument is enough to drive Lady Sophia mad and
kill her in four days.[61] Again, I suggest that we beware of discarding
such talk as a mere figure of speech. Instead we should take seriously
the possibility that sometimes people adopt ideas but sometimes ideas
adopt people—and sometimes with devastating results.

## PATHOLOGIES OF DEBATE

On the eve of the French Revolution, Hannah More already was deriding proud talk of enlightenment. "In vain do we boast of the enlightened eighteenth century, and conceitedly talk as if human reason had not a manacle left about her, but that philosophy had broken
down all the strongholds of prejudice, ignorance, and superstition":
this, she snorted, in a world where Mesmer became fabulously
wealthy touting animal magnetism, where Londoners flocked to a
fortune-teller, where people believed in Lavater's zany theories of
physiognomy and in divining rods, where ministers cast out devils—
and where slavery had its defenders in print and in Parliament.[62] The
*Anti-Jacobin Review* smirked at popular gullibility, with people willing
to pay fourteen shillings to read stale bits of recycled Hazlitt.[63] "In
this age of reason, anything rather than reason has ruled," opined the

[59] Southey, *History of the Peninsular War,* 1:12.

[60] Robert Southey, *Sir Thomas More,* 2:110. Compare *The Statesman's Manual* [1816],
in *Works of Coleridge,* 6:22.

[61] Sophia King, *Waldorf; or, The Dangers of Philosophy: A Philosophical Tale,* 2 vols. (London, 1798; reprint ed. New York: Garland, 1974), 1:117–27.

[62] Hannah More to Horace Walpole, September 1788, in Roberts, *Memoirs of
Hannah More,* 2:120.

[63] *Anti-Jacobin Review* (December 1819) 57:312.

*Quarterly Review;* "it ought to be called the age of political quacks and mountebanks. . . ."[64] The *Times* sardonically saluted a troupe of trained fleas as evidence that the schoolmaster was indeed abroad.[65]

If it was the age of political quacks and mountebanks—and what age cannot claim that estimable title?—it wasn't just because it enjoyed its share of human folly, as though something called human nature is bound to peep out through the cracks in the thin veneer of civility. It was threatened, in Southey's typically understated view, by a "new evil," "the supremacy of popular opinion . . . the worst evil with which, in the present state of the world, civilized society is threatened."[66] Some conservative rhetoric here is easily dismissed as the whining of sourpusses. Some of it is unpersuasive, proceeding all too rapidly from the abstract account of social order to fear and loathing at the rise of the lower orders, a terrifying feast of misrule or carnival inversion brazenly persevering long past its appointed time, what Cruikshank once labelled "the scum uppermost."[67] Much of it, though, is arrestingly intelligent and provocative, not refuse that democrats can afford to ignore. Conservatives paid resolutely unblinking attention to what we might call, adopting their obsessive concern with sickness and poison, pathologies of debate. Their aim was to deny that we should be confident in the rational credentials of democratic debate. I want now to catalogue some of their complaints; I will sometimes add observations by writers not themselves conservative.

Take first balkanization. Preparing an article on (what else?) the French Revolution for the *Quarterly,* Southey was forlorn: "The evil is, that it is writing to those readers who are in the main of the same way of thinking. Our contemporaries read, not in the hope of being instructed, but to have their own opinions flattered."[68] "Nobody reads

[64] *Quarterly Review* (January 1831) 44:266, (October 1822) 28:111. See too *The Greville Memoirs 1814–1860,* ed. Lytton Strachey and Roger Fulford, 8 vols. (London: Macmillan, 1938), 2:278 [1 April 1832].

[65] Richard D. Altick, *The Shows of London* (Cambridge, MA: Belknap Press, Harvard University Press, 1978), p. 306.

[66] Robert Southey, *Sir Thomas More,* 1:234; see too 2:209.

[67] *BMC* no. 13248 [17 July 1819]. This splendid cartoon is reproduced on the cover of William Godwin, *Enquiry Concerning Political Justice,* ed. Isaac Kramnick (Harmondsworth: Penguin, 1985).

[68] Southey to John Rickman, 18 May 1812, *Life and Correspondence of Southey,* 3:344. See too Louis Simond, *Journal of a Tour and Residence in Great Britain, during the Years 1810 and 1811, by a French Traveller,* 2 vols. (Edinburgh, 1815), 1:61–62 [30 March 1810].

any thing but what coincides with his wishes," agreed *Blackwood's;* "the arguments are followed which fall in with preconceived opinions; none other so much as looked at."[69] Willie Semple's Club in Kilmarnock furnishes a choice specimen of artisans plunged into the invigorating world of democratic debate. They met three nights a week, reading the *Black Dwarf* and the *Glasgow Chronicle,* arguing about politics. Yet all of them (except Willie) were weavers, all radical republicans. Not that they spent all their time cooing in sweet concord. Only some favored the redistribution of property.[70] Still, they weren't poring over the *Anti-Jacobin* or the *Quarterly* or *Blackwood's,* conscientiously striving to come to terms with the challenges posed by divergent political visions. Nor did they count in their midst any loyalists or for that matter moderates or those genuinely undecided. Similarly, one day in July 1793, the Crown and Anchor Tavern was positively bursting with political talk. Upstairs was a meeting of the radical LCS. Downstairs was a meeting of Reeves's Association for Preserving Liberty and Property against Republicans and Levellers.[71] There's no evidence that they all sat down together and politely tried to thrash out their differences.[72]

Next is intolerance. Suppose a relatively like-minded group abruptly refuses to consider some political view. *John Bull* reprinted one troubling story from a Macclesfield newspaper. In the midst of labor disturbances in 1827, the weavers met to discuss what they should do. They advertised "that every man should be heard *quietly,* and be at liberty to declare his sentiments freely, and *without interruption.*" But when one weaver suggested the merits of meeting one's contractual obligations before heading out to strike, these champions

---

[69] *Blackwood's Edinburgh Magazine* (March 1831) 29(178):442. See too *Quarterly Review* (April 1822) 27:136; Lewis Goldsmith, *Observations on the Appointment of the Right Hon. Geo. Canning to the Foreign Department,* in *Pamphleteer* (1823) 22(44):300; *The Autobiography, Times, Opinions, and Contemporaries of Sir Egerton Brydges,* 2 vols. (London, 1834), 2:356–57.

[70] Paterson, *Autobiographical Reminiscences,* pp. 65–70.

[71] Draft of LCS to Hertford, 31 July 1793, in *The Second Report from the Committee of Secrecy to the House of Commons,* 4th ed. (London, 1794), app. E.

[72] Some take such segmentation to indicate the existence of separate public spheres: see for instance Jon P. Klancher, *The Making of English Reading Audiences, 1790–1832* (Madison, WI: University of Wisconsin Press, 1987); Geoff Eley, "Nations, Publics, and Political Cultures: Placing Habermas in the Nineteenth Century," in *Habermas and the Public Sphere,* ed. Craig Calhoun (Cambridge, MA: MIT Press, 1992). Provided there is sufficient vigorous exchange at the boundaries of these segmented groups, though, we can still sensibly refer to one public sphere. An internally differentiated sphere, allowing separate groups to refine their views, could even be more intelligent.

of free speech pulled him away "and *rolled him in the mud.*"[73] I suppose they felt betrayed; they might have wondered if he was put up to this spineless display by the masters. I suppose, too, that rolling the hapless speaker in the mud helped cement their own solidarity. But if there was anything intelligent in what he was saying, they weren't going to figure it out.

Consider, third, problems surrounding deference and imitation, or what we might call bandwagon effects. One repentant former radical penned a scathing indictment of radicals forming reading clubs "to furnish themselves with the heavy artillery of Voltaire, Godwin, &c." They might claim to be shrugging off the mantle of prejudice and donning that of reason. "But still, so it happened, that those who despised the labour of reading, took their creeds implicitly, from the extemporaneous effusions of others, whose talents were comparatively above their own. And yet these people were invariably in the habit of ridiculing Christians, in concert with the orators, for being blindly led by priests."[74] Not rational autonomy, but unthinking submission continued to be the lot of these benighted workers. Their great triumph was to substitute the reviled word of Godwin for the revealed word of God. Why not label the spread of such opinions contagion? "Thus it is in revolutions," snapped Arthur Young, "one rascal writes, and an hundred thousand fools believe."[75] One defender of Mary Wollstonecraft complained about those who never even had glanced at her works but offered confident views about them.[76]

Fourth comes the debased currency of political debate, the irrational absurdities of the very language deployed. In 1797, Richard Dinmore set out to vindicate the cause of the English Jacobins. De-

---

[73] *John Bull* (16 December 1827) 7(366):399.

[74] William Hamilton Reid, *The Rise and Dissolution of the Infidel Societies in This Metropolis* (London, 1800), p. 8.

[75] Arthur Young, *Travels in France during the Years 1787, 1788 & 1789*, ed. Constantia Maxwell (Cambridge: Cambridge University Press, 1950), p. 185 [24 July 1789]. See too *The Principles of Moral and Political Philosophy* [1785], in *The Works of William Paley, D.D. Archdeacon of Carlisle*, 2 vols. (London, 1828), 1(2):212; *Anti-Jacobin Review* (October 1812) 43:153–54; *Quarterly Review* (January 1818) 18:305.

[76] *A Defence of the Character and Conduct of the Late Mary Wollstonecraft Godwin* (London, 1803), pp. 42–43. The anonymous *Defence*, pp. 51–54, criticizes William Godwin's *Memoirs of the Author of a Vindication of the Rights of Woman* (London, 1798) as indiscreet and inept, but the *Defence*'s style and substance are, shall we say, uncannily reminiscent of Godwin's work. This pamphlet isn't listed in Halkett and Laing.

spite their monstrous image, he averred, they embraced neither Robespierre nor despotism. "I call them jacobins because their enemies chose so to call them, with a view to confound the public mind; to render it incapable of distinguishing their merits from the brutal cruelty" of their French namesakes.[77] Writing from Italy in 1820, Mary Shelley had no desire to return to England. English subjects were "the slaves of King Cant whose dominion I fear is of wider extent in England than any where else." Reading that cant even "double distilled" in a foreign periodical "makes one almost sick."[78] Dinmore's worry is that the reigning concepts betray the stamp of viciously narrow partisanship. Shelley's worry is that they animate vacuous slogans which stand in the way of serious thought. Both worries might be right; in fact, both might fairly apply to the very same concepts.

Fifth are worries about the judicious impartiality of the press. Trying to understand why the *Courier* and *Morning Herald* were full of "contemptible trash" and staffed by people of "extreme stupidity," the *Anti-Jacobin* lit on the view that these jobs were plums, handed out to reward incompetents who became raving Jacobins.[79] Brougham was appalled that not a single newspaper dared to report that the Prince of Wales was greeted with savage hissing at public affairs. Perhaps some were bribed, he mused, and perhaps others buckled to flattering attention from the royal household.[80] Newspapers were "bound to the car of party by chains stronger than those of iron," offered the *Quarterly*, no doubt blithely exempting themselves.[81] One writer concluded that "there is no country perhaps where the truth in political matters is to be discovered with such difficulty as in England. The

[77] Richard Dinmore, Jr., *An Exposition of the Principles of the English Jacobins*, 2d ed. (Norwich, 1797), pp. 6–7. See too John Thelwall's heated denunciation of Coleridge in Burton Pollin, assisted by Redmond Burke, "John Thelwall's Marginalia in a Copy of Coleridge's *Biographia Literaria*," *Bulletin of the New York Public Library* (1970) 74(2):93–94.

[78] Mary Shelley to Marianne Hunt, 24 March 1820, *The Letters of Mary Wollstonecraft Shelley*, ed. Betty T. Bennett, 3 vols. (Baltimore, MD: Johns Hopkins University Press, 1980–1988), 1:137.

[79] *Anti-Jacobin* (12 March 1798) no. 18, p. 138.

[80] Henry Brougham to Leigh Hunt, May 1814, *The Correspondence of Leigh Hunt*, ed. Thornton Hunt, 2 vols. (London, 1862), 1:94–95; Brougham to Hunt, 10 June 1814, *Correspondence of Hunt*, 1:95. See too Michael J. Murphy, *Cambridge Newspapers and Opinion 1780–1850* (Cambridge: Oleander Press, 1977), p. 32.

[81] *Quarterly Review* (October 1822) 28:203.

freedom of the press . . . diverts or obstructs our view by the constant misrepresentation of party feeling."[82]

Opposite the overheated issues of party are boring technicalities, the sort making coffeehouse readers' eyes glaze over. Take matters of funding the budget deficit or disputes about the financial implications of Pitt's sinking fund. The Earl of Lauderdale apologetically commenced a pamphlet on such dismal subjects. "There is no task more discouraging, from its repeated failure, than any attempt to attract public attention to the Finances of the country. It is a subject understood by few, and amusing to none." We might agree that such matters are more important than Caroline's sexual peccadilloes, but that doesn't mean the public will pay attention to them. Lauderdale didn't think this blind spot in public scrutiny provided an opportunity for a responsible political elite to work out rational views. He thought it permitted corrupt leaders to plunder the treasury.[83]

Seventh on my motley list of pathologies is the pedestrian business of ignoring what one's opponent is actually saying, whether from inability to comprehend it or from a strategic desire to score points with one's audience. Countless millions of words were printed and uttered in this period on the topic of equality. Here is a long-running and vibrant public debate on a pressing political question. To the bitter end, though, partisans flaunted the same tired misconceptions or strategic deceptions. One conservative writer after another insisted that political equality was a pernicious or impossible fantasy because—people were different! In the tracts they dispensed for the consumption of the lower orders, the Association for Preserving Liberty and Property drove home this profound and penetrating observation. "You have heard a great deal too about one man's being equal to another. Now to my mind, the folk that talk so, talk as foolish as if they were to say, that a Man of five feet high were as tall as a Man of six feet; that the People down in our Church could sing as well as the choir in the Gallery; that a pack of Boys could ring and play at cricket as well as our ringers and

---

[82] *What is a Revolution?* in *Pamphleteer* (1819) 14(27):48. See too William Wordsworth to Lord Lonsdale, 24 May 1819, *The Letters of William and Dorothy Wordsworth*, 2d ed., ed. Ernest de Selincourt, rev. Chester L. Shaver and others, 8 vols. (Oxford: Clarendon, 1967–1993), 3:544.

[83] James Maitland, Earl of Lauderdale, *Thoughts on Finance, Suggested by the Measures of the Present Session* (London, 1797), p. 1. See too William Morgan, *An Appeal to the People of Great Britain, on the Present Alarming State of the Public Finances, and of Public Credit* (London, 1797), p. 1.

cricket club. . . ."[84] (More promising were *reductios* of equality: why not embrace the rights of brutes? or the rights of waters?[85]) In a revealing sign of the stupidities engendered by the pressures of political debate, in 1792 conservative journalist John Gifford would approvingly reproduce a 1774 dialogue on the inevitability of inequality, not bothering to mention that the original text was archly mocking the chief speaker as a sententious Methodist.[86]

Radicals succumbed to the same illicit temptations. "I would wish to let the reader into a momentous secret," whispered Godwin. "Kings are born to their stations, but are not made of a different mould from common men."[87] But whoever suggested that they were? Whose views even implicitly depended on such a goofy premise? This wasn't a momentous secret, but something banally obvious to which virtually everyone assented. The ordinary conservative position was not that some are naturally superior, whatever that would mean, but that social order requires hierarchy. Queen Charlotte herself solemnly instructed the Prince of Wales that "we are all equal," so he had better be considerate to his servants.[88]

---

[84] *Association Papers* (London, 1793), pt. 2, no. 7, p. 6. See too pt. 2, no. 1, pp. 1–2; pt. 2, no. 2, p. 5; pt. 2, no. 3, p. 9; pt. 2, no. 5, p. 15. More generally, see William Combe, *Plain Thoughts of a Plain Man, Addressed to the Common Sense of the People of Great Britain* (London, 1797), p. 12; Richard Hey, *Happiness and Rights,* abridged ed. (York, 1792), pp. 36–37; John Moore, *A Journal, during a Residence in France,* 2 vols. (Boston, 1794), 2:254 [23 November 1792]; *Liberty and Equality; a Dialogue between a Clergyman and His Parishioner* (London, 1794), p. 15; Basil Montagu, *Thoughts on Liberty, and the Rights of Englishmen,* 3d ed. (London, 1822), in *Pamphleteer* 21(41):88–89; Walter Scott, *Life of Napoleon Buonaparte* [1827], in *The Prose Works of Sir Walter Scott, Bart.,* 28 vols. (Edinburgh, 1834–1836), 8:197; *Bristol Job Nott* (31 May 1832) no. 25, p. 97. For a trenchant complaint about the Association's reliance on this line of argument, see Robert Hall, *An Apology for the Freedom of the Press, and for General Liberty,* 2d ed. (London, 1793), pp. 26–27.

[85] Thomas Taylor, *A Vindication of the Rights of Brutes* (London, 1792; reprint ed. Gainesville, FL: Scholars' Facsimiles & Reprints, 1966); William C. Smith, *Two Political Allegories; Written in the Year 1793, and Now Revised for the Pamphleteer,* in *Pamphleteer* (1820) 16(32):470–72.

[86] John Gifford, *Plain Address to the Common Sense of the People of England* (London, 1792), pp. 45–46, quoting from Richard Graves, *The Spiritual Quixote; or, The Summer's Ramble of Mr. Geoffry Wildgoose,* 2d ed., 3 vols. (London, 1774), 2:272–75.

[87] William Godwin, "Interview of Charles I & Sir William Davenant" [*circa* 1809], in *Shelley and His Circle 1773–1822,* ed. Kenneth Neill Cameron and Donald H. Reiman, 8 vols. (Cambridge, MA: Harvard University Press, 1961–1986), 1:449.

[88] Queen Charlotte to the Prince of Wales, 12 August 1770, *The Correspondence of George, Prince of Wales 1770–1812,* ed. A. Aspinall, 8 vols. (London: Cassell, 1963–1971), 1:5–6.

Some didn't bother misrepresenting their opponents' positions. Instead they kept repeating themselves. The *Edinburgh Review* complained that proslavery writers were tireless boxers, always pummelled and always cheerfully bouncing back for more of the same:

> There are no limits to the power of restating the same arguments which have been refuted, and repeating the same falsehoods which have been disproved; and to do this without at all noticing the decisive answers which have been given, or the conclusive evidence which has been adduced against them, is the constant policy of these writers.
>
> We lament to say, that it is an artifice by no means useless to that bad cause, on behalf of which it is employed.[89]

Bad enough that readers parroted what they read. These writers parroted their own prior performances.

Perhaps some of these pathologies could be cured, or, dropping the contentious medical categories, perhaps these problems could be solved. Or perhaps they could be redescribed as innocuous or even choiceworthy. I want only to emphasize that the conservative armory included an intimidating battery of objections to the world of enlightenment. Facing them, only the incurably smug could remain sure that we should use *reason* to refer to the likes of alehouse debate and newspaper reading.

Again, the irreversibility thesis didn't make conservatives collapse. William Wilberforce hoped in 1798 that "men of authority and influence" would teach the young so that "an antidote may be provided for the malignity of that venom, which is storing up in a neighbouring country."[90] True, agreed the Bishop of Llandaff in 1821, the "moral infection" was lethal and had spread swiftly. But things were looking up; one could hope "that the disease is not irremediable"; perhaps an "effective antidote" could be found.[91] Both were betting on the prospects of rededicating the nation to Christianity. That was one strategy among many. I turn now to the enchanting variety of antidotes hawked with abandon.

[89] *Edinburgh Review* (July 1806) 8(16):358.

[90] William Wilberforce, *A Practical View of the Prevailing Religious System of Professed Christians, in the Higher and Middle Classes of This Country, Contrasted with Real Christianity,* 6th ed. (London, 1798), pp. 428–29.

[91] William, Lord Bishop of Llandaff, *A Charge Delivered to the Clergy of the Diocese of Llandaff* (London, 1821), in *Pamphleteer* (1821) 19(38):304.

## REPRESSION

The state made abortive efforts to control or even shut down the burgeoning realm of democratic discussion. They paid special attention to the writers and printers of seditious materials. They were egged on by a host of angry onlookers stunned by what seemed to them cavalier inactivity in the face of a poisonous onslaught. No doubt the authorities were caught unawares by some of the sweeping changes. It's worth remembering, too, that their efforts were curtailed by the relatively limited state capacities of the day and by a quintessentially British regard for legal procedure. Not that they couldn't act at all; not that they didn't engineer some legally irregular proceedings now and again. But we need to beware projecting the ruthless policies of twentieth-century fascist and communist states back into this period.

The most dramatic episodes in the seamy history of repression are from the tense 1790s. A royal proclamation sets the tone. Issued in May 1792, just a few months after the publication of the second part of Paine's *Rights of Man,* the proclamation frets that "wicked and seditious writings have been printed, published, and industriously dispersed, tending to excite tumult and disorder, by endeavouring to raise groundless jealousies and discontents in the minds of our faithful and loving subjects" and that a revolutionary agenda is being advanced by correspondence with "sundry persons in foreign parts," a polite but transparent reference to detestable France. It urges subjects to "guard against all such attempts which aim at the subversion of all regular government within this kingdom, and which are inconsistent with the peace and order of society"; it commands magistrates to "make diligent enquiry in order to discover the authors and printers of such wicked and seditious writings," and, "from time to time, to transmit to one of our Principal Secretaries of State, due and full information" about the offenders.[92]

In November, one correspondent beseeched Pitt to take action. Pondering thousands of "hardy fellows, strongly impressed with the new doctrines of equality, and at present composed of such combustible matter that the least spark will set them in a blaze, I cannot help

---

[92] *London Chronicle* (19–22 May 1792) 71:488.

thinking the supineness of the magistrates very reprehensible."[93] Later that month, John Reeves's newly organized Association for Preserving Liberty and Property urged the organization of local societies "to check the circulation of seditious publications of all kinds . . . by discovering and bringing to justice not only the authors and printers of them, but those who keep them in shops, or hawk them in the streets for sale. . . ."[94] Wary of vigilante action, the group urged that members cooperate with magistrates. Brandishing the irreversibility thesis, radicals argued that such efforts would prove impotent. A Patriot wrote to Reeves,

> I find myself at a loss to determine what were your ideas on publishing such contemptable threatenings you would greatly oblige me & no doubt the public at large by informing us if you can how it is possible for a society like yours to quench the ardour of investigation which now fires the breasts of Englishmen & mankind at large is it possible for a society like yours to prevent the different societies formed for political information from meeting or to prevent the circulation of political publications if so you are powerful indeed but as this seems to me impossible what your scandalous advertisements aim at is to me a mystery which I am not able to unravel—[95]

Perhaps A Patriot's anger betrays an edgy sense that repression might succeed.

That December, dutifully responsive to their worthy constituents, some parliamentary figures sought a harsher crackdown. Subjects, explained Windham, couldn't follow arguments. They could only submit to bald assertions. So it wasn't clear what the point of free discussion could be.

---

[93] Thomas Powditch to William Pitt, 3 November 1792, in *The Early English Trade Unions: Documents from the Home Office Papers in the Public Record Office,* ed. A. Aspinall (London: Batchworth, 1949), p. 13.

[94] *Association Papers,* no. 1, pp. 7–8 [24 November 1792]. It's unclear to what extent the government knew and approved of Reeves's establishment: H. T. Dickinson, "Popular Conservatism and Militant Loyalism 1789–1815," in *Britain and the French Revolution, 1789–1815,* ed. Dickinson (New York: St. Martin's Press, 1989), pp. 121–22. For instances of prosecutions spurred by the Association, see Austin Mitchell, "The Association Movement of 1792–3," *Historical Journal* (1961) 4(1):67–69.

[95] A Patriot to John Reeves, 30 November 1792, British Library, Add. Mss. 16919, f. 167.

Nor could he see the harm there was of preventing all endeavours to explain to a poor, illiterate fellow, whose extent of powers was but barely adequate to the task of procuring food for his own subsistence, points which had divided the opinions of the ablest writers. He saw no great loss to society from putting an end to public-house political clubs, and ale-house debates on politics; in short, he saw no reason why they should not be altogether suppressed.[96]

"A sort of inquisition now prevails in this country," warned an anxious pamphleteer that same month; "the freedom of the press and of conversation is invaded; the fury of the ruling party brands even moderate men with the name of levellers; Englishmen are degraded into spies upon their brethren. . . ."[97] In February 1793, France declared war on England and England generously reciprocated the favor. To no avail, Sheridan would rise in March to assault a "system of delusion," what he saw as a duplicitous effort to terrify people into loyal submission. The publicans of London, he complained, faced heavy-handed threats by magistrates that if they took in the wrong newspapers, they were likely to lose their licenses—and be punished for circulating such offensive materials to their customers. The publicans of Cambridge, he charged, had been forced to swear that they wouldn't permit any political conversation in their alehouses and that they would tell the authorities everything they could about the local republicans.[98]

In April 1794, the LCS mounted a huge outdoor meeting at Chalk Farm. In May, Pitt would deliver a hair-raising speech on the dangers posed by the LCS and other radical groups: "So formidable a conspiracy had never before existed."[99] He would receive the report of the Committee on Secrecy, which found that the Society for Constitutional Information too was doggedly pursuing the subversion of the constitution. The Committee produced decisive evidence: the Society had embraced a project for publishing a cheap edition of Paine's

[96] Windham, *Speeches*, 1:221 [13 December 1792].

[97] *Is All We Want Worth a Civil War? or, Conciliatory Thoughts upon the Present Crisis* (London, 1792), p. 25. For December support of government crackdowns, see *Declaration of the Noblemen and Gentlemen Assembled at St. Alban's Tavern* (London, 1792).

[98] *Speeches of the Late Right Honourable Richard Brinsley Sheridan (Several Corrected by Himself)*, ed. A Constitutional Friend, 5 vols. (London, 1816), 3:92, 3:96 [4 March 1793].

[99] *Speeches of Pitt*, 2:32 [16 May 1794].

*Rights of Man.*[100] (In 1791, a pamphleteer had shuddered at the prospect of a few zealous radicals so circulating Paine's text: "If they at an abated price, send it like a cheapened drug through the inferior classes of society . . . it might happen that a deluded people would swallow the mental poison, and in the delirious moments of its operation they might overturn and deface the collected wisdom of ages. . . ."[101]) Despite an eloquent speech by Fox,[102] Parliament promptly voted to suspend habeas corpus; it remained suspended until July 1795. Indeed, habeas corpus would be suspended repeatedly in these years. ("The suspension of the Habeas Corpus Act is a measure approved by all the well disposed," approvingly purred a well-disposed Wordsworth in 1817, a month after it had been suspended again and weeks after Sidmouth directed a circular to the magistrates enjoining more stringent action.[103] Sidmouth explained that he'd examined "misguided delinquents" and found "that they had been well-disposed members of society, until their principles were corrupted by the poison instilled by those who had enlisted blasphemy in the service of sedition."[104])

In August 1794, London endured a week of riots protesting crimping, the practice of seizing men to serve in His Majesty's Navy. In September, a popgun plot to assassinate the king was uncovered.[105] In June 1795, the LCS held another open-air meeting. That July, London endured another week of crimping riots.[106] At the end of October, George III was attacked in his open carriage.[107] Prudently react-

---

[100] *The First Report of the Committee of Secrecy of the House of Commons, on the Papers Belonging to the Society for Constitutional Information, and the London Corresponding Society, Seized by Order of Government, and Presented to the House by Mr. Secretary Dundas, on the 12th and 13th of May 1794* (London, 1794), pp. 4–5.

[101] *Defence of the Rights of Man; Being a Discussion of the Conclusions Drawn from Those Rights by Mr. Paine* (London, 1791), p. 24.

[102] *The Speeches of the Right Honourable Charles James Fox, in the House of Commons,* 6 vols. (London, 1815), 5:289 [17 May 1794].

[103] William Wordsworth to Daniel Stuart, 7 April 1817, *Letters of William and Dorothy Wordsworth,* 3:375. Habeas corpus was restored 28 January 1818 and not suspended again.

[104] Pellew, *Life and Correspondence of Addington,* 3:176 [12 May 1817].

[105] *Papers of the London Corresponding Society,* pp. 220–23.

[106] See *Reflections on the Pernicious Custom of Recruiting by Crimps; and on Various Other Modes Now Practised in the British Army* (London, 1795), an Eaton production.

[107] For descriptions, *Autobiography of Place,* pp. 145–47; James Woodforde, *The Diary of a Country Parson,* ed. John Beresford, 5 vols. (London: Oxford University Press,

ing to this abhorrent development—or opportunistically capitalizing on it—Pitt's government immediately introduced two bills, one for better securing the king's person and government, one against seditious meetings.[108] (The next year, remembering the permeability of legal barriers, the government bulletproofed George's state coach.[109]) The former extended treason to include such offences as inciting hatred of the king. The latter required that magistrates be given advance notice of all public meetings with more than fifty present and gave the magistrates broad-ranging powers to combat them.

Fox privately retorted that the attack was a pretext and that the bills would "prohibit all public discussion, whether in writing or in speaking, of political subjects."[110] The Whig opposition fought back, maybe gamely, maybe lamely, but surely ineffectively. In May 1797, Grey's motion for parliamentary reform was defeated. Fox and his followers would boycott parliamentary proceedings until February 1800. After one inflammatory speech Fox gave in 1798, Pitt seriously contemplated jailing the great Whig in the Tower.[111]

In October 1798, the *Anti-Jacobin Review* called for sterner measures against the debating societies.[112] In April 1799, Pitt again girded himself for combat, obligingly promising he would move against the societies, busy corrupting their audiences. English law embraced the freedom of the press and militated against prior restraint, he agreed. But new tactics were required to deal with "the plan of disseminating hand-bills, tending to poison the minds of the people," so he proposed regulations making it easier to hold authors and publishers of

---

1926–1931), 4:240–42; *Truth and Treason! or A Narrative of the Royal Procession to the House of Peers, October the 29th, 1795* (London, 1795).

[108] 36 Geo. III, c. 7; 36 Geo. III, c. 8. For a brief but passionate outcry against these measures, published within days of their introduction as bills, see *Ten Minutes Advice to the People of England, on the Two Slavery-Bills Intended to Be Brought into Parliament the Present Sessions* (n.p., 1795).

[109] Roger Wells, "English Society and Revolutionary Politics in the 1790s: The Case for Insurrection," in *The French Revolution and British Popular Politics*, ed. Mark Philp (Cambridge: Cambridge University Press, 1991), p. 189.

[110] Charles James Fox to Lord Holland, 15 November 1795, in Fox, *Memorials and Correspondence*, ed. Lord John Russell, 3 vols. (London, 1853–1854), 3:123–24.

[111] Pitt to Lord Grenville, 5 May 1798, *Report on the Manuscripts at Dropmore*, 4:187.

[112] *Anti-Jacobin Review* (October 1798) 1:478. On the impact of repression on the debating societies, see Mary Thale, "London Debating Societies in the 1790s," *Historical Journal* (1989) 32(1):57–86.

such dubious texts responsible. Once again he assaulted "the existence of secret societies totally unknown in the history of this or any other country," "totally repugnant to the genius of this constitution . . . clearly of foreign growth."[113]

In 1816, Southey was still distressed by the prospects of political arson. He wanted those found guilty of sedition to be transported to Australia: not vindictively, he insisted, but just to expel them from the body politic.[114] The familiar medical imagery led him to cast repression as safeguarding the public health. "We have laws to prevent the exposure of unwholesome meat in our markets, and the mixture of deleterious drugs in beer," he noted. "We have laws also against poisoning the minds of the people, by exciting discontent and disaffection," he added. Then came the plaintive punchline: "Why are not these laws rendered effectual and enforced as well as the former?"[115] In 1819, the government passed a seditious and blasphemous libel act prescribing transportation for the guilty. In 1821, *John Bull* promised to keep squawking until they succeeded in directing the magistrates' attention to the coffeehouses.[116] In 1823, Southey anticipated that finally the law would be put to work against the radical press.[117] But this new law was never once deployed.[118] It was repealed in 1830.[119] In Parliament the next year, Macaulay crowed over its failure.[120]

The script has become hackneyed: dangerous conflicts in foreign affairs, demonized radicals at home, a state whittling away at civil liberties. Was all this repression successful? That depends on what would count as failure and what would have happened had such measures not passed—not to mention debates on just how repressive the repression was in the first place.[121] Despite some well-publicized

[113] *Speeches of Pitt,* 3:71–79 [19 April 1799].

[114] Robert Southey to Grosvenor Charles Bedford, 10 September 1816, *New Letters of Robert Southey,* ed. Kenneth Curry, 2 vols. (New York: Columbia University Press, 1965), 2:142; see too Southey to Bedford, 7 September 1816, *Letters,* ed. Warter, 3:43.

[115] Robert Southey, *Essays, Moral and Political,* 2 vols. (London, 1832), 1:420 [1816].

[116] *John Bull* (6 May 1821) no. 21, p. 164.

[117] Southey to Bedford, 27 January 1823, *Life and Correspondence of Southey,* 5:132.

[118] A. Aspinall, *Politics and the Press c. 1780–1850* (London: Home & Van Thal, 1949), p. 383.

[119] 2 Geo. IV and 1 Wm. IV, c. 73.

[120] Thomas Babington Macaulay, *The Works of Lord Macaulay Complete,* ed. Lady Trevelyan, 8 vols. (London, 1875), 8:59 [10 October 1831].

[121] Clive Emsley, "The Home Office and Its Sources of Information and Investigation 1791–1801," *English Historical Review* (July 1979) 94:532–61; Emsley, "Repression, 'Terror,' and the Rule of Law in England during the Decade of the French Revolution," *English Historical Review* (October 1985) 100:801–25.

acquittals, though, the state managed to convict some of its chief tormentors.

## POLITICAL TRIALS

In the autumn of 1794, a few months after Pitt's parliamentary indictment of the LCS, the state launched criminal proceedings against some of the LCS's ringleaders. Thomas Hardy was put on trial 25 October and acquitted 5 November.[122] Horne Tooke was put on trial 17 November and acquitted 22 November.[123] These acquittals were publicly celebrated humiliations for the authorities. Unwilling to lose again, they released the others they had charged on 1 December. The episode is sometimes taken as demonstrating English juries' fierce devotion to freedom of the press.

So, too, the authorities struck out in December 1817 when they put William Hone on trial for blasphemy three times, three days in a row. Hone had published stinging and hilarious parodies, using the structure and rhythms of such parts of the liturgy as the Athanasian Creed to mock corrupt ministers. Defending himself, querulously making much of his fatigue and unfamiliarity with the law, like many radicals before him vehemently insisting on the rights of juries to nullify the law, maintaining that he was the victim of selective prosecution, wondering why George Canning's and John Reeves's right-wing parodies of religious texts had been amply rewarded, tenaciously citing one celebrated parody after another, feuding with the presiding judge, Hone emerged not just innocent, but a triumphal hero.[124] A public meeting celebrated the liberty of the press and raised funds to support Hone and his struggling family.[125]

---

[122] *The Trial of Thomas Hardy for High Treason*, rep. Joseph Gurney, 4 vols. (London, 1794–1795).

[123] *The Trial of John Horne Tooke, for High Treason*, rep. Joseph Gurney, 2 vols. (London, 1795).

[124] *The First Trial of William Hone*, 4th ed. (London, 1817); *The Second Trial of William Hone* (London, 1817); *The Third Trial of William Hone*, 4th ed. (London, 1817). For the story of Hone's arrest and refusal to plead, *Hone's Reformist Register* (10 May 1817) 1(16):481–500, dated 8 May from King's Bench Prison. Hone would repeat his charges against Reeves in *A Slap at Slop and the Bridge-Street Gang* (London, 1822), p. 13, in Hone, *Facetiae and Miscellanies* (London, 1827).

[125] *Trial by Jury and Liberty of the Press: The Proceedings at the Public Meeting, December 29, 1817, at the City of London Tavern, for the Purpose of Enabling William Hone to Surmount the Difficulties in Which He Has Been Placed by Being Selected by the Ministers of the Crown as the Object of Their Persecution*, 5th ed. (London, 1818).

Yet the authorities were stubbornly persistent and sometimes racked up notable successes. Again, though Tom Paine eluded the authorities by going to France in September 1792, he was charged in December with seditious libel for the second part of his *Rights of Man*. The attorney general testified to the power of Burke's schism between the polite argument of the political nation and the untutored loyalty of vulgar subjects. Given his overt paternalism and his troubled sense that the lower orders were taking a prurient interest in political debate, we might call this the not-in-front-of-the-children motif. He'd not prosecuted the first part, though "it was highly reprehensible," because he imagined "it would be confined to the judicious and discriminating," who could refute it themselves. But the second part "was printed at a very low price, for the express purpose of its being read by the lowest classes of the people," who "possessed not the power of discussing abstract propositions, or of finding an antidote against the baneful poison." Why, it even had candies stuffed inside to tempt children.[126] The jury, appropriately aghast, prevailed on the attorney general not to bother making a closing address, on the judge not to bother summing up. They were already satisfied Paine was guilty.[127]

In Edinburgh in August 1793, Thomas Muir was convicted of sedition: he'd exhorted such ignominious locals as his hairdresser to purchase and read the *Rights of Man*.[128] Reporter William Woodfall was struck by parliamentary discussion of the presiding judge's admission that he hadn't realized that the sentence, fourteen years' transportation to Botany Bay, would include servitude. "As my reports sell so

---

[126] *The Trial of Thomas Paine, for Certain False, Wicked, Scandalous and Seditious Libels Inserted in the Second Part of the Rights of Man, before the Right Hon. Lord Kenyon and a Special Jury, at Guildhall, on Tuesday the 18th December, 1792* (London, n.d.), pp. 16–18. More briefly, *The Whole Proceedings on the Trial of an Information Exhibited ex Officio by the King's Attorney General against Thomas Paine . . . Tried by a Special Jury in the Court of King's Bench, Guildhall, on Tuesday, the 18th of December, 1792*, rep. Joseph Gurney, 2d ed. (London, 1793), p. 47; far more briefly, *The Trial of Thomas Paine, before Lord Kenyon and a Special Jury, at Guildhall, on Tuesday, the 17th of December 1792; When He Was Convicted of a Libel, Published in the Second Part of His Rights of Man* (London, 1792), pp. 3–4.

[127] *Trial . . . for Certain False . . . Libels*, pp. 64–65; *Whole Proceedings*, pp. 195–96; *Trial . . . before Lord Kenyon*, pp. 63–64.

[128] *An Account of the Trial of Thomas Muir . . . before the High Court of Justiciary, at Edinburgh, on the 30th and 31st Days of August, 1793, for Sedition*, ed. James Robertson (Edinburgh, 1793).

well, and will get into the libraries as a book of reference," he put special effort into commemorating just what had transpired.[129] In 1796, an LCS bookseller was sentenced to a year's hard labor and a bond of £1,000 for life for publishing the cheap edition of the first part of Paine's *Age of Reason*.[130]

Daniel Isaac Eaton, the mischievous and prolific radical publisher, was resigned to the occasional prison term as a cost of doing business: he moved his family near the jail so they could visit him more conveniently.[131] The authorities were relentless, but not always successful. Eaton found himself indicted in June 1793 for publishing the second part of Paine's *Rights of Man*. He was acquitted.[132] He found himself back in court in February 1794 for a scurrilous libel in his own racy periodical, *Politics for the People*. The prosecution warned the jury that it was aimed not at "any gentleman such as you: but it is calculated to find its way among the lowest of the people, to excite them to discontents and commotions."[133] Once again, he was acquitted. In March 1812, Eaton found himself yet again in court for publishing the third part of Paine's *Age of Reason*, a spirited exercise in Christianity-bashing. This time, Eaton was sentenced to one and a half years in prison and an hour in the pillory.

Cobbett must have relished reporting the resulting fiasco. Some twelve to twenty thousand people attended. An elderly Eaton emerged from prison and was stuffed into the pillory, at which the crowd burst into applause—for him, not the officials. The crowd tried to offer him food and succeeded in wiping the sweat from his face.[134] The authorities must have noticed this additional sign that public opinion had all the powers of sorcery. It was apparently

[129] William Woodfall to Lord Auckland, 16 April 1794, *The Journal and Correspondence of William Lord Auckland*, ed. Bishop of Bath and Wells, 4 vols. (London, 1861–1862), 3:205.

[130] J. Ann Hone, *For the Cause of Truth: Radicalism in London 1796–1821* (Oxford: Clarendon, 1982), p. 223.

[131] Joseph Ritson to the editor, 29 November 1793, *The Letters of Joseph Ritson, Esq.*, 2 vols. (London, 1833), 2:34.

[132] *The Proceedings, on the Trial of Daniel Isaac Eaton, upon an Indictment, for Selling a Supposed Libel, 'The Second Part of the Rights of Man, Combining Principle and Practice,' by Thomas Paine*, 2d ed. (London, 1793).

[133] *The Trial of Daniel Isaac Eaton, for Publishing a Supposed Libel, Comparing the King of England to a Game Cock in a Pamphlet Intituled Politics for the People . . . at Justice Hall in the Old Bailey, February Twenty Fourth, 1794* (New York, 1794), p. 15.

[134] *Political Register* (13 June 1812) 21(24):748.

capable of transforming a solemn legal punishment into a public honor.[135]

Cobbett probably took especial pleasure in this report because he wrote it from jail, where he was almost done serving a two-year sentence for publishing a stinging attack in the *Political Register* on the military's use of flogging.[136] Contemporaries were appropriately puzzled as to why the regime would bother locking up offending journalists and then allow them to continue producing and marketing their poisons.[137] The practice offered more public relations victories for the radicals: Cobbett opened the eighteenth volume of the *Register* with a cloying tribute to himself and his predecessors in suffering oppression.[138] In July 1831, Cobbett was again put on trial for an inflammatory issue of the *Register,* its "Rural War" understood to foment violence.[139] The jury couldn't reach a verdict, so he was dismissed.[140]

Facing prosecution, Thomas Wooler of the *Black Dwarf* boasted, "I do not mean to let any apprehension of the sting of these political musquitos, interrupt me in my course," a resolution leaving him in the luxurious position of writing from Warwick gaol.[141] Carlile, Cobbett's nemesis on the left (or one of them, anyway), made a point of printing a dateline on his articles in the *Republican.* Dorchester Gaol may not have been the trendiest address around, but it must have gained the inveterate atheist a good deal of affectionate regard, perhaps some awe too, among his faithful readers. Carlile was jailed in 1819 for publishing Paine's *Age of Reason*—Wilberforce encouraged the attorney general to hurry[142]—and not released until November 1825.[143]

[135] On these dynamics, consider *Principles of Penal Law,* in *The Works of Jeremy Bentham,* ed. John Bowring, 11 vols. (Edinburgh, 1843), 1:466.

[136] For the offending text, *Political Register* (1 July 1809) 15(26):993–94.

[137] Simond, *Journal of a Tour,* 2:274 [5 September 1811].

[138] *Political Register* (14 July 1810) 18(1):1.

[139] For the offending text, *Political Register* (11 December 1830) 70(24):929–51.

[140] *A Full and Accurate Report of the Trial of William Cobbett, Esq. (Before Lord Tenterden and a Special Jury,) on Thursday, July 7, 1831, in the Court of King's Bench, Guildhall* (London, 1831), p. 45.

[141] *Black Dwarf* (9 May 1821) 6(19):645. For the first dateline from Warwick gaol, *Black Dwarf* (13 June 1821) 6(24):845. Wooler was released 26 July 1822: *Black Dwarf* (31 July 1822) 9(5):143.

[142] William Wilberforce to Henry Bankes, 1 November 1819, in Robert Isaac Wilberforce and Samuel Wilberforce, *The Life of William Wilberforce,* 5 vols. (London, 1838), 5:39.

[143] *Vice versus Reason: A Copy of the Bill of Indictment, Found at the Old Bailey Sessions,*

Carlile was already in jail when he began publishing the *Republican*. He began the journal in response to the Peterloo massacre of 16 August 1819, when, as he later put it in his scrupulously fair-minded way, a legal assembly of peaceable reformers "were attacked, and barbarously mutilated and murdered, by a bloody and ferocious armed banditti of despotic desperadoes, acting under the sanction, and enjoying the subsequent approbation of the Government. . . ."[144] Tens of thousands eager for parliamentary reform had attended an outdoor rally in Manchester, where they were to be addressed by Henry Hunt, whose stentorian voice earned him the nickname "Orator." Hunt barely had begun speaking when the soldiers on horseback charged and opened fire. A dozen were killed, hundreds more wounded.[145]

The bloody debacle provoked the usual comments. With a conspicuous lack of trepidation, Shelley heard "the distant thunders of the terrible storm which is approaching," that of revolution.[146] Some Tories managed an air of serenity, too, if for different reasons. Even if the magistrates had acted impetuously, urged Walter Scott, no "friend of good order" should be lending aid and comfort to the radicals. "It is an obvious thing that 50,000 men are not a deliberative body," he insisted. "They cannot be assembled for any proper or useful purpose and they are in the case in hand avowedly assembled for the overthrow of the constitution."[147] Not only assembled, but "marching in regular order" with banners in an ominous paramilitary display, warned Peel in defending the magistrates—and supporting new legislation against seditious meetings.[148] Who was responsible for the

---

*January 16, 1819, against Richard Carlile, for Publishing Paine's Age of Reason* (London, 1819).

[144] *Republican* (29 December 1820) 4(18):616, (6 February 1824) 6(9):176.

[145] Malcolm Bee and Walter Bee, "The Casualties of Peterloo," *Manchester Region History Review* (1989) 3:43–50.

[146] Shelley to Thomas Love Peacock, 9 September 1819, *Letters of Percy Bysshe Shelley*, 2:119.

[147] Scott to James Ballantyne, 12 September 1819, *The Letters of Sir Walter Scott*, ed. H. J. C. Grierson, 12 vols. (London: Constable & Co., 1932–1937), 5:485–86.

[148] *The Speeches of the Late Right Honourable Sir Robert Peel, Bart. Delivered in the House of Commons*, 4 vols. (London, 1853; reprint ed. New York: Kraus Reprint Co., 1972), 1:136 [2 December 1819]. Peel would return to the banners in addressing Hunt's imprisonment: *Speeches*, 1:184–85 [24 April 1822]. The worry about paramilitary displays surfaced in the Gordon riots of 1780: see *The Trial of George Gordon, Esquire, Commonly Called Lord George Gordon: For High Treason at the Bar of the Court of King's Bench, on Monday, February 5th, 1781*, rep. Joseph Gurney, 3d ed. (London, 1781).

bloodshed? Tories couldn't concede that the authorities were to blame, and they had their usual skepticism about the agency of the multitude. So George Canning pointed an accusing finger at the rally's organizers: "To *them* the widowed mother and orphan child must trace their miseries! On *their* heads be for ever fixed the responsibility of all the blood that has been shed!"[149]

But contemporaries did more than round up the usual suspects, more too than generate pamphlets and reprint primary documents to try to illuminate this dark affair.[150] Litigious in their way, they turned to the courts to identify the true culprits. Henry Hunt and a small band were hauled to prison on charges of criminal conspiracy.[151] The prosecutor asked the jury "whether such an immense number of labourers and mechanics as were assembled together on that day, could fail to produce the most serious alarm in the minds of men of property. . . ."[152] Assault charges brought against members of the charging cavalry led to sustained debate on those banners. Were they, as the defense insisted, "insurrectionary and revolutionary banners"? Or were they, as the plaintiff's lawyer insisted, innocent signals to prevent people from different towns from getting lost?[153]

As poet laureate, Southey saluted the death of George III with a fulsome *Vision of Judgment.* George ascends to Heaven; his accusers are exposed as the impotent tools of Satan; his princely virtues are extolled and he is welcomed.[154] Byron promptly published a biting

[149] *The Speeches of the Right Honourable George Canning,* ed. R. Therry, 6 vols. (London, 1828), 4:174 [24 November 1819].

[150] Among them: Francis Philips, *An Exposure of the Calumnies Circulated by the Enemies of Social Order, and Reiterated by Their Abettors, against the Magistrates and the Yeomanry Cavalry of Manchester and Salford* (London, 1819); *Peterloo Massacre, Containing a Faithful Narrative of the Events Which Preceded, Accompanied, and Followed the Fatal Sixteenth of August, 1819,* ed. An Observer (Manchester, 1819); John Wade, *Manchester Massacre!! An Authentic Narrative of the Magisterial and Yeomanry Massacre, at Manchester* (London, n.d.); *An Impartial Narrative of the Late Melancholy Occurrences in Manchester* (Liverpool, 1819).

[151] *An Impartial Report of the Proceedings in the Cause of the King versus Henry Hunt, Joseph Johnson, John Knight, James Moorhouse, Joseph Healey, John Thacker Saxton, Robert Jones, Samuel Bamford, George Swift, and Robert Wilde, for a Conspiracy, Tried before Mr. Justice Bayley, and a Special Jury, at York Spring Assizes, on the 16th, 17th, 18th, 20th, 21st, 22d, 23d, 24th, 25th, and 27th of March, 1820* (Manchester, 1820).

[152] *Impartial Report,* p. 12.

[153] *In the King's Bench: Between Thomas Redford, Plaintiff; and Hugh Hornby Birley, Alexander Oliver, Richard Withington, and Edward Meagher, Defendants: for an Assault on the 16th of August, 1819,* rep. Mr. Farquharson (Manchester, 1822), pp. 237, 4–5.

[154] Robert Southey, *A Vision of Judgement* (London, 1821).

and aesthetically superior *Vision of Judgment.* Satan brands George III "this old, blind, mad, helpless, weak, poor worm"; St. Peter chimes in, dismissing George as "this royal Bedlam bigot." That unabashedly hypocritical prostitute, Robert Southey, dragged up to Heaven by Asmodeus, who sprains his left wing in the process, is ready to read his *Vision* when the heavenly host flees and St. Peter knocks him over.[155] Byron was safely ensconced in Italy. But for publishing his audacious *Vision* in *The Liberal,* John Hunt was found guilty of libel.[156]

It matters that the LCS ringleaders got off scot-free, that Hone was acquitted repeatedly, that Eaton sometimes managed to evade the jailer's warm embrace. But it matters, too, that others were convicted: not only in assessing the state and political culture of the period, but also in remembering some of the chilling effects surrounding such repression. We know that John Wolcot, author of the sassy Peter Pindar odes, almost departed for America.[157] We know that Joseph Ritson demurred, "I find it prudent to say as little as possible upon political subjects, in order to keep myself out of Newgate."[158] We know that Jeremy Bentham couldn't find anyone willing to publish a second edition of his *Plan of Parliamentary Reform* after his first publisher, scared of prosecution, backed out.[159] We know that many booksellers refused to carry *The Liberal,* "so full of Atheism and Radicalism and other noxious *isms.*"[160]

We don't know how many others kept their lips buttoned and their pens dry, prudently refusing to take their chances in the lottery of political prosecution. Nor do we know how much journalistic activity was curtailed by the infamous "taxes on knowledge" that required

[155] *The Vision of Judgment* [1822], in Byron, *The Complete Poetical Works,* ed. Jerome J. McGann and Barry Weller, 7 vols. (Oxford: Clarendon, 1980–1993), 6:325.

[156] For abbreviated proceedings, *Black Dwarf* (21 January 1824) 12(3):83–96.

[157] John Taylor, *Records of My Life,* 2 vols. (London, 1832), 1:299–300, 2:231.

[158] Ritson to Mr. Wadeson, 16 January 1793, *Letters of Ritson,* 2:7. See too Christopher Wyvill to the Earl of Buchan, 27 February 1799, in Wyvill, *Political Papers,* 6 vols. (York, 1794–1805), 6(1):317–18.

[159] Bentham to "Imlac," 15 August 1817, *The Correspondence of Jeremy Bentham,* ed. Timothy L. S. Sprigge and others, 10 vols. to date (London: Athlone Press; Oxford: Clarendon, 1968–), 9:43. See too Percy Shelley to Charles Ollier, 11 December 1817, *Letters of Shelley,* 1:579.

[160] Thomas Carlyle to Jane Baillie Welsh, 28 October 1822, *The Collected Letters of Thomas and Jane Welsh Carlyle,* ed. Charles Richard Sanders and others, 22 vols. to date (Durham, NC: Duke University Press, 1970–), 2:190; see too Thomas Carlyle to Alexander Galloway, 6 November 1822, *Collected Letters,* 2:195.

periodicals to pay for stamped paper and the like.[161] (By the 1830s, though, a rash of "unstamped" radical papers braved the threat of prosecution.[162]) One of the measures, charged the radical *Poor Man's Guardian,* was designed to suppress Cobbett's *Political Register.*[163] Canning defended the stamp duty, warning the House of Commons against "letting out a stream of vile pollution which has happily been dammed up."[164] Also defending it, Lord Ellenborough was happy to affirm a *reductio* in the House of Lords. "If he was asked whether he would deprive the lowest classes of society of all political information? he would say, that he saw no possible good to be derived to the country from having statesmen at the loom and politicians at the spinning jenny."[165] "A reduction in the duty would be more than compensated by an increase in the circulation of papers," drily noted John Wade; "but then the object of the government has been not so much to realize revenue as to *control public opinion.*"[166] An economist might notice that by driving up the cost of political publications, the government encouraged readers to band together in alehouses and libraries to do their reading—and talking.

## POLITICS AND MARKETS

The taxes on knowledge straddle the frontier between politics and markets: they're repressive, but they work by raising the price. Or, better, they undercut facile distinctions between politics and markets: as if one were the realm of power, forever diminishing freedom by closing off various possibilities, the other the realm of voluntary transactions, forever enhancing freedom by opening up new possibilities. Other measures, too, might serve as a useful precaution against thinking of politics and markets that way.

[161] For a scathing description, *Tait's Edinburgh Magazine* (February 1833) 2(11):608–17.

[162] Patricia Hollis, *The Pauper Press: A Study in Working-Class Radicalism of the 1830s* (London: Oxford University Press, 1970).

[163] 60 Geo. III c. 9; *Poor Man's Guardian* (19 January 1833) 2(85):17.

[164] *Speeches of Canning,* 6:258 [1 June 1827].

[165] *Parliamentary Debates* (29 December 1820) 41:1591.

[166] John Wade, *The Extraordinary Black Book: An Exposition of Abuses in Church and State, Courts of Law, Representation, Municipal and Corporate Bodies; with a Précis of the House of Commons, Past, Present, and to Come,* new ed. (London, 1832), p. 388. Note too *Westminster Review* (April 1830) 12(24):417.

Alarmed by the flood of radical journalism, some suggested that the state subsidize a conservative press or even establish an official press outlet. William Playfair reminded the Home Office of the internal threats posed by impudent radicals spouting Paine. True, coffeehouses and alehouses might contain people willing to speak out and oppose the radicals, but they were unarmed. The government funded national defense; shouldn't it also find a way of supporting these helpful allies, of slipping government-funded arguments into their hands?[167] In 1812, a memorial delivered to the royal household urged "that the *poison* of the Press should be counteracted by the *antidote* of the Press." The government should establish an official newspaper, not to offer controversial policy support but to ensure the supply of authoritatively honest accounts of the news.[168] Just a few weeks after the government withdrew the Bill of Pains and Penalties against Caroline, one career bureaucrat urged the prime minister to "counteract the poison now raging" by establishing a newspaper to reprint and offer wider circulation to properly loyal sentiments.[169] *Blackwood's* didn't mince words or hide behind the veil of objectivity. They wanted "a Conservative militia to combat the force of anarchy with its own weapons," a conservative press that would be officially established and funded for just the same reason there was an established church: left to their own devices, "people choose wrong."[170] In 1830 and 1831, a small group of leading Tories made incessant efforts to purchase control of leading newspapers.[171]

In fact, the government carried on a brisk trade in journalistic integrity. For ten years after the French Revolution, the editor of the *Times* received payments for supporting the government and inserting paragraphs for them.[172] Secret service money helped found two

[167] William Playfair to the Home Office, 24 April 1794, in Aspinall, *Politics and the Press*, p. 437.

[168] Memorial Respecting the Present State of the British Press, 17 September 1812, *The Letters of King George IV 1812–1830*, ed. A. Aspinall, 3 vols. (Cambridge: Cambridge University Press, 1938), 1:146.

[169] George Harrison to Lord Liverpool, 30 November 1820, in Aspinall, *Politics and the Press*, pp. 151, 99–100.

[170] *Blackwood's Edinburgh Magazine* (September 1834) 36(226):383; see generally 373–91.

[171] Robert Stewart, *The Foundation of the Conservative Party 1830–1867* (London: Longman, 1978), pp. 73–76.

[172] *Correspondence of George, Prince of Wales*, 2:68 n. 1. Aspinall, *Politics and the Press*, chap. 3 reviews the extensive government subsidies of the press in England.

loyalist newspapers, the *True Briton* and the *Sun*.[173] William Gifford, editor of the *Anti-Jacobin* and later of the *Quarterly,* earned a couple of government jobs. John Gifford, editor of the *Anti-Jacobin Review,* became a police magistrate. John Bowles, loyalist pamphleteer, got another government job.[174] Hone was half right about John Reeves: in 1799, he became King's printer, overseeing the printing of Bibles and prayer books through England; from 1803 to 1814, he was Superintendent of Aliens.[175] (But half wrong: he neglected to report that Reeves was prosecuted for his *Thoughts on English Government* of 1795, a constitutional—or, as its critics had it, an unconstitutional— extravaganza arguing that the houses of Parliament were mere branches that safely could be "lopped off" from the tree of monarchy.[176]) It's not as if indefatigable government scoundrels forever were entrapping innocent journalists. William Jerdan, then editor of the *Sun,* later recalled being "in constant and familiar communication with the Treasury and Secretary of State's departments" around 1813.[177] He also offered his services to Canning, then prime minister, in 1827.[178] Canning had his private secretary instruct Jerdan that it was imperative that ministers be able credibly to deny that they illicitly were influencing the press.[179] With more pointed disdain, Wellington turned down a couple of similar offers.[180]

[173] Gregory Claeys, *Thomas Paine: Social and Political Thought* (Boston: Unwin Hyman, 1989), p. 141.

[174] Aspinall, *Politics and the Press,* p. 176 n. 2.

[175] James J. Sack, *From Jacobite to Conservative: Reaction and Orthodoxy in Britain, c. 1760–1832* (Cambridge: Cambridge University Press, 1993), p. 104; J. R. Dinwiddy, *Radicalism and Reform in Britain, 1780–1850* (London: Hambledon Press, 1992), p. 162.

[176] John Reeves, *Thoughts on English Government: Addressed to the Quiet Good Sense of the People of England* (London, 1795), pp. 12–13. I suspect Reeves was deliberately inverting Blackstone's suggestion that the royal prerogative had been reined in: "Some invidious, nay dangerous, branches of the prerogative have since been lopped off" (William Blackstone, *Commentaries on the Laws of England,* 4 vols. [Oxford, 1765–1769; reprint ed. Chicago: University of Chicago Press, 1979], 4:432). On this episode see A. V. Beedell, "John Reeves's Prosecution for a Seditious Libel, 1795–6: A Study in Political Cynicism," *Historical Journal* (December 1993) 36(4):799–824.

[177] *The Autobiography of William Jerdan,* 4 vols. (London, 1852–1853), 1:43.

[178] Jerdan to Canning, 19 April 1827, *Some Official Correspondence of George Canning,* ed. Edward J. Stapleton, 2 vols. (London, 1887), 2:367; see too Jerdan to Canning, 5 May 1827, *Correspondence of Canning,* 2:368–70.

[179] A. G. Stapleton to Jerdan, 7 May 1827, *Correspondence of Canning,* 2:370.

[180] Alfred Mallalieu to Wellington, 3 March 1833, in *Wellington Political Correspondence,* pp. 95–98; Wellington to Mallalieu, 5 March 1833, *Wellington Political Correspondence,* p. 101; James Amphlett to Wellington, 24 January 1834, *Wellington Political Corre-*

We now recoil from such sordidly commercial dealings between the government and the press. In fact, the parties involved in them did their best to keep them secret: some will say that that shows they knew their dealings were shameful. Justifiable as our instincts may be, I want only to emphasize that the simple view of politics and markets prevents our noticing how such state intervention may enhance democratic debate by offering a wider range of views. Not to mention less impious links: there is something unsettling today in first seeing the front pages of these newspapers, completely covered with advertisements; but arguably that advertising revenue enabled the press to command what political independence it could.[181]

But, some will complain, we are still in the realm of state action. What, then, about private action undertaken to clean up the squalid filth of radical prose? "The successful zeal of Lady Howard" prevailed upon six shops to stop carrying the "vicious trash" of radicalism.[182] How did Lady Howard exercise her zeal? Did she impress the booksellers with her avid loyalty and persuade them that no right-thinking British subject ought to be poisoning the wells of popular sentiment? Or did she threaten them by suggesting in passing that they wouldn't want to suffer Lord Howard's ill will or reminding them of the ever-lurking dangers of criminal prosecution? Suppose she persuaded them. Does it follow that they have acted voluntarily? that no power has been exercised? that there are more possibilities than there were previously?

## GOOD READING

In one book they reviewed, the *British Critic* was pleased to find "an Appendix, in which is a very useful enumeration of authors on religious and political subjects, the reading of which two hours a day . . . will effectually cure infidelity and democracy."[183] Some conservatives

---

spondence, pp. 434–35; Wellington's draft reply, 26 January 1834, *Wellington Political Correspondence*, p. 435. Note too the Rev. Arthur Henry Glasse to Wellington, 23 October 1834, *Wellington Political Correspondence*, p. 698, seeking £50 for the *Argus*.

[181] Ivon Asquith, "Advertising and the Press in the Late Eighteenth and Early Nineteenth Centuries: James Perry and the *Morning Chronicle* 1790–1821," *Historical Journal* (1975) 18(4):703–24.

[182] Hannah More to Zachary Macaulay, 6 January 1796, in Roberts, *Memoirs of Hannah More*, 2:457.

[183] *British Critic* (May 1798) 11:558.

decided they might as well dive into the brackish pool of popular literacy and contribute sound and healthful prose. So the *Bristol Job Nott,* excoriating "the most exciting newspapers and pamphlets" which left "the people's minds . . . continually heated and fired," bit the bullet: "If Job Nott could *extinguish* this fever of curiosity, he would willingly do so; but seeing this is impossible, the next best thing that can be done is to endeavour to *alter the diet.*"[184] So the *White Dwarf* was created as a cleansing agent to combat the filthy discharge from the *Black Dwarf.* Carlile jeered, though, that once patrons no longer distributed the *White Dwarf* into coffeehouses and alehouses for free, it disappeared.[185] Consumer demand issued its political verdict.

The Bishop of London prevailed upon Hannah More to take up the cudgels against Paine and write something specifically for the lower orders. "In an evil hour, against my will and my judgment, on one sick day, I scribbled a little pamphlet called *Village Politics, by Will Chip*": though More hoped to escape identification, she didn't.[186] The bishop was delighted with the results, telling More that the work was "greatly admired" at court and that the attorney general had suggested that Reeves's Association distribute it around the country, which they did.[187] For the Association didn't merely promote the detection of seditious authors; they also promulgated good reading, sometimes offending authors and publishers by cavalierly ignoring copyright.[188]

More's pamphlet is an ingenuous dialogue, the best representative of the genre.[189] Tom Hod, a hotheaded mason, apparently has just read Paine's *Rights of Man* and discovered he is unhappy. Jack Anvil, a

---

[184] *Bristol Job Nott* (26 January 1832) no. 7, p. 26.

[185] *Republican* (8 December 1820) 4(15):525.

[186] Hannah More to Mrs. Boscawen, 1793, in Roberts, *Memoirs of Hannah More,* 2:378.

[187] Beilby Porteus to Hannah More, 1793, in Roberts, *Memoirs of Hannah More,* 2:348. The pamphlet is in *Association Papers,* pt. 2, no. 9.

[188] Eugene Charlton Black, *The Association: British Extraparliamentary Political Organization 1769–1793* (Cambridge, MA: Harvard University Press, 1963), p. 268.

[189] Compare for instance Solomon Searchem, *Modern Madmen; or, The Constitutionalists Dissected* (London, 1792); *A Dialogue between Mr. Worthy and John Simple, on Some Matters Relative to the Present State of Great Britain* (London, 1792); John Bowles, *Dialogues on the Rights of Britons, between a Farmer, a Sailor, and a Manufacturer,* 2 pts. (London, 1792); *Equality, as Consistent with the British Constitution, in a Dialogue between a Master-Manufacturer and One of His Workmen* (London, 1792); *Liberty and Equality: A Dialogue between a Clergyman and His Parishioner* (London, 1794); *The Street Politicians, or A Debate about the Times* (Manchester, 1817). For a dialogue supporting equality, see A Friend to Equality, *Political Dialogues, upon the Subject of Equality,* 2d ed. (London, 1792), in which Lord Despotism, after speaking with Citizen Equality, becomes Mr. Convert.

wise blacksmith, teases him: how unhappy could he have been if he needed to read a book to discover it? Tom is off and running on a radical tirade: he craves the rights of man, a new constitution, equality. But Jack patiently expounds time-honored conservative wisdom. Equality would mean chaos and disorder; hierarchy is in everyone's interests; Sir John, the local lord, is a benevolent paternalist, paying for Sunday schools and the local hospital. It takes just a dozen pages for Tom greedily to gulp down a beautifully crafted antirevolutionary catechism:

TOM. What then does thou take French *liberty* to be?

JACK. To murder more men in one night, than ever their poor king did in his whole life.

TOM. And what dost thou take a *Democrat* to be?

JACK. One who likes to be governed by a thousand tyrants, and yet can't bear a king.

TOM. What is *Equality?*

JACK. For every man to pull down every one that is above him, till they're all as low as the lowest.

TOM. What is the *new* RIGHTS *of* MAN?

JACK. Battle, murder, and sudden death.

TOM. What is it to be an *enlightened people?*

JACK. To put out the light of the gospel, confound right and wrong, and grope about in pitch darkness.[190]

By dialogue's end, Tom is ready to burn his copy of Paine and then start a bonfire. But Jack is no fan of church-and-king mobs, either. He urges Tom to mind his own business and the newly docile mason agrees. It's easy to see why Reeves's Association distributed this text. It's easy, too, to see why More herself spearheaded the writing and publication of the Cheap Repository Tracts for "the inferior ranks," "such wholesome aliment as might give a new direction to their taste, and abate their relish for those corrupt and inflammatory publications which the consequences of the French revolution have been so fatally pouring in upon us."[191] Why, then, did More rue the day she wrote *Village Politics?*

[190] Hannah More, *Village Politics: Addressed to All the Mechanics, Journeymen, and Day-Labourers, in Great Britain,* 5th ed. (York, 1793), p. 15; with variations in *Works of Hannah More,* 2:233.

[191] *Tales for the Common People,* advt., in *Works of Hannah More,* 1:249. Many of the tracts are available in the Opie Collection, 002:020 and 002:021.

The English Jacobins often snickered at the efforts of conservatives
to inject good sense into coffeehouse politicians and alehouse de-
baters. As they saw it, the resulting vivid controversy fanned the
flames of political discussion. Burke should have kept silent, advised
one wryly, "for it is notorious that Mr. Burke himself has done more to
excite enquiry" than all of London's radical organizations could have
done in twenty years.[192] John Thelwall had contempt for Burke, a
"State Juggler" intent on deluding the people; but he also was grateful
to Burke for the explosion of radical writing and reading: "We are to
look upon him as the great father and first propagator of the principles of democracy in this country."[193] Parliament repeatedly ordered
the publication of the reports of its Committees on Secrecy, bulging
with sordid details and internal documents of radical groups.[194] Publication was meant to stir up popular vigilance and alarm. No doubt it
did. But it also gave the radical groups greater publicity than they
could have hoped for on their own.

Conservatives once again were caught by a vicious paradox. They
couldn't very well stand by and leave the coffeehouses and alehouses
to the mercy of relentless Jacobin attacks. But their intercession

[192] Charles Pigott, *Strictures on the New Political Tenets of the Rt. Hon. Edmund Burke*
(London, 1791), pp. 50–51 n. †. See too United Constitutional Societies meeting, 24
March 1792, resolutions to Society for Constitutional Information, in *The Second Report
from the Committee of Secrecy to the House of Commons*, 4th ed. (London, 1794), app. D;
William Williams, *Rights of the People; or, Reasons for a Regicide Peace* (London, 1796),
pp. ii–iii.

[193] *Tribune* (9 September 1795) no. 25, in *The Politics of English Jacobinism: Writings of
John Thelwall*, ed. Gregory Claeys (University Park, PA: Pennsylvania State University
Press, 1995), pp. 220–21. Godwin, *Enquiry Concerning Political Justice*, 2:124–41 [1798],
"Of Political Imposture," acutely explores some of the intractable problems facing a
nameless writer who is obviously Burke. See too Thomas Walker, *A Review of Some of the
Political Events, Which Have Occurred in Manchester, during the Last Five Years* (London,
1794), p. 5; *Extermination, or An Appeal to the People of England, on the Present War, with
France* (London, 1793), pp. 18–19 n.

[194] See *The First Report of the Committee of Secrecy of the House of Commons; The Second
Report from the Committee of Secrecy to the House of Commons; The First Report from the Commit-
tee of Secrecy Appointed by the House of Lords to Inspect the Report and Original Papers, and the
Book Sealed up in a Bag, Delivered on Monday the 19th of May Last, by a Message from the
Commons*, 4th ed. (London, 1794); *The Second Report from the Committee of Secrecy Appoin-
ted by the House of Lords to Inspect the Report and Original Papers, and the Book Sealed up in a
Bag, Delivered on Monday the 19th of May Last, by a Message from the Commons* (London,
1794); *Supplement to the Second Report from the Committee of Secrecy, to Whom the Several
Papers Referred to in His Majesty's Message of the 12th Day of May 1794, and Which Were
Presented (Sealed up) to the House of Commons, by Mr. Secretary Dundas, upon the 12th and
13th Days of the Said Month, by His Majesty's Command, Were Referred* (London, 1794).

looked self-defeating: it encouraged further reading, the corrosion of prejudice, precisely what they wanted to avoid. This is just a sharper version of the paradox of timing. Thelwall archly scolded Burke for unloosing his frenzied Jacobin attack on the Duke of Bedford in the *Letter to a Noble Lord*. Burke, recall, had impeached Bedford by revisiting the dismal origins of his house and title in Henry VIII's dissolution of the monasteries. But, remarked Thelwall, this attack promised to provoke searching public discussion into the legitimacy of aristocratic property rights. "Mr. *Burke* has done an irreparable injury to the cause of aristocracy by provoking this discussion; and, if an antidote is not applied, which I trust it will, by fair and manly exposition of the subject, has set a poison in circulation most dangerous to the health and existence of the social frame."[195] Thelwall's isn't a simple inversion. He doesn't pose as the defender of veils against Burke's rude unmasking. His antidote will be fair and (here's that funny appeal to gender again) manly discussion. Tradition, loyalism, and aristocracy joined in titanic combat against reason, criticism, and the rights of man: but which was the poison, which the antidote?

## THE POLITICS OF NECESSITY

We can exacerbate the dilemma. What was reason, anyway? In one interpretation, *reason* referred to the world of coffeehouse discussion, a move enabling the valiant attacks on the rationality of such discussion. But there are other interpretations. Hannah Arendt once asked rhetorically, thinking I suppose of Burke, "And which conservatism worth its salt has not been romantic?"[196] The question has a perfectly good answer. I want to explore the terribly shrewd rhetoric of Thomas Malthus, which introduces not just another antidote to the poison of revolutionary argument but also a distinctive conservatism, utterly at odds with that of Burke.

Burke posed as the lover of veils and pleasing illusions. His Jacobin opponents posed as stern unmaskers, ripping aside those veils and illusions in the name of reason. Malthus's sly genius is to unmask the unmaskers, to expose their radical agenda as itself a fatuous illusion.

---

[195] John Thelwall, *Sober Reflections on the Seditious and Inflammatory Letter of the Right Hon. Edmund Burke, to a Noble Lord,* 3d ed. (London, 1796), p. 43; on pp. 16–17, Thelwall declares that he himself never has seen fit to raise such dangerous questions.

[196] Hannah Arendt, *On Revolution* (New York: Viking, 1963), p. 198.

The *Essay on Population* now figures in the history of demography, but it was intended and received as a political polemic. The agenda is already clear in the preface to the first edition, where a detached Malthus ruminates on his work in the third person: "He professes to have read some of the speculations on the future improvement of society, in a temper very different from a wish to find them visionary; but he has not acquired that command over his understanding which would enable him to believe what he wishes, without evidence, or to refuse his assent to what might be unpleasing, when accompanied with evidence."[197] No fantasies permitted.

I won't attempt a reconstruction of the infamous argument of the *Essay*.[198] A brief rehearsal or reminder: Malthus holds that the supply of food tends to increase arithmetically, while population tends to increase geometrically. So something must be restraining population growth. In the first edition, Malthus is adamantly bleak: misery and vice do the job. What would otherwise be excess population yields to war, starvation, and the like, or is choked off by such moral horrors as infanticide. Any scheme of utopian improvement crumbles in the face of this grim necessity. If we imagine somehow reaching a relatively affluent society, we see that population growth would again explode, bringing grinding poverty and worse in its wake. But the analysis means that we can't reach such a society even temporarily, because population always already must be bumping up against the constraints of misery and vice.

I want to draw attention to just one aspect of the argument, its appeal to necessity. Malthus doesn't argue that on the merits, Jacobin schemes are a bad idea. He argues instead that they are ruled out by impersonal laws of nature, so there's no point in daydreaming about them. The strategy suggests an abstract but crucial similarity between Malthus and Burke. Even if one mocks illusion and the other embraces it, even if one turns to ecological and biological mechanisms and the other to claims about history and cognition, both argue that the scope of political agency is dramatically limited. This is a deep structural prop in conservative politics. Similarly, democrats offer in-

---

[197] *Essay on the Principle of Population* [1798], in *The Works of Thomas Robert Malthus*, ed. E. A. Wrigley and David Souden, 8 vols. (London: William Pickering, 1986), 1:ii.

[198] For an analytically meticulous and historically informed account, see A. M. C. Waterman, *Revolution, Economics and Religion: Christian Political Economy, 1798–1833* (Cambridge: Cambridge University Press, 1991).

toxicatingly expansive accounts of the scope of political agency. Much of the rhetoric of popular sovereignty denies that nature or history or Providence—or, maybe, much of anything—limits what the people can do.

This analysis departs from a standard reading of the period, indeed from one contemporary self-understanding. In that view, Malthus as a political economist naturally joins ranks with the liberals surrounding the *Edinburgh Review,* opposed on one side by the Tories of the *Quarterly Review* and (to a lesser extent) by the radicals and utilitarians of the *Westminster Review.* True, Southey despised Malthus's theory: "It is my heart's desire to put his rascally book to death and damnation."[199] True, the radical Cobbett loathed him: "I have, during my life, detested many men; but never any one so much as you."[200] But the standard reading conceals some striking political affinities. For a while, the *Quarterly* enthusiastically endorsed Malthus.[201] So did *Blackwood's.*[202] And young conservative Cobbett adored his views.[203]

On an innocent reading, how wide the scope of political agency actually is—what we can accomplish, what lies within our collective control—is an empirical question. Perhaps conservatives are right; perhaps democrats are. Or perhaps it depends on the issue at hand. Much criticism was levelled at Malthus, much of it wildly off the mark. But his shrewdest critics had a field day exposing his claims of necessity as illusory. They argued that Malthus effortlessly ruled out genuine possibilities without bothering to venture any reasoned defense of his politically controversial views.

Malthus can barely bring himself to allude to birth control and abortion, which he sees as unnatural and repulsive.[204] This wasn't idiosyncratic. Some of his critics agreed with him.[205] Others wrongly

---

[199] Southey to John Rickman, 27 July 1803, *Selections from the Letters of Southey,* 1:225.

[200] *Political Register* (8 May 1819) 34(33):1019. For a scathing account of the political uses to which Malthus could be put, see especially Cobbett's inimitable comedy, *Surplus Population,* in *Political Register* (28 May 1831) 72(9):493–511, also in *Cobbett's Two-Penny Trash; or, Politics for the Poor* (June 1831) 1(12):265–92.

[201] For instance, *Quarterly Review* (July 1817) 17:402, (October 1821) 26:168.

[202] *Blackwood's Edinburgh Magazine* (November 1818) 4(20):208.

[203] Cobbett to George Hibbert, 29 December 1805, in Lewis Melville, *The Life and Letters of William Cobbett in England & America,* 2 vols. (London: John Lane, The Bodley Head, 1913), 1:292–93; *Political Register* (18 January 1806) 9(3):65.

[204] *Essay on Population* [1798], in *Works,* 1:57; "Population" [1824], in *Works,* 4:203.

[205] For instance, Michael Thomas Sadler, *The Law of Population,* 2 vols. (London, 1830; reprint ed. London: Routledge/Thoemmes Press, 1994), 2:160. Compare the

accused him of supporting such measures.[206] But some, including Carlile the atheist and Place the tailor, urged the merits of birth control—and worked hard to promulgate knowledge of the requisite techniques, Carlile offering a calmly antiseptic discussion of vaginal sponges.[207] Birth control and abortion may be objectionable. But it's illusory to pretend they aren't possible.

Or again: in the second edition, Malthus introduced a new check, moral restraint. People might prudently decide to marry late and remain chaste in the meantime. This new check—"a snivelling interpolation,"[208] scoffed Hazlitt; "an amendment that entirely overthrew all the conclusions of the first"[209] edition, in the verdict of the *Quarterly*—eviscerates the unrelenting gloom of the earlier argument, since it implicitly returns to human agency what had been assigned to natural necessity.

Or again: Hazlitt was furious that "Mr. Malthus's gospel is preached only to the poor!"[210] They were the source of excess population, since they didn't possess enough assets to support all their children. But what role did existing property rights play in Malthus's argument? "It has appeared," he pronounced, "that from the inevitable laws of our nature, some human beings must suffer from want. These are the unhappy persons who, in the great lottery of life, have drawn a blank."[211] Or, embellishing the ornaments of his argument:

---

aghast silence of John Berkeley Monck, *General Reflections on the System of the Poor Laws, with A Short View of Mr. Whitbread's Bill, and a Comment on It* (London, 1807), p. 44.

[206] For instance, James Grahame, *An Inquiry into the Principle of Population* (Edinburgh, 1816; reprint ed. London: Routledge/Thoemmes Press, 1994), pp. 19, 21.

[207] Note Richard Carlile to John Finch, 31 August 1829, *Lion* (4 September 1829) 4(10):290–91; Carlile, *Every Woman's Book; or, What Is Love?*, 4th ed. (London, 1826), a revision of *Republican* (6 May 1825) 11(18):545–69; Francis Place, *Illustrations and Proofs of the Principle of Population*, ed. Norman E. Himes (London: George Allen & Unwin, 1930). See too William Thompson, *An Inquiry into the Principles of the Distribution of Wealth Most Conducive to Human Happiness* (London, 1824; reprint ed. New York: Augustus M. Kelley, 1963), p. 550. For a review of the beginnings of birth control, see Dudley Miles, *Francis Place 1771–1854: The Life of a Remarkable Radical* (Sussex: Harvester Press, 1988), chap. 9.

[208] *A Reply to the Essay on Population, by the Rev. T. R. Malthus* [1807], in *The Complete Works of William Hazlitt*, ed. P. P. Howe, 21 vols. (London: J. M. Dent and Sons, 1930–1934), 1:227.

[209] *Quarterly Review* (April 1831) 45:125.

[210] *Reply* [1807], in *Works of Hazlitt*, 1:356.

[211] *Essay on Population* [1798], in *Works*, 1:74; and see *Essay on Population* [1826], in *Works*, 3:567 for more with this imagery.

A man who is born into a world already possessed, if he cannot get subsistence from his parents on whom he had a just demand, and if the society do not want his labour, has no claim of *right* to the smallest portion of food, and, in fact, has no business to be where he is. At nature's mighty feast there is no vacant cover for him. She tells him to be gone, and will quickly execute her own orders, if he do not work upon the compassion of some of her guests. If these guests get up and make room for him, other intruders immediately appear demanding the same favour. The report of a provision for all that come, fills the hall with numerous claimants. The order and harmony of the feast is disturbed, the plenty that before reigned is changed into scarcity; and the happiness of the guests is destroyed by the spectacle of misery and dependence in every part of the hall, and by the clamorous importunity of those, who are justly enraged at not finding the provision which they had been taught to expect. The guests learn too late their error, in counteracting those strict orders to all intruders, issued by the great mistress of the feast, who, wishing that all her guests should have plenty, and knowing that she could not provide for unlimited numbers, humanely refused to admit fresh comers when her table was already full.[212]

There are agents in this account, but they are bumblers of the most inept sort. The poor, lacking property to feed themselves, are cast in the thankless role of boors crashing a party. The more affluent guests are well-intentioned but naive. Their efforts to accommodate the poor can only encourage a further supply of boors and give rise to complaints about legitimate expectations. This is nature's feast, after all, and those lucky enough to win an invitation should mind their manners and submit to the rules that their not astonishingly generous hostess has dictated for the occasion.

One critic denied that the existing property regime was dictated by nature. Ireland's population problems, he argued, stemmed from the ignoble history of repressive English legislation. Absentee landlords plundered the countryside; legally imposed tithes forced Catholics to support a Protestant ministry they found useless. No wonder the country was desperately poor. So why blame nature?[213] Another critic

[212] *Essay on Population* [1803], in *Works*, 3:697–98. For an acrid rejoinder, see *Quarterly Review* (December 1812) 8:327.

[213] George Ensor, *An Inquiry Concerning the Population of Nations* (London, 1818; reprint ed. London: Routledge/Thoemmes Press, 1994), pp. 267, 420–21. See generally pt. 2, chap. 5, pp. 260–96.

concurred. "Human institutions are the real cause of all the misery with which we are surrounded, and he who in the arrogance of his folly would trace them to any other source, as he renders hopeless all improvement of our condition, is equally an enemy to man whom he oppresses, and to God whom he maligns."[214]

These disputes about contingency and necessity weren't central only to the debate about population. They were replayed endlessly, democrats gravitating to defenses of contingency, conservatives to necessity. To take one dramatic example, the same dispute swirled around the pathologies of debate, the stupidities of democracy. Were the masses ineducable or merely uneducated? These people rioted in the streets and heaved bricks through the windows of their betters at the slightest provocation. Who could imagine permitting such crude ruffians to vote? But consider the *Gorgon*'s acid jest: "We certainly should recommend that every individual be put into the immediate possession of his elective franchise. The unrepresented part of society would not then be under the necessity of expressing their opinion of public men by spittle, brick-bats, and breaking of windows, they might do it in a much more silent and effectual manner, by a vote at a general election."[215]

Here the putatively natural deficiencies taken to preclude political participation are recast as the contingent outcome of denying citizenship. Was it merely pious hope? A much reprinted and lurid account of the gypsies of London portrayed the entirely sober election of a new gypsy king.[216] If such despicable rabble could flourish under elective monarchy, why not the English?

---

[214] Piercy Ravenstone, *A Few Doubts as to the Correctness of Some Opinions Generally Entertained on the Subjects of Population and Political Economy* (London, 1821; reprint ed. London: Routledge/Thoemmes Press, 1994), p. 120. See too Charles Hall, *The Effects of Civilization on the People in European States* (London, 1805; reprint ed. London: Routledge/Thoemmes Press, 1994), pp. 130–37.

[215] *Gorgon* (11 July 1818) no. 8, p. 62. See too George Grote, *Statement of the Question of Parliamentary Reform; with a Reply to the Objections of the Edinburgh Review, No. LXI* (London, 1821), pp. 86–87; Earl of Durham in House of Lords, 22 May 1832, in Stuart J. Reid, *Life and Letters of the First Earl of Durham 1792–1840,* 2 vols. (London: Longmans, Green, 1906), 1:291–92. Compare Mark Harrison, *Crowds and History: Mass Phenomena in English Towns, 1790–1835* (Cambridge: Cambridge University Press, 1988), p. 221.

[216] *The Life and Adventures of Bampfylde-Moore Carew, Commonly Called the King of the Beggars* (London, 1793), pp. 58–61. There are editions as early as 1745–1749, but the original figure seems to have had no contact with gypsies: see *The King of the Beggars: Bampfylde-Moore Carew,* ed. C. H. Wilkinson (Oxford: Clarendon, 1931), pp. viii–x.

Those fearful of political poison tended to gravitate toward Burke, champion of illusion and veils. Those fond of necessity tended to gravitate toward Malthus, grim unmasker. But they shared a knack for making controversial political judgments invisible. If the masses are being poisoned, they need diagnosis and cure, as if feverish political discussion were a public health problem. If no one can alter the structure of private property or poverty, they're outside the scope of political agency, so there's no point fussing about them.

We could conceive of one thread through this knotty material as a dialectic of enlightenment, if not the one Horkheimer and Adorno had in mind, which leads inexorably from brave enlightenment crusades for liberty to fascist and bourgeois repression, not to mention poor kinky de Sade.[217] To put it in utterly stylized terms: Burke celebrates prejudice; the Jacobins rip aside his veils in the name of reason; Malthus strips their arguments bare and reveals fatuous illusion. We can imagine just one more step in the dialectic, though not one I've found explicitly stated during the period.

Suppose that Malthus is wrong, that Hazlitt and the others are right in unmasking him in turn and finding contingent political practices where he found natural necessity. The way is then clear for the argument to come full circle, at least in the spiralling way dialectical arguments do, back to a position reminiscent of Burke's. For even if Malthus's argument is an illusion, it might turn out to be politically beneficent. Workers who came to believe that nature doomed their fondest radical dreams would have accepted a bad argument. Nonetheless, they'd lapse back into political quiescence, just as if they were still in the thralls of prejudice and illusion. The vibrant world of coffeehouse reading and alehouse debate was supposed to rouse the sleepy subjects; the irreversibility thesis was supposed to ensure that once awake they'd never sleep again. But now it seems that bad arguments can be a surrogate for tradition. Those accepting them may be nominally awake, or, to unpack the metaphor, they may be participating in vigorous argument. But they might as well be sleepwalking.

[217] Max Horkheimer and Theodor Adorno, *Dialectic of Enlightenment* [1944], trans. John Cumming (New York: Seabury Press, 1977).

# FOUR

# THE POLITICS OF REASON

———— ⊗⊗⊗ ————

R UBBING SHOULDERS with strangers in London disgusted Tobias
Smollett. "In a word," he complained in 1753, "this metropolis is
a vast masquerade, in which a man of stratagem may wear a thousand
different disguises, without danger of detection."[1] These shapeshifters continued to rankle in Smollett's belligerently Tory imagination. "In short," he complained in 1771, "there is no distinction or
subordination left—The different departments of life are jumbled
together—The hod-carrier, the low mechanic, the tapster, the publi-
can, the shop-keeper, the pettifogger, the citizen, and courtier, all
tread upon the kibes of one another"[2] in a shatteringly promiscuous
riot of status confusion.

But the same urban anonymity could be repackaged as a promising
glimpse of democratic sociability. Pierce Egan parlayed a breezy prose
style and a disturbing intimacy with London lowlife into a career as
one of the early nineteenth century's popular writers. He had a keen
sociological imagination, too. Consider his account of one coffeehouse, emphatically not the silent sort:

> The *groupes* to be met with in the Coffee room . . . are highly *characteristic*
> of the different grades of life—abounding with ORIGINALS of all sorts—
> a kind of Masquerade, with this difference only, where the *characters* play
> their parts without resorting to the assistance of masks; yet, nevertheless,
> a great many persons "pop in on the sly," who have not courage to ac-
> knowledge who they are; and who are equally cautious, if possible, to
> prevent recognition. But there is no need of this display of *sensitive* feel-

---

[1] Tobias Smollett, *The Adventures of Ferdinand Count Fathom* [1753], ed. O. M. Brack,
Jr. (Athens, GA: University of Georgia Press, 1988), p. 145.
[2] Tobias Smollett, *The Expedition of Humphry Clinker* [1771], ed. O. M. Brack, Jr.
(Athens, GA: University of Georgia Press, 1990), pp. 87–88.

ing; the visitor may be as quiet as a mouse; or as talkative as a clown outside a show if he has any desire to amuse the company. You may be seated next to an M.P. without being aware of *that* honor; and you may likewise *rub* against some noble lord without committing a breach of privilege. You may meet poets on the look out for a hero; artists for subjects; and boxers for customers.[3]

Or, as Egan put it of another coffeehouse, "Every body is welcome, first come, first served—there is no distinction of persons, it is all 'hail fellow, well met;' and the only acknowledged great man amongst them is the chairman, whose hammer is omnipotent."[4]

Masquerades make Smollett uneasy; he wants to know who people really are, where they stand in the status hierarchy. Masquerades make Egan jolly; he beams at people casually letting down their hair. For Smollett, "no distinction or subordination" summons up frightful disorder. For Egan, "no distinction of persons" summons up convivial egalitarianism.

I wouldn't recommend taking Egan literally. Surely clothing, accent, and the like, not to mention an expansive presentation of self, flagged the M.P.s and aristocrats in the crowd. But Egan was no dimwit. He's dramatizing the contrast between the easygoing equality of the coffeehouse, where people are relatively free to ignore status distinctions, with other social settings in which those distinctions have ominous clout. If the boxer, somehow alerted to the real identity of the M.P., were to deign to swing by his residence to continue their conversation, the servant would curtly inform him that the great man is not at home.

So we can construe the masquerade with no masks as an injunction to those seated in the coffeehouse: yes, you can figure out who is the noble lord, who the hapless artisan. But you must blind yourself to that fact, because it's irrelevant in this context. The M.P. must not presume on his status, say by trying to bully his interlocutors into meek submission. Nor, for that matter, may the artisan presume on his status (and just what would count as presumption here?). Egan

---

[3] *Pierce Egan's Book of Sports, and Mirror of Life: Embracing the Turf, the Chase, the Ring, and the Stage Interspersed with Original Memoirs of Sporting Men, Etc.* (London, 1832), p. 73.

[4] *Pierce Egan's Book of Sports,* p. 100. Note Ian R. Christie, *Stress and Stability in Late Eighteenth-Century Britain: Reflections on the British Avoidance of Revolution* (Oxford: Clarendon, 1984), pp. 58–59.

doesn't magically invent this injunction. He discovers it in surveying the actual practices of coffeehouse discussion and trying to decipher the rules of the game. Not that the players always obey the rules, any more than they do in any other game. Imagine the M.P., lips pinched and nostrils flared, asking the poet, "Do you realize who you are talking to?" Or imagine him not needing to ask the question aloud at all. Imagine a contemptuous glare, even an airy wave of the hand or a quizzical glance, doing potently dismissive work. Perhaps the coffeehouse patrons recognize distinctions of persons all the time, but they know they shouldn't.

Other observers didn't focus so narrowly on the coffeehouse. In a brief entry on *conversation,* the 1797 *Encyclopedia Britannica* did nothing but offer rules to ensure a pleasant experience for all. So for instance it advised, "Talk often, but not long. The talent of haranguing private company is insupportable."[5] "The advantages of rank or fortune are no advantages in argumentation," declared Richard Cumberland; "neither is an inferior to offer, or a superior to extort the submission of the understanding on such occasions; for every man's reason has the same pedigree; it begins and ends with himself."[6] People ought to listen carefully and speak civilly, he added. "In the name of freedom, what claim hath any man to be the tyrant of the table? As well he may avail himself of the greater force of his fists as of his lungs."[7] There's a glimpse here of a conception of democratic debate as—to spoof it only a bit—disembodied rationality, or more seriously as the priority of reason to politics, a conception I mean to challenge.

## A MOMENT SURROUNDED

It's a mistake to try to isolate reasonable speech from the other aspects of democratic debate and politics. Alehouses and coffeehouses were frequently the sites of political plotting. A March 1799 raid on London's Royal Oak was supposed to round up Irish revolutionaries.

---

[5] *Encyclopedia Britannica,* 3d ed., 18 vols. (Edinburgh, 1797), 5:385–86 s.v. *conversation.* See too *Encyclopedia,* 15:486 s.v. *prejudice.*

[6] Richard Cumberland, *The Observer: Being a Collection of Moral, Literary and Familiar Essays,* 5th ed., 6 vols. (London, 1798), 1:181, italics inverted.

[7] Cumberland, *The Observer,* 3:283.

It failed to do that, but it did turn up impressive documentary evidence of a plot.[8] To keep secret his identity as principal writer for *John Bull*, Theodore Hook arranged to meet the proprietors in various coffeehouses.[9] In 1831, William Benbow convened a meeting at his own coffeehouse. There, Francis Place recorded with wondering disdain, "the most unprincipled" radicals planned a public meeting to which "it was openly proposed that every man should come armed to preserve the peace," armed with staves a good twenty inches long, suitable for fracturing skulls.[10] If the authorities were dismayed by the flags at Peterloo, we can imagine how they would have greeted these peace-preserving implements. (A radical shoemaker was hauled before the Privy Council in 1817 to answer questions about such weapons. "Pikes, pikes? Oh yes!" he shot back impudently; "we cleaned them, boiled them, and me and my family eat them with melted butter."[11] He was dismissed.)

Contemporaries struggled over when they might justifiably have recourse to violence. "I have been three days ago most horridly abused in a news paper," confessed Goldsmith in 1773, "so like a fool as I was I went and thrashed the Editor."[12] A lawsuit followed. In 1809, Canning and Castlereagh fought a duel after Canning's threatened resignation led to a cabinet shake-up.[13] In 1823, there was a fiery exchange on the floor of Parliament between Canning and Brougham. Brougham assailed Canning's motives and behavior; Canning rose to give him the lie, in the day's splendid phrase; the house fell into a stunned silence. After some fancy footwork about whether Canning's public or private character had been assailed, the exchange blew

[8] Marianne Elliott, *Partners in Revolution: The United Irishmen and France* (New Haven, CT: Yale University Press, 1982), pp. 254–55.

[9] R. H. Dalton Barham, *The Life and Remains of Theodore Edward Hook*, 2 vols. (London, 1849), 1:215.

[10] *London Radicalism 1830–1843: A Selection from the Papers of Francis Place*, ed. D. J. Rowe (London: London Record Society, 1970), p. 54.

[11] *Life and Opinions of Thomas Preston, Patriot and Shoemaker* (London, 1817), p. 32. I've corrected the punctuation of the original text.

[12] Oliver Goldsmith to James Boswell, 4 April 1773, *The Correspondence of James Boswell with Certain Members of the Club*, ed. Charles N. Fifer (New York: McGraw-Hill, 1976), p. 26. See too John Clare to John Taylor, 24 February 1821, *The Letters of John Clare*, ed. Mark Storey (Oxford: Clarendon, 1985), p. 159.

[13] *The Later Correspondence of George III*, ed. A. Aspinall, 5 vols. (Cambridge: Cambridge University Press, 1962–1970), 5:340–70.

over. It didn't lead to a duel and afterwards parliamentary insults were more acceptable.[14] In 1833, there was a fracas at another newspaper when the printer refused to identify the author of a handbill.[15]

Indeed, speech and action aren't mutually exclusive categories. We know from Austin and others that sometimes to say something is to do something; we know from Geertz and others that sometimes to do something is to say something.[16] But even where performatives and symbolic actions aren't in play, coffeehouse discussion drifts insensibly from speech to action. One aspect—a moment, for those who admire Hegelian language—of heated political debate is an attempt to sort out what ought to be done. But another is planning to do it. In 1800, authorities were confronted with the grotesque spectacle of radical graffiti on city walls in London and Manchester. "The Public Eye is dayly saluted with Sedition in Chalk Characters on our Walls," complained one Manchester justice. "And Whether the subject regards Bread or Peace NO KING introduces it. This is a shocking Idea to be thus familiarised." The police were duly issued sponges to remove the offending slogans.[17] Is posting the graffiti speech or action? Or again: Place organized a run on the banks to overwhelm Wellington's staunch resistance to the Reform Bill of 1832. Placards emblazoned, "TO STOP THE DUKE, GO FOR GOLD": speech or action?[18]

---

[14] *Parliamentary Debates* (17 April 1823) new series, 8:1089–1104.

[15] *John Bull* (24 November 1833) 13(676):370.

[16] J. L. Austin, *How to Do Things with Words*, ed. J. O. Urmson and Marina Sbisà, 2d ed. (Cambridge, MA: Harvard University Press, 1975); Clifford Geertz, *The Interpretation of Cultures* (New York: Basic Books, 1973), esp. chaps. 1, 15.

[17] Roger Wells, *Insurrection: The British Experience 1795–1803* (Gloucester: Alan Sutton, 1983), p. 185; Thomas Butterworth Bayley to Portland, 30 November 1800, quoted in Wells, *Wretched Faces: Famine in Wartime England 1793–1801* (Gloucester: Alan Sutton, 1988), p. 150. For more radical graffiti, see *Diaries of William Johnston Temple 1780–1796*, ed. Lewis Bettany (Oxford: Clarendon, 1929), p. 137 [20 August 1795]. Reeves's correspondents worried about such graffiti: see A Well-Wisher to John Reeves, 12 December 1792, British Library, Add. Mss. 16922, f. 24, wondering "Whether it would not be proper to employ a quiet & confidential person privately to wipe out what is chalked on the Walls by ill-meaning Persons," and Woolwich Association to Reeves, 16 January 1793, Add. Mss. 16924, f. 94, reporting such graffiti as *"Damn the King"* and wondering what legal steps might be taken.

[18] For Place's account of his 12 May 1832 invention of this slogan, see *London Radicalism*, ed. Rowe, pp. 89–90; note too Place to John Cam Hobhouse, 18 May 1832, in Dudley Miles, *Francis Place 1771–1854: The Life of a Remarkable Radical* (Sussex: Harvester Press, 1988), pp. 198–99, for concerns about how far this campaign should be pressed.

So, too, there's a blurry boundary between political debate and moneymaking. Irish alehouses would hire "a regular Patriot, who goes about among the publicans talking violent politics & so helps to sell the beer—"[19] Elsewhere, coffee ordinarily was adulterated to cut costs.[20] That's fraudulent, but it doesn't threaten the integrity of coffeehouse conversation. The brewer's patriot does. His spirited talk is driven by the desire to sell more beer, not by his independent judgment, but the other patrons don't know that. Cash infiltrated parliamentary debates, too, or at least insiders often claimed it did. A veteran porter of the House of Commons defined *reasons* as "weighty and convincing proofs given to the different Members in favor of a motion, and generally conveyed by the *Secretaries* of the *Treasury*."[21]

And of course principled debate was infected by government manipulation. Recall such everyday intrusions as secret service payments to writers and newspapers. One more incident: the government commissioned a scurrilous and—how to put this delicate point?—highly inventive biography of Tom Paine, paying George Chalmers £500.[22] Chalmers was fiendishly deceptive. He published his *Life of Thomas Pain* under a pseudonym. To attract the right readers, those enamored of Paine, he added a subtitle: *with A Defence of His Writings*. The "defense" included, for instance, a scornful catalogue of Paine's grammatical errors, a sign of his vulgar incapacity to participate in learned political debate.[23] Chalmers's biography was recycled by others.[24] Or again: the government infiltrated many radical workers'

[19] *The Journal of Thomas Moore*, ed. Wilfred S. Dowden and others, 6 vols. (Newark: University of Delaware Press, 1983–1991), 3:1328 [21 September 1830].

[20] *Life & Struggles of William Lovett in His Pursuit of Bread, Knowledge, and Freedom* [1876], intro. R. H. Tawney (London: G. Bell and Sons, 1920), pp. 89–90.

[21] Joseph Pearson, *Pearson's Political Dictionary; Containing Remarks, Definitions, Explanations, and Customs, Political, and Parliamentary* (London, 1792), p. 44. See too Walter Savage Landor, *Imaginary Conversations of Literary Men and Statesmen*, 2d ser., 2 vols. (London, 1829), 1:71–72; *Lord Eldon's Anecdote Book*, ed. Anthony L. J. Lincoln and Robert Lindley McEwen (London: Stevens & Sons, 1960), pp. 51–52.

[22] Gregory Claeys, *Thomas Paine: Social and Political Thought* (Boston: Unwin Hyman, 1989), p. 20.

[23] Francis Oldys, *The Life of Thomas Pain, the Author of The Rights of Man: with A Defence of His Writings*, 2d ed. (London, 1791), pp. 27–29. The Paine family had varied the spelling of their name, and Tom himself used "Pain" as a young man: see John Keane, *Tom Paine: A Political Life* (Boston: Little, Brown, 1995), pp. xv, 16–17, 54.

[24] See for instance Charles Harrington Elliot, *The Republican Refuted; in a Series of Biographical, Critical and Political Strictures on Thomas Paine's Rights of Man* (London, 1791), in *Political Writings of the 1790s*, ed. Gregory Claeys, 8 vols. (London: William

groups with spies who helped justify their pay by peddling alarming stories to the Home Office and maybe by entrapping the workers. The infamous Oliver seems to have done just this.[25]

Coffeehouses and alehouses, then, were the setting of political debate. But that debate was forever penetrated by what we might be inclined to think of as disruptive intrusions, by political plotting and market dynamics and government manipulation. So we should reject Jürgen Habermas's view that the "bourgeois" public sphere worked well but was later corrupted. Habermas has a specific kind of decay in mind: the emergence of the social welfare state, he holds, gave citizens pressing material interests in taxation and other policy decisions, thus distracting their attention from disinterested considerations of the common good. So Habermas argues that politics was refeudalized.[26]

## INTEREST, PRINCIPLE, AND AFFECTION

Leave aside the empirical retorts one might offer: as if, for instance, frantic preoccupations with rising poor law rates didn't motivate much of this period's politics. Consider instead the contrast between interest and principle. Much democratic theory lyrically extols principled judgment on the common good and assaults pluralist accounts of democratic politics as the push and pull of interest groups.[27] What should we make of this?

---

Pickering, 1995), 5:312–14; John Gifford, *Plain Address to the Common Sense of the People of England* (London, 1792), pp. 15–21.

[25] On Oliver, see E. P. Thompson, *The Making of the English Working Class* (New York: Vintage Books, 1966), pp. 649–69. For an indictment of Edwards, another infamous spy, see Thomas Preston, *Letter to Lord Viscount Castlereagh; Being a Full Developement of All the Circumstances Relative to the Diabolical Cato Street Plot* (London, 1820).

[26] Jürgen Habermas, *The Structural Transformation of the Public Sphere: An Inquiry into a Category of Bourgeois Society*, trans. Thomas Burger with Frederick Lawrence (Cambridge, MA: MIT Press, 1989), pp. 222–35. The decline of the public sphere here ironically coincides with—and is caused by?—the expansion of the franchise, with the introduction of class diversity to democratic politics. Cavils aside, I am indebted to Habermas's sociological account of the public sphere: see *Structural Transformation;* Habermas, "Further Reflections on the Public Sphere," in *Habermas and the Public Sphere*, ed. Craig Calhoun (Cambridge, MA: MIT Press, 1992); Habermas, *Between Facts and Norms: Contributions to a Discourse Theory of Law and Democracy*, trans. William Rehg (Cambridge, MA: MIT Press, 1996), pp. 360–84.

[27] See for instance John Dunn, *Western Political Theory in the Face of the Future*, Canto edition (Cambridge: Cambridge University Press, 1993), chap. 1, dourly taking Athens as a model, and Joshua Cohen, "Deliberation and Democratic Legitimacy," in *The Good*

Those captivated by economic models of social life, those collapsing everything into the pursuit of self-interest or utility, may find it
hard to grasp the shape of this dilemma. Consider a richer typology,
not just a quaint period piece but on the merits a more incisive bit of
social theory than the economist's model: the distinction between
interest, principle, and affection.[28] Here's a rough gloss. One acts
from interest in pursuing something that will further one's ends; typically, those ends are taken to be self-interested, and not in the vacuous sense that makes utility-maximization coextensive with voluntary action. (For all his obsession with interest, even Bentham
forswore this vacuous sense.[29]) So instrumental rationality is the key.
One acts from principle in complying with a rule one accepts; typically, the rule is taken to be an impartial moral demand. One acts
from affection in more or less impulsively gratifying a passion or
weaker desire.

To take a modern example: the Ku Klux Klan act from interest as they
protect the jobs of marginal white workers, from principle as they
pursue racial purity, and from affection as they relish marching around
in those goofy outfits. In this case, all three sorts of motives lead to the
same actions. But they can conflict. Then the scheme leaves emphatically open the question of which motive will prevail. This scheme isn't
exhaustive. It's not obvious, for instance, that action from habit falls
neatly into any of the three categories. We might wonder, too, about
shoving a finicky concern for honor and status into the category of
affection. Regardless, this typology is invoked constantly in the literature of the eighteenth and nineteenth centuries.

Consider a few examples. Economists today like to show how the
methodical pursuit of interest links up with perverse incentives to
produce socially irrational outcomes. Contemporaries offered similar
but richer arguments. So Brougham instructed the House of Lords
that the poor laws promoted the loss of chastity and the growth of
population: a woman's sexual passion was assisted by the interest she

---

Polity: Normative Analysis of the State, ed. Alan Hamlin and Philip Pettit (Oxford: Basil
Blackwell, 1989), optimistic about deliberation and the common good.

[28] For a canonical statement, see "Of Parties in General," in David Hume, Essays:
Moral Political and Literary [1741–1742] (Oxford: Oxford University Press, 1963).

[29] Jeremy Bentham, Of Laws in General, ed. H. L. A. Hart (London: Athlone Press,
1970), pp. 70–71 n. p.

had in gaining poor law support and the principled appeal of being honorably married, also imposed by the law.[30] I don't endorse this argument or any of the others I'm presenting; I want only to emphasize their structure.

In 1792, Joel Barlow sounded as though he'd read James Madison. "I hope I shall not be understood to mean, that the nature of man is totally changed by living in a free republic. I allow that it is still *interested* and *passionate* men, that direct the affairs of the world. But in national assemblies, passion is lost in deliberation, and interest balances interest; till the good of the whole community combines the general will."[31] Barlow assumes that democratic politics ought to be a matter of principle. Perhaps wary of Robespierre's campaigns, he denies that democracy then requires transforming human nature. Well-designed institutional machinery will do the trick.

In 1806, Fox moved "that this House, conceiving the African slave trade to be contrary to the principles of justice, humanity, and sound policy, will, with all practicable expedition, proceed to take effectual measures for abolishing the said trade," a resolution that passed overwhelmingly, in part because it left entirely vague how and when this happy state of affairs would come to pass.[32] Shrewdly—or fatuously—Fox argues that justice (principle), humanity (passion), and policy (interest) are simultaneously served. Earlier he had recognized an apparent conflict between commercial interest and justice and argued, heroically or implausibly, that "nothing could be the true interest of any description of men that revolted against the principles of justice and humanity."[33] Trying valiantly to resolve the same problem

[30] *Speeches of Henry Lord Brougham*, 4 vols. (Edinburgh, 1838), 3:522–23 [21 July 1834].

[31] Joel Barlow, *Advice to the Privileged Orders, in the Several States of Europe, Resulting from the Necessity and Propriety of a General Revolution in the Principle of Government*, pt. 1 (London, 1792), pp. 73–74, also in *The Works of Joel Barlow*, ed. William Bottorff and Arthur L. Ford, 2 vols. (Gainesville, FL: Scholars' Facsimiles & Reprints, 1970), 1:165–66.

[32] *The Speeches of the Right Honourable Charles James Fox, in the House of Commons*, 6 vols. (London, 1815), 6:662–63 [10 June 1806].

[33] *Speeches of Fox*, 3:390–91 [9 May 1788]. On Fox's view, see Josiah Conder, *Wages or the Whip: An Essay on the Comparative Cost and Productiveness of Free and Slave Labour* (London, 1833), pp. 1–2. Contrast the appeals in Thomas Clarkson, *An Essay on the Impolicy of the African Slave Trade* (Philadelphia, 1789), p. 132, and Clarkson, *The History of the Rise, Progress, & Accomplishment of the Abolition of the African Slave-Trade, by the British Parliament*, 2 vols. (Philadelphia, 1808), 2:96.

in protesting slavery, a student of slavery warned that God might well intercede to punish nations that dared to prefer national interest to justice.[34]

Those misnamed realists want to unmask principle as a mask for interest. Sometimes that's right. But Lord Holland, for instance, fought for the abolition of the slave trade and slavery despite his own extensive holdings in Jamaica.[35] There may be a clever account about how this fight was a devious route to securing his interests, but it's incredible that we can always furnish such accounts, let alone that they'll always be true.[36] Those who forever seek such accounts are too clever by half. They also miss some more perplexing combinations. Burke tried to exhibit principle as a mask for passion: "I never will allow, that enormous aggregate of Crime and Madness, called the French System, to stand for principle in any Man. The attachment to it is a proof of a malignant and wicked disposition; and this is all that can be truly said of it."[37] Consider the other permutations: affection as a mask for principle, for instance, or interest as a mask for affection.

Hazlitt contemplated the bizarre twists and turns of English policy towards America and Ireland:

> The behaviour of governments to their dependencies would be indeed in many cases a riddle, if states, any more than individuals, were influenced by right reason, and did not suffer their passions, their prejudices, and idle humours constantly to prevail not only over justice but policy. The habit of treating others ill seems by degrees to confer the right: there is no hatred equal to that we feel towards those we have injured; and the conscious incapacity to govern finds obvious relief in the resolution to oppress.[38]

[34] James Stephen, *The Slavery of the British West India Colonies Delineated*, 2 vols. (London, 1824–1830), 1:xli.

[35] *The Life and Times of Henry Lord Brougham Written by Himself*, 3 vols. (Edinburgh, 1871; reprint ed. Westmead: Gregg International Publishers, 1972), 3:447.

[36] These matters remain central in the historiography of slavery and its abolition: see particularly C. Duncan Rice, "'Humanity Sold for Sugar!' The British Abolitionist Response to Free Trade in Slave-Grown Sugar," *Historical Journal* (1970) 13(3):402–18.

[37] Burke to Lord Loughborough, 28 November 1792, *The Correspondence of Edmund Burke*, ed. Thomas W. Copeland, 10 vols. (Chicago: University of Chicago Press, 1958–1978), 7:304.

[38] *The Life of Napoleon Buonaparte* [1828], in *The Complete Works of William Hazlitt*, ed. P. P. Howe, 21 vols. (London: J. M. Dent and Sons, 1930–1934), 13:26.

Here affection triumphs over interest and principle. Adam Smith already had argued not just that England's colonies served the interests of a well-organized few against the interests of a more diffuse many, but also that English passions were gratified by holding colonies. This unholy alliance meant that even "the most visionary enthusiast" couldn't seriously propose that England voluntarily divest herself of her colonies. "Such sacrifices, though they might frequently be agreeable to the interest, are always mortifying to the pride of every nation"—yet he closed the *Wealth of Nations* by proposing just that.[39] It's not how we usually think of imperial ventures, but maybe it's right.

The grammar of interest, principle, and affection exposes a fundamental ambiguity in thinking of democratic debate as reason. Is it instrumental rationality, the calculated pursuit of interest? Or is it a more principled practical rationality, focussed on categories like the common good? This grammar also makes it easier to get a grip on Habermas's elegy for the bourgeois public sphere, more generally on tirades against interest-group pluralism and pleas for the common good. Should democratic debate be a relentlessly disinterested discussion of issues of principle? Should we cordon off passion and interest?

To be blunt: no.[40] It's easy enough to deride the whimsical irrationalities that infect democratic debate. Yet it doesn't follow that a public debate without passion would be desirable. Take appeals to the sympathies and compassion of one's audience, intensely evocative sketches of the suffering of the subordinate and pariahs. Or take the attempt to summon up simmering resentment, even boiling rage, at some injustice. Or the gleefully adolescent pursuit of puncturing the bloated bubbles of complacency, hypocrisy, and pomposity. Do we really want a politics purged of such appeals to affection?

The leading statesmen of the day testified to the intensely emotional nature of political debate. "I was nearly overcome," recorded Canning. But he collected himself. The stakes were high; "anger too, and indignation against the person who was playing his anticks to

[39] Adam Smith, *An Inquiry into the Nature and Causes of the Wealth of Nations* [1776], ed. R. H. Campbell, A. S. Skinner, and W. B. Todd, 2 vols. (Oxford: Clarendon, 1976), 2:616–17, 2:946–47.

[40] I'm indebted to Bernard Yack, *The Problems of a Political Animal: Community, Justice, and Conflict in Aristotelian Political Thought* (Berkeley: University of California Press, 1993), esp. chaps. 2, 4.

perplex me—all conspired at once." His speech was a triumph, Pitt's and Dundas's "countenances smirking and glittering," Canning himself overwhelmed with pleasure. He learned afterward that in his theatrical abandon he had struck Lord Bayham with considerable violence and that Pitt and Dundas had dodged.[41] The young Gladstone was in agony searching for an opportune moment to take the floor.[42] John Cam Hobhouse, smarting under Canning's repeated insults, delivered "a portrait of a political adventurer" to a House of Commons hanging on every word. Canning "turned all colours, pulled his hat over his eyes," yet despite speculation didn't pursue a duel.[43] After one of Macaulay's assaults, "Peel looked as if sweating blood."[44] On the campaign stump, Disraeli "gave it to them for an hour and 1/4. I can give you no idea of the effect. I made them all mad. A great many absolutely *cried*."[45] Politicians and their audiences may be wringing handkerchiefs or necks even without any appeals to affection. But those appeals are surefire ways to inspire emotion.

Similarly, it's easy to mock the pluralist's impoverished vision of politics, pressure groups buffeting legislatures that perform vector addition. But it doesn't follow that a resolutely impartial commitment to the common good should replace the pursuit of interest. One plausibly could argue that nothing could count as a just solution to a social conflict that required trampling on the interests of some part of the community, so permitting heated discussions of interest (and forcibly suggesting that there is no just solution to many of our conflicts). Or one could remember those who present private grievances

[41] *The Letter-Journal of George Canning, 1793–1795*, ed. Peter Jupp (London: Offices of the Royal Historical Society, 1991), pp. 58, 60 [31 January 1794]. The speech was indeed a triumph: see Lady Stafford to Granville Leveson Gower, 1 February 1794, *Lord Granville Leveson Gower (First Earl Granville): Private Correspondence 1781 to 1821*, ed. Castalia Countess Granville, 2 vols. (London: John Murray, 1916), 1:78; Gower to his mother, 22 February 1794, *Granville Correspondence*, 1:86–87. For a slightly earlier case of an emotionally saturated parliamentary speaking experience, see Gilbert Elliot to Lady Elliot, 13 December 1787, *Life and Letters of Sir Gilbert Elliot First Earl of Minto from 1751 to 1806*, ed. Countess of Minto, 3 vols. (London, 1874), 1:176–80.

[42] William Ewart Gladstone, *The Gladstone Diaries*, ed. M. R. D. Foot and H. C. G. Matthew, 11 vols. (Oxford: Clarendon, 1968–1990), 2:32 [31 May 1833].

[43] John Cam Hobhouse, Baron Broughton, *Recollections of a Long Life*, ed. Lady Dorchester, 6 vols. (New York: Charles Scribner's Sons, 1909–1911), 2:145 [14 April 1821], 2:147 [17 April 1821], 2:148–49 [17–19 April 1821].

[44] Broughton, *Recollections*, 4:155 [16 December 1831].

[45] Disraeli to Sara Austen, 10 June 1832, in Benjamin Disraeli, *Letters: 1815–1834*, ed. J. A. W. Gunn and others (Toronto: University of Toronto Press, 1982), p. 289.

on a public stage, trying to show that their interests have been trampled on in unjust ways.[46] But I have a cruder point in mind. The
dissonant intertwining of principle and interest gives our political
conflicts depth and seriousness of purpose. A politics of genuinely
disinterested pursuit of the common good wouldn't be cause for celebration. It would be unpleasantly reminiscent of an interminable
Sunday school class or a boring graduate seminar.

So it's not that only a visionary enthusiast could seriously propose
getting rid of affection and interest, that unfortunately they're here
to stay, so we might as well grit our teeth and learn to live with them.
It's that they're inherently choiceworthy features of political life. Particular appeals to affection and interest are objectionable. But so are
particular appeals to principle. Or, to put the point differently, debate over principle, over the common good and justice, is a distinctive
and invaluable moment of political life, a recurring focus of democratic debate. But it should remain a moment surrounded—by interest and affection, by plotting and action. And we should resist the
inclination to think of it as a pearl surrounded by muck.

## PATHS TO EQUALITY

However weighty their differences, Egan and Cumberland both notice a principle of equality internal to argument, or at least coffeehouse argument. Bringing that principle into focus is tricky. We
might begin provisionally with this maxim: Pay attention only to the
merits of the argument, not the status of the speaker. (Does that
mean we shouldn't be bothered by the brewer's patriot?) It's a tempting maxim, sassy and briskly dismissive about the claims of learned
windbags and exalted magnates. It seems to hold out the promise of
bringing our political disputes to the bar of reason, resolving them
impartially and on the merits. Consider two more routes that led contemporaries to some such principle of equality in debate.

[46] For instance, John Cartwright, *A Letter to the Duke of Newcastle* (London, 1792);
Hugh Lord Sempill, *A Short Address to the Public, on the Practice of Cashiering Military
Officers without a Trial; and A Vindication of the Conduct and Political Opinions of the Author*
(London, 1793); William Tatham, *A Collection of Sundry Casual Documents, Addressed to
the Reflection of His Relations and Particular Friends* (London, 1797); Arthur Anderson,
*Important to Every Person Who Rents a House! A Caution to Tenants against the Injustice and
Legal Chicanery to Which They Are Exposed* (London, 1833).

"I have not any great notion of the advantage of what the 'free discussion' men, call the 'collision of opinions,' it being my creed that Truth is *sown* and germinates in the mind itself, and is not to be struck *out* suddenly like fire from a flint by knocking another hard body against it," sniffed one skeptic in 1833. Amusingly, the skeptic was none other than John Stuart Mill.[47] It would be easy to construct a prehistory of those anticipating (to put it teleologically, that is, badly) the doctrines of *On Liberty*. Already in 1793, for instance, one liberal had suggested that free speech would sort out the value of competing views, even those "of a mixed nature, where truth is often blended with falsehood," so controversy ought to be embraced as socially productive.[48] Anyway, Mill may have been caustically echoing the words of Hazlitt's celebration of free speech:

> There can be no true superiority but what arises out of the presupposed ground of equality: there can be no improvement but from the free communication and comparing of ideas. Kings and nobles, for this reason, receive little benefit from society—where all is submission on one side, and condescension on the other. The mind strikes out truth by collision, as steel strikes fire from the flint![49]

Reflecting on negotiating with patrons about commissions, the artist Constable too held that great men couldn't profit from frank conversation. "They are always angered—and their reasoning powers being generally blinded by their rank, they have no other idea of a refusal than that it is telling them to kiss your bottom."[50] Peel cautioned the House of Commons that "it would tend to impede the freedom of discussion, and prevent the discovery of truth, if the arguments advanced by men of superior abilities were exempted, through the deference or apprehensions of others, from being fully and minutely

---

[47] John Stuart Mill to Thomas Carlyle, 18 May 1833, *The Earlier Letters of John Stuart Mill 1812–1848*, ed. Francis E. Mineka, 2 vols. (Toronto: University of Toronto Press, 1963), 1:153.

[48] Robert Hall, *An Apology for the Freedom of the Press, and for General Liberty*, 2d ed. (London, 1793), pp. 3–4. See too Mary Hays, *Memoirs of Mary Courtney*, 2 vols. (London, 1796; reprint ed. New York: Garland, 1974), 1:6–7 (of preface); *The Periodical Press of Great Britain and Ireland: or An Inquiry into the State of the Public Journals, Chiefly as Regards Their Moral and Political Influence* (London, 1824), pp. 7–8.

[49] *Table-Talk* [1822], in *Works of Hazlitt*, 8:208.

[50] John Constable to C. R. Leslie, 5 July 1831, in John Constable, *Correspondence*, ed. R. B. Beckett, 6 vols. (Ipswich: Suffolk Records Society, 1962–1968), 3:41.

canvassed."[51] Here it's not that conversation or argument strictly speaking requires treating one's interlocutor as an equal. It's rather that it works better on those terms.

Take another trope. In 1739, David Hume referred offhandedly to "the republic of letters," a phrase that I suppose already had a distinguished history.[52] Hume seems to have had in mind learned writers, but in 1757, Goldsmith turned to the phrase in thinking about mushrooming popular literacy. "Never was the Republic of Letters so copiously supplied from the press as at present," he observed, so granting readers citizenship.[53] Byron, not the most modest figure to grace the canon of English literature, rejected one syrupy tribute from a group of admirers. "I cannot accept what it has pleased your friends to call their *homage,* because there is no sovereign in the republic of letters; and even if there were, I have never had the pretension or the power to become a usurper."[54]

The republic of letters: merely a bookish republic, to be sure, its citizens not the bloody-minded ruffians who would topple French monarchy. The temptation is to neglect the explicitly political language, to cast the republic, like Egan's coffeehouse, as the site of rational discussion, not any kind of political formation. So Paine promised that "the republic of letters brings forward the best literary productions, by giving to genius a fair and universal chance," making it a sort of impartial equal opportunity meritocracy.[55] It's still a republic, though, and one with its own political problems. By 1762, Goldsmith's view of the republic of letters had grown intemperate. "Every member of this fancied republic is desirous of governing, and none

[51] *The Speeches of the Late Right Honourable Sir Robert Peel, Bart. Delivered in the House of Commons,* 4 vols. (London, 1853; reprint ed. New York: Kraus Reprint Co., 1972), 1:75 [9 May 1817].

[52] David Hume, *A Treatise of Human Nature* [1739–1740], ed. L. A. Selby-Bigge, rev. P. H. Nidditch, 2d ed. (Oxford: Clarendon, 1978), p. 17. See too Smith, *Wealth of Nations,* 2:678.

[53] *Monthly Review* (July 1757) in Oliver Goldsmith, *Collected Works,* ed. Arthur Friedman, 5 vols. (Oxford: Clarendon, 1966), 1:81. See too James Boswell, *The Hypochondriack,* ed. Margery Bailey, 2 vols. (Stanford, CA: Stanford University Press, 1928), 1:105 [October 1777].

[54] Byron to J. J. Coulmann, 7? July 1823, *Byron's Letters and Journals,* ed. Leslie A. Marchand, 13 vols. (London: John Murray, 1973–1994), 10:207. Contrast John Holland and James Everett, *Memoirs of the Life and Writings of James Montgomery,* 7 vols. (London, 1854–1856), 3:259.

[55] *Rights of Man* [1792], in *The Life and Works of Thomas Paine,* 10 vols. (New Rochelle, NY: Thomas Paine National Historical Association, 1925), 6:264.

willing to obey," he reported. "They calumniate, they injure, they despise, they ridicule each other"; "instead of uniting like the members of a commonwealth, they are divided into almost as many factions as there are men; and their jarring constitution instead of being stiled a republic of letters should be entituled, an anarchy of literature."[56]

But maybe this is just bickering. Maybe we can imagine a republic of letters without political strife. Take another seductive image, reason as umpire. With sufficient time for debate, thought Priestley, an overwhelming majority would converge on one view. "Thus will *reason* be the umpire in all disputes, and extinguish civil wars as well as foreign ones. The empire of reason will ever be the reign of peace."[57] Maybe we should be cynical about the prospect of such sweet reasonableness. Maybe people will fiercely defend their interests, stubbornly digging in their heels instead of considering arguments on the merits. But wouldn't reasoned debate provide an alternative to political conflict? Isn't it a sensible aspiration?

It would help to have on the table a reasonably crisp account of politics. It's too easy to construe politics as the stuff with which the modern state is entrusted. That makes it impossible to discuss the politics of stateless societies, an illuminating topic.[58] Worse, it makes it impossible to discuss the politics of everyday life, the ways in which the workplace and the family and the university are the sites of political conflict. As a first pass, suppose we take politics as the sphere of controversy over authority. Then we can accommodate the view that the modern state is centrally preoccupied with politics, but we can also accommodate the intuition that other social settings may be political. For employers, parents, and teachers all claim authority over their charges. And we can resist the charge that leaving the state behind threatens to make all of social life political. Authority may be lurking in lots of social settings, but it isn't centrally implicated in

---

[56] *The Citizen of the World* [1762], in Goldsmith, *Works*, 2:85. See too *Covent-Garden Journal* (4 January 1752) no. 1, in Henry Fielding, *The Covent-Garden Journal and A Plan of the Universal Register Office*, ed. Bertrand A. Goldgar (Middletown, CT: Wesleyan University Press, 1988), p. 15; William Godwin, *Fleetwood: or, The New Man of Feeling*, 3 vols. (London, 1805), 2:117.

[57] Joseph Priestley, *Letters to the Right Honourable Edmund Burke, Occasioned by His Reflections on the Revolution in France, &c.* (Birmingham, 1791), pp. 146–47.

[58] See for instance M. I. Finley, *The World of Odysseus*, 2d ed. (Harmondsworth: Penguin, 1979); William Ian Miller, *Bloodtaking and Peacemaking: Feud, Law, and Society in Saga Iceland* (Chicago: University of Chicago Press, 1990).

everything we do. Notice that when we take the state as a wooden bureaucracy and focus on technical issues of administration, we usually don't think we're focusing on politically interesting matters.

Something needs to be said in turn about authority. A familiar view casts power as the ability to command, authority as the right to command. Helpfully, this view orients our attention to struggles over legitimacy. Authorities, we sometimes complain, are abusing their authority. They exceed its scope, claiming legitimacy when all they really have is brute power. Or they act within the scope of their authority but act stupidly or wrongly. Then we protest that their actions are illegitimate.

But this familiar gloss on authority is unhelpful in other ways. Suppose that we say that Adela is an authority on Victorian literature, or, as we might also put it, that she really knows what she's talking about, that she speaks authoritatively, that we ought to take her word for it. Surely we don't mean that she has the right to command us to believe what she says or that we're obliged to submit to her. So is it a purely prudential ought? is it that it serves our interests to believe what she says? Perhaps, depending on how we characterize our relevant interests. Recall here the troubles plaguing the pragmatists' promising suggestion that we take *true* as something like *useful to believe*. It might be useful for my daughters to believe that there's a bear in the closet that will eat them if they don't go to sleep on time. But that doesn't mean it's true. To which pragmatists want to respond, wearily, that that wasn't the sense of *useful* they had in mind. Fair enough: but what was? Finessing such questions, let's say that Adela has epistemic authority, or, better, that we ascribe such authority to her. It's sensible to defer to her when questions about Victorian literature come up, at least for those of us who can't claim any particular expertise.

So consider competing accounts of epistemic authority. Whom should we believe? In what social settings? About what issues? Answers to these questions are controversial. But that means that they are political. And that means that there is something faulty in the picture of turning to reason, to public debate, to resolve our political disputes, in thinking that reason is somehow prior to politics. For *reason* is itself the name of a series of political disputes. I don't mean to labor over the trivial point that reason is one way of settling disputes, head banging another, so opting for the authority of reason is controversial. I mean instead that there are inescapable controversies about authority internal to any conceivable practice of public debate. Let's consider some.

## "THE WHOLE HERD OF PECULATORS, IMPOSTORS, AND HIRELING SCRIBES"[59]

Criticized on the floor of Parliament by Dundas for his radical activities, John Harrison turned author in 1794 to offer an extended self-defense. Consider his introduction, an artful bid for epistemic authority:

> And as J. H. is only a plain rustic, he hopes his country will not be displeased with his plebeian and artless manner of reasoning.—How far he may succeed in taking off the odium which has been cast upon him, he will with due regard and respect, leave to the good opinion of a great and generous people to determine.—He promises to be brief and plain, as his abilities are not great:—only he wishes first to say,—he is no hireling;—he possesses no place or pension;—has no four and ten thousands a year squeezed out of the blood and sweat of the labouring part of the people:—no eighty-one thousands a year to squander about to his relations; in short;—he is unbought;—unbiassed by any other motives than the good of his country; as all the labouring part of the nation must be, who can neither expect places, nor pensions! but must assuredly pay the pipers, even if they pipe to the ruin of the people!!![60]

No fancy talker, he: like Socrates, he will stumble along in his unpretentious way and trust his audience. Like Socrates, too, he strikes a pose of innocence that isn't all that innocent. He isn't only flattering the reader in evoking "the good opinion of a great and generous people"; he's also nudging the reader and reminding him of the solemn and judicial task he shoulders in picking up the pamphlet. In fact, before turning to his self-defense he already has insinuated that any reasonable reader will have to vindicate him against Dundas's charges.

He performs this trick by impeaching Dundas's epistemic authority and staking his own claims to such authority. Unlike Dundas, he isn't

---

[59] *Gorgon* (23 May 1818) no. 1, p. 1.

[60] John Harrison, *A Letter to the Right Hon. Henry Dundas, M.P. Secretary of State, &c. &c. or, An Appeal to the People of Great-Britain* (London, 1794), pp. 1–2. See too Edward Tatham, *An Address to the Right Honourable Lord Grenville, Chancellor of the University of Oxford, upon Great and Fundamental Abuses in That University* (Oxford, 1811), p. 42.

cashing in on the public fisc. A political daredevil, Harrison leaps audaciously to the conclusion that he must be motivated only by the public good: as if nothing but place or pension could corrupt such lofty impartiality. Whatever we make of the leap, the insinuation is devastatingly clear. Don't believe what Dundas says, Harrison instructs his reader, because Dundas is a base hireling. He exercises no impartial judgment. He says whatever he must to safeguard the gurgling flow of tax receipts into his outstretched hands and those of his family. So too Hazlitt produced one of the finest slashing invectives in the history of English prose, a *Letter to William Gifford* exhibiting the editor of the *Quarterly Review* as a lickspittle wretch doing the dirty work of his political employers.[61] Gifford had forfeited not just his integrity, urged Hazlitt, but his credibility.

With a reasonably straight face, I'd suggested that we might see the state promotion of conservative prose as contributing to the rationality of democratic debate by putting additional positions on the table for the clash of critical judgment. One radical who fled England saw it differently:

> I have often amused myself, by perusing the laboured productions of these mercenary hirelings. Misrepresented facts—premeditated fallacies—and plausible deceptions—occupy the pens of these wretched pamphleteers, who propound their own problems, and give their own reply, with such a seeming facility, that while they betray a self-conviction, they have an influence upon the minds of those persons for whom such books are intended—they are concealed as much as possible from the well-informed, and as industriously circulated, gratis, among the vulgar, and put into the hands of every peasant.—Does not all this plainly denote a defect, which, if known to the bulk of the community, must militate against the interest of an intriguing faction? Is it not a proof, that the drift of the ministry is to conceal their deformity, by keeping the people in gross ignorance, stopping their eyes, mouths, and ears, and winding their imaginations in the obscurity of political mysteries?[62]

---

[61] *A Letter to William Gifford, Esq.* [1819], in *Works of Hazlitt*, 9:11–59.

[62] John Butler, *The Political Fugitive: Being a Brief Disquisition into the Modern System of British Politics; and the Unparalleled Rigor of Political Persecution: Together with General Miscellaneous Observations on the Abuses and Corruptions of the English Government* (New York, 1794), pp. 47–48.

Pay no attention to hireling prose. It throws up a cloud and blocks the blazing sun of demystifying enlightenment.

Ought we believe hirelings? or even pay attention to what they say? That's a controversial question about ascribing epistemic authority, so it's a political question. In the background are further controversies about objectivity. Briefly, distinguish a psychological conception of objectivity from a sociological one. In the psychological view, objectivity requires that each and every individual strive for a dispassionate and disinterested judgment. ("THIS examination is made in the cause of truth," opened one 1797 pamphlet. "It disclaims parties of all descriptions; and it appeals only to the dispassionate people of England. . . ."[63]) Hirelings and other partisans are then obviously untrustworthy; we shouldn't pay even perfunctory attention to their stridently one-sided views. But this is to reject or refine the tempting democratic maxim that we should pay attention only to the merits of the argument, not the status of the speaker.

In the sociological view, objectivity requires a relatively detached audience capable of sorting out arguments pressed by partisans. (Lawyers will recall traditional defenses of the adversary system.) Instead of disparaging their political enthusiasm, we can capitalize on it: they're motivated to search out every error made by their opponents, to marshal all the resources of their own case as forcibly as they can. And the broader the range of views defended, the less homogeneous the audience, the better: a parochial or insular community, however much its members strive for impartiality, isn't in a very good position to figure out what's wrong with its current views.

Skeptics about psychological objectivity will wonder if we are capable of setting aside our own commitments. Skeptics about sociological objectivity will wonder if the audience is attentive and knowledgeable enough to sort through the blizzard of arguments offered by the partisans. Both conceptions could (and should) be refined. The conceptions can be blended, too. We might want to require, for instance, that rabid partisans respect norms of civility and fairness, that they refuse to misrepresent the facts as they best understand them or that they forthrightly engage with objections instead of sweeping them aside. Notice here the appeal of Egan's great man with the omnipo-

[63] Manasseh Dawes, *An Examination into the Particulars of the Two Last Elections for the Borough of Southwark, in May and November 1796* (London, 1797), p. iii. See too Richard Watson, *An Address to the People of Great Britain*, 7th ed. (London, 1798), pp. 1–2.

tent hammer, the chairman of coffeehouse discussion. If things get out-of-bounds, he can rule authoritatively. Wouldn't such a politically nonpartisan moderator be helpful?

## BENTHAM'S MODEST PROPOSAL, THE AD HOMINEM FALLACY, AND THE POLITICS OF DEBATE

In 1800, indefatigable Jeremy Bentham generated yet another reform proposal. "Debate *beside* the question, or even *without* a question, consuming a large proportion of the time of every deliberative assembly as yet known," parliamentary debate was horribly inefficient. To enhance efficiency, he went on, Parliament should post the language of whatever proposal was being debated in letters large enough for every member to read. Better, if this amendment could withstand fear of innovation and ridicule, would be adding two tables, one a list of the rules of debate, the other a list of political fallacies. Should a member begin to stray from the mandated focus of debate, should he begin to break a rule or commit a fallacy, the chair would point with a rod to issue a stern reminder.[64] Presumably this would keep the member in line, else further sanctions would follow.

It's easy to reject Bentham's proposal out of hand. But just what's wrong with it? Maybe it would be imprudent to trust a parliamentary chair with such powers. Maybe he wouldn't exercise them impartially: he'd wink at the incursions of members of his own party against the rules, but be severe with members on the other side of the aisle. Or maybe it underestimates the vital place in parliamentary proceedings of obstructionist tactics.

Maybe, but I want to press a different objection. There will be disputes about the substance of the rules. What counts as straying from the motion on the table? What ought to be on the tables listing rules of debate and political fallacies? The rules, after all, are supposed to make sure the members address only the matter at hand. But we need to beware this deceptively plausible formulation. A reason, say, putting it roughly, is (something taken to be) a relevant consideration. But we frequently dispute whether some consideration is relevant to the matter at hand. Such disputes mean that the authority of the

---

[64] Bentham to Henry Addington, 24 July 1800, *The Correspondence of Jeremy Bentham*, ed. Timothy L. S. Sprigge and others, 10 vols. to date (London: Athlone Press; Oxford: Clarendon, 1968–), 6:336.

chair is political, even if we call him a parliamentarian, even if we're confident in his lofty and judicious sensibilities, his exquisite care in refusing to favor either party.

Not that all political disputes are at bottom disputes about epistemic authority or the rules of debate. The *Edinburgh Review*'s charge that proslavery writers blithely ignored refutations and kept repeating their views was hurled back by one Jamaican minister infuriated by Wilberforce's endless attacks on slavery: "Is it candid to repeat, as facts, what have been a thousand times refuted?"[65] Writers on slavery might have been bringing rival epistemic norms to bear but failing to notice their importance, which would explain this mutual frustration about their debate. But maybe one side was shamelessly repeating their lies. (On what grounds are we so sure we know which side that was?) People with sharp disagreements about the advisability of some piece of legislation may be agreed on epistemic norms and rules of debate. So there is a sense in which we could describe them as submitting their political disagreements to the bar of reason. And it's tempting to insist that no reasonable person could object to placing a series of logical fallacies on Bentham's table. It's tempting, but it's misguided.

Consider the plight of poor Thersites. His ugliness a sign of his contemptibly low status, he dares to rise at the assembly in the second book of the *Iliad*. Agamemnon, he holds, already has gained plenty of prizes—the Achaians first hand over their plunder to him—and manifestly shouldn't be dishonoring Achilles, his superior. The faceless soldiers ought to demonstrate how much Agamemnon needs them by setting sail, leaving him sitting outside Troy, pondering his prizes. Odysseus doesn't answer Thersites on the merits. He instructs him that because he is the worst of men, he should keep his mouth shut. Then he beats him up. Cowed, Thersites slinks off and cries. The assembly laughs approvingly.

Contemporaries recognized the *ad hominem* fallacy, that of inferring the falsehood of a statement from the vicious motives or bad character of the speaker.[66] Is Odysseus guilty of the *ad hominem* fallacy? That depends on how we represent his comments. "You are the

---

[65] George Wilson Bridges, *A Voice from Jamaica; in Reply to William Wilberforce*, 2d ed. (London, 1823), p. 47.

[66] For instance, see James Mill, *The History of British India*, 3 vols. (New Delhi: Associated Publishing House, 1972), 2:137 [1820]; *Speeches of Peel*, 1:230 [17 April 1823].

worst of men; therefore, what you say is false": that's a logical fallacy. "You are the worst of men; therefore, you shouldn't dare to talk at the assembly and no one should bother answering what you say": that's no fallacy. It rejects the attractive democratic injunction that we should pay attention only to the merits of the argument, not the status of the speaker. Yet it's child's play to furnish plausible rationales for this reading of Odysseus's move. One would focus on the economics of information. Time is scarce and it's unlikely that such oafs as Thersites are going to advance the discussion. Another would focus on status and social order. It's degrading to engage in public dispute with the likes of Thersites. The very fact of such dispute, regardless of its content, does politically debilitating work. It shreds the fabric of social order.

No wonder, then, that contemporaries appealed to Thersites's inglorious moment on the public stage. For one foe of democracy in 1796, Thersites was the model of a malcontent English Jacobin, the laughing troops loyal English subjects: "In Thersites, the chieftain Ulysses checks the licence of a seditious demagogue. The people though free, loyal, and attached to the king, from whom they experience protection, approve of the castigation of a person who attempted to excite their dissatisfaction with their sovereign."[67] Byron mocked Brougham—this is a radical's distaste for a Whig—as a "Thersites of the House" of Commons, shamelessly stupid enough to mistake others' dismissive "Scorn for awe."[68] Lambasting Cobbett's harangues on the floor of the Commons, *Fraser's* declared, "He bawled and swaggered like another Thersites in the tent of Agamemnon."[69]

I doubt that even the ultra-Tories of *Fraser's* wanted Cobbett to be thrashed on the floor: who would have played Odysseus? But they did want him dismissed out of hand. If we construe their position as a

[67] Robert Bisset, *Sketch of Democracy* (London, 1796), p. 24.

[68] *Don Juan*, in Byron, *The Complete Poetical Works*, ed. Jerome J. McGann and Barry Weller, 7 vols. (Oxford: Clarendon, 1980–1993), 5:86 [1819]. The lines are from some stanzas unincorporated in the first canto.

[69] *Fraser's* (July 1831) 3(18):746. For further deployments of Thersites, see Elliot, *Republican Refuted*, in *Political Writings*, 5:360; *British Critic* (April 1795) 5:389; Sheridan to the editor of the *Oracle*, 18 February 1802, *The Letters of Richard Brinsley Sheridan*, ed. Cecil Price, 3 vols. (Oxford: Clarendon, 1966), 2:171; "Vivian" [1809], in Maria Edgeworth, *Tales and Novels*, 10 vols. (London, 1848), 5:314; *Black Dwarf* (23 January 1822) 8(4):123; Robert Southey, *Sir Thomas More: or, Colloquies on Progress and Prospects of Society*, 2 vols. (London, 1829), 2:231; *Blackwood's Edinburgh Magazine* (August 1831) 30(184):408.

mere logical fallacy, we miss its deep political significance and we're more likely to suppose that surely Bentham's tables could be filled out in some suitable way. All we receive in return is a bit of misguided complacency about the status of our own democratic convictions. True, some assailed the practice of impeaching the status of one's opponents. "When unable to refute an argument," complained one pamphleteer, opponents of the rights of man "descend to personal invective, and rack their invention to stigmatize the BIRTH and EDUCATION of those they are unable to oppose."[70] And some sighed at their failure to gain a respectful hearing. "I know some ministers, whom I have been ordered to write to, have treated my letters with contempt, and would not give them a hearing,—to think that a person unlearned should instruct them that are learned," admitted Joanna Southcott.[71] But people who reject egalitarian norms of debate aren't making a logical mistake.[72]

Nor are those doing what they can to sway political decisions. Local notables often were thought to enjoy some legitimate influence during elections, influence easier to exert since polls were open for days on end and ballots weren't secret.[73] Desperate to secure Sheridan's

[70] *The Political Crisis; or, A Dissertation on the Rights of Man* (London, 1791), p. vi.

[71] Joanna Southcott to Thomas P. Foley, 19 July 1801, in Southcott, *Letters, &c.* (London, 1801), p. 12.

[72] Nor a mistake about language. Habermas has intermittently flirted with a transcendental derivation of democratic debate, softening the view from an *a priori* "theoretical certainty" (Habermas, *Knowledge and Human Interests,* trans. Jeremy J. Shapiro [Boston: Beacon Press, 1971], p. 314) to an assertoric hypothetical imperative (*The Theory of Communicative Action,* trans. Thomas McCarthy, 2 vols. [Boston: Beacon Press, 1984–1987], 1:397). The general thought is that language use presupposes that we make sense of justification by submitting our claims to criticism in an ideal speech situation, where everyone affected participates on a basis of equality, in principle with no limits whatever on time, motivated only by the quest for truth. This is a regulative ideal, not a concrete social practice. See for instance Habermas, *Communication and the Evolution of Society,* trans. Thomas McCarthy (Boston: Beacon Press, 1979), chap. 1, esp. pp. 23–25; Habermas, *Legitimation Crisis,* trans. Thomas McCarthy (Boston: Beacon Press, 1975), p. 108; Habermas, *Moral Consciousness and Communicative Action,* trans. Christian Lenhardt and Shierry Weber Nicholsen (Cambridge, MA: MIT Press, 1990), pp. 31, 44, 163; Habermas, *Justification and Application: Remarks on Discourse Ethics,* trans. Ciaran Cronin (Cambridge, MA: MIT Press, 1993), pp. 49–50. My own view, which I won't defend here, is that there is no sound argument for the transcendental derivation. Habermas, *Postmetaphysical Thinking: Philosophical Essays,* trans. William Mark Hohengarten (Cambridge, MA: MIT Press, 1992), p. 82 argues that other sorts of language use are parasitic on critical debate but succeeds in showing only that they are different.

[73] For a helpful sketch of the mechanics of influence, see E. Anthony Smith, "Earl

election in 1812, one local notable reported, "I have declared open hostility against every tenant who holds, and against every Man who expects to hold land, and who opposes Sheridan—I think by great personal exertion I can muster near one hundred votes, which will decide the balance in our favour."[74] Some voters, though, insisted on "every freeholder exercising his right of voting in the choice of a representative in parliament, unawed by rank and power, and uninfluenced by hope of reward, or fear of injury."[75]

But power can also arise within democratic debate, without any pushy landlords making threats.[76] Remember Brougham's unsettling threat: should the king approach victory in his legal action against Queen Caroline, he would have no choice but to explore the king's own history of sexual infidelity. Or take issues of timing. In 1830, staunch Tory Harriet Arbuthnot fretted that the Whigs were managing to draw Peel into debate early, leaving Brougham the triumphant opportunity of replying and having the last word in debate.[77] She wanted to ensure that a couple of other leading Tories take the floor, so allowing Peel to wait for Brougham to take the floor first. I see no reason to take such power dynamics as unhappy defects in democratic politics.[78]

---

Fitzwilliam and Malton: A Proprietary Borough in the Early Nineteenth Century," *English Historical Review* (January 1965) 80:51–69.

[74] Edward Jerningham to Lady Bedingfield, 4 October 1812, *The Jerningham Letters (1780–1843)*, ed. Egerton Castle, 2 vols. (London, 1896), 2:23–24. For the record, Sheridan lost the election and never returned to Parliament. See too John Golby, "A Great Electioneer and His Motives: The Fourth Duke of Newcastle," *Historical Journal* (1965) 8(2):204.

[75] Resolutions of independents at Wiltshire, 1818, quoted in Frank O'Gorman, *Voters, Patrons, and Parties: The Unreformed Electoral System of Hanoverian England 1734–1832* (Oxford: Clarendon, 1989), pp. 277–78. See the similar language of the Reading independents in 1820, in O'Gorman, *Voters,* p. 266.

[76] For contemporary studies of the manipulative side of political life, see William Gerard Hamilton, *Parliamentary Logic* [1808] (Cambridge: W. Heffer and Sons, 1927); *The Political Primer; or, Road to Public Honours* (London, 1826). Note the Habermasian rejoinder to Hamilton in *Edinburgh Review* (October 1809) 15(29):170.

[77] Harriet Arbuthnot, *The Journal of Mrs. Arbuthnot 1820–1832,* ed. Francis Bamford and the Duke of Wellington, 2 vols. (London: Macmillan, 1950), 2:398 [4 November 1830].

[78] Habermas has insisted that the ideal speech situation "excludes all force—whether it arises from within the process of reaching understanding itself or influences it from the outside—except the force of the better argument" (*Theory of Communicative Action,* 1:25). This is pointedly unhelpful, perhaps downright incoherent.

## NORMS OF CIVILITY

I can further expand the scope of what's political in reason. Suppose next that there is no one answering to Egan's or Bentham's chair, but the community has a rough and ready sense of what the norms of debate are, how one ought to speak, which issues are fair game and which are out-of-bounds, when people transgress, and the like. Suppose too that there is controversy about these norms. Some deny they are the right norms in the first place; others dispute their rightful interpretation. There is a controversy about authority here. Those who transgress risk all kinds of sanctions. Jeers, hisses, denunciations, glares, disapproving shakes of the head: the list is endless. Only those fixated on state-imposed sanctions will think that these aren't serious, even devastating, sanctions.

A wistful libertarian fantasy has it that we could enjoy the entire realm of speech. But we can't. It's not just that we effortlessly prohibit criminal conspiracy, suborning perjury, commercial fraud, and the like. It's that any imaginable practice of free speech is governed by norms. And norms are enabling constraints. By closing off some possibilities in the realm of speech, they open up others.[79] Every such constraint is a sign of an antinomy: free speech demands abolishing such constraints *and* free speech demands maintaining them.[80] "As politics spoil all conversation," Walpole, Hannah More, and the rest of their social circle bound themselves not to mention it.[81] The framework-knitters of Nottingham did the same to ensure they could discuss their trade (and, I suppose, to steer clear of government spies hungry for news of political plotting).[82] There's nothing special about excluding politics in the name of permitting casual fraterniz-

---

[79] This generalizes the argument of Stephen Holmes, *Passions and Constraint: On the Theory of Liberal Democracy* (Chicago: University of Chicago Press, 1995), chap. 7. On enabling constraints, see Bernard Yack, "Toward a Free Marketplace of Social Institutions: Roberto Unger's 'Super-Liberal' Theory of Emancipation," *Harvard Law Review* (June 1988) 101(8):1967–68.

[80] I'm indebted here to Robert C. Post, *Constitutional Domains: Democracy, Community, Management* (Cambridge, MA: Harvard University Press, 1995), though I doubt he would assent to my analysis.

[81] Hannah More to her sister, 8 March 1784, in William Roberts, *Memoirs of the Life and Correspondence of Mrs. Hannah More*, 2d ed., 4 vols. (London, 1834), 1:311.

[82] Malcolm I. Thomis, *Politics and Society in Nottingham 1785–1835* (Oxford: Basil Blackwell, 1969), p. 100.

ing or labor organizing. These are just instances of the general structure of norms.

Take minimal norms of civility: no one may interrupt, say, or more modestly yet, interruptions should be occasional and never used to overwhelm one's opponent. Even these modest restrictions take the form of enabling constraints. Despite their image as frenetic, radical groups were scrupulously careful to insist on norms of civility. The LCS, for instance, turned away members who showed up drunk and expelled those routinely showing up drunk. Members removed their hats as a sign of respect. Interruptions were forbidden, except to call a member back to the topic on the floor; members addressed the chair; they took turns speaking, and no one could speak more than twice.[83] The Birmingham Society for Constitutional Information also excluded drunks and authorized the chair to dismiss those disrupting meetings with heated debate.[84] The Society of Spencean Philanthropists granted free admission "to all persons of decorous demeanour" and prohibited personal attacks "or calumnious aspersions on the established form of government or religion."[85]

So workers intent on radical reform were mannered, even prissy, in hashing out their differences. Some of these rules reflect a prudent acknowledgment of those ubiquitous spies: I doubt that the Spenceans actually worried all that much about maligning the church or the government. But some of these rules don't lend themselves to that sort of cynical reading. "We know debates often lead to warmth; and, that when disputants wax warm, they generally grow tumultuous and irregular," explained Maurice Margarot at his trial. In his closing statement, he was reviewing the rules of the British Convention of the Delegates of the People, Associated to Obtain Universal Suffrage and Annual Parliaments, yet another radical group with scrupulously polite rules, ordinarily requiring that no one speak twice until everyone who wanted to had already spoken once. Margarot needed to dislodge the ominous image of overheated radicals from the minds of the jury. Where had the Convention learned about the dangers of

---

[83] *Selections from the Papers of the London Corresponding Society 1792–1799*, ed. Mary Thale (Cambridge: Cambridge University Press, 1983), p. xxvi; *The Autobiography of Francis Place (1771–1854)*, ed. Mary Thale (Cambridge: Cambridge University Press, 1972), pp. 131, 131–32 n. 2.

[84] Birmingham Society for Constitutional Information, *Address* (Birmingham, 1792), p. 16. See too *London Radicalism*, ed. Rowe, p. 33 [4 June 1831].

[85] *Address of the Society of Spencean Philanthropists to All Mankind, on the Means of Promoting Liberty and Happiness* (London, n.d.), p. 20.

warmth, "these tumults and this riotous manner of debating"? Amusingly, from the House of Commons. Nice try, but Margarot was convicted and sentenced to fourteen years' transportation.[86]

Convention or Commons, the familiar rule requiring that members address the chair, not each other, is another enabling constraint. Face-to-face confrontations, the worry is, shed more heat than light. But the members and their audience pay a price for this proscription. Not a significant price in the dubious pleasures of emotional confrontation. Even with the stylized mediation of the chair, Canning was turning colors and Peel was sweating blood. Consider, too, all the tones—icy, leering, loftily sardonic, and many more—in which one may refer to one's opponent as "the honorable member" or "the learned gentleman," norms of civility generating new possibilities of incivility. But the mediation may detract from the immediacy of two partisans slugging it out, especially if it's coupled with a rule against repeatedly taking the floor until others have spoken. That rule, of course, is designed to widen the range of views entertained, as well as express respect for each and every member. But it may also diffuse and blur discussion; it may allow meretricious arguments and bruised speakers to live to fight another day, even the same day, the failures of their position not registering as they otherwise might.

Or take civility as politeness and restraint. That, too, keeps the channels of communication open. But it also prevents the frank expression of contempt: as if no one ever blurt out something so stupid that a blunt dismissal be richly warranted. Lost in Mackintosh's elaborate prose, James Mill sputtered, "It is very disgusting to follow such a man as this through his labyrinth of jargon. It is, however, useful; both for the exposure of such a case of imposture; and as a practical lesson to the young; to whom nothing is of more importance than the art of detecting want of meaning, or foolish meaning, or bad meaning, under foggy expressions."[87] Then again, William Paley wanted "to restrain the circulation of ridicule, invective, and mockery, upon religious subjects," fearing that such leering words would corrupt readers and corrosively undercut the authority of religion.[88] But proponents

---

[86] *The Trial of Maurice Margarot, before the High Court of Justiciary, at Edinburgh, on the 13th and 14th of January, 1794, on an Indictment for Seditious Practices*, rep. Mr. Ramsey (New York, 1794), pp. 130–37, 164.

[87] James Mill, *A Fragment on Mackintosh* (London, 1835), p. 194.

[88] *The Principles of Moral and Political Philosophy* [1785], in *The Works of William Paley, D.D. Archdeacon of Carlisle*, 2 vols. (London, 1828), 1(2):256.

of religious invective thought they needed to break through a thick crust of unreflective deference that precluded criticism.[89] Here, too, we cannot enjoy all the benefits of both polite and impolite speech.

### ANONYMITY, THE AUTHORIAL PERSONA, AND PUBLIC AND PRIVATE

Consider next anonymous publications. Anonymity appears to be a plausible strategy for implementing the maxim that we pay attention only to the merits of the argument. In fact, though, anonymity raises thorny dilemmas. One harks back to epistemic authority. Sir Brooke Boothby explained that he had intended to publish his thoughts on Burke and Paine anonymously, but had demurred. "In the discussion of characters and facts, something must always rest upon the supposed integrity and judgment, and knowledge of the Authour," so his readers were entitled to know his identity and his sources of information.[90] Priestley found himself unable to adopt the literary mask of an unbeliever; he even had qualms about addressing published letters to a character of his own invention.[91] Yet that name on the title page permits or invites other kinds of deference and defiance.

The reviews published in the day's leading quarterlies were anonymous. For Walter Scott, this policy was imperative. It left writers free to venture difficult critical judgments without fear of hostile response.[92] Others thought it left critics free to be cavalier and spiteful, irresponsible and unaccountable. So Boswell and Walpole made a general rule of refusing to respond to anonymous criticisms.[93] Ano-

[89] But for William Hone's pleasure in being treated civilly in a dispute on religion, see *Reminiscences Personal and Bibliographical of Thomas Hartwell Horne* (London, 1852), pp. 39–40.

[90] Sir Brooke Boothby, *Observations on the Appeal from the New to the Old Whigs, and on Mr. Paine's Rights of Man* (London, 1792), advt. For more arguments from character to credibility, see Capt. Macarty, *An Appeal to the Candour and Justice of the People of England, in Behalf of the West India Merchants and Planters, Founded on Plain Facts and Incontrovertible Evidence* (London, 1792), intro., esp. pp. xii–xiv.

[91] Priestley's memoirs, in John Towill Rutt, *Life and Correspondence of Joseph Priestley,* 2 vols. (London, 1831–1832), 1:38.

[92] *Biographical Memoirs of Eminent Novelists* [1825], in *The Prose Works of Sir Walter Scott, Bart.,* 28 vols. (Edinburgh, 1834–1836), 3:220; see too Scott to Charles Kirkpatrick Sharpe, 30 December 1808, *The Letters of Sir Walter Scott,* ed. H. J. C. Grierson, 12 vols. (London: Constable & Co., 1932), 2:143.

[93] *Public Advertiser* (27 July 1785), in *Boswell: The Applause of the Jury 1782–1785,* ed. Irma S. Lustig and Frederick A. Pottle (New York: McGraw-Hill, 1981), p. 328; Walpole

nymity, thought one friend, explained the fits of spleen and contra-
dictions punctuating Hazlitt's work.[94] "Under the shade of an anonymous character," offered Boothby apologetically, "I have perhaps expressed myself with somewhat less reserve of men and things than I
might have been inclined to use in my own person," but the prospect
of rewriting was too distressing to confront.[95]

Anonymity had its temptations, though, even for authors who usually signed their works. Malthus flippantly rejected Godwin's painstak-
ing response to his *Essay on the Principle of Population*. Because of its
stinging personal abuse and its denial of "the most glaring and best-
attested facts," "I am quite sure every candid and competent inquirer
after truth will agree with me in thinking that it does not require a
reply."[96] But Malthus already had replied to Godwin—in the *Edinburgh Review*, skulking under the cloak of anonymity and maybe stooping to personal abuse of his own. Perhaps Godwin was no longer talented or perhaps he never had been. But his *On Population* "appears
to us, we confess"—ah, that *we*, the first person royal, ready prerogative of any and every individual speaking as corporate voice of the
*Review*—"to be the poorest and most old-womanish performance that
has fallen from the pen of any writer of name, since we first commenced our critical career. . . ."[97] Wordsworth sent his son "a sonnet
which I shall not print in my collection, because my poems are wholly
as I wish them to continue, without *personalities* of a vituperative character. If you think it worth being printed, pray have it copied and sent
to the *Cantabridge Chronicle*, without a name. . . ."[98] Here the fellow

---

to Lady Ossory, 17 July 1792, *The Yale Edition of Horace Walpole's Correspondence*, ed. W. S.
Lewis, 48 vols. (New Haven, CT: Yale University Press, 1937–1983), 34:150; Walpole to
John Pinkerton, 17 September 1785, *Walpole's Correspondence*, 16:278–79.

[94] *The Diary of Benjamin Robert Haydon*, ed. Willard Bissell Pope, 5 vols. (Cambridge,
MA: Harvard University Press, 1960–1963), 3:130 [3 August 1826].

[95] Boothby, *Observations*, advt. See too *Westminster Review* (January 1833) 18(35):202.

[96] *An Essay on the Principle of Population* [1826], in *The Works of Thomas Robert Malthus*,
ed. E. A. Wrigley and David Souden, 8 vols. (London: William Pickering, 1986), 3:623.

[97] *Edinburgh Review* (July 1821) 35(70):362, also in *Works of Malthus*, 4:161. See too
James Mill to Ricardo, 13 November 1820, *The Works and Correspondence of David Ricardo*,
ed. Piero Sraffa with M. H. Dobb, 11 vols. (Cambridge: Cambridge University Press for
the Royal Economic Society, 1951–1973), 8:291–92.

[98] William Wordsworth to John Wordsworth, 10 March 1838, *The Letters of William
and Dorothy Wordsworth*, 2d ed., ed. Ernest de Selincourt, rev. Chester L. Shaver and
others, 8 vols. (Oxford: Clarendon, 1967–1993), 6:530.

Wordsworth protects the author Wordsworth from having his sterling reputation besmirched by a blackguard sonnet by poet Wordsworth.

Too many Wordsworths, it seems, and maybe too many Malthuses, too. Yet isn't there always some gap between author and authorial persona? Even in a solemn tome, that is, can't we show that the narrator's voice is an unreliable guide to the author's identity? Walter Scott vowed early on to laugh at pointed criticism, to step aside instead of valiantly shielding his text with his emotions and integrity. This policy, he happily explained, had gained him "the personal friendship of my most approved contemporaries of all parties."[99] The markedly less jovial Southey drew a similar distinction. "To Jeffrey as an individual I shall ever be ready to show every kind of individual courtesy; but of Judge Jeffrey of the Edinburgh Review I must ever think and speak of as a bad politician, a worse moralist, and a critic, in matters of taste, equally incompetent and unjust."[100]

The norms here raise difficult political questions. On one hand, we have the appeal of sincerity and integrity, the text that faithfully mirrors its author. This makes for confident imputations of character and epistemic authority. On the other, we have another image of civility, a realm of public debate made bearable by the ability of authors to escape from their textual creatures. So we also have deep controversies over the shape and cogency of the distinction between public and private. In 1808, unrepentant radical Godwin met truculent turncoats Coleridge and Wordsworth not for angry political denunciations, but for tea and discussion of the ancients, Spenser, and Milton.[101] Was he selling out? Or again, that gifted pamphleteer William Hone staggered when Bentham pointed out the actual Lord Castlereagh, butt of his zesty attacks, playing with his children. "My conscience flew in my face," he confessed.[102] Was Hone naive?

---

[99] *The Lay of the Last Minstrel*, intro. [1830], *The Poetical Works of Sir Walter Scott, Bart.*, 12 vols. (Edinburgh, 1833–1834), 6:16. For instance, see Scott to Robert Surtees, April 1808, *Letters of Scott*, 2:54.

[100] Southey to Walter Scott, 8 December 1807, *The Life and Correspondence of Robert Southey*, ed. Charles Cuthbert Southey, 6 vols. (London, 1849–1850), 3:125.

[101] Godwin's diary, 3 March 1808, Abinger Mss., reel 1. For Worsdworth's political shifts, see especially Wordsworth to William Mathews, 23 May 1794, *Letters of William and Dorothy Wordsworth*, 1:119; Wordsworth to James Losh, 4 December 1821, *Letters*, 4:96–98.

[102] Frances Rolleston, *Some Account of the Conversion from Atheism to Christianity of the Late William Hone*, 2d ed. rev. (London, 1853), pp. 51–52.

Wordsworth found it easy to distinguish between attacks on persons and attacks on opinions.[103] "A public man's public foibles are fair game!" But it was degrading to peer into the private lives of even public figures.[104] Others weren't so sure. "No man has a right to pry into his neighbour's private concerns," agreed Cobbett. Should that neighbor turn public figure, though, "his opinions, his principles, his motives, every action of his life, public or private, become the fair subject of public discussion."[105] Hazlitt conceded that he had abused Malthus (without the veil of anonymity), but insisted that the abuse was merited. Still, "if I could have attacked the work successfully, without attacking the author, I should have preferred doing so. But the thing was impossible. Whoever troubles himself about abstract reasonings, or calm, dispassionate inquiries after truth? The public ought not to blame me for consulting their taste."[106] Others didn't hesitate. "It behoves us at all times to inquire into the private character and circumstances of those who aspire to take the lead in political disputes," one pamphleteer declared. He went on to offer a lengthy questionnaire: "Is he gentle to his servants? . . . Is he fond of sneering at religion in company? . . . Is he married? And is he a constant husband and tender father? . . . will a banker discount a bill on him without hesitation?"[107] The *Age* gloried in their uncivil personal attacks. "GOD forgive us for it! we were bred in a school where we were taught to consider a rascally action to be the act of a rascal, and have

[103] Wordsworth to John Thelwall, mid-January 1804, *Letters of William and Dorothy Wordsworth*, 1:433.

[104] Wordsworth to Robert Southey, May 1833, *Letters of William and Dorothy Wordsworth*, 5:618. See too Wordsworth to Viscount Lowther, 6 October 1818, *Letters*, 3:489; Wordsworth to Lowther, 23 October 1818, *Letters*, 3:504; Robert Peel to Mr. Gregory, 10 June 1814, *Sir Robert Peel from His Private Papers*, ed. Charles Stuart Parker, 3 vols. (London, 1891–1899), 1:116.

[105] William Cobbett, *Observations on Priestley's Emigration* [1794], in *Porcupine's Works*, 12 vols. (London, 1801), 1:151–52.

[106] *A Reply to the Essay on Population* [1807], in *Works of Hazlitt*, 1:179, with a typographical error corrected from *A Reply to the Essay on Population* (London, 1807), pp. 1–2, italics reversed. See too *Boswell's Life of Johnson: Together with Boswell's Journal of a Tour to the Hebrides and Johnson's Diary of a Journey into North Wales*, ed. George Birkbeck Hill, rev. L. F. Powell, 6 vols. (Oxford: Clarendon, 1934–1950), 2:444 [20 March 1776]; James Boswell, *The Journal of a Tour to the Hebrides, with Samuel Johnson, Ll.D.* [1786], in *Life of Johnson*, 5:29 [15 August 1773].

[107] A Friend to Liberty, Property, and Reform, *An Address to the People of Great Britain; Containing a Comparison between the Republican and Reforming Parties, in Their Sentiments and Intentions with Respect to the British Constitution* (Edinburgh, 1793), in *Political Writings*, ed. Claeys, 7:344–45.

not yet sufficiently progressed with the march of intellect, as to perceive that we were educated upon a wrong principle." They added that they still clung to unvarnished honesty, so their vocabulary might not always be terribly polite.[108]

The invention of the author, as it's been styled, is then neither a sign of an unfolding ensemble of practices of social control depending on individual discipline nor another nasty bit of possessive individualism. Or anyway we can situate it in less macabre contexts. It's an attempt to eke out some space for democratic accountability between the hazards of anonymous irresponsibility and the terrors of a more sweeping personal and private accountability. But this way of putting it is just to endorse one controversial view of the norms in play.

The disputes here made for wholly admirable possibilities. In the run-up to Peterloo, A Patriot cautioned the residents of Manchester against taking Henry Hunt as their guide.

> In giving this caution, I do not advert to his private character, for it is nothing to us, whether he is a good husband or a bad one; whether he does or does not live in open Adultery with the wife of another Person;—though to be sure, it would strengthen your Cause, if you could with truth boast of the Virtues of your leaders. It is nothing to you, if he did make Oath that he used nothing but Malt and Hops in his Brewhouse, or that almost on the eve of the Oath, he should stand convicted of using Unwholesome Drugs in the fabrication of the Beer which he sold to the inhabitants of Bristol;—for though he might be a little careless in what he *swore*, he may be very conscientious in what he *says* to you; and you know, *you* did not drink the Beer which the law pronounced pernicious. You must not therefore suspect him because his *Private Life* is said to have been a little incorrect.[109]

Norms enable transgressions: I don't mean that norms elicit deviance; I mean instead that actions can't count as transgressions in the

---

[108] *Age* (13 December 1829), p. 396. See too *Political Register* (22 December 1804) 6(25):1021.

[109] Placard from A PATRIOT, 14 August 1819, quoted in Robert Walmsley, *Peterloo: The Case Reopened* (Manchester: Manchester University Press, 1969), p. 119. I don't know about the beer, but for the record Hunt did leave his wife for Mrs. Vince: John Belchem, *'Orator' Hunt: Henry Hunt and English Working-Class Radicalism* (Oxford: Clarendon, 1985), pp. 17, 22. Compare William Combe, *A Letter from a Country Gentleman, to a Member of Parliament, on the Present State of Public Affairs* (London, 1789), pp. 23–24, flirting with impeaching Fox's character.

absence of norms. Norms also enable shrewd and ironic play. A Patriot's innuendoes mock the distinction between public and private he pretends to respect.

## EQUALITY AND STATUS

These norms don't link up in any straightforward way with the political disputes joined by conservatives and democrats. Other norms do. Egan's masquerade with no masks, the republic of letters, and the like suggested that democratic debate should proceed on terms of equality, that participants should blind themselves to extraneous facts about social status. But norms of equality would put conservatives, with their affection for hierarchy, at a profound structural disadvantage in debate. In fact, they managed to insist on conducting debate on inegalitarian terms, on refusing to appear in Egan's masquerade.

One conservative was incensed by Sheridan's suggestion "that all names appended to any petition are of equal value": as if, he snorted, the lofty judgment of great landholders and London's leading merchants ought to have no more weight in Parliament than that of radical "wretches" milling about at an outdoors rally.[110] Robert Peel was proud to introduce a petition graced with signatures "of the very first respectability," their social status a guarantee of their impartiality.[111] Petitions aren't usually celebrated for their careful arguments; they're just supposed to indicate the fact of popular sentiment. But whose sentiment? Weighted how? Bentham's "everybody to count for one, nobody for more than one"[112] isn't trivial; it's a substantive and radical bit of egalitarianism.

Or take controversies about respect: not just the civility that we might suppose any speaker is entitled to, but special acknowledgment for special characters. One pamphleteer, hawking *An Antidote to the Poison Now Vending by the Transatlantic Republican Thomas Paine*, was

[110] Edmund Malone to William Windham, 29 November 1795, *The Windham Papers*, 2 vols. (London: Herbert Jenkins, 1913), 1:319–20.

[111] *Speeches of Peel*, 1:94 [6 April 1818].

[112] This famous slogan is attributed to Bentham by John Stuart Mill in *Utilitarianism* [1861], in *Essays on Ethics, Religion and Society*, ed. J. M. Robson and others (Toronto: University of Toronto Press, 1969), p. 257. The sentiment is surely Bentham's—see for instance *An Introduction to the Principles of Morals and Legislation* [1789], ed. J. H. Burns and H. L. A. Hart (London: Athlone Press, 1970), pp. 39–40—but as far as I know he never published the words.

unhappy with the bellicose tone Paine adopted toward Burke. "Modesty and deference are always due from inferiors to their superiors. It would have become Mr. Paine to have behaved to so eminent a character with decorum and respect."[113] More striking, Godwin agreed that Wollstonecraft's response to Burke was similarly blameworthy. "Marked as it is with the vehemence and impetuousness of its eloquence, it is certainly chargeable with a too contemptuous and intemperate treatment of the great man against whom its attack is directed."[114]

Or take a common bid for epistemic authority, that of cluttering one's title page with a list of one's degrees. Thomas Beddoes appended "M.D." to his name, then opened his book by musing over what difference his being a doctor made if he wanted to write about politics.[115] Richard Watson signed his response to Paine's assault on Scripture as "R. Watson, D.D. F.R.S. LORD BISHOP OF LANDAFF, AND REGIUS PROFESSOR OF DIVINITY IN THE UNIVERSITY OF CAMBRIDGE."[116] The title page implicitly insists that the reader pay exquisite attention to status, not just to the merits of Watson's arguments. Did it matter that Watson was a Doctor of Divinity and Fellow of the Royal Society? That, again, was the stuff of political controversy. Writing pseudonymously, A Deist was irritated by Watson's lofty tone of superiority to Paine. "The long and short of the matter is, Thomas Paine and you, write on the same subject. You meet fairly and equally as men; nothing more need be said about it."[117] But the terms on which Paine and Watson might meet are the subject of political controversy. Is it man meeting man? or unlettered mechanic being chastened by erudite divine? The Deist forged on—coherence be damned—to suggest that Watson's status undercut his credibility. Priests aren't impartial, "having *selfish views* and *pecuniary* purposes to

113 Isaac Hunt, *Rights of Englishmen: An Antidote to the Poison Now Vending by the Trans-atlantic Republican Thomas Paine* (London, 1791), p. 39.

114 William Godwin, *Memoirs of the Author of a Vindication of the Rights of Woman* (London, 1798), p. 76.

115 Thomas Beddoes, *Essay on the Public Merits of Mr. Pitt* (London, 1796), t.p., chap. 1.

116 Richard Watson, *An Apology for the Bible, in a Series of Letters, Addressed to Thomas Paine* (London, 1796), t.p.

117 A Deist, *Thomas Paine Vindicated: Being a Short Letter to the Bishop of Landaff's Reply to Thomas Paine's Age of Reason* (London, 1796), p. 2.

answer, which the *Layman* cannot have upon this subject."[118] Himself writing pseudonymously as A Layman, Thomas Williams took a different view: "A capital crime this! that men who have devoted their lives to the service of Christianity should defend it!"[119]

For conservatives, polite conversation was reserved for those variously denominated the world, the fashion, or polite society. Take Mrs. West:

> It has been remarked, that though in this age of equalization one rank slides into another in the articles of dress, luxury, and amusement, conversation still preserves its *aristocratical* distinctions; and I am afraid that my inveterate dislike of democracy will be deduced from the observation I am going to make, that it would have been well for society, if the politeness and accommodation of our superiors were as imitable, as the form of their attire or the arrangements of their tables.[120]

Was conversation—in person and in print—still properly aristocratic? That is, did it still mark in its very inflections a regard for social status? Perhaps that of R. Watson, D.D. F.R.S. and all the rest, did. Perhaps that of Edmund Burke, M.P., with its sesquipedalian vocabulary and majestically tangled syntax, did. ("He then quite ranted with eloquent bombast," recorded Horace Walpole of one speech.[121]) Not, though, the spunky stuff dished out by Tom Paine: unless we want to think of that as a creature of aristocracy, its pert or impertinent cadences available only to a gifted and bitter underling.

One antislavery writer tried to have it both ways. "The name and authority of an author have perhaps greater weight with some readers than his arguments," he conceded. He buttressed his case with quotations from "works of acknowledged merit" for their sake. But he vaunted in his own independence of mind. "Yet, as a citizen of the *free* republic of letters, I reserve, in the fullest extent, the right of private judgment," a right worth clinging to in a literature full of mystified nonsense provided by philosophers. "By the authority of those

[118] A Deist, *Thomas Paine Vindicated*, p. 8.

[119] Thomas Williams, *The Age of Infidelity: Part II: In Answer to the Second Part of the Age of Reason*, 2d ed. (London, 1796), p. v.

[120] Jane West, *Letters to a Young Lady*, 3d ed., 3 vols. (London, 1806), 3:11–12.

[121] *The Last Journals of Horace Walpole: During the Reign of George III from 1771–1782*, ed. A. Francis Steuart, 2 vols. (London: John Lane, The Bodley Head, 1910), 1:55 [16 March 1772].

writers, or indeed of any description of writers, I do not think myself
bound to be governed, except in so far as they appear to me to have
been governed by unbiassed reason and philosophy."[122]

## BURKE'S SCHISM AND COLERIDGE'S TWO MORALITIES
## OF DISCUSSION

Recall Burke's schism between the political nation, required to shoulder the burden of critical debate, and subjects, better consigned to
the dreamland of pleasing illusions. Recall the attorney general's
comment that he didn't bother prosecuting the first part of Paine's
*Rights of Man* because it looked as if it would be left to an intelligent
reading public to reject it, but that he launched proceedings against
the second part because it was published cheaply and spirited into the
hands of the gullible lower orders. This position was echoed by the
solicitor general at Robert Wedderburn's May 1820 sentencing for
blasphemy: "If he had but delivered his sentiments in a cautious, decent, and guarded manner, this prosecution would never have been
instituted, but such language as his, addressed to the lower orders of
the community, can never be tolerated."[123] I've cast this schism as the
boundary between citizens and subjects. It has also served as the basis
for adopting two moralities of discussion, a bifurcation of the norms
of debate depending on the audience.

Democratic equality here collides with the conservative account of
social order. According to one Swedish traveller, the Royal Institution
sought "to serve each and every seeker after knowledge without dif-
ferentiation of class or persons. Therefore workmen from the lowest
classes of the populace are also admitted to the lectures; for the comfort of themselves and others, they have their special seats."[124] None
of the unruffled camaraderie of Egan's coffeehouse here. The polite
"others" would just as soon keep their distance from the scruffy

---

[122] William Dickson, *Letters on Slavery . . . to Which Are Added, Addresses to the Whites,
and to the Free Negroes of Barbadoes; and Accounts of Some Negroes Eminent for Their Virtues
and Abilities* (London, 1789), pp. iii–iv.

[123] Robert Wedderburn, *The Horrors of Slavery and Other Writings*, ed. Iain McCalman
(Edinburgh: Edinburgh University Press, 1991), p. 140 [9 May 1820]. So too at the
initial trial: *The Trial of the Rev. Rob*. *Wedderburn, (A Dissenting Minister of the Unitarian
Persuasion,) for Blasphemy*, ed. Erasmus Perkins (London, 1820), pp. 19–20.

[124] Eric T. Svedenstierna, *Svedenstierna's Tour Great Britain 1802–3*, trans. E. L.
Dellow (Newton Abbot: David & Charles, 1973), p. 12.

workers—and the workers would just as soon keep their distance, too. A diverse audience consumes the same information, but any ensuing discussion is balkanized. Right-wing journals didn't even nod in the direction of equality. The *Anti-Jacobin* found room for a Latin letter and poem from Etonensis.[125] The *Anti-Jacobin Review* closed their lengthy run with a Greek sentence; this from a journal which routinely ran Latin poetry, as well as text in Hebrew and French.[126] Even Shelley, putative radical, kept his *Refutation of Deism* expensive to keep it out of the hands of the lower orders.[127]

Yet subjects weren't supposed to be left to their own devices, especially when they were drinking in sedition at alehouses. The imperative but loathsome business of addressing the inferiors was already Coleridge's obsession in 1795:

> In the disclosal of Opinion, it is our duty to consider the character of those, to whom we address ourselves, their situations, and probable degree of knowledge. We should be bold in the avowal of *political* Truth among those only whose minds are susceptible of reasoning: and never to the multitude, who ignorant and needy must necessarily act from the impulse of inflamed Passions.[128]

Once again, the higher one's social status, the greater one's capacities for deliberative rationality. Speakers and writers had better tailor their words accordingly; equality would be sociologically naive and politically pernicious.

Still, in 1809, Coleridge began his abortive periodical, *The Friend*, as an attempt to educate the English: they were, he thought, riveted on calculating interest and blind to lofty principle.[129] He professed himself a lover of "free enquiry of the boldest kind"—as long as that enquiry "is evidently intended for the perusal of those only, who may be presumed to be capable of weighing the arguments," not tossed

---

[125] *Anti-Jacobin* (2 July 1798) no. 35, pp. 278–79.

[126] *Anti-Jacobin Review* (December 1821) 61:359.

[127] *A Refutation of Deism* [1814], in *Shelley's Prose or The Trumpet of a Prophecy*, ed. David Lee Clark, corrected ed. (Albuquerque: University of New Mexico Press, 1966), pp. 118–19.

[128] *Conciones ad Populum* [1795], in *The Collected Works of Samuel Taylor Coleridge*, ed. Kathleen Coburn, Bart Winer, and others, in progress (Princeton, NJ: Princeton University Press, 1969–), 1:51. See too the opening formulation of *Aids to Reflection* [1831], *Works of Coleridge*, 9:5.

[129] Coleridge to John Prior Estlin, 3 December 1808, *Collected Letters of Samuel Taylor Coleridge*, ed. Earl Leslie Griggs, 6 vols. (Oxford: Clarendon, 1956–1971), 3:129.

out to tease and seduce the lower orders.[130] But the desire to educate
the English didn't square well with his magisterial, not to say obtuse,
prose. Soon Southey berated him about the stringent intellectual demands he was making on his hapless readers: "All brains, Sir, were not
made for thinking. . . ."[131] By 1810, Coleridge was fretting: "these are
AWEFUL TIMES!", he moaned, unnerved by the excessive popular taste
for reading.[132] By 1816, Coleridge was snarling:

> I would that the greater part of our publications could be thus *directed,*
> each to its appropriate class of Readers. But this cannot be! For among
> other odd burs and kecksies, the misgrowth of our luxuriant activity, we
> have now a READING PUBLIC—as strange a phrase, methinks, as ever
> forced a splenetic smile to the staid countenance of Meditation; and yet
> no fiction! For our Readers have, in good truth, multiplied exceedingly,
> and have waxed proud. . . . From a popular philosophy and a philo-
> sophic populace, Good Sense deliver us![133]

More savagely yet, in 1817 he wondered what really answered to popular literacy. "For as to the devotees of the circulating libraries, I dare
not compliment their *pass-time,* or rather *kill-time,* with the name of
*reading.* Call it rather a sort of beggarly daydreaming," an aimless activity belonging in a class with "gaming, swinging, or swaying on a
chair or gate; spitting over a bridge; smoking; snuff-taking; tete a tete
quarrels after dinner between husband and wife; conning word by
word all the advertisements of the daily advertizer in a public house
on a rainy day, &c. &c. &c."[134] His earlier reservations about a genuinely educational public discourse apparently had hardened into bitter rejection of that fateful prospect. "You begin with the attempt to

[130] *The Friend* [10 August 1809], in *Works of Coleridge,* 4(2):42.

[131] Southey to Coleridge, *circa* October 1809, *Life and Correspondence of Southey,*
3:263.

[132] Coleridge to Thomas Poole, 28 January 1810, *Letters of Coleridge,* 3:281.

[133] *The Statesman's Manual* [1816], in *Works of Coleridge,* 6:36–38. In a footnote, Coleridge added a joke too terrible to quote: for the joke and reactions, see *The Statesman's
Manual* [1816], in *Works of Coleridge,* 6:37–38 n; *Melincourt* [1817], in *The Works of
Thomas Love Peacock,* Halliford edition, ed. H. F. B. Brett-Smith and C. E. Jones, 10 vols.
(London: Constable & Co., 1924–1934), 2:339 n. ‡; *Edinburgh Review* (December 1816)
27(54):457; *Political Essays, with Sketches of Public Characters* [1819], in *Works of Hazlitt,*
7:126.

[134] *Biographia Literaria* [1817], in *Works of Coleridge,* 7(1):48.

*popularize* learning and philosophy," he warned menacingly in 1818; "but you will end in the *plebification* of knowledge."[135]

These formulations echo and affirm Burke's schism but overlook Coleridge's steady conviction that still there was vital pedagogical work to be done. In 1812, he roundly rejected the position of "statesmen, who survey with jealous dread all plans for the education of the lower orders," deeming their agenda impolitic and dishonest.[136] In 1819, he continued to worry about the dangers of popular education: "There are in every Country times when the few, who knew the truth, cloathed it for the Vulgar and addressed the Vulgar, in the vulgar language and modes of conception, in order to convey any part of the Truth." Sadly, the process corrupted the "Illuminati": "the Teachers of the Vulgar . . . became a part of the Vulgar—"[137] Still, the task couldn't be shunted. *On the Constitution of the Church and State,* his tangled skein of political musings from 1830, insisted on the central role of those Coleridge dubbed the clerisy. Not just churchmen but intellectuals more generally, the clerisy had to educate the lower orders. The goal was emphatically not to introduce them to the fevered world of coffeehouse reading and alehouse discussion, but to cultivate a sober respect for Christianity and inequality. The subject matter of their education was to be different from that of the higher orders. So was the style in which it was to be delivered.

## THE POLITICS OF PUBLIC OPINION

Even such dull bromides as the reminder that public opinion is important in democratic politics mask political disputes. After fleeing England but before his trial, Paine informed the attorney general that only a packed jury could convict him. "I have gone into coffeehouses, and places where I was unknown, on purpose to learn the currency of opinion, and I never yet saw any company of twelve men that condemned" his *Rights of Man.*[138] At the trial, the attorney gen-

[135] *The Friend* [1818], in *Works of Coleridge,* 4(1):447. This passage didn't appear in the initial periodical version of the work.

[136] Robert Southey, *Omniana, or Horae Otiosiores,* 2 vols. (London, 1812), 1:189–90 (starred in table of contents, an indication of a contribution from Coleridge).

[137] *The Notebooks of Samuel Taylor Coleridge,* ed. Kathleen Coburn, in progress (New York: Pantheon Books, 1957–), 4:4597 21½.75 [1819].

[138] Paine to Archibald Macdonald, 11 November 1792, in *Works of Paine,* 7:288.

eral derisively quoted these words to the jury, adding, "Whether the sense of this *nation* is to be had in some pot-houses and coffee-houses in this town of his own choosing, is a matter I leave to your judgment."[139] Their judgment, again, convicted Paine. But there were other judgments.

What counts as authoritative public opinion? Whose views? Forged how? One could reconstruct a host of intriguing views, but I'll restrict myself to two basic alternatives. The first depends on publicity and free speech. Parliamentary representatives, thought the *Edinburgh Review*, could "call down the steady vengeance of public execration, and the sure light of public intelligence, for the repression and redress of all public injustice." They could do so because of the links between Parliament, press, and public discussion, all depending on "our precious talisman of Publicity" and its enlightening illuminations penetrating the corrupt political darkness of veils and illusions.[140] (Meanwhile, a series of judges worried that publicity would disturb sound legal procedure at their trials.[141]) So the possibility of public opinion depends on background social practices: a free press, free speech, unvarnished coverage of political authorities, and so on. Absent such practices, a society has no public opinion at all: surveys of popular attitudes are another matter. So the *Black Dwarf* lectured Cobbett: "The man who would *divide* the public, in effect *destroys* the public mind. It only exists in a free communication."[142]

[139] *The Whole Proceedings of the Trial of an Information Exhibited ex Officio by the King's Attorney-General against Thomas Paine . . . Tried by a Special Jury in the Court of King's Bench, Guildhall, on Tuesday, the 18th of December, 1792*, rep. Joseph Gurney, 2d ed. (London, 1793), p. 81.

[140] *Edinburgh Review* (September 1818) 30(60):468–69, (March 1819) 31(62):548. See too James Mill, "Jurisprudence" [1819–1823], in *Political Writings*, ed. Terence Ball (Cambridge: Cambridge University Press, 1992), p. 88; *Securities against Misrule* [1822], in Jeremy Bentham, *Securities against Misrule and Other Constitutional Writings for Tripoli and Greece*, ed. Philip Schofield (Oxford: Clarendon, 1990), pp. 44–47; *An Essay on Political Tactics*, in *The Works of Jeremy Bentham*, ed. John Bowring, 11 vols. (Edinburgh, 1843), 2:310–17.

[141] For instance, *The Trial of Colonel Quentin, of the Tenth, or, Prince of Wales's Own Regiment of Hussars*, rep. William Brodie Gurney (London, 1814), p. 6; *The First Trial of William Hone*, 4th ed. (London, 1817), p. 47; *The Trials of Jeremiah Brandreth, William Turner, Isaac Ludlam, George Weightman, and Others, for High Treason*, 2 vols. (London, 1817), 1:316–19; *Pierce Egan's Account of the Trial of John Thurtell and Joseph Hunt* (London, 1824), p. 92.

[142] *Black Dwarf* (5 March 1817) 1(6):91. See too *Letters on a Regicide Peace* [1796–1797], in *The Works of the Right Honorable Edmund Burke*, 9th ed., 12 vols. (Boston: Little, Brown, 1889), 5:449, 6:67.

But then we can expect a riposte. Those worried about political poison groped their way to theories of the silent majority as the true bearers of public opinion. "You are not to infer because a drunken scoundrel may have chalked upon a wall some seditious words, that the town is disaffected," cautioned An Officer.[143] Wordsworth disdained "the clamour of that small though loud portion of the community, ever governed by factitious influence, which, under the name of the PUBLIC, passes itself, upon the unthinking, for the PEOPLE."[144] A lengthy analysis distinguished public opinion and popular clamor, associating the former with the upper and middle classes, the latter with the lower.[145] One stubborn opponent of the Reform Bill of 1832 insisted that "the people of England are not 'the people' of the Bill. The cry for the Bill might even have been ten times greater, yet not the cry of the people, but the rabble."[146] However interpreted, these distinctions indicate some subterranean political disputes.

We're used to thinking of deliberation as a central category of democratic theory, but it's Janus-faced.[147] Conservatives use it to plead for lingering over alternatives, defying the gusts of popular passion. So the *Quarterly Review*, still betting in the final months of the melodrama that delaying the progress of the Reform Bill of 1832 would mean destroying it, yearned for the House of Lords to hit the brakes:

> It has never been denied by any person professing to belong to the
> conservative party, and certainly not by us, that on this, as on all other
> subjects of moment, *public opinion*, (by which we mean, the prevailing
> opinion of persons competent to form a sound judgment on such mat-

---

[143] An Officer, *Letter on the Present Associations, Interspersed with Various Remarks, Highly Interesting; Particularly at This Most Alarming Crisis* (London, 1793), p. 5.

[144] William Wordsworth, *Essay, Supplementary to the Preface* [1815], in *Shorter Poems, 1807–1820,* ed. Carl H. Ketcham (Ithaca, NY: Cornell University Press, 1989), p. 657. See too William Wordsworth to George Beaumont, February 1808, *Letters of William and Dorothy Wordsworth,* 2:194.

[145] William A. MacKinnon, *On the Rise, Progress, and Present State of Public Opinion, in Great Britain, and Other Parts of the World* (London, 1828; reprint ed. Shannon: Irish University Press, 1971), pp. 15, 17, 115–16. Note too *Edinburgh Weekly Journal* (8 February 1820), in *Prose Works of Sir Walter Scott,* 4:331; Asa Briggs, "The Language of 'Class' in Early Nineteenth-Century England," in *Essays in Social History,* ed. M. W. Flinn and T. C. Smout (Oxford: Clarendon, 1974), pp. 161–62.

[146] John Eagles, *The Bristol Riots, Their Causes, Progress, and Consequences* (Bristol, 1832), pp. 25–26.

[147] For connected arguments, see Lynn M. Sanders, "Against Deliberation," *Political Theory* (June 1997) 25(3):347–76.

ters,) must, in the present state of society, sooner or later overcome all obstacles that may be set up against it. And it has been justly described as one of the most important branches of the conservative duty of the Peers, to take care that due time be afforded in all cases for this opinion being deliberately formed and clearly ascertained,—and, in particular, that no measure like this, to which their own judgments refuse assent, shall, out of mere deference to what may be supposed to be the popular sentiment, be permitted to pass their house, at least until it shall first have been put beyond all doubt, that such is really the well-considered and deliberate opinion of those classes of society, who have a right to claim such a deference;—to take care, in brief, that, under the pretext of yielding to public opinion, the nation be not sacrificed to popular clamour.[148]

If the rabble are unreflective, uninformed, tempestuous, they don't deliberate. But then deliberation can require excluding whole segments of the community. All we need do is gloss public opinion as the deliberative judgment of the community, politely keeping in the background the devastating premise that the lower orders don't deliberate.[149]

Radicals too fulminated against the patent irrationalities of public opinion. "There is not a more mean, stupid, dastardly, pitiful, selfish, spiteful, envious, ungrateful animal than the Public." "The public is as envious and ungrateful as it is ignorant, stupid, and pigeon-livered—" These formulations, and others every bit as serene, are Hazlitt's.[150] They sound suspiciously like sentences from *Blackwood's* on "the great grey-goggle-eyed public . . . gluttonously devouring whatever rumour flings into her maw. . . ."[151]

These bitter sentiments suggest that radicalism is just the parlor game of literary intellectuals, pious hypocrisy from Outs not so secretly wishing they were Ins. Sometimes that seems exactly right. Shelley could assure one poor friend that he was "a worshipper of equality" who would never presume on the perquisites of rank; a couple of

[148] *Quarterly Review* (January 1832) 46:602–3.

[149] Less harshly, *Fraser's* (March 1831) 3(14):185–86 flirts with miracle-of-aggregation arguments.

[150] *Table-Talk* [1821], in *Works of Hazlitt*, 8:97, 8:99. See too "On Consistency of Opinion" [1821], in *Works of Hazlitt*, 17:27; *Characteristics* [1823], in *Works of Hazlitt*, 9:181; "On Public Opinion" [1828], in *Works of Hazlitt*, 17:303–13.

[151] *Blackwood's Edinburgh Magazine* (December 1828) 24(147):811.

months later, he could try to sting his father's lawyer with this: "Mr. S. commends Mr. W. when he deals with gentlemen (which opportunity perhaps may not often occur) to refrain from opening private letters, or impudence may draw down chastisement upon contemptibility."[152]

But recall the politics of contingency. In the conservative indictment, usually the stupidity of the lower orders is taken as natural and necessary. In the radical indictment, usually it's taken as a sign of defective social practices—priestcraft, statecraft, lack of education— which can and should be reformed. That is surely what Hazlitt had in mind.[153] Now this suggests another sort of bad faith, the inability to accept that the people might fairly consider one's case on the merits and reject it. We'll see, however, that not everyone on the left took this line.

To count as properly authoritative, then, perhaps public opinion had to be deliberative; perhaps it had to emerge from a society free of priestcraft and statecraft; and so on. It had to be rational—but what would qualify as rationality was hotly debated. This explains why it's tricky to decide whether church-and-king mobs, the sort burning down Priestley's house, were autonomous or victims of false consciousness. The background intuition, cantankerously elaborated by Kant, is that their actions count as autonomous only if they're rational. But that's a matter of political controversy. And this explains why it's tricky to decide whether Jeremiah Brandreth was responsible for leading an abortive insurrectionary march against London in 1817. The structure of *mens rea* aside, the background intuition is that responsibility too depends on rationality.

Most important, this explains why it begs the question to cast Burke's conservatism as prejudice, Paine's democracy as reason. Like the attorney general, Burke vehemently rejects Paine's confidence in the rationality of coffeehouse discussion. He fears "the pernicious consequence of destroying all docility in the minds of those who are not formed for finding their own way in the labyrinths of political theory," the black magic promising to transform subjects into citizens.[154] True, Burke himself deploys the language of veils, illusion,

---

[152] Shelley to Elizabeth Hitchener, 19 August? 1811, *The Letters of Percy Bysshe Shelley*, ed. Frederick L. Jones, 2 vols. (Oxford: Clarendon, 1964), 1:136; Shelley to William Whitton, 30 October 1811, *Letters*, 1:165.

[153] Note especially *The Plain Speaker* [1826], in *Works of Hazlitt*, 12:243–44.

[154] *An Appeal from the New to the Old Whigs*, 2d ed. [1791], in *Works*, 4:202.

and prejudice. But we should see that language as searing in its irony, part of Burke's literary stockpile of snide antidemocratic weaponry. Burke doesn't uncritically endorse something he sees as illusion. He is mordantly consumed with the palpable folly of those who dare to poison the minds of the lower orders and baptize their handiwork *reason*. Finally and most deeply, the dialectic of enlightenment is a dispute over what social practices embody or realize the demands of rationality.

Assign no epistemic authority to popular discussion, urges Burke; the gradual accretion of wisdom in organically developing social institutions is more worthy of credence. Or that along with a much more limited discussion, that of the political nation, especially that of Parliament. But radicals showered with abuse the thought that parliamentary debates were rational. One much reprinted advertisement cast William Pitt as Signor Gulielmo Pittachio, a wizard from the corrupt land of Italy who led hypnotized M.P.s by the nose—and kept the audience in the dark, so they could be mystified.[155] Electoral corruption, the mad scramble of placemen and pensioners for their share of the cash oozing from tax coffers, petty personality and sexual intrigue: these were the central features of debate in the political nation and Parliament. Or so claimed radicals. Here again, it's unhelpful to suggest that we turn to reason to adjudicate our political disputes. For one of our central political disputes is deciding what answers to reason.

These disputes about the rationality of public opinion didn't budge a weighty dilemma. However little it deserved epistemic deference, public opinion would prevail. So concurred a host of observers from across the ideological spectrum.[156] Some harked back to Hume's

[155] *BMC* no. 8500 [28 November 1794]; *Politics for the People* 2(25):388–89, 2(26):406–7 [1795]; *Black Dwarf* (10 February 1819) 3(6):92–93. Note too Harrison, *Letter to Dundas*, pp. 30–31; Charles Pigott, *A Political Dictionary: Explaining the True Meaning of Words* (London, 1795), p. 84 s.v. *necromancer; BMC* no. 9056 [*circa* 1797]; Marcus Wood, *Radical Satire and Print Culture 1790–1822* (Oxford: Clarendon, 1994), pp. 82–85.

[156] For instance, William Godwin, *An Account of the Seminary that Will Be Opened* (London, 1783), p. 2, in *Four Early Pamphlets (1783–1784)*, ed. Burton R. Pollin (Gainesville, FL: Scholars' Facsimiles and Reprints, 1966), p. 150; Joseph Priestley, *Political Dialogues: Number I: On the General Principles of Government* (London, 1791), p. 31; Dugald Stewart, *Elements of the Philosophy of the Human Mind* [1793], in Stewart, *Collected Works*, ed. William Hamilton, 10 vols. (Edinburgh, 1854–1858), 2:228; William Playfair to the Home Office, 24 April 1794, in Aspinall, *Politics and the Press*, p. 437; *Gorgon* (4 July 1818) no. 7, p. 50; David Ricardo to Hutches Trower, 18 September 1818, *Works and Correspondence of Ricardo*, 7:298; *The Speeches of the Right Honourable George Canning*, ed. R. Therry, 6 vols. (London, 1828), 6:405 [1822]; Southey, *Sir Thomas More*, 2:209; John Wade, *The Extraor-*

view, echoed by Burke, that all government rests in opinion.[157] Others thought this a new development, one of the implications of popular enlightenment.[158]

Why could Southey style public opinion, "whether right or wrong, more powerful with a British ministry than any or all other considerations"?[159] For the same reason motivating Wooler's derisive salvo:

> The House of Lords has talked much about its contempt for public clamour. This carries with it an air of great bravado; but what is its import? Literally nothing! The noble lords may value *public opinion* as little as they please; but they cannot disguise from themselves that they do fear public determination. They must fear it, or they must be strange ideots. They must know that public fury is *irresistible*.[160]

For the same reason that the magistrates of Norfolk recommended "the general disuse of THRESHING MACHINES as a friendly concession on the part of the Proprietors to public opinion," a concession, that is, not to sober discussion but to the arson campaigns associated with the dread name of Captain Swing.[161] For the same reason that Lord Ellenborough nervously recorded incidents of popular disorder: raids on bakeries, riots, mobs breaking windows, arson, and murder.[162] For the same reason that Peterloo wasn't a dress rehearsal for Tiananmen Square: the repressive capacities of the British state were

---

dinary *Black Book: An Exposition of Abuses in Church and State, Courts of Law, Representation, Municipal and Corporate Bodies; with a Précis of the House of Commons, Past, Present, and to Come,* new ed. (London, 1832), pp. xiii, 472; Southey to John May, 1 March 1833, *The Letters of Robert Southey to John May 1797 to 1838* (Austin, TX: Jenkins Publishing Co., The Pemberton Press, 1976), p. 255.

[157] "Of the First Principles of Government," in Hume, *Essays* [1741–1742], p. 29; "Speech on a Motion Made in the House of Commons" [7 May 1782], in Burke, *Works,* 7:91.

[158] For both views, see John Moore, *A View of the Causes and Progress of the French Revolution,* 2 vols. (London, 1795), 1:39, 1:317–18. MacKinnon, *Public Opinion,* pp. 191–93 emphasizes the latter.

[159] Robert Southey, *History of the Peninsular War,* 3 vols. (London, 1823–1832), 3:125.

[160] *Black Dwarf* (15 November 1820) 5(20):711. See too Edmund Phipps, *Memoirs of the Political and Literary Life of Robert Plumer Ward, Esq.,* 2 vols. (London, 1850), 2:21–22 [diary, 15 November 1819].

[161] 1830 Norfolk magistrates' address, quoted in E. J. Hobsbawm and George Rudé, *Captain Swing* (New York: W. W. Norton, 1975), p. 155.

[162] Edward Law, Lord Ellenborough, *A Political Diary 1828–1830,* 2 vols. (London, 1881), 2:33 [7 May 1829]; *Three Early Nineteenth Century Diaries,* ed. A. Aspinall (London: Williams and Norgate, 1952), pp. 89 [29 April 1831], 149 [11 October 1831], 150 [13 October 1831], 153 [31 October 1831], 159–60 [29 November 1831].

severely limited. If the people were angry enough to take to the streets and persevere, they would prevail.

Here is public opinion as brute power, not rationality. This conception cements the appeal of loyal and unthinking subjects, the terrors of the scum uppermost. It underlines the importance of one central illusion: popular sovereignty might be an ineluctable fact, but it might be better to cast it as a misguided "normative" position. (Southey didn't claim that divine right was true, but he did endorse it as "a wholesome opinion both for prince and subject; impressing upon both a sense of duty, from which no ill could follow, but much good might arise."[163]) And it helps explain the appeal of the irreversibility thesis, as well as the tactics of those conservatives who made their troubled peace with popular education and entered the fray with beneficent arguments.

## CONTEMPTUOUS DISMISSAL AND A STRUCTURAL IMPASSE

Consider one last set of political controversies at the heart of reason. Champions of civility aspire to a world where we can temperately discuss all our political disputes. But many will be unwilling to dignify some of their opponents with the recognition that such temperate discussion in public entails. They will respond with searing contempt. Or, also contemptuously, they will refuse to respond at all. And their opponents won't be happy. Even Satan bridled at being treated with contempt in his disputations with Joanna Southcott.[164]

We may be able to command widespread allegiance to the view that there is a wide range of opinions that can be held in good faith and are worthy of respectful attention. But people won't agree on whether particular views fall inside or outside that range. Ridiculing "affected civility" and "cowardly compromise with malice and with treason," Cobbett proudly avowed "my most unqualified contempt" for Priestley.[165] "Treat the busy, meddling, seditious zeal of reforming associations with the contempt they deserve," counselled A True-

---

[163] *Southey's Common-Place Book,* ed. John Wood Warter, 4 vols. (London, 1849–1851), 4:665.

[164] Joanna Southcott, *A Dispute between the Woman and the Powers of Darkness* (London, 1802), p. 43.

[165] *Porcupine's Gazette* (September 1798), in *Porcupine's Works,* 9:248–49.

Born Englishman.[166] The *Edinburgh Review* dismissed one learned foray into the history and politics of parliamentary reform. "On such crude plans and meagre speculations, it would be an insult on the understanding of our readers, to offer a single word of comment."[167] Those crusading atheists, Richard Carlile and Robert Taylor, often met with outright rejection—and gloried in it, taking it as a sign of how intellectually bankrupt Christians were. But when the *Leeds Intelligencer* congratulated "the good people of Huddersfield" on dismissing the two "with utter contempt," the paper wasn't furtively thinking that public debate would embarrass Christianity by revealing how nonsensical its justifications were. It was thinking that atheism was beyond the pale.[168]

"But ridicule and contemptuous criticism are dangerous weapons," admonished Godwin.[169] No doubt. Still, speakers and writers frequently recur to them. It's too easy to impeach their democratic credentials: as though we ourselves prize earnest public discussion with Nazis and racists; as though we wouldn't rather demonize them; as though our doing so is a lamentable character flaw, not a sign of our devotion to fundamental norms of equality and respect that help define democracy. Contemptuous dismissal isn't found only in the conservative arsenal.

Yet Burke fired off his dismissals with expert precision, mocking the masses' fledgling efforts in political theory, "their crude undigested and vulgar conceptions": "They look on those things as discoveries because no one had hitherto been so absurd as to spit out such nonsense."[170] Burke harbored special contempt for Tom Paine, "that Jacobin incendiary."[171] So he refused to argue against Paine. In the *Appeal from the New to the Old Whigs*, Burke quotes for some pages from Paine, only occasionally interspersing comments on such Jacobin notions. "I will not attempt in the smallest degree to refute them,"

---

[166] A True-Born Englishman [William Combe], *A Word in Season to the Traders and Manufacturers of Great Britain,* 6th ed. (London, 1792), p. 14. See too William Wordsworth, *Essay, Supplementary to the Preface* [1815], in *Shorter Poems,* p. 643.

[167] *Edinburgh Review* (June 1816) 26(52):338–39 on T. H. B. Oldfield, *The Representative History of Great Britain and Ireland,* 6 vols. (London, 1816).

[168] *Leeds Intelligencer* (17 September 1829), as triumphantly reprinted in *Lion* (25 September 1829) 4(13):394.

[169] William Godwin, *Lives of Edward and John Philips, Nephews and Pupils of Milton* (London, 1815), p. 146.

[170] Burke to Sir Lawrence Parsons, 7 March 1793, *Correspondence,* 7:359.

[171] Burke, *Observations on the Conduct of the Minority* [1793], in *Works,* 5:20.

he concludes. "This will probably be done (if such writings shall be thought to deserve any other refutation than that of criminal justice) by others. . . ."[172] Privately, he reiterated the point:

> You talk of Paine with more respect than he deserves: He is utterly inca-pable of comprehending his subject. He has not even a moderate por-tion of learning of any kind. . . . Payne possesses nothing more than what a man whose audacity makes him careless of logical consequences, and his total want of honour and morality makes indifferent as to politi-cal consequences, may very easily write. They indeed who seriously write upon a principle of levelling ought to be answered by the Magistrate—and not by the Speculatist.[173]

Opening the second part of *Rights of Man*, a swaggering but wounded Paine complains that Burke hasn't responded to him. His tone in these pages is hectoring, indignant, but also petulant, that of a schoolyard bully not fully poised or confident but nonetheless mis-chievously thrusting himself in his opponent's face, trying to provoke a confrontation. "I will meet Mr. Burke whenever he please," he promises. "It was himself that opened the controversy, and he ought not to desert it."[174] He also proposes that a properly authoritative jury be convened to decide the controversy between the two of them. And Paine himself resorts to contemptuous dismissal. Burke's suggestion that the settlement of 1688 bound posterity "is now become too de-testable to be made a subject for debate; and, therefore, I pass it over with no other notice than exposing it."[175]

Could Paine and Burke publicly have discussed their political dif-ferences? Could they have brought them to the bar of reason? One of Paine's opponents complained about Burke's proposed recourse to criminal prosecution. "If Mr. Paine has erred let him be nationally confuted, but not criminally convicted."[176] But this is saccharine, even maudlin; it fails to do justice to the depth and vehemence of the political conflicts at stake. Who could judge this dispute? For his im-partial jury, Paine proposed an elected popular convention fairly rep-

---

[172] Burke, *Appeal from the New to the Old Whigs*, in *Works*, 4:161.

[173] Burke to William Cusac Smith, 22 July 1791, *Correspondence*, 6:303–4.

[174] *Rights of Man* [1792], in *Works*, 6:225–26.

[175] *Rights of Man* [1792], in *Works*, 6:321; note too *Rights of Man* [1791], in *Works*, 6:172.

[176] *Constitutional Letters, in Answer to Mr. Paine's Rights of Man* (London, 1792), p. 24.

resenting the whole nation.[177] But of course Burke would have had principled objections to submitting his case to them—or to workers in alehouses or auditors at mechanics' institutes or readers in coffee-houses. Burke might have been happy (ignoring qualms about the onslaught of Jacobin corruption represented by the Duke of Bedford) to submit the dispute to the House of Lords or to landed aristocrats. But Paine would have seen them as a shamelessly self-interested bunch of rogues fearing that the rights of man would eviscerate their wealth and power.

It's not a matter of Burke's acerbic rage or Paine's snotty adolescence; it's not that more civility would help. The structure of their political views leads not to constructive engagement but to impasse, an impasse replayed frequently between right and left. Burke has deeply principled reasons to despise Paine, to refuse any public debate with him. Paine, as we'll see, can readily justify the same sort of contempt for Burke. For contempt, I want next to argue, isn't only central to norms of debate. It's a furiously contested battleground of modern politics.

[177] *Rights of Man* [1792], in *Works*, 6:227.

# CONTEMPT

Hᴀʀᴅ ᴀꜱ ɪᴛ ᴍᴀʏ ᴀᴘᴘᴇᴀʀ in individual instances, dependent poverty ought to be held disgraceful."[1] Or so held Malthus, worried about the disincentives created by the poor laws. If people are paid not to work, they'll stop working. "The greater is the provision that is made for the poor," agreed Priestley, "the more poor there will be to avail themselves of it; as, in general, men will not submit to labour if they can live without it."[2] Worse—and here is Malthus's special concern—they will marry and have children, paying no heed to the savage discipline of poverty. So it would be prudent to ensure that only the genuinely desperate accept the payment of poor rates from the parish, to make accepting that payment costly, to make it disgraceful.

So Malthus urged the repeal of the poor laws. True, "no man of humanity could venture to propose their immediate abolition."[3] Too many people had become too dependent on them. So the benevolent parson preferred their "*very gradual* abolition,"[4] generously allotting two years to accomplishing that end. Malthus proposed that no legitimate child born one year later, and no illegitimate child born two years later, be eligible for support. (I don't know why he was willing to be more generous with the latter.) In the interests of legal notice and to impress the stern message on the minds of the poor, local clergymen would take the occasion of publishing marriage banns to read an address explaining the new rules and their rationale. Afterwards, "if any man chose to marry, without a prospect of being able to support a family, he should have the most perfect liberty to do so." (Why are women missing here?) But he would have to shoulder the crushing

---

[1] *Essay on the Principle of Population* [1798], in *The Works of Thomas Robert Malthus*, ed. E. A. Wrigley and David Souden, 8 vols. (London: William Pickering, 1986), 1:33. See too Thomas Peregrine Courtenay, *Copy of a Letter to the Rt. Hon. William Sturges Bourne*, in *Pamphleteer* (1817) 11(22):388.

[2] Joseph Priestley, *Lectures on History, and General Policy*, 2 vols. (Philadelphia, 1803), 2:54.

[3] *Essay on the Principle of Population* [1826], in *Works of Malthus*, 3:514. The proposal is fully in place in the second edition of 1803.

[4] *Essay on the Principle of Population* [1826], in *Works of Malthus*, 3:381.

burden of responsibility. "He should be taught to know, that the laws of nature, which are the laws of God, had doomed him and his family to suffer for disobeying their repeated admonitions; that he had no claim of *right* on society for the smallest portion of food, beyond that which his labour would fairly purchase," and that he should be hugely grateful for any private charity he received.[5] But could children be held responsible for the imprudence of their parents? "The infant is, comparatively speaking, of little value to the society, as others will immediately supply its place."[6] (Witness the deft touch of the economist, suitably impartial and attentive to fungibility and opportunity cost. Those finding it heartless will be reassured to learn that it softens the judgment of an earlier edition that the infant is "of no value."[7]) Malthus warned, too, that even private charity should be offered only with the most gingerly care. Private or public, payments for the poor would create a flood of beseeching claimants.[8]

Why hadn't that flood already overwhelmed England? Poor law payments did rise steadily.[9] In a mechanically thrumming refrain, commentators worried that formerly the poor, devoted to the dignity of labor, found dependence shameful, but now that devotion was collapsing—or already had collapsed or would soon collapse—under the insidious assault of the poor laws. The timing was sadly uncertain, the trend ominously clear. In 1786, Joseph Townsend declared that "the shame and reproach of being relieved by a parish" had averted the laws' worst consequences, "but these have long since ceased to operate."[10] In 1798, Malthus thought that the poor still clung to a "love of independence," but that the poor laws would eviscerate that noble sentiment.[11] "They do not trust to their own industry for support. They

---

[5] *Essay on the Principle of Population* [1826], bk. 4, chap. 8, in *Works of Malthus*, 3:514–23, especially 3:515–17. Note too Miss Morgan of Clifton, *Hints towards the Formation of a Society, for Promoting a Spirit of Independence among the Poor* (Bristol, n.d.), p. 14.

[6] *Essay on the Principle of Population* [1826], in *Works of Malthus*, 3:517.

[7] *Essay on the Principle of Population* [1803], in *Works of Malthus*, 3:517 n. 23.

[8] *Essay on the Principle of Population*, in *Works of Malthus*, 3:498 [1826], 3:516 n. 14 [1803].

[9] John Rule, *Albion's People: English Society, 1714–1815* (London: Longman, 1992), p. 129.

[10] Joseph Townsend, *A Dissertation on the Poor Laws by a Well-Wisher to Mankind* [1786], foreword by Ashley Montagu, afterword by Mark Neuman (Berkeley: University of California Press, 1971), pp. 49–50.

[11] *Essay on the Principle of Population* [1798], in *Works of Malthus*, 1:27. See too *Essay on the Principle of Population* [1826], in *Works of Malthus*, 3:543.

grow insolent," snarled William Holland, like Malthus a parson of the Church of England, in 1800. "Subordination is lost and [they] make their demands on other people's purses as if they were their own."[12] "There was formerly found an unconquerable aversion to depend on the parish," agreed Arthur Young in 1801. "That spirit is annihilated. . . ."[13] "Until of late years," opined Cobbett in 1808, "there was, amongst the poor, a horror of becoming chargeable to the parish." But no longer: "The barrier, shame, has been broken down. . . ."[14] "The manly and honest pride of independence is gone," went one 1816 lament. "The sense of shame is extinguished."[15] "Twenty years ago," The Wife of a Clergyman reported in 1825, workers found the prospect of support humiliating. "But where now shall we look for the labourer who feels or cares for these things? So much is the scene reversed, and so *entirely* departed are those feelings of independence, that the struggle now is to get from the parish" whatever one can.[16] An 1833

[12] *Paupers and Pig Killers: The Diary of William Holland, a Somerset Parson 1799–1818*, ed. Jack Ayres (Gloucester: Alan Sutton, 1984), p. 47 [13 October 1800]. See too Thomas Gisborne, *An Enquiry into the Duties of Men in the Higher and Middle Classes of Society in Great Britain, Resulting from Their Respective Stations, Professions, and Employments*, 5th ed. corrected, 2 vols. (London, 1800), 1:437.

[13] *An Inquiry into the Propriety of Applying Wastes to the Better Maintenance and Support of the Poor* [1801], in *Arthur Young and His Times*, ed. G. E. Mingay (London: Macmillan, 1975), p. 130. See too John Hill, *The Means of Reforming the Morals of the Poor, by the Prevention of Poverty; and A Plan for Meliorating the Conditions of Parish Paupers, and Diminishing the Expence of Maintaining Them* (London, 1801), p. 12; Thomas Rudge, *General View of the Agriculture of the County of Gloucester* (London, 1807), p. 346.

[14] *Political Register* (16 July 1808) 14(3):73. See too *Political Register* (28 September 1816) 31(13):390. Compare Cobbett's earlier view that the poor laws guaranteed the sturdy dignity of the poor: *Priestley's Charity Sermon for Poor Emigrants*, in William Cobbett, *Porcupine's Works*, 12 vols. (London, 1801), 9:396 n. [May 1801; for date, 9:410].

[15] W. Peter, *Thoughts on the Present Crisis, in a Letter from a Constituent to His Representative*, 2d ed., in *Pamphleteer* (1816) 8(15):225. See too J. T. Barber Beaumont, *An Essay on Provident or Parish Banks*, in *Pamphleteer* (1816) 7(14):476; A Country Overseer, *The Poor Laws England's Ruin* (London, 1817), p. 7; George Glover, *Observations on the Present State of Pauperism in England* (London, 1817), pp. 3–4, reprinted in *Pamphleteer* (1817) 10(20):373; Walter Scott to Robert Southey, 23 March [1818], *The Letters of Sir Walter Scott*, ed. H. J. C. Grierson, 12 vols. (London: Constable & Co., 1932–1937), 5:114–15; John, Earl of Sheffield, *Observations on the Impolicy, Abuses, and False Interpretation of the Poor Laws*, in *Pamphleteer* (1818) 13(25):115–16; *Manchester Mercury* (14 September 1819), in G. B. Hindle, *Provision for the Relief of the Poor in Manchester 1754–1826* (Manchester: Manchester University Press for the Chetham Society, 1975), p. viii.

[16] The Wife of a Clergyman, *Some Account of the Utility, as Practically Exemplified, of Small Clubs, in Country Villages* (Bath, 1825), pp. 3–4. See too J. W. Cunningham, *A Few Observations on Friendly Societies, and Their Influence on Public Morals*, 2d ed., in *Pamphleteer* (1823) 22(43):157.

pamphlet reported, "The spirit of independence is not entirely, but nearly gone."[17]

Malthus wasn't alone or original in urging the abolition of the poor laws.[18] It's easy enough to ridicule this project or to suggest that it exposes the gracious nub of conservatism, the meanspirited desire of skinflints to keep their wallets shut. Or maybe it's a different nub, the appeal to natural necessity that we've already seen in Malthus's defense of property rights. Neither nature nor the poor themselves, charged one critic, but the rich were responsible for the plight of the poor: the rich, idlers "who have never produced any part of all they have consumed."[19]

Score another easy triumph for the left. Yet the ideological cleavages here aren't what one might expect. Carlile, that disciple of Tom Paine, himself urged the abolition of the poor laws.[20] *Blackwood's,* the *Age,* and *Fraser's* sprang to their defense.[21] The *Quarterly* flip-flopped.[22] And Malthus was obdurate in his conviction that the poor laws were making the poor worse off, increasing population, decreasing wages, driving up the price of food. Nor do I doubt the sincerity of his indictment of the poor laws as "grating, inconvenient and tyrannical," his denunciation of the tawdry business of trying to hustle future claimants, even claimants yet unborn, across parish boundaries. "The

[17] *The Abolition of the Poor Laws, the Safety of the State* (London, 1833), p. 13; note too pp. 3–4, 15. See too *Speeches of Henry Lord Brougham,* 4 vols. (Edinburgh, 1838), 3:496–97 [21 July 1834].

[18] See for instance Townsend, *Dissertation,* p. 63; George Dyer, *The Complaints of the Poor People of England* (London, 1793; reprint ed. Oxford: Woodstock Books, 1990), pp. 155–69; Marquis of Lansdown to Jeremy Bentham, 4 April 1796, *The Correspondence of Jeremy Bentham,* ed. Timothy L. S. Sprigge and others, 10 vols. to date (London: Athlone Press; Oxford: Clarendon, 1968–), 5:195; the resolutions of the Society for the Gradual Abolition of the Poor's Rate, 23 April 1806, in John Bone, *The Principles and Regulations of Tranquillity* (London, 1806), pp. xxi–xxiv; David Ricardo, *On the Principles of Political Economy and Taxation* [1821], in *The Works and Correspondence of David Ricardo,* ed. Piero Sraffa with M. H. Dobb, 11 vols. (Cambridge: Cambridge University Press for the Royal Economic Society, 1951–1973), 1:106; Harriet Martineau, *Illustrations of Political Economy,* 9 vols. (London, 1832–1834), 9(2):67.

[19] Charles Hall, *The Effects of Civilization on the People in European States* (London, 1805; reprint ed. London: Routledge/Thoemmes Press, 1994), p. 341.

[20] *Republican* (4 August 1826) 14(4):119–27, especially p. 126.

[21] *Blackwood's Edinburgh Magazine* (June 1828) 23(140):923–36, especially pp. 932–33; *Age* (7 October 1827) 3(125):140; *Fraser's* (April 1833) 7(40):499.

[22] *Quarterly Review* (October 1827) 36:484, (March 1828) 37:540, (February 1831) 44:511–54, (October 1832) 48:66, (December 1832) 48:336, (January 1834) 50:359.

parish persecution of men whose families are likely to become chargeable, and of poor women who are near lying-in, is a most disgraceful and disgusting tyranny."[23]

Notice, anyway, an enviable choice: the lot of the poor is disgrace or disgust, come what may. Dependent poverty ought to be held disgraceful; the tyranny of the poor laws is disgraceful and disgusting; and, added an M.P., "The sight and the importunities of miserable and shocking poverty, are what the most inhumane cannot but feel extremely disgusting. . . ."[24] The unflagging emphasis on disgrace and disgust isn't a superficial trapping of a social welfare program that could have done without it. One deliberate goal of the poor laws—the old poor laws every bit as much as the harsher new poor laws of 1834—was to undercut human dignity and social status.

In some parishes, the poor were bundled off to workhouses, typically run on a contractual basis. The master of the house received a flat fee from the parish and pocketed whatever was left after he housed, fed, and clothed the poor and extracted labor from them. Like the tax farming of an earlier day, this arrangement gave the master an incentive to be harsh. Clean or dirty, some workhouses resembled prisons.[25] Social control, or, in haunting cadences already sounded in Tudor England, the maintenance of "good order," was a pressing issue. Instead of eating dinner, one found guilty of telling lies at some houses sat on a stool in the middle of the dining room with a paper identifying him as an "INFAMOUS LIAR."[26] In some parishes, those on the rates had to wear badges.[27] One popular ballad, "The New Starvation Law Examined," branded the workhouses "New British Bastilles" and ridiculed the dreary clothing the poor were saddled with:

[23] *Essay on the Principle of Population* [1798], in *Works of Malthus*, 1:35–36.

[24] George Rose, *Observations on the Poor Laws, and on the Management of the Poor* (London, 1805), pp. 10–11.

[25] Frederic Morton Eden, *The State of the Poor*, 3 vols. (London, 1797; reprint ed. Bristol: Thoemmes Press, 1994), 2:536–37, 2:678.

[26] Eden, *State of the Poor*, 2:470, 3:756, 3:854–55.

[27] Eden, *State of the Poor*, 2:688, 3:783. In the House of Commons, Addington opposed the use of badges: George Pellew, *The Life and Correspondence of . . . Henry Addington, First Viscount Sidmouth*, 3 vols. (London, 1847), 1:474 [24 November 1801].

> Of their uniform, too, you something shall hear,—
> In strong Fearnaught jackets the men do appear;
> In coarse Grogram gowns the women do shine,
> And a ninepenny cap,—now won't they be fine?[28]

The poor fought back, sometimes spectacularly. The governess of Knighton's workhouse was beaten by her charges.[29] One overseer of the poor outside Manchester was treated to a dousing of boiling water and sulfuric acid.[30]

"Who can view these mansions of misery without horror?" demanded another M.P.[31] The horror was accentuated by the endless possibilities of moral corruption, with say prostitutes, "the very dregs of the streets . . . filthy and beastly beyond imagination," promiscuously mixing with the virtuous needy.[32] But the horror of the workhouses was entirely deliberate, the rational response to fears of disincentives. "Every poor house should be so ordered as to be a place irksome and abhorrent to every able-bodied pauper within its walls," patiently explained one writer.[33] The campaign to degrade the status of the dependent poor had its more gruesome aspects. In some parishes, paupers were treated as livestock. Cobbett warmed to the theme in a public lecture:

> People have been drawing wagons, chained or harnessed together like beasts of burden. In Nottinghamshire I met twenty men harnessed in this way, and in Sussex, in Hertfordshire, and in Hampshire, it has been common. Gentlemen, we ought to blush to speak about such things,

---

[28] Martha Vicinus, *Broadsides of the Industrial North* (Newcastle upon Tyne: Frank Graham, 1975), p. 49. The *OED* defines *fearnought* as coarse woolen cloth, *grogram* as a coarse cloth of silk or wool and mohair mixed with silk and stiffened with gum. The broadside isn't dated, but its title suggests that it's a response to the new poor law of 1834.

[29] Eden, *State of the Poor,* 3:901.

[30] *The Early English Trade Unions: Documents from the Home Office Papers in the Public Record Office,* ed. A. Aspinall (London: Batchworth, 1949), p. 367 n. 1.

[31] *The Speech of J. C. Curwen, Esq. M.P. in the House of Commons, on the 28th of May, 1816,* 2d ed., in *Pamphleteer* (1816) 8(15):16.

[32] *Further Observations on the Improvements in the Maintenance of the Poor, in the Town of Kingston-upon-Hull* (Hull, 1801), p. 20. For a more sympathetic glimpse of a prostitute, see Samuel Bamford, *Early Days* (London, 1849), pp. 221–22.

[33] A. Barnett, *The Poor Laws, and Their Administration; Being an Enquiry into the Causes of English Pauperism, and the Failure of Measures Intended for Its Relief* (London, 1833), chap. 9.

unless we call upon the people to make an effort to get rid of them. They talk about the hardships of negro slaves, why it is enough to fill us with indignation to hear them whine over the sorrows of a fat and greasy negro in Jamaica—by the way, they moan over his fate while they are sipping the sugar and the coffee produced by his labour—but it fills us with indignation to see their sympathies called forth in behalf of the well-fed negroes, while their own countrymen are found in such a condition under their very eyes. (Applause.) Oh, yes, while talking about the poor dear negroes they can look out of the window, and say, "Oh, it's only some men drawing a wagon."[34]

(I'll be turning to those fat and greasy Negroes soon enough, but Cobbett wasn't alone in dwelling gloomily on the comparative predicaments of Jamaican blacks and the English poor. "No WHITE SLAVERY!" proclaimed London placards opposing the new poor law of 1834.[35]) Recalling respectful funerals provided for those dying while needy, one distinguished historian is suffused with wistful holiday cheer: "Poverty or not, human dignity was preserved, and the sense of human social status maintained."[36] Yet even after death, paupers were dehumanized. A shortage of cadavers for those learning medicine gave rise to grave robberies and even murder. Urging that publicity be avoided, Bentham shepherded through Parliament an 1832 bill providing that the unclaimed bodies of the poor would be handed over to the anatomists.[37] The authorities proved suitably aggressive in denying that some families were capable of providing an appropriate burial for their kin. Longstanding popular belief that resurrection required the physical integrity of one's corpse redoubled the horror with which this legislation was received.

[34] William Cobbett, *Eleven Lectures on the French and Belgian Revolutions, and English Boroughmongering* (London, 1830), lec. 3, p. 11. Note too Ian Dyck, *William Cobbett and Rural Popular Culture* (Cambridge: Cambridge University Press, 1992), pp. 152–54.

[35] *Age* (3 August 1834), p. 245.

[36] Ian Christie, *Stress and Stability in Late Eighteenth-Century Britain: Reflections on the British Avoidance of Revolution* (Oxford: Clarendon, 1984), p. 107.

[37] Ruth Richardson, *Death, Dissection and the Destitute* (London: Penguin, 1988), pp. 111, 198–200. Others had the same idea: *London Debating Societies, 1776–1799*, comp. Donna T. Andrew (Great Britain: London Record Society, 1994), pp. 386–87 [4 March 1799]; John Abernethy, *The Hunterian Oration for the Year 1819* (London, 1819), pp. 35–36; William Mackenzie, *An Appeal to the Public and to the Legislature, on the Necessity of Affording Dead Bodies to the Schools of Anatomy, by Legislative Enactment* (Glasgow, 1824), p. 29; John Wade, *A Treatise on the Police and Crimes of the Metropolis* (London, 1829), pp. 202–3. *John Bull* (24 May 1829) 9(441):164 scorns the idea.

Suppose we distinguish being a human being, a biological organism catalogued as *homo sapiens,* from being a person, a social actor enjoying dignity. Take food, conveyor of nutritive fuel and social status. Cobbett loathed the potato, "this worse than useless root," because he doubted its nutritive value and because he took it to be "soul-degrading" food for mere animals.[38] Then we can see the poor laws as grudgingly nourishing human beings but moving decisively to undercut persons. If only idle, recommended a writer on slavery, the poor "should have a scanty coarse fare, and clothes made up of patches, to make their situation irksome to them."[39] "When bread is given it should not be of the first quality," urged A Country Overseer. "Care should be taken to ascertain the least quantity of food that could be given to an individual without endangering his health,"[40] safeguarding the biological organism but shredding his dignity. The poor of Derbyshire somberly lined up for stewed ox's head, publicly receiving food others defined as waste.[41]

Not everyone chimed in with the line of argument I've sketched. One liberal attributed the poor's degradation to their lack of education.[42] Arthur Young thought that distributing land to the poor would be a huge help.[43] (Though Wordsworth worried that parish relief, giving the poor a right to others' assets, was tantamount to such redistribution.[44]) One overseer began with the usual conceptions

---

[38] *Political Register* (18 November 1815) 29(7):193; *Cobbett's Two-Penny Trash* (April 1831) 1(10):221. See too William Cobbett, *Cottage Economy,* new ed. (London, 1826), §107; *Political Register* (31 May 1828) 46(9):517–20.

[39] James Ramsay, *An Essay on the Treatment and Conversion of African Slaves in the British Sugar Colonies* (London, 1784), p. 42 n.

[40] A Country Overseer, *The Poor Laws England's Ruin,* p. 10.

[41] *The Reports of the Society for Bettering the Condition and Increasing the Comforts of the Poor,* 5 vols. (London, 1798–1800), 1:81–85, 1:328–29. For a more efficiency-minded concern with food, see A Physician, *Practical Oeconomy: or A Proposal for Enabling the Poor to Provide for Themselves: with Remarks on the Establishment of Soup Houses* (London, 1801); *Thoughts on the Best Modes of Carrying into Effect the System of Economy Recommended in His Majesty's Proclamation* (London, 1801). Compare the defense of the quality of the food given to the poor in *Seventh Report of the General Committee of the Association for the Suppression of Mendicity in Dublin* (Dublin, 1824), p. 25.

[42] Robert Hall, *An Apology for the Freedom of the Press, and for General Liberty,* 2d ed. (London, 1793), p. 110.

[43] Young's diary, 6 June 1801, *The Autobiography of Arthur Young with Selections from His Correspondence,* ed. M. Betham-Edwards (London, 1898), pp. 365–66.

[44] William Wordsworth to Daniel Stuart, 22 June 1817, *The Letters of William and Dorothy Wordsworth,* 2d ed., ed. Ernest de Selincourt, rev. Chester L. Shaver and others,

about the lazy irresponsibility of the poor. But he learned on the job and denied that "men capable of working and able to procure work. . . . look forward, with a kind of longing desire, to get, and remain, on the list of paupers."[45] (People of color, he thought, were another matter: threatening to overwhelm the country, they were "among the very worst and most depraved characters"; the state ought to sequester them near the ports they entered by and try to expel them.[46]) *Blackwood's* rejected the familiar economic story about disincentives and held that the real problem was that no jobs were available.[47] One writer, speaking for the Society for Bettering the Condition and Increasing the Comforts of the Poor, wondered plaintively why the poor had to be piled into dismal hovels. Couldn't they be given gardens?[48] Endearing or pathetic, these were minority voices swept away in fierce political gales.

Disgrace and disgust, not humanity and dignity: the poor laws singled out the unfortunate to serve as the butt of contempt. Bad enough, explained a letter in Cobbett's *Political Register,* that the poor were "naturally despised." Malthus had aggravated their plight. "He has fairly hunted them down, he has driven them into his toils, he has thrown a net over them, and they remain as a prey to the first invader, either to be sacrificed without mercy at the shrine of cold, unfeeling avarice, or to linger out a miserable existence under the hands of ingenious and scientific tormentors." Once their status was lowered, they were fair game. "But, it is neither generous nor just, to come in aid of the narrow prejudices and hard-heartedness of mankind, with metaphysical distinctions and the cobwebs of philosophy."[49] Neither generous nor just, but seductive and devastating.

---

8 vols. (Oxford: Clarendon, 1967–1993), 3:386–87. But see too Wordsworth to George Huntly Gordon, 1 December 1829, *Letters,* 5:182.

[45] Samuel Roberts, *A Defence of the Poor Laws, with A Plan for the Suppression of Mendicity, and for the Establishment of Universal Parochial Benefit Societies* (Sheffield, 1819), pp. 27, 33.

[46] Roberts, *Defence,* pp. 41–42.

[47] *Blackwood's Edinburgh Magazine* (June 1828) 23(140):923, 932–33.

[48] Bernard Thomas, *A Letter to . . . the Lord Bishop of Durham . . . on the Principle and Detail of the Measures Now under the Consideration of Parliament, for Promoting and Encouraging Industry, and for the Relief and Regulation of the Poor* (London, 1807), p. 56.

[49] *Political Register* (14 March 1807) 11(11):397–98.

# FIVE

# THE POLITICS OF
# THE EMOTIONS

—⚬❧⚬—

Y<small>OU DROP BY</small> a friend's apartment one day. Your friend is beaming as she answers the door, and to your wryly perplexed amusement, you notice that she is strutting as she heads toward the couch and gestures toward the chair. You sit down and wait for her good news.

"I feel great!" she exclaims.

"I figured that out," you respond drily. "What's up?"

"I have a red bicycle," she announces, "and I am *very* proud of myself." Her chin is turned up and her eyes are defiant. She hustles you over to the back stairs and there it is, bright and shiny, fire-engine red frame, two wheels, chain, derailleur, the whole bit: yes, a red bicycle. But proud of a red bicycle? Surely something is wrong here.

So you search for a context that will make sense of her pride. Perhaps the bicycle was a prize for winning a race. Or maybe she recently figured out in therapy that her childhood bicycle accident still loomed large in her unconscious, and so she has decided to work through her anxieties by getting a bike just like that old one. Or it's actually her old rusty blue bicycle, newly restored, and she is pleased with herself for doing a professional job, with no stray splotches of paint disfiguring the wheels. Or she has taken a dare to shoplift an implausibly conspicuous item and succeeded fabulously. Or. . . .

Indefinitely many stories would make sense of her pride. But not any story will do. So suppose she sits shaking her head, even chortling, at one conjecture after another. "Give up?" she finally demands. "Okay, I'll tell you. I'm proud of my new red bike because it cost exactly two hundred dollars." Now this too is baffling, so once again you start hunting for a context that will make sense of pride. Maybe she was intent on for once respecting the limits of her budget, and she'd managed to do so while still getting a splendid bicycle. Or. . . .

But now she looks pained, baffled herself, wondering why you think there has to be a further story. A red bike, and it cost two hundred dollars, and she's proud, and that's that. "Look," she appeals, "I'm proud of it, okay?" And manifestly she is proud. Or is she?

### Justifying Emotions

The emotions aren't freefloating moods or affects or feelings. Instead, they're richly cognitive. So, in a view long familiar from work in philosophy and psychology, the possibility of experiencing an emotion depends on one's background beliefs. So too the possibility of attributing an emotion to others depends on being able to attribute a relevant set of beliefs to them. The case of the red bicycle is puzzling because it seems we can't get an appropriate set of beliefs on the table.

How might we proceed? Here are a few possibilities. One: we might doubt her sincerity. Perhaps it's all an elaborate hoax. Two: we doubt her command of the language. She's not a native speaker, and now and then her vocabulary is eccentric or incomprehensible. Three: we might simply override her claim to be proud. Granted, she says she's proud; she looks proud; she does the sorts of things that proud people do, such as showing off the bicycle. So we might concede that she has the same feeling that people who are proud have. Still, it doesn't qualify as pride unless the relevant set of beliefs is in place. So is the emotion an additive construct, beliefs plus a feeling? Or are beliefs and feeling linked in internally complex ways, so that it's hard to interpret the claim that she has the same feeling as someone who actually is proud?

Picture this: "The bike was a prize for winning a ten-kilometer race. But that's not why I'm proud of it." Here we have a belief plus a feeling, but not yet pride, or anyway not yet a conventional or unequivocal case of pride. Or this: "I won it as a prize, and I guess that makes me proud. Not sure why it does, though." If we construe this as demure self-deprecation—winners of races might think it inappropriate to exult in their victories—we have a clear case of pride. (We also have a nested emotion: being ashamed of being proud; or, if that's too strong, diffident about being proud.) Or we could construe it as token piety, an acknowledgment that others might think it rude to exult. But we could also construe it as acknowledging the wrong sort of link between belief and feeling, a purely causal link. Pride here would require that she feel good about herself because she won the race. But that *because* is a matter of reasons and justification, not a causal link that she wouldn't affirm on reflection.

Four: so now we have a dispute about whether she genuinely has good grounds for being proud. Suppose again that she's sincere, a fully competent speaker of the language, and that no intelligible background story seems to make sense of her being proud. Again, we might simply override her claim to being proud. Whatever she is, we might say, it doesn't fall within the scope of the concept. But instead we might concede that she is proud but insist that it's weird to be proud just because you have a red bicycle. She shouldn't be proud. She has nothing to be proud of.

Now we have two ways of securing the crucial place of justificatory beliefs in understanding the emotions. Absent such beliefs, in one view, we can't invoke the emotion in the first place: she isn't really proud at all. Absent such beliefs, in another view, we can challenge people and engage them in critical argument: why should she be proud? For my purposes, it doesn't much matter which route we take. And sometimes it's difficult to distinguish them. Suppose that your small child is proud of defecating, not because she's finally learned to use the potty. And suppose that, on the anxious and repressive side in these matters, you override her: "It's nothing to be proud of," you mutter. You may not know and you may not care whether she sees her turds as a precious extension of self, a gift to you. Are you teaching her something about the meaning of *pride*? or are you teaching her what one ought to take pride in?

Let's say, then, that we need to be able to *make sense* of being proud, where that locution covers both routes. What sort of justificatory account makes sense of pride? Perhaps pride requires the belief that one has done something valuable, acquitted oneself well, performed admirably. Winning a race would ordinarily qualify (but not, perhaps, if the opponents were all pathetically slow; or not if you cheated; or not if you were the coach, sadistically demonstrating that you were still faster than your student). So would successfully navigating all the fiendishly difficult passages in that Bartók sonata (but not if you already were esteemed as a master, in which case you can't earn pride just by playing all the right notes—then we demand interpretive insight and clarity, higher hurdles you must surmount before you can be proud—but you can earn humiliation by failing).

So doing something valuable makes sense of pride. Tendentious accounts of what's valuable will then create further dispute: consider being proud of washing one's car twice a day. So will tendentious accounts of the agent who's done the deed: consider being proud because one's second cousin is opening on Broadway (not proud of her, which raises other difficulties, but proud oneself, basking in the glow of her accomplishment, appealing to the family connection to take the accomplishment as in some sense one's own); or consider the Jew who's proud of centuries of scriptural commentary, the black who's proud of the history of jazz, and so on.

But is it necessary to *do* something valuable? Maybe it's enough to *be* something valuable or to *have* something valuable. Take the vain man admiring his chiseled chin. He's not thinking that he struggled valiantly to overcome a history of obesity that obscured his chin in rolls of fat. He cheerfully confesses that he happened to inherit the genes that gave him such an admirably handsome chin, but anyway there it is and he's proud of it. Or take the eldest son of the aristocrat who comes of age and saddles up the stallion to survey his dominions. He hasn't done anything at all. He was just born lucky, in the right role to profit from the social practices of aristocracy and primogeniture. And he's managed not to die young, but he agrees that he has no reason to be especially proud of that. Still, he is proud of his new estates; their expansive wealth and power reflect back on him.

Are these two proud? Should they be proud? Some will think it's not enough to be or to have something valuable, that we should hold out for doing something valuable. Call this the bourgeois model of pride. (There's that funny adjective—or is it an epithet?—again.) In this view, there are still tricky judgment calls at the frontiers of the concept, but they concern various ways of falling short of the valuable accomplishment: take being proud of giving it your best shot even if you fail. But the chin and the estate don't make sense of pride. Others will say that surely the bourgeois model is too narrow, that we should recognize other kinds of pride. Still others will be ambivalent about the chin and the estate. True, they'll agree, people are proud of such things, but they shouldn't be. (And these same others might not want to concede that the woman is proud of her red bicycle.)

Now we have a debate about the legitimacy of an emotion, with rival norms in the background serving as contestable sources of authority, buttressing or undercutting the appeals of various partisans. (Consider: does successful shoplifting make sense of pride?) So we have one way of unpacking a topic that might seem puzzling, the politics of the emotions. We will soon see others.

## CONDESCENSION, INSOLENCE, AND IMPUDENCE

In 1832, John Payne Collier was working in the Duke of Devonshire's library when the duke brought him his lunch. A duke performing the duties of a servant: the occasion was notable and Collier recorded it in his diary. "He always does his utmost to lessen the distance between us, and to put me at my ease, on a level with himself," he mused. "I do not call it condescension (he will not permit the word), but kindness, and I should be most ungrateful not to make all the return in my power."[1] Why call this condescension? Isn't condescension a matter of being patronizing, looking down on another as if he were inferior? And if it is somehow condescending, why be grateful for it? Isn't condescension a repulsive vice? Or take Mr. Bennet, alarmed by Lizzy's impending marriage to Darcy. "I have given him my consent," he confesses to his daughter. "He is the kind of man, indeed, to whom I should never dare refuse any thing, which he condescended to ask."[2] What could this mean?

In one contemporary understanding, condescension was a virtue, the act of a great man who graciously lowers himself to deal with inferiors on a footing of equality. Consider the language of a constituent addressing a parliamentary representative: "We are all greatly obliged to you for the trouble you have taken in giving us your sentiments, and for the condescending deference you pay to the opinions of your Constituents, regarding a point about Parliaments."[3] Today this would be sarcastic. But where representatives tended to claim much more lofty independence, this language was sincere. The representative condescended by bringing himself down to the level of his

---

[1] John Payne Collier, *An Old Man's Diary, Forty Years Ago,* 4 vols. (London, 1871–1872), 1:36 [6 March 1832].

[2] *Pride and Prejudice* [1813], in *The Novels of Jane Austen,* ed. R. W. Chapman, 3d ed., 6 vols. (Oxford: Oxford University Press, 1987), 2:376.

[3] Gamaliel Lloyd to Sir G. Savile, 29 May 1780, in Christopher Wyvill, *Political Papers,* 6 vols. (York, 1794–1805), 3:259–60, italics removed.

constituents (or indeed lower, so that he can defer to them); they appreciated the opportunity to deal with him as an equal. So too, one of the Cheap Repository Tracts offered a colonel who "condescended to speak to Wells, as kindly as if he had been his equal," a cheerful vision of social hierarchy made palatable by the grace of the superior—published the same year as London's second crimping riot.⁴ Similarly, those writing to George III fell all over themselves applauding "the marks of condescending goodness from your Majesty that I have been honour'd with," "the very gratious and condescending manner in which your Majesty has often been pleased to recollect my father and to mention his name," "the condescension of your Majesty's personal and confidential kindness"⁵—and this is just a sampling from the summer of 1801. Fanny Burney was a condescension junkie, her happiest moments in the royal household spent luxuriating in its coils.⁶

George IV, a decidedly less attractive character than his father, even apart from the dismal episode with Caroline, elicited the same lavish thanks for his condescension. "Your Royal Highness has condescended in your letter to address me as *your friend*. I am penetrated with a due sense of your condescension and goodness," slobbered Dundas.⁷ More token piety, perhaps, another verbal form to be ob-

---

⁴ *The Two Soldiers* (London, 1795), p. 23.

⁵ Thomas Coutts to George III, 9 June 1801, *The Later Correspondence of George III*, ed. A. Aspinall, 5 vols. (Cambridge: Cambridge University Press, 1962–1970), 3:551; Earl of Malmesbury to George III, 16 June 1801, *Later Correspondence*, 3:555; Earl of Hardwicke to George III, 25 August 1801, *Later Correspondence*, 3:597.

⁶ For instance, *The Early Journals and Letters of Fanny Burney*, ed. Lars E. Troide and Stewart J. Cooke, 3 vols. to date (Oxford: Clarendon, 1988–), 1:231 [16 January 1773]; *Diary & Letters of Madame D'Arblay*, ed. Charlotte Barrett, with preface and notes by Austin Dobson, 6 vols. (London: Macmillan, 1904–1905), 2:457 [12 August 1786], 4:223 [13 January 1789], 4:441 [December 1790], 4:452 [April 1791], 4:477 [5 June 1791]; *The Journals and Letters of Fanny Burney (Madame D'Arblay)*, ed. Joyce Hemlow and others, 12 vols. (Oxford: Clarendon, 1972–1984), 4:18 [3 November 1797], 5:302 [4 May 1802], 8:218 [10–20 June 1815], 9:191 [24 August 1816], 9:217 [22 September 1816], 10:810 [9 March 1818], 11:58–59 [*circa* 27 February 1819], 11:70 [4 March 1819], 12:974–75 [2 April 1827]. But see too Burney, *Cecilia, or Memoirs of an Heiress* [1782], ed. Peter Sabor and Margaret Anne Doody (Oxford: Oxford University Press, 1988), p. 98.

⁷ Henry Dundas to Prince of Wales, 3 March 1795, *The Correspondence of George, Prince of Wales 1780–1812*, ed. A. Aspinall, 8 vols. (London: Cassell, 1963–1971), 3:39. See too Lieutenant-Colonel Gerard Lake to Prince of Wales, 23 January 1795, *Correspondence of George, Prince of Wales*, 1:44; Duke of Portland to Prince of Wales, 21 January 1793, *Correspondence of George, Prince of Wales*, 2:331; Earl of Moira to Prince of Wales,

served, not an expression of any underlying emotion. Once George
exacted his rightful share of deference, though, he could condescend
with the best of them. When he nominated a Mr. Garrow for a government post, Garrow dropped by Carleton House and left his card. This
gesture was an insufficiently polite acknowledgment, he was crisply
informed, so he dutifully returned in formal dress and thanked the
prince in person. "The Prince then said 'Now Mr. Garrow we are
friends, (meaning now we may talk with equality) but nothing that
properly belongs to my situation shall be given up by me.' " By contrast, George's brother, the Duke of Gloucester, was known for subjecting others "to a tedious attention to ceremonious personal respect
to him" and never permitting them to relax.[8]

Forced to choose between Prince of Wales and Duke of Gloucester,
then, one might well prefer the Prince of Wales. In either case,
though, inequality and deference are still in the background. Without them, there is no possibility of this sense of condescension. (In
one of the *Waverley Novels*, Scott imagines a sixteenth-century knight
incongruously dueling with someone beneath his status. The knight
proposes nicknames for himself and his opponent: Condescension
and Audacity.[9] In another story, Scott has King Richard condescend
by sucking the poison from the wound of a black slave.[10]) Yet that
explains why others found condescension irritating. Remember too
that the duke wouldn't permit Collier to call his actions condescending. That's a sign that condescension is not an unmitigated good. In a
biting sketch, Samuel Johnson summoned up the smoldering annoy-
ances of visiting Prospero, an old friend who had become rich. "The
best apartments were ostentatiously set open, that I might have a distant view of the magnificence which I was not permitted to approach;
and my old friend receiving me with all the insolence of condescen-

---

12 September 1808, *Correspondence of George, Prince of Wales*, 6:310; Richard Ryder to
Prince Regent, 13 February 1811, *Correspondence of George, Prince of Wales*, 7:232; Marquis Conyngham to George IV, 30 January 1820, *The Letters of King George IV 1812–1830*,
ed. A. Aspinall, 3 vols. (Cambridge: Cambridge University Press, 1938), 2:302–3;
George Canning to George IV, 11 April 1826, *Letters of George IV*, 3:144.

    8 *The Diary of Joseph Farington*, ed. Kenneth Garlick, Angus Macintyre, and Kathryn
Cave, 16 vols. (New Haven, CT: Published for the Paul Mellon Centre for Studies in
British Art by Yale University Press, 1978–1984), 10:3834–35 [25 December 1810].

    9 Walter Scott, *The Monastery* [1820], in *Waverley Novels*, 48 vols. (Edinburgh, 1829–
1833), 19:54–64.

    10 *The Talisman* [1825], *Waverley Novels*, 38:345–46.

sion at the top of the stairs, conducted me to a back room, where he told me he always breakfasted when he had not great company."[11] This is a manipulative condescension, designed to rub Johnson's nose in his own inferiority, to accentuate inequality while pretending to abandon it.

Yet even authentic condescension had its critics. In Elizabeth Inchbald's *Simple Story*, Rushbrook balks at the marriage that his doting uncle, Lord Elmwood, has arranged for him. (He happens to be in love with another woman.) He enlists Sandford to plead for a delay of a year or two. The lord is Rushbrook's only friend, Sandford assures him. This assurance baffles Elmwood:

> "Then why will he not submit to my advice; or himself give me some substantial reason why he cannot?"
> "Because there may be friendship without familiarity—and so it is between him and you."
> "That cannot be; for I have condescended to talk to him in the most familiar terms."
> "To condescend, my lord, is *not* to be familiar."
> "Then come, sir, let us be on an equal footing through you.—And now speak out *his* thoughts freely, and hear mine in return."[12]

The condescending man leaves behind his august status—but not entirely. The equality he creates remains partial, tentative, something like the as-if masquerade of Egan's coffeehouse. Even when he brings the lunch to the library, the duke is still a duke and there's still a tinge of icy distance. Collier noted that the duke wasn't the sort to let others toy with him: "If he thinks any persons presuming, and disposed to make too free, his noble nostrils dilate like those of a finely-bred racer, and he at once looks the fools down to their level."[13] So in the midst of their putative equality, Collier owes the duke a bit of gracious deference and he knows full well the consequences of with-

---

[11] *Rambler* (15 February 1752), no. 200, in *The Yale Edition of the Works of Samuel Johnson*, ed. Herman W. Liebert and others, in progress (New Haven, CT: Yale University Press, 1958–), 5:278–79.

[12] Elizabeth Inchbald, *A Simple Story* [1791], ed. J. M. S. Tompkins (Oxford: Oxford University Press, 1988), p. 317.

[13] Collier, *Diary*, 1:37 [6 March 1832]. See too Ann Radcliffe, *The Italian: or The Confessional of the Black Penitents* [1797], ed. Frederick Garber (Oxford: Oxford University Press, 1981), p. 114; *Memoirs of the Lady Hester Stanhope, as Related by Herself in Conversations with Her Physician*, 3 vols. (London, 1845), 2:38.

holding it. "Slave," growls Frankenstein's monster in a less decorous context, "I before reasoned with you, but you have proved yourself unworthy of my condescension. Remember that I have power; you believe yourself miserable, but I can make you so wretched that the light of day will be hateful to you. You are my creator, but I am your master;—obey!"[14]

Like pride, condescension depended on a background set of beliefs, in this case clustering around the claim that the condescending man is voluntarily lowering his status. If the servant of the duke's household comes in to serve Collier lunch, we can't make sense of the claim that he's condescending, even if he assures us that he shares the duke's feelings. Notice, though, that insofar as the background beliefs refer to status, they tie the emotion and practice of condescension to a particular social order. A society that doesn't articulate an account of status hierarchy can't give rise to this sense of condescension. This is why we now take condescension as a vice, a matter of being patronizing. The would-be great man who now tries to lower himself to the level of his interlocutor is met by the claim that the two of them were already equal, so it's insulting for him to pretend that he needs to lower himself in the first place. The background transformation in our commitment to equality doesn't merely turn the same emotion into a vice. It changes the emotion itself: for now the condescending must be haunted by the uneasy sense that they are repulsively arrogant snobs, not refreshingly unpretentious gentlemen.

The background beliefs that refer to contingent social practices immediately give the emotions a history. As the practices change, the emotions change with them. Indeed it seems possible for an emotion to wither and die if the practices required to support the beliefs change and aren't replaced by something reasonably close. Such referents also supply another way of grasping the politics of the emotions: if the legitimacy of those practices is contested, so too will be the emotions.

Return to Johnson's claim that Prospero treated him "with all the insolence of condescension." Why insolence? In 1712, the *Spectator* singled out insolence as "the Crime of all others which every Man is most apt to rail at" yet a surprisingly common one, cautioning readers

---

[14] Mary Shelley, *Frankenstein or The Modern Prometheus* [1818], ed. James Rieger (Chicago: University of Chicago Press, 1982), p. 165.

against men of wealth absorbed in "the Support of Pomp and Luxury" and indifferent to others' sufferings. "It is indeed the greatest Insolence imaginable, in a Creature who would feel the Extremes of Thirst and Hunger if he did not prevent his Appetites before they call upon him, to be so forgetful of the common Necessity of humane Nature as never to cast an Eye upon the Poor and Needy."[15] Chesterfield, whose fastidious sense of etiquette made him an invaluable ethnographer, noted scornfully in 1748 that "low people in good circumstances, fine clothes, and equipages, will insolently show contempt for all those who cannot afford as fine clothes, as good an equipage, and who have not (as their term is) as much money in their pockets. . . ."[16] Notice how the parenthesis assigns Chesterfield the upper hand: these vulgar people's coarse language reveals how shaky their claim to imposing status is.

Cobbett entertained and inflamed one laughing audience by rehearsing the tale of a magistrate who had lectured a drunken auditor of one of his previous lectures. "These seditious lectures ought to be put down by the parish authorities," had intoned the magistrate. "The insolence of this man is great enough," exploded Cobbett; "the *insolence*, that he should dare to speak thus of me—and, by-the-by, he called those who came here rabble." Reminding the audience of the magistrate's "thumping salary, paid out of our labour," that is from the state's tax coffers, Cobbett concluded with a flourish: "It is something beyond insolence; it is ingratitude, and audacity added to it."[17] Charles Greville bickered with Lady Holland. "She was insolent, so I was fierce, and then She was civil, as She usually is to those who won't be bullied by her."[18]

These passages stretch out over some twelve decades, but they offer a consistent view of insolence, one we've since lost. The insolent man makes more of his high status than he ought to; he's presumptuous. He swaggers or is oblivious to the underlings. In 1751, Chesterfield

[15] *Spectator* (6 February 1712), no. 294, in *The Spectator*, ed. Donald F. Bond, 5 vols. (Oxford: Clarendon, 1965), 3:47.

[16] Chesterfield to his son, 29 October OS 1748, *The Letters of Philip Dormer Stanhope, 4th Earl of Chesterfield*, ed. Bonamy Dobrée, 6 vols. (London: Eyre and Spottiswoode, 1932), 4:1246.

[17] William Cobbett, *Eleven Lectures on the French and Belgian Revolutions, and English Boroughmongering* (London, 1830), lec. 6, p. 1.

[18] *The Greville Memoirs 1814–1860*, ed. Lytton Strachey and Roger Fulford, 8 vols. (London: Macmillan, 1938), 2:392 [12 July 1833].

urged his son to be gentle with his servants, to "soften, as much as possible, the mortifying consciousness of inferiority": "If I bid my footman bring me a glass of wine in a rough, insulting manner, I should expect that in obeying me he would contrive to spill some of it upon me; and I am sure I should deserve it."[19] In 1816, An Englishman delivered the very same advice. "All I complain of is a degree of indelicate assumption . . . which frequently prevails in the manner of the master or mistress, and which makes those towards whom it is adopted painfully sensible of their dependence." No "harshness and superciliousness of manner" were permissible.[20] Neither passage mentions insolence by name, but that is centrally their target.

Making sense of insolence, like condescension, requires beliefs about status and hierarchy. The political controversies arise when we ask what sort of superiors are entitled to what sort of superiority, just when is it that they tiptoe across the apparently evanescent but extraordinarily powerful and intricate boundaries that define the perquisites of their social position, what counts as a transgression. Tickled by Robert Peel's manners, George IV would amuse himself by beckoning the great Tory. "Now, I shall call Peel over to me—watch him, as he comes—he can't even walk like a gentleman." The story made its way to incensed poet Thomas Moore, a political maverick but surely no sort of Tory, who roundly condemned George and his snickering associates. "These people, in their insolence, attribute this want of gentleman-like air in Peel to his birth. As if some of the highest among themselves had not the looks & minds of *waiters*—"[21] Who should be sneering here? Who should be ashamed? That depends on what finally counts as appropriately high. And maybe ambitious and accomplished Peel, with his family textile fortune in the background, is more meritorious than those making a joke of his gait. Maybe their august status masks base character. These are politically controversial matters. (So for that matter is Moore's passing swipe at waiters.) Arguments about what emotions George and Peel do and should experi-

19 Chesterfield to his son, March 1751, *Letters*, 4:1691.

20 An Englishman, *Brief Remarks on English Manners, and An Attempt to Account for Some of Our Most Striking Peculiarities* (London, 1816), pp. 94–95. See too *Porcupine's Gazette* (2 June 1797), in William Cobbett, *Porcupine's Works*, 12 vols. (London, 1801), 6:6.

21 *The Journal of Thomas Moore*, ed. Wilfred S. Dowden and others, 6 vols. (Newark: University of Delaware Press, 1983–1991), 3:1189–90 [18 February 1829].

ence in this endearing exchange are already arguments about the claims of royal and aristocratic status and the career open to talents.

Or again, Johnson remained a bitter opponent of equality: recall his arch suggestion that republican Catherine Macaulay invite her footman to join them for dinner. But only the superficial, he insisted, would succumb to thinking of high and low here in terms of social status.

> Contempt and admiration are equally incident to narrow minds: he whose comprehension can take in the whole subordination of mankind, and whose perspicacity can pierce to the real state of things through the thin veils of fortune or of fashion, will discover meanness in the highest stations, and dignity in the meanest; and find that no man can become venerable but by virtue, or contemptible but by wickedness.[22]

So Prospero's condescension is insolent: his putative superiority lies in his wealth, not virtue. For Johnson, that means his condescension is swaggering, transgressing the proper boundaries in such affairs.

Then again, Johnson was delighted—it "gratified his monarchical enthusiasm," as Boswell put it—when he was working in the queen's library and George III stopped by to chat. Absorbed in his studies, Johnson was jolted into awareness when the librarian nudged him. "His Majesty approached him, and at once was courteously easy." (Notice the fine-grained modulations that these actors have to master: with very little change in his demeanor, the king could have been flippantly easy or haughtily easy.) They talked for some minutes, the king asking about various authors and periodicals and praising Johnson. "During the whole of this interview, Johnson talked to his Majesty with profound respect, but still in his firm manly manner, with a sonorous voice, and never in that subdued tone which is commonly used at the levee and in the drawing-room." Afterwards he styled the king "the finest gentleman I have ever seen." Yet he also insisted, "it was not for me to bandy civilities with my Sovereign."[23] George's condescension is more appealing than Prospero's. Is it that as king of England, he's unequivocally high and so does Johnson a very great boon by being "courteously easy"? Or is it that his style reveals consid-

---

[22] *Idler* (26 June 1753) no. 67, in *Works of Johnson*, 2:386.

[23] *Boswell's Life of Johnson: Together with Boswell's Journal of a Tour to the Hebrides and Johnson's Diary of a Journey into North Wales*, ed. George Birkbeck Hill, rev. L. F. Powell, 6 vols. (Oxford: Clarendon, 1934–1950), 2:33–40 [February 1767].

erable personal virtue? To what extent is his fine gentility a matter of conventional status, to what extent a matter of his way of executing the role? Recall the woman who broke down sobbing while reminiscing on a celebration for George III: "Not so much for a being he was a King, but because they said as a was such a worthy Gentleman. . . ." Lovers of monarchy were never comfortable with a sharp distinction between person and office.

We could convict Johnson of some blatant inconsistencies by suggesting that his monarchical enthusiasm obscured his inexorable devotion to virtue. Better, though, to enlist the episode as a reminder that contemporaries could draw on competing accounts of high and low. So they could offer competing accounts of who could appropriately condescend and who was insolent. So, too, they could offer competing accounts of impudence. Sometimes *impudence* appears as an apparent synonym for *insolence:* I take Cobbett's sneer at "the impudent and insolent Rush"[24] as a bit of deliberate redundancy, hammering home its point with assonance. Usually, though, impudence is the vice of the saucy underling who doesn't offer an appropriately studied deference. Recall Shelley's blistering warning to his father's lawyer "to refrain from opening private letters, or impudence may draw down chastisement upon contemptibility." Or ponder one glowing portrait of the West Indies' interracial population:

> All Mongrels, male and female, have a vast share of pride and vanity, baseness and ingratitude in their compositions: their delicacy and ignorance being such, that they despise and degrade their parents and relations inclining to the sable race; the men, if born to estates or properties (as many are), are much of the same nature of the illiterate white Creole men; not much inferior, but of course more negrofied; and when they are not kept at a proper distance and under due subjection, are often very insolent and impudent.[25]

Far from innocent repetition, the closing words register the conflicting imperatives of class and race. As wealthy men lording it over others, the mongrels are insolent; as uppity colored men refusing to submit, they're impudent. This leaves them in an unhappy double

---

[24] *Rush-Light* (March 1800) no. 3, in *Porcupine's Works,* 11:340. See too *Political Register* (7 December 1833) 82(10):588.

[25] J. B. Moreton, *Manners and Customs in the West India Islands* (London, 1790), pp. 123–24.

bind, facing the demand that they simultaneously send whole-heartedly grovelling signals about race and reasonably proud signals about property.

Or contrast an exchange from Charlotte Smith's *Old Manor House* of 1793. Monimia is beautiful, virtuous, and helplessly in the clutches of her aunt, grouchy Mrs. Lennard, who is grooming her for domestic service. Mrs. Lennard is artfully playing a ticklish game, supervising the household of frail Mrs. Rayland, pleasing her mistress with duplicity while struggling to serve her own interests. Staying up late at night to share precious secret hours with her beloved Orlando, then tossing and turning in anxiety over his imminent departure, Monimia is increasingly bedraggled. Confronted with her appearance, she pleads that she is trying to learn to read. Mrs. Lennard is adamant:

> "I'd be glad to know what good your reading does you, but give you a
>     hankering after what you've no right to expect? An improved lady
>     will be above helping me, I suppose, very soon."
> "When I *am*, my dear aunt," answered Monimia, "it will be time enough
>     for you to forbid my reading; but, till then, pray don't be angry if I
>     endeavour to obtain a little common instruction."
> "Don't be impertinent," exclaimed Mrs. Lennard; "don't be insolent—
>     for if you are, Miss, this house is no place for you.—I see already
>     the blessed effects of your reading—you fancy yourself a person of
>     consequence: but I shall take care to put an end to it. . . ."[26]

When Smith has Mrs. Lennard brand Monimia impertinent and insolent, it isn't repetition. As lowly servant refusing to accept correction from her superior, Monimia is impertinent (or impudent). Then again, Monimia's new literacy makes her a social climber, like those Cockney linen drapers' assistants skewered in the *Age*. The dignity bequeathed by literacy gives her some claim to being "a person of consequence." Worse yet, Mrs. Lennard knows all too well that Monimia is virtuous and beautiful. Her own crankiness about status reveals her annoyed sense that there are realms in which Monimia towers

---

[26] Charlotte Smith, *The Old Manor House* [1793], ed. Anne Henry Ehrenpreis (Oxford: Oxford University Press, 1989), p. 177. See too Thomas Holcroft, *Knave; or Not? A Comedy* (London, 1798), p. 43, reprinted in *The Plays of Thomas Holcroft*, ed. Joseph Rosenblum, 2 vols. (New York: Garland, 1980); Walter Scott to Joanna Baillie, 4 April 1812, *The Letters of Sir Walter Scott*, ed. H. J. C. Grierson, 12 vols. (London: Constable & Co., 1932–1937), 3:99.

over her. So Monimia is also insolent. Her poise in the face of Mrs.
Lennard's attack betrays her unwillingness to give the duties of domestic service what Mrs. Lennard sees as their rightful due. It suggests
that she is willing to credit Mrs. Lennard only with the brute fact of
power, not with legitimate authority.

The impudent or impertinent servant was for centuries a stock figure in dramatic comedies, appealing both to the lower orders in the
pit, who rejoiced in his publicly scolding fine ladies and gentleman,
and to those fine ladies and gentlemen themselves, who ruefully recognized the tensions of their own domestic governance. Here's a
plodding example from Thomas Holcroft's *Love's Frailties*. Sir Gregory is fed up with his servant, James, and his facetious quips. "How
dare you, fellow, reptile, slave, comment on my actions?" he demands.

> SIR GREGORY. I'll dismiss you instantly—
>
> JAMES. So you have said a thousand times.
>
> SIR GREGORY. For your infernal impudence.
>
> JAMES. No; 'tis for that you keeps me. I shouldn't suit your honour if I
>     hadn't a bit o'brass.[27]

Yet even this tired old scenario could be invigorated. In *The Dreamer
Awake*, Jenny is Sir David Drowsy's new maid.

> *Enter* JENNY, *crossing the stage.*
>
> SIR DAVID. I think that's our new maid—yes—she's a fine girl really—
>     come, come hither, my dear!
>
> JENNY. Sir! Did you speak?
>
> SIR DAVID. Yes truly—but don't be abashed—step nearer to me.
>
> JENNY. He can do me no harm, so I'll even play the fool with him
>     [*aside*]. What's your pleasure, Sir. [*curtsies and comes forward.*]
>
> SIR DAVID. What's my pleasure? Why to kiss every pretty girl, like you,
>     my sweet one. [*Kisses her.*]
>
> JENNY. La, Sir! if you kiss every girl like me, you kiss very bad indeed!
>
> SIR DAVID. What an impudent baggage!

Drowsy tries to intimidate her, then says that he'll excuse her if she
will wait for him in a private room. In another sly aside, she tells the
audience she won't do it. He gives her a silver penny and kisses her

---

[27] Holcroft, *Love's Frailties: A Comedy* (London, 1794), p. 32, reprinted in *Plays*. See
too Richard John Raymond, *Cherry Bounce! A Farsetta, in One Act, as Performed for the First
Time on Monday, August 27th, 1821 at Sadler's Wells Theatre* (London, 1821), p. 11.

again.[28] This is the stuff of pedestrian farce, not anguished sermon, but its unflinching depiction of what we now think of as sexual harassment may well invite the contemporary audience to reflect on who's really being impudent.

Condescending duke, insolent Prospero, impudent mongrel: each demonstrates the intimate connections between emotion, social practice, and political controversy. None can get off the ground without a social grammar or code offering an account of high and low, and none of those accounts can escape political controversy. Insolence and impudence, once antonyms, have drifted into vague synonyms for rudeness. Why? Because our official commitments to democracy leave us hesitant in our ability to recover understandings of high and low.

For that matter, none of them can get off the ground without two parties. You need someone else to condescend to, to be insolent to, to be impudent to. (Or at least an imagined other.) There's a residual discomfort labelling them emotions in the first place, which might be explicated this way. Each refers centrally to the social interaction between the pair, not to any feelings either is experiencing. And each sometimes refers only to a relatively detached account of the action: one can condescend or be insolent or impudent without intending to, without noticing that one's actions might be interpreted that way. But when the duke brings Collier his lunch and at the same time prohibits him from calling that action condescending, when Collier is recording such pithy reflections on the episode, we have more than detached actions in play. We have specific emotions.

So consider an otherwise unremarkable Christian homily against the deadly sin of pride:

> Survey the man who is intoxicated by pride of birth. Forgetful that the long line of his ancestry may have been conspicuous rather for success than for desert, for talents than for virtue: forgetful that the glory of their success, the praise of their desert, was due not to themselves but to Him, from whom is every good and perfect gift: forgetful that the merit of ancestors assures not hereditary excellence to their descendent, but renders its absence more degrading: forgetful that the humblest of his menials, the most despised of the beggars whom he passes in the street,

[28] Edmund John Eyre, *The Dreamer Awake; or, Pugilist Matched: A Farce* (Shrewsbury, 1791), pp. 8–10. See too *The Child of Providence*, 4 vols. (London, 1792), 1:57.

claim a pedigree which terminates in Adam, may look back on paradise as the natal seat of their progenitors: he scorns the mass of his fellow-creatures as men of yesterday; and deems himself entitled to homage as though he were a being of a higher nature; a being who had condescended to step down from a superior orb, to receive for a time the respect and admiration of the inhabitants of this lower sphere.[29]

Framed by this homily is a telling snapshot of condescension, understood specifically as an emotional state. The intoxicated man isn't merely proud or arrogant or haughty. Imbued with a pleasing sense of his own superiority, of how generous he's being in dealing with the lowly mortals surrounding him, he's condescending. We immediately grasp the intoxicated man's facial expression, his bodily posture, and his mental states. He condescends to a generalized other, not any particular actor, but we know how his victims might look and hold themselves and feel, too.

I've been exploring how the emotions are dependent on background beliefs that in turn refer to social practices. Yet the expressive dimensions of political policies and practices provide another way of understanding the politics of the emotions. The *Edinburgh Review* protested the legal disabilities imposed on Catholics, "the process by which all such sweeping proscriptions extend as *insult,* much further than they actually reach as *injury,* begetting, on the one side, a general habit of insolence and contempt, and, on the other, a feeling of resentment and degradation. . . ."[30] One expert on colonial affairs remarked that the laws of St. Lucia prevented free "persons of colour"—the phrase refers to what we might style the "racially mixed" offspring of "black" and "white," in whatever "proportion" of "blood"—from wearing the same clothes as whites and prohibited referring to them in any legal document with the minimal honorific "Mr." or "Madam," however wealthy they were. "Thus every paper they were parties to bore proof of the contempt with which they were viewed; and it is scarcely conceivable how much ill blood this single unmeaning distinction—this wanton and paltry insult—

---

[29] Thomas Gisborne, *Sermons,* 5th and 6th ed., 2 vols. (London, 1809–1811), 2:134–35.

[30] *Edinburgh Review* (November 1810) 17(33):2. See too Earl of Moira to Prince Regent, 19 August 1811, *Correspondence of George, Prince of Wales,* 8:99.

engendered."[31] Here the link between policy and emotion is even tighter. The policy is itself an emotionally loaded message.

## NATURAL EQUALITY, SOCIAL HIERARCHY, AND EMOTIONAL INVESTMENT

We've already encountered Queen Charlotte's instruction to the Prince of Wales: "We are all equal," so he had better be considerate to his servants. Now we can see here yet another injunction against insolence. For all his devotion to courtly etiquette, Chesterfield agreed with Charlotte. "The lowest and the poorest people in the world, expect good breeding from a gentleman," he warned his godson, "and they have a right to it; for they are by nature your equals, and are no otherwise your inferiors than by their education and their fortune."[32]

It might seem surprising that conservatives took this line. But they had no choice: such a view was thrust on them by Christianity, by the time-honored view that all God's creatures are "of one clay."[33] Horsley, the bishop notorious for holding that the mass of subjects had nothing to do with the laws but obey them, weighed the sublime spectacle of judgment day, Christ judging one soul after another, all of humanity in attendance, "the whole angelic host," too. "As no elevation of rank will then give a title to respect, no obscurity of condition shall exclude the just from public honour, or screen the guilty from public shame." He kept flitting back to equality, a vision of repellent allure, his obsessively echoing language stressing the anomalies. "The rich and the poor will indeed strangely meet together; when all the inequalities of the present life shall disappear," God's perspective will be revealed. And God, it turns out, is something of a Jacobin. "The characters and actions of the greatest and the meanest have in truth been equally important, and equally public; while the

---

[31] John Jeremie, *Four Essays on Colonial Slavery* (London, 1831), p. 30.

[32] Chesterfield to his godson, 1762, *Letters,* 6:2411. See too the maxims enclosed in a letter of 15 January 1753, *Letters,* 5:2000; Chesterfield to his godson, 1768, *Letters,* 6:2838; "Speech on Mr. Fox's East India Bill" [1 December 1783], in *The Works of the Right Honorable Edmund Burke,* 9th ed., 12 vols. (Boston: Little, Brown, 1889), 2:439; "Speech in Opening the Impeachment of Warren Hastings" [15 February 1788], in *Works,* 9:455–56.

[33] Mary Ann Hanway, *Ellinor; or, The World as It Is,* 4 vols. (London, 1798; reprint ed. New York: Garland, 1974), 2:50.

eye of the omniscient God hath been equally upon them all,—while all are at last equally brought to answer to their common Judge, and the angels stand around spectators, equally interested in the dooms of all."[34] Ironically, the day's democrats were flirting with atheism, while conservatives were resolute in their Christianity, a tradition saddling them with some uncomfortable views about equality.

The social distance between God and man dwarfed that between king and subject. Still, God could be inserted into the same emotional economy I've been exploring. For one deeply pious preacher, "the great Shepherd's condescending care" was cause for rapturous gratitude and submission.[35] Think of how much further Christ had to stoop than did the Duke of Devonshire. A dourly acerbic divine acknowledged "the Power in whose eye pyramids, palaces, and the worms whose toil has formed them, and the worms who toil out their existence under their shadow or their pressure, are perhaps all alike contemptible," God's colossal distance making everything on earth insignificant.[36]

Anyway, the stock conservative wisdom is that even though we're naturally equal, hierarchy is crucial for maintaining social order. No doubt the view is logically coherent (an easy enough standard to meet), but it raises a puzzle. If people are naturally equal and if we're not trying to conceal that behind the veil of secrecy, how successfully can they carry off the routines of deference and hierarchy? Why won't their role-playing always be ironic, detached, not fully sincere or committed? And if their role playing isn't sincere, won't the social drama of inequality collapse?

Take Dr. Johnson's views on sexual infidelity, a classic statement of the double standard. No sensible wife, in his view, would much mind her husband having sex with others. The real crime centers on uncertainty about who has fathered the family's children, and that, thought Johnson, requires only the sexual fidelity of wives. (But why not the fidelity of men from outside the household?) So adultery had to be an extraordinary crime for married women. "I asked him," reports

---

[34] Samuel Horsley, *Sermons*, 2 vols. (New York, 1811), 1:31.

[35] *Some Account of the Life and Religious Labours of Sarah Grubb* (Dublin, 1792), p. 198 [March 1790]. See too An Englishman, *A Rejoinder to Mr. Paine's Pamphlet, Entitled, Rights of Man* (London, 1791), pp. 47–49.

[36] Charles Maturin, *Melmoth the Wanderer* [1820], ed. Douglas Grant (Oxford: Oxford University Press, 1989), p. 30.

Boswell, "if it was not hard that one deviation from chastity should so absolutely ruin a woman." "Why, no, Sir," parried Johnson; "the great principle which every woman is taught is to keep her legs together. When she has given up that principle, she has given up every notion of female honour and virtue, which are all included in chastity."[37] (Boswell later found himself squirming when a married woman suggested that this rationale would leave her free to "intrigue" when she was pregnant.[38]) Boswell also asked Johnson if it would be permissible to legitimate children born outside wedlock by marrying after the fact. "I think it a bad thing," declared Johnson, "because the chastity of women being of the utmost importance, as all property depends upon it, they who forfeit it should not have any possibility of being restored to good character. . . ."[39]

Distinguish accepting a norm from being emotionally invested in it.[40] Accepting a norm, say, means believing that it's right and ordinarily being willing to act on it. Being emotionally invested in it means also caring about it, registering appropriate pleasures when it's observed, resentments when it's violated. It's one thing to accept the norm that adultery is wrong for women, to shrug and concede that it's all terribly unfortunate but insist nonetheless that fallen women be excluded from polite society. It's another thing to be emotionally invested in it, even to be passionately committed to it, to have a visceral reaction of rage or loathing when a fallen woman has the audacity to persevere in the quest for social acceptance. One would expect that a community emotionally invested in the norm will do a better job enforcing it—and sustaining it over time. One would expect that a community merely accepting the norm is already on the road to winking at violations, perhaps eventually suspending or abolishing the norm itself. Recall John Bowles's lament for the loss of "that con-

[37] *Boswell in Search of a Wife 1766–1769,* ed. Frank Brady and Frederick A. Pottle (New York: McGraw-Hill, 1956), pp. 155–56 [28 March 1768].

[38] *Boswell: The Ominous Years 1774–1776,* ed. Charles Ryskamp and Frederick A. Pottle (New York: McGraw-Hill, 1963), p. 320 [5 April 1776].

[39] *Life of Johnson,* 2:457 [22 March 1776]. A more forgiving line was taken by Jane West, *Letters to a Young Lady,* 3d ed., 3 vols. (London, 1806), 2:310–11; *Biographical Memoirs of Eminent Novelists* [1825], in *The Prose Works of Sir Walter Scott, Bart.,* 28 vols. (Edinburgh, 1834–1836), 3:457.

[40] Contrast the distinction between accepting a norm and being in its grip in Allan Gibbard, *Wise Choices, Apt Feelings: A Theory of Normative Judgment* (Cambridge, MA: Harvard University Press, 1990), pp. 68–75.

servative pride of character" that once marked women. Flabbergasted
at the "astonishing condescensions" of virtuous women willing to mingle with those "not clothed in the fair robe of unsullied reputation,"
Bowles wondered if female modesty and chastity were to be
discarded.[41]

The puzzle, then, is whether a belief in natural equality makes it
hard to be emotionally invested in norms of social hierarchy. If it
does, can social hierarchy endure? (Maybe the slow but steady march
of Jacobin orthodoxies is to be understood in precisely this way: Christian commitments to equality undercut the time-honored wisdom
about God's good order. This would be a case—not the first, not the
last—of a political theory imploding, not yielding to critical attack
from outside.) If it doesn't, why not? (Maybe our equality in God's
eyes makes it easier to accept everyday social inequality, for rich and
poor alike. The rich salve their guilty consciences; the poor console
themselves with parables about camels and needles' eyes.)

Benjamin Robert Haydon, the painter, echoed the injunction
against insolence to servants. "Cruel is he who uses a servant ill or
stretches his authority to a wanton pitch, or takes advantage of the
slavery of their minds to degrade them into greater dependence."
Unlike Chesterfield and Charlotte, though, he fretted over their very
existence. "There is something in the Fate of Servants that always
makes me melancholy. Born to a lower station, destined to have their
views narrowed to the will of others," dining "on coldish meat &
colder potatoes," they spent their lives running and jumping at the
beck and call of others. "Why should a set of human creatures start up
when another knocks?"

Haydon imagined that the servants were oblivious to these matters.
"They see us daily take our wine & eat our tarts, and yet their minds
are so influenced as to act under the impression that such things are
not for them."[42] If there's reassuring false consciousness here, surely
it's on Haydon's part, not his servants'. Common parlance bequeathed the title of *catch fart* on the footboy, "so called from such
servants commonly following close behind their master or mis-

---

[41] John Bowles, *Reflections at the Conclusion of the War* (London, 1800), in *Political Writings of the 1790s,* ed. Gregory Claeys, 8 vols. (London: William Pickering, 1995), 8:404.

[42] *The Diary of Benjamin Robert Haydon,* ed. Willard Bissell Pope, 5 vols. (Cambridge, MA: Harvard University Press, 1960–1963), 2:223–24 [11 April 1819].

tress."[43] The language, not the very model of decorous submission, forcibly suggests that servants weren't austerely self-denying in thinking about hierarchy. So do the reports of more trenchant observers of the social scene. In agony, Hazlitt cast the domestic household as the setting of frightful turmoil, with servants dishing out an unrelenting diet of unabashed hostility and cunning deception, not loving benevolence or dutiful service. "Any real kindness or condescension only sets them the more against you," he brooded. "They feel themselves like a degraded *caste,* and cannot understand how the obligations can be all on one side, and the advantages all on the other."[44] In either account, the clear-sighted, whoever they are, cannot reconcile natural equality and social inequality.

In either account, emotions loom large. For all his droning on about property rights and political obligation, moral responsiblity and causal determinism, Godwin was shrewd enough to seize on the emotions as a crucial lever for social and political transformation.

> In England at the present day there are few poor men who do not console themselves, by the freedom of their animadversions upon their superiors. The new-fangled gentleman is by no means secure against having his tranquillity disturbed by their surly and pointed sarcasms. This propensity might easily be encouraged, and made conducive to the most salutary purposes. Every man might, as was the case in certain countries upon record, be inspired with the consciousness of citizenship, and be made to feel himself an active and efficient member of the great whole. The poor man would then perceive, that, if eclipsed, he could not be trampled upon; and he would no longer be stung with the furies of envy, resentment, and despair.[45]

Despairing subjects could become dignified citizens just by poking fun at gentlemen. For all its gravity, for all its aura of natural necessity, hierarchy was enchantingly fragile. A series of pinpricks administered

[43] Pierce Egan, *Grose's Classical Dictionary of the Vulgar Tongue, Revised and Corrected* (London, 1823), s.v. *catch fart.*

[44] *Table-Talk* [1822], in *The Complete Works of William Hazlitt,* ed. P. P. Howe, 21 vols. (London: J. M. Dent and Sons, 1930), 8:308. The anxiety effect is also in play: contrast Swift's amused awareness of insubordinate misbehavior in *Directions to Servants* [1745], in *The Prose Works of Jonathan Swift,* ed. Herbert Davis, 14 vols. (Oxford: Basil Blackwell, 1939–1968), 13:1–65.

[45] William Godwin, *Enquiry Concerning Political Justice and Its Influence on Morals and Happiness,* ed. F. E. L. Priestley, 3 vols. (Toronto: University of Toronto Press, 1946), 3:141 [1793]. Godwin dropped this passage from the tamer edition of 1798.

with adolescent glee would deflate it. Or so Godwin seems to suggest here. Call it the Tinkerbell effect: if we don't believe in it, it stops existing.

Godwin might have been cribbing from Paine's assault on aristocratic titles: "If a whole country is disposed to hold them in contempt, all their value is gone, and none will own them. It is common opinion only that makes them any thing or nothing, or worse than nothing."[46] It's easy to overstate the political promise of such campaigns, or, in our own jargon, to think that if hierarchy is socially constructed, it isn't real. Citizenship may be crucially caught up with sentiments of dignity and independence, but it's also caught up in social practices and for that matter legal doctrines enforced by the state, which can't be changed just by shrugging and sneering. Aristocratic titles may be caught up with haughty pride and fawning and scraping, but they too entitle their holders to specific legal rights backed by the state. Then again, it's also easy to underplay the political promise of such campaigns. Embolden the despairing poor, make insecure the gentlemen, and neither may remain emotionally invested in the norms defining their roles. That may be helpful, even crucial, to those who want those roles to crumble.

Tweaking the notion of emotional investment supplies yet another gloss on the politics of the emotions. Sometimes the emotions neither depend on nor reinforce social hierarchy. Sometimes they help create or even constitute that hierarchy. The world of emotional display is also a world of strategic maneuvering for power and ascendancy. Ann Radcliffe's *Mysteries of Udolpho,* perhaps the greatest of the Gothic novels, supplies a nice example. Desperately helpless Emily (need I add that she is beautiful and virtuous?) is in remote and corrupt Italy; worse, in the clutches of implacably cold Montoni, the evil genius presiding over the household. (But not yet the worst, in what will become one of literature's stereotypical dark foreboding castles, Udolpho, full of mysterious corridors, shadowy figures, maybe even dead bodies.) Montoni is eager to marry her off to Count Morano, whom she finds nauseating, and misunderstands (or pretends to misunderstand) a note she has written as indicating her resignation to her fate. Meeting to his amazement with yet another stern rejection,

---

[46] *Rights of Man* [1791], in *The Life and Works of Thomas Paine,* 10 vols. (New Rochelle, NY: Thomas Paine National Historical Association, 1925), 6:93.

Morano indignantly announces that he will hold Montoni accountable for an explanation.

"From me, sir! you shall have it;" muttered Montoni, "if your discern-
ment is indeed so far obscured by passion, as to make explanation necessary. And for you, Madam, you should learn, that a man of honour is not
to be trifled with, though you may, perhaps, with impunity, treat a *boy*
like a puppet."

This sarcasm roused the pride of Morano, and the resentment which
he had felt at the indifference of Emily, being lost in indignation of the
insolence of Montoni, he determined to mortify him, by defending her.

"This also," said he, replying to Montoni's last words, "this also, shall
not pass unnoticed. I bid you learn, sir, that you have a stronger enemy
than a woman to contend with: I will protect Signora St. Aubert from
your threatened resentment. You have misled me, and would revenge
your disappointed views upon the innocent."

"Misled you!" retorted Montoni with quickness, "is my conduct—my
word"—then pausing, while he seemed endeavouring to restrain the
resentment, that flashed in his eyes, in the next moment he added, in a
subdued voice, "Count Morano, this is a language, a sort of conduct to
which I am not accustomed: it is the conduct of a passionate boy—as
such, I pass it over in contempt."

"In contempt, Signor?"

"The respect I owe myself," rejoined Montoni, "requires, that I should
converse more largely with you upon some points of the subject in dispute. Return with me to Venice, and I will condescend to convince you
of your error."

"Condescend, sir! but I will not condescend to be so conversed with."

Montoni smiled contemptuously. . . .[47]

The two are sizing one another up, circling and feinting, jostling for
the upper hand. It is not merely a contest of will, though Montoni's
grim self-assurance ought not be underestimated. The two must
reckon with Morano's title, norms of gallantry toward women, norms
of honor and integrity among gentlemen, norms of debate, all part of
a social context that they have to take as more or less given but that
they can also navigate within—and use. (So the episode is a home-

[47] Ann Radcliffe, *The Mysteries of Udolpho* [1794], ed. Bonamy Dobrée (Oxford: Oxford University Press, 1991), p. 201.

spun example of what social theorists label the dialectic of structure
and agency.) Montoni's insolence, condescension, and contempt
don't depend on the already fixed judgment that Morano is an inferior. Instead they help make Morano an inferior.

## SERVANTS, CHILDREN, AND DEFERENCE

"Throw from you the doctrine of equality, as you would the poisoned
chalice." William Cobbett rattled off rhetorical questions cataloguing
equality's pernicious effects. Among them: "Would you teach servants
to be disobedient to their masters, and children to their parents?" So
Cobbett warned repeatedly.[48] If order requires hierarchy, it requires
willing deference. Only underlings emotionally invested in norms of
hierarchy and deference will reliably perform their allotted parts. No
point smattering a touch of insouciant irony over the proceedings.
That, again, would be a sign of the rot setting in. So William Holland
noted "a serious Rumpus among the Servants. That tribe of beings
are much altered of late years, no subordination among them. The
Glorious Effects of the French Revolution."[49] Although it's couched
as a claim about genuine change, this is best understood as an example of the anxiety effect. The English had complained forever that
their servants weren't deferential enough, but the stakes seemed
higher after 1789.

Masters, we've seen, weren't supposed to be insolent; servants
weren't supposed to be impudent. One servant lost her job after leaving the back door open for the chimney sweep and then being saucy
about it.[50] Betty, on the saucy side herself in *The Old Manor House*,
tries to soothe an apprehensive Monimia, fearing one of Mrs. Lennard's tongue-lashings after being late. "As for a few angry words, I've
no notion of minding 'em, not I: 'tis hard indeed if one's to be always
a slave, and never dares to stir ever so little;—one might as well be a
negur."[51] Then, too, there were cases too grand and horrible to qual-

[48] Cobbett, *The Bloody Buoy, Thrown Out as a Warning to the Political Pilots of All Nations*, 3d ed. (London, 1797), pp. 147–48, reprinted in *Porcupine's Works*, 3:171 [1796];
Cobbett, *Democratic Principles Illustrated*, pt. 2, 5th ed. (Dublin, 1798), p. 14.

[49] *Paupers and Pig Killers: The Diary of William Holland, a Somerset Parson 1799–1818*,
ed. Jack Ayres (Gloucester: Alan Sutton, 1984), p. 91 [5 October 1803].

[50] *Mary Hardy's Diary*, intro. B. Cozens-Hardy (Norfolk: Norfolk Record Society,
1968), p. 95 [2 May 1797].

[51] *Old Manor House*, p. 82.

ify as mere impudence or insubordination. One fifteen-year-old servant murdered the family's infant: "Her mistress called her a slut, and she resolved to spite her."[52]

One rival to the permutations of insolence and impudence was supplied by easygoing, frank equality. English servants, reported Mary and Percy Shelley, tended to lapse from familiarity into impudence. French servants, though, were as unruffled and polite as "the most well-bred English; they treat you unaffectedly as their equal, and consequently there is no scope for insolence." (Is *insolence* here a synonym for *impudence*, so that the servants can't be saucy in their inferiority? But why then wouldn't their stance of equality be the worst impudence of all? Or, as I suspect, is the point that since the French servants already have adopted a stance of equality, there's no incentive for their masters to be brusque and abusive?) Cultures clashed when "haughty English ladies," "greatly disgusted with this consequence of republican institutions," scolded their Genevan servants. The servants, not used to such abusive treatment, complained bitterly.[53]

Equality isn't the only alternative to insolence and impudence. Instead, domestic service might revolve around affable authority and courteous deference. "Servants are, in general, ignorant and cunning," declared none other than Mary Wollstonecraft. "The same methods we use with children may be adopted with regard to them": it was crucial to be consistent in enforcing rules, to be firm, not to be angry. "We cannot make our servants wise or good, but we may teach them to be decent and orderly; and order leads to some degree of morality."[54] In his pensive recollections of Wollstonecraft, Godwin remarked, "to her servants there never was a mistress more considerate or more kind."[55] There is no contradiction here. Wollstonecraft was firm, exercising a judicious authority and disciplining the wayward. That's just what it means to be considerate and kind.

[52] *Hertfordshire 1731–1800 as Recorded in the Gentleman's Magazine*, ed. Arthur Jones (Hatfield: Hertfordshire Publications, 1993), p. 143 [20 June 1800].

[53] Mary Wollstonecraft Shelley and Percy Bysshe Shelley, *History of a Six Week's Tour* (London, 1817; reprint ed. Oxford: Woodstock Books, 1989), pp. 9, 103.

[54] *Thoughts on the Education of Daughters* [1787], in *The Works of Mary Wollstonecraft*, ed. Janet Todd and Marilyn Butler, assistant ed. Emma Rees-Mogg, 7 vols. (London: William Pickering, 1989), 4:38–39.

[55] William Godwin, *Memoirs of the Author of a Vindication of the Rights of Woman* (London, 1798), p. 43.

Servants, after all, were festering sewers of pollution. Reflecting on the crucial matter of earning parents' trust, one governess of a girls' school boasted that all her teachers were from "respectable families." Better yet, the students were forbidden from communicating directly with the servants: "All necessary orders were given to them by myself and the teachers." That way, the girls' morals remained pure. Yes, once a student picked up some coarse language from a servant "unworthy of confidence." But it was outrageous to suggest that her students exchanged sexual *double-entendres*.[56] Wollstonecraft too, eager to "prevent their acquiring nasty, or immodest habits," warned that "many girls have learned very nasty tricks, from ignorant servants"; better, then, not to mix them together.[57] We might wonder why masturbation or lesbianism is thought to be the province of the lower orders. The answer, presumably, is that it's because they are the lower orders, never disciplined enough, their very sexuality summoning up the specter of a decimated order.

Coleridge assaulted "the indifference of the Clergy in general to the manifest depravity of the lower orders": thousands of servant girls tramped the streets of London "without characters," that is with sexual availability. Once, he imagined forlornly, the household was a loving family unit, the servants diligently steeping themselves in moral and religious principles, "the Inequalities of Society not only mitigated and made a light and easy Yoke for the inferior classes but actually transmitted into a golden Chain of Unity, elevating a people into a true Community. . . ." Now all that was left was the impersonal cash nexus of an arm's-length contractual relationship.[58] Accepting that same ugly cash mortified poor Fanny Burney, eager to see herself as a loved dependent of the royal household. She gratefully reported that the man paying her was "as awkward and embarrassed how to present me my salary as I felt myself in receiving it," that nice as it might be to have and spend money, "I can never take possession of it without a secret feeling of something like a degradation. . . . it made me feel so like—what I am, in short—a servant!"[59] Adoring conde-

---

[56] Frances Broadhurst, *A Word in Favor of Female Schools*, in *Pamphleteer* (1827) 27(54):464.

[57] *Vindication of the Rights of Woman* [1792], in *Works of Wollstonecraft*, 5:197.

[58] *The Notebooks of Samuel Taylor Coleridge*, ed. Kathleen Coburn, in progress (New York: Pantheon Books, 1957–), 4:5059 30.91 [1823–1824].

[59] *Diary & Letters of Madame D'Arblay*, 3:142–43 [December 1786]. For the custom of servants collecting tips in the early 1790s, see *Recollections of the Life of John Binns: Twenty-*

scension, she was in no position to seize on whatever intimations of equality and independence surrounded wage labor.

Others embraced the sorts of emotional warmth that depended on inequality. Here's Claire Clairmont, mother of Allegra, writing imploringly to the child's father, Byron:

> I have observed one thing in you which I like; it is this. Let a person depend on you, let them be utterly weak and defenceless, having no protector but yourself and you infallibly grow fond of that person. How kind & gentle you are to Children! How good-tempered & considerate towards your Servants; how accommodating even to your dogs! And all this because you are sole master & lord; because there is no disputing your power you become merciful & just: but let any one more on a par with your self enter the room you begin to suspect & be cautious & are consequently very often cruel.[60]

Clairmont would learn an agonizing lesson about relying on such regal warmth: Byron would hurl her into an abyss of agony by depositing Allegra in a convent without asking her permission.

So the nature and scope of a master's authority over his servants was contested; that makes it fall squarely within my gloss on politics. Yet the contest is already a contest about the range of emotions appropriate to both master and servant, about the pitfalls of insolence and impudence, the charms and dangers of casual Genevan equality, the dignity and degradation of the cash nexus.

So, too, with parents and children. Godwin wanted the parents of adult children to bow to the claims of equality. "There is no more unequivocal exhibition of imbecility, than the behaviour of a parent who, in his son now become a citizen at large, cannot forget the child; and who exercises, or attempts to exercise, an unseemly authority over him." Better, he thought, to confide in children, to treat them as friends, to respect them, even to defer to them.[61] (Needled during these years by his mother on his apparent lack of religious faith, Godwin dashed off a typically officious letter instructing her that he was

---

*Nine Years in Europe and Fifty-Three in the United States* (Philadelphia, 1854), pp. 37–38.

[60] Claire Clairmont to Byron, 12 January 1818, *The Clairmont Correspondence: Letters of Claire Clairmont, Charles Clairmont, and Fanny Imlay Godwin*, ed. Marion Kingston Stocking, 2 vols. (Baltimore, MD: Johns Hopkins University Press, 1995), 1:109.

[61] William Godwin, *The Enquirer: Reflections on Education, Manners, and Literature* (London, 1797), p. 118.

satisfied with his own position.[62] Fifteen years later, a more rueful Godwin contemplated his tangled relationship with daughter Mary, who would run off with Shelley a couple of years later. "There can never be a perfect equality between father & child," he conceded. Fathers were prone to command "in a way somewhat sententious & authoritative"; children wouldn't confide in them, but would treat them with "awe & restraint."[63]) David Ricardo lectured his father-in-law, urging him to relinquish his older, fierce style of parenting, that of "an eastern monarch ruling over abject slaves."[64] Byron was eager to escape from "maternal bondage," sick of his mother's upbraiding him with the alleged vices of his father's family. "Am I to call this woman mother? Because by natures law she has authority over me, am I to be trampled upon in this manner? Am I to be goaded with insult, loaded with obloquy, and suffer my feelings to be outraged on the most trivial occasions?" He owed her respect, he conceded, but not reverence or affection.[65]

But one critic of newfangled educational ideas denounced such dangerous sentiments. "Do not suppose that *any* situation or period of life exempts us from the reverence that is due to our parents." God, she reminded her readers, had adopted the name of Father. Yet families "in this revolutionary age" were scrambling to topple the laws of nature and God. Parents were deferring to children, mothers more attentive to teenaged daughters than to husbands. The emotional harvest of such monstrous husbandry revealed the political errors: "Caprice, discontent, and a restlessness of disposition" awaited these spoiled children.[66] Here again, a dispute about the legitimacy of pa-

---

[62] William Godwin to Ann Godwin, undated, Abinger Mss., reel 15, in the midst of a series of letters from her to him.

[63] Godwin to W. T. Baxter, 8 June 1812, in *Shelley and His Circle 1773–1822*, ed. Kenneth Neill Cameron and Donald H. Reiman, 8 vols. (Cambridge, MA: Harvard University Press, 1961–1986), 3:101.

[64] Ricardo to Edward Wilkinson, 12 September 1803, *The Works and Correspondence of David Ricardo*, ed. Piero Sraffa with M. H. Dobb, 11 vols. (Cambridge: Cambridge University Press for the Royal Economic Society, 1951–1973), 10:120.

[65] Byron to Augusta Byron, 18 August 1805, *Byron's Letters and Journals*, ed. Leslie A. Marchand, 13 vols. (London: John Murray, 1973–1994), 1:76; Byron to Augusta Byron, 11 November 1804, *Byron's Letters and Journals*, 1:55–56; Byron to Augusta Byron, 23 April 1805, *Byron's Letters and Journals*, 1:66.

[66] Mary Cockle, *Important Studies for the Female Sex, in Reference to Modern Manners; Addressed to a Young Lady of Distinction* (London, 1809), pp. 27, 54–55.

rental authority is already a dispute about the range of emotions appropriate to parents and children alike.

Unruly servants and unruly children needed a stiff dose of deference and submission. So did plenty of other subjects, their time-honored insubordination raising new anxieties after the French Revolution. John Skinner, the pompous and hot-tempered Somerset rector, constantly faced such insubordination. In 1821, he threatened to fire his clerk, who'd neglected to return the church key. The clerk was unmoved by this threat, even nonchalant. "He replied, he did not care if I did so, that it was no great matter to him; that I had dismissed him once before and might do so again if I chose," and he denied that Skinner had ever instructed him to return the key.

> I told him the reason I had dismissed him before was for being impudent, and that his tongue would get him into the same mischief it then did. He replied he was flesh and blood as well as myself, and if I spoke to him he should answer me. I said I perceived he was of the Radical School, and he might see whether that School would profit him. I would not permit that kind of insubordination as long as I had any authority.

But Skinner didn't fire him. The next day, the clerk obstinately repeated his claim that he hadn't been told to return the key and Skinner chose to take it as a valid excuse. He consoled himself with anguish: "It is not merely in the microcosm of this Parish that the lower orders are striving to supplant their superiors, the whole Kingdom is exactly in the same situation," he wrote, gloomily anticipating civil war breaking out in the next few years.[67]

The next year, another of his servants failed to monitor the tithing. Skinner, worried that he wasn't receiving his fair share, reproved him. Didn't he remember how Skinner had tended to him on his sickbed? Whom did he expect to tend to him next time he was stricken? "Instead of being recalled to any grateful recollection by this apostrophe he replied, many a parson might groan in hell, which was still worse."[68] Discipline and affection alike were wasted on such stony soil. This time Skinner did fire the servant.

[67] John Skinner, *Journal of a Somerset Rector 1803–1834*, ed. Howard and Peter Coombs (Bath: Kingsmead, 1971), pp. 172 [17 September 1821], 173 [18 September 1821].

[68] Skinner, *Journal*, p. 191 [11 June 1822].

Edgy again about tithing two years later, Skinner headed out to the fields and found himself face-to-face with Samuel Day. Day, a Catholic, couldn't have been too happy about tithing in the first place. Skinner objected to the work done so far. The cocks, receptacles for the barley being separated, weren't fully separated, so he wasn't getting his fair share. "I then said that I knew not what Mr. Day's religion taught him, but mine instructed me to do unto others what I should expect them to do unto me, and that Mr. Day, if he were in my place, would not wish his tithe to be set out in this manner." Skinner ordered the carter to stop hauling and tithing: he wanted his servants to come and serve as witnesses that the division was unfair. "You go and tithe it, never mind what that fellow says!" Day ordered. Faced with conflicting imperatives, the carter deferred—to Day.

Watching his authority crumble before his eyes, Skinner complained—appealed?—to Day, urging that still the cocks were too close together. Day denied it. "The air of the man was in the extreme menacing; he put his face quite up to mine, shaking his head." Plunging ahead, Skinner accused him of lying.

> He said he was not so much a liar as myself. I was scarcely able to restrain myself from striking him. However, I did not, and stepped aside, saying, if I were his equal I should very well know what to do with him, but it was beneath me to take notice of such a mongrel. He asked me what I meant by mongrel, I replied a low-bred fellow who would insult his superiors, knowing he could do so with impunity, but he would not do so to his equals, for they would probably chastise him. He said he did not know what I meant by low bred and his equals; that his father and mother were honest people and as good as mine, and as for himself he was in every respect my equal.

The two exchanged increasingly heated words. Along the way, Skinner impeached Catholicism as "a religion of tricks." Day, "endeavouring by words and actions to irritate me to the utmost of his power," thrust himself close to Skinner. "Scoundrel," seethed Skinner; "rascal," fired back Day. Beside himself, ignoring the golden rule and Christian charity, dismissing the unequivocal demands of his position as rector, forgetting that he was in his early fifties, Skinner slammed Day twice in the face, leaving him with a bloody nose. "This is what I have been wishing for," crowed Day, summoning the carter as witness.

Realizing that Day intended to launch legal proceedings against him, Skinner indulged in some bravado: he would show, he announced, that he'd been provoked and Day had gotten no more than he deserved.[69] Day promptly indicted him for assault; vacillating as ever, Skinner decided not to contest the action.[70] The jury found against him and levelled damages of £50. "My name went forth to the world with all these malicious stigmas hanging to it," mourned Skinner. "I am tied hands and feet, and placed in a pillory to be pelted at," hapless victim of a world turned upside down, of deference shattered and impudence on the roam.[71]

Making sense of Skinner's emotions partly demands coming to terms with his idiosyncratic personality. Not all rectors were subject to such indignities. But it also demands coming to terms with his social context and its political controversies. The uneasy position of an Anglican rector compelling a Catholic to grant him tithes isn't available to anyone with Skinner's irascible temper. Similarly, Day's ability to claim that he is "in every respect" Skinner's equal—and not to sound hopelessly eccentric or insane in doing so—summons up the 1790s' debates on equality. So the links between social and political life and the "inner" mental life are very tight. We have, in short, another reading of the slogan that the personal is political.

## CONTEMPT: SOME PRELIMINARY CONSIDERATIONS

I want now to start zeroing in on the emotion that will occupy us for some time, contempt. Just as the *Spectator* singled out insolence as an especially hideous vice, Henry Fielding singled out contempt. "There is not in Human Nature a more odious Disposition, than a Proneness to Contempt." No good man would permit himself the sensation. Nor could anyone rest secure in the belief that he was superior, holding others in contempt but immune to being held in contempt himself. "Contempt is, generally at least, mutual, and . . . there is scarce any one Man who despises another without being at the same Time despised by him," evidence of reciprocity among knaves.[72] ("Nothing is

---

[69] Skinner, *Journal*, pp. 272–74 [18 September 1824].
[70] Skinner, *Journal*, p. 275 [19 September 1824].
[71] Skinner, *Journal*, p. 283 [7 April 1825].
[72] *Covent-Garden Journal* (29 August 1752) no. 61, in Henry Fielding, *The Covent-Garden Journal and A Plan of the Universal Register Office*, ed. Bertrand A. Goldgar (Mid-

so contagious as contempt!" Fanny Burney's Cecilia would hold, decades later.[73])

That reciprocity might suggest that contempt is an amorphous hostility, freely available to any and all comers. That's surely one way to interpret talk of despising, the same concept the 1797 *Encyclopedia Britannica* invoked to define *contempt*.[74] Crucially, though, contempt requires some background scheme of high and low, the sort supplied by schemes of social hierarchy. Contempt is what the high may feel toward the low; it's simply unavailable to the low. Or, better, to the low insofar as they're low. Again, though, there are competing accounts of status hierarchy. Prospero is rich but morally shabby, Monimia poor but beautiful and virtuous. So Fielding's mischievous parade of examples of reciprocal contempt hangs on the ability of the putative underling to substitute a status hierarchy in which he's on top.[75]

More helpful, the *Encyclopedia Britannica* painstakingly described the facial expression of the contemptuous man.

> In contempt and derision, the upper lip is raised at one side and exposes the teeth, while the other side of the lip moves a little and wears the appearance of a smile. The nostril on the elevated side of the lip shrivels up, and the corner of the mouth falls down. The eye on the same side is almost shut, while the other is open as usual; but the pupils of both are depressed, as when one looks down from a height.[76]

Here the contemptuous man sneers. He radiates hostility, to be sure, but he's also bitterly amused by the lowly object of his contempt. Those eyes that glare down are beautifully expressive of his judgment of the other's inferior status.

---

dletown, CT: Wesleyan University Press, 1988), pp. 328, 330. This essay was reprinted in *The Gleaner: A Series of Periodical Essays,* ed. Nathan Drake, 4 vols. (London, 1811), 2:233–40. Note too the strictures against contempt in *Bristol Job Nott* (20 September 1832) no. 41, p. 164.

[73] Burney, *Cecilia,* p. 557.

[74] *Encyclopedia Britannica,* 3d ed., 18 vols. (Edinburgh, 1797), 5:380 s.v. *contempt.*

[75] I'd offer the same analysis of the cases examined in William Ian Miller, "Upward Contempt," *Political Theory* (August 1995) 23(3):476–99. But upward contempt might still be distinctive because the would-be superior knows that he's been cast as the inferior.

[76] *Encyclopedia Britannica,* 10:517 s.v. *man.* See too the depiction of scorn in *Encyclopedia,* 14:15 s.v. *passions, in painting.*

The *OED*'s first instance of *contempt*, already summoning up the judgment that something is vile or of little worth, is from 1393.[77] That judgment remains central in the history of the concept, including one picturesque example which the *OED* doesn't mention. "Boys do now cry 'Kiss my Parliament' instead of 'Kiss my arse,' so great and general a contempt is the Rump come to among all men, good and bad," recorded Pepys in 1660.[78] Pepys was referring to the Rump Parliament, so dubbed after Cromwell disbanded the House of Lords and Colonel Pride purged insufficiently zealous members from the Commons. That this clever play on words indicates contempt for the Parliament displays again the central role of a politically controversial judgment in making sense of an emotion. This Parliament is low, base, undignified, unworthy of respect. Like Shakespeare's Bottom, it inherits all the disreputable and buffoonish aspects of its namesake, so even bad men can hold themselves superior to it.

Like condescension, insolence, and impudence, then, contempt centrally requires an account of high and low; like them, too, it often takes that account from the conventions of social status and hierarchy. Boswell's brother David held Glasgow in contempt because it was "filled with a set of unmannerly, low-bred, narrow-minded wretches"; a shame, because it was "really pretty"; perhaps the city could be rescued by drowning its occupants.[79] Slaves ought to be emancipated gradually, urged one sensitive soul, moved not by Burkean skepticism about innovation but by the appeal of dismantling a pernicious emotional economy. "In this way would be gradually abolished all that contempt, and insolence of conduct in superiors to inferiors, which the mind of man can never digest—and with it would cease the hatred and malice of inferiors which are its necessary consequences."[80]

And like condescension, insolence, and impudence, contempt mirrors controversies about schemes of social status. Carlile's *Republican* scornfully published a loyalist diatribe from a True Briton.

---

[77] *OED* s.v. *contempt.*

[78] *The Diary of Samuel Pepys*, ed. Robert Latham and William Matthews, 11 vols. (London: G. Bell and Sons; Bell & Hyman, 1970–1983), 1:45 [7 February 1660].

[79] David Boswell to James Boswell, 30 October 1767, *Boswell in Search of a Wife*, p. 99.

[80] James Anderson, *Observations on Slavery; Particularly with a View to Its Effects on the British Colonies, in the West-Indies* (Manchester, 1789), p. 19.

We insert the following precious *morceau*, to show the writhings of one of corruption's tools, or some member of the Vice Society. We can only add that we hope the writer will see it in print, that he may learn what is our contempt for him and his own impotence. If we might judge by the handwriting, we should say the writer was some official reptile that lives on the public plunder.[81]

That reptile's handwriting was presumably neatly rounded, elegant, not full of the crabbed misspellings that saturated many workers' painful efforts at handwritten prose. As the reptile presumably sees it, his elegant handwriting is a sign of high status. As the *Republican* sees it, Britain's status hierarchy inverts a scale of moral worth. Those with wretched handwriting, even the illiterate, are exploited saints. So too Bentham proudly inverted the conventional status hierarchy: "Never is the day labourer, never is the helpless pauper, an object of contempt to me: I can not say the same thing of the purse-proud aristocrat: I can not say the same thing of the ancestry-proud aristocrat: I can not say the same thing of the official bloodsucker: I can not say the same thing of the man covered with the tokens of factitious honor: least of all can I say the same of a King."[82]

The centrality of hierarchy suggests a crude distinction between anger and contempt. One is angry at a rough equal, not a patent inferior. ("But you can be angry with a small child, with a pet, with the stone that makes you stumble!" Yes, but notice how easy it is to rein in your anger by reminding yourself of the status of its object.) Imagine being betrayed by a friend, a colleague, a beloved family member. You are bitter, sad, angry. But then you reflect on what sort of person could have done you such a debilitating injury. If you revise her status downward ("only a worm could have done that"), your anger will fade into contempt.[83]

---

[81] *Republican* (29 September 1820) 4(5):161.

[82] "Jeremy Bentham to Greek Legislators" [1823], in Jeremy Bentham, *Securities against Misrule and Other Constitutional Writings for Tripoli and Greece*, ed. Philip Schofield (Oxford: Clarendon, 1990), p. 194. See too Bentham, *Official Aptitude Maximized; Expense Minimized* [1830], ed. Philip Schofield (Oxford: Clarendon, 1993), p. 234; *A Manual of Political Economy*, in *The Works of Jeremy Bentham*, ed. John Bowring, 11 vols. (Edinburgh, 1843), 3:73. But contrast "Miscellaneous Fragments" [1774–1776?], in Bentham, *A Comment on the Commentaries and A Fragment on Government*, ed. J. H. Burns and H. L. A. Hart (London: Athlone Press, 1977), pp. 316–17.

[83] Note *Life of Dryden* [1821], in *Prose Works of Sir Walter Scott*, 1:164.

The centrality of hierarchy also suggests a bifurcation between nasty and amiable forms of contempt. Usually, we think of despising the lowly objects of contempt. Sometimes, though, we patronize them; we look after their interests, or anyway we flatter ourselves that we are doing so, steadily maintaining that they are after all contemptibly low. "To be the object of pity is a situation very humiliating," thought Boswell. Pity might be akin to love. Still, "there is no doubt at the same time such an inferiority in being pitied as is not consistent with dignity of character. *Poor man—I am sorry for him—I pity him*—are lessening expressions, and *pitiful* is as much a contemptuous as it is a lamentable epithet."[84] So *contempt* is doing double duty, referring both to the dismissive lowering of status and to the hostility that might but need not ensue.

This amiable version of contempt illuminates the political alliance between working-class radicals and paternalistic Tories, on fine display in the struggle for limiting the working day to ten hours. It also explains the friction in such alliances. The impatience of workers eager to be recognized as dignified and independent agents, not charges forever in need of benevolent care, collides with the betrayed sense of their would-be sponsors that their charges are ungrateful.

Finally, the centrality of hierarchy suggests a link between contempt and indifference. The underling is pathetically weak, so contempt can take the form of airily dismissing him. Think of the haughty aristocrat confronted with an ardent complaint from a silly clown, to use the apt locution of Tudor England. He might first be tickled at the clown's audacity, but then he quickly tires of the spectacle, waves the man away, and turns his back. This is a display of contempt, but it is emotionally quite cold. Hobbes's gloss on contempt nicely captures its frigid indifference: "Those things which we neither Desire, nor Hate, we are said to *Contemne:* CONTEMPT being nothing else but an immobility, or contumacy of the Heart, in resisting the action of certain things," incidentally making it tricky for Hobbes to distinguish contempt from death.[85] For some, this syndrome of stolid inertia arises in confronting someone or something beneath contempt. In 1730, Jonathan Swift permitted himself some savage irony:

[84] James Boswell, *The Hypochondriack*, ed. Margery Bailey, 2 vols. (Stanford, CA: Stanford University Press, 1928), 1:325 [February 1780].

[85] Thomas Hobbes, *Leviathan* [1651], ed. C. B. Macpherson (Harmondsworth: Penguin, 1984), p. 120.

"I do not despise All Squires," he reported blithely. "It is true I despise the bulk of them. But, pray take notice, that a Squire must have some merit before I shall honor him with my contempt. For, I do not despise a Fly, a Maggot, or a Mite."[86] Stubbornly virtuous Mr. Tyrold of Burney's *Camilla* gently chides his abjectly miserable daughter Eugenia, who has finally realized that her disfiguring smallpox invites raucous derision. "Wretches who in such a light can view outward deficiencies cannot merit a thought, are below even contempt, and ought not to be disdained, but forgotten."[87] Being beneath contempt here isn't an intensifier, a way of underlining just how contemptible those deriding a smallpox victim are. Instead the point is that they are so very low that even contempt would be wasted on them.

But if one is more anxious about the underlings, if they aren't obviously weak, they can't be written off safely with an airy dismissal and a turned back. The scheme of social status requires that they be meek and deferential, that should they forget themselves in a moment of impudence, a firmly disapproving look of contempt will bring them quickly to heel; but astonishingly, perversely, unsettlingly, the putative underlings don't relent. Here, I conjecture, contempt becomes more heated, closer to venomous fury. As the question of the underlings' inferiority becomes pressingly open, the boundary between contempt and anger becomes fluid. Coupled with what I've styled the anxiety effect, the conjecture explains why so much contempt after the French Revolution is so very heated. Fifteen-year-old Princess Charlotte, ill-fated daughter of George and Caroline, explained that no cold dismissal would do for her loathsome sub-governess. "*Contempt* is not *sufficient* for her, for I now *dislike* & I am *disgusted* with her. . . ."[88]

So far we have *amiable* and *nasty* contempt, *contempt* and *beneath contempt*, and *hot* and *cold* contempt. Closely associated is a further distinction. Sometimes we single out the objects of contempt for our studied attention; sometimes we make them socially invisible. When it comes to contemptuous dismissal in democratic debate, for instance, sometimes we single out others' comments for derisive attention. But

[86] Jonathan Swift to Robert Percival, 3 January 1730, *The Correspondence of Jonathan Swift*, ed. Harold Williams, 5 vols. (Oxford: Clarendon, 1963–1965), 3:368.

[87] Fanny Burney, *Camilla, or A Picture of Youth* [1796], ed. Edward A. Bloom and Lillian D. Bloom (Oxford: Oxford University Press, 1983), p. 302.

[88] Princess Charlotte to Mercer Elphinstone, 23 October 1811, *Letters of the Princess Charlotte 1811–1817*, ed. A. Aspinall (London: Home and van Thal, 1949), p. 11.

sometimes we simply ignore what they say. So too with the detestable figures of low status: we can draw attention to their contemptible features, even their contemptible selves, or we can breeze by them.

I will be dwelling in morbidly loving detail on those singled out for contemptuous attention. Here let me briefly note the everyday business of compulsively noticing who's Jewish. "On our arrival at Venice," noted one diarist, "Mr. Ellis was dangerously ill of a putrid fever. He recovered by the care of a Jew doctor."[89] Why note that he was a Jew doctor? (Or, as we would say, a Jewish doctor: not that he was a doctor in the business of curing Jews.) Or another diarist: "This morning I went immediately after breakfast to a Jew dentist, C——, who put in a natural tooth in the place of one I swallowed yesterday."[90] Why a Jew dentist? Why not any of the indefinitely many other characteristics of the dentist which could have been singled out for attention? (Perhaps because the dentist assured him that the tooth came from the battlefield of Waterloo and was far preferable to an artificial tooth, and Jews had a reputation for being unscrupulous.) Nothing said so far establishes that there's anything contemptuous in this attention. Perhaps the diarists are congratulating themselves on their great good fortune. Perhaps the doctor and dentist themselves made much of their Judaism. Perhaps not. One Jew complained of "the extreme publicity that is at all times given to crimes committed by Jews." Why, he asked, weren't other suspects identified as Protestants or Catholics or Baptists, as French or Dutch or Italian?[91] Indeed, *John Bull*'s police reports routinely identified criminal suspects as Jews.[92]

Consider, too, the flap over Burke's comment that the king of Great Britain "holds his crown in contempt of the choice of the Revolution Society," much as those Jacobin scoundrels would like to organize an electoral college, and that his successors would hold their crowns "with the same contempt."[93] Was Burke—or Burke's king—

[89] *The Journal of Elizabeth Lady Holland*, ed. Earl of Ilchester, 2 vols. (London: Longmans, Green, and Co., 1908), 1:15 [2 August 1792].

[90] *Diary, Reminiscences, and Correspondence of Henry Crabb Robinson*, ed. Thomas Sadler, 2 vols. (Boston, 1869), 1:327 [9 January 1816].

[91] Barnard Van Oven, *An Appeal to the British Nation on Behalf of the Jews* (London, 1830), pp. 46–47.

[92] For instance, *John Bull* (11 March 1821) no. 13, p. 103; (28 October 1821) no. 46, p. 363; (17 November 1822) no. 101, p. 803; (14 November 1824) 4(46):371; (16 November 1828) 8(414):366; (6 September 1829) 9(456):283.

[93] Burke, *Reflections on the Revolution in France* [1790], in *Works*, 3:250–51.

simply ignoring subjects or drawing contemptuous attention to them? Paine mockingly quoted the claim, inviting his readers to see the perverse lengths to which Burke had been driven by the radicals' measured presentation of common sense. "Government with insolence is despotism; but when contempt is added, it becomes worse. . . ."[94] Kings who ruled in contempt of their subjects: what more vicious and absurd fantasy could one imagine? An Oxford Graduate responded to Paine's lampoon.

> The idea of defiance and disdain is not always conveyed under the words, *in contempt*, they often intimate no more, than a right in one, not liable to the controul of another; and which may be exercised independent of all. Was not such the right of our Sovereign, his kingdom would cease to be hereditary. Used in a softened, and qualified sense, the words are properly, and with justice, applied by Mr. B.[95]

As a reading of the legal implications of Burke's doctrine, this seems eminently fair. But it isn't a knockout blow against Paine. For still we might wonder how a king gaining his throne with no regard for the views of his subjects might come to view them or how attentive he might be to their interests.[96] We might wonder what emotional investments the pageantry of monarchy requires: fretting about the casual stance of William IV, Lord Eldon wrote, "I hear the condescensions of the K. are beginning to make him unpopular. In that station, such familiarity must produce the destruction of respect."[97] For that matter, we might wonder whether hereditary monarchy itself expresses contempt for subjects. Then again, conservatives might wonder whether the caustic ridicule of Paine and his allies posed a lethal threat to the English government. "All authority, in a great degree, exists in opinion: royal authority most of all," warned Burke. "The supreme majesty of a monarch cannot be allied with contempt."[98]

---

[94] *Rights of Man* [1792], in *Works of Paine*, 6:163–66.

[95] An Oxford Graduate, *A Rod in Brine, or A Tickler for Tom Paine* (Canterbury, 1792), p. 60. Note too *Letters to Thomas Paine; in Answer to His Late Publication on The Rights of Man: Shewing His Errors on That Subject; and Proving the Fallacy of His Principles as Applied to the Government of This Country* (London, 1791), pp. 77–80.

[96] Consider Jeremy Bentham, *First Principles Preparatory to Constitutional Code* [1822], ed. Philip Schofield (Oxford: Clarendon, 1989), pp. 165–71.

[97] Lord Eldon to Lord Stowell, Michaelmas day 1830, in Horace Twiss, *The Public and Private Life of Lord Chancellor Eldon, with Selections from His Correspondence*, 3 vols. (London, 1844), 3:117.

[98] *Letters on a Regicide Peace* [1796–1797], in *Works*, 6:55.

Bentham derided all such reverence for king and Parliament, which he saw as part of the apparatus of repression. "Was it in a mad house that this theory was hatched, or in a den of thieves: a question not unapt for a debating club, were it not that under and by virtue of it all debating clubs, all meetings that can produce discussion on topics the most interesting to human happiness, are silenced."[99]

We might wonder, too, whether there are any structural affinities between political theories and contempt. Conservatism, after all, provides a robust account of high and low in its image of social order as a unified hierarchy. Contempt is perennially available for those installed toward the top of that hierarchy as they look down on their inferiors—and not merely available, but required, if emotional investment is required to keep norms and practices in place. Democrats, though, disavow talk of high and low in the name of equality. Democrats assail cringing and cowering, posturing and pretentiousness; they applaud the simple dignity of the world of citizens. "It is beyond all controversy," insisted Godwin, "that men who live in a state of equality, or that approaches equality, will be frank, ingenuous and intrepid in their carriage; while those who inhabit where a great disparity of ranks has prevailed, will be distinguished by coldness, irresoluteness, timidity and caution"—not to mention condescension, insolence, impudence, and contempt.[100] Here's an inference to tempt anyone with complacent democratic sentiments: conservatives are committed to contempt for subjects, that is for ordinary men and women, while democrats are committed to human dignity.

The inference is too hasty. As we've seen, Johnson insisted as strenuously as anyone that "order cannot be had but by subordination." As we've also seen, he reserved contempt for the vicious, holding that virtuous subjects were dignified, even venerable. Or consider Mrs. West, whose conservative credentials can't be questioned. She too offered a paean to natural equality: "The soul of the mistress is not more *intrinsically* valuable, than that of her handmaiden, in the eyes of God; her nature is not less corrupted, nor is her ultimate destination more exalted. Each has her appointed station in the great drama of life, and each is accountable for her conduct in discharging her

---

[99] Bentham, *First Principles*, p. 276.

[100] Godwin, *Enquiry Concerning Political Justice*, 1:49 [1798]; see too 2:119 [1798]. Also see William Cobbett, *Cottage Economy*, new ed. (London, 1826), §144.

relative functions."[101] So conservatives can appeal to a formally egalitarian standard, that of competently acquitting oneself in one's role. Such a standard might allow an illiterate hairdresser to look down on a polished lord, provided that the hairdresser admirably performed his duties and the lord bobbled his. More important, it would preclude the thought that those consigned to the bottom of the status hierarchy are automatically contemptible.

Nor can democrats claim a happy immunity from contempt. For one thing, meritocracy and equal opportunity seem applicable not just to jobs and the splendid things in life, but to the allocation of nasty things, too. Democrats might want, indeed might need, an account of fairly earned contempt. Take the individual who flouts the minimal rules defining membership in his community: the scientist who cynically peddles junk science as an expert witness in the courtroom, say, or the professor who plagiarizes a paper or harasses his students. Perhaps these individuals seem as contemptible for Johnson and West as for any patrons of the career open to talents. For another, then, consider a line of argument worked up most pointedly by Carl Schmitt.[102] For democratic equality to amount to anything, it can't be extended universally. One can't qualify as a citizen, a full member of the community, unless one is surrounded by subjects or metics or aliens or other inferiors. Otherwise, the thought is, the contrasts necessary to give membership shape and meaning can't get off the ground. I don't say—in fact, I don't believe—that this analysis is right. But it's premature to say that it's wrong: recall Cobbett's effort to secure the status of workers thrown on the tender mercies of the parish by mocking fat and greasy Negroes. And if it is right, we face an apparent paradox: democrats seem to be committed to contempt because of their commitment to equality.

In diving into the pestilent swamp of materials on contempt, we'll find conservatives and democrats alike seething with contempt, condemning contempt, bemused by contempt. That's not to say that contempt has no political significance, not even that it doesn't have deeply structural connections to both conservatism and democracy. It's just to offer a caution against the perils of glib and moralistic generalizations. So the exploration will also require suspending our

---

[101] West, *Letters to a Young Lady,* 3:214.

[102] Carl Schmitt, *The Crisis of Parliamentary Democracy,* 2d ed. [1926], trans. Ellen Kennedy (Cambridge, MA: MIT Press, 1988), pp. 9–13.

tendency rapidly to dismiss the astonishingly nasty things people say and do to each other. We need to devote ourselves to contempt with the same care that we usually devote to political obligation, property rights, and other such grand topics in political theory.

If conservatives and democrats alike traffic in contempt, we can administer a gentle pinprick to one of the more fatuous complacencies haunting political theory: I mean laments for the collapse of community. The empirical credentials of the stale script of our decline and fall from some prior state of grace and unity are bankrupt, since it's child's play to show that the good old days weren't what we now imagine them to be. Then, too, community is thriving in the modern world. It just happens not to take the inspiring form of devotion to virtue and republican self-government. It takes the sordid form of visceral contempt, weirdly uniting political adversaries. Call it unholy community. Here's just one specimen: the *Age*, aggressively impolite and conservative, reported on "NEWS FOR NIGGERS"; *Tait's Edinburgh Magazine*, exuberantly unconventional and radical, reported on "HONOUR AMONG THE NIGGERS!"[103] And if we are willing, as we should be, to conceive community as leaving plenty of room for conflict, we can note that this unholy community sweeps up the objects of contempt, too. It charts the magnificent terrain on which they're forced to play. (Or the terrain as seen by the men of polite society, revealingly called *the world*. It's a disturbingly open question to what extent the objects of contempt saw the terrain the same way.) The stakes are dizzyingly high: so this is deep play, implicating the social status and very selves of the players, even if it's not particularly enjoyable.

[103] *Age* (19 September 1830), p. 299; *Tait's Edinburgh Magazine* (December 1833) 4(21):377–78.

# SIX

# A GUIDE TO THE MENAGERIE:
# WOMEN AND WORKERS

—⧈—

COBBETT LIKED TO fume about "those who have now the insolence to call the mass of the People of England the '*Lower Orders.*'"[1] He preferred to identify that mass as workers and adamantly refused to refer to them as "the poor," the definite article suggesting that they were "a distinct race of beings," as one might refer to "the sheep, the pigs, the fowls, the moles, and the worms. I, on behalf of the labourers, reject this appellation with scorn," the name itself enabling a dismissive contempt for the despondent plight of the workers Cobbett prized.[2]

But there were other ways of identifying the lower orders. Perhaps they were subjects, not citizens. Or take Coleridge: "With the exception of the Jews on the Stock-exchange & their compeers, the lower classes are demoralized by low wages. . . ."[3] Despite the invocation of class, the lower orders here aren't defined in economic terms, for those wealthy Jews are unequivocally in their ranks. (Contemporaries tended to use *class, rank,* and *order,* in singular and plural forms, interchangeably.[4])

Whoever they were, the lower orders could serve as objects of contempt. Whoever they were, the upper orders could be accused of inso-

---

[1] *Political Register* (6 December 1817) 32(35):1092–93.

[2] *Political Register* (22 December 1832) 78(12):728.

[3] Coleridge to Daniel Stuart, 12 October 1827, *Collected Letters of Samuel Taylor Coleridge,* ed. Earl Leslie Griggs, 6 vols. (Oxford: Clarendon, 1956–1971), 6:704.

[4] For instance, Helen Maria Williams, *Julia, A Novel,* 2 vols. (London, 1790), 1:172; William Playfair, *An Inquiry into the Permanent Causes of the Decline and Fall of Powerful and Wealthy Nations* (London, 1805), pp. 218–19; *The Diary of Benjamin Robert Haydon,* ed. Willard Bissell Pope, 5 vols. (Cambridge, MA: Harvard University Press, 1960), 2:250–51 [4 December 1819]; Robert Southey, *History of the Peninsular War,* 3 vols. (London, 1823–1832), 2:263; *Westminster Review* (October 1827) 8(16):330–31.

lence in their treatment of the lower orders. Provisionally, then, we could invert these observations and say that whoever served as an object of contempt could constitute the lower orders and whoever got away with expressing contempt could constitute the upper orders. Here I want to launch a reconstruction of contemporary views about women, workers, blacks, and Jews. Not merely to show that all of them were held in contempt—no surprise there, and we have less complacent things to do than point accusing fingers at the dead—but to investigate contempt itself. Other groups might be chosen: the Irish, for instance, came in for their fair share of abuse; the gypsies remained a "degraded and despised people."[5] But enough is enough— a book ought not to resemble a toxic waste dump—and these four groups will suffice. Anyway I want to resist one shibboleth of identity politics, the view that there's some special honor in being singled out for study as a pariah.

## Sex and Gender

"Is the effeminate Man, or the Masculine Woman the more contemptible character?" So enquired one London debating society in 1780.[6] Innocent or offensive, the question has some knotty presuppositions worth untangling. It seems to depend on a distinction between sex and gender. Suppose, roughly, that we take sex as a category of biology, what distinguishes male and female members of the human species. And suppose, again roughly, that we take gender as a category of culture or society or politics, what counts as appropriately masculine and feminine behavior. So put, gender is logically parasitic on sex: males are supposed to be masculine, females feminine. (Could we live without gender? or are we stuck with bickering about its content?) But it doesn't always work out that way, which provided the debating society the occasion for their weighty discussion.

The distinction opens two pressing but independent questions. First is a causal question: do the facts of sex explain the rules of gen-

---

[5] James Crabb, *The Gipsies' Advocate; or Observations on the Origin, Character, Manners, and Habits, of the English Gipsies*, 3d ed. (London, 1832), p. 28. But for "the wonderful physical perfection" of the "extraordinary race" of gypsies, see William Hone, *The Table Book*, 2 vols. (London, 1827–1828; reprint ed. Detroit: Gale Research Co., 1966), 1:210.

[6] *London Debating Societies, 1776–1799*, comp. Donna T. Andrew (Great Britain: London Record Society, 1994), pp. 86–87 [5 April 1780].

der? (If for instance women are supposed to be submissive, did that arise because they are on average physically weaker?) Second is a justificatory question: does sex provide good reasons for gender? (So what if women are weaker: why should they be submissive?)

Still, the distinction might be thought unwelcome or useless from at least two points of view. If the goal is to maintain familiar gender norms, to resist innovation, then it might be helpful to keep both questions obscured. Or, less manipulatively, if sex massively explains and justifies gender, there's no point in opening the distinction in the first place. A more recent challenge focuses on our ability to get our hands on the facts of sex in the first place. The political stakes in our grasp of human bodies—for that matter in the bodies themselves—are huge. Nor, in some accounts, is it possible to sweep aside those stakes: not because we're in the clutches of ideology, but because the scientific categories are indeterminate and our interpretations will always invest them with political content.[7]

Talk of the facts of biology is ambiguous. It might mean our collection of statements about life, the body of knowledge appearing in textbooks. Or it might mean the actual state of affairs in the world, whatever that is, the way chromosomes and whatever else really work. If we take *sex* in the first sense, it may well be that we can never give a plausible account of sex not already caught up in gender. The second sense might seem to supply firmer footing. Yet the second sense invites a classic skepticism about our grasp of things in themselves. Or, in less Kantian and more pragmatist terms, it invites reminders about the world well lost.[8] In this context, we might construe those reminders as a caution against taking sex as somehow more real than gender. Social construction isn't the opposite of reality. It's one way in which things become perfectly real.But back to the debating society's

[7] On (what we might style in a palpably gendered way) gender penetrating sex, see for instance Denise Riley, *"Am I That Name?": Feminism and the Category of "Women" in History* (Minneapolis: University of Minnesota Press, 1988), chap. 5; Judith Butler, *Gender Trouble: Feminism and the Subversion of Identity* (New York: Routledge, 1990); Thomas Laqueur, *Making Sex: Body and Gender from the Greeks to Freud* (Cambridge, MA: Harvard University Press, 1990); Londa Schiebinger, "Why Mammals Are Called Mammals: Gender Politics in Eighteenth-Century Natural History," *American Historical Review* (April 1993) 98(2):382–411. More generally, see the dazzling account of Donna Haraway, *Primate Visions: Gender, Race, and Nature in the World of Modern Science* (New York: Routledge, 1989). For a helpful recent discussion, see Linda Nicholson, "Interpreting Gender," *Signs* (Autumn 1994) 20(1):79–105.

[8] To borrow a phrase from Richard Rorty, *Consequences of Pragmatism: Essays, 1972–1980* (Minneapolis: University of Minnesota Press, 1982), chap. 1.

question. Maybe it has no knotty presuppositions at all ("It's just a question!"); maybe theorists just like cluttering the terrain with their own fabrications. Still, contemporaries frequently seem to have had something suspiciously like this distinction between sex and gender in mind. Let's turn, then, to discussions that tilt *woman* in the direction of sex, not gender. Obsessed with Malthusian worries about excess population, contemporaries sometimes saw women as lethally fecund reproducers threatening social order. So the Isle of Wight's workhouse dealt severely with single women bearing second illegitimate children. They were hauled before the justice of the peace; in the workhouse, they were denied meat and forced to "wear coarse yellow coats or gowns, or other disgraceful distinctions," as the authorities saw fit.[9] Carlile didn't only offer advice on birth control. He also insisted that the best equality would be sexual equality and protested vigorously against "treating women as the mere breeding machines for the human race, and men as the directing lords of the aggregate machinery."[10] Malthus himself indicted the "silly and unjust ridicule" directed at old maids, proposing that they be applauded as heroines.[11]

Or consider Wordsworth, whose famed appreciation of nature reached its emphatic limit at a social gathering of the illustrious. Caroline was there, but that's not what riveted Wordsworth's attention. One woman, he informed his wife, was graced with "a tolerable face and features, but in her native bosom so huge and tremendous, that had you seen her enter a room in that condition I am sure the soul of modest womanhood in you would have shrunk almost as with horror." The bigger the breasts, the more womanly the woman—but so much so that this woman appears to Wordsworth as a loathsome caricature, one of the "many most disgusting objects" at the gathering. His own wife—here sex is creeping insensibly into gender—is enabled to be a properly modest woman because she isn't cursed with such repellent but fascinating giant breasts. Wordsworth must have been staring. "Her Breasts were like two great hay-cocks or rather hay stacks, protruding themselves upon the Spectator, and yet no body

[9] Frederic Morton Eden, *The State of the Poor,* 3 vols. (London, 1797; reprint ed. Bristol: Thoemmes Press, 1994), 2:236.

[10] *Lion* (4 April 1828) 1(14):425.

[11] *Principles of Political Economy* [1826], in *The Works of Thomas Robert Malthus,* ed. E. A. Wrigley and David Souden, 8 vols. (London: William Pickering, 1986), 3:498. For a more conventional defense of old maids, see the contribution of An Old Maid to *The Indicator* (21 February 1821) no. 72, pp. 154–56.

seemed to notice them—"[12] That is, presumably, that the others present didn't find her breasts all that interesting or at least they were managing to be minimally civil about it. But they too might have thought that something profound about being a woman was on display.

Or consider: women are vulnerable to rape. (Is this a physiological fact about women? or a reflection on social practices?) Ann Radcliffe capitalized on the fact to generate dramatic tension.[13] A comic playwright, by contrast, made it fuel odd bantering.[14] John Skinner returned home to discover "one of my female servants much indisposed in consequence of a brutal assault made on her by Mr. Stephens's gardener during my absence. . . ." Skinner didn't expect Stephens to do anything about it, "knowing his own sentiments on this head." So he decided he would have to pursue it himself, chalking up the episode as "a little drawback to my satisfaction" in his recent trip.[15] The cavalier attitude—Skinner's every bit as much as Stephens's— qualifies as contempt, surely, even if it's not so emotionally heated as was Benjamin Robert Haydon on being told that Byron's wife had refused to have sex with him. "If I had been Byron, I would have smacked her bum first, and prostrated her by force!—at any rate a man can't be hung for a rape on his wife. . . . I always hated her before, & now I hate her 50 times more."[16]

I turn to issues more tempting to describe in terms of gender. The ever pedantic John Bennett denounced the newly fashionable riding habits donned by women. They "conceal every thing that is attractive in a woman's person, her figure, her manner, and her graces. They wholly *unsex* her, and give her the unpleasing air of an Amazon, or a virago."[17] The tricky tightropes one must walk in the name of gender:

---

[12] William Wordsworth to Mary Wordsworth, 1 June [1812], *The Letters of William and Dorothy Wordsworth*, 2d ed., ed. Ernest de Selincourt, rev. Chester L. Shaver and others, 8 vols. (Oxford: Clarendon, 1967–1993), 8:104.

[13] Ann Radcliffe, *The Romance of the Forest*, 2d ed., 3 vols. (London, 1792), 3:4–5. Radcliffe also had a rapist bemoan that his victim "did not even condescend to conceal her disdain": *The Italian: or The Confessional of the Black Penitents* [1797], ed. Frederick Garber (Oxford: Oxford University Press, 1981), p. 340.

[14] Frederick Reynolds, *The Dramatist: or Stop Him Who Can!* (London, 1793), pp. 46–47.

[15] John Skinner, *Journal of a Somerset Rector 1803–1834*, ed. Howard and Peter Coombs (Bath: Kingsmead, 1971), p. 21 [6 October 1804].

[16] *Diary of Haydon*, 4:100 [17 June 1833].

[17] John Bennett, *Letters to a Young Lady, on a Variety of Useful and Interesting Subjects*, 2 vols. (Warrington, 1789), 1:241.

women could fail, too, by a more assertively erotic and thus immodest presentation of self, like that of frightful bare-bosomed Caroline. Not to mention poisoning themselves—their bodies, not their minds— with makeup based on lead and mercury to whiten their skin in the pursuit of attractiveness.[18] Why white skin, instead of our coveted suntan? Is this a change in fashion? Not exactly: thanks to the vast increase in indoors work, both their fair skin and our bronzed skin proclaim that the wearer is above the base necessity of working. To say the obvious, this little bit of class semiotics is designed for whites.

Worse than wearing a riding habit was riding. Charlotte Lennox's *Euphemia* offers Lady Cornelia Classick and her sidekick, "the fearless huntress Miss Sandford," single at age forty-five and bragging about "her wonderful art in keeping the men at a distance." Sandford "mounts her steed with most masculine agility, to escort her female friend." "Talents so masculine, and so ostentatiously displayed," laments Mr. Harley, "place them above those attentions and assiduities to which the charming sex have so just a claim, and which we delight to pay. Women should always be women; the virtues of our sex are not the virtues of theirs." Lennox's narrator agrees: "How absurd does it seem in our sex to step out of nature, in order to be more agreeable!"[19] Surely we are entitled to see in this curiously emphatic rejection of horseback-riding women a play on mounting, the position of ordinary sexual intercourse redolent of dominance and submission.

Women should always be women: not a tautology, but an injunction to respect one's assigned gender identity. Are Classick and Sandford lesbians?[20] Would that suffice to disqualify them as women? Their conspicuous and masculine talents, says Mr. Harley, place them above the assiduous attentions due to women. Not outside, not below, but above. Here's a perverse wrinkle in contempt: if women assume a higher status, they become contemptible.

---

[18] *Thraliana: The Diary of Mrs. Hester Lynch Thrale (Later Mrs. Piozzi) 1776–1809*, ed. Katharine C. Balderston, 2d ed., 2 vols. (Oxford: Clarendon, 1951), 1:393 [1779]; Cowper to William Unwin, 3 May 1784, *The Letters and Prose Writings of William Cowper*, ed. James King and Charles Ryskamp, 5 vols. (Oxford: Clarendon, 1979–1986), 2:243.

[19] Charlotte Lennox, *Euphemia*, 4 vols. (London, 1790), 2:159–65. This novel is light years from Lennox, *The Female Quixote or The Adventures of Arabella* [1752], ed. Margaret Dalziel (Oxford: Oxford University Press, 1989). See too the account of Emma Beagle, later Lady Fearnought, in Pierce Egan, *Sporting Anecdotes* (London, 1820), pp. 120–29.

[20] Compare the account of sisters Mary and Sarah Spencer, dubbed Captain Sally and her Man Mary, in Eden, *State of the Poor*, 1:626 n.

Another horseback-riding woman, Lady Sarah Savage, is heard offstage promising to whip and gallop her horses. "She'll whip and gallop them!" gasps demure Clara. "There now!—this is one of the modern breed of fine ladies, who, instead of being feminine and tender,
have the Rage for confidence and boldness—Look at her dress—
she's more like a man than a woman, and her language is as masculine as her manners." Gingham is blunter: "Damme, it's another
man in woman's clothes!" At play's end, he ritually couches the same
crass sentiment in verse:

> —May manners masculine no more deface
> The charms, that constitute each female grace.
> To man be bold and daring schemes confin'd;
> Woman for softer passions was design'd,
> And by meek virtue—to subdue mankind![21]

The thought, drearily familiar from Rousseau, is that a woman's
meekness is power, her bold confidence weakness. So, too, Maria
Edgeworth's *Leonora,* one of the day's studies—or lampoons—of
Mary Wollstonecraft's vision of gender relations, plays on paradoxes
of strength and weakness. Actually a conniving seductress, Olivia is
forever spouting putatively feminist sentiments. Her misfortune is being born a woman, she proclaims, the slave of society; it's degrading
even to occupy a female body.[22] Reviewing the spectacle, the duchess
concedes that Olivia affects a "manly soul," a "masculine spirit," but
she also notes how overwrought Olivia tends to be. Olivia exhibits a
"more than female tenderness of heart. I have observed," she adds
tartly, "that the ladies who wish to be men, are usually those who have
not sufficient strength of mind to be women."[23]

This was the milieu in which Wollstonecraft had the audacity to
suggest that women should become masculine. "From every quarter
have I heard exclamations against masculine women; but where are
they to be found?" She wouldn't promote "hunting, shooting, and
gaming"—horseback riding is presumably unspeakable—but if it was

[21] Frederick Reynolds, *Rage* [1795], in *The Modern Theatre; A Collection of Successful
Modern Plays,* ed. Elizabeth Inchbald, 10 vols. (London, 1811), 1:78, 1:118, 1:142.
[22] Compare *The Wrongs of Women* [1798], in *The Works of Mary Wollstonecraft,* ed. Janet
Todd and Marilyn Butler, assistant ed. Emma Rees-Mogg, 7 vols. (London: William
Pickering, 1989), 1:88.
[23] *Leonora* [1805], in Maria Edgeworth, *Tales and Novels,* 10 vols. (London, 1848),
8:255.

a matter of "the imitation of manly virtues," she would wish that women "would every day grow more and more masculine."[24] If women as a rule became masculine, the logic of gender would collapse. (Though for some time, the meaning of masculinity could be secured by memories of those feminine figures of the past.)

We need also to remember how tangled a thicket gender provides, how excruciatingly fine-grained and contradictory its dictates can be. One last masculine woman, Lady John Dareall, exemplifies the point. The narrator introduces her to parents "to prevent their reversing the order of nature, by making their girls masculine, and their boys feminine. . . ." Lady John is nothing like the novel's protagonist, Ellinor. But Lady John is one of Ellinor's great benefactors, taking her in after a scoundrel sets up an assignation and then attempts to rape her.[25] Perhaps this episode inspires the narrator to modify her assessment: "under a rough and rigid exterior" and despite her fierce manners and strong body, she explains apologetically, Lady John was deeply compassionate.[26] So she was a real woman all along, unfortunately stuck with a hideously masculine presentation of self. But doesn't her fierce strength enable her to save poor Ellinor? Would a properly submissive woman have dared to intercede? But maybe a suitably manly man wouldn't have proved compassionate enough to intercede. Maybe it takes Lady John's odd gender-bending blend of traits to be so virtuous.

To prevent the sloppy habit of thinking that gender applies only to women (or race only to blacks, or . . . ), let me say just a bit about effeminate men. Radicals assailed the "paltry gaudiness and affected finery" of soldiers, suggesting that they were frivolous and effeminate.[27] The radical *Black Dwarf* worked up a lather in a piece on the rights of women. The subject, emblematic of gender confusion, instantly brought to mind the disgusting antics of dandies.

[24] *Vindication of the Rights of Woman* [1792], in *Works*, 5:74.

[25] Mary Ann Hanway, *Ellinor; or, The World as It Is*, 4 vols. (London, 1798; reprint ed. New York: Garland, 1974), 2:114–15, 2:280–83.

[26] Hanway, *Ellinor*, 2:313–14, 2:332. See too Augusta's judgment, 4:313. Compare Keats to Charles Brown, August? 1820, *The Letters of John Keats*, ed. Hyder Edward Rollins, 2 vols. (Cambridge, MA: Harvard University Press, 1958), 2:327.

[27] *Reflections on the Pernicious Custom of Recruiting by Crimps; and on Various Other Modes Now Practised in the British Army* (London, 1795), p. 6. See too *Vindication of the Rights of Woman* [1792], in *Works of Wollstonecraft*, 5:86, 5:92–93; John Butler, *Brief Reflections upon the Liberty of the British Subject* (Canterbury, *circa* 1792), in *Political Writings of the 1790s*, ed. Gregory Claeys, 8 vols. (London: William Pickering, 1995), 3:383.

Their gender is not yet ascertained, but as their principal ambition seems to be *to look as pretty as women,* it would be most uncharitable to call them *men.* One of them the other day dropped his glove, and seemed quite astonished that one of the passing male brutes did not pick it up for her, or him. And indeed it was quite shocking to see the poor thing distressed in attempting to stoop for itself.[28]

The *Dwarf*'s fumbling for the correct pronoun is a nicely understated bit of invective. Him or her or it, the dandy was contemptible, a thing out of nature, every bit as pernicious and nonsensical as the rights of women.

Other men managed to escape the usual rules of gender without facing such scathing ripostes. Male lovers, Boswell reported—he must have been thinking of polite society—were permitted sighs, tears, protestations of helplessness, declarations that they were enslaved by their passions. He wondered at the anomaly: "It is peculiar to the passion of Love, that it supports with an exemption from disgrace, those weaknesses in a man which upon any other occasion would render him utterly contemptible."[29] But this was love before marriage, as a series of slapstick comedians reported. "What! on your knees?" blusters Sir Edward, finding Lindor kneeling to his daughter, Clara. "Aye, aye, all supple enough before marriage; I was so myself; but whether it was because I was married during the hard frost, and caught cold by celebrating my wedding on the ice, or what else I can't tell, but I could never get the muscles of my knees to give way afterwards."[30]

The man with the bent knee lowers himself, physically expressing deference. No such deference was expected—or permitted—when women appeared as wives. Now their job was to submit to husbands, who had to avoid the perils of petticoat government. Her husband had become "completely odious," explained Richard Graves's Mrs. Booby, from his belief in male superiority "and the arbitrary notions he entertained of the authority of the husband over us poor domestic

[28] *Black Dwarf* (9 September 1818) 2(36):573.

[29] James Boswell, *The Hypochondriack,* ed. Margery Bailey, 2 vols. (Stanford, CA: Stanford University Press, 1928), 1:186–87 [September 1778].

[30] James Fennell, *Lindor and Clara; or, The British Officer: A Comedy* (London, 1791), p. 4. Note too Gaylove's crack, p. 40; Elizabeth Inchbald, *Every One Has His Fault,* 2d ed. (London, 1793), pp. 82–83.

animals, called wives."[31] Wilberforce chided one woman for "a certain quickness of reply which is unbecoming the submissive obedient demeanour which certainly should distinguish the wife towards her husband."[32] Patrick Malooney, servant to Cumberland's *Passive Husband,* curses the turn in his luck: "My poor master, in the folly of his dotage, tackled himself to a tear-cap of a wife, and suffer'd her to hoist the petticoat on the flag-staff of his citadel. Out upon him for it! By the life of me, this poor passive Sir Toby Truckle has no more manhood in him than my mother."[33]

"A husband thus under command," announced Cobbett, "is the most contemptible of God's creatures." "A beggarly dependent under his own roof," he has no property of his own; he might as well kill himself.[34] The law of coverture meant that ordinarily married women had no property in their own names, but Cobbett failed to see anything troubling in the logical symmetry. Couples sporting such perniciously inverted gender relations might still meet the centuries-old public sanction of skimmingtons, their neighbors parading and banging on pots and pans to call them to order—or drive them out of the community.[35] The *Pioneer* dismissed the tiresome refrain on the dangers of petticoat government as "mere twaddle."[36] The journal wasn't alone, but its position wasn't crowded, either.

No authority for wives: and authority more generally was dangerous for women. Marianne Hudson's *Almack's,* a barely fictional portrait of the terribly clever London club managed by an incestuous coterie of

[31] Richard Graves, *The Spiritual Quixote: or, The Summer's Ramble of Mr. Geoffry Wildgoose,* 2d ed., 3 vols. (London, 1774), 1:294. See too Henry Home, Lord Kames, *Sketches of the History of Man,* 2d ed., 4 vols. (Edinburgh, 1778), 2:3.

[32] Wilberforce to ———, 3 November 1804, *The Correspondence of William Wilberforce,* ed. Robert Isaac Wilberforce and Samuel Wilberforce, 2 vols. (London, 1840), 1:337. See too Mrs. Richard Trench to Richard Trench, 29 April 1809, *The Remains of the Late Mrs. Richard Trench, Being Selections from Her Journals, Letters, & Other Papers,* 2d ed. rev., ed. Dean of Westminster (London, 1862), p. 232.

[33] *The Passive Husband,* in *The Posthumous Dramatic Works of the Late Richard Cumberland, Esq.,* 2 vols. (London, 1813), 1:231, reprinted in *The Plays of Richard Cumberland,* ed. Roberta F. S. Borkat, 6 vols. (New York: Garland, 1982), vol. 6. See too Fanny Burney, *The Wanderer; or, Female Difficulties* [1814], ed. Margaret Anne Doody and others (Oxford: Oxford University Press, 1991), p. 24.

[34] William Cobbett, *Advice to Young Men, and (Incidentally) to Young Women, in the Middle and Higher Ranks of Life* (London, 1829), §184.

[35] For a 1790 skimmington, see E. P. Thompson, *Customs in Common* (New York: New Press, 1991), p. 475.

[36] *Pioneer* (26 April 1834) no. 34, p. 322.

women, its "fair legislators," might be taken as a study of the backbiting and trivial nature of petticoat government outside the household.[37] No wonder citizenship for women struck so many as preposterous on its face. Women had to remain subjects, not just in electoral politics but in every social setting, lest they forfeit their very womanhood. Even independent thought might be too much for them. "Power made men of" Queen Elizabeth and Catherine of Russia, thought Charlotte Bury. "Otherwise, as it is the interest of the stronger sex to subdue women, mentally and personally—at least, they imagine that it is so—all display of vigorous intellect in them is charged with folly, if not with crime."[38]

## PUBLIC AND PRIVATE

The danger of authority is the deepest source of the time-honored appeal of consigning women to the private sphere, making domestic affairs their special preserve. Embracing "tender Mothers and faithful Wives," disdaining "furious Partizans" (of the female sort), the *Spectator* laid down the law: "Female Virtues are of a Domestick turn. The Family is the proper Province for Private Women to Shine in."[39] Whatever talents women had, emphasized Cumberland, "they should never be put forward in such a manner as to overshadow and keep out of sight those feminine and proper requisites, which are fitted to the domestic sphere. . . ."[40] "They ought to mind home," scribbled Byron in his journal, "and be well fed and clothed—but not mixed in society. Well educated, too, in religion—but to read neither poetry nor politics—nothing but books of piety and cookery."[41] These

[37] Marianne Spencer Stanhope Hudson, *Almack's*, 2d ed., 3 vols. (London, 1826), 3:104.

[38] Lady Charlotte Bury, *Diary Illustrative of the Times of George the Fourth*, new ed., 4 vols. (London, 1838–1839), 1:360 [17 June 1814]. On Elizabeth, consider *Kenilworth* [1821], in Walter Scott, *Waverley Novels*, 48 vols. (1829–1833), 23:56.

[39] *Spectator* (2 June 1711) no. 81, in *The Spectator*, ed. Donald F. Bond, 5 vols. (Oxford: Clarendon, 1965), 1:349.

[40] Richard Cumberland, *The Observer: Being a Collection of Moral, Literary and Familiar Essays*, 5th ed., 6 vols. (London, 1798), 4:297. See too John Bowles, *Remarks on Modern Female Manners, as Distinguished by Indifference to Character, and Indecency of Dress* (London, 1802), p. 24.

[41] *Byron's Letters and Journals*, ed. Leslie A. Marchand, 13 vols. (London: John Murray, 1973–1994), 8:15 [6 January 1821]. See too Scott, *Count Robert of Paris* [1831], in *Waverley Novels*, 47:94.

writers knew perfectly well the implications of what they were saying. The domestic sphere, reported Thomas Gisborne, "admits far less diversity of action" than "the widely differing professions and employments" enjoyed by men: but that meant it saved women from temptation.[42]

Many women echoed these formulations. Mrs. West was alarmed by talk of female independence: "The propriety of our seclusion from public affairs is necessarily interwoven with domestic subjection."[43] Mrs. Sandford's mechanical recital of the catechism could have been lifted from dozens of sources: "Domestic life is a woman's sphere, and it is there that she is most usefully as well as most appropriately employed." "There is, indeed," she continued, "something unfeminine in independence. It is contrary to nature, and therefore it offends."[44] An Englishwoman, paradoxically appearing in public or at least in print, scolded "the Females of Great Britain" for their unprecedented intrusions in public. The military, politics, the law, science, business: these were reserved for men. "To woman, the secluded scenes of domestic life" were destiny.[45]

Nor can we dismiss such women as a scattering of hidebound conservatives. Some radical women adopted the same views. Women must not mix in "the public haunts of men," insisted Priscilla Wakefield. "The sphere of feminine action is contracted by numberless difficulties, that are no impediments to masculine exertions."[46] Wollstonecraft declared, "Whatever tends to incapacitate the maternal character, takes woman out of her sphere."[47] Mary Hays, unjustly neglected as a sidekick of Wollstonecraft, relished the prospect of women's demystification: "Thus awakened to a sense of their injuries, they would behold with astonishment and indignation, the arts which had been employed, to keep them in a state of PERPETUAL BABYISM." "A wife is neither more, nor less, than—a great baby in leading-strings—" but no longer. Instead women "ought to be considered as

---

[42] Thomas Gisborne, *An Enquiry into the Duties of the Female Sex,* 5th ed. corrected (London, 1801), p. 2.

[43] Jane West, *Letters to a Young Lady,* 3d ed., 3 vols. (London, 1806), 1:132.

[44] Mrs. John Sandford, *Woman, in Her Social and Domestic Character* (London, 1831), pp. 4, 13.

[45] *John Bull* (12 May 1833) 13(648):149.

[46] Priscilla Wakefield, *Reflections on the Present Condition of the Female Sex; with Suggestions for Its Improvement* (London, 1798; reprint ed. New York: Garland, 1974), p. 9.

[47] *Vindication of the Rights of Woman,* in *Works,* 5:248.

the companions and equals, not as the inferiors,—much less as they virtually are,—as the slaves of men." This brave beginning gave way to a drearily long list of exceptions. No "warlike enterprises" for women; no participation in law or divinity; no "active part in popular assemblies"; maybe no practicing medicine or surgery, certainly not on male patients; and, most striking, in a conflict any other pursuits must give way to the duties of "daughter, sister, wife, or mother," thanks to "that attention to domestic concerns, which is beyond all dispute the duty of every woman."[48] Radical men, too, faltered. In a loopy novel imagining the emancipation of women, James Lawrence insisted on freedom, equality, and property for women. But not political power: "It would be absurd should the affairs of state be interrupted while her excellency the prime ministress was in the straw," that is, menstruating.[49]

Such sentiments have inspired impatience with the distinction between public and private. And not just sentiments, but the accompanying practices: the "female friends" of one poet were "necessarily precluded from being present" when a public dinner was held in his honor.[50] My inclination is to say that the distinction is invaluable, though I have zero interest in endorsing these sentiments about the domestic sphere being woman's special preserve. The distinction rolls together two basic strands. So something is public if it's open to the view of others, private if it's hidden—or if they shouldn't be looking, even if they can. ("Don't do that in public!" we exhort small children blithely masturbating. Think about the neighbor who discovers that if she tilts her mirror she can see into your living room. Or think about coming to a stop at the red light and discovering that the driver in the adjacent car is industriously picking his nose.) Or again, something is public if one must consult the interests of others, private

---

[48] Mary Hays, *Appeal to the Men of Great Britain in Behalf of Women* (London, 1798; reprint ed. New York: Garland, 1974), pp. 97, 281–82, 127, 193–203, 240.

[49] James Lawrence, *The Empire of the Nairs; or, The Rights of Women*, 4 vols. (London, 1811), 1:xxviii. The *Lion* (21 November 1828) 2(21):653–72 reprinted Lawrence's introduction; the *Lion* (5 December 1828) 2(23):717 published Percy Bysshe Shelley to James Henry Lawrence, 17 August 1812, endorsing Lawrence's book: see too *The Letters of Percy Bysshe Shelley*, ed. Frederick L. Jones, 2 vols. (Oxford: Clarendon, 1964), 1:322–23. *Blackwood's Edinburgh Magazine* (August 1826) 20(116):297 also takes menstruation and pregnancy to preclude women from exercising political power.

[50] Rowland Hodgson to James Montgomery, 2 November 1827, in John Holland and James Everett, *Memoirs of the Life and Writings of James Montgomery*, 7 vols. (London, 1854–1856), 4:226.

if one may suit oneself; public if one is accountable to others, private if one owes no justification or apology for one's actions. (So arise the unhappy predicaments of government officials found with their hands stuck in the till.) Both notions admit a shifting account of who counts as a relevant other. Consider picking your nose in front of your spouse or your child or your best friend or your colleague. Or take the firms of a capitalist economy. In one sense, they're all private. But we also distinguish the private firms from the public ones in which anonymous strangers may buy shares of stock.[51]

So cast, the distinction between public and private doesn't require consigning women to the domestic sphere. Or, if you like, what's offensive isn't the distinction itself, but the now infamous mapping, public man, private woman.[52] Nor does the distinction require thinking that what's public is political, what's private nonpolitical. For authority is exercised in such classically private settings as family and workplace, and there are controversies about its legitimacy.

### GENDER AGAIN: THE SEX OF SOULS AND BEYOND

"I am sure, I do not mean it an Injury to Women, when I say there is a Sort of Sex in Souls. I am tender of offending them," apologized the *Tatler* in 1710, rushing to deny that men were better than women. Still, the truth had to be affirmed. "The Virtues have respectively a Masculine and a Feminine Cast."[53] One might wonder whether souls are the sorts of things one could attribute sex or gender to. This is the territory of blasphemy, though. So let's just say that as the basis for a claim about gendered virtue, the sexed soul is sadly obscure. Wollstonecraft deliberately made short work of the matter: if women had souls at all, they were part of mankind.[54] Mary Shelley, daughter of Wollstonecraft and Godwin, wistfully reflected on her own tentative

[51] Crucial here is Georg Simmel's brief but powerfully suggestive account of "The Stranger" in *The Sociology of Kurt Simmel*, trans. and ed. Kurt H. Wolff (New York: Free Press, 1950), pp. 402–8.

[52] Jean Bethke Elshtain, *Public Man, Private Woman: Women in Social and Political Thought* (Princeton, NJ: Princeton University Press, 1981).

[53] *Tatler* (13–16 May 1710) no. 172.

[54] *Vindication of the Rights of Woman*, in *Works*, 5:88. Unpersuaded, Coleridge suspected there was indeed sex in souls: *The Notebooks of Samuel Taylor Coleridge*, ed. Kathleen Coburn, in progress (New York: Pantheon Books, 1957–), 3(1):3531 L.44 [July–September 1809].

intellect and character. "My Mother had more energy of character—still she had no sufficient fire of imagination—in short my belief is—whether there be sex in souls or not—that the sex of our material mechanism makes us quite different creatures—better though weaker but wanting in the higher grades of intellect."[55]

Others' views on the matter demonstrate yet again the depth—and scope—of gender. "Woman is but a man of another shape," held Priscilla in the *Republican:* notice how much is at stake in accepting this claim.[56] "I give no credit to the opinion of a sexual excellence," wrote Catherine Macaulay. Still, men and women shouldn't receive the same education. It was necessary to "form the female mind to the particularity of its situation."[57] A distinction without a difference? Surely not, if there's an ensuing argument about the imperatives of eliminating or modifying those particular—peculiar—situations. Maybe not, if there's an amorphous background thought about the difference between inborn nature and social role, so that naturally similar men and women must nonetheless cultivate different roles and so need different virtues.

Nature or politics: that was the dilemma. Here's the *Quarterly Journal of Education,* one of the organs of the Society for the Diffusion of Useful Knowledge, dodging political controversy not by turning to geology or linguistics but by echoing time-honored wisdom:

> Women are adapted by nature to regulate the (apparently) minor affairs of life; *details* fall under their direction; these necessarily demand a training different from that which enables men to contend with and overcome the difficulties which they encounter in the world. The qualities which render a woman amiable, would often make a man contemptible; those faculties which often lead him to eminence would unsex her.[58]

But the very idea of a sexual excellence, objected the *Westminster Review,* was a pernicious prejudice arising from the desire of husbands to win irrationally boundless admiration from their wives.

---

[55] Mary Shelley to Maria Gisborne, 11 June [1835], *The Letters of Mary Wollstonecraft Shelley,* ed. Betty T. Bennett, 3 vols. (Baltimore, MD: Johns Hopkins University Press, 1980–1988), 2:246.

[56] *Republican* (3 December 1824) 10(22):690.

[57] Catherine Macaulay Graham, *Letters on Education: with Observations on Religious and Metaphysical Subjects* (London, 1790; reprint ed. New York: Garland, 1974), p. 216.

[58] *Quarterly Journal of Education* (October 1834) 8(16):215.

It is considered meritorious in a man to be independent: to be sufficient to himself, not to be in a constant state of pupillage. In a woman, help-lessness, both of mind and of body, is the most admired of attributes. A man is despised, if he be not courageous. In a woman, it is esteemed amiable to be a coward. To be entirely dependant upon her husband for every pleasure, and for exemption from every pain; to feel secure, only when under his protection; to be incapable of forming any opinion, or of taking any resolution without his advice and aid; this is amiable, this is delicate, this is feminine: while all who infringe on any of the preroga-tives which man thinks proper to reserve for himself; all who can or will be of any use, either to themselves or to the world, otherwise than as the slaves and drudges of their husbands, are called masculine, and other names intended to convey disapprobation.[59]

The illicit desires of vain husbands aren't enough to begin to compre-hend, let alone explain, these matters. They are part of what needs explanation. Six years later, the *Review* abruptly wheeled about and held that nature was behind the observed physical, mental, and social differences between men and women. "It is an evil thing to have a man emasculated by an effeminate education, or a woman forced into an amazon by a masculine one."[60]

To cast a social contingency as an unalterable natural fact is deftly to eliminate the possibility of criticism. So Malthus tried to show that poverty and private property were inevitable and Hazlitt tried to show that Malthus was concealing valuable political possibilities. In this context, though, Hazlitt stubbornly maintained, "The character of women (I should think it will at this time of day be granted) differs essentially from that of men, not less so than their shape or the tex-ture of their skin." He remembered that "the fair and eloquent au-thoress of the Rights of Women was for establishing the masculine pretensions and privileges of her sex on a perfect equality with ours."[61] But his language shows how ludicrous he thought her view. *Fair authoress* are words chosen by this master craftsman of prose to hammer home her sex, and he capitalizes on the archaism of giving

[59] *Westminster Review* (April 1824) 1(2):526. The *Review* went on to charge that the *Edinburgh Review* "has never stood up manfully [!] to resist this prejudice," but see *Edinburgh Review* (January 1810) 15(30):299–315.

[60] *Westminster Review* (July 1830) 15(29):86–87.

[61] *The Plain Speaker* [1826], in *The Complete Works of William Hazlitt*, ed. P. P. Howe, 21 vols. (London: J. M. Dent and Sons, 1930), 12:234.

*author* a feminine ending to make it look faintly ludicrous. Hazlitt boasted sterling misogynist credentials.[62]

Other defenders of traditional gender roles were drawn to talk of natural necessity, too.[63] (There were appeals to other justificatory sources. Scripture was perennially available.[64] Creatively, not to say whimsically, Southey turned to Latin grammar and the traditional view that female fetuses were ensouled later than male ones.[65]) But there were other ways to deploy the notoriously ambiguous concept of nature. Burke, for instance, remained fond of teleology. Female beauty, he explained, "almost always carries with it an idea of weakness and imperfection. Women are very sensible of this; for which reason they learn to lisp, to totter in their walk, to counterfeit weakness, and even sickness. In all this they are guided by nature."[66] It's not that women necessarily or automatically lisp and totter. It's that they flourish when they do. An odd flourishing, no doubt, that dictates mastering the routines of weak delicacy and even sickness. But one would expect only an odd flourishing for such an odd organism. Then again, nature wasn't always comporting with the dictates of gender. Take Blake's glum query: "O Albion why didst thou a Female Will Create?"[67]

---

[62] See for instance "Standard Novels and Romances" [1815], in *Works,* 16:22; "Education of Women" [1815], in *Works,* 20:41–42; Hazlitt to William Hazlitt, Jr., February or March 1822, *The Letters of William Hazlitt,* ed. Herschel Moreland Sikes, assisted by Willard Hallam Bonner and Gerald Lahey (New York: New York University Press, 1978), pp. 231–35; "Common Places" [1823], in *Works,* 20:126; *Characteristics* [1823], in *Works,* 9:212–13; *Conversations of James Northcote* [1830], in *Works,* 11:218.

[63] For instance, Thomas Gisborne, *An Enquiry into the Duties of Men in the Higher and Middle Classes of Society in Great Britain, Resulting from Their Respective Stations, Professions, and Employments,* 5th ed. corrected, 2 vols. (London, 1800), 2:465. For nature and Scripture, see William Ewart Gladstone, *The Gladstone Diaries,* ed. M. R. D. Foot and H. C. G. Matthew, 11 vols. (Oxford: Clarendon, 1968–1990), 2:127 [5 September 1834].

[64] John Bennett, *Strictures on Female Education* (London, 1787), pp. 120–24; John Whitaker, *The Real Origin of Government* (London, 1795), pp. 7–8; Gisborne, *Enquiry,* 2:465.

[65] Robert Southey, *Omniana, or Horae Otiosiores,* 2 vols. (London, 1812), 1:22.

[66] *A Philosophical Inquiry into the Origin of Our Ideas of the Sublime and Beautiful,* 2d ed. [1757], in *The Works of the Right Honorable Edmund Burke,* 9th ed., 12 vols. (Boston: Little, Brown, 1889), 1:188. Consider the use of Burke's sentiment in *The Inheritance* [1824], in *The Works of Susan Ferrier,* Holyrood edition, 4 vols. (London: Eveleigh Nash & Grayson, 1929), 2:40.

[67] William Blake, *Jerusalem: The Emanation of the Giant Albion* [1804], ed. Morton D. Paley (Princeton, NJ: The William Blake Trust / Princeton University Press, 1991), p. 221.

Hannah More could easily generate a laundry list of differences between men and women.[68] But these differences didn't arise spontaneously. They required discipline.

> Girls should be led to distrust their own judgment; they should learn not to murmur at expostulation; they should be accustomed to expect and to endure opposition. It is a lesson with which the world will not fail to furnish them; and they will not practise it the worse, for having learnt it the sooner. It is of the last importance to their happiness, even in this life, that they should early acquire a submissive temper and a forbearing spirit.[69]

More was a staunch evangelical Christian, so we might interpret this injunction as a reminder of original sin. Pride, remember, is the deadliest of the seven sins, so it will take hard work to scale these sublime heights of self-mutilation. (Enduring oral readings of More's *Hints toward Forming the Character of a Young Princess,* chock full of similar advice, Princess Charlotte confessed herself unutterably bored: "This I believe is what makes me find the hours so long. I *am not quite good enough* for that yet."[70])

Consider how wide-ranging gender turns out to be. To take an apparently innocent case: Cobbett noticed that it was puzzling to "apply the term *gender* to things destitute of all sexual properties," but somehow ships and workers' own special implements were called *she.* "And, you know, that our country folks in Hampshire call almost everything *he* or *she.*"[71] It's tantalizing that such usages appear in English, lacking as it does the gendered articles of other languages. Characteristically, Bentham found the matter not tantalizing but nonsensical. Equating gender with sex, not thinking too hard about word choice, he branded the sort of usage Cobbett noticed "replete with absurdity and pregnant with inconvenience."[72] But Bentham moved too

[68] *Essays on Various Subjects, Principally Designed for Young Ladies* [1777], in *The Works of Hannah More,* 9 vols. (London, 1840–1843), 6:264–65.

[69] *Strictures on the Modern System of Female Education* [1799], in *Works of Hannah More,* 3:106.

[70] Princess Charlotte to Mercer Elphinstone, 16 November 1812, *Letters of the Princess Charlotte 1811–1817,* ed. A. Aspinall (London: Home and van Thal, 1949), p. 38.

[71] William Cobbett, *A Grammar of the English Language* [1823] (Oxford: Oxford University Press, 1984), pp. 21–22.

[72] *Fragments of Universal Grammar,* in *The Works of Jeremy Bentham,* ed. John Bowring, 11 vols. (Edinburgh, 1843), 8:346; see too Jeremy Bentham, *Chrestomathia* [1817], ed. M. J. Smith and W. H. Burston (Oxford: Clarendon, 1983), pp. 404–5.

quickly. Even such linguistic usages might well have deep and systematic causal or symbolic connections with political matters.

Or recall the typology between interest, principle, and affection.
Contemporaries turned to it in thinking about men and women. Take
Southey: "Perhaps the female heart is more alive to affection than
mans and the dangerous error entailed upon them by education is—
that they almost act from their feelings and not from fixed principles. . . ."[73] Take Haydon: "The great difficulty is to find a woman of
exquisite susceptibility, curbed & directed by principle. Many there
are who tremble with love at every pore but whose very feeling is a
cause of their vice. . . ."[74] (A further wrinkle: for women, *principle* just
means monogamous sexual fidelity.) Take Godwin: "Woman is the
weaker vessel, and more a slave to passion."[75] Reason was quintessentially masculine. One conversationalist held out for the view that
women don't reason. Another, "agreeing generally, said He knew one
woman now in Paris, who has an understanding of most masculine
strength."[76] "A man of the ordinary notions," that is not the progressive notions of the *Westminster Review,* "no sooner hears of an instructed woman, than he conjures up the idea of an ugly, arrogant,
unattractive pedant. . . ."[77] Novelists showed how the masculinity of
reason made brainy women unattractive. Lady Cornelia Classick,
friend or lover of Miss Sandford, earns her own scolding for masculine talents by being "learned and scientific," prone to lecturing on
the ancient Greeks.[78] Anthelia reveals, "In our sex a taste for intellectual pleasures is almost equivalent to taking the veil; and though not
absolutely a vow of perpetual celibacy, it has almost always the same

[73] Southey to Grosvenor Charles Bedford, 12 May 1795, *New Letters of Robert Southey,*
ed. Kenneth Curry, 2 vols. (New York: Columbia University Press, 1965), 1:96.

[74] *Diary of Haydon,* 1:320 [26 August 1813].

[75] William Godwin, *Of Population: An Enquiry Concerning the Power of Increase in the
Numbers of Mankind, Being an Answer to Mr. Malthus's Essay on That Subject* (London,
1820), pp. 532–33.

[76] *The Diary of Joseph Farington,* ed. Kenneth Garlick, Angus Macintyre, and Kathryn
Cave, 16 vols. (New Haven: Published for the Paul Mellon Centre for Studies in British
Art by Yale University Press), 10:3684 [3 July 1810]. See too Mary Wollstonecraft to
Jane Arden, May?–June? 1778, in *Shelley and His Circle 1773–1822,* ed. Kenneth Neill
Cameron and Donald H. Reiman, 8 vols. (Cambridge, MA: Harvard University Press,
1961–1986), 2:966.

[77] *Westminster Review* (July 1831) 15(29):72.

[78] Lennox, *Euphemia,* 2:159, 2:165.

practical tendency."[79] Here Hannah More was less stringent—or more discriminating about the ways in which reason was masculine. Her Coelebs, on one of literature's more dogged searches for a wife, explained that a woman knowledgeable in classics would be fine, but "one who was always dabbling in chemistry, and who came to dinner with dirty hands from the laboratory" wouldn't do.[80]

Can we say that the scheme of interest, principle, and affection is itself gendered? or that the category of reason is? Something is gendered if it is logically dependent on gender norms. Take for instance being a wimp, impossible without the conceptual backdrop of masculinity. Or something is gendered if it is causally dependent on gender norms, so that it couldn't arise without them. So one might argue, for instance, that private property is gendered, if one could show that it depends not just on distinguishing public from private but on consigning women to the private sphere. (And so one might reject my facile suggestion that it's easy to pry apart the public/private distinction from gender, if one could make a similar showing.) Or, more simply, these categories could be gendered because of the monotonously frequent associations between affection and women, reason and men, so that even when they're deployed in other domains, they carry along these other associations. Now the way is clear to disconnect gender from sex: for so too we might come to think, say, of an emotionally drenched Mahler symphony as feminine, a crisply geometric Bach fugue as masculine. We could repeat the analysis for a host of other categories routinely associated with femininity and masculinity but then invoked in other domains. Contrast Walter Scott's reference to "the true negroe-driving principle of self-interest"[81] or the *Age*'s pun that if the Jews were admitted to Parliament, "we may hope to see something like pure and independent *principal* in every speech, and the *interests of the peoples calculated* in every de-

[79] *Melincourt* [1817], in *The Works of Thomas Love Peacock*, Halliford edition, ed. H. F. B. Brett-Smith and C. E. Jones, 10 vols. (London: Constable & Co., 1924–1934), 2:166–67. See too Anne Romilly to Maria Edgeworth, 6 October 1817, *Romilly-Edgeworth Letters 1813–1818*, ed. Samuel Henry Romilly (London: John Murray, 1936), p. 176; Charles Maturin, *Women; or, Pour et Contre*, 3 vols. (Edinburgh, 1818; reprint ed. New York: Garland, 1979), 3:31, 3:39.

[80] *Coelebs in Search of a Wife* [1808], in *Works of Hannah More*, 7:292.

[81] *The Journal of Sir Walter Scott*, ed. W. E. K. Anderson (Oxford: Clarendon, 1972), p. 81 [8 February 1826].

bate."[82] Whatever we make of these comments, it doesn't seem as though the categories are always stamped with the signatures of race or slavery and religion.

## THE SECRETS OF SEXISM

So what about contempt for women? Some observers said forthrightly that women were worse than men. Fanny Burney's admiral is impressed with Juliet. "Not that one ought to expect perfection; for a woman is but a woman," he tells her, "which a man, as her native superiour, ought always to keep in mind. . . ."[83] "You will be glad to hear that my child proves to be of the more worthy gender," cackled Southey.[84] "A really sensible woman," opined Mrs. Sandford, "feels her dependence. She does what she can, but she is conscious of inferiority, and therefore grateful for support."[85] These writers would have hastened to add that men owed these inferior women benevolent care, not snarling hostility. Even assigning women a low status, then, can trigger affection for them. So again, what about contempt?

Recall Boswell's formulation: "*Pitiful* is as much a contemptuous as it is a lamentable epithet." Wollstonecraft suggested that women were figures of pity, verging on contempt.[86] The low can invite (patronizing) affection and gentle care. They can also invite dismissive neglect or hostile abuse. But contempt, recall, does double duty, indicating not just neglect and abuse but also the assignment of low status in the first place. So those holding that women are inferior exhibit contempt for women in their very affection for them. Consider Coleridge, reduced to tears in stammering through his weighty grievance against his wife, declaring that he couldn't go on living with her if she didn't refrain from her vicious behavior. What had she dared to do?

[82] *Age* (25 April 1830), p. 134.

[83] Fanny Burney, *The Wanderer*, p. 831.

[84] Southey to John Rickman, 13 October 1806, *The Life and Correspondence of Robert Southey*, ed. Charles Cuthbert Southey, 6 vols. (London, 1849–1850), 3:53. See too Southey, *The Life of Wesley; and The Rise and Progress of Methodism*, 2 vols. (London, 1820), 2:299; Southey to Grosvenor Charles Bedford, 28 March 1829, *New Letters of Southey*, 2:335; *Morning Post* (16 April 1800), in *The Collected Works of Samuel Taylor Coleridge*, ed. Kathleen Coburn, Bart Winer, and others, in progress (Princeton, NJ: Princeton University Press, 1969–), 3(1):239; Byron to Augusta Leigh, 30 November 1808, *Byron's Letters and Journals*, 1:179.

[85] Sandford, *Woman*, p. 13.

[86] *Vindication of the Rights of Woman*, chap. 5, in *Works*, 5:147.

She'd insisted that on icy mornings he get up and light the fire before she rose with their baby.[87]

Then again, some observers maintained that women were men's superiors. I don't mean the mandatory romantic salutations of angels and goddesses.[88] The ecstatic worship of woman as romantic love object was (too?) easily discarded as pretense: "In your fictitious characters as lovers you endeavour to make us believe that we are exalted above human weaknesses; but, in your real characters, as men, you more honestly demonstrate to us, that you place us even below your own level, and deny us the equal truth and justice that belongs alike to all intelligent beings."[89] And for every breathy invocation of angelic women, we can find deflating sentiments delivered with asperity: "Everything's the better for a little beating, as I tells my wife," leers a ruffian explaining how he has trained a bullfinch in Burney's *Camilla*.[90]

But there were more measured claims that women were superior. Wrathful over the degradation and beating of some Indian women that he traced to Hastings's corrupt administration, Burke reminded the Lords that women, "the better and more virtuous part of mankind," had sensitive moral natures.[91] Discussing domestic squabbles, Mrs. West permitted herself a wry sneer: "Conciliatory measures are first expected from our sex; and I pique myself upon this tacit acknowledgment of what I have always pleaded for, the intrinsic,

[87] John Payne Collier, *An Old Man's Diary, Forty Years Ago*, 4 vols. (London, 1871–1872), 3:81–82 [11 June 1833].

[88] For instance, Boswell to Temple, 26 June 1767, *Boswell in Search of a Wife 1766–1769*, ed. Frank Brady and Frederick A. Pottle (New York: McGraw-Hill, 1956), p. 76; Fanny Burney, *Evelina, or The History of a Young Lady's Entrance into the World* [1778], ed. Edward A. Bloom and Lillian D. Bloom (Oxford: Oxford University Press, 1982), p. 107; Charlotte Smith, *The Old Manor House* [1793], ed. Anne Henry Ehrenpreis (Oxford: Oxford University Press, 1989), pp. 264, 476; Thomas Carlyle to Jane Baillie Welsh, 1 July 1823, *The Collected Letters of Thomas and Jane Welsh Carlyle*, ed. Charles Richard Sanders and others, 22 vols. to date (Durham, NC: Duke University Press, 1970–), 2:390; Carlyle to Welsh, 25 November 1823, *Letters*, 2:419–20. Thomas Hamilton, *The Youth and Manhood of Cyril Thornton*, 3 vols. (Edinburgh, 1827) offers a moral and mortal combat between a feverish romantic love and a sedate companionate love.

[89] Joseph Richardson, *The Fugitive*, 3d ed. (London, 1792), p. 63.

[90] Fanny Burney, *Camilla, or A Picture of Youth* [1796], ed. Edward A. Bloom and Lillian D. Bloom (Oxford: Oxford University Press, 1983), p. 492. See too Thomas Holcroft, *Love's Frailties* (London, 1794), p. 29.

[91] "Speech in General Reply" [12 June 1794], in *Works*, 12:164. See too *A Note-Book of Edmund Burke*, ed. H. V. F. Somerset (Cambridge: Cambridge University Press, 1957), pp. 52–54.

though not ostensible, superiority of women."[92] In a lyrical rapture only partly indebted to sentiments of romantic love, *Blackwood's* insisted that "any mind unbesotted by sex" would agree that women were "infinitely superior." "Men for the most part are such worthless wretches, that we wonder how women condescend to allow the world to be carried on; and we attribute the phenomenon solely to the hallowed yearnings of maternal affection. . . ."[93]

If women are more valuable, even precious angels, does it make sense to say they are held in contempt? There might be more rewarding situations than being perched up on a pedestal, but it matters that it's up, not down. We might think about why so much effort went into ensuring that women stayed where they belonged: cynics will say this is rather too reminiscent of the paradise of East Berlin, whose inhabitants got shot if they dared try to escape its rarefied pleasures.[94] Or we might take our lead from the young and still radical Southey. Not yet enshrining men as the more worthy gender, Southey averred that "of the two animals woman is the best," yet he managed to make sense of contempt without attributing to others the mistaken view that they were worse. He did so by railing against secluding women in the domestic sphere. "There is not a part of the civilized world where the female mind is not murdered by the customs of society, and thus to immure them is to render them wretched as well as contemptible."[95] Southey wants to exploit the difference between human worth and social status. Women have great human worth, but their low social status justifies the claim that they are contemptible.

But there was further debate about the judgment that women occupied a low social status. Was the domestic sphere the magical preserve of life's most rewarding activities? Were men stuck with the thankless task of heading off to the dusty battlefields of work and politics? Or was the domestic sphere mindlessly repetitive, full of "unimportant events,"[96] but work and politics richly rewarding? These questions

---

92 West, *Letters to a Young Lady*, 3:161. See too *Boswell, Laird of Auchinleck 1778–1782*, ed. Joseph W. Reed and Frederick A. Pottle (New York: McGraw-Hill, 1977), p. 160 [6 January 1780].

93 *Blackwood's Edinburgh Magazine* (September 1831) 30(185):485.

94 I owe this formulation to Danielle LaVaque-Manty.

95 Robert Southey, *Letters Written during a Short Residence in Spain and Portugal*, 2d ed. (Bristol, 1799), p. 221.

96 "The Elder Son" [1834], in Mary Wollstonecraft Shelley, *Collected Tales and Stories*, ed. Charles E. Robinson (Baltimore, MD: Johns Hopkins University Press, 1976), p. 265.

motivate what is already visible in the eighteenth century as a dispute
about difference and dominance.[97] Celebrants of difference prized
the social status of women: "If the delicacy of their constitution, and
other physical causes, allow the female sex a smaller share of some
mental powers, they possess others in a superior degree, which are no
less respectable in their own nature, and of as great importance to
society."[98] Coleridge jeered at Wollstonecraft's "foolish book"; women
had better taste, but men had better minds, and this very comple-
mentarity, supplied by Providence, qualified as "the most perfect
equality."[99] The value of distinctively female traits and the possibility
of seeing equality hang on the background assessment of how valuable women's work is.

Critics—and celebrants—of dominance depended on competing
assessments. "From the laws and dispositions of men," explained a
remarkable 1784 pamphlet, "women are almost in every respect
made a second sort of beings. . . ." "It was men who made the laws,
and those give a man an unlimited power over his wife." (Bentham
later echoed the claim in denouncing the law's presumption that
property should be inherited by male descendants: "The strongest
have had all the preference. Why? Because the strongest have made
the laws."[100]) That power included the right forcibly to restrain one's
wife at home, to beat her, to "insult and torment her," to parade in
public with a prostitute and introduce her as one's wife, to squander
the family assets on prostitutes.[101] Despite assiduous pleas, Hannah
More refused even to read Wollstonecraft's *Vindication*. She already
knew that "there is perhaps no animal so much indebted to subordination for good behaviour, as woman."[102] On marrying, Cobbett

[97] Catharine A. MacKinnon, *Feminism Unmodified: Discourses on Life and Law* (Cambridge, MA: Harvard University Press, 1987), chap. 2.

[98] John Robison, *Proofs of a Conspiracy against All the Religions and Governments of
Europe, Carried on in the Secret Meetings of Free Masons, Illuminati, and Reading Societies*, 2d
ed. (London, 1797), pp. 246–47.

[99] *1813 Lectures on Shakespeare and Education*, in *Works of Coleridge*, 5(1):594–95.

[100] *Principles of the Civil Code*, in *Works of Bentham*, 1:335.

[101] *Letters from a Peeress of England to Her Eldest Son* (London, 1784), pp. 9, 14–15,
120–21. Note the echoes of this analysis and its application to black slavery in William
Thompson, *An Inquiry into the Principles of the Distribution of Wealth Most Conducive to
Human Happiness* (London, 1824; reprint ed. New York: Augustus M. Kelley, 1963),
p. 303.

[102] Hannah More to Earl of Orford [Horace Walpole], 1793, in William Roberts,
*Memoirs of the Life and Correspondence of Mrs. Hannah More*, 2d ed., 4 vols. (London,
1834), 2:371.

agreed, a woman offered her husband "an absolute surrender, of her liberty . . . and, above all, she surrenders to him *her person*."[103]

Three literary women offered equally chilling assessments. Mary Wollstonecraft was unabashed: "What a fine thing it is to be a man!"[104] At sixty, Mary Berry remembered her views at twenty-one: "What regrets I felt then at having been born a woman, and deprived of the life and position which, as a man, I might have had in this world! But I am calm and resigned now. I will say no more about it."[105] Mary Shelley wasn't exactly resigned. "Most women I believe wish that they had been men—so do not I—change my sex & I do not think that my talents would be greater"—she would be just another "selfish unkind" man. "Did not the memory of those matchless lost ones"—she meant Percy Shelley, drowned a couple of years before, and Byron, just deceased—"redeem their race, I should learn to hate a sex who are strong only to oppress—moral only to insult—"[106]

The *Westminster Review* was deliberate: "Men are generally accustomed to treat women much in the same manner in which a superstitious votary treats the image of his saint; they approach them with reverence, bestow upon them, in words, great homage and adoration, and invariably manifest, by their actions, a most contemptuous opinion of their intellect."[107] This claim provoked *Blackwood's* into furious sarcasm. The "worthy contemporary, who enlightens the world four times per annum" and produced such dubious gems must be a tailor. After quoting the offending passage, *Blackwood's* responded: "Stop, Snip—not so fast if you please. MEN are not accustomed to do any such thing—they do, indeed, treat women so far like saints, that they do not take the measure of them for stays, or even a riding-habit. . . ." The reverence expressed for women, they insisted, was utterly authentic, the result of courtesy and feeling.[108]

---

[103] Cobbett, *Advice to Young Men*, §178.

[104] Wollstonecraft to Godwin, 10 June 1797, *Godwin & Mary: Letters of William Godwin and Mary Wollstonecraft*, ed. Ralph M. Wardle (Lawrence, KS: University of Kansas Press, 1966), p. 94.

[105] *Extracts from the Journals and Correspondence of Miss Berry from the Year 1783 to 1852*, ed. Lady Theresa Lewis, 2d ed., 3 vols. (London, 1866), 3:332 [16 March 1823].

[106] *The Journals of Mary Shelley 1814–1844*, ed. Paula R. Feldman and Diana Scott-Kilvert, 2 vols. (Oxford: Clarendon, 1987), 2:487–88 [3 December 1824].

[107] *Westminster Review* (January 1827) 7(13):50.

[108] *Blackwood's Edinburgh Magazine* (June 1827) 21(126):645.

Now gender is the name of a swarm of controversies: over the capacities of men and women, the value of those capacities, the value of domestic seclusion, and more. Were women held in contempt? That's not a simple descriptive question, as if there's a fact of the matter hidden inside the heads of those long dead, and if only we could somehow crawl inside and inspect them, we'd finally know for sure. Making sense of contempt, just like making sense of pride, depends on our ability to attribute a range of background beliefs to the relevant actors. The very terms those beliefs are expressed in are politically controversial. I suspect that many groped their way to this sort of view: "The idea of the equality of the sexes is truly ridiculous. Man is the natural protector of woman; and the shade of subordination is so delicate as to be almost imperceptible. Let the fair-sex meekly enjoy their privileges, and leave imperial man in possession of his prerogatives."[109] There is room here for genuine and deep affection, for love, both a love built around care and deference and, thanks to the delicacy of the subordination, a love on a rough footing of equality. At the very same time, because equality is ridiculous and meek women are deferring to imperial men, there is room for contempt: both the assignment of low status and a kind of hostility or dismissiveness based on it. So too with sexual intercourse itself: in Boswell's view, "genuine reciprocal amorous affection with an amiable woman" was a paramount pleasure for man, in part because "in this enchanting union he exults with a consciousness that he is the superior person. The dignity of his sex is kept up."[110]

Examining pride, I imagined people who tell us they're proud and then asked if we could make sense of their pride. Now, though, I am attempting something sneakier: attributing contempt to those who would strenuously disavow the very possibility. They feel affection, an expansive sense of their own largesse, maybe some of the pleasures of being in control, but surely not contempt. It's one thing to hold that an emotion isn't merely a feeling, but depends on a set of background beliefs. But should we admit that there can be an emotion without a feeling?

---

[109] John Corry, *A Satirical View of London*, 4th ed. (London, 1809), p. 149 n.

[110] *Boswell's London Journal 1762–1763*, ed. Frederick A. Pottle (New York: McGraw-Hill, 1950), p. 84 [14 December 1762]. See too *Boswell in Holland 1763–1764*, ed. Frederick A. Pottle (London: William Heinemann, 1952), pp. 224–25 [20 April 1764].

I suppose not. But you can treat others with contempt without intending to and without experiencing yourself as doing so. Other emotions double in this way, too: you can be humiliated, that is in a state of humiliation, without feeling the least bit humiliated.[111] Take a man who appends to a letter, "My wife sends all those sort of message which womenfolk deal in." Or who thinks it's especially unfortunate for the male head of the household to get sick: "Women and children are the natural prey of the Apothecary, but a man has something else to do than to keep his chamber & look delicate."[112] Suppose he sincerely denies that he means to be dismissive. Suppose he believes in the superior status of women and their allotted domestic role. Suppose he thinks that men have something else to do precisely because they're drudges or drones, and their wives are really queen bees. Or take John Byng, peeved at the ugly and disheveled women of Wales, lumping pretty women together with gardens and flowers as "beauties of nature," longing for his return home: "The sight of a smart English waiting maid will be delightful."[113] Suppose he assures us that he reverences women, that he is in awe of natural beauty, that he knows full well that women are human and flowers are plants. Or suppose he embraces eccentric views about the competing worth of flora and fauna. Suppose he denies that somehow it's working-class women who turn him on.

Even if these men are sincere, we are free to say they are contemptuous toward women. Doing so involves making some politically controversial judgments of our own. But so does denying that they are contemptuous. Either way, again, we have far more than an innocent factual dispute about what's going on inside their heads. Those still tempted by the view that there must be such a decisive fact might consider what they'd say about the character who declares, "I look upon woman to be a valuable piece of household furniture," the sort a man will want to steal if he's forbidden to purchase it.[114] Woman as

---

[111] William Ian Miller, *Humiliation and Other Essays on Honor, Social Discomfort, and Violence* (Ithaca, NY: Cornell University Press, 1993), pp. 136–39.

[112] John Fisher to Constable, 31 August 1820, in John Constable, *Correspondence*, ed. R. B. Beckett, 6 vols. (Ipswich: Suffolk Records Society, 1962–1968), 6:55; Fisher to Constable, 7 February 1823, in Constable, *Correspondence*, 6:109.

[113] John Byng, *The Torrington Diaries*, ed. C. Bruyn Andrews, 4 vols. (London: Eyre & Spottiswoode, 1934–1938), 3:277–78 [5 August 1793], 3:301 [15 August 1793].

[114] Archibald MacLaren, *The New Marriage Act; or, Look before You Leap* (London, 1822), p. 3.

commodity: now surely this is contemptuous. Or is it not contemptuous if he believes furniture is more admirable than people? Can he say and think and feel whatever he likes, or is the meaning of what he says and thinks and feels partly dependent on social facts not in his control?

### THE DIGNITY OF LABOR?

Workers inherited a long and dismal history of contempt. The lowest of the three estates or the feet of the body politic, those who fetched and hewed were readily disregarded by polite society, that is, when they weren't serving as absurdly comic figures. By comparison with the thicket of gender, contempt for workers seems attractively simple in its structure, though here too we will find some inviting complications.

Sometimes what was salient about workers was their work, in all its sheer physicality and degrading splendor. "How many by inhuman toil debased," lamented the young Wordsworth, "Abject, obscure, and brute to earth incline / Unrespited, forlorn of every spark divine?"[115] The time-honored routines of rural life were familiar enough, but there were new developments to grapple with. Blake's "dark Satanic Mills"[116] and the rest of the new industrial landscape loomed large. The odious cotton mills themselves were explored in the sad tale of Robert Blincoe, a desperately exploited waif.[117] Posing as a Spanish traveller, Southey bared the underbelly of English prosperity by leading his readers through an alarming visit to Birmingham. "Every where around us, instead of the village church whose steeple usually adorns so beautifully the English landscape; the tower of some manufactory was to be seen in the distance, vomiting up flames and smoke, and blasting every thing around with its metallic vapours." Filth was strewn and spewing everywhere, the people themselves filthy, some

---

[115] William Wordsworth, *Salisbury Plain* [1793–1794], in *The Salisbury Plain Poems*, ed. Stephen Gill (Ithaca, NY: Cornell University Press, 1975), pp. 35–36.

[116] *Milton* [1804], in *William Blake's Writings*, ed. G. E. Bentley, Jr., 2 vols. (Oxford: Clarendon, 1978), 1:318.

[117] John Brown, *A Memoir of Robert Blincoe, an Orphan Boy* (Manchester, 1832). The *Memoir* was serialized in the *Lion*. Consider too "The Factory" [1835], in *Poetical Works of Letitia Elizabeth Landon "L.E.L."*, ed. F. J. Sypher (Delmar, NY: Scholars' Facsimiles & Reprints, 1990), pp. 569–71.

adults boasting grotesque "red eyes and green hair," the children "in rags, and their skins encrusted with soot and filth."[118]

Such scenes produced poignant images of dehumanization. Some observers thought workers had been turned into animals. "I cannot pretend to say," Southey reported somberly, "what is the consumption here of the two-legged beasts of labour; commerce sends in no return of its killed and wounded."[119] Godwin attacked child labor in the production of silk threads. "Numbness and vacancy of mind are the fruits of such an employment. It ultimately transforms the being who is subjected to it, into quite a different class or species of animal."[120] "The dull routine of a ceaseless drudgery, in which the same mechanical process is incessantly repeated," explained one student of urban poverty, was stupefying. The worker lost sight of genuinely human pursuits and gained "the habits of an animal," living wretchedly and pursuing mere sensory gratification.[121] Maybe workers had sunk lower than the animals. Mary Shelley found another arresting formulation of the dehumanization implicit in poverty: "*As well be a cabbage as poor.*"[122]

Other observers thought that workers had left the kingdom of the living altogether and entered the realm of inanimate equipment. Less intelligent workers "are regarded by their employers as parts of the machinery," disclosed Elizabeth Hamilton.[123] *Blackwood's* gloomily agreed: "The lower orders—for godsake quarrel not with the word lower, for they are as low as tyranny can tread them down—are in many places as much parts of the machinery as are spindles."[124] The indictment comes from right and left, Southey and Godwin alike, just as it echoes back to Adam Smith and forward to Karl Marx alike.[125]

---

[118] Robert Southey, *Letters from England* [1807], ed. Jack Simmons (London: Cresset Press, 1951), pp. 203, 197, 203.

[119] Southey, *Letters from England*, p. 197.

[120] William Godwin, *Fleetwood: or, The New Man of Feeling*, 3 vols. (London, 1805), 1:265–66.

[121] James Phillips Kay, *The Moral and Physical Condition of the Working Classes Employed in the Cotton Manufacture in Manchester*, 2d ed. (London, 1832; reprint ed. London: Frank Cass, 1970), p. 22.

[122] *Journals of Mary Shelley*, 2:516 [1 December 1830].

[123] Elizabeth Hamilton, *A Series of Popular Essays, Illustrative of Principles Essentially Connected with the Improvement of the Understanding, the Imagination, and the Heart*, 2 vols. (Edinburgh, 1813), 1:129.

[124] *Blackwood's Edinburgh Magazine* (April 1833) 33(206):419–20.

[125] For Smith, see *An Inquiry into the Nature and Causes of the Wealth of Nations* [1776],

Now surely this indictment isn't contemptuous. Here the distinction between human worth and social status is deep and sincere, and there are no bleak ironies about policing Berlin's boundaries. That is, all these writers wanted to alleviate the plight of industrial workers, to make them more fully human, though of course they had wildly disparate views about how to accomplish that—and, perhaps, about what would have qualified as fully human. All of them cast the evils of industrial poverty as contingent, as within the scope of political agency. So too the *Black Dwarf* was appalled by the predicament of the homeless, of "thousands of miserable, half-famished beings, in the shape of free-born Englishmen, who wander about in search of a miserable pittance, and that nightly take shelter upon the bridges, and outhouses, till death gives relief, by putting an end to their sufferings."[126] The journal clung to its regard for workers reduced to such misery. Their plight too was contingent, it insisted, the product of harsh taxation.

Others disagreed. Pride of place goes to Burke, never one to pull his punches, though he couldn't have had in mind the same daunting scenes of industrialism that later commentators did. Incensed by France's confiscation of the church's massive property holdings, Burke fumes,

> The monks are lazy. Be it so. Suppose them no otherwise employed than by singing in the choir. They are as usefully employed as those who neither sing nor say,—as usefully even as those who sing upon the stage. They are as usefully employed as if they worked from dawn to dark in the innumerable servile, degrading, unseemly, unmanly, and often most unwholesome and pestiferous occupations to which by the social economy so many wretches are inevitably doomed.[127]

That *unmanly* oughtn't be overlooked—in turning to class we haven't left behind gender—and I'll return to it later. Another cruel neces-

ed. R. H. Campbell, A. S. Skinner, and W. B. Todd, 2 vols. (Oxford: Clarendon, 1976), 2:781–85; *Lectures on Jurisprudence,* ed. R. L. Meek, D. D. Raphael, and P. G. Stein (Oxford: Clarendon, 1978), pp. 539–41 [1766]. The universality of the indictment was noticed in *England and America* [1833], in *The Collected Works of Edward Gibbon Wakefield,* ed. M. F. Lloyd Prichard (Glasgow: Collins, 1968), p. 338.

[126] Juvenis to the editor, *Black Dwarf* (16 February 1820) 4(6):211–12.

[127] *Reflections on the Revolution in France* [1790], in *Works,* 3:445. For a response, see Thomas Beddoes, *Hygëia: or Essays Moral and Medical, on the Causes Affecting the Personal State of Our Middling and Affluent Classes,* 3 vols. (Bristol, 1802–1803), 1(2):58–61.

sity, outside the scope of political agency, consigns workers to a grim fate. We should admire Burke's bravado—or is it gall?—in asserting that a singing monk is every bit as useful as these indispensable workers. Compare Arthur Young, touring France just before the Revolution, outraged by the sight of the wealthiest abbey of the kingdom: "What a noble farm would the fourth of this income establish! What turnips, what cabbages, what potatoes, what clover, what sheep, what wool! Are not these things better than a fat ecclesiastic?"[128] Young's unbudging emphasis on instrumental rationality makes a mockery of the profoundly expressive practices of the *ancien régime*. But Burke isn't posturing. Monks who sing all day help consecrate religion and lend the church an imposing status. If Christianity is a crucial prop in maintaining social order, who can say their work is useless?

The other sort of useful workers themselves needed some decent drapery and veils, not the harsh glare of public discussion. Exasperated by talk of the laboring poor, Burke urged that they be treated compassionately: "But let there be no lamentation of their condition. It is no relief to their miserable circumstances; it is only an insult to their miserable understandings."[129] Other sorts of relief were available, anyway: unlike those disturbed by the unseemly antics of workers in the alehouse, Burke embraced alcohol as "a medicine for the mind."[130] There weren't many rich people anyway, so slitting their throats and redistributing their assets wouldn't appreciably improve the plight of the poor. It would, though, shatter civilization. The rich "are trustees for those who labor"; "deducting some very trifling commission and discount," their assets redound to the welfare of the poor.[131] (Hazlitt found this laughable.[132]) Here the low status of workers is unalterable fact, and that tends to corrode any independent sense of their human worth.

---

[128] Arthur Young, *Travels in France during the Years 1787, 1788 & 1789*, ed. Constantia Maxwell (Cambridge: Cambridge University Press, 1950), p. 81 [14 October 1787].

[129] *Thoughts and Details on Scarcity* [1795], in *Works*, 5:135. Note too *Letters on a Regicide Peace* [1796–1797], in *Works*, 5:466. Burke to Charles O'Hara, 30 December 1762, *The Correspondence of Edmund Burke*, ed. Thomas W. Copeland, 10 vols. (Chicago: University of Chicago Press, 1958–1978), 1:162 does refer to "the wretched poor whose Burthens are already so lamentably heavy."

[130] *Thoughts and Details on Scarcity*, in *Works*, 5:164.

[131] *Thoughts and Details on Scarcity*, in *Works*, 5:134. See too *Association Papers* (London, 1793), pt. 2, no. 8, p. 7.

[132] *Political Essays, with Sketches of Public Characters* [1819], in *Works of Hazlitt*, 7:108–9.

Sometimes what was salient about workers was their poverty, taken as choiceworthy, even crucial. Social order itself required poverty, according to Soame Jenyns. A wealthy worker, if one could imagine such an odd fellow, would be threatening in just the same way an educated worker was: "Had all been rich, none could have submitted to the commands of another, or the drudgeries of life; thence all governments must have been dissolved, arts neglected, and lands uncultivated; and so an universal penury have overwhelmed all, instead of now and then pinching a few."[133] Dr. Johnson thought it a mistake to raise the wages of ordinary workers. Instead of improving their lives, the additional money would make them idle, "and idleness is a very bad thing for human nature."[134] "The greatest of evils to agriculture," explained one patient observer, "would be to place the labourer in a state of independence, and thus destroy the indispensable gradations of society."[135] The same sensibility was evinced by a critic of the poor laws who spied "a law of nature, that the poor should be to a certain degree improvident, that there may always be some to fulfil the most servile, the most sordid, and the most ignoble offices in the community." This happy fact let "the more delicate" escape doing the dirty work.[136]

Workers may not have invested emotionally in their inferior status, but it was enforced anyway. London workers were feisty and independent minded, reported one sketch, but still they had to put up with insults from their employers, lest they be fired.[137] For once, the lower orders were responsible agents:

> But poverty with most who whimper forth
> Their long complaints, is self-inflicted woe,
> The effects of laziness or sottish waste.[138]

[133] *A Free Inquiry into the Nature and Origin of Evil* [1758], in *The Works of Soame Jenyns, Esq.*, 4 vols. (London, 1790), 3:59–60.

[134] *Boswell's Life of Johnson: Together with Boswell's Journal of a Tour to the Hebrides and Johnson's Diary of a Journey into North Wales*, ed. George Birkbeck Hill, rev. L. F. Powell, 6 vols. (Oxford: Clarendon, 1934–1950), 4:176–77 [30 March 1783].

[135] Thomas Rudge, *General View of the Agriculture of the County of Gloucester* (London, 1807), p. 48.

[136] Joseph Townsend, *A Dissertation on the Poor Laws by a Well-Wisher to Mankind* [1786] (Berkeley: University of California Press, 1971), p. 35.

[137] *Modern London; Being the History and Present State of the British Metropolis* (London, 1804), pp. 135–36.

[138] *The Task* [1784], in *The Works of William Cowper*, ed. Robert Southey, 15 vols. (London, 1836–1837), 9:180.

One poetaster looked back at her days in the workhouse, shuddered, and did her best to eke out some distance between herself and the loathsome creatures she'd dwelt among:

> Within these dreary walls confin'd,
> A lone recluse, I live,
> And, with the dregs of human kind,
> A niggard alms receive.
>
> Uncultivated, void of sense,
> Unsocial, insincere,
> Their rude behaviour gives offence,
> Their language wounds the ear.[139]

If unemployment is structural, there's no point singling out particular unemployed people for blame: this is the left's version of an appeal to necessity.

In 1792, William Paley produced *Reasons for Contentment, Addressed to the Labouring Part of the British Public*.[140] The poor, Paley argues, are better off than the rich, even forgetting their happy afterlife. The poor are busy working, bustling with physical and mental vitality, cheerful and serene, "free from many heavy anxieties which rich men feel . . . fraught with many sources of delight which they want."[141] Paley labors so intensively to establish the choiceworthiness of poverty that it becomes mysterious why the rich don't try to foist off their assets on unsuspecting poor people, or for that matter why they don't bury or burn them. Paley's Christianity wasn't the hellfire-and-brimstone sort, but perhaps he would have appealed to our corrupt fallen natures to explain this mystery. Like More's Cheap Repository Tracts, his tract was much reprinted, doing its bit to soothe the in-

---

[139] Ann Candler, *Poetical Attempts* (Ipswich, 1803), p. 53.

[140] *Reasons for Contentment; Addressed to the Labouring Part of the British Public* (Carlisle, 1792), also in *The Works of William Paley, D.D. Archdeacon of Carlisle*, 2 vols. (London, 1828), 2(1):216–22.

[141] *Reasons for Contentment*, p. 21; in *Works of Paley*, 2(1):222. Compare *Rambler* (6 October 1750) no. 58, in *The Yale Edition of the Works of Samuel Johnson*, ed. Herman W. Liebert and others, in progress (New Haven, CT: Yale University Press, 1958–), 3:309–13; William Burdon, *Advice, Addressed to the Lower Ranks of Society; Useful at All Times, More Especially in the Present* (Newcastle upon Tyne, 1803), pp. 3–4, 15; Elizabeth Hamilton, *The Cottagers of Glenburnie: A Tale for the Farmer's Ingle-Nook* (Edinburgh, 1808; reprint ed. New York: Garland, 1974), pp. 49, 253–54.

flamed lower orders: Paley himself offered it to Reeves's Association for Preserving Liberty and Property against Republicans and Levellers for broader circulation.[142] In 1817, William Hone noticed an advertisement in the *Times:* the tract was being distributed yet once more. "*It is false,*" he thundered, "that whilst some have exhorbitant fortunes, the rest are happy." Circulating such views "in the midst of desolation and ruin" was outrageous, "mocking the poor man's sorrow—jesting upon his misery."[143] Two years later the *Black Dwarf* reported a morsel of news sounding as though it came straight from Elizabethan England. "Five poor miserable wretches" had been dragged through the streets of Newington and then whipped for daring to beg. It was an attempt, urged the journal, "to create a courtly contempt for the rights and feelings of the poor" and to make whipping acceptable routine. "Whatever Paley and Malthus, or other arrogant and full fed priests" might say, though, the compassionate English would continue to relieve the needy.[144] Yet in 1825, *John Bull* reprinted Paley's tract. It was a dangerous time, they warned, "when the servant turns upon his master, and the shopman claims to be a philosopher," a time calling for Paley's perennial wisdom.[145]

There were indeed prejudices in favor of the rich, reported Johnson. No matter how many moralists denounced the habit, no matter how often people were reminded that sterling virtue was "obscured by indigence," "poverty still continues to produce contempt. . . ."[146] Charlotte Smith's Ethelinde screws up her courage to renounce her beloved: "Do you think then that I could bear to see Montgomery, the descendant of so many heroes—himself the worthiest, the most truly noble of his race—degraded for my sake to the abject condition of labouring for bread, or humbling himself to the drudgery of a mechanic?"[147] (Such frightful prospects, endemic in the contemporary

[142] I assume this is the "short tract" offered in William Paley to John Reeves, 14 December 1792, British Library, Add. Mss. 16922, f. 93; it appears in *Association Papers,* pt. 1, no. 6. See Robert Faulder to John Reeves, 13 February 1793, Add. Mss. 16925, f. 26, complaining that he is the proprietor of *Reasons for Contentment* and Reeves has no permission to reprint it.

[143] *Hone's Reformist Register* (19 April 1817) 1(13):393–94.

[144] Peter Playfair to editor, *Black Dwarf* (19 May 1819) 3(20):317–18.

[145] *John Bull* (9 October 1825) 5(41):325–26. See too *Bristol Job Nott* (4 October 1832) no. 43, pp. 170–71.

[146] *Rambler* (19 October 1751) no. 166, in *Works of Johnson,* 5:116.

[147] Charlotte Smith, *Ethelinde, or The Recluse of the Lake,* 2d ed., 5 vols. (London, 1790), 3:132–33.

novel, help stamp it as a middle-class genre.) The radical essayists of Norwich's Society of Gentlemen complained of the "insolent superiority" assumed by the rich, the "cold and supercilious contempt" they exhibited toward their brothers, the poor—and marvelled at the sight of poor people assenting in their own inferiority.[148] The radicals of Willie Semple's Club set the refrain to music:

> 'Tis hard to bear a rich man's look,
> The pride, contempt, the jeer o't,
> He measures worth by length o'purse,
> An' kens ye've no your share o't.[149]

Facing this traditional barrage of contempt, some observers fought valiantly to articulate and defend the dignity of labor. They needed to turn the world upside down, to expose the ghastly anomalies in enshrining the leisured aristocracy as the pinnacle of social hierarchy. In Tom Paine's caustic pun, the nobility emerged as the no-ability, rudely stripped of any legitimate claim to their wealth, power, and social status.[150] A radical wondered why labor "is held in the utmost contempt by the useless great, though at the same time they derive all their luxury and exclusive advantages from the exertions of the industrious poor."[151] One workers' journal held that "usefulness and utility are the only badges which ought to entitle a fellow creature to respect . . . that the scavenger, the chimney sweep, the washerwoman and the spunkmaker, if their behaviour be consistent, are infinitely more worthy of the thanks and respect of society than my lord who has nothing to recommend him but the thousands of acres which his birth entitles him to. . . ."[152] Years later, one radical sadly recalled the "really contemptible feeling of class-ism, the curse of England and Englishmen," the rich who spurned social contact with the poor and so "filled the working classes with a fierce contempt and hatred of

---

[148] A Society of Gentlemen, *The Cabinet,* 3 vols. (Norwich, 1795), 1:35–36. See too William Cobbett, *Cottage Economy,* new ed. (London, 1826), §§5–6.

[149] James Paterson, *Autobiographical Reminiscences* (Glasgow, 1871), p. 68 [*circa* 1820].

[150] *Rights of Man* [1791], in *The Life and Works of Thomas Paine,* 10 vols. (New Rochelle, NY: Thomas Paine National Historical Association, 1925), 6:138.

[151] Charles Pigott, *A Political Dictionary: Explaining the True Meaning of Words* (London, 1795), p. 67 s.v. *Labour.* See too Godwin, *Of Population,* p. 586.

[152] *Herald to Trades Advocate* (16 October 1830), quoted in Patricia Hollis, *The Pauper Press: A Study in Working-Class Radicalism of the 1830s* (London: Oxford University Press, 1970), pp. 22–23.

every one wearing a decent coat." Wouldn't it be better, he asked plaintively, for everyone to meet on terms of dignified equality?[153]

But these champions of the dignity of labor also needed to distance workers from those poor enough to find themselves supported by the parish, lavished with the disgrace and disgust deliberately created by the poor laws. The so-called Speenhamland system, adopted in May 1795 but essentially practiced for many decades already,[154] supplemented the wages of poor workers to keep them independent or offered them foodstuffs at below-market prices. Suppose that these payments brought the worker's net income to precisely the same level that a higher wage would have. Then it might seem—to an economist— that it made no difference whether the wage was raised or the parish supplemented it. Workers disagreed. Some Norfolk workers turned to Scripture.[155] "The Labourer is worthy of his Hire," they insisted. "Selling him flour under the market price, and thereby rendering him an object of a parish rate, is . . . an indecent insult on his lowly and humble situation. . . ."[156] One clergyman attributed the infamous crumbling independence of the poor to this very system: it was all too demoralizing for workers to find themselves already on the rates, so they succumbed to passivity.[157]

Especially beguiling was drawing invidious distinctions within the ranks of labor, refusing to believe that workers as such were dignified, securing the dignity of some by denying that of others. So painters looked down on engravers, whom they cast as mere mechanics.[158] It was imperative, insisted another writer, to retain the distinction between artists and artisans. Painters and engravers alike qualified as dignified artists, along with architects and sculptors. But not masons,

[153] Samuel Bamford, *Passages in the Life of a Radical,* 2 vols. (London, 1844), 2:89–90.

[154] John Knott, *Popular Opposition to the 1834 Poor Law* (London: Croom Helm, 1986), pp. 16–20; Mark D. Neuman, "A Suggestion Regarding the Origins of the Speenhamland Plan," *English Historical Review* (April 1969) 84:317–22.

[155] *Luke* 10:7.

[156] *Norfolk Chronicle* (14 November 1795), quoted in Roger Wells, *Wretched Faces: Famine in Wartime England 1793–1801* (Gloucester: Alan Sutton, 1988), p. 163.

[157] Wells, *Wretched Faces,* p. 332.

[158] *Diary of Farington,* 4:1573 [5 July 1801]; see too *Diary of Haydon,* 3:651–53 [19 October 1832]. See John Barrell, *The Political Theory of Painting from Reynolds to Hazlitt: 'The Body of the Public'* (New Haven, CT: Yale University Press, 1986), chap. 1, esp. pp. 12–16, emphasizing the centrality of the liberal/mechanic distinction in the civic humanist vocabulary of art.

bricklayers, carpenters, smiths, and housepainters, lowly artisans all. "Too long have artisans, however able in their own trades, usurped the titles and immunities of artists, which honorable name should scarcely be allowed to the practisers of the lower departments of the fine arts; by how much less, then, to those artisans, who thus so shamelessly assume it."[159]

Alexander Somerville rebelled at what he saw as the intolerable tyranny of masons over their laborers. Apprentices and others working to master a trade were supposed to be deferential.[160] But Somerville thought that the radical principles of parliamentary reform adopted by many workers ought to apply to the workplace, too, replacing a dismal pageant of swaggering and self-abasement with the uplifting routines of dignified equality.[161] Social distinctions, he discovered to his chagrin, were present everywhere, not just in such familiar cases as the relation between noble lord and tenant farmer. "Look for them also between the artizan who has long tails to his coat, and the humbler labourer who has short tails to his coat; between the engine-maker, who is a free member of his trade, and the blacksmith, who has not been apprenticed to engine-making." Indeed the barriers to social mobility were far more imposing in such cases. "No matter how high the ability of the blacksmith may be, nor how willing the master-mechanic may be to promote him and make use of his superior abilities, he is doomed to remain a blacksmith; he cannot pass the boundary which rigorously excludes him from rising above the level of the blacksmith class."[162]

Revealingly, when the gruffly affectionate *Bristol Job Nott* wanted to say something reassuring about the plight of workers, the paper turned to the domestic household. "I don't know a more respectable title for a labouring person, than that of 'an old servant.'" Old servants were "looked up to with respect in the family," gratefully remembered by the children for their good work.[163] No condescension and insolence here, just the sort of paternal affection dictated by many decades of homilies—and, I'm sure, faithfully offered by many

[159] James Elmes, *A Letter to Thomas Hope, Esq.,* in *Pamphleteer* (1814) 3(6):331–32.

[160] See for instance Henry George Watkins, *Affectionate Advice to Apprentices, on Their Being Bound at Weavers' Hall* (London, 1827).

[161] Alexander Somerville, *The Autobiography of a Working Man* (London, 1848), pp. 145–48.

[162] Somerville, *Autobiography*, pp. 179–80.

[163] *Bristol Job Nott* (22 August 1833) no. 89, p. 353.

family heads and other employers, too. Yet again, that paternal affection was made possible only by assigning the servant a lower status. And again, that lower status made possible some rather less savory emotions and treatment.

I want to assign the last word on these matters to Francis Place, the radical tailor who lost a slew of customers when they discovered he had the effrontery to assemble a library for himself. E. P. Thompson detested Place—he saw him as pandering to the utilitarians, or, as Thompson sweetly put it, "sitting to James Mill for his own portrait as the White Man's Trusty Nigger"[164]—and Place did take a less radical line on the politics of labor than the cherished heroes of Thompson's morality play. (Place was also instrumental in the 1824 repeal of the combination laws that had made workers' unions illegal, a change hustled through Parliament with minimal publicity and debate.[165]) But Place thought long and hard and acutely about contempt for the lower orders. "Francis Place is a superior man, but why will he always wear a coat of bristles when he is in company with those who, by the accident of station, are his superiors in society?" wondered the Earl of Durham. "He is equal to them in reality, and yet he seems to think himself always called upon to evince his sturdy independence and his contempt for artificial distinctions."[166] There again is the slippery distinction between social superiors and "real" equals, a distinction that preoccupied, even tortured, Place himself. This white man's nigger was moved by the plight of those workers who scrimped and saved and worked and struggled and learned that their hopes of improvement were "but too often illusory," then plunged into despair and an early death. "None but such as they can tell how disappointment preys on them, how as the number of their children increases, hope leaves them, how their hearts sink as toil becomes useless, how adverse circumstances force on them those indiscribable feelings of their own degradation which sinks them gradually to the extreme of wretchedness." Many more, intent not on climbing the greased pole of prosperity but only on holding their own, also slipped into poverty.

[164] E. P. Thompson, *The Making of the English Working Class* (New York: Vintage Books, 1966), p. 154.

[165] Dudley Miles, *Francis Place 1771–1854: The Life of a Remarkable Radical* (Sussex: Harvester Press, 1988), p. 164.

[166] Stuart J. Reid, *Life and Letters of the First Earl of Durham 1792–1840,* 2 vols. (London: Longmans, Green, 1906), 1:346–47 [n.d.].

I have seen a vast many such, who when the evil day has come upon them, have kept on working steadily but hopelessly more like horses in a mill, or mere machines than human beings, their feelings blunted, poor stultified moving animals, working on yet unable to support their families in any thing like comfort, frequently wanting the common necessaries of life, yet never giving up until "misery has eaten them to the bone," none knowing none caring for them, no one to administer a word of comfort, or if an occasion occured which might be of service to them, none to rouse them to take advantage of it. All above them in circumstances, calumniating them, classing them with the dissolute, the profligate and the dishonest, from whom the character of the whole of the working people is taken. Yet I have witnessed in this class of persons, so dispised so unjustly judged of by their betters, virtues which I have not seen, to the same extent as to means, among any other description of the people. Justice will never perhaps be done to them because they may never be understood, because it is not the habit for men to care for others beneath them in rank, and because they who employ them will probably never fail to look grudgingly on the pay they are compelled to give them for their services, the very notion of which produces an inward hatred of them, a feeling so common that it is visible in the countenance and manners in nearly every one who has to pay either journeymen, labourers, or servants.[167]

Fanny Burney, remember, found the ceremony of lining up to receive her salary as servant to the royal family utterly dispiriting. The cash nexus, so brazenly displayed, was degrading. She was heartened by the awkward embarrassment of the man paying her. It never occurred to her that those paying her might have shared her sentiments, might have found her degraded, their easy condescension and undoubted amiability accompanying sentiments of ready hostility and unvarnished contempt. It's too easy to think that the *Bristol Job Nott* captured the sentiments of some employers, Place those of others; just as it's too easy to think that some men prized women while others despised them. All these sentiments are intricately woven together. That helps explain why contempt is as intractable, as irresistible, and as loathsome as it is.

[167] *The Autobiography of Francis Place (1771–1854)*, ed. Mary Thale (Cambridge: Cambridge University Press, 1972), pp. 127–28.

# SEVEN

# A GUIDE TO THE MENAGERIE: BLACKS AND JEWS

—◦◦◦—

I T'S TRICKIER, though not impossible, to find sneaking admiration for blacks combined with nasty contempt. Now we're up against something closer to unmitigated disgust. The blacks of coastal Africa, wrote one defender of slavery, were

> stupid and unenlightened Hordes, immersed in the most gross and impenetrable glooms of barbarism, dark in mind as in complexion, prodigiously populous, impatient of all control, profoundly ignorant, unteachable, lazy, ferocious as their own congenial tigers, nor in any respect superiour to these rapacious beasts in intellectual advancement; but distinguished only by a rude and imperfect organ of speech, which is abusively employed on the utterance of dissonant and inarticulate jargons.[1]

Africans had no history: "The natives neither admit nor even know of innovation, their manners remaining from age to age invariably the same. . . ."[2] (So were Africans the very model of loyal conservative subjects, uninterested in heated political discussion and Jacobin radicalism, stolidly attached to their past traditions?) "Their intellect has stood still for many thousand years," agreed *Blackwood's,* "and has, up to this moment, done absolutely NOTHING—"[3]

These blacks manage somehow to be simultaneously inert and loathsome. In the imaginations of these angry and bemused commentators, they are strictly speaking subhuman, or as we would see it

---

[1] *Slavery No Oppression; or, Some New Arguments and Opinions against the Idea of African Liberty* (London, 179–), p. 12.

[2] Miss Tully, *Narrative of a Ten Years' Residence at Tripoli in Africa,* 2d ed. (London, 1817), p. iii.

[3] *Blackwood's Edinburgh Magazine* (December 1823) 14(83):652.

dehumanized more rudely, more unequivocally, than workers and women. Some of that depends on the demographic context. One historian offers 10,000 as a ceiling estimate for Britain's black population through the eighteenth century.[4] So they weren't everywhere, like workers. Nor were they ordinarily living in one's home, though some were servants; nor on terms of sexual intimacy, though again some were, if not precisely as wives were. They were usually slaves in the Caribbean and prospective slaves in Africa, victims or targets or beneficiaries of vitriolic contempt and paternal benevolence, both crucially offered at a whopping geographic—and social—distance. Racial hierarchy was straightforward. Social status in Europe, reported one aristocrat, was "a science which requires a particular study," shot full of niggling difficulties and the possibility of embarrassing mistakes. In Saint Domingo, though, "it is only necessary to have eyes, to be able to place every individual in the class to which he belongs."[5]

Blacks' inferiority was manifest in their stupidity. In vain did their defenders point to Phyllis Wheatley and Ignatius Sancho as evidence of the natural aptitudes of blacks.[6] In vain did one wealthy Jamaica landholder insist that they learned mechanics and science with the same ease and tenacious attention as European whites.[7] In vain did the king of Haiti protest that critics of "the African race" failed to see that contingent facts about civilization explained the lesser achievements of blacks.[8] One traveller through southern Africa, William Bur-

---

[4] Folarin Shyllon, *Black People in Britain 1555–1833* (London: Oxford University Press for the Institute of Race Relations, 1977), p. 102.

[5] Francis Alexander Stanislaus, Baron de Wimpffen, *A Voyage to Saint Domingo, in the Years 1788, 1789, and 1790,* trans. J. Wright (London, 1797), pp. 42–43 [February 1789].

[6] Thomas Burgess, *Considerations on the Abolition of Slavery and the Slave Trade upon Grounds of Natural, Religious, and Political Duty* (Oxford, 1789), p. 133; J. G. Stedman, *Narrative of a Five Years' Expedition against the Revolted Negroes of Surinam, in Guiana, on the Wild Coast of South America; from the Year 1772, to 1777,* 2 vols. (London, 1796), 2:259–61. See too William Greenfield, *A Defence of the Surinam Negro-English Version of the New Testament* (London, 1830), p. 51.

[7] William Beckford [d. 1799], *A Descriptive Account of the Island of Jamaica,* 2 vols. (London, 1790), 2:351. See too *The Diary of the Rev.ᵈ· William Jones 1777–1821,* ed. O. F. Christie (London: Brentano's, 1929), p. 19 [6 May 1778].

[8] King Henry to the Emperor Alexander, 20 March 1819, *Henry Christophe & Thomas Clarkson: A Correspondence,* ed. Earl Leslie Griggs and Clifford H. Prator (Berkeley: University of California Press, 1952), pp. 134–35. See too *Edinburgh Review* (July 1805) 6(12):335.

chell, wanted to learn how bright—and how human—the Bushmen women were, so he posed some elementary moral questions. But his interpreter balked: "He declared they were so stupid that it was not in his power to make them comprehend at all."[9] "And as to the fact of inferiority in intellect, is it not now proved?" demanded William Cobbett. Not, he hastened to add, that their inferiority justified cruel treatment, any more than it would be legitimate to mistreat a puppy. (On another occasion, Cobbett asserted that a greyhound hunting hares displayed reason, "a great deal more than many a Negro that I have seen."[10]) This textbook instance of benevolent paternalism, the affection and regard made possible by a contemptuous assignment of low status, comes from the fully mature and radical Cobbett of 1830.[11] The *Anti-Jacobin Review* was already triumphantly on record in 1804 insisting that Africans had "a torpidity of understanding, and indolence of disposition which fits them for slavery." Nor could their inferiority itself be chalked up to slavery. "We believe the slave trade an effect of African inferiority, and not a cause," held the *Review*.[12] In 1807, the slave trade was abolished. Almost two decades later, though, *Blackwood's* stubbornly held on. Slavery and the slave trade hadn't produced "African ignorance, barbarity, and degradation," they explained; they were their results.[13]

Blacks' inferiority was manifest in their odor. In vain did Thomas Winterbottom protest that African women were extraordinarily attentive to personal cleanliness, that their smell came from anointing themselves with scented oil.[14] They had a "bestial or fetid smell," reported one observer of Jamaica, Edward Long, so strong that it could linger a full fifteen minutes after they had departed.[15] Bushmen

[9] William J. Burchell, *Travels in the Interior of Southern Africa*, 2 vols. (London, 1822–1824), 1:461 [17 November 1811].

[10] William Cobbett, *Rural Rides* [1830], ed. George Woodcock (Harmondsworth: Penguin, 1985), p. 62.

[11] *Political Register* (26 June 1830) 69(26):819. Compare an uncertain Henry Home, Lord Kames, *Sketches of the History of Man*, 2d ed., 4 vols. (Edinburgh, 1778), 1:50, 1:64–65.

[12] *Anti-Jacobin Review* (May 1804) 18:47–48. But see *Anti-Jacobin Review* (October 1818) 55:105–6.

[13] *Blackwood's Edinburgh Magazine* (December 1826) 20(120):891.

[14] Thomas Winterbottom, *An Account of the Native Africans in the Neighbourhood of Sierra Leone*, 2 vols. (London, 1803; reprint ed. London: Frank Cass, 1969), 1:102–3.

[15] Edward Long, *The History of Jamaica*, 3 vols. (London, 1774; reprint ed. London: Frank Cass, 1970), 2:352–53.

women, reported Burchell, were so revoltingly filthy that "the odor with which they tainted the air, kept me at the distance of a couple of yards, the nearest at which a person having any delicacy of smell, could endure their presence."[16]

Blacks' inferiority was manifest in their color. In vain did Dr. Johnson, a staunch foe of slavery,[17] argue that this was purely conventional.[18] (Johnson raised eyebrows when he left his black servant Frank a handsome bequest.[19]) The *Edinburgh Review* was unmoved by thought experiments about the reactions of Africans to a white woman deemed beautiful in England. "With great deference to the present chevaliers of Tombuctoo," they sneered, "we cannot help thinking, that the colour of the Europeans is intrinsically superior to that of their sable rivals."[20] Coleridge was intrigued to learn that "the Negroes often console themselves in their cruel punishments, that their wounds will become *white* / and looking on this as a grand Progression in their rank of Nature, spite of their abhorrence of the cruelty of white men." Africans loved white, he continued, even those of the interior who never had seen white men. Why, even their gods loved white. This wasn't just titillating travel gossip. By providing evidence for "permanent Principles of *Beauty*," by rebutting the kind of view offered by Dr. Johnson, the tale helped secure the objectivity of aesthetic judgments.[21] Skipping the obvious rejoinders about the slippage between white and the skin color of the people we refer to as white, I note only how intimately a racist fantasy gets embedded in a lofty account of aesthetics, another instance of the seamy and seamless copulation of low and high.

How did this racism arise? For some, the question would have been confounding. No special explanatory account was needed: this was

[16] Burchell, *Travels*, 1:460 [17 November 1811].

[17] *Taxation No Tyranny* [1775], in *The Yale Edition of the Works of Samuel Johnson*, ed. Herman W. Liebert and others, in progress (New Haven, CT: Yale University Press, 1958–), 10:454; *Boswell's Life of Johnson: Together with Boswell's Journal of a Tour to the Hebrides and Johnson's Diary of a Journey into North Wales*, ed. George Birkbeck Hill, rev. L. F. Powell, 6 vols. (Oxford: Clarendon, 1934–1950), 3:200–201 [23 September 1777].

[18] *Idler* (10 November 1759) no. 82, in *Works of Johnson*, 2:257.

[19] William Johnston Temple to Boswell, 6 January 1785, *The Correspondence and Other Papers of James Boswell Relating to the Making of the Life of Johnson*, ed. Marshall Waingrow (New York: McGraw-Hill, 1969), p. 39.

[20] *Edinburgh Review* (January 1806) 7(14):300–301.

[21] *The Notebooks of Samuel Taylor Coleridge*, ed. Kathleen Coburn, in progress (New York: Pantheon Books, 1957–), 2:2604 18.194 [June 1805].

just the transparently correct response to the patent inferiority of blacks. Those on the other side of the debate needed a story about how these entrenched beliefs in black inferiority had arisen. Usually, they appealed to slavery. "Contempt and degradation" clung tightly to blacks, explained one observer of the Caribbean, because they were slaves.[22] Blackness itself, insisted the *Edinburgh Review* in a more cosmopolitan mood, was no more contemptible than "the cut and colour of a prison uniform." True, they conceded, even blacks in the free states of America were "regarded with disgust and contempt." It was naive to think that all the pernicious effects of slavery would evaporate instantly on its repeal. Yet the *Review* was confident that after emancipation, "a very few generations" would do the trick.[23] *John Bull* derided the humanitarian idiocy of thinking these problems might have political solutions. Here, too, the scope of political agency was narrow:

> I sing the March of Intellect,
>   Which banish'd Slav'ry's rigours,
> And much more *free* than *welcome* made
>   Those idle dogs the NIGGERS.[24]

For thankless yet intransigent years, evangelical conservative William Wilberforce led the parliamentary battle against the slave trade. He offered a curious variant on the view that slavery produced contempt:

> In the minds of Europeans in general, more especially in vulgar minds, whether vulgar from the want of education, or morally vulgar, (a more inwrought and less curable vulgarity,) the personal peculiarities of the Negro race could scarcely fail, by diminishing sympathy, to produce impressions, not merely of contempt, but even of disgust and aversion. But how strongly are these impressions sure to be confirmed and augmented, when to all the effects of bodily distinctions are superadded all those arising from the want of civilization and knowledge, and still more, all the hateful vices that slavery never fails to engender or to aggravate.

[22] Bryan Edwards, *An Historical Survey of the French Colony in the Island of St. Domingo* (London, 1797), pp. 6–7.

[23] *Edinburgh Review* (March 1827) 45(90):389, 394.

[24] *John Bull* (5 October 1834) 14(721):317.

With the dexterity of a practiced politician, Wilberforce manages to avoid saying that blacks are naturally inferior. The problem with slavery is that it gives "to a contemptuous aversion for the Negro race the sanction of manners and of law," underwriting a racism that might be described as natural.[25]

A more provocative variant on the familiar position was offered by Thomas Clarkson, who tirelessly led the extraparliamentary campaign against the slave trade. In 1819, he referred to "that unhappy distinction between black and white, which originated in the execrable Slave Trade," meaning that not just racism but race itself was a product of slavery.[26] As far as I know, Clarkson nowhere pursues this suggestion. It's not hard to see how it might be pursued, though. If we want to exploit some group of people, it's helpful to eviscerate all sympathy for them, to make them the targets of a withering contempt. Lumping them together as an inferior race is an inviting way to do that. (Is this an invidiously functionalist explanation? Not if we imagine the ideologists of race self-consciously inventing and deploying the concept to serve this end. More indirect stories would evade functionalist fallacies, too, but that would take me too far afield.)

If contempt for blacks might quickly be glossed as racism, it would be helpful to have an account of race, which seems the logically prior notion. (But not necessarily: the superficial syntax aside, perhaps *race* will turn out to be whatever group is the target of an independently defined racism, which would then emerge as the primary notion.) In grappling with their contempt for blacks, contemporaries generated a surprisingly wide range of accounts of race, to which I now turn.

## "THESE INHUMAN DISTINCTIONS OF COLOURS"[27]

In an apparently innocent usage, *race* could refer to more or less any group of people. When Fanny Burney's Mr. Monckton denounces "a

[25] William Wilberforce, *An Appeal to the Religion, Justice, and Humanity of the Inhabitants of the British Empire, in Behalf of the Negro Slaves in the West Indies,* new ed. (London, 1823), p. 9.

[26] Thomas Clarkson to King Henry, 28 June 1819, *Henry Christophe & Thomas Clarkson: A Correspondence,* p. 141.

[27] John Stuart [Cugoano] to Granville Sharp, *circa* 1791, in Ottobah Cugoano, *Thoughts and Sentiments on the Evil and Wicked Traffic of the Slavery and Commerce of the Human Species, Humbly Submitted to the Inhabitants of Great-Britain* (London, 1787; reprint ed. London: Dawsons of Pall Mall, 1969), p. xxii.

jealous, vindictive, and insolent race," he's referring to the distinguished Delvile family and their obnoxious head.[28] Burney herself refers to "the male Race" (and ironically imagines herself being born one of its members as punishment for her sins).[29] Take Bentham's generous encomium to England's lawyers:

> A passive and enervate race, ready to swallow any thing, and to acquiesce in any thing: with intellects incapable of distinguishing right from wrong, and with affections alike indifferent to either: insensible, short-sighted, obstinate: lethargic, yet liable to be driven into convulsions by false terrors: deaf to the voice of reason and public utility: obsequious only to the whisper of interest, and to the beck of power.[30]

Cowper demurred that even though he was a Whig, he agreed that "the mad-caps of France" were "a terrible race."[31] A defender of London's newly projected police force assured skeptics that the police would restrict their attention "to the idle, desultory, profligate and marauding race of freebooters" responsible for London's troubles.[32] Thomas Creevey dined "with the ugliest and most dismal race I ever beheld," apparently as arbitrary a grouping as whoever happened to show up that evening at Fitzwilliam's.[33] The Romans, according to one aristocrat, were "not worth knowing. They are a dull, sulky, ill-

---

[28] Fanny Burney, *Cecilia, or Memoirs of an Heiress* [1782], ed. Peter Sabor and Margaret Anne Doody (Oxford: Oxford University Press, 1988), p. 765 (and see p. 462). See too Charlotte Smith, *Celestina*, 4 vols. (London, 1791), 1:12; Ann Constable to John Constable, 8 May 1810, in John Constable, *Correspondence*, ed. R. B. Beckett, 6 vols. (Ipswich: Suffolk Records Society, 1962–1968), 1:43; John Constable to Thomas Dunthorne, 19 April 1833, *Correspondence*, 1:274.

[29] *The Early Journals and Letters of Fanny Burney*, ed. Lars E. Troide and Stewart J. Cooke, 3 vols. to date (Oxford: Clarendon, 1988–), 1:250 [1773].

[30] *A Fragment on Government* [1776], in Jeremy Bentham, *A Comment on the Commentaries and A Fragment on Government*, ed. J. H. Burns and H. L. A. Hart (London: Athlone Press, 1977), p. 402.

[31] Cowper to Walter Bagot, 4 March 1793, *The Letters and Prose Writings of William Cowper*, ed. James King and Charles Ryskamp (Oxford: Clarendon, 1979–1986), 4:302. See too *The Diary of Joseph Farington*, ed. Kenneth Garlick, Angus Macintyre, and Kathryn Cave, 16 vols. (New Haven, CT: Published for the Paul Mellon Centre for Studies in British Art by Yale University Press, 1978–1984), 13:4668 [12 July 1815]; Robert Southey, *Journal of a Tour in the Netherlands in the Autumn of 1815* (Boston: Houghton, Mifflin and Company, 1902), pp. 70–71.

[32] George B. Mainwaring, *Observations on the Present State of the Police of the Metropolis*, 2d ed., in *Pamphleteer* (1822) 20(39):232.

[33] Creevey to Elizabeth Ord, 2 June 1834, *The Creevey Papers*, ed. Herbert Maxwell (New York: E. P. Dutton, 1904), p. 619.

bred, ignorant, inhospitable people—from high to low, the worst race in Europe with which I have any acquaintance."[34] A leading citizen of Birmingham inveighed against "this degenerate race" of London prostitutes.[35]

We may want to discard these cases, to say that even if they happen to use the word *race,* it's not the same concept we're after, that this is a mere homonym. I'm not so sure that's right: at least other cases can't be so easily finessed. Take Coleridge: "Men of genius are rarely much annoyed by the company of vulgar people; because they have a power of looking at such persons as objects of amusement, of another race altogether."[36] A race of vulgar or stupid people: is that a genuine or merely metaphoric race? Does a concept as nefarious and slippery as that of race admit of a genuine or innocent or primary usage and then parasitic and metaphoric usages? Or are there no clear core cases to which it applies? If there is a clear core, does it have to do with something revolving around blood or genetics? Or, as Coleridge seems to suggest, around hierarchy and contempt?

Or take a characteristically arch comment from Charles Lamb. Finally, he insisted, there were "two distinct races, *the men who borrow,* and *the men who lend.*" All the other races—white, black, red, Gothic, Celtic, you name it—finally reduced to these two. "The infinite superiority of the former, which I choose to designate as the *great race,* is discernible in their figure, port, and a certain instinctive sovereignty. The latter are born degraded." As we'll see, Lamb's conjuring up moneylenders would have led his readers to think about Jews: Bentham thought that disdain for the "odious" ways of Jewish moneylenders helped explain what he took to be irrational opposition to collecting interest.[37] And plenty of those readers were ready to classify Jews as a race. But suppose we take Lamb at face value. Race is built around hierarchy and domination. That domination makes the lender "lean and suspicious, contrasting with the open, trusting, gen-

[34] Lord Dudley to Mary Berry, 10 May 1824, *Extracts from the Journals and Correspondence of Miss Berry from the Year 1783 to 1852,* ed. Lady Theresa Lewis, 2d ed., 3 vols. (London, 1866), 3:351.

[35] W. Hutton, *A Journey from Birmingham to London* (Birmingham, 1785), p. 77.

[36] *Table Talk,* in *The Collected Works of Samuel Taylor Coleridge,* ed. Kathleen Coburn, Bart Winer, and others, in progress (Princeton, NJ: Princeton University Press, 1969–), 14(1):429 [17 August 1833].

[37] *Defence of Usury* [1816], in *The Works of Jeremy Bentham,* ed. John Bowring, 11 vols. (Edinburgh, 1843), 3:16.

erous manners of the other."[38] Once again, is this not "really" about race? Why ever not?

Brougham warned the House of Commons that if England were ever held accountable for her stewardship of Ireland, she would be found sorely wanting. Under English governance, he charged, the Irish had become "a wretched, suffering, degraded race—without a motive for exertion—starving in the midst of plenty."[39] The Duke of Northumberland was wrong, Harriet Arbuthnot confided in her diary. He "thinks the Catholics are the oppressed race, whereas they are the most numerous, the most barbarous & the most turbulent, & our only chance of civilizing Ireland is by coercing them."[40] Are Irish Catholics a race? What kind of question is this, anyway? What would count as a reasonable answer? What criteria sensibly govern application of the concept? Brougham may have the apparently innocent usage in mind, the one making *race* any kind of grouping at all. Not so, I suspect, Arbuthnot. Not so, I'm sure, Southey, who thought Ireland inhabited "by a race of ignorant and ferocious barbarians, who can never be civilized till they are regenerated—till their very nature is changed."[41] The unholy mix of uncivilized savages and a defective nature seems intuitively to cut close to the bone of the concept of race.

In their efforts at popular education, Hannah More and her sister Martha saw themselves as missionaries who didn't have to venture abroad to discover exotic foreigners in need of English civilization and Christianity. One town was full of "savages," of "more ignorance than we supposed existed anywhere in England." Some parents apparently believed that if the Mores had their children for seven years they'd gain the right to "send them beyond sea. I must have heard this myself," marvelled Hannah, "in order to have believed that so much ignorance existed out of Africa." Glassworkers, recorded Martha, were the worst yet: "Both sexes and all ages herding together; voluptuous beyond belief"; the factories themselves, crammed full of

[38] *Elia* [1823], in *The Works of Charles and Mary Lamb,* ed. E. V. Lucas, 6 vols. (New York: Macmillan, 1913), 2:26.

[39] *Speeches of Henry Lord Brougham,* 4 vols. (Edinburgh, 1838), 4:46 [26 June 1823].

[40] *The Journal of Mrs. Arbuthnot 1820–1832,* ed. Francis Bamford and the Duke of Wellington, 2 vols. (London: Macmillan, 1950), 2:302 [3 September 1829].

[41] Robert Southey, *Journal of a Tour in Scotland in 1819,* ed. C. H. Herford (London: John Murray, 1929), p. 137. See too W. R. Ward, *Religion and Society in England 1790–1850* (London: B. T. Batsford, 1972), p. 210.

"half-dressed, black-looking beings," offering "a most infernal and horrible appearance," shades of Blake's dark Satanic mills. Even colliers, she noted later with relief, "are abundantly more human than the people of the glass-houses."[42] There's no explicit mention of race here, but it's lingering in the margins.

We needn't suspect the Mores of any invidious preconceptions because of their evangelical conservatism. Richard Carlile pressed similar complaints:

> For want of more attention to the health of the people who work in cotton mills, a very diminutive and degenerate race of people is growing up in Lancashire, that promises to degrade our national character. Indeed, the cotton people, as a whole, in Lancashire, form a new race of people, below, in wretched appearance, any that have been known to live within the temperate zone.[43]

In turning to class, I noted, we didn't leave behind gender; now I can add that in turning to race, we haven't left behind class. Did the punitive turmoils of early industrialism create a new degenerate race of English? Could they do such a thing? Take the whole package of bruising assaults, the occupational hazards and physical defects and illnesses and filth and poverty and desperate lack of education. Were their victims maltreated English, obviously still of the same racial stock they always had been? Or were they transmuted into a new race? Is this another of the wondrous alchemies of capitalism? Isn't it illuminating, if grisly, that one writer in the 1820s fantasized about eugenics programs for improving the peasantry—"I cannot help thinking that, if the same pains were taken in breeding mankind that gentlemen have bestowed upon the breeding of horses and dogs, human nature might, as it were, be new modelled"—and suggested that an aristocrat pursuing such an inspired project would gain immortality?[44]

[42] Martha More's journal, October 1789, *Mendip Annals,* ed. Arthur Roberts (New York, 1859), p. 23; Hannah More to Wilberforce, *circa* 1792, *Mendip Annals,* p. 51; Martha More's journal, 1792, *Mendip Annals,* pp. 61–63.

[43] *Lion* (29 February 1828) 1(9):283. See too William Godwin, *Fleetwood: or, The New Man of Feeling,* 3 vols. (London, 1805), 1:264–66; An Honorary Director, *Letters to John Probert . . . upon the Advantages and Defects of the Montgomery and Pool House of Industry* (London, 1801), pp. 42–43; Sydney Smith to Francis Jeffrey, 7 August 1821, *Letters of Sydney Smith,* ed. Nowell C. Smith, 2 vols. (Oxford: Clarendon, 1953), 1:378.

[44] *A Memoir of Thomas Bewick, Written by Himself,* ed. Austin Dobson (London, 1887), pp. 47–48 [1822–1828].

Let's turn to the contemporary accounts of blacks or Africans as a race. First, recall the great chain of being: the same theoretical structure informing conservative accounts of social order guided thinking about race. It even served as the basic framework of a scientific research program. Why should man alone be found in unbroken uniformity? All other animals came in a neatly ascending chain of variety, expostulated Long. So in fact did all of creation, with its "regular order and gradation," links connecting everything from "mere inert matter" to the highest animals. Any plausible standard of epistemic coherence thus demanded assigning Africans a subordinate status.[45] "I know it is urged by writers on this subject, that all mankind are by nature free and equal, and that no one has a right to subjugate the person of another to slavery," acknowledged another African explorer, John Matthews. Yet this idea flew in the face of a view common in moral philosophy and theology, "that though man, of created beings, holds the first link, yet that there are different degrees of excellence in the human race, as there are in every other animal, or descending link, of the great chain of nature." And that view dovetailed elegantly with his experience of Africa, where "you find a constant and almost regular gradation in the scale of understanding, till the wretched Cafre sinks nearly below the Ouran Outang."[46]

This theory shaped the studiously scientific research of Charles White. From microscopic reptile to man himself, "Nature exhibits to our view an immense chain of beings, endued with various degrees of intelligence and active powers, suited to their stations in the general system." White painstakingly measured an African skeleton and about fifty blacks and found their lower arms were proportionally longer than those of Europeans. Everything from cartilage to muscles, sweat to "rank smell," testes to clitoris, size of brain to reason fit the same continuum. White moved effortlessly from that continuum to a hierarchy on the grounds that Europeans had departed further from the rest of the animal kingdom than had Africans. The verdict: "In whatever respect the African differs from the European, the particularity brings him nearer to the ape."[47]

[45] Long, *History of Jamaica*, 2:356.

[46] John Matthews, *A Voyage to the River Sierra-Leone, on the Coast of Africa* (London, 1788), pp. 158–59.

[47] Charles White, *Account of the Regular Gradation in Man, and in Different Animals and Vegetables, and from the Former to the Latter* (London, 1799), pp. 1, 52, 63–64, 67.

We might wonder about the mix of politics and empiricism that fuels this dispiriting conclusion. The great chain of being doesn't dictate such overt racism. Yet another African explorer, John Barrow, was enchanted by the Kaffers (transliteration being what it is, these are apparently the same as the Cafres who so disgusted John Matthews). "There is perhaps no nation on earth, taken collectively, that can produce so fine a race of men as the Kaffers: they are tall, stout, muscular, well made, elegant figures." A comparative anatomist would find it hard to place them in the great chain. Were it not for their black color, taken again as a badge of inferiority, the Kaffers "might have ranked among the first of Europeans."[48]

The principle of plenitude dictated that the great chain of being should be smoothly continuous and each level should be full. Yet people seemed abruptly separate from apes. This conceptual background motivates the time-honored search for the missing link: Haydon conjectured that on an ascending scale from brute creation to intellectual beings were located first monkeys, then blacks.[49] A lot of diabolical play about blacks and monkeys was indebted to the great chain of being. Ever sensible, Charlotte Smith's Desmond angrily rejects the view of an M.P. with a West Indies estate that actually Negroes were monkeys. "Monkies! I believe, indeed, they are a very distinct race from the European—So also is the straight-haired and fine formed Asiatic—So are the red men of North America—But where, amid this variety, does the man end, and the monkey begin?"[50] The Malays themselves, Burchell wrote, "look down on the Hottentots as a very inferior race, who, they say, are descended from orang-outangs."[51] Fond as usual of bashing Christianity, Carlile aimed squarely at the ludicrous spectacle of Wesleyan missionaries pursuing "the salvation of the blubber-lip and copper-coloured souls of the Chimpanzes and ourang-outangs" but ignoring the damnation of English infidels such as himself.[52] Taking their own stab at racial anatomy, *Fraser's* offered a glowing description of the Caucasian skull and a less flattering de-

---

[48] John Barrow, *An Account of Travels into the Interior of Southern Africa,* 2 vols. (London, 1801–1804; reprint ed. New York: Johnson Reprint, 1968), 1:204–6.

[49] *Examiner* (1 September 1811) no. 192, pp. 566–68. For the attribution, *The Diary of Benjamin Robert Haydon,* ed. Willard Bissell Pope, 5 vols. (Cambridge, MA: Harvard University Press, 1960–1963), 1:210 n. 2.

[50] Charlotte Smith, *Desmond,* 3 vols. (London, 1792), 3:163*.

[51] Burchell, *Travels,* 1:32 [1 January 1811].

[52] *Lion* (12 June 1829) 3(24):741.

scription of the Negro skull, which "will be observed to bear a striking affinity to the head of the ape and monkey tribes."[53] No wonder one traveller to Africa reported with a straight face that the Negroes themselves had reported that orangutans would sometimes "manifest an ardent passion for black women," though he noted that others didn't believe this.[54] No wonder one diarist wasn't sure what to make of a friend's story that he had ordered a slave with a tail from Cairo. "Is this a quip?" he wondered.[55]

### CLIMATE, SKIN COLOR, AND BIBLICAL DESCENT

Trying to figure out if blacks might be whites in disguise, contemporaries investigated climate. (We can learn something about the structure of racism by asking why that way of putting it has quite different force from asking if whites are blacks in disguise.) Even skin color in all its immediacy, suggested Gilbert Imlay, should be understood as superficial and contingent. "The difference is not fixed in nature, but is the mere effect of climate. . . ."[56] Crucially, the claim is not that climate explains the now deep and natural and necessary differences between white and black. The claim is that there are no such differences. Compare Winterbottom's suggestion that Jews, who didn't usually intermarry, had everywhere the same facial features, but their complexions depended on where they happened to be living.[57] This raises questions about the status of those facial features.

Still, no one believed that the effect of climate on skin color was instantaneous, that if a black moved to England, she would quickly

[53] *Fraser's* (December 1832) 6(36):673–74. See too Harriet Martineau, *Illustrations of Political Economy*, 9 vols. (London, 1832–1834), 5(2):102. See too the whimsical William Thomson, *Mammuth; or, Human Nature Displayed on a Grand Scale: in a Tour with the Tinkers, into the Inland Parts of Africa*, 2 vols. (London, 1789), 2:118.

[54] G. Mollien, *Travels in the Interior of Africa, to the Sources of the Senegal and Gambia*, ed. T. E. Bowdich (London, 1820; reprint ed. London: Frank Cass, 1967), p. 286.

[55] Sylvester Douglas, *The Glenbervie Journals*, ed. Walter Sichel (London: Constable & Co., 1910), p. 125 [16 April 1811]. For the claim that Spaniards believed that Jews had tails, see *Journal of Mrs. Arbuthnot*, 1:214 [7 February 1823], reporting the views of Lord FitzRoy.

[56] Gilbert Imlay, *A Topographical Description of the Western Territory of North America*, 2d ed. (London, 1793), p. 207. Here Imlay is pursuing a polemic against Thomas Jefferson's account of race. Compare the bantering of "Cool Reflections during a Midsummer Walk," in Robert Southey, *Metrical Tales and Other Poems* (London, 1805), p. 131.

[57] Winterbottom, *Account of the Native Africans*, 1:187.

turn white. These discussions are shot through with wild fantasies, but they're sometimes attentive to glaringly obvious facts, too. What about racial characteristics besides skin color? Henry Meredith believed that the characters of blacks—suspicious and carefully calculating, neither brave nor energetic, their passions quickly roused and quickly subdued—stemmed from African heat.[58] Did these characters somehow sink in and become fixed?

Not just a routine suntan or a passionate character could become inbred: so too could the most elaborate and contingent facts about society, culture, and politics. Here's Southey thinking aloud to a friend:

> Timbuctoo is not very much better than the other collections of negrosties which are called cities in Africa. The state of society in Negroland puzzles me. We read of cities, and courts, and palaces, and kings—and kings they are to all intents and purposes; yet when we think of one of these King Toms, with a captain's old coat, a pair of Monmouth-street red breeches, a tye-wig, playing with his brass buttons, or with a rattle, one wonders how the devil they came by the forms of a regular government. They look to me like a degraded race, as if they had been civilised once, and had sunk into the dotage, the second childhood, of society.[59]

Is this second childhood a description of the current social practices of Africa? Or does it penetrate the very nature of Africans? Coleridge unequivocally adopted the latter view. Assuming that blacks weren't descended from orangutans and that God hadn't created "Five Pairs of Adams & Eves," a stunning consequence had to be faced: "That Individual Depravity in a nation of depraved individuals may sink so deep & diffuse itself thro' all the acts, affections, faculties, passions and habits of the Man as at length to master the formative principle itself & involve the generative power in it's sphere of influence—."[60]

[58] Henry Meredith, *An Account of the Gold Coast of Africa* (London, 1812; reprint ed. London: Frank Cass, 1967), p. 20.

[59] Southey to C. W. Williams Wynn, 28 September 1803, *Selections from the Letters of Robert Southey*, ed. John Wood Warter, 4 vols. (London, 1856), 1:238. See too Southey to John Rickman, 23 December 1803, *The Life and Correspondence of Robert Southey*, ed. Charles Cuthbert Southey, 6 vols. (London, 1849–1850), 2:243.

[60] Coleridge to J. H. Green, 25 January 1828, *Collected Letters of Samuel Taylor Coleridge*, ed. Earl Leslie Griggs, 6 vols. (Oxford: Clarendon, 1956–1971), 6:723. See too Thomas Bankes, *A Modern, Authentic and Complete System of Universal Geography* (London, 1797), p. 315.

This political Lamarckianism makes a mockery of any facile distinction between nature and nurture.

Others found additional evidence that blacks and whites must be different species. Attractive as mulattoes were, reported Long, their marriages among themselves were usually "defective and barren. They seem in this respect to be actually of the mule-kind, and not so capable of producing from one another as from a commerce with a distinct White or Black."[61] That impassive scientist Charles White was unable to accept that climate could lead to the extensive variations he'd catalogued—or even provide a satisfactory account of the variation in skin color. So he urged that "the opinion that all people descended from one pair at first cannot be maintained," a barely veiled way of saying that the biblical account would have to go.[62] Carlile taunted a rabbi: the fact of different races—and the appeal of contempt—made nonsense of the biblical account. "You, I presume, would pause before you say that the Jew and the Hottentot were alike descended from Noah."[63]

Here scientific speculation had gone too far, at least for those secure in revealed religion. So the *British Critic* rejected White's findings. His evidence was scanty, they charged—he didn't have too many Negro skeletons—and anyway he'd not appreciated the profound effects of environment throughout the animal kingdom.[64] The *Encyclopedia Britannica,* offered in part as a devout counterpart to the dread *Encylopédie* of Diderot and the rest, affirmed the biblical account. Until the deluge, everyone was white. Only "infidel ignorance" would think that perceived racial differences couldn't be squared with the biblical account.[65]

---

[61] Long, *History of Jamaica,* 2:335. The *Encyclopedia Britannica* adopted the same test for qualifying as an independent species, but reported that in fact mulattoes could reproduce: *Encyclopedia Britannica,* 3d ed., 18 vols. (Edinburgh, 1797), 12:795 s.v. *Negro.*

[62] White, *Account,* p. 124; see generally pp. 124–35.

[63] *Republican* (13 February 1824) 9(7):199. The *Republican* did throw open its columns to an extended defense of the Jews: see "Israel Vindicated," *Republican* (6 September 1822) 6(15):455–77, (13 September 1822) 6(16):499–512, (27 September 1822) 6(18):564–76, (4 October 1822) 6(19):607–8, (25 October 1822) 6(22):694–704, (1 November 1822) 6(23):717–30, (8 November 1822) 6(24):755–68, (15 November 1822) 6(25):790–99, (29 November 1822) 6(27):857–63; see too *Republican* (16 May 1823) 7(20):634–35. But see too *Republican* (13 February 1824) 9(7):193.

[64] *British Critic* (October 1799) 14:422. See too Winterbottom, *Account of the Native Africans,* 2:254–74.

[65] *Encyclopedia Britannica,* 12:796 s.v. *Negro;* George Gleig, *Supplement to the Third Edi-*

But the biblical account was also taken to explain racial difference. Blacks were the descendants of Ham, cursed for daring to look at his naked and drunken father, Noah.[66] The account had venerable credentials in England, going back at least as far as 1577.[67] Johnson noticed it as a plausible conjecture in 1763.[68] Blacks, noted one of Wilberforce's many critics, were "the wretched descendants of Ham."[69] One proslavery poet provided "The Negro's Address to His Fellows":

> We're children of Cham! He his father offended,
> Who gave him the curse, which to us is descended.

Not to worry, though: the address is exultant at the Negroes' great good fortune at being packed off to work as slaves,

> Belov'd by our masters, kindly treated, esteemed,
> And, in God's own due time, from Cham's curse quite redeem'd.[70]

If not Ham, maybe Cush, his eldest son.[71] Or maybe Cain.[72]

Some were exasperated by turning to these passages to make sense of race.[73] Surely all Christians had to agree that blacks, even if cursed,

---

tion of the *Encyclopedia Britannica*, 2 vols. (Edinburgh, 1801), 2:164 s.v. *Man.* For the devout purposes of the *Encyclopedia,* see Gleig, *Supplement,* 1:iv. See too Winterbottom, *Account of the Native Africans,* 1:182.

[66] *Genesis* 9:20–26.

[67] Peter Fryer, *Staying Power: Black People in Britain Since 1504* (Atlantic Highlands, NJ: Humanities Press, 1984), p. 143.

[68] *Boswell's Life of Johnson,* 1:401 [25 June 1763].

[69] William Knox, *A Letter from W.K. Esq. to W. Wilberforce, Esq.* (London, 1790), p. 5.

[70] *Instructions for the Treatment of Negroes, &c. &c. &c.* (London, 1797), p. 133.

[71] Gilbert Francklyn, *An Answer to the Rev. Mr. Clarkson's Essay on the Slavery and Commerce of the Human Species, Particularly the African* (London, 1789; reprint ed. Miami, FL: Mnemosyne Publishing, 1969), pp. 31–33; responding to the reading of Scripture in Thomas Clarkson, *An Essay on the Slavery and Commerce of the Human Species, Particularly the African; Translated from a Latin Dissertation Which Was Honoured with the First Prize in the University of Cambridge for the Year 1785,* 2d ed. rev. (London, 1788), pp. 126–35.

[72] James Stewart, *Plocacosmos: or The Whole Art of Hair Dressing* (London, 1782), p. 177 rejects this view; Leah Wells Sumbel, *Memoirs of the Life of Mrs. Sumbel, Late Wells,* 3 vols. (London, 1811), 3:88 affirms it.

[73] For instance, Thomas Gisborne, *The Principles of Moral Philosophy Investigated, and Applied to the Constitution of Civil Society,* 4th ed. (London, 1798), pp. 210–11. Compare a jocular John Courtenay, *Philosophical Reflections on the Late Revolution in France, and the Conduct of the Dissenters in England, in a Letter to the Rev. Dr. Priestley,* 2d ed. with additions (London, 1790), pp. 25–32. For Courtenay's assisting Boswell's poetic efforts on this front, see James Boswell, *No Abolition of Slavery; or The Universal Empire of Love: A Poem* (London, 1791), p. 12; *The Correspondence of James Boswell with Certain Members of the Club,* ed. Charles N. Fifer (New York: McGraw-Hill, 1976), p. 418.

were the children of God, that all human beings were. Consider Ignatius Sancho's prayer: "Son of the Most High God—who died for the sins of all—all—Jew, Turk, Infidel, and Heretic;—fair—fallow—brown—tawny—black—and you and I—and every son and daughter of Adam."[74] In his passionate quest to bring justice to the people of India, Burke described them as "a set of people, who have none of your Lillies and Roses in their faces; but who are the images of the great Pattern as well as you and I. I know what I am doing; whether the white people like it or not," he added tersely."[75] Notice that even if we think that conservatives have to be emotionally invested in social hierarchy, that they have to find some groups to hold in contempt, it doesn't follow that they have to be racists. Notice too that this heartening bit of Christian egalitarianism makes trouble for the great chain of being, whose smoothly gradual ascent is interrupted by the apocalyptic divide between creatures without immortal souls and creatures with them.

### WILLIAM COBBETT, JEW-HATER

I turn to another apocalyptic divide, that between Christian and Jew. We've seen that William Cobbett was no slouch when it came to racism and that he was a garden-variety misogynist. In the annals of anti-Semitism, though, Cobbett can stand tall. One needn't be excessively fastidious to acknowledge his signal contributions; indeed one has to be excessively agile to avoid them. There's an ignoble historiographical tale to be told about life on the academic left: E. P. Thompson and Raymond Williams embraced Cobbett with nary a mention of his scurrilous views.[76] But I won't tell that tale. Instead, let me review some of the historical evidence itself.

[74] *Letters of the Late Ignatius Sancho, an African*, 5th ed. (London, 1803; reprint ed. London: Dawsons of Pall Mall, 1968), p. 99 [25 August 1777]. See too Cugoano, *Thoughts and Sentiments*, p. 119.

[75] Burke to Mary Palmer, 19 January 1786, *The Correspondence of Edmund Burke*, ed. Thomas W. Copeland, 10 vols. (Chicago: University of Chicago Press, 1958–1978), 5:255. See too William Dickson, *Letters on Slavery . . . to Which Are Added, Addresses to the Whites, and to the Free Negroes of Barbadoes; and Accounts of Some Negroes Eminent for Their Virtues and Abilities* (London, 1789), p. 57.

[76] E. P. Thompson, *The Making of the English Working Class* (New York: Vintage Books, 1966); Raymond Williams, *Culture and Society 1780–1950* (New York: Columbia University Press, 1958), pp. 12–20; and, most remarkable, Raymond Williams, *Cobbett* (Oxford: Oxford University Press, 1983). George Spater, *William Cobbett: The Poor Man's Friend*, 2 vols. (Cambridge: Cambridge University Press, 1982), 1:199, 2:441 notices Cobbett's anti-Semitism only in passing; so too Ian Dyck, *William Cobbett and Rural Popular Culture* (Cambridge: Cambridge University Press, 1992), p. 10. But see W. D.

In an 1806 piece on "Jewish Predominance," Ethnicus informed the readers of the *Political Register* that "'till lately, the richest Jews amongst us affected poverty for fear of envy, and eat their unleavened cakes and counted their usuries in secret. But now they are the companions of our feasts, the pride of our assemblies, the arbiters of our amusements."[77] The pariah unashamedly in control: Cobbett continued to rage at the hideous inversion through all his ideological transformations and he became more obsessed with it as he became more radical.

By 1822, Cobbett was protesting to the Earl of Chichester that even as the common people were becoming steadily more disreputable, "the race of loan-jobbers, stock-jobbers, jews, and paper-money makers, and nabobs, have been hugged to your very bosoms!"[78] He was unfazed by the possibility of disturbing the currency market: "The whole race of Jews and Jobbers would disappear, as the slugs do before the face of a scorching sun. To that corrupt, that cormorant, that infernal race, it might be total ruin!"[79] These are the Jewish stockjobbers and moneylenders of popular lore, spiced with a dash of Cobbett's inimitable prose, also cast—jubilant prospect, this—as disgusting animals to be exterminated. But I don't want to deny Cobbett his own macabre creativity. Stockjobbers, he announced in 1823, owned over 80 percent of the London newspaper press. "No small part of them are, perhaps, literally Jews"; "it is my real belief, that a very large part of the London newspaper press is owned, really owned, by the sons of Israel." Here's a new reason for worrying about the explosion of newspaper reading poisoning the minds of the lower orders: for the "poisonous touch" of this press is administered by Jews with shamelessly self-interested motives, their eyes riveted on the bottom line and their interest payments from the war debt, not by impartial guardians of public debate or principled critics of the government.[80] "Nine tenths of this press, which ought to be the guardian of public

---

Rubenstein, *Elites and the Wealthy in Modern British History: Essays in Social and Economic History* (Sussex: Harvester Press, 1987), chap. 11.

[77] *Political Register* (6 September 1806) 10(10):404.

[78] *Political Register* (19 January 1822) 41(3):141. For similar plaints against Jews and jobbers, see Cobbett, *Rural Rides*, pp. 34, 37, 119, 221, 344, 480.

[79] *Political Register* (20 July 1822) 43(3):170.

[80] *Political Register* (8 February 1823) 45(6):377–79. See too *Political Register* (31 January 1824) 49(5):294–95.

morals, which ought to be the support of public spirit, which ought to prevent the nation from being cheated or deluded. Nine tenths of this press, or at least a very large part of it, is absolutely in the pay of the Jews."[81]

Nor do I want to deny Cobbett his stubborn pursuit of righteousness. He crusaded against "the Extortions and the Insolence of the Turnpike-Toll Collectors and Renters" in part because theirs was an "impudent system of Jewish extortion." "These extortioners were a nest of Jews. I had no idea of this. I did not think that we were Jew-ridden to this extent." So Cobbett took one collector to court. Outraged by the man's calling him an atheist, Cobbett responded by calling him a "JEW DOG."[82] Or so he proudly told his readers. The account of the proceedings in *John Bull* has Cobbett turning to Mr. Levy, a lessee of the Kensington Trust Turnpike-road, and saying, "You are a Jew, I suppose." "I am a Jew, it is true," responds Levy; "but you are neither Jew, Christian, nor any other religion. You are an Atheist, as every body knows." In this account, though, there's no brave rejoinder from Cobbett, who merely "smiled, and observed, that what he had advanced in this office was strictly true." In some further witty repartée, Cobbett managed to cast himself as a reluctant understudy to Jesus Christ, righteously defending the downtrodden tollpayers but not willing to be crucified.[83]

Jews were unrepentant Christ-killers. "Do not they boast of being descended from the murderers of Christ? Do not they, in their blasphemous assemblies called synagogues, call Jesus Christ an impostor, and treat his faith and doctrine with the utmost contempt?"[84] (I wonder if Cobbett knew that he was joined in this particular belief about Jews by the dotty religious enthusiast, Joanna Southcott: "I know the religion of our nation is mocked by them," she calmly reported.[85]) The doughty radical recoiled from "the horrible orgies of the blas-

---

[81] *Political Register* (5 January 1828) 65(1):22.

[82] *Political Register* (25 October 1823) 48(4):193, 194, 206, 213.

[83] *John Bull* (19 October 1823) no. 149, p. 331. For a nuisance follow-up suit with the same characters, see *John Bull* (11 September 1825) 5(37):290.

[84] *Political Register* (25 October 1823) 48(4):217.

[85] Joanna Southcott, *An Account of the Trials on Bills of Exchange, wherein the Deceit of Mr. John King and His Confederates, under the Pretence of Lending Money, is Exposed, and Their Arts Brought to Light* (London, 1807), p. 37. See too John Allen, *Modern Judaism: or, A Brief Account of the Opinions, Traditions, Rites, and Ceremonies, of the Jews in Modern Times* (London, 1816), chap. 14.

pheming Jews."[86] He finally screwed up his courage and almost named these ineffable horrors, denouncing "their blasphemous rites, repeating in effigy (as on certain days is said to be their custom) the bloody deed for which their race has been condemned to wander throughout the earth."[87]

Stockjobbers and Christ-killers fused in an effervescent display of Cobbett's literary imagination. In 1822, he denounced the extortioners making outrageous profits from Britain's war debt. The fundowner became personified greed. "With Jewish rigour, with Jewish hypocrisy, with Jewish cruelty, he is now meting out a Jewish justice to his country. Let the very same justice be measured back to himself," urged Cobbett.[88] Lecturing at Manchester in 1832, decrying the injustice of saddling tiny children with debts, Cobbett urged that the debt not be repaid. But he warned his audience that escaping it wouldn't be easy. All the might of the government would be exerted on behalf of "the atrocious Jews, whether calling themselves Christians or not, who now come and demand from us the pound of flesh in virtue of their bond. . . ." These aren't Jews ineptly trying to pass as Christians: these are Christians who might as well be Jews, who automatically become Jews when they become moneylenders. We are vanishingly close to Marx's claims about the real content of Judaism; I'll return to this motif. Anyway,

> The Jew, who comes and lends money to this Government, is to come, when the people have got the power of altering the law which enabled the Government to do this, and tell them; the blaspheming Jew is to come, and tell them that they are bound in conscience to pay back the money that he lent for the purpose of keeping them down, and to threaten to have them crucified, if they hold back a farthing of his demand. . . .[89]

In court, Cobbett slyly cast himself as Christ. Now the long-suffering public, those poor workers groaning under the heavy taxes supporting war with France and Jewish moneylenders, are cast as the Messiah

---

[86] *Political Register* (12 June 1830) 69(24):752.

[87] William Cobbett, *Good Friday; or, The Murder of Jesus Christ by the Jews* (London, 1830), p. 10.

[88] *Political Register* (30 November 1822) 44(9):566.

[89] *Cobbett's Manchester Lectures, in Support of His Fourteen Reform Propositions* (London, 1832), pp. 92–94; also in *Political Register* (4 February 1832) 75(6):361–62.

on the cross. A pedant might complain that it's not immediately obvious what answers to the threat of crucifixion (withholding further
loans?). But Cobbett aimed well: his audience must have welcomed
the invitation to blame their ills on nameless foes who turned out to
be the incarnation of blasphemous evil.

Cobbett went on relentlessly. He even discovered an unswerving
law of political doom: "Every nation, that has fostered the Jews, has
become miserable in proportion to their numbers and influence."[90]
His bravura performance inspired his son, who approved of Rome's
sequestering Jews in a ghetto.[91] (The practice already had been rejected fiercely by such humanitarians as Hazlitt.[92]) But this elegant
business of Jew-hating wasn't merely a Cobbett family affair. I turn to
the broader cultural scene.

## RACE, NATION, TRIBE, PERSUASION, POLITICAL ARTIFACT

Again, the demographic context is noteworthy. In the early 1800s,
London supported just six synagogues.[93] One contemporary estimated the city's Jewish population at 20,000—"the majority are notorious sharpers"[94]—but a modern historian suspects the city didn't
have more than 15,000 Jews until the 1820s.[95] Contemporary estimates for Britain's Jewish population in this period range from 12,000
to 25,000.[96] Like blacks, then, Jews were a tiny handful of Britain's

[90] *Political Register* (5 January 1828) 65(1):23.

[91] James P. Cobbett, *Journal of a Tour in Italy, and Also in Part of France and Switzerland*
(London, 1830), pp. 268–69. Note the spirited criticism in *Westminster Review* (January
1831) 14(27):179–80.

[92] *Notes of a Journey through France and Italy* [1826], *The Complete Works of William
Hazlitt*, ed. P. P. Howe, 21 vols. (London: J. M. Dent and Sons, 1930), 10:233. See too
Johann Wilhelm de Archenholz, *A Picture of Italy*, trans. Joseph Trapp, 2 vols. (London,
1791), 2:125.

[93] *Modern London; Being the History and Present State of the British Metropolis* (London,
1804), p. 126; William Henry Pyne and William Combe, *The Microcosm of London*, 3 vols.
(London, 1808–1811), 3:167; David Hughson, *Walks through London* (London, 1817),
p. 1; Edward Wedlake Brayley, *London and Its Environs; or, The General Ambulator, and Pocket
Companion for the Tour of the Metropolis and Its Vicinity*, 12th ed. (London, 1820), pt. 1, p. 56.

[94] John Corry, *A Satirical View of London*, 4th ed. (London, 1809), p. 40.

[95] Todd Endelman, *The Jews of Georgian England 1714–1830: Tradition and Change in
a Liberal Society* (Philadelphia: Jewish Publication Society of America, 1979), p. 172.

[96] *John Bull* (2 August 1829) 9(451):246; Apsley Pellatt, *Brief Memoir of the Jews, in
Relation to Their Civil and Municipal Disabilities* (London, 1829), p. iv.

millions. Surely it's easier airily to dismiss a group, to brand them "sheenies,"[97] to have a less tortured and ambivalent contempt for them, when they are mostly exotic and faceless others, not the familiar figures of everyday life, as women and workers were. Unfamiliarity breeds contempt. Or unfamiliarity makes for strident and one-dimensional contempt.

Recalling a prior history of even more pointed contempt, contemporaries congratulated themselves on their humanity. A 1753 parliamentary attempt to relieve the Jews of their legal disabilities had been turned back by popular outrage.[98] "The legal condition of Jews has not altered," conceded one writer; "but the people no longer view them with rancour, or mistrust, or unbrotherly emotions."[99] "Within memory it was customary among the lowest classes of the populace to hunt the Jews, and shamefully maltreat them," recalled another, but no more.[100] Francis Place winced at the dreadful years in which Jews were abused publicly for fun. "Dogs could not now be used in the streets, in the manner, many jews were treated."[101] Even Jewish experts were unsure of the extent of their remaining legal disabilities.[102] And Jews themselves generated homespun expressions of loyalty. We can't easily discard these as opportunistic posturing: many were published in Hebrew.[103] Perhaps Jews, attentive to the available alternatives in other European nations, were indeed fiercely loyal to England. Let's survey England's new humanity.

[97] Pierce Egan, *Boxiana*, 4 vols. (London, 1818–1824), 4:528, 4:644.

[98] See Thomas W. Perry, *Public Opinion, Propaganda, and Politics in Eighteenth-Century England: A Study of the Jew Bill of 1753* (Cambridge, MA: Harvard University Press, 1962). For a more concentrated dose of popular invective, see G. A. Cranfield, "The 'London Evening-Post' and the Jew Bill of 1753," *Historical Journal* (1965) 8(1):16–30.

[99] W. Button, *The Rise, Fall, and Future Restoration of the Jews: to Which Are Annexed, Six Sermons, Addressed to the Seed of Abraham by Several Evangelical Ministers* (London, 1806), pt. 1, p. 49.

[100] John Thomas Smith, *Ancient Topography of London* (London, 1815), p. 20.

[101] *The Autobiography of Francis Place (1771–1854)*, ed. Mary Thale (Cambridge: Cambridge University Press, 1972), pp. xxiv–xxv.

[102] Compare Francis Henry Goldsmid, *Remarks on the Civil Disabilities of British Jews* (London, 1830), pp. 4, 7–14, 20; John Elijah Blunt, *A History of the Establishment and Residence of the Jews in England; with An Enquiry into Their Civil Disabilities* (London, 1830), p. vi n, 111–29.

[103] See the collection in Israel Abrahams, "Hebrew Loyalty under the First Four Georges," *Transactions of the Jewish Historical Society of England* (1918–1920) 9:103–30.

In 1712, the *Spectator* identified Jews as a race.[104] The suggestion lingered. Travelling through Poland in 1786, Jeremy Bentham indignantly reported that innkeeping had been monopolized by "the race of Israel: a people by inbred filthiness the worst qualified, and by religious scruples, one should think the least disposed, to engage in such a business."[105] J. B. Moreton punctuated his account of Jamaica with fury. The Jews, "Christ-killing dogs," were forever cheating upright Christians. "Ever since the murdering of God Almighty, they are remarkably fond of gold and silver . . . these foreskin-clipped scoundrels have clipped and sweated almost all the coin," so travellers had better take care in trafficking with them. Moreton was glad to report that Jews couldn't hold public office in Jamaica, sad to report that they were permitted to testify in court: for money, he complained, they would happily testify to anything. "I was credibly informed that the legislature, not twenty years ago, were about enacting a law to allow them no further privileges than mungrels; and it is to be lamented that it was not carried into execution, for they are a vile race."[106]

In one insanely tangled Gothic extravaganza, Don Fernan reveals his Jewish identity to his son: "I am one of that unhappy race every where stigmatized and spoken against," he announces.[107] However odd this fictional language seems, actual Jews deployed it themselves. An anonymous pamphleteer protested "the long-endured contempt cast upon our race."[108] Hyman Hurwitz became professor of Hebrew language and literature at University College. At his 1828 inaugural lecture, he marvelled that one with "the name and *characteristic distinction* of my Race" could attain such a position.[109] One Jewish doc-

---

[104] *Spectator* (27 September 1712) no. 495, in *The Spectator*, ed. Donald F. Bond, 5 vols. (Oxford: Clarendon, 1965), 4:255.

[105] Jeremy Bentham to Jeremiah Bentham, 6/17 January–10/21 February 1786, *The Correspondence of Jeremy Bentham*, ed. Timothy L. S. Sprigge and others, 10 vols. to date (London: Athlone Press; Oxford: Clarendon, 1968–), 3:454. Compare Bentham's diary, 11 December 1787, *Correspondence of Bentham*, 3:606.

[106] J. B. Moreton, *Manners and Customs in the West India Islands* (London, 1790), pp. 65–67.

[107] Charles Maturin, *Melmoth the Wanderer* [1820], ed. Douglas Grant (Oxford: Oxford University Press, 1989), p. 247.

[108] *A Letter from a Jew to a Christian, Occasioned by the Recent Attacks on the Bible*, in *Pamphleteer* (1820) 16(32):280.

[109] Leonard Hyman, "Hyman Hurwitz: The First Anglo-Jewish Professor," *Transactions of the Jewish Historical Society of England* (1962–1967) 21:233.

tor hammered away at the point: Jews were "a despised and degraded race," "a degraded and despised race."[110] Yet, he insisted, "*I will dare to call myself*" an Englishman.[111]

Are Jews a race? Could they be a race? Is *race* something like shared physical or mental characteristics, genetically transmitted, or, as contemporaries would have said, in the blood? Consider the young man "in His countenance the very essence of judaism distilled from a thousand Jews."[112] Or is it something like being held in contempt? I suggest that we couple the two notions, that we think of race as conjuring up inherited characteristics and contempt.[113] I say *conjuring* because much of this terrain is shot through with lurid fantasies; *contempt,* and not say being the object of contempt, because of course one can refer to the white race. But then we conceive of the white race as in a superior position, atop a hierarchy, looking down on contemptible other races. Absent such relations of contempt and hierarchy, we haven't got the concept of race at all: at least not at this historical juncture. Blacks are noteworthy not as the sole or even paradigm case of race, but as perhaps the extreme instance of contempt. Bentham bemoaned the dehumanization: "Colour still determines whether, by men, a man shall be dealt with as a man or as a beast."[114] It is not clear that his utilitarianism, generously including animals—"The question is not, Can they *reason?* nor, Can they *talk?* but, Can they *suffer?*"[115]—can make fully intelligible what is at stake in such dehumanization.

So, depending on one's beliefs about such groups, the vulgar, the stupid, and the Irish can qualify as races. Not metaphoric races, not races that stretch the concept away from its presumptively legitimate core case of blacks, but perfectly legitimate instances of race. Or instances as legitimate as any other: for any candidate group, we might

---

[110] Barnard Van Oven, *An Appeal to the British Nation on Behalf of the Jews* (London, 1830), pp. 16, 20.

[111] Van Oven, *An Appeal,* p. 34.

[112] *Diary of Farington,* 10:3583 [12 October 1809].

[113] Such a view seems to me to escape the critique that race is unreal: see for instance Kwame Anthony Appiah, *In My Father's House: Africa in the Philosophy of Culture* (New York: Oxford University Press, 1992), chap. 2.

[114] *Rid Yourselves of Ultramaria* [1821], in Jeremy Bentham, *Colonies, Commerce, and Constitutional Law: Rid Yourselves of Ultramaria and Other Writings on Spain and Spanish America,* ed. Philip Schofield (Oxford: Clarendon, 1995), p. 130.

[115] Jeremy Bentham, *An Introduction to the Principles of Morals and Legislation* [1789], ed. J. H. Burns and H. L. A. Hart (London: Athlone Press, 1970), p. 283 n. b.

have our doubts about the inherited characteristics, and even if we accept them we might reject hierarchy and contempt. Or we might have doubts about what sort of inheritance is at stake: if Bentham's lawyers become contemptibly passive and enervate as their minds are "poisoned with the study of the law,"[116] can they qualify as a race? Or take the Duke of Wellington's impatience with poets: "I hate the whole race. I have the worst opinion of them. There is no believing a word they say—your professional poets, I mean—there never existed a more worthless set than Byron and his friends for example. Poets praise fine sentiments and never practise them. . . ."[117] Perhaps we should say that at the frontiers of the concept of race, inherited characteristics shade off into shared characteristics, however acquired. That would more easily accommodate such cases as Lamb's borrower and lender. But perhaps we should construe such cases as metaphoric or parasitic on those of genuinely inherited characteristics.

Now contrast another common usage: "O Lord and heavenly Father, look down, we pray Thee, with compassion on the whole race of mankind," prayed Anglicans in communion.[118] This bit of officially imposed Christianity is amusingly close to Jacobin cosmopolitanism and fraternity. If it's the human race, not the black and white and Jewish and countless other races, there is no conceptual room for the peculiar nastiness engendered by the interface of inherited characteristics and contempt. (There is still room, though, for the human race to exercise dominion over brute nature. Are the higher animals contemptible or strictly speaking beneath contempt?) So too Harriet Martineau's Dr. Sneyd comes to the defense of a "little negro boy, stunted in form and mean in countenance," being mistreated by his son-in-law. "As one of the same race with this boy, I have a right to call you to account for making property of that which is no property," and he summarily orders that the lad's chains be removed.[119] Dr. Sneyd

---

[116] *Rationale of Judicial Evidence* [1827], in *Works of Bentham*, 6:123, repeated at 7:188.

[117] Carola Oman, *The Gascoyne Heiress: The Life and Diaries of Frances Mary Gascoyne-Cecil 1802–39* (London: Hodder and Stoughton, 1968), p. 91 [26 September 1833]. So too Thomas Denman branded country gentlemen a "timid, selfish, and purse-proud race": Denman, "The Year 1820," in Joseph Arnould, *Life of Thomas, First Lord Denman*, 2 vols. (Boston, 1874), 1:114.

[118] *A Form of Prayer to Be Used . . . on Wednesday the Eighth Day of February 1809, Being the Day Appointed by Proclamation for a General Fast and Humiliation before Almighty God* (London, 1809), p. 11.

[119] Martineau, *Illustrations of Political Economy*, 8(1):28–29. See too James Mill, *The*

isn't seizing the opportunity to divulge that he's black. He is deliberately introducing a vocabulary that makes his son-in-law's noxious pursuits unjustifiable, even unintelligible.

Shared characteristics triggering contempt: like blacks', Jews' inferiority was manifest in their odor. Bursting with erudition, Southey surveyed the history of this time-honored belief.[120] Isaac D'Israeli's Jewish philosopher muses on the tradition and suggests that it's because Christians managed to convert only filthy Jews from the streets: the magic wrought by holy water was the same accomplished by an ordinary bath, so inherited characteristics had nothing to do with it.[121] In 1802, Coleridge complained bitterly to his wife about a ride he'd taken on the mail coach to London. "A horrible stinking Jew crucified my Nose the whole way—It is fact, that I never knew what a true *foul* stench was, before—O it was a STINKING JEW!"[122] Cobbett as Christ, the taxpaying public as Christ, and now, implausibly enough, Coleridge's nose as Christ: these Christ-killing dogs provoked luxurious or megalomaniacal fantasies of divinity.

Blacks slipped off into the kingdom of the apes; other animals were selected for Jews. In the perennially popular *Love a la Mode*, Sir Archy MacSarcasm can't accept that Mordecai's wealth might be enough to make him socially acceptable: "The fellow is wealthy, 'tis true; yes, yes, he is wealthy, but he is a reptile, a mere reptile!"[123] In another of the books patterned after Pierce Egan's rollicking tours through London, Principal tours the stock exchange. "The bashaw in block yonder, who rests his elephantic trunk against a pillar of the Exchange . . . is the *Hebrew* star—the *Jewish luminary*, a very *Shiloh* among the *peoples* of his own persuasion, and, I am sorry to say, much too potent with the orthodox ministers of George the Fourth." Ruminating on this sorry spectacle, Principal goes on to offer some choice poetry indicting Jews as "reptiles and vermin" breeding in the filthy heap of the national debt.[124]

---

*History of British India* [1820], 3 vols. (New Delhi: Associated Publishing House, 1972), 1:47, 1:161.

[120] Robert Southey, *Roderick, the Last of the Goths* (London, 1814), pp. ix–x.

[121] Isaac D'Israeli, *Vaurien: or, Sketches of the Times; Exhibiting Views of the Philosophies, Religions, Politics, Literature, and Manners of the Age*, 2 vols. (London, 1797), 2:236–37.

[122] Coleridge to Mrs. S. T. Coleridge, 8 November 1802, *Letters of Coleridge*, 2:880.

[123] Charles Macklin, *Love a la Mode* (London, 1793), p. 8.

[124] Bernard Blackmantle [Charles Molloy Westmacott], *The English Spy*, 2 vols. (London, 1825–1826), 2:144–46.

But Jews also were cast as a nation, not a race, a category pointing in an emphatically different direction. One diarist was disgusted by the Old Testament and its tale of the chosen people, perplexed too by the ongoing attention to this curious text, where despite tradition one had to strain to find anything connected to the Gospels. "Posterity will wonder that all the nations of Europe s^d be better acquainted with the history of this vile execrable people than with their own," he wrote. Then he went back, crossed out "people," and replaced it with "nation."[125] Intent on doing "justice to a humble remnant of a once highly favoured state," William Dickson reported that the Jews of Barbados, "the HEBREW NATION," were disproportionately generous donors to a charity for the sick poor. "Sir, this despised, (not to say *oppressed*) but peaceable, loyal and, I will add, *venerable,* people, still remember, as they were commanded, the affliction of their forefathers, in the land of Egypt."[126] Here the focus is on a people, once a political community, who have lost their land, their political organization. We are close to the infamous wandering Jew, circling back to Christ-killing dogs. In his poetic rendition of the tale, Shelley has the Jew recall the mob, "Infuriate for Deicide," and his own repulsive zeal: "I mocked our Saviour, and I cried, / 'Go! go!' "[127] We are also close to the elemental disbelief greeting the claim that Jews might be British subjects, even citizens, in good standing. Not only did Britain have to remain a Protestant or anyway a Christian nation, but these Jews were aliens, wanderers of the great Diaspora, enjoying whatever limited privileges they were accorded as a matter of condescending generosity, not inflexible justice.

So Jews were routinely exhibited in literature and on stage with an uncouth Eastern European accent. Thomas Love Peacock's rapier wit, usually deployed to skewer conservative cruelties, etched a portrait of Levi Moses. Here are the opening stanzas:

> MA name'sh Levi Moshesh: I tink I vash born,
>   Dough I cannot exactly remember,
> In Roshemary-Lane, about tree in de morn,
>   Shome time in de mont of November.

---

[125] *Diaries of William Johnston Temple 1780–1796,* ed. Lewis Bettany (Oxford: Clarendon, 1929), p. 18 [3 March 1781].

[126] Dickson, *Letters on Slavery,* p. 138.

[127] *The Wandering Jew* [1810], in *The Complete Poetical Works of Percy Bysshe Shelley,* ed. Neville Rogers, 2 vols. to date (Oxford: Clarendon, 1972–), 1:201.

> Ma fader cried "*clothesh,*" trough de shtreetsh ash he vent,
>   Dough he now shleeping under de shtone ish,
> He made by hish bargains two hundred per shent,
>   And dat vay he finger'd de monish.[128]

These aren't the Jews of the stock exchange or moneylending fame.
They are Jews trafficking in rags and old clothes, hawking their wares
in the streets and defrauding their customers, also assembling for the
daily Rag Fair, a bustling and dangerous convocation.[129] (But the social distance between the two sorts of Jews could vanish in an instant:
one cartoonist exhibited the mighty Rothschild himself purveying old
rags.[130]) *Figaro in London* sternly pursued these "low and filthy Jews,"
"filthy unshorn loathsome animals," in a crusade to purify London's
streets.[131] Even wealthy Jews were represented with the same harsh
accent. Audiences of one of Holcroft's comedies were treated to this
verse in the epilogue:

> I lend my moneesh, 'cause I love de Nation
> I join, mit all my art, to pay taxation.
> De Var and Peesh to me be quite all von,
> Give me but von goot shlish from dat great loaf—de Loan![132]

Eager vocalists turning to *The Universal Songster* could learn the words
to some fifty songs featuring Jews, among them the ever memorable
"Cent. per Cent.; or, Pargains to Puy," "The Jew Pedlar Selling a Pig,"
"Jabesh Ham; or, The Catastrophe of a Pork-Chop Dinner," and "De
Chinkling of de Cash."[133] Somehow these aren't the sort of deep sea

---

[128] "Levi Moses" [1806], in *The Works of Thomas Love Peacock,* Halliford edition, ed.
H. F. B. Brett-Smith and C. E. Jones, 10 vols. (London: Constable & Co., 1924–1934),
6:87.

[129] Richard Phillips, *Modern London* (London, 1804), plate and description of "Old
Clothes" at end of volume; *Real Life in London; or, The Rambles and Adventures of Bob
Tallyho, Esq. and His Cousin, the Hon. Tom. Dashall, through the Metropolis,* 2 vols. (London,
1824), 1:474–75; Ann Taylor, *City Scenes, or A Peep into London* (London, 1828), pp. 21–
22; John Wade, *A Treatise on the Police and Crimes of the Metropolis* (London, 1829), p. 337.

[130] *BMC* no. 15523 [March 1828].

[131] *Figaro in London* (30 August 1834) 3(143):138, (6 September 1834) 3(144):
142–43.

[132] Thomas Holcroft, *The Man of Ten Thousand: A Comedy* (London, 1796), p. 87.

[133] *The Universal Songster; or, Museum of Mirth,* 3 vols. (London, 1825–1826), 1:108,
1:135–36, 2:135, 2:360.

treasures that surface when social historians want to wax romantic about popular culture.

Close to *nation* is *tribe,* also emphasizing a wandering political community—but, with its echoes of Africa, circling back toward race, so maybe a shade or six more disreputable than *nation.* We can observe the bleaker emotional associations of *tribe* and its summoning up race in the sources. Edward Long managed in one sentence to summon up "the poorer and more knavish tribe" and "their nation" to refer to Jews.[134] Moreton, that fount of human kindness, disdained Jamaica's Jews as "a numerous tricking tribe" as well as a vile race.[135] The new bride of Edgeworth's *Castle Rackrent,* a Jewess, isn't just of a novel "tribe or nation." "Mercy upon his honour's poor soul," commiserates the narrator; "what will become of him and his, and all of us, with his heretic blackamoor at the head of the Castle Rackrent estate!"[136] "We have in London very respectable persons of the Jewish nation, whom we will keep," intoned Burke; "but we have of the same tribe others of a very different description,—housebreakers, and receivers of stolen goods, and forgers of paper currency, more than we can conveniently hang."[137] These he graciously offered to send to France.

Most gently, Jews might be those of the Jewish persuasion. However facetious the phrase's later history, it has a centrally humanizing thrust: all that separates the Jew from the Christian is religious belief, not anything as deep and unyielding as race. The Duke of Kent was pained to learn that "some of the most respectable persons of the Jewish persuasion" found offensive the efforts of the London Society for Promoting Christianity among the Jews—the same group that congratulated itself on rescuing "two infants . . . from the baneful influence of Jewish prejudice in their early years. . . ."[138] William Hone met the common complaint that "A JEW IS A THIEF!" by sympathetically rehearsing the plight of "an individual of the Jewish persuasion," a victimized 93-year-old of dignity and virtue.[139] One auto-

[134] Long, *History of Jamaica,* 2:296.

[135] Moreton, *Manners and Customs,* p. 65.

[136] *Castle Rackrent* [1800], in Maria Edgeworth, *Tales and Novels,* 10 vols. (London, 1848), 4:14.

[137] *Letter to a Member of the National Assembly* [1791], in *The Works of the Right Honorable Edmund Burke,* 9th ed., 12 vols. (Boston: Little, Brown, 1889), 4:15.

[138] *Jewish Repository* (May 1813) 1:195, (April 1813) 1:152.

[139] William Hone, *The Everyday-Book,* 2 vols. (London, 1827; reprint ed. Detroit:

biographer recalled an old friend "of the Jewish persuasion, but with a truly Christian disposition."[140] Politely declining to support admitting Jews to Parliament, Sidmouth assured Isaac Goldsmid that "I regard the members of the Jewish persuasion with no feelings of disfavour: on the contrary I have frequently had occasion to admire in those with whom I have been acquainted, and others whom I have met in society, great liberality of disposition, and a warm and impartial benevolence"; but that didn't qualify them to legislate for a Christian nation.[141] (A few months later, Goldsmid would become an organizer of the Jewish Association for Obtaining Civil Rights and Privileges.[142])

Money might not humanize Jewish reptiles, but baptism could work its magic on those of the Jewish persuasion. One pamphleteer bewailed the criminal negligence of Christians in spreading the good news. "Oh be it so no longer!—let every christian unite in heart and hand to extend the glorious light of Christianity, till it shine in every heart, upon Jew and Pagan to the extremity of the world."[143] So arose the London Society for Promoting Christianity among the Jews, which came in for spirited criticism and ridicule. Their former printer published an exposé arguing that the Society had succeeded only in assembling a rogues' gallery of nominally converted poor Jews in it for the money—converts received cash payments—and a Jerusalem rabbi fond of brothels. Perhaps he took his lead from the Society's chief missionary among the Jews, allegedly fond not just of brothels but of attempting to take liberties with married women, also attempting to purchase sexual services from them.[144] The Reverend

---

Gale Research Co., 1967), 2:533–36. Note the temperate tone of Hone, *The Year Book* (London, 1832; reprint ed. Detroit: Gale Research Co., 1967), col. 1384. See too *The Memoirs of the Life of Daniel Mendoza* [1816], ed. Paul Magriel (London: B. T. Batsford, 1951), p. 18.

[140] John Taylor, *Records of My Life*, 2 vols. (London, 1832), 2:214.

[141] Lord Sidmouth to I. L. Goldsmid, 31 July 1833, in Lionel Abrahams, "Sir I. L. Goldsmid and the Admission of the Jews of England to Parliament," *Transactions of the Jewish Historical Society of England* (1899–1901) 4:167.

[142] Bill Williams, *The Making of Manchester Jewry 1740–1875* (Manchester: Manchester University Press, 1976), p. 78.

[143] *An Appeal to the Humanity of the English People in Behalf of the Jews* (Dunstable, 1812), pp. 18–19. See the more chaste tones of M. J. Mayers, *A Brief Account of the Zoharite Jews* (Cambridge, 1826), pp. i–vi.

[144] B. R. Goakman, *The London Society for Promoting Christianity amongst the Jews, Examined; and the Pretensions of the Converted Jew, Investigated* (London, 1816), esp. pp. 19–22, 58. See too *Black Dwarf* (31 January 1821) 6(5):157–60.

H. H. Norris, a staunch proponent of converting the Jews,[145] published a slashing attack on the Society for defiling that uplifting project. Approving Norris's attack, Southey discarded the whole enterprise of converting the Jews as insanity.[146] Even the converted Jew,
however, might retain traces of Judaism in the wary eyes of Christians.
When Ricardo argued in parliament for tolerating religious debates
in the press, *John Bull* guffawed: "What fellows those reporters are!
only conceive, that in the Debates of Wednesday night, they have got
MR. RICARDO's name stuck to a speech about *Christianity!*"[147] Not
given to guffawing, Wilberforce lamented Ricardo's mistake. "I had
hoped," he sighed, "that Ricardo had become a Christian; I see now
that he has only ceased to be a Jew."[148]

One last approach to the elusive business of identifying a Jew: for
some, the Jew was the creation of a legislative history, perhaps a sustained social and cultural assault, anyway a political artifact. (Not a
social construction, for race and nation and tribe and persuasion are
all social constructions.) Were Jews sordidly devoted to moneylending? What else could one expect at the end of a history preventing
Jews from owning land and Christians from charging interest? Did
Jews cluster in such undignified occupations as selling old clothes?
"The causes of such pursuits have been studiously concealed,"
charged that Jewish doctor; "the causes consist in the laws of the
country, and the municipal regulations which have hitherto disqualified them from all more honourable pursuits, and have compelled
them into the lowest walks of trade. The laws have placed a badge on
them, and the populace taunt them that they wear a badge."[149] "We
throw in the teeth of the Jews that they are prone to certain sordid
vices. If they are vicious it is we who have made them so," insisted

[145] H. H. Norris, *The Origin, Progress, and Existing Circumstances, of the London Society
for Promoting Christianity amongst the Jews: An Historical Inquiry* (London, 1825),
pp. 493–94.

[146] Southey to Herbert Hill, 10 March 1826, *Selections from the Letters*, 3:533. For Jews
critically addressing the Society, see Williams, *Making of Manchester Jewry*, pp. 45–47.

[147] *The Works and Correspondence of David Ricardo*, ed. Piero Sraffa with M. H. Dobb,
11 vols. (Cambridge: Cambridge University Press for the Royal Economic Society,
1951–1973), 5:280 [26 March 1833]; *John Bull* (30 March 1823) no. 120, p. 100, some
small capitals removed.

[148] Robert Isaac Wilberforce and Samuel Wilberforce, *The Life of William Wilberforce*,
5 vols. (London, 1838), 5:173, filling in Ricardo's name.

[149] Van Oven, *An Appeal*, pp. 42–43. Note too Joshua van Oven to Patrick
Colquhoun, 24 March 1801, *Anglo-Jewish Letters (1158–1917)*, ed. Cecil Roth (London:
Soncino Press, 1938), pp. 211–12.

Hazlitt. "Shut out any class of people from the path to fair fame, and you reduce them to grovel in the pursuit of riches and the means to live."[150] Is this the most humane approach of all? That depends in part on what one thinks of its apparently denying any agency to Jews themselves.

I don't mean that speakers or writers were careful in deciding whether to describe Jews as a race, nation, tribe, persuasion, or political artifact—or even that they made a decision. In one passage, Walter Scott shifts effortlessly from race to persuasion to tribe.[151] In one sentence in his *Ivanhoe*, artless and not subversive, the Jews are a race and possess a national character.[152] Still, the logic or social grammar of these constructs matters. However conscious or in control of their language individual speakers are, however aware their audiences, the concepts focus attention on some perspectives and obscure others. Transforming Jews from race to persuasion, to take a mindlessly cheery description of what we've done in this terrain, makes a difference.

## Monotonous Refrains

Then again, one might argue that in daily practice, it made precious little difference what abstract category Jews were dumped into: they were unsavory regardless. Consider the traveller through the fashionable resort town of Brighton, appalled by the teeming population of Jews. "Hook Noses, Mosaical Whiskers and the whole tribe of Benjamin occupy every shop, every donkey-cart, and every seat in Box, Pitt, and Gallery. I am very tired of them, and shall probably take flight at the end of the week to Worthing."[153] Did it make any differ-

---

[150] "Emancipation of the Jews" [1831], in *Works of Hazlitt*, 19:321. See too "Party Spirit" [1830], in *Works of Hazlitt*, 20:323; *Edinburgh Review* (January 1831) 52(103):369, with variations in Thomas Babington Macaulay, *The Works of Lord Macaulay Complete*, ed. Lady Trevelyan, 8 vols. (London, 1875), 5:464. Privately, Macaulay referred to Jews as "unbelieving dogs": Macaulay to Hannah Macaulay, 23 May 1833, *The Letters of Thomas Babington Macaulay*, ed. Thomas Pinney, 6 vols. (Cambridge: Cambridge University Press, 1974–1981), 2:244.

[151] *Biographical Memoirs of Eminent Novelists* [1825], in *The Prose Works of Sir Walter Scott, Bart.*, 28 vols. (Edinburgh, 1834–1836), 3:212–13.

[152] *Ivanhoe* [1817], in Walter Scott, *Waverley Novels*, 48 vols. (Edinburgh, 1829–1833), 16:65–66.

[153] Archibald Macdonald to John Spencer-Stanhope, 7 August 1819, in A. M. W. Stirling, *The Letter-Bag of Lady Elizabeth Spencer-Stanhope*, 2 vols. (London: John Lane, The Bodley Head, 1913), 1:342.

ence to him whether Jews were race, nation, tribe, persuasion, or political artifact?

Killing Christ is enough to earn an especially contemptible status. The British of this period didn't invent the view that the Jews were still collectively responsible for deicide, but they didn't forget it, either.[154] "Your fathers murdered the Lord of Glory," the Jews were instructed gravely in one sermon.[155] Samuel Horsley charged the Jews with this particularly outrageous disobedience in his sermons—but he also urged that everyone's noxious passions "were, more truly than the Jews, the murderers of our Lord."[156]

Christ-killing Jews figured not just as figures of contempt and dread, but as resources in political argument. Since the Jews had crucified Christ, explained one loyalist pamphlet published by the Association for Preserving Liberty and Property against Republicans and Levellers, they hadn't been good enough to deserve a king. So they enjoyed equality—a divine imposition to punish them. Why would republicans emulate them? "We should be just where the Jews are; a proverb to all Nations; a monument of the Divine wrath; and a disgrace to the world."[157] In his polemic against utilitarianism, Macaulay imagined James Mill as director of police, "as great a receiver of stolen goods as Ikey Solomons himself."[158] (Solomons was a notorious fence; *John Bull* faithfully reported his tireless doings in their police columns.[159]) Christ-killing Jews yielded resources in fund-

---

[154] Granville Sharp, *Remarks on the Use of the Definitive Article in the Greek Text of the New Testament,* 3d ed. (London, 1803), p. 97 (and see p. vi); William Van Mildert, *An Historical View of the Rise and Progress of Infidelity, with A Refutation of Its Principles and Reasonings,* 2 vols. (London, 1806), 1:106; Robert Southey, *Letters from England* [1807], ed. Jack Simmons (London: Cresset Press, 1951), p. 393; *Anti-Jacobin Review* (February 1811) 38:174–75.

[155] Button, *Rise, Fall, and Future Restoration,* pt. 2, p. 78.

[156] Samuel Horsley, *Nine Sermons on the Nature of the Evidence by Which the Fact of Our Lord's Resurrection Is Established; and on Various Other Subjects: to Which Is Prefixed a Dissertation on the Prophecies of the Messiah Dispersed among the Heathen* (New York, 1816), pp. 156, 200–201.

[157] *Association Papers* (London, 1793), pt. 2, no. 1, p. 4. Contrast Charles Hall, *The Effects of Civilization on the People in European States* (London, 1805; reprint ed. London: Routledge/Thoemmes Press, 1994), pp. 275–76, arguing that "the whole history of the Jewish nation" demonstrates the possibility of an egalitarian distribution of property.

[158] *Edinburgh Review* (June 1829) 49(98):289, reprinted in *Utilitarian Logic and Politics: James Mill's 'Essay on Government', Macaulay's Critique and the Ensuing Debate,* ed. Jack Lively and John Rees (Oxford: Clarendon, 1978), p. 167.

[159] J. J. Tobias, *Prince of Fences: The Life and Crimes of Ikey Solomons* (London: Valentine, Mitchell, 1974). See for instance *John Bull* (27 May 1827) 7(337):168, (23 September 1827) 7(354):298, (10 February 1828) 8(374):48, (20 April 1828) 8(384):126, (26

raising, too: the Society for the Conversion of the Jews didn't mind turning to them to drum up enthusiastic support.[160] Who wouldn't hand over some pence or pounds to help rid the planet of the Messiah's murderers—and so accelerate the arrival of judgment day?

The Jews wouldn't: their voracious appetite for money was legendary, their unscrupulous tactics infamous. Cheated by a moneychanger abroad, Boswell recited, as if from a prayer book, "O Israel! Why art thou ever so dishonest?"[161] In court, the Earl of Mansfield snorted at counsel asking a wealthy Jew if he could furnish bail of £50. "Why do you ask him that question?" demanded Mansfield. "Don't you see he would burn for twice the sum?"[162] "The Jews are the lowest of mankind," fumed Coleridge; "they of the lower orders have not a principle of honesty in them; to grasp and be getting moneys for ever is their one occupation."[163] They would take any risk to make money, agreed Southey.[164] "Any thing for money, in contempt of their own law as well as of the law of the country;—the pork-butchers are commonly Jews." "Ordinary profits do not content them," he added.[165]

Nor, according to some observers, did ordinary work. Jewish labor wasn't dignified: stockjobbers or beggars, thieves or peddlers, Jews didn't know the meaning of an honest day's work. Their rabbis taught them, charged one pamphleteer, that labor was dishonorable.[166] One collection of periodical stories echoed the charge: "No one ever saw a labouring Jew, *i.e.* a Jew employed in honest labour—they are, indeed, mere vermin on the body-politic."[167] German Jews, warned one account of England, were tireless crooks: "I believe few burglaries,

---

July 1829) 9(450):237, (7 March 1830) 10(482):80, (8 May 1831) 11(543):152, (21 October 1832) 12(619):339.

[160] Extract from an address at a Jewish Contributors' Meeting, August 1822, in Norris, *Origin, Progress, and Existing Circumstances*, app., p. ci.

[161] *Boswell on the Grand Tour: Germany and Switzerland 1764*, ed. Frederick A. Pottle (New York: McGraw-Hill, 1953), p. 165 [2 November 1764].

[162] William Seward, *Anecdotes of Distinguished Persons, Chiefly of the Present and Two Preceding Centuries*, 4th ed., 4 vols. (London, 1798), 2:431.

[163] *Table Talk*, in *The Collected Works of Samuel Taylor Coleridge*, ed. Kathleen Coburn, Bart Winer, and others, in progress (Princeton, NJ: Princeton University Press, 1969–), 14(1):102 [13 April 1830].

[164] Southey to John Rickman, 22 March 1805, *Life and Correspondence*, 2:319.

[165] Southey, *Letters from England*, p. 397. See too *John Bull* (19 June 1825) 5(25):197.

[166] *A Peep into the Synagogue, or A Letter to the Jews* (London, 178–), p. 24.

[167] *The Rebellion; or, All in the Wrong*, 2d ed. (London, 1809), p. 44 [13 October 1809].

robberies, and false coinages are committed, in which some of them are not, in one shape or other, concerned."[168] Jews were prominent in the ranks of the day's empiric or quack doctors, who cheerfully capitalized on popular credulity by hawking preposterous cure-alls.[169] "Educated in idleness from the earliest infancy" but also socially consigned to it, Jews had "no alternative but to resort to those tricks and devices which ingenuity suggests, to enable persons without an honest means of subsistence to live in idleness."[170]

A mordantly ironic rage at the Jewish moneylenders who cashed in on others' distress was central to Byron's obsessive refrains. He had plenty of experience in these matters,[171] experience he turned to good use in his poetry, sprinkled with passing references to the Jews' "double-damned post-obits"[172] and the like, with sustained discussion too:

> How rich is Britain! not indeed in mines,
> Or peace, or plenty, corn, or oil, or wines,
> No land of Canaan, full of milk and honey,
> Nor (save in paper shekels) ready money:
> But let us not to own the truth refuse,
> Was ever Christian land so rich in Jews?[173]

---

[168] Fred. Aug. Wendeborn, *A View of England towards the Close of the Eighteenth Century*, 2 vols. (London, 1791), 2:471. Similarly, on the Jews of Tunis note Bankes, *System of Universal Geography*, p. 412.

[169] Corry, *Satirical View*, pp. 112–25; Daniel Lysons, *The Environs of London: Being an Historical Account of the Towns, Villages, and Hamlets, within Twelve Miles of That Capital*, 2d ed., 2 vols. (London, 1811), 2(2):717 n. 191.

[170] *Real Life in London*, 1:477.

[171] Byron to John Hanson, 10 March 1806, *Byron's Letters and Journals*, ed. Leslie A. Marchand, 13 vols. (London: John Murray, 1973–1994), 1:90–91; Byron to Hanson, 25 June 1809, *Letters and Journals*, 1:207; Byron to Samuel Rogers, 25 March 1813, *Letters and Journals*, 3:30; Byron to John Cam Hobhouse, 26 January 1815, *Letters and Journals*, 4:259; Hobhouse to Byron, 9 February 1815, *Byron's Bulldog: The Letters of John Cam Hobhouse to Lord Byron*, ed. Peter W. Graham (Columbus, OH: Ohio State University Press, 1984), p. 160; Byron to Douglas Kinnaird, 29 November 1823, *Letters and Journals*, 11:58; Byron to Kinnaird, 10 October 1822, *Letters and Journals*, 10:48; Byron to Kinnaird, 23 October 1822, *Letters and Journals*, 10:67; Byron to Kinnaird, 30 October 1822, *Letters and Journals*, 10:74.

[172] *Don Juan* [1819], in Byron, *The Complete Poetical Works*, ed. Jerome J. McGann and Barry Weller, 7 vols. (Oxford: Clarendon, 1980–1993), 5:48.

[173] *The Age of Bronze* [1823], in *Complete Poetical Works*, 7:22. See too *Don Juan* [1819], in *Complete Poetical Works*, 5:109; *Don Juan* [1823], in *Complete Poetical Works*, 5:496.

These overabundant Jews furnished one of the day's stock phrases, *rich as a Jew.*[174] When John Thorpe, one of Jane Austen's boors, abruptly blurts out to refined Catherine Morland that "Old Allen is as rich as a Jew—is not he?" she's baffled—but only because she refers to him as "Mr. Allen." True, she is too delicate to repeat the phrase— "Yes, I believe, he is very rich"—but it's not clear that she takes any offense at it. Or that Austen does.[175] The same overabundant Jews faced a quota: only twelve of them could serve as brokers on London's stock exchange and they had to pay off the mayor for the privilege.[176] The quota survived until 1830.[177] The same overabundant Jews kept Shylock on the minds and tongues of many.[178] The essayist who ventured a defense of Shylock and tried to set aside whatever

---

[174] For instance, *Letters from Mrs. Elizabeth Carter, to Mrs. Montagu, between the Years 1755 and 1800,* 3 vols. (London, 1817; reprint ed. New York: AMS Press, 1973), 2:106 [8 July 1771]; William Hutton, *An History of Birmingham,* 2d ed. (Birmingham, 1783; reprint ed. Wakefield: EP Publishing, 1976), pp. 128*–123; Charles Dibdin, *Hannah Hewit; or, The Female Crusoe,* 3 vols. (London, 1792), 1:55; "The Lottery" [1799], in Maria Edgeworth, *Tales and Novels,* 10 vols. (London, 1848), 2:165; *Paupers and Pig Killers: The Diary of William Holland, a Somerset Parson 1799–1818,* ed. Jack Ayres (Gloucester: Alan Sutton, 1984), p. 180 [25 October 1809]; Jeremy Bentham to Samuel Bentham, 19 July 1814, *Correspondence of Bentham,* 8:404; *Ormond* [1817], in Edgeworth, *Tales and Novels,* 9:284; *The Blues* [1823], in Byron, *Complete Poetical Works,* 6:299; *The Journal of Sir Walter Scott,* ed. W. E. K. Anderson (Oxford: Clarendon, 1972), p. 471 [8 May 1828]; *Bristol Job Nott* (20 June 1833) no. 80, p. 320.

[175] *Northanger Abbey* [1818], in *The Novels of Jane Austen,* 3d ed., ed. R. W. Chapman, 6 vols. (Oxford: Oxford University Press, 1987), 5(1):63.

[176] Sholto Percy and Reuben Percy [Joseph Clinton Robertson and Thomas Byerley], *London: or Interesting Memorials of Its Rise, Progress & Present State,* 3 vols. (London, 1824), 3:76–77; *Diary of Farington,* 12:4349 [13 May 1813].

[177] Blunt, *History of the Establishment,* p. 119 n. §; Endelman, *Jews of Georgian England,* p. 22. Cecil Roth, *A History of the Jews in England,* 3d ed. (Oxford: Clarendon, 1964), p. 247 apparently is mistaken in claiming the limit was dropped in 1828. See too Chaim Bermant, *The Cousinhood: The Anglo-Jewish Gentry* (London: Eyre & Spottiswoode, 1971), p. 68.

[178] For instance, Horace Walpole to George Selwyn, 11 October 1757, *The Yale Edition of Horace Walpole's Correspondence,* ed. W. S. Lewis, 48 vols. (New Haven, CT: Yale University Press, 1937–1983), 30:141; Richard Cumberland, *The Jew: A Comedy,* 2d ed. (London, 1794), p. 6; Mary Ann Hanway, *Ellinor; or, The World as It Is,* 4 vols. (London, 1798; reprint ed. New York: Garland, 1974), 1:231–32; *The Age of Bronze* [1823], in Byron, *Complete Poetical Works,* 7:22; Susan Ferrier to Miss Clavering, 26 September 1809, in *The Works of Susan Ferrier,* Holyrood edition, 4 vols. (London: Eveleigh Nash & Grayson, 1929), 4:62–63; *The Rebellion,* p. 41 [11 October 1809]; Percy Bysshe Shelley to Thomas Love Peacock, 6 November 1818, *The Letters of Percy Bysshe Shelley,* ed. Frederick L. Jones, 2 vols. (Oxford: Clarendon, 1964), 2:46; *Political Register* (25 January 1834) 83(4):212.

prejudice happened to attach to his being Jewish had a tough row to hoe.[179]

Jews as Christ-killers and moneygrubbers: they are ubiquitous in political debate, literature, diaries, letters, and casual conversation, so much part of the backdrop of daily life that bitter political adversaries could chorus in sweet concord over them. Burke, we've seen, loathed Jews. Like Cobbett, he shuddered at the vision of a Britain over-whelmed by them. "The next generation of the nobility," he proph-esied grimly, "will resemble the artificers and clowns, and money-jobbers, usurers, and Jews, who will be always their fellows, sometimes their masters."[180] Yet Richard Price, the Dissenting minister whose affection for the nascent French Revolution so enraged Burke, was no friend of the Jews, either. "What was the love of their country among the Jews, but a wretched partiality to themselves and a proud con-tempt of all other nations?"[181] Here Price wants to belittle narrow patriotism and applaud generous cosmopolitanism. So the political purposes aren't Burke's, but those wretched Jews, plastic, even pro-tean, are available to both writers, who embrace in unholy commu-nity. Similarly, Tom Paine adduced aristocrats and Jews as examples of how inbreeding makes the human species degenerate.[182] Not that Burke would have suggested that the aristocracy were racially inferior; not that he would have minded sneering at the Jews. Or again, God-win deplored the "most unheard of barbarities, and . . . unrelenting persecution" that Jews had suffered for centuries in their starring role as Christ-killers.[183] But he didn't mind letting the narrator of one of

[179] *Essays by a Society of Gentlemen, at Exeter* (Exeter, 1796), pp. 552–73.

[180] *Reflections on the Revolution in France* [1790], in *Works,* 3:295. Contrast J. G. A. Pocock, "Edmund Burke and the Redefinition of Enthusiasm: The Context as Counter-Revolution," in *The Transformation of Political Culture 1789–1848,* ed. François Furet and Mona Ozouf (Oxford: Pergamon Press, 1989), p. 31: "That Burke does not break out in invectives against Freemasons and Jews is a thing to be grateful for; he is not far from doing so." But see *Parliamentary History* (14 May 1781) 22:223–26, (4 December 1781) 22:775, (4 February 1782) 22:1023–26.

[181] *A Discourse on the Love of Our Country* [1789], in Richard Price, *Political Writings,* ed. D. O. Thomas (Cambridge: Cambridge University Press, 1991), p. 179. Note too *Britain's Happiness and the Proper Improvement of It* [1759], in Price, *Writings,* pp. 8–9.

[182] *Rights of Man* [1791], in *The Life and Works of Thomas Paine,* 10 vols. (New Rochelle, NY: Thomas Paine National Historical Association, 1925), 6:98. For a re-sponse, see *Considerations on Mr. Paine's Pamphlet on the Rights of Man* (Edinburgh, 1791), pp. 39–40. See too *Age of Reason* [1795], in *Works of Paine,* 8:173 n, 8:174, 8:254–55.

[183] William Godwin, *History of the Commonwealth of England,* 4 vols. (London, 1824–1828), 4:243.

his novels find "considerable entertainment" in talking to a Jewish peddler.[184] Nor did he mind reporting that throughout Europe Jews were "universally distinguished . . . for extortion."[185]

These contemptuous asides sometimes met with rebuttals or protestations of affection for Jews. Even the apparent affection, though, often depended on a contemptuous assignment of low status or was otherwise tangled up with demeaning sentiments. The unremarkable ancient Jews, after all, worked out monotheism—but perhaps this was a sign of providential intervention.[186] "They are the very ants of the mercantile world," reported *The Scourge*, unselfconsciously putting animal imagery to humanizing work, "ever busy, ever thriving: let us hold them up as examples of patience and perseverance scarcely ever equalled in Christian society. . . ."[187] Southey was willing to credit their role in world history with some happy unintended consequences: "The great services which, in their pursuit of gain, this most unfortunate and persecuted people rendered to civilisation, to science, and to literature, has scarcely yet been acknowledged with sufficient gratitude."[188] A few pages after reminding their readers that the "degenerate" Jews had slaughtered Christ, the *Anti-Jacobin Review* credited them with "peaceable and orderly behaviour" and suggested that perhaps they were different only in religious ceremonies. As usual, the turn to religious persuasion mollified hostility. Still, it didn't eliminate contempt. "May this consideration obtain from the reflecting part of the world a generous confidence, and properly Christian feelings of commiseration, towards the despised Jews!"[189]

These despised Jews were legendary for their sheer endurance in the face of centuries of unyielding contempt. "Though they are universally reduced to a state of the lowest subjection, and even exposed to hatred, contempt, and persecution," their numbers didn't dimin-

---

[184] William Godwin, *Mandeville: A Tale of the Seventeenth Century in England,* 3 vols. (Edinburgh, 1817), 1:140–41.

[185] William Godwin, *Enquiry Concerning Political Justice and Its Influence on Morals and Happiness,* ed. F. E. L. Priestley, 3 vols. (Toronto: University of Toronto Press, 1946), 1:101 [1798].

[186] Elizabeth Hamilton, *Letters, Addressed to the Daughter of a Nobleman, on the Formation of Religious and Moral Principle,* 2d ed., 2 vols. (London, 1806), 2:12–13.

[187] *Scourge* (1 March 1814) 7:240.

[188] Robert Southey, *Lives of the British Admirals, with An Introductory View of the Naval History of England,* 5 vols. (London, 1833–1840), 1:140.

[189] *Anti-Jacobin Review* (February 1811) 38:175, 38:178. See too Allen, *Modern Judaism,* pp. vi–viii.

ish.[190] "Buffeted and spurned," agreed another writer, Jews "persist inflexibly in the doctrines of their fathers."[191] Perhaps contempt helped cement Jewish solidarity. When one intelligent Jew abroad was asked "whether the odium frequently cast on the Jews operated as a temptation to embrace Christianity," he explained that Jews were "trained to return contempt with hatred. All those I love are Jews. Were I to go over to your church, I should become an object of hatred and contempt to all I love."[192] That weighty penalty couldn't be offset by gaining the esteem of the hated Christians—especially when their esteem would be guarded, anyway.

Is rote contempt for Jews genuine? Are speakers emotionally invested in such stock phrases as *rich as a Jew*? This question could be posed about any putative subordinates. When Cruikshank addresses his beloved as "my chick a biddy my Buttermilk & whisky . . . Dear little Lambkin,"[193] does he think she is an animal or a comestible? Or are these just innocent terms of affection? Is she delighted or indignant on receiving his letter? But she was just thirteen years old at the time: so how should she feel? Regardless of how she does feel or should feel, what is it like to be a woman and navigate a social world in which such expressions are routine, in which they somehow happen not to be directed by women to men?

In 1830, Coleridge regaled his dining companions:

> I once sat in a coach opposite a Jew—a symbol of Clothes Bags—an Isaiah of Hollywell Street—he would close the window—I opened it—he closed it again—Upon which I looked gravely at him and said—"Son of Abraham! thou smellest! Son of Isaac! thou art offensive! Son of Jacob! thou stinkest damnably! See the man in the Moon! He is holding his nose at thee at that distance: Dost thou think that I sitting here can

[190] William Belsham, *Essays, Philosophical, Historical, and Literary* (London, 1789), p. 87.

[191] Thomas Newte, *Prospects and Observations; on a Tour in England and Scotland: Natural, Oeconomical, and Literary* (London, 1791), p. 370. See too William Henry Pyne and William Combe, *The Microcosm of London*, 3 vols. (London, 1808–1811), 3:161; Henry Hart Milman, *History of the Jews*, 2d ed., 3 vols. (London, 1830), 1:3–4, 3:91–92; Isaac D'Israeli, *The Genius of Judaism* (London, 1833), pp. 4, 219.

[192] *Diary, Reminiscences, and Correspondence of Henry Crabb Robinson*, ed. Thomas Sadler, 2 vols. (Boston, 1869), 1:66 [1801].

[193] George Cruikshank to Mary Ann Walker, 11 September 1820, in Robert L. Patten, *George Cruikshank's Life, Times, and Art: 1792–1835* (New Brunswick, NJ: Rutgers University Press, 1992), p. 216.

endure it any longer?" The Jew was astounded—opened the window himself, and said "he was sorry he did not know before I was so great a shentleman!!"[194]

If the story sounds suspiciously familiar, it's because I already quoted the skeletal version Coleridge had recounted to his wife some twenty-eight years earlier. Over those years, he embellished the story: the great artist busily transmuting a tawdry pedestrian tale into, shall we say, a slightly longer tawdry pedestrian tale. Yet the details are telling. The Jew's closing remark might sound sarcastic, as if he were demanding who Coleridge thought he was, what imaginary status gave him the right to shower such patrician contempt down on others. Still, the Jew dutifully opens the window. Coleridge's huffing and puffing in his best King James Bible English succeeds in extorting deference.

How many times did Coleridge ride in a coach with a Jew? One, I presume. (But maybe zero.) How many times did Coleridge tell this story? I can imagine only one answer: dozens. Like the garrulous buffoon at the annual party of one's extended family, he must have launched eagerly into this little gem of a narrative at every opportunity, boring some and making others giggle, some at the Jew, maybe some at him. Maybe Coleridge and his audience enjoyed the luxury of recalling the event with serene hilarity. Maybe their great good cheer on the occasions of his recital wasn't colored by any particular contempt for Jews. Surely we are emotional worlds away from Cobbett's frantic paranoia or Moreton's disgusted fury.

Now consider: how many times did the Jew tell the story? Could he have told it triumphantly? (But maybe he too embroidered it. Maybe at the end of his version, the window remained closed. And— assuming this enchanting incident actually took place—where did the window in fact end up?) How would he have felt upon learning that Coleridge was telling it endlessly, that others were chortling over it? Would he have felt any less forlorn if he learned that none of them intended to express any contempt for Jews?

Perhaps an audaciously confident Jew could have laughed off the episode. But the background social script casting Jews as low would make that difficult. Contrast the case in which an aristocrat learns that the workers in the alehouse are mocking him. Perhaps that will

---

[194] *Table Talk*, in *Works of Coleridge*, 14(1):176–77 [7 July 1830].

sting: suppose he happens to be insecure. (But perhaps the worry is that they are manly men and he is effeminate, so they have found a status hierarchy assigning them the upper hand.) Still, the aristocrat can more easily marshal more social resources to maintain his equanimity. Coleridge's Jew would have a tougher time of it. And one crucial social resource is precisely the use of everyday language, familiar sneers and jeers, whether rote or heartfelt.

So it matters politically that Charles Dickens could refer to the police as "such a rascally set of *Negurs.*"[195] It matters politically that Carlyle could recall that Harriet Martineau was "full of Nigger fanaticisms. . . ."[196] Not because we need to figure out whether Dickens or Carlyle was a racist: I don't much care. But because if we want to understand the implications of trafficking in contempt, the obstacles faced by blacks in their daily lives, we need to focus on the nefarious weaving together of slavery and racism and such apparently offhand comments. And if we want to understand the significance of Dickens's and Carlyle's comments, we don't need to peer deeper into their inner mental lives. We need to fan out, to think about the range of views promulgated by others and the background social practices that help cash out the referents of their language.

So consider a conjecture about the relationship between understated contempt and blunt contempt. Spokesmen for understated may take pride in distancing themselves from their ugly. This may be pretense; they may secretly thrill in their de on unvarnished contempt while seeming to stay po- he fray. Or it may be heartfelt. Either way, the salience of contempt is partly caught up in expressions of snarling to mention the background practices of hierarchy and n. Whatever he happened to think of it, the meaning of enticing vignette is partly defined by Cobbett's scabrous rants, by legal disabilities, by a history of physical assaults in the streets.

[195] Dickens to H. W. Kolle, January? 1833, *The Letters of Charles Dickens*, Pilgrim edition, ed. Graham Storey and others, 7 vols. to date (Oxford: Clarendon, 1965–), 1:14.

[196] Thomas Carlyle, *Reminiscences*, ed. James Anthony Froude, 2 vols. (London, 1881), 2:213 [1866].

## EIGHT

# SELF AND OTHER

W HEN Joanna Baillie's Mrs. Betty, a maid, loses her patience at her mistress's insolent treatment, she exclaims, "Does she think I am going to live in her service to be call'd names so, and compared to a blackamoor too?"[1] True, the line she wanted to insist on was fragile, and not just because many English blacks worked as household servants: *slavey* was a popular term for servant maids.[2] But it was still worth insisting on. Whatever dignity she could muster as a servant depended on distancing herself from blacks, on claiming the payoffs of racial solidarity with her mistress. Mrs. Betty's heartfelt belief, I conjecture, is that contempt for blacks is different in kind, not just degree, from contempt for servants. More generally, the contempt that women, workers, blacks, and Jews suffer isn't merely the same damned thing over and over. Instead contempt's structure depends on the target group. Blacks and Jews don't end up on any pedestals. Prosperous white Englishmen might wish to live among attractive women but have no interest in hobnobbing with workers. A worker who struck it rich might escape some of the contempt attaching to his ignoble origins; a Jew might remain a reptile despite his wealth.

But what about individuals who fall into multiple categories? Contempt for black women, say, isn't a simple additive construct of con-

---

[1] *The Tryal: A Comedy,* in Joanna Baillie, *A Series of Plays* (London, 1798; reprint ed. Oxford: Woodstock Books, 1990), p. 248.

[2] Pierce Egan, *Life in London; or, The Day and Night Scenes of Jerry Hawthorn, Esq. and His Elegant Friend Corinthian Tom, Accompanied by Bob Logic, the Oxonian, in Their Rambles and Sprees through the Metropolis* (London, 1821), pp. 174 n. 5, 364; Pierce Egan, *Grose's Classical Dictionary of the Vulgar Tongue, Revised and Corrected* (London, 1823), s.v. *slavey;* Pierce Egan, *The Finish to the Adventures of Tom, Jerry, and Logic, in Their Pursuits through Life in and out of London* [1828] (London, 1887), p. 111; *The Memoirs of James Hardy Vaux, Including His Vocabulary of the Flash Language,* ed. Noel McLachlan (London: Heinemann, 1964), p. 265 s.v. *slavey.*

tempt for blacks and contempt for women.[3] It has its own quirky structure. In some regions of Africa, reported one traveller, women had vaginal labia so elongated that they were easily mistaken for penises. Their rear ends were grotesquely large. Their breasts were "disgustingly large and pendant; the usual way of giving suck, when the child is carried on the back, is by throwing the breast over the shoulder."[4] This putatively deformed body, a caricature of English femininity, was put on public display when the Hottentot Venus became a kind of circus exhibition in London in 1810.[5] (Do we dignify her by using her surviving proper name, Saartjie Baartman, stamped as it is with Dutch imperialism?) People purchased tickets to gape and prod. Cobbett grabbed the opportunity to reprint a letter in guttural dialect purporting to be from her to Lord Grenville (or, as "she" had it, Grinwell).[6] The Hottentot Venus was no freak, another traveller to Africa assured the British reading public. Or, as he saw it, no more a freak than thousands of African women who "scarcely yielded to her in any point of beauty."[7] But nothing said so far about women or blacks raises the specter of this pointedly contemptuous—and contemptibly pointed—focus on anatomy. So contempt for black women can't be reduced to contempt for blacks and contempt for women.

Or consider the interface between class and gender. "A woman should never be seen eating or drinking," Byron instructed Lady Melbourne, "unless it be *lobster sallad & Champagne,* the only truly feminine & becoming viands."[8] But this means that a considerable amount of wealth is required to become a woman, that the delicacy of the lady is definitive of the gender role. Mothers aside, held Mary

[3] For a sharp recent statement, see Kimberle Crenshaw, "Mapping the Margins: Intersectionality, Identity Politics, and Violence against Women of Color," *Stanford Law Review* (July 1991) 43:1241–1299.

[4] John Barrow, *An Account of Travels into the Interior of Southern Africa,* 2 vols. (London, 1801–1804; reprint ed. New York: Johnson Reprint, 1968), 1:278–82, 1:390. See too Andrew Sparrman, *A Voyage to the Cape of Good Hope,* 2 vols. (London, 1785; reprint ed. New York: Johnson Reprint, 1971), 1:188.

[5] Richard D. Altick, *The Shows of London* (Cambridge, MA: Belknap Press, Harvard University Press, 1978), pp. 269–73. For a sketch of her later history, culminating in dissection in Paris, see Stephen Jay Gould, "The Hottentot Venus," *Natural History* (October 1982) 91(10):20–27.

[6] *Political Register* (17 November 1810) 18(29):937–38.

[7] Cowper Rose, *Four Years in Southern Africa* (London, 1829), pp. 102–3.

[8] Byron to Lady Melbourne, 25 September 1812, *Byron's Letters and Journals,* ed. Leslie A. Marchand, 13 vols. (London: John Murray, 1973–1994), 2:208.

Hays, "women are considered in two ways only.—In the lower classes as necessary drudges—In the higher as the ornaments of society, the pleasing triflers, who flutter through life for the amusement of men, rather than for any settled purpose with regard to themselves. . . ."[9] So this eighteenth-century feminist is acutely aware that a class division lies at the heart of the category *woman*, raising now familiar and sticky issues about how gender and misogyny are and are not general.

Here too, social practices helped fix the meaning of politically volatile terms. Aristocrats and wealthy men seeking divorce could turn to Parliament for a private act. In the early 1800s, the lower orders continued a venerable if infrequent English tradition which peaked in these years: they sold their wives. Typically a husband needing to unload a wife would lead her by a rope to the marketplace and auction her off to the highest bidder, often already understood to be in love with her.[10] Of no legal force, the ceremony routinely was accepted by the locals but frowned on by high-minded commentators. ("A disgraceful exhibition," sniffed *John Bull* of one such occurrence in 1826.[11]) Wife sales help underline the class cleavage in the contemporary experience and understanding of gender. But—wives are sold, not husbands, and wives show up in the market with halters around their necks, as if they were livestock, just like the poor law beneficiaries saddled up to drag heavy agricultural equipment through the fields—the practice does more than illuminate or modify gender. It's already about class, gender, and commodification, all messily interwoven. If we focus on contempt for women or contempt for workers, we'll miss the significance of wife sales.

Similarly, if we conceive of contempt as prejudice or stereotype, a nasty attitude or a bit of mental shorthand, we'll miss its structure. Not so momentarily forgetting about Christian fraternity, parson William Holland confided in his diary, "I am not very partial to West

[9] Mary Hays, *Appeal to the Men of Great Britain in Behalf of the Women* (London, 1798; reprint ed. New York: Garland, 1974), p. 160.

[10] For instance, John Ashton, *Social England under the Regency*, 2 vols. (London, 1890), 1:373–75 [1815]; *John Bull* (9 December 1827) 7(365):390, (21 November 1830) 10(519):371; Ashton, *When William IV. Was King* (London, 1896), pp. 297–303; *John Bull* (7 July 1833) 13(656):215. See Samuel Pyeatt Menefee, *Wives for Sale: An Ethnographic Study of British Popular Divorce* (Oxford: Basil Blackwell, 1981). For skepticism about the prevalence of the practice, see Lawrence Stone, *Road to Divorce: England 1530–1987* (Oxford: Oxford University Press, 1995), pp. 143–48.

[11] *John Bull* (21 May 1826) 6(284):167.

Indians, especially to your Negro Half Blood people."[12] That sounds like prejudice, probably the emotion of contempt: decidedly unattractive, no doubt, but just a private fault, nothing of public or political significance; only the militant would reproach Holland. Or so it might seem. Yet I want to insist again that the emotion of contempt is partly dependent on background beliefs and a range of social practices that make it public and political. Hazlitt once watched the Duke of Cumberland leave the palace for a promenade, graciously reciprocating the doffed hats of passersby by bowing to each in turn. Then the duke encountered a predicament: "a negro sweep. If human at all,—which some people doubted,—he was pretty nearly as abject a representative of our human family divine as can ever have existed." Equality under the law this "paralytic nigger" was entitled to, but a bow from a member of the royal family? "Ought a son of England, could a son of England, descend from his majestic pedestal to gild with the rays of his condescension such a grub, such a very doubtful grub, as this?" Scrutinized by the expectant crowd, forced to act without guidance in this delicate affair of state, the prince took out his purse but didn't bow. The crowd burst into applause. "The black swore that the prince gave him half-a-crown," but Hazlitt didn't care. Alone against the applauding crowd, he thought that the prince owed the black a bow.[13] We can't understand this drama by wondering if the Duke of Cumberland was prejudiced.

Or recall the cheery democratic sociability of Pierce Egan's coffeehouse, the masquerade with no masks, no distinction of persons. Egan also depicted "the unsophisticated Sons and Daughters of Nature," disreputable patrons of an alehouse or club energetically dancing. "The parties *paired off* according to *fancy;* the eye was pleased in the choice, and nothing thought of about birth and distinction. All was *happiness,*—every body free and easy, and freedom of expression allowed to the very echo." On offer here isn't breezy egalitarian political debate, but interracial coupling, with for instance "*African Sall*" dancing with "*nasty Bob,*" and *no distinction of persons* bearing on more than norms of debate.[14] The practice is at the intersection of class,

[12] *Paupers and Pig Killers: The Diary of William Holland, a Somerset Parson 1799–1818,* ed. Jack Ayres (Gloucester: Alan Sutton, 1984), p. 106 [25 January 1805].

[13] "Notes on Gilfillan's Literary Portraits" [1845–1846], in *The Collected Writings of Thomas de Quincey,* ed. David Masson, 14 vols. (Edinburgh, 1889–1890), 11:348–49.

[14] Egan, *Life in London,* p. 286, with facing Cruikshank plate, "Lowest 'Life in Lon-

race, and gender. It isn't somehow "fundamentally" about any one of those categories. And it is very much about citizenship, once again a category not exhausted by the legal rules defining the franchise. Less casual than Egan, young Cobbett brandished some news from Virginia: a black man was sentenced to castration for attempting to rape a white woman. "This was very unjust," he leered. "Why should this poor fellow be thus served for wishing to enjoy the *Rights of Man*?"[15]

Here I turn to demonizing the other, inflating one's own social status or self-esteem by taking some loathsome other as a convenient foil. This is the world in which we know it's wonderful to be a white English upper-class male precisely because we know it's contemptible not to be one. It's the world of in-group and out-group, us and them, the pure and the defiled—and defiling, the orderly and the dissolute. Some have always suspected that those magically fertile distinctions, with all their rotten fruits, are endemic to the human condition. Their content may be wildly contingent, but the same simple binary oppositions structure social life everywhere. Maybe so: but maybe we should learn to detect in that suspicion another conservative bid to limit the scope of political agency.

## SOCIAL DISTANCE AND SYMPATHY

Lower a group's status and you can safely abuse them. That, remember, is what a correspondent in Cobbett's *Political Register* accused Malthus of doing to the poor. An especially sharp statement of the view came from the son of King Naimbanna of Rohanna, baptized Henry Granville in England. This African prince exploded at the mention of someone who had "publicly asserted something very degrading to the general character of Africans" and impatiently brushed aside the dutiful Christian advice that he forgive his enemies.

> "If a man should rob me of my money, I can forgive him; if a man should shoot at me, or try to stab me, I can forgive him; if a man should sell me

---

don'." Note Cruikshank's "Courtiers Carousing in a Cadgers Ken," in Bernard Blackmantle [Charles Molloy Westmacott], *The English Spy*, 2 vols. (London, 1825–1826), facing 2:33, for more jolly racial mixing among the lower orders. So too "A View of the Exchange Coffee House," in Charles Varlo, *Nature Display'd* (London, 1794), p. 304, takes the coffeehouse as the site of international shoulder-rubbing.

[15] *Porcupine's Gazette* (21 September 1797), in William Cobbett, *Porcupine's Works*, 12 vols. (London, 1801), 7:183–84.

and all my family to a slave-ship, so that we should pass all the rest of our days in slavery in the West Indies, I can forgive him;—but" (added he, rising from his seat with much emotion,) "if a man takes away the character of the people of my country, I never can forgive him. . . . if any one takes away the character of Black people, that man injures Black people all over the world; and when he has once taken away their character, there is nothing which he may not do to Black people ever after. That man, for instance, will beat Black men, and say, *Oh, it is only a Black man, why should not I beat him?* That man will make slaves of Black people; for when he has taken away their character, he will say, *Oh, they are only Black people—why should not I make them slaves?*"[16]

Hazlitt approvingly quoted the passage as an explanation for the increasingly scurrilous treatment of English workers.[17] The *Quarterly Journal of Education*, one of the organs of the Society for the Diffusion of Useful Knowledge, echoed the analysis years later and gestured toward the lethally powerful work it could do. "Men feel little compunction in tormenting and exterminating those whom they consider as a degraded race."[18]

Genocide and the petty cruelties of everyday life share this structure. A Jew tried to board a coach in Kensington, but the inside was packed. Riding outside was dangerous, so he didn't want to, but the travellers were exasperated. "They couldn't understand why a Jew should be ashamed of travelling on the outside; anyway, as they said, he was nothing but a Jew!"[19] Travelling in Hamburgh, Dorothy and William Wordsworth watched a woman being beaten on the street; "this brutal treatment did not excite the smallest indignation in the breast of the spectators."[20] Two days later, they watched "a surly-

---

[16] Prince Hoare, *Memoirs of Granville Sharp* (London, 1820), pp. 368–69 n.

[17] *Edinburgh Review* (July 1821) 35(70):317–18, reprinted as "Capital Punishments" in *The Complete Works of William Hazlitt*, ed. P. P. Howe, 21 vols. (London: J. M. Dent and Sons, 1930), 16:218–19.

[18] *Quarterly Journal of Education* (April 1834) 7(13):271. See too Piercy Ravenstone, *A Few Doubts as to the Correctness of Some Opinions Generally Entertained on the Subjects of Population and Political Economy* (London, 1821; reprint ed. London: Routledge/Thoemmes Press, 1994), p. 210.

[19] Carl Philip Moritz, *Journeys of a German in England in 1782*, trans. and ed. Reginald Nettel (New York: Holt, Rinehart and Winston, 1965), p. 105 [20 June 1782]. For the hazards of riding outside, note pp. 178–79. See too "The Good Aunt" [1801], in Maria Edgeworth, *Tales and Novels*, 10 vols. (London, 1848), 1:172.

[20] *Journals of Dorothy Wordsworth*, ed. E. de Selincourt, 2 vols. (New York: Macmillan, 1941), 1:27 [28 September 1798], in William's handwriting. For other foreign cruelties, see F. W. Chesson, *The Treatment of Women in Italy* (London, 1815).

looking German" use foul language—and a stick—to drive along a
Jew. This "insolence," they learned, was supported by the law and
public opinion; "the countenances of the by-standers expressed cold
unfeeling cruelty."[21] No one interceded in either case, including the
distraught Wordsworths, paralyzed perhaps by their status as foreigners. Less brutally but just as insidiously, Lambeth's Asylum for
orphan girls excluded Negroes and mulattoes.[22] These pariahs might
taint their betters—or even other pariahs. "There was a great difficulty in getting a place, after living with Jews," one servant
remembered.[23]

There's a sinister link between social status and sympathetic regard,
already noticed by Adam Smith.[24] Put bluntly, human beings as such
don't necessarily qualify as persons or instantiations of Kantian rational nature. They don't necessarily extort respect from other rational
agents as such. If they are sufficiently remote—in social, not geographic, space—others will gaze on them with wondering indifference or worse. Conservatives deployed the analysis to suggest that
the poor didn't resent the rich. In her *Memoirs of Modern Philosophers,*
an antic sendup of the English Jacobins, Elizabeth Hamilton has a
meddling idiot, Bridgetina Botherim, spout radical pieties at every
turn. (Hamilton conscientiously offers the appropriate footnotes to
Godwin.) Confronting some "rustic" workers in the countryside,
Botherim is off and running on a ferocious tirade about social injustice and degradation. But the workers themselves are nonplussed—
"What should make me wretched?" demands one—and judicious
Mrs. Martha assures her that the poor are happy. They "see the equi-

---

[21] *Journals of Dorothy Wordsworth,* 1:29 [30 September 1798].

[22] Daniel Lysons, *The Environs of London: Being an Historical Account of the Towns,
Villages, and Hamlets, within Twelve Miles of That Capital,* 2d ed., 2 vols. (London, 1811),
1(1):226. This kind of restriction seems not to be routine; compare for instance
Lysons, *Environs,* 1(2):517 on an asylum at Greenwich. But this depends on an argument from silence: compare William Henry Pyne and William Combe, *The Microcosm of
London,* 3 vols. (London, 1808–1811), 1:25–31 on Lambeth's Asylum and 2:61–78 on
the Foundling Hospital.

[23] *Life of a Licensed Victualler's Daughter* (London, 1844), p. 41.

[24] Adam Smith, *The Theory of Moral Sentiments* [1759], ed. D. D. Raphael and A. L.
Macfie (Oxford: Clarendon, 1976), p. 55; *Lectures on Rhetoric and Belles Lettres,* ed. J. C.
Bryce (Oxford: Clarendon, 1983), p. 124 [14 January 1763]; *An Inquiry into the Nature
and Causes of the Wealth of Nations* [1776], ed. R. H. Campbell, A. S. Skinner, and W. B.
Todd, 2 vols. (Oxford: Clarendon, 1976), 2:794. Essentially the same analysis is central
in Richard Rorty, *Contingency, Irony, and Solidarity* (Cambridge: Cambridge University
Press, 1989).

page of my lord and lady with the same indifference that they behold
the flight of a bird; and would as soon think of grieving at the want of
wings as at the want of a carriage."[25] Yet radicals were inclined to run
the analysis the other way, that is to deplore the lofty contempt displayed by social superiors. The demand for equality is a bid to bridge
these yawning social chasms, simultaneously to change social structure and emotional repertoires. Conservatives have long claimed that
the demand for equality is a base expression of envy. We might instead think of it as the exalted aspiration to make envy possible.

Once again, there's all too much room in these matters for ambiva-
lence, just because there are competing accounts of hierarchy. Walter
Scott took painting lessons from "a little Jew animalcule—A Smouch
called Burrell, a clever sensible creature though."[26] When the ani-
malcules are clever and sensible, it's not clear how much sympathy
they generate: one wonders just how Scott treated his teacher—and
how his teacher endured it.

There's also room for a relatively benevolent form of contempt, a
quizzical amusement at the silliness of the socially remote inferior. Or
a relaxed fascination with the inferior's exotic ways or very being. In
1788, patrons of one Birmingham theatre were treated to "a new Pan-
tomime Dance called 'The Drunken Dancing Jews', which has never
been performed in Birmingham," the Jews' peculiarities not disqual-
ifying them from public regard but shaping the regard they might
attain.[27] Respectable people dropped by to observe Jewish services.
One found a Jewish wedding quite odd.[28] "The service without dignity, and in no way imposing," reported a disdainful Mary Berry.[29]
Elizabeth Wynne found these ceremonies risible. At one wedding,
"the two rabies sung a most ridiculous thing which made it very difficult for me to keep from laughing."[30] The viewing is akin to ogling

[25] Elizabeth Hamilton, *Memoirs of Modern Philosophers*, 3 vols. (London, 1800; reprint
ed. New York: Garland, 1974), 1:207–12.

[26] *The Journal of Sir Walter Scott*, ed. W. E. K. Anderson (Oxford: Clarendon, 1972),
p. 100 [1 March 1826]. The *OED* defines *smouch* as a Jew; one presumes it's a pejorative.

[27] John Money, *Experience and Identity: Birmingham and the West Midlands 1760–1800*
(Montreal: McGill—Queen's University Press, 1977), p. 93.

[28] Henry Seymour Conway to Walpole, 4 September 1751 NS, *The Yale Edition of
Horace Walpole's Correspondence*, ed. W. S. Lewis, 48 vols. (New Haven, CT: Yale University
Press, 1937–1983), 37:311–12.

[29] *Extracts from the Journals and Correspondence of Miss Berry from the Year 1783 to 1852*,
ed. Lady Theresa Lewis, 2d ed., 3 vols. (London, 1866), 3:62 [7 June 1815].

[30] Elizabeth Wynne's diary, 29 July 1795, *The Wynne Diaries*, ed. Anne Fremantle, 3

the Hottentot Venus. Or the spotted boy, transported from the West
Indies for the delectation of English observers.[31] Or the Portuguese
dwarf, not quite three feet high, "really not very ugly," observed by
Eugenia Wynne.[32] Or an albino black girl on display at Bartholomew
Fair, the social stakes captured in the barker's pitch: "The white
negro, the greatest curiosity ever seen—the first that has been exhibited since the reign of George the Second—look at her head and
hair, ladies and gentleman, and feel it; there's no deception, it's like
ropes of wool."[33]

## MANLY AND DESPICABLE BOXERS, WOMANLY AND DESPICABLE WORKERS

These are pariahs observed and recollected in tranquillity, under the
impassive gaze of those secure in their own full humanity, seeking
diversion in the spectacles of local color. Other spectacles inspired
more anxiety. Consider boxing.

Under contemporary rules, boxers fought with no gloves and fights
could stretch on and on. One 1818 bout went for 125 rounds.[34] The
sport produced its casualties. Reporting one 1817 death, *Blackwood's*
urged the magistrates to crack down.[35] Reporting one 1833 death,
the *Poor Man's Guardian* indicted "those brutal exhibitions so disgraceful to this country"[36]—polite Tory monthly and impolite radical
weekly lining up in the name of humanity. Others, too, indicted the
sport as appalling savagery. One debating society called for its aboli-

---

vols. (London: Oxford University Press, 1935–1940), 2:39. Note too *Wynne Diaries,* 1:94
[25 December 1791].

[31] *The Oakes Diaries: Business, Politics and the Family in Bury St Edmunds 1778–1827,* ed.
Jane Fiske, 2 vols. (Suffolk: Boydell Press, 1990), 2:148–49; *Gentleman's Magazine*
(March 1813) 13:287. For context, see Altick, *Shows of London,* chaps. 3, 19, 22, and
pp. 250–51.

[32] Eugenia Wynne's diary, 24 April 1805, *Wynne Diaries,* 3:165.

[33] William Hone, *The Every-Day Book,* 2 vols. (London, 1827; reprint ed. Detroit:
Gale Research Co., 1967), 1:1188–89.

[34] Pierce Egan, *Boxiana,* 4 vols. (London, 1818–1824), 2:447. I have been unable to
obtain vol. 3 of *Boxiana.*

[35] *Blackwood's Edinburgh Magazine* (July 1817) 1(4):435. But see too *Blackwood's Edinburgh Magazine* (March 1820) 6(36):609–11.

[36] *Poor Man's Guardian* (8 June 1833) 2(105):182.

tion in 1788.[37] *John Bull* loathed "this detestable traffic in human flesh," on a par with the slave trade.[38] In these years magistrates increasingly did crack down on prizefighting.[39]

But others embraced boxing. Another debating society applauded the magistrates "for their prudence in not too violently opposing public taste and winking at what affords much amusement and keeps up the spirit and courage of the company."[40] The actual content of that spirit and courage wasn't kept covert. For William Windham, boxing secured English masculinity. "Will it make no difference in the mass of a people, whether their amusements are all of a pacific, pleasurable, and effeminate nature, or whether they are of a sort that calls forth a continued admiration of prowess and hardihood?" he demanded.[41] Windham liked to attend the matches.[42] In fact, he was an amateur boxer.[43] Egging Windham on, Cobbett inveighed against the humanitarian critique of boxing, an indictment for murder after another boxing casualty, and the judges "afraid of displeasing the well-dressed, lisping, soft-tongued rabble," as so much pathetic effeminacy.[44] Here, longstanding fears that commerce and prosperity lead to an emasculating refinement issue in a plea for boxing as public therapy.[45] Egan introduced his own volumes on boxing with a sarcas-

[37] *London Debating Societies, 1776–1799,* comp. Donna T. Andrew (Great Britain: London Record Society, 1994), p. 218 [30 January 1788].

[38] *John Bull* (12 December 1824) 4(50):404.

[39] Robert W. Malcolmson, *Popular Recreations in English Society 1700–1850* (Cambridge: Cambridge University Press, 1973), p. 145.

[40] J. C. Reid, *Bucks and Bruisers: Pierce Egan and Regency England* (London: Routledge & Kegan Paul, 1971), p. 39.

[41] Windham to A. Hudson, 17 August 1809, *The Windham Papers,* 2 vols. (London: Herbert Jenkins, 1913), 2:352. For a somewhat more complex analysis, see Windham to Boswell, 26 October 1792, *The Correspondence of James Boswell with Certain Members of the Club,* ed. Charles N. Fifer (New York: McGraw-Hill, 1976), p. 378.

[42] *The Diary of the Right Hon. William Windham 1784 to 1810,* ed. Mrs. Henry Baring (London, 1866), pp. 138 [9 June 1788], 180 [6 July 1789], 450 [20 July 1805].

[43] John Taylor, *Records of My Life,* 2 vols. (London, 1832), 1:344.

[44] Cobbett to Windham, 2 August 1805, *Letters of William Cobbett,* ed. Gerald Duff, *Romantic Reassessment* (Salzburg: Institut für Englische Sprache und Literatur, 1974), 35:16–18; *Political Register* (10 August 1805) 8(6):193–202, (21 September 1805) 8(12):417–25.

[45] For the context, see Albert O. Hirschman, *The Passions and the Interests: Political Arguments for Capitalism before Its Triumph* (Princeton, NJ: Princeton University Press, 1977); Hirschman, *Rival Views of Market Society and Other Recent Essays* (New York: Viking, 1986), chap. 5. Note too John Bowles, *A Dispassionate Inquiry into the Best Means of*

tic snipe at the fragile souls who shrank from the likes of rain showers.[46] "The practice of BOXING through the means of the *prize-ring*," he emphasized on another occasion, "is one of the corner stones towards preventing EFFEMINACY from undermining the good *old character* of the people of England. . . ."[47]

The boxers doing their bit to preserve English manhood were disproportionately blacks and Jews. Bill Richmond, Tom Molineaux, Sam Robinson, and Henry Sutton graced the lists as blacks and men of color (the latter locution usually indicated those of mixed race); Daniel Mendoza, Elisha Crabbe, Dutch Sam, and Abraham Belasco as Jews. So Windham's spectators are vampires, greedily sucking in the potent masculinity displayed by despised blacks and Jews, presumably struggling to contain a bit of furtive anxiety about the transaction. Perhaps they consoled themselves in their undead languor by capitalizing on the cultural force of the mind/body distinction. Perhaps, that is, the very physicality of these triumphant displays of masculinity let the spectators console themselves in their superior status. The fighters' brute energy, quintessentially male or masculine, placed them close to animal nature. Or, if you like, here man is to woman as nature is to culture.[48] Yet women too occasionally took to the ring, several of them Jewish.[49] The singer of "The Jew Beauties" glumly recounted how his courtship collapsed in the face of his beloved's pugilistic expertise.[50] One can only marvel at the intricate gender-bending possibilities.

Egan urged boxing fans to adopt this maxim: "Impartial to *colour*, giving praise to each feat, / 'BUT NE'ER BE UNMINDFUL TO BRAVE MEN IN DEFEAT!' "[51] *Blackwood's* recalled witnessing Molineaux knock down England's own Tom Cribb. "At once all distinction of colour was lost." The collapsing of social distance and of contempt led to a flurry of antislavery sentiments: "We saw before us two human beings—and

*National Safety* (London, 1806), pp. 31–54; Joseph Priestley, *Lectures on History, and General Policy*, 2 vols. (Philadelphia, 1803), 2:276–77.

[46] Egan, *Boxiana*, 1:iv.

[47] Pierce Egan, *Sporting Anecdotes* (London, 1820), p. vi.

[48] Contrast Sherry Ortner, "Is Female to Male as Nature Is to Culture?" *Feminist Studies* (Fall 1972) 1(2):5–31.

[49] Todd Endelman, *The Jews of Georgian England 1714–1830: Tradition and Change in a Liberal Society* (Philadelphia: Jewish Publication Society of America, 1979), p. 220.

[50] *BMC* no. 10681 [12 August 1806].

[51] Egan, *Boxiana*, 2:561. Compare *Boxiana*, 1:358, 1:481.

our hearts beat for the cause of liberty all over the world."[52] Still, Egan reported, "the sporting world preferred having a *white* to a *black* pugilistic champion," so there was great rejoicing when Cribb finally defeated Molineaux in 1810. (Yet the fans showered Molineaux with gifts.[53]) The internal norms of athletic competition define the sparring partners as equals, but those norms collide with racism. At an 1811 rematch with Cribb, Molineaux received fair play. But he "had to contend against a prejudiced multitude, the pugilistic honour of the country was at stake, and the attempts of MOLINEAUX were viewed with jealousy, envy, and disgust"—and this, Egan claims, not because he was a black struggling against a white, but because he was an American pitted against an Englishman.[54] No doubt Molineaux's reign made the fans fond of him. But I suspect that their fondness was always a bit uneasy. I suspect too that when they showered him with gifts after his defeat at Cribb's hands, the fans were secretly relieved that his days in the sun were over.

Is this contempt? Don't the fans look up to Molineaux and Cribb alike? Aren't we already seeing the sports champion as popular hero? Thomas Spence struck a commemorative coin of Daniel Mendoza.[55] But consider: would Windham want his own son to become not just an amateur boxer, but a prize-fighter? Or consider other grudging formulations of what we might call equality at a distance. "*I* should be happy to *enlighten* the lower classes," mused Haydon, "but not to *dine* with them."[56] "I have, in the abstract, no disrespect for Jews," declared Charles Lamb. "But I should not care to be in habits of familiar intercourse with any of that nation." His reservations promptly brought him to confess that he found much to admire in the faces of blacks. "But I should not like to associate with them, to share my meals and my good-nights with them—because they are black."[57] One can imagine respecting, even admiring, the pariah—at an anti-

[52] *Blackwood's Edinburgh Magazine* (October 1820) 8(43):64.

[53] Egan, *Boxiana,* 2:233–34.

[54] Egan, *Boxiana,* 1:367.

[55] *Trial of Thomas Spence in 1801 together with His Description of Spensonia, Constitution of Spensonia, End of Oppression, Recantation of the End of Oppression, Newcastle on Tyne Lecture Delivered in 1775, Also, A Brief Life of Spence and a Description of His Political Token Dies,* ed. Arthur W. Waters (Leamington Spa: privately printed at the Courier Press, 1917), p. 20.

[56] *The Diary of Benjamin Robert Haydon,* ed. Willard Bissell Pope, 5 vols. (Cambridge, MA: Harvard University Press, 1960–1963), 4:33 [24 January 1833].

[57] *Elia* [1823], in *The Works of Charles and Mary Lamb,* ed. E. V. Lucas, 6 vols. (New York: Macmillan, 1913), 2:70–72.

septic distance. The Jew and black in the ring are one thing, at the dinner table another.

In 1809, Jewish boxers left the ring and were greeted with howls of contempt. Drury Lane Theatre had burned down at the end of February. Rebuilding, the management installed private boxes and raised ticket prices. Reviling these purported gestures of financial prudence, the theater-going public launched the O.P. (for "old prices") riots.[58] Night after night, rowdy audiences interrupted plays with their hoarse screams.[59] Sheridan, part owner and playwright, lingered ironically in verse on this stupendous victory for free speech.[60] (Here's another enabling constraint: the norm that the audience remain silent or applaud only intermittently makes it possible to enjoy the speech of the actors and actresses.) John Kemble, head of the theater, tried in vain to defuse the riots by opening his books to an impartial committee and publicizing the results of their inspection.[61] The management turned for assistance to London's Jews. Some were given free tickets to show up and support the theatre; their "Israelitish avidity of turning the *monish*" made the scheme backfire, since they scalped the tickets and undercut box office prices, and those buying the tickets had no reason to express loyalty to management.[62] But the theater also hired a crew of Jewish boxers, including Mendoza and Dutch Sam, to roam the theater and intimidate their opponents into silence.

"*Turn out the fighting Jews,*" cried the audience. They began to show up flaunting handbills. Among them: "Oppose Shylock and the whole tribe of Israel"; "Genius of Britain, espouse our cause, / Free us from Kemble and Jewish laws"; "Britons, be true and brave, / Never be to Jew or Kemble, slave."[63] These Jewish boxers inspired no admiration.

[58] Marc Baer, *Theatre and Disorder in Late Georgian London* (Oxford: Clarendon, 1992), is a very fine study of the riots.

[59] But for the customary level of audience noise in contemporary theater, consider *A Regency Visitor: The English Tour of Prince Pückler-Muskau Described in His Letters 1826–1828,* trans. Sarah Austin, ed. E. M. Butler (London: Collins, 1957), pp. 83 [23 November 1826], 275 [28 November 1827].

[60] "O.P.—A New Song," *The British Press* (19 September 1810), in *The Letters of Richard Brinsley Sheridan,* ed. Cecil Price, 3 vols. (Oxford: Clarendon, 1966), 3:340.

[61] *The Rebellion; or, All in the Wrong,* 2d ed. (London, 1809), pp. 24–27.

[62] *Covent Garden Journal,* 2 vols. (London, 1810), 1:80–81. This is an invaluable primary source on the riots.

[63] *The Rebellion,* pp. 40 [10 October 1809], 41 [11 October 1809], 47 [16 October 1809], 63 [1 November 1809].

The audience didn't greedily ingest their masculinity. Instead the deployment of "tribes of Jew-ruffian pugilists" struck onlookers as a crass attempt to muzzle public opinion.[64] In a mischievous carnival inversion, O.P. rioters dressed as Jews, one as a rabbi whose fellow rioters demanded that he be turned out.[65]

It's not just that Jewish boxers in a theater are out of place, that this is a routine instance of social discomfort of the sort surrounding any role confusion. (Compare: at your parents' dinner table, you take notes on the conversation and yawn. Or at the restaurant, you genuflect to the waiter and murmur in Latin.) Instead, the ordinary loathsomeness of the Jew reasserts itself, the boxing ring not present to work its reasonably sanitizing spell. In fact, the Jews' loathsomeness rubbed off on the theater management. Audiences feasted on caricatures endowing Kemble with a large nose.[66]

In ring and theater alike, these masculine boxers offer a convenient foil for framing a story about English identity. The sturdy English subject isn't American: that much is trivially obvious. But he isn't black or Jewish either. Invited to rally to the genius of Britain by rejecting slavery to Jews, he effortlessly slides into the familiar Manichean economy, his social status and self-esteem underwritten by the repulsive credentials of his Jewish opponents. The O.P. rioters had other concerns: they worried that the new private boxes concealed sexual intrigue and that the foreign Mme Catalani, a celebrity of the day, was grossly overpaid. But a major appeal of the endless brawling must have been celebrating their identity as pure and virtuous Englishmen. For similar reasons, Cobbett found the census returns lacking. "I would have dispensed with the distinction of male and female, and some others, if I could have obtained, in lieu of them, a pretty accurate account of the number of *foreigners,* distinguishing particularly, *Jews, Negroes,* and *Mulattoes;* for, when I reflect on the vast number of these that I see in and about this town," he found it hard to congratulate himself on booming English prosperity.[67]

In addition to slurping down the bold masculinity of the boxers, virtuous Englishmen liked to distance themselves from the most effeminate in their ranks. Wondering why cooks and tailors were

[64] *The Rebellion,* p. 46 [14 October 1809].
[65] Baer, *Theatre and Disorder,* pp. 173, 215.
[66] Baer, *Theatre and Disorder,* p. 216.
[67] *Political Register* (16 June 1804) 5(24):935.

"looked upon with an unaccountable contempt," Boswell lit upon "the effeminacy of these employments, compared with others where more strength is required. . . ."[68] Once, reported a historian of the cotton industry, workers hurled themselves into athletic recreations. But enlightenment had corrupted them: "It is to be regretted that the present pursuits and pleasures of the labouring class are of a more effeminate cast—They are now Pigeon-fanciers, Canary-breeders and Tulip-growers."[69] So the dignity of labor had to be secured against idle aristocrats and the helpless poor thrown on the parish—and the unpleasantly effeminate workers in their midst.

Much was made of the man-milliner. "Which is the most ridiculous Character, a Man Milliner or a Military Fop?" enquired one debating society in 1786. A "very small majority" came down against the milliner.[70] At a similar debate later that year, where one speaker indicted the new tendency of "the sexes to exchange situations with each other," the man-milliner was deemed more "exceptionable" than the libertine or the miser.[71] Meeting London refinement head on, Fanny Burney's Evelina chortles over the man-milliners: "Such men! so finical, so affected! they seemed to understand every part of a woman's dress better than we do ourselves; and they recommended caps and ribbands with an air of so much importance, that I wished to ask them how long they had left off wearing them!"[72] "I look upon a Man Milliner not only as one of the most despicable members of society, but as one of the most injurious," spat out Southey. At the sight of the monstrous figure, "anger will mingle itself with the feeling of contempt, for the employment that degrades this animal might have preserved a woman from prostitution."[73]

[68] James Boswell, The Hypochondriack, ed. Margery Bailey, 2 vols. (Stanford, CA: Stanford University Press, 1928) 1:223–24 [February 1779].

[69] Richard Guest, A Compendious History of the Cotton-Manufacture; with a Disproval of the Claim of Sir Richard Arkwright to the Invention of Its Ingenious Machinery (Manchester, 1823), pp. 38–39.

[70] London Debating Societies, 1776–1799, comp. Donna T. Andrew (Great Britain: London Record Society, 1994), p. 179 [6 March 1786].

[71] London Debating Societies, p. 193 [27 December 1786].

[72] Fanny Burney, Evelina, or The History of a Young Lady's Entrance into the World [1778], ed. Edward A. Bloom and Lillian D. Bloom (Oxford: Oxford University Press, 1982), p. 27. See too Colonel Floyd to Doctor Bell, 4 October 1792, in Robert Southey and Charles Cuthbert Southey, The Life of the Rev. Andrew Bell, 3 vols. (London, 1844), 1:439.

[73] Robert Southey, Letters Written during a Short Residence in Spain and Portugal, 2d ed. (Bristol, 1799), p. 223.

*John Bull* repeatedly singled out "the most anomalous of beings called human, a man-milliner."[74] Aghast at learning that the man-milliners were clamoring for education, the paper averred, "There is no class of persons who ought to be so perfectly satisfied as those monopolizers of women's work, the dandy men-milliners of this metropolis." These "hugeous he fellows" ought to find demanding physical labor instead of subjecting women customers to "impertinent familiarities."[75] Impertinent familiarities indeed: the paper later exploded that a woman accused of shoplifting in a man-milliner's shop had been strip-searched. "Ladies are not to be outraged, even by men-milliners," it insisted, and encouraged women to patronize only women.[76]

Pity the poor conservatives of the day, forced to admire the masculinity of contemptible blacks and Jews, to condemn the effeminacy of once stout and hardy English workers. In this brave new world of gender confusion, with the sexes gaily exchanging their rightful roles, the lower orders couldn't safely be cordoned off and dismissed. They were everywhere. So who could claim unequivocally to be high? And how secure could any contemptuous emotional investment in social hierarchy finally be?

### ERRANT SEXUALITIES

Again, if intelligence finally distinguishes the human from the animal world, it's tempting to fasten subordinate status on the dehumanized by emphasizing their animal physicality. Brawny biceps sufficed for boxers; rude carnal desires sufficed for many others. (For the boxers, too, or anyway the black ones: Egan noticed their remarkable amorous appetites.[77])

Jews and blacks, the story went, had such voracious sexual appetites that they ignored the rules regulating such matters: here too they were primitive animals. In one 1784 play, a Jew turns to a woman he's been lending money to and suggests, "We will settle Accounts upon your Beauty; you shall accept my Draft upon your Virtue and pay me with your Honour. . . ." Indignantly, she announces that she would rather surrender her life than her virtue and she will never consent.

[74] *John Bull* (1 August 1830) 10(503):247.
[75] *John Bull* (28 August 1825) 5(35):277.
[76] *John Bull* (19 January 1834) 14(684):18.
[77] Egan, *Boxiana*, 2:202, 2:333–34.

He announces that he will rape her and tries to drag her offstage. But a valiant young Quaker, willing to exchange blows in this cause, saves her.[78] For Cobbett, slave revolts featured the horrifying rape of white women.[79] African slaves were pleased to offer voluntary sexual service, even to European clergy, reported one traveller.[80] In his manual on the proper care of slaves, Dr. Collins cautioned planters that "negro women have ardent constitutions, which dispose them to be liberal of their favours," their steamy promiscuity actually lowering their birth rate.[81] One student of the West Indies ridiculed the suggestion that slaves be allowed to marry. Black men and women alike, he explained, "would consider it as the greatest exertion of tyranny, and the most cruel of all hardships, to be compelled to confine themselves to a single connection," so legally enforced monogamy would be in vain.[82]

The not-so-secret subtext of these comments on black sexuality was the uncanny propensity of slaveholding males to indulge themselves sexually with their chattels. However ugly the bodies of black women were supposed to be, travellers to Africa managed to find them devastatingly attractive.[83] On the middle passage, one slave kept repulsing the captain's lewd advances; "furious with disappointment," he "murdered his unfortunate and unoffending victim with the most savage cruelty, the details of which are too horrible to be conceived, far less described!"[84] White planters developed insatiable hunger for sexual contact with their female slaves. In Jamaica, charged one observer, "the general profligacy, in this respect, is perfectly notorious and un-

[78] John O'Keeffe, *The Young Quaker* (Dublin, 1784), pp. 32–34.

[79] Cobbett to Windham, 10 June 1802, in Lewis Melville, *The Life and Letters of William Cobbett in England & America*, 2 vols. (London: John Lane, The Bodley Head, 1913), 1:159.

[80] J. G. Stedman, *Narrative of a Five Years' Expedition against the Revolted Negroes of Surinam, in Guiana, on the Wild Coast of South America; from the Year 1772, to 1777*, 2 vols. (London, 1796), 1:25–26.

[81] A Professional Planter [Dr. Collins], *Practical Rules for the Management and Treatment of Negro Slaves* (London, 1811; reprint ed. Freeport, NY: Books for Libraries Press, 1971), p. 133.

[82] Bryan Edwards, *The History, Civil and Commercial, of the British Colonies in the West Indies*, 2d ed., 3 vols. (1794–1801), 2:82.

[83] Rose, *Four Years*, pp. 186–90; note too the transition from *The Niger Journal of Richard and John Lander*, ed. Robin Hallett (London: Routledge and Kegan Paul, 1965), p. 52 [27 March 1830] to pp. 97 [24 May 1830], 242–43 [5 November 1830].

[84] Peter Leonard, *Records of a Voyage to the Western Coast of Africa* (Edinburgh, 1833), p. 141.

disguised," a whopping 95 percent of white males indulging themselves within one month of landing on the island.[85] And these white
men, not blacks, had no interest in marrying. Or, as another observer
put it, "No White man of decent appearance, unless urged by the
temptation of a considerable fortune, will condescend to give his
hand in marriage to a Mulatto! The very idea is shocking."[86] Condescension may have been a virtue, but one could stoop only so far. So
whites displaced their anxieties about their own illicit sexualities by
projecting them onto blacks; the fantasy of the prodigious animal
sexuality of blacks created a bogus white purity and superiority. And
contempt makes possible not just benevolent paternalism but also
lust.

Opponents of slavery tried to capitalize on the sexual stakes of the
practice. In the arch words of the *Black Dwarf:* "I would ask, why the
whites in the Colonies, who insist upon it that the Negroes are mere
cattle, ought not to be indicted, aye, and executed, for BESTIALITY,
for their promiscuous sexual intercourse with the *females* among *these
brutes.*" Or if they admitted that blacks were human, the planters
could be prosecuted for rape. But surely they should be prosecuted
for something.[87] "However much Europeans may have doubted
whether negroes were men," sneered the *Westminster Review,* "there
has never been a difference of opinion as to whether negresses were
women."[88] Regardless of the intentions of the authors in offering
these comments, their audiences may well have interpreted their
words as summoning up a tinge of nausea at miscegenation.

The perils of miscegenation were nothing new. In 1753, one writer
protesting the removal of the Jews' legal disabilities claimed, "Their
very breed is in general of the lowest, basest, and most contemptible
kind, distinguishable to the eye by peculiar marks, odious for that
distinction, and what, if once communicated to a family, becomes
indelible"; "the wise politician," he added, "would most rigidly punish

[85] Thomas Cooper, *Facts Illustrative of the Condition of the Negro Slaves in Jamaica* (London, 1824), pp. 8–9. See too James Stephen, *The Slavery of the British West India Colonies
Delineated,* 2 vols. (London, 1824–1830), 2:336.

[86] Bryan Edwards, *History,* 2:22. See too *The Diary of the Rev^d. William Jones 1777–
1821,* ed. O. F. Christie (London: Brentano's, 1929), p. 52 [21 April 1779]; J. B.
Moreton, *Manners and Customs in the West India Islands* (London, 1790), p. 124.

[87] *Black Dwarf* (3 March 1824) 12(9):265–66.

[88] *Westminster Review* (April 1826) 5(10):335. See too Sharp's marginalia in Hoare,
*Memoirs of Granville Sharp,* app. no. 4, p. x.

every carnal trespass."[89] But these perils usually showed up when commentators shifted their attention from white men and black women to black men and white women. The Duchess of Queensberry alarmed the conventional with her curious relationship with Soubise.[90] One social critic dreaded "a vile mongrel race of people" that would degrade England if the slaves were emancipated.[91] More specifically, the perils of miscegenation surface overwhelmingly in discussions of the alleged infatuation of working-class white women with black men. "The lower class of women in *England*, are remarkably fond of the blacks, for reasons too brutal to mention," scoffed one 1772 pamphleteer; "they would connect themselves with horses and asses, if the laws permitted them."[92] In 1785, another writer fretted over "the great number of negroes at present in England, the strange partiality shewn for them by the lower orders of women, and the rapid increase of a dark and contaminated breed. . . ."[93] Cobbett deplored what he saw as the prestige accorded to English blacks, with the rich preferring blacks to the white middle class: "Is it astonishing that the daughters of poor people should cohabit and marry with negroes?" He professed himself eager to defend these women, but unable to: "Their own conduct is foul, unnatural, and detestable."[94]

It's an imperialist or colonizing vision of sexual dominion, of white men eager to maintain rights of sexual access to white and black women alike. When Lord Pembroke told Boswell about exhausting himself in a London whorehouse full of black women, he wasn't glumly confessing his foul, unnatural, and detestable conduct.[95] He

[89] James Ralph's *Protester,* quoted in Thomas W. Perry, *Public Opinion, Propaganda, and Politics in Eighteenth-Century England: A Study of the Jew Bill of 1753* (Cambridge, MA: Harvard University Press, 1962), p. 108.

[90] *Reminiscences of Henry Angelo,* 2 vols. (London, 1830), 1:446–52; Folarin Shyllon, *Black People in Britain 1555–1833* (London: Oxford University Press for the Institute of Race Relations, 1977), pp. 41–43.

[91] Clara Reeve, *Plans of Education; with Remarks on the Systems of Other Writers: in a Series of Letters between Mrs. Darnford and Her Friends* (London, 1792; reprint ed. New York: Garland, 1974), pp. 90–91.

[92] A Planter [Edward Long], *Candid Reflections upon the Judgement Lately Awarded by the Court of King's Bench, in Westminster-Hall, on What Is Commonly Called the Negroe-Cause* (London, 1772), pp. 48–49.

[93] James Tobin, *Cursory Remarks upon the Reverend Mr. Ramsay's Essay on the Treatment and Conversion of African Slaves in the Sugar Colonies* (London, 1785), p. 118 n.

[94] *Political Register* (16 June 1804) 5(24):935–37. See too *Political Register* (27 August 1803) 4(8):280.

[95] *Boswell: The Ominous Years 1774–1776,* ed. Charles Ryskamp and Frederick A. Pottle (New York: McGraw-Hill, 1963), p. 118 [3 April 1775].

was gloating about new territory for sexual conquest, no doubt trying to entice Boswell into accompanying him on another foray. The singer of "Black Brown & Fair," patron of another interracial whorehouse, assures his dear Mary that after his frolics he surely will return to her.[96] Or take affable Sir Simon of one 1785 play. He is forever exchanging sexual innuendoes with his black servant, Blanchee. Reasonably secure in her status in the household, Blanchee resists the injunction of Israel the Jew that she leave while he talks to Sir Simon. Finally he canes her. Sir Simon is unruffled: "Ha, ha, ha, the Jew beats the Pagan. I am sorry you should take such trouble. I am afraid you have heated your blood."[97] His august status isn't threatened by his relationship with Blanchee. Nor is his effortless calm disturbed by Israel's tantrum. He is master of all he surveys, of black woman and Jew alike. This entrenched social script provides one authoritative context, not under the control of any individual. I suspect that the Wynne sisters disguised themselves as Negroes for masquerades, went to gawk at a newly arrived mulatto family from Barbados, and enjoyed exchanging covert glances "with a nice handsome negro at a window" in the same spirit—not exactly innocent, but not all that sexually charged—that they took in Jewish services and the Portuguese dwarf.[98] But third parties might have perceived shocking differences.

Meanwhile, miscegenation was making a mockery of the cataclysmic divide between white and black. One contemporary after another solemnly classified the offspring of interracial couplings, their names depending on their shares of white and black blood. So there were samboes, mulattoes, quadroons or quarterons, demi-quarterons or metis, and so on.[99] But the fruits of interracial reproduction and the conceptual pressures exerted by the great chain of being on behalf of smooth continuity didn't undercut the binary distinction be-

96 *BMC* no. 10925 [6 May 1807].

97 *The Israelites; or, The Pampered Nabob* [1785], in H. R. S. Van der Veen, *Jewish Characters in Eighteenth Century English Fiction and Drama* (USA: Ktav Publishing House, 1973), pp. 276, 281, 280.

98 Elizabeth Wynne's diary, 4 October 1789, *Wynne Diaries*, 1:10; 31 January 1792, *Wynne Diaries*, 1:104; Thomas Fremantle to Elizabeth Wynne, 21 March 1801, *Wynne Diaries*, 3:36; Elizabeth Wynne's diary, 17 December 1801, *Wynne Diaries*, 3:64; Harriet Wynne's diary, 15 March 1805, *Wynne Diaries*, 3:161.

99 For instance, Moreton, *Manners and Customs,* pp. 123–25; Francis Alexander Stanislaus, Baron de Wimpffen, *A Voyage to Saint Domingo, in the Years 1788, 1789, and 1790,* trans. J. Wright (London, 1797), pp. 60–61 [March 1789]; Reeve, *Plans of Education,* pp. 90–91; Stedman, *Narrative,* 1:296, 1:326–27; *Encyclopedia Britannica,* 3d ed., 18 vols. (Edinburgh, 1797), 12:795–96 s.v. *Negro.*

tween white and black. That distinction was maintained by a familiar
pollution model, according to which the mixture of even a bit of
black blood made one black or a person of color. "Mongrels, though
thirty generations distant from blacks blood, cannot be real
whites."[100]

Yet dread of miscegenation wasn't universal. "The race of man in
all his animal powers is decidedly improved by mixture," declared
the *Quarterly Review*.[101] Southey looked forward to the emergence of
a mixed race suited for industrious life in the tropics, one inheriting European intelligence and African endurance to heat.[102] In
1828, one bureaucrat drafted an official report suggesting that after
emancipation, the races would freely intermingle and so destroy
racism. "Where the difference is from white to black, antipathies
and jealousies may arise. . . . But where there will be every shade of
colour and complexion, white, tawny, mustee, copper, red, or black,
none enjoying exclusive privileges, colour will be no more considered than size." He conceded that this process might take some
time.[103] Even so, this proposal is as breathtakingly ingenuous as the
suggestion that a little girl's racism might be eliminated by having
her play with gorgeous black and white dolls, both stuffed with rags,
showing that their differences are only superficial.[104] Or that a student's racism might be eliminated by locking him up for a month
with an African.[105]

## PARIAHS IN POLITICS

The contempt slathered on pariah groups rubbished dreams of their
humanity, their equality, their dignity, their citizenship. One of *John
Bull*'s correspondents cleverly impeached the epistemic authority of a
reform leader: "COHEN, a *Jew*, who has been three times publicly
thrashed for publishing libellous accounts of individuals in a Radical

---

[100] Moreton, *Manners and Customs*, p. 123.

[101] *Quarterly Review* (November 1810) 4:471.

[102] Southey to John May, 1 July 1814, *Selections from the Letters of Robert Southey*, ed.
John Wood Warter, 4 vols. (London, 1856), 2:358.

[103] John Jeremie, *Four Essays on Colonial Slavery* (London, 1831), pp. 69–70.

[104] Mary Russell Mitford, *Our Village*, 5 vols. (London, 1824–1832), 4:265–70.

[105] Mary Lamb (?), "Conquest of Prejudice," in *Poetry for Children* [1809], in *Works of
Charles and Mary Lamb*, 3:476–78.

newspaper, twice convicted of libel on private persons, and who was Gazetted a bankrupt," was assuredly not a reliable guide to thinking about politics.[106] And it's not just that he was given to vicious speech or financially irresponsible. First on the list of charges is that he's COHEN, a *Jew*, the type faces chosen to highlight his inadequacies. *John Bull* traverses the road from contempt to bankrupt epistemic authority to the absurdities of citizenship at dizzying speed. So too the *Bristol Job Nott:* "It was the *public opinion* of the Jews and their rulers, that decreed the crucifixion of the Saviour of the world."[107] Who, then, could endorse public opinion? Putting blacks on juries, scowled the *Age*, "is about as reasonable as if we were to extend the same privileges to baboons—they are absolutely not fit for them."[108]

Here's a sustained burst of opulent imagery from *John Bull*, a bit of vicious speech which led to no thrashings or convictions. I need to quote it in hideously pornographic detail.

IT appears to us that the Advocates of Negro Emancipation have never yet carried their speculations connected with the success of that important measure half as far as they ought to have done, in order fully to comprehend the benefits of the system—emancipating the slaves will of course lose us the Colonies, but that is merely a secondary consideration when put in competition with the vast advantages which will accrue to our black brothers, and the elevation which it will naturally give them in the scale of society.

Emancipate the race of slaves—give to the black an entire equality of right with his white relations, and there is no knowing where his improvement will stop. If they are to remain toiling in sugar plantations, cutting and cropping, and baking and boiling, they might as well (and as *we know,* much better) remain slaves as they are; but as that is not to be the case, they are to participate of course in every advantage the world affords for their enjoyment, of which their minds may be rendered capable. They will of course no longer confine themselves to the islands in which their career would continue to be that of menial labourers; education and refinement will fit them for better things, and in another century we shall have importations of talent from the West Indies as common as they now are from Ireland and Scotland.

[106] *John Bull* (20 May 1832) 12(597):167.
[107] *Bristol Job Nott* (15 November 1832) no. 49, p. 195.
[108] *Age* (12 May 1833), p. 148.

Suppose the slaves are emancipated in 1835—in the course of one hundred years from that period, cultivation, freedom, foreign travel, and general study, will have rendered them perfectly equal to the whites, between whom and themselves no difference shall remain, except in *colour.* Well—in the year 1935, then, our descendants will read of the Old Bailey trials before my Lord Chief Justice QUASHEE, whose fine sable countenance (powerfully contrasted with the whiteness of his Lordship's wig) exhibited marks of deep affliction while he passed sentence of death upon a prisoner, who had been ably defended by Mr. Sergeant QUAMINABASH and two white Counsel. They will be told that the elegant Mrs. MUMBO JUM had a splendid ball at her house in some yet unknown square, which was numerously attended by a party of fashionables, black and white—that Massa FAMAGOO acted *Romeo* at Drury-lane Theatre with the happiest effect, and that Doctor SWIMMING MUCK was the most popular physician in London.

This is the consummation to which the advocates of Emancipation ought to look forward; and certainly, when society has arrived at such a pitch, that DAY and MARTIN's bottles[109] supersede GATTIE and DELCROIX on the toilette of the *fair,* everything will go on extremely well, because the prejudice about colour is quite absurd. Mrs. SNOB of Peckham, or Mrs. HOG of Clapham, or any of those ladies, would, we are quite sure, at this very moment prefer having a black accoucheur to a white one, and would select for choice a negress as nurse, in preference to a great coarse woman all red and white, like the English. As for the husbands of the ladies, a party of five talented niggers in July, in a small dinner-parlour, with a southern aspect, on the Clapham-road, would be the real feast of reason; white men and women might wait upon them, and do the menial duties of the house; but for society, our enlightened and emancipated brethren would undoubtedly bear away the bell.

Conceive the popular painter of the day, having his gallery thronged with the persons and portraits of the rescued race—fancy a jury-box dotted black and white like a Danish coach dog—or cast your eye over the Opera pit, looking like a vast chess-board covered with alternate squares—or, imagine ALMACK's peopled with niggers in the height of the season, in the full activity of a gallopade.

---

[109] A black shoe polish so easy to apply at home that it destroyed the trade plied in public: William Hone, *The Table Book* (London, 1827–1828; reprint ed. Detroit: Gale Research Co., 1966), 2:436.

Now all this seems very preposterous—but what is the reflection to which it gives rise? It is not for us to presume to question the inscrutable ways of Providence, or to discuss the reasons why a certain portion of GOD's creatures are black, and another portion white; but it *is* the province of common sense to shew that an attempt to emancipate generally a race like those whom Mr. WILBERFORCE, and the Claphamites, and the Peckhamites, and the Balamites, and the Wandsworthites, and the Nag's-head-laneites, and the Nightingaleites, and all the rest of the new *lites,* call "*Men and Brothers,*" must fail—that it is absurd to attempt to contravene the will of GOD, or attempt to "change the colour of the Ethiopian"—and without it, we only put the question—Is it likely—is it possible, that negroes would, even under any circumstances whatever, become equal participators in the rights of a white population? We mean, that nature has decreed a distinction so decided, and prejudice has rendered that distinction so unconquerable, that if it were possible to produce an effect at all resembling that which we have laughingly anticipated, the black never could, and never would attain an equal footing in European society, however humble and low the sphere in which he might attempt to move.

A coal black judge in a snow-white wig—a tall nigger, carrying his purse as Lord Chancellor to the bar of the Lords to receive a bill from a flight of Parliamentary crows—a charity sermon at St. James's by a sable bishop—or the enactment of *Juliet* by a delicate piccannini, the colour of one's hat: Is it not clear that all this is impossible?—that the black is an inferior being to the white, and that he is doomed to be so?[110]

The passage inculcates its simmering rage and frenzied disbelief with carefully studied detail. The writer—I assume it is Theodore Hook, editor of the paper, strident adversary of Queen Caroline, celebrated in his day as an extemporaneous wit—is seduced by his own imagery. Coming up for air at the sixth paragraph, indignantly accosting the reader and demanding his assent to the view that all this is impossible, he suddenly dives back in and returns to plumbing the grisly depths of the racist imagination. Equality, warns the newspaper, knows no

[110] *John Bull* (10 January 1830) 10(474):12; see too *Age* (4 September 1825) no. 17, p. 132. Hook also sketched life in 1926 to imagine the absurd lack of deference of the servants: *John Bull* (26 March 1826) 6(276):101, reprinted in Theodore Hook, *The Choice Humorous Works, Ludicrous Adventures, Bon Mots, Puns and Hoaxes* (London, 1873), pp. 395–400, also in R. H. Dalton Barham, *The Life and Remains of Theodore Edward Hook,* 2 vols. (London, 1849), 2:297–304.

boundaries, no limits. There is finally no possibility of equality at a distance, no living in a world where the lower orders are enlightened but don't appear at one's dining table. So emancipated blacks will cross the Atlantic and invade English society, taking over courts and churches, clubs and homes. More appalling, baffled whites won't have the integrity and intelligence to recognize this invasion of filth. This is not a vision of white civilization destroyed, dragged down to the savage level of reprobate blacks. It's a vision of the unspeakably low inexorably on the march, infiltrating the prestigious and powerful preserves of the once superior. Indeed it is a vision of their incipient superiority, of a world where white servants wait on talented black husbands married to the philanthropic white women who always lusted after them anyway, where blacks finally have taken over Parliament. If we don't enslave the blacks, warns the newspaper—its audience here must be white men—they'll beat us at our own game. Conservatives repeatedly have sought to expose democrats' demand for equality as the expression of a base and sullen resentment of superiority, an envious or spiteful desire to drag down the high into the muck of their own inferiority. What, then, should we say about the psychology of conservatives who fear not being dragged down, but the successful rise out of the muck of those very inferiors?

The passage exploits a fatiguingly familiar, if valiantly contradictory, logic of social criticism: racial equality is absolutely pernicious and absolutely impossible. So the consolation is that no one ever will awake to this nightmare, not even in the unimaginably remote year of 1935. The good evangelicals of Clapham, radiating saintly Christian brotherhood in their struggles for the emancipation of the benighted blacks, are actually at war with God's manifest will in history. Providence and nature, underwritten by prejudice, have gutted political agency.

But then what's the point of all this trenchant fury? (The writer assures us he spins this macabre tale "laughingly," but even if we're impious enough to admit the possibility of his eliciting a chuckle, it would have to be an awfully grim chuckle.) It's not as though the poor confused Claphamites are running pell-mell over the edge of a cliff and hoping to fly. Then *John Bull* might feel sorry for them. Or even if the paper mocked them, it would rest sanguine in the impotence of their puny display. It wouldn't scare up any agony over lurid social disorder. So the real worry about Wilberforce and those

Claphamite evangelicals is that they might in fact prevail. At the very same time the passage derides the view that race, finally, is no deeper than skin color, it betrays an anxiety that maybe that's all race is, that its nightmare could in fact greet those waking up in 1935.

Some of the fury directed at Wilberforce, then, is instrumental. He is working for outcomes that his opponents loathe. And some of it depends on his saintly credentials, which earn at best a grudging respect, and the tired history of English hatred of Puritans: how many M.P.s could publish a plump book priggishly scolding contemporaries for their failures to take Christianity seriously?[111] Both sentiments are in play in the *Anti-Jacobin Review*'s stance: "We respect Mr. Wilberforce as a *moralist*, but, as a *statesman*, we must despise him. The adoption of his contracted and fantastical notions would convert us into a set of the most degraded beings that now vegetate upon the face of the earth!"[112]

But there is more to this fury. One Gillray cartoon portrayed Wilberforce finding solace at the failure of his parliamentary maneuvers with a black woman, her ample breasts billowing right out of her dress.[113] (Also here is a fiendish voyeurism revelling in sex with pariahs. Or among them: another cartoon pictured a rabbi and a Dissenting minister cupping the breasts of a grinning black woman.[114]) *John Bull* gleefully reported that at one rally, Wilberforce's speech was interrupted by a woman "holding up a mulatto child at the moment—'God bless Massa Wilbyfoss, *him fader of us all.*' "[115] Some of this is more stock anti-Puritanism, a matter of puncturing saintly pretense. But these materials lend themselves to a decidedly different reading, one connected to the frequent charge that Wilberforce had no interest in the political travails of white people. On learning that the French Convention had made Wilberforce a citizen, the Whig wag Courtenay warned them, "If you make Mr. W. a citizen, they will take you for an assemblage of negroes, for it is well known he never favoured the liberty of any white man in all his life."[116] If I'm right in

[111] William Wilberforce, *A Practical View of the Prevailing Religious System of Professed Christians, in the Higher and Middle Classes in This Country, Contrasted with Real Christianity*, 6th ed. (London, 1798).

[112] *Anti-Jacobin Review* (November 1802) 13:336.

[113] *BMC* no. 8793 [4 April 1796].

[114] *BMC* no. 13112 [1817–1819].

[115] *John Bull* (11 May 1828) 8(387):149.

[116] *The Journal of Thomas Moore*, ed. Wilfred S. Dowden and others, 6 vols. (Newark:

spotting a glimpse of icy contempt for Wilberforce, not just adolescent snickering at his hypocrisy, how might we understand it?

A blissfully flattened reading of Hegel's analysis of lord and bondsman might run this way: like any self, the lord seeks recognition and affirmation from the other, but the degraded bondsman is in no position to provide that recognition. This flattened reading seems to entail that hierarchy tends to crumble. True, it is the workaday lament of conservatives that hierarchy is always already collapsing. Yet the flattened reading seems badly broken.

To repair it, all we need to do is add a few more social actors—one, for those mad about parsimony. So suppose that two would-be lords can affirm one another as valuable selves by sharing contempt for a bondsman. Then there's nothing contradictory or perverse in demoting a self in the pursuit of recognition. Instead, they recognize one another as members of the community that hold this third self in contempt. As Mary Wollstonecraft put it, struck by how badly treated Swedish men were in some occupations, "The men stand up for the dignity of man, by oppressing the women."[117]

This simple scheme helps explain why racists are so infuriated by whites who fraternize with blacks, why tough guys sneer at less masculine males as wimps and fags, and so on. To take the first example: the white who presents himself as a racial egalitarian raises a disquieting challenge to the club of white racists who define and validate themselves by their contempt for blacks. Not that the club members need to have noticed this unsavory fact about their club. It may dawn on them only when they notice their irritation at the challenge. It may not dawn on them even then. On even this schematic analysis of identity and recognition, that challenge can't be dismissed as embodying a mistaken belief about blacks, even as a pernicious political program. Instead the challenge threatens to undercut their identity, by making it less easy to meet each other and take pride in knowing that they are the whites who stomp on blacks. So the traditional solution is to hurl contempt at those other whites as nigger-lovers. Again,

---

University of Delaware Press, 1983–1991), 2:799 [12 January 1825]. See too, for instance, *Black Dwarf* (18 March 1818) 2(11):165–67; *Republican* (21 January 1820) 2(2):42.

[117] *Letters Written during a Short Residence in Sweden, Norway, and Denmark* [1796], in *The Works of Mary Wollstonecraft*, ed. Janet Todd and Marilyn Butler, assistant ed. Emma Rees-Mogg, 7 vols. (London: William Pickering, 1989), 6:253.

in part Wilberforce is being ribbed as another Tribulation Whole-some, a pious hypocrite. But the barely suppressed rage for him de-pends on the challenge he implicitly poses to the terms on which British whites affirm each other.

Yet equality for pariahs made its way onto the legislative agenda.

> Who hold the balance of the World? Who reign
> O'er congress, whether royalist or liberal?

So asked a dyspeptic Byron. His answer was that bankers did, partic-ularly "Jew Rothschild."[118] The *Age* bitterly anticipated the Jews' ad-mission to Parliament: "It would rejoice us to see the Leviathan of the Stock Exchange—that behemoth of a banker—ROTHSCHILD (Lord! the man's name strikes upon our tympanum like the crash of a mil-lion sovereigns!) in the Commons House." (The figure of crashing sovereigns puns on collapsing governments and jingling coins.) The thought of watching the ministers nervously conduct their business before the impassive face of the man who really made the decisions was cause for mordant pleasure.[119] And like *John Bull* cowering before the specter of 1935, like Burke unveiling a grotesque Jew-ridden fu-ture, *Blackwood's* conjured up its own nightmare. "In the dark vista of futurity, we behold a rapacious Jew administering the finances of this once flourishing and fortunate empire." And not only futurity: "Sev-eral Ministers of State are said to have been already converted; and of one high in office, in particular, it is rumoured, that the price of his return for a certain Jewish borough was his consenting forthwith to undergo the odious ceremony of circumcision."[120] The underlings were on the march, already prowling inside the secret recesses of Brit-ish government. Jews in power: a spectacle every bit as nauseating as that of emancipated blacks infesting one valued preserve after another.

Part of the genius of the hallowed settlement of 1688 was ensuring that no more crypto-Catholics could gain the throne of England. Nor could Catholics even enter Parliament, an exclusion guaranteed by

---

[118] *Don Juan* [1823], in Byron, *The Complete Poetical Works,* 7 vols., ed. Jerome J. McGann and Barry Weller, 7 vols. (Oxford: Clarendon, 1980–1993), 5:496.

[119] *Age* (24 February 1833), p. 61.

[120] *Blackwood's Edinburgh Magazine* (June 1829) 25(153):702. See too Jesse Foot, *The Life of Arthur Murphy, Esq.* (London, 1811), pp. 52–59, approvingly reprinting *Gray's-Inn Journal* (14 July 1753), imagining an England ruled by intolerant Jews.

administering oaths. English identity was Protestant, better yet Anglican. In 1813, one Birmingham mob trashed the city's Methodist chapel, its synagogue, and its Baptist chapel in an ecumenical display of
hostility toward religious deviance.[121] Yet in April 1829, after many
years of struggle and debate, the Catholics were emancipated: Britain
moved with solemn legal formality from being a Protestant state to
being a Christian one. Was this another sign of the rot setting in, a
drastic innovation spurning ancestral wisdom? Less than a year later,
Robert Grant introduced a bill to repeal the civil disabilities of the
Jews.[122] And O'Connell, the Irish Catholic agitator, made common
cause with the Jews. In these years, then, the terms of inclusion in the
polity were scrutinized.[123]

In 1812, Byron rose in the House of Lords to rebut the already
familiar *reductio:* if the Catholics were to be emancipated, why not the
Jews? His response, on the slippery side, was that compassion for Jews
was one thing, but that this question was just a sneer at Catholics—of
the sort that Shylock might offer.[124] *John Bull* met the discussion of
Grant's bill with another *reductio:* "We are encouraged to hope that
the attention of Ministers will be speedily drawn to the absolute necessity of putting another equally meritorious and even more suffering race of people upon an equal footing in society—we mean the
long persecuted gipsies. . . ."[125] Or why not the atheists?[126] By 1833, a
weary *Age* had accepted the logic of such appeals: "Any Legislative
Assembly in which a Papist appears cannot be disgraced by the presence of a Jew." Those Papists—the word summons up England's fes-
tive history of Popery-bashing—now polluting the House of Lords
were so disgusting that "we might as well have the old clothesmen,
who are of an older lineage, of greater loyalty, and of far superior
intellect" than the new Catholic peers.[127]

---

[121] Robert K. Dent, *Old and New Birmingham: A History of the Town and Its People,* 3
vols. (Birmingham, 1879; reprint ed. Yorkshire: EP Publishing, 1972–1973), 2:364.

[122] For the text, see Israel Abrahams, "Text of Mr. Robert Grant's Bill, 1830," *Transactions of the Jewish Historical Society of England* (1908–1910) 6:249–53.

[123] A useful overview is U. R. Q. Henriques, "The Jewish Emancipation Controversy
in Nineteenth-Century Britain," *Past & Present* (July 1968) no. 40, pp. 126–46.

[124] Byron in Lords, 21 April 1812, in Byron, *The Complete Miscellaneous Prose,* ed.
Andrew Nicholson (Oxford: Clarendon, 1991), p. 39.

[125] *John Bull* (11 April 1830) 10(487):116.

[126] *John Bull* (25 April 1830) 10(489):132.

[127] *Age* (4 August 1833), p. 244.

Deciding where the floodgates finally had been thrown open to the contemptible was ticklish business. More than willing to live with Catholic emancipation, like Burke harboring deep-seated reservations about the Reformation, Cobbett was livid at Grant's bill and thought it imperative that Catholics immediately disavow any interest in it.[128] "If they pray for the passing of that bill which is now before the Commons, they pray, in effect, for the degradation of the memory of Jesus Christ," since the bill would declare the Jews every bit "as worthy of credence, trust, power, and honour" as Christians. So it would ascribe epistemic authority to scoundrels. Worse, it would contaminate the English political nation. "The Jews assert, that Jesus Christ was an impostor, a liar, a cheat, and that he deserved to be nailed upon the cross."[129] How defiling to admit such blasphemers to the dignities and power of seats in Parliament!

To be sure, Cobbett offered his own humanitarianism, if a somewhat pinched and austere one. "Do I call upon you to destroy them, or to hunt them from the land like beasts of prey?" No, for that would reject Christian charity.[130] Others had more unabashedly humanitarian impulses. "It is not the business of the Jews to petition for justice," insisted Hone, "but it is the duty of Christians to be just."[131] Hazlitt blithely remarked, "The Emancipation of the Jews is but a natural step in the progress of civilisation."[132] In 1833, the Commons was again debating Jewish emancipation. Macaulay quite deliberately attacked Cobbett, then M.P. for Oldham, as a mean-spirited bigot.[133] Cobbett slinked out of the chamber.

Were the Jews excluded because they were contemptible? Or were they contemptible because they were excluded? "If persons of the Jewish persuasion"—there's the emphatically humanizing tag again—

[128] For Cobbett's views on Catholicism and the Reformation, see *Cobbett's Legacy to Parsons*, 2d ed. (London, 1835), pp. 15–18. I haven't been able to obtain what is apparently the crucial text on point, Cobbett's *A History of the Protestant Reformation in England and Ireland* (London, 1829).

[129] *Political Register* (22 May 1830) 69(20):672. See too *Political Register* (12 June 1830) 69(24):752–53; Cobbett, *Good Friday; or, The Murder of Jesus Christ by the Jews* (London, 1830), pp. 14–15.

[130] Cobbett, *Good Friday*, p. 21.

[131] Hone, *Every-Day Book*, 1:298.

[132] "Emancipation of the Jews" [1831], in *Works of Hazlitt*, 19:320.

[133] Macaulay in Commons, 17 April 1833, in *The Works of Lord Macaulay Complete*, ed. Lady Trevelyan, 8 vols. (London, 1875), 8:100–110. For Cobbett's March 1833 manuscript notes for his own speech, see Melville, *Life and Letters of Cobbett*, 1:21.

"were declared by law entitled to the same benefit of the constitution as Dissenters and Catholics, they would be no longer deemed fit objects for general hatred and oppression," insisted one of their defenders; "but so long as they are debarred from full civil rights, they will be a marked and degraded people."[134] Invoking a judicious conservative skepticism about the scope of political agency, *Fraser's* raucously rejected such views.

> But why should any body think, that making Jews members of parliament is removing them from being a taunt and a by-word? We have often heard of the omnipotence of the House of Commons; but that the fact of becoming an M.P. is to release a whole nation from the curse of God, surpasses any thing we ever heard attributed to it. There might be 658 Jews in the House of Commons, and the scheme of God be perfect nevertheless. The contempt might stick to them with as cleaving a vengeance as ever.[135]

Jews can't be purified by entering Parliament, but Parliament can be soiled. Their ban from politics is a sign of the contempt they're held in, but there's no reason to think that that contempt would evaporate if only the ban were lifted.

## Christian Cosmopolitans and Their Jacobin Foes

So it was crucial to exclude pariahs from politics—but not from political scrutiny or even political care. Some conservatives, remember, recoiled from the unflinching abuse dished out by the likes of *John Bull.* Christianity dictated that the low were equal human beings. Their superiors were charged with solemn obligations of trusteeship. So keep the blacks from barging into Parliament, but by all means have Parliament pay attention to them—at a comfortable distance. So the crusade against the slave trade, and later against slavery, was led by Christian evangelicals, conservatives in very good standing.

One might expect concern for slaves from the Jacobins, famed for their cosmopolitanism, their universalist accounts of the rights of man. Thomas Hardy, leader of the London Corresponding Society,

[134] Apsley Pellatt, *Brief Memoir of the Jews, in Relation to Their Civil and Municipal Disabilities* (London, 1829), p. 22.
[135] *Fraser's* (June 1830) 1(5):546–47.

accosted a clergyman in 1792: surely his opposition to the slave trade
meant that he ought to support the LCS agenda on the rights of man.
But it doesn't yet follow that Hardy himself was interested in antislavery politics. Then again, Olaudah Equiano, fearless black agitator,
himself joined the LCS.[136] And *John Bull* wasn't alone in expressing
conservative antagonism toward Wilberforce's agenda. "What, in the
name of God, is this whole business of slave-snapping to us?" demanded the *Age*. "Have we no white misery at home to mind?"[137]

Usually, though, Jacobin radicals disdained interest in slavery. As a
young conservative, Cobbett was denouncing "the hypocritical sect of
negro-loving philanthropists";[138] the mature radical Cobbett still
found Wilberforce insufferable. "I feel a degree of indignation that is
impossible for me to express, when I see an Englishman thus dead to
the sufferings, the indescribable sufferings, the real torments of half
the nation," devoting himself instead to the welfare of "a fat and lazy
Negro that laughs from morning to night!"[139] One "notorious Radical . . . laughed most vociferously" at the campaign to help the slaves
of the West Indies "and begged us first to emancipate the slaves at
home, and then cross the Atlantic at our leisure."[140] "Human suffering is equally painful to bear," conceded John Wade, "whether inflicted on this or the other side of the globe, on black or white men, and
we should be sorry, even for the sake of economy, that any measures
should be adopted tending to revive the hellish traffic in Negroes.
But, after all, we ought to look *at home*." It was intolerable to permit
the campaign against slavery to distract attention from the abuses of
the factory system, at least as horrible, in Wade's view, as the infamous
middle passage.[141]

Wilberforce and his parliamentary allies fretted that they were being smeared as patrons of the rights of man, their holy pursuits mis-

[136] Peter Fryer, *Staying Power: Black People in Britain Since 1504* (Atlantic Highlands,
NJ: Humanities Press, 1984), pp. 106–7, reads Hardy's letter more generously than
I do.

[137] *Age* (11 December 1831), p. 396. See too *Blackwood's Edinburgh Magazine* (October 1823) 14(81):438.

[138] William Cobbett, *Letters to the Right Honourable Henry Addington* (London, 1802),
p. 6.

[139] *Political Register* (13 December 1823) 48(11):677.

[140] *Memoirs of a West-India Planter,* ed. John Riland (London, 1827), p. 166.

[141] John Wade, *The Extraordinary Black Book: An Exposition of Abuses in Church and
State, Courts of Law, Representation, Municipal and Corporate Bodies; with a Précis of the House
of Commons, Past, Present, and to Come,* new ed. (London, 1832), p. 382.

cast as helping to import the French plague.[142] As they were: the Earl of Abingdon rose in the House of Lords to denounce "that new philosophy, as it is called, which is gone abroad; containing like Pandora's box of old, all the evils and vices that human nature can be inflicted with." Having triggered the usual anxieties, he went on to charge, "What does the abolition of the slave trade mean more or less in effect, than liberty and equality? what more or less than the rights of man? and what is liberty and equality; and what the rights of man, but the foolish fundamental principles of this new philosophy?"[143] Yet like any other good paternalists, Wilberforce and his allies were moved by stories of exploitation. No devout Christian, they thought, could stomach learning of the slave who was endlessly flogged for daring to attend a Wesleyan chapel.[144] No devout Christian could stomach learning that a woman had stamped on a slave's head with her heel and "*bruised her head almost to a jelly*" to punish her for not bringing back enough money as a prostitute.[145] No devout Christian could stomach learning that another woman had forced her slave "to swallow a glass of rum mixed with human excrement."[146] No devout Christian could stomach learning that a young female slave had been tied up hanging naked, the man punishing her holding a torch "to all the parts of her body" as she swung helplessly.[147] No devout Christian could stomach learning that a jealous Jewess had plunged a red-hot poker into the body "of a young and beautiful Quadroon girl" and

---

[142] Samuel Hoare to Wilberforce, 20 February 1792, *The Correspondence of William Wilberforce*, ed. Robert Isaac Wilberforce and Samuel Wilberforce, 2 vols. (London, 1840), 1:89–90; Wilberforce to Lord Muncaster, October 1792, in Robert Isaac Wilberforce and Samuel Wilberforce, *The Life of William Wilberforce*, 5 vols. (London, 1838), 1:343. See too John Hampson, *Observations on the Present War, the Projected Invasion, and a Decree of the National Convention, for the Emancipation of the Slaves in the French Colonies* (Sunderland, 1793), pp. 20–21.

[143] *Parliamentary History* (11 April 1793) 30:653–54. See too Bryan Edwards, *An Historical Survey of the French Colony in the Island of St. Domingo* (London, 1797), pp. xix–xxi; *Anti-Jacobin Review* (February 1813) 44:128–29.

[144] Mary Reckord, "The Colonial Office and the Abolition of Slavery," *Historical Journal* (1971) 14(4):726–30; see too Alexander Knox to Lord Castlereagh, 15 July 1803, *Memoirs and Correspondence of Viscount Castlereagh*, ed. Charles Vane, 12 vols. (London, 1848–1853), 4:289.

[145] *An Abstract of the Evidence Delivered before a Select Committee of the House of Commons in the Years 1790, and 1791, on the Part of the Petitioners for the Abolition of the Slave-Trade* (London, 1791), p. 75.

[146] John Marjoribanks, *Slavery: An Essay in Verse* (Edinburgh, 1792), p. 17 n.

[147] *The Speeches of the Right Honourable Charles James Fox, in the House of Commons*, 6 vols. (London, 1815), 4:189 [19 April 1791].

murdered her, that a Jew had beaten a young black woman in chains "till the blood streamed out of her head, her arms, and her naked sides," though the horror of Jewish miscreants has to modulate the compassion for the slaves.[148] No devout Christian could stomach learning that to amuse himself, one slaveholder "would have a couple of Negroe boys during his dinner with their eyes nailed to the Table by a fork, to the music of whose cries he eat his dinner."[149] These expressions of visceral contempt were out-of-bounds; they were themselves contemptible. Samuel Horsley assured the Lords that the Christian opponents of the slave trade "proceed upon no visionary notions of equality and imprescriptible rights of men; we strenuously uphold the gradations of civil society." But those gradations could never permit the cavalier trampling on others' interests so sadly characteristic of slavery.[150] "GOD despises not labourers on account of their poverty, or negroes on account of their colour," warned one of the Cheap Repository Tracts: this sentiment, not regard for the rights of man, spurred on Wilberforce and his allies.[151] It meant according blacks decent care, not offering them citizenship.

This territory makes for prickly exploration; in it, contempt is ubiquitous. Cobbett is spraying his fire at Wilberforce and blacks alike, his contempt for one redoubling his contempt for the other. The Jacobins neglecting oppressed blacks are surely exhibiting a kind of contempt. But so too are the evangelicals showering them with benevolent concern: for that concern is wrapped up with the sense that blacks are inferior. And maybe they're simultaneously demonstrating contempt for English workers: "Preposterous attempts are made to civilize African savages, while our own peasantry, who are the foundation and uphold of the state, are abandoned, as of inferior consideration in the political scale of society, to abject poverty and unmerited contempt."[152] Again, a contemptuous assignment of low status enabled both the caustic hostility of *John Bull* and the stately sympathy of

---

[148] Stedman, *Narrative*, 1:126–27; see too 1:325–26.

[149] *The Notebooks of Samuel Taylor Coleridge*, ed. Kathleen Coburn, in progress (New York: Pantheon Books, 1957–), 3(1):3369 13.13 [September 1808].

[150] *The Speeches in Parliament of Samuel Horsley* (Dundee, 1813), pp. 196–97 [5 July 1799].

[151] *Babay: A True Story of a Good Negro Woman* (London, 1795), p. 12.

[152] John Hill, *The Means of Reforming the Morals of the Poor, by the Prevention of Poverty; and A Plan for Meliorating the Condition of Parish Paupers, and Diminishing the Enormous Expence of Maintaining Them* (London, 1801), p. 75.

Wilberforce. Not to mention the bizarre genius of the pamphleteer wracking his brains for new arguments on behalf of abstaining from sugar consumption: "How difficult," he moaned, "to persuade some, that when they eat Sugar, they figuratively eat the Blood of the Negro." But how easy to persuade them that they might literally be doing so: he described the unsanitary conditions of sugar production and catalogued the sickening bodily fluids of blacks that might be in the sugar.[153]

And, I daresay, contempt enabled some of the rapturous poetry of William Blake. Perhaps the least innocent of his *Songs of Innocence* is "The Little Black Boy," a childlike recital.

> My mother bore me in the southern wild,
> And I am black, but O! my soul is white.
> White as an angel is the English child:
> But I am black as if bereav'd of light.

The little black boy looks forward to arriving in heaven:

> When I from black and he from white cloud free,
> And round the tent of God like lambs we joy;
>
> Ill shade him from the heat till he can bear,
> To lean in joy upon our fathers knee.
> And then I'll stand and stroke his silver hair,
> And be like him and he will then love me.[154]

This looks like a dream of the obliteration of race: the two boys are to be free of the clouds of white and black. But it's actually a dream of racial assimilation. In Blake's engraving, the boys unmistakably remain white and black in heaven. Even in heaven, the black boy's appointed role, his self-appointed role in fact, is to shield the white boy from the brilliant sun. (Perhaps he capitalizes on the hardy constitution which, according to proslavery writers, uniquely suited blacks for the arduous work of sugar plantations.) What it will take for the white boy to love the black boy is for the black boy to be like him. The black

---

[153] Andrew Burn, *A Second Address to the People of Great Britain: Containing a New, and Most Powerful Argument to Abstain from the Use of West India Sugar* (Rochester, 1792), pp. 6–10.

[154] "The Little Black Boy" [1789] in William Blake, *Songs of Innocence and of Experience*, ed. Andrew Lincoln (Princeton, NJ: The William Blake Trust / Princeton University Press, 1991), plates 9–10, p. 148.

boy's are the defects, the departures, that need to be remedied. The poem doesn't summon up the leering cadences of *John Bull*'s disquisition on racial equality. But it doesn't summon up any images of respect, equality, or dignity either. William Davidson, radical mulatto from Jamaica, son of the attorney general, found himself making the same sort of arguments in court as he tried to extricate himself from responsibility in the Cato Street conspiracy of 1820. "One man of colour," he reminded the jury, "may be mistaken for another," adding, "Although I am a man of colour, that is no reason that I should be guilty of such a crime. My colour may be against me, but I have as good and as fair a heart as if I were a white."[155]

## HAPPY SLAVES AND SOCIAL STRUCTURE

"Degrade a Man in his own opinion, stigmatize him by legal Suspicion, take for granted that he has no Character to lose, and you go the sure way to work to make him in reality what you believe him to be. We have done so by the Jews."[156] No wonder some Jews tried to pass. Making her way as a popular singer, the young Miss Romanzini couldn't observe the sabbath. Not just because she needed to work on Saturdays, but because she needed to avoid the insidious charge, pressed by "a wicked Wag," that she was Jewish. (As she was.) So she spent Saturday afternoons sitting by her window and sewing, flouting the sabbath. So, too, she had her mother go buy a pig and broadcast the news that they were to dine on it.[157] Talk about being trapped: Romanzini wants to escape from contempt, but her attempt is contemptible, both in being puerile and in opportunistically renouncing her identity. (But what if she didn't really care about that identity?— But wouldn't it depend on why she didn't care? Suppose she didn't care because she didn't relish living a life colored by contempt.) So contempt works: it turns its victims into what it claims they already

---

[155] George Theodore Wilkinson, *An Authentic History of the Cato-Street Conspiracy* (London, 1820; reprint ed. New York: Arno Press, 1972), pp. 321–22.

[156] Thomas Cooper, *A Reply to Mr. Burke's Invective against Mr. Cooper, and Mr. Watt, in the House of Commons, on the 30th of April, 1792,* 2d ed. (London, 1792), p. 71.

[157] Joseph Haslewood, *The Secret History of the Green Room,* 2d ed., 2 vols. (London, 1792), 1:235–39. George Raymond, *Memoirs of Robert William Elliston Comedian,* 2d ed., 2 vols. (London, 1846; reprint ed. New York: Benjamin Blom, 1969), 2:72–73 tells essentially the same story, but has her mother forcing her to go buy the pig.

are. But does it really work? And if it does, or to the extent it does, just how does it work?

Perhaps those endlessly showered with contempt begin to believe in their own horrid inferiority. Perhaps they become happy slaves, cheerfully insisting on their own subordination. "SLAVERY so far degrades man," warned the radical *Politics for the People*, "that he at length becomes enamoured with it."[158] *Toad-eater* was the picturesque phrase for such a lickspittle wretch, eagerly complicit in his own degradation.[159] Fear that subjects or women or other such groups were happy slaves, even scorn that they were, pop up frequently.[160] Mary Hays held that if "men should never, or but rarely, be tempted to abuse their authority," women would "submit contentedly to the yoke; and not from a mistaken and ridiculous pride, differ about a mere

---

[158] *Politics for the People* 1(11):150 [1793]. See too *Politics for the People* 2(25):385 [1795].

[159] Walpole to Rev. William Mason, 23 March 1774, *Walpole's Correspondence*, 28:139; *Porcupine's Gazette* (January 1799), in Cobbett, *Porcupine's Works*, 10:83–84; *Political Essays, with Sketches of Public Characters* [1819], in *Works of Hazlitt*, 7:148.

[160] For instance, Romilly to John Roget, 10 November 1781, in *Memoirs of the Life of the Sir Samuel Romilly, Written by Himself*, ed. his sons, 3 vols. (London, 1840), 1:176–77; Catherine Macaulay Graham, *Letters on Education: with Observations on Religious and Metaphysical Subjects* (London, 1790; reprint ed. New York: Garland, 1974), pp. 204–5; *Vindication of the Rights of Woman* [1792], in *Works of Wollstonecraft*, 5:145 n. 13, 5:189; Isaac D'Israeli, *Domestic Anecdotes of the French Nation, during the Last Thirty Years: Indicative of the French Revolution* (London, 1794), p. 2; Coleridge to Southey, 3 November 1794, *Collected Letters of Samuel Taylor Coleridge*, ed. Earl Leslie Griggs, 6 vols. (Oxford: Clarendon, 1956–1971), 1:68; *Notebooks of Coleridge*, 3(1):3505 L.17 [April–July 1809]; Charles Pigott, *A Political Dictionary: Explaining the True Meaning of Words* (London, 1795), p. 74 s.v. *Man;* A Society of Gentlemen, *The Cabinet*, 3 vols. (Norwich, 1795), 2:194–95; Southey, *Letters Written . . . in Spain and Portugal*, p. 217; Robert Southey, *Letters from England* [1807], ed. Jack Simmons (London: Cresset Press, 1951), pp. 197–98 [1807]; George Pinckard, *Notes on the West Indies*, 3 vols. (London, 1806), 2:204–9, 2:353, 3:255–56; *An Address to the Irish People* [1812], in Percy Bysshe Shelley, *Shelley's Prose or The Trumpet of a Prophecy*, ed. David Lee Clark, corrected ed. (Albuquerque: University of New Mexico Press, 1966), p. 54; *A Proposal for Putting Reform to the Vote throughout the Kingdom* [1817], in *Shelley's Prose*, p. 159; *A Philosophical View of Reform* [1820], in *Shelley's Prose*, p. 258; *Political Essays* [1819], in *Works of Hazlitt*, 7:149; *The Life of Napoleon Buonaparte* [1828–1829], in *Works of Hazlitt*, 13:308, 14:305, 14:354; "Lines on the Entry of the Austrians into Naples, 1821," in *The Poetical Works of Thomas Moore*, ed. A. D. Godley (London: Oxford University Press, 1915), p. 536; *Black Dwarf* (8 August 1821) 7(6):187; William Thompson, *Appeal of One Half the Human Race, Women, against the Pretensions of the Other Half, Men, to Retain Them in Political, and Thence in Civil and Domestic, Slavery; in Reply to a Paragraph of Mr. Mill's Celebrated "Article on Government"* (London, 1825), p. 103; William Cobbett, *Cottage Economy*, new ed. (London, 1826), §§5–6 [19 July 1821]; *Edinburgh Review* (September 1831) 54(107):18, reprinted in *Works of Macaulay*, 5:516; *Pioneer* (21 September 1833) no. 3, p. 24.

name."[161] As if subjugation were unjust or insulting only because of considerations of welfare, not autonomy. Mary Prince, testifying on her experience of West Indian slavery, emphasized both in rejecting the frequent claim that chattel slaves were happy: "I am often much vexed, and I feel great sorrow when I hear some people in this country say, that the slaves do not need better usage, and do not want to be free. . . . they put a cloak about the truth. It is not so. All slaves want to be free—to be free is very sweet."[162] (A lawsuit ensued when *Blackwood's* denounced Prince's tale as fabrication and insinuated that her sponsor and publisher was sleeping with her.[163])

It seems plausible that people can internalize noxious signals, especially when those signals are public and reiterated. But consider another story about how those contemned might become contemptible. Women in the family, workers in the workplace, Jews industriously making money, and blacks in slavery: each group has its special social location or two. This suggests a strategy for generalizing the familiar mapping, public man, private woman, one happily allowing us to say nothing about the public/private gap, one of the great tar babies of political theory. If modern society is highly differentiated, if being fully human, vibrantly colorful and alive, requires the ability to move freely from one social setting to another, then contempt takes a particular social-structural form: the figure of contempt is locked away in some social settings, barricaded from entering others.[164] Then indeed the contemptible group will come to seem a narrow or pinched representation of what it is to be fully human: and then others are free to point at their narrowness in justifying ongoing contempt.

This focus on social structure allows a different approach to the vexing topic of how anyone might in any respect, to any extent, come to be complicit in her own subordination, even cheerful about it. It's not just that she is subjected to a deafening roar constantly instructing her that she is inferior, and so willy-nilly comes to adopt that belief, as though a message bombarded frequently enough finally im-

[161] Hays, *Appeal to the Men*, p. 275.

[162] *The History of Mary Prince, a West Indian Slave: Related by Herself*, 2d ed. (London, 1831), pp. 22–23.

[163] *Blackwood's Edinburgh Magazine* (November 1831) 30(187):744–52; *John Bull* (24 February 1833) 13(637):59.

[164] The key text remains "On the Characteristics of Total Institutions," in Erving Goffman, *Asylums: Essays on the Social Situation of Mental Patients and Other Inmates* (Chicago: Aldine, 1961).

prints itself on the target. It's that she finds herself in a role, with a job to do. In doing it, in digging in and negotiating the daily demands of her work, she develops certain character traits, works up an account of the world she lives in, gains characteristic virtues and vices. She exercises agency. And she may sculpt herself into a happy slave, cheerfully contemptible. No stranger to misogyny, Dr. Johnson seems provocatively to have grasped the plight of women in this way: "The custom of the world seems to have been formed in a kind of conspiracy against them, though it does not appear but they had themselves an equal share in its establishment. . . ."[165] Maybe not its establishment, and maybe not equal, but maybe its maintenance.

[165] *Rambler* (31 July 1750) no. 39, in *The Yale Edition of the Works of Samuel Johnson,* ed. Herman W. Liebert and others, in progress (New Haven, CT: Yale University Press, 1958–), 3:211. See too *Irene* [1749], in *Works of Johnson,* 6:134.

# NINE

# FACES IN THE MIRROR

W E'VE SEEN a dismissive contempt, exhibited at a proud distance from the despicable inferiors. Here contempt and social practices are in good working order. One can safely ignore the low, brush past them with disdain, or feast upon their inferiority to buttress one's own self-esteem. And we've seen a more edgy contempt, laced with resentment, even fury, as those inferiors boldly trespass the boundaries cordoning them off from a full share of dignity and humanity— or even as it seems that they might. Contempt grows angrier not despite visions of equality but because of them. If social hierarchy is under attack, it calls for vivid new emotional investments that always betray the fear that hierarchy is doomed, or at least that it will never again be what it used to be.

Now I want to investigate some of the oddest wrinkles on the politics of contempt, quirks driven not by the fearful prospect that the low are strutting provocatively in the midst of the high, but by the haunting doubt entertained by the high that they themselves are already indistinguishable from the low, that the nominally low might actually be superior. One mischievous cartoonist portrayed the Hottentot Venus gravely meeting a nude Lord Grenville, himself renowned for his large posterior, and offered a sneaky pun on broad bottom, standing in for their distended rear ends and for the name of Grenville's faction, which promised wide coalitional support instead of narrow partisanship.[1] Now women, workers, Jews, blacks, and others, sometimes fastidiously sorted out to receive their structurally different kinds of contempt, haphazardly blur into each other: here Mrs. Betty has good reason to despair when her mistress compares

[1] *BMC* no. 11577 [15 November 1810].

her to a blackamoor. Here the social grammars defining high and low are incoherent, the social practices defining hierarchy irremediably in disrepair. Contempt doesn't collapse—the contemptible we shall have with us always; the trick is merely identifying them—but it becomes perverse. The high confront what they have to see as a richly deserved self-contempt.

Thomas Gisborne gently scolded his Christian readers for their contempt for the Jews. Jews, too, were the children of God; "human nature is in all men the same"; there was no reason to believe that their "contemptuous disregard" for God was any different from what Christians would have exhibited. "When we contemplate the enormities of the chosen people; we contemplate the course which we should ourselves have been no less disposed to pursue. The history of Israel is a mirror, which reflects our own likeness."[2] Yet Gisborne joined the wearying refrain: these very same Jews were Christ-killers. "The Jews refused to receive Jesus Christ; and completed their guilt by crucifying him."[3] Then the Christians themselves would have killed Christ. So their contempt for Jews has to rest on nothing firmer than the distinction between indicative and subjunctive, on knowing that the Jews did kill Christ, while they only would have.

Christians peering into a mirror and seeing deicide Jews: a grotesque mirror belonging in a political fun-house. But also an illuminating mirror, revealing unsavory facts a more innocent mirror might conceal, just as a cartoonist's caricature might capture something genuine that would be missing or obscured in a photograph. That mirror turned out to be fiendishly inventive, reflecting one repellent image after another, mocking the aristocratic male's bid to be the socially fairest of them all.

## ANGELIC LITERARY JEWS

Let's canvass some literary depictions of Jews with sterling virtues, appearing in print and on stage as another kind of mirror image, an inversion of their usual grubby and vicious selves. "That honest Hebrew" gracing one of Tobias Smollett's whimsical novels is a

[2] Thomas Gisborne, *Sermons*, 5th and 6th ed., 2 vols. (London, 1809–1811), 1:156–57.

[3] Gisborne, *Sermons*, 1:197.

charged presence.[4] He has to be charged, regardless of Smollett's private views, because he is thrown into bold relief by the swarms of unscrupulous moneylenders surrounding him, some in literature and some, according to contemporaries, on the streets.

In 1792, Charles Dibdin interrupted himself to recommend that someone put a Jew on stage. Not just any old Jew—no novelty there—but a Jew like the one of his novel, a moneylender "publickly execrated as a Jew, and a devil" but embraced by those who knew him for his abundant virtues.[5] Two years later, Richard Cumberland staged *The Jew.* "Old Sheva, the rich Jew, the meerest muck-worm in the city of London," blessed with the routine guttural accent and broken syntax, stars as a miserly moneylender.[6] Frederic Bertram has angered his father by spurning an arranged marriage worth £10,000. Instead, he secretly marries poor Eliza Ratcliffe. As requested, Sheva lends Bertram £300.

So far, Sheva plays to type. But he loses his patience when Bertram tells him that everyone knows he is wealthy. "I live sparingly and labor hard, therefore I am called a miser—I cannot help it—an uncharitable dog, I must endure it—a blood-sucker, an extortioner, a Shylock—hard names, Mr. Frederic, but what can a poor Jew say in return, if a Christian chuses to abuse him?" In a bit of ironically reflexive play, he continues by assaulting longstanding dramatic practice. "If your playwriters want a butt or a buffoon, or a knave to make sport of, out comes a Jew to be baited and buffetted through five long acts for the amusement of all good Christians—Cruel sport, merciless amusement!" (Cumberland may ruefully be recollecting his own dramatic practice, studded with passing swipes at Jews, though no Jews beleaguered for all of five acts.[7]) "How can you expect us to shew kindness, when we receive none?"[8] Anti-Semitism isn't just a failure of

[4] Tobias Smollett, *The Adventures of Ferdinand Count Fathom* [1753], intro. and notes by Jerry C. Beasley, ed. O. M. Brack, Jr. (Athens, GA: University of Georgia Press, 1988), p. 339; see too pp. 225–27, 335.

[5] Charles Dibdin, *Hannah Hewit; or, The Female Crusoe*, 3 vols. (London, 1792), 2:79–80.

[6] Richard Cumberland, *The Jew: A Comedy*, 2d ed. (London, 1794), p. 4. The first edition, which seems identical, is reprinted in *The Plays of Richard Cumberland*, ed. Roberta F. S. Borkat, 6 vols. (New York: Garland, 1982), vol. 5.

[7] See for instance Cumberland, *The Fashionable Lover; A Comedy*, new ed. (London, 1772), p. 16, reprinted in *Plays of Cumberland*, vol. 2; Cumberland, *The Critic* [1779], pp. 12–13, in *Plays of Cumberland*, vol. 2.

[8] *The Jew*, pp. 6–7.

Christian brotherhood; it flouts the civility and reciprocity so basic to social life.

Outraged by the marriage, Bertram's father, Sir Stephen, turns indignantly on Sheva, who protests that it wasn't his fault. "Wretch, miser, usurer!" fumes Sir Stephen; "you never yet let loose a single guinea from your gripe, but with a view of doubling it at the return." "I pray you, goot Sir Stephen," retorts Sheva, "take a little time to know my heart, before you rob me of my reputation. I am a Jew, a poor defenceless Jew; that is enough to make me miser, usurer—Alas! I cannot help it."[9] Now it turns out that Sheva is indebted to Ratcliffe's family. Her brother Charles, an old friend of Frederic, has rescued Sheva from a mob; he learns later that her mother is "the widow of my preserver from the inquisitors of Cadiz."[10] Without telling a soul, Sheva makes over a deed of—no prizes for the correct guess—£10,000 to Eliza Ratcliffe. Driven by an exquisite sense of honor, Charles proceeds to duel Frederic to salve the disgrace of a secret marriage. Interceding, Sheva professes himself a stranger to these dubious customs of honor and hustles the two of them off to his house to help a wounded Charles. Meanwhile, Sir Stephen, newly smitten with Eliza's finances, assures her that he would gladly accept her as his daughter-in-law even if she were penniless. But she rejects his wild tale of the £10,000 and disavows any knowledge of Sheva: "No Jew of that or any other name do I know; nay, I question if I ever exchang'd a word with any one of the nation in my life."

This salvo persuades Sir Stephen that she is penniless. This lamentable fact should disqualify her from his son's matrimonial regard: aristocratic fortune is not to be squandered. But the proud lass's belligerent innocence of Jews charms him: "Your merit then, and not your fortune, shall endear you to me," he declares.[11] And now Sheva is marched onstage by a beaming Charles, who supplies him a glowing encomium as "the widow's friend, the orphan's father, the poor man's protector, the universal philanthropist." Embarrassed, he sheepishly throws his hands over his face. But Charles is inexorable. Too long, he instructs Sheva, has he hidden all his good deeds. "You must now face the world, and transfer the blush from your own cheeks to their's, whom prejudice has taught to scorn you. For your

9 *The Jew*, p. 39.
10 *The Jew*, pp. 5–6, 53.
11 *The Jew*, p. 70.

single sake we must reform our hearts, and inspire them with candor towards your whole nation." "Enough, Enough!" protests Sheva; "more than enough—I pray you spare me: I am not used to hear the voice of praise, and it oppresses me: I shou'd not know myself, if you were to describe me; I have a register within, in which these merits are not noted."[12]

Actually, Sheva isn't just embarrassed in the face of such testimonials. He is abashed, even stricken, and he grovels. When Sir Stephen learns of the splendid grant of £10,000 and apologizes, Sheva is taken aback: "I pray you, goot Sir Stephen, say no more; you'll bring the blush upon my cheek, if you demean yourself so far to a poor Jew, who is your very humble servant to command."[13] So Cumberland's play doesn't hurl any ferocious admonitions at its audience. It lobs an emotional cream puff at them instead. They can maintain their views about the degraded status of Jews; they're invited only to substitute the amiable version of contempt for the nasty one. A bit of a wizard, a Christ figure himself, this one humble Jew will redeem the rest of his race. He'll also permit the audience to keep believing that one fictional Jew's implausible charities don't challenge what they know perfectly well are the facts about the real Jews outside the theater. Scoffing at mercenary Jews afforded its dramatic pleasures, but so did embracing pathetic philanthropist Sheva. "Sheva's Creed" became a popular song.[14]

Thomas Dibdin introduced his 1800 farce, *The Jew and the Doctor,* by assuring the public that he'd been oblivious to Cumberland's play when he wrote his own, indeed that he had solicited comments from Cumberland when he learned about *The Jew* and had pruned offendingly similar passages.[15] Like Cumberland, Dibdin offered a secretly virtuous Jew. Abednego is forever insisting, "I must take care of de main chance," that is attend to self-interest, but he has brought up foundling Emily as a Christian and invested money for her. Her grate-

---

[12] *The Jew*, p. 73–74.

[13] *The Jew*, p. 42.

[14] *The Memoirs of J. Decastro, Comedian*, ed. R. Humphreys (London, 1824), p. 90; Louis Zangwill, "Richard Cumberland Centenary Memorial Paper," *Transactions of the Jewish Historical Society of England* (1911–1914) 7:177–79. See too George Raymond, *Memoirs of Robert William Elliston Comedian*, 2d ed., 2 vols. (London, 1846; reprint ed. New York: Benjamin Blom, 1969), 1:78, 1:88.

[15] Thomas Dibdin, *The Jew and the Doctor: A Farce, in Two Acts* (London, 1800), advt.; see too *The Reminiscences of Thomas Dibdin*, 2 vols. (London, 1837), 1:218–19.

ful father reclaims her and asks Abednego how he can thank him. "I'll tell you how to *pay* me," answers Abednego, pandering to the audience's preconceptions but turning to offer a transparent sermon. "If ever you see a helpless creature vat needs your assistance, give it for ma sake—And if de object should even not be a Christian, remember that humanity knows no difference of opinion; and that you can never make your own religion look so well, as when you shew mercy to de religion of others."[16] Abednego throws into bold relief the asymmetric structure of the audience's sympathies. Nice of him to have the decency to raise a helpless Christian girl, but could any of them imagine raising a helpless Jewish girl? and respecting her religion?

Dibdin returned to the fray the following year with his *School for Prejudice*. Poor Ephraim is another moneylender, whipped and addressed as "mongrel" by arrogant Squire Chace.[17] But actually Ephraim is benevolent and honest. He even refuses to hang onto the imposing sum of—yes, £10,000.[18] One such singular action gives rise to a colloquy:

> RACHEL. Well-a-daisy! that's a good-natur'd old soul! Ah! if he was but one of us.
>
> MARIAN. Why, is he *not* one of us?
>
> RACHEL. What, he? a Jew! Why, miss, they are not, no, not even Christians.
>
> MRS. HOWARD. Certainly not, Rachel; but they are men.
>
> RACHEL. True, ma'am; but not like us. My poor, dear husband used to say they were fit for nothing, but to lend money, wear long beards, and buy bad shillings.
>
> MRS. HOWARD. But, Rachel, you shou'd recollect, that if the Christians didn't furnish, by their extravagance, the ground of Jewish usury, the sons of Israel wou'd be more respected.
>
> RACHEL. Ah, I dare say what you tell me is right—Dear me! a Jew one of us! Bless us, how a body may live and learn! [*Exit muttering.*[19]

Refined Mrs. Howard instructs the audience on their new duties. Even crude Rachel, unwilling to concede that a Jew might be "one of

---

16 Dibdin, *Jew and the Doctor,* p. 31.

17 Thomas Dibdin, *School for Prejudice* [1801], in *The Modern Theatre; a Collection of Successful Modern Plays,* ed. Elizabeth Inchbald, 10 vols. (London, 1811), 4:355, 4:357.

18 Dibdin, *School for Prejudice,* in *Modern Theatre,* 4:408–9.

19 Dibdin, *School for Prejudice,* in *Modern Theatre,* 4:345–46.

us," recognizes Ephraim's virtues. Then again, Rachel's sarcastic closing jibe allows the audience to exhale again and revile the Jew. Perhaps again the point is to replace nasty with amiable contempt, to
recognize the role of Christian financial indiscipline in producing
Jewish moneylenders. This play, too, was popular. In 1825, Dibdin
turned it into an opera, *The Lawyer, the Jew, and the Yorkshireman*.[20] A
handbill from Sadler's Wells, site of popular if vulgar entertain-
ments, cast this new production as "a most whimsical burletta, which
sends people home perfectly exhausted from uninterrupted ris-
ibility. . . ."[21] I don't know what the audience found laughable.

Maria Edgeworth painstakingly sculpted one last model literary Jew
in 1817 after years of churning out the usual inglorious variety. Solomon the Jew is the scoundrel of one of her 1801 stories, Mr. Carat
"the wily Jew" of another.[22] In 1802 she has a couple of Jews sell some
chests of clothing carrying the plague.[23] (Anything for money, indeed: some Jews actually attempted this scam in 1786, according to
one report.[24]) And so on, one disreputable Jew after another making
their ritual appearances in the endless pages of her works. Edgeworth
was dissuaded from continuing the parade, perhaps, by a letter she
received from one Rachel Mordecai, an American Jew, in 1815. Mordecai demanded how Edgeworth could exhibit such consistently liberal sentiments on other matters but continually exhibit Jews as
wretches. "Can it be believed that this race of men are by nature
mean, avaricious, and unprincipled?"[25]

A chastened Edgeworth penned *Harrington*. Its eponymous protagonist commences a Jew-hater, if an innocent victim. His nursery
maid would threaten him that Simon the Jew would carry him away in
a bag of used rags if he misbehaved.[26] And he recoiled from a Pari-

[20] *Reminiscences of Thomas Dibdin*, 2:318.

[21] William Hone, *The Every-Day Book*, 2 vols. (London, 1827; reprint ed. Detroit:
Gale Research Co., 1967), 1:1200.

[22] "The Prussian Vase" [1801], in Maria Edgeworth, *Tales and Novels*, 10 vols. (London, 1848), 1:111–43; "The Good Aunt" [1801], in *Tales and Novels*, 1:191.

[23] "Murad the Unlucky" [1802], in *Tales and Novels*, 2:262, 2:274.

[24] Miss Tully, *Narrative of a Ten Years' Residence at Tripoli in Africa*, 2d ed. (London,
1817), p. 107 [12 January 1786].

[25] Rachel Mordecai to Maria Edgeworth, 7 August 1815, *The Education of the Heart:
The Correspondence of Rachel Mordecai Lazarus and Maria Edgeworth*, ed. Edgar E. Mac-
Donald (Chapel Hill, NC: University of North Carolina Press, 1977), p. 6.

[26] Maria Edgeworth, *Harrington, a Tale; and Ormond, a Tale*, 3 vols. (London, 1817),
1:3–5; in *Tales and Novels*, 9:2–3.

sian Jew who sold pork pies, "but it was found out at last, that the pies were not pork, they were made of the flesh of little children," saving the Jew from the everyday taunt that he didn't cleave to kosher foods.[27] Harrington finds himself falling in love with Jewish Miss Montenero. He wonders—this is profound, not laughable—if it is possible to marry a Jewess.[28] Offering no explanation, her father insists that it's not.[29] Perplexed, Harrington finally realizes that her father suspects he is engaged to Lady Anne Mowbray and is merely toying with his daughter.[30] Harrington's father, himself a Jew-hater, relaxes his own opposition when Montenero wields his considerable financial resources to extricate him from causing a run on a bank.[31] But Montenero's opposition remains inflexible—until Lord Mowbray turns out to be practicing a sleazy deception.[32] So it is possible to fall in love with a Jewess, even to marry her, at least in a novel that pedantically marches the reader along from Harrington's own anti-Semitism to his impending marriage. Does the prospect induce too much anxiety, even nausea? Is the marriage of Jew and Christian a display of rampant disorder, not a moment of exalted fraternity? Never fear: in this too happy of endings, it suddenly turns out that Berenice Montenero, like her mother, is a Protestant.[33] Like Abednego, Montenero has dutifully brought her up without tampering with her religion.

Disappointed, Mordecai dashed off another letter to Edgeworth to ask why she had concluded her novel this way. Mordecai reported that her father had suggested it was intended as further evidence of the goodness of Jews.[34] "I wish you would thank your kindhearted father for the reason he gave for my making Berenice turn out to be a Christian," responded Edgeworth after sagely pondering the matter

[27] *Harrington,* 1:5; *Tales and Novels,* 9:2–3.

[28] *Harrington,* 1:281; *Tales and Novels,* 9:110.

[29] *Harrington,* 1:363–64; *Tales and Novels,* 9:144.

[30] *Harrington,* 1:409; *Tales and Novels,* 9:162.

[31] *Harrington,* 1:432–33; *Tales and Novels,* 9:173.

[32] *Harrington,* 1:479–503; *Tales and Novels,* 9:189–99.

[33] *Harrington,* 1:509; *Tales and Novels,* 9:203. Compare Karl Spindler, *The Jew,* 3 vols. (London, 1832), 3:149, 3:166. Contrast the reductionist reading of Catherine Gallagher, *Nobody's Story: The Vanishing Acts of Women Writers in the Marketplace, 1670–1820* (Berkeley: University of California Press, 1994), p. 325, which singles out Edgeworth's anxieties about her odd relationship with her father.

[34] Rachel Mordecai to Maria Edgeworth, 28 October 1817, *Education of the Heart,* p. 16.

for several years. "It was a better reason than I own I had ever thought up."[35] The concession might be construcd as a challenge to some bromides about the crucial role of authorial intent in interpretation.

But Edgeworth's other readers weren't baffled by Berenice's turning out to be Christian. One renowned novelist was relieved: "I own I breathed more freely when I found Miss Montenero was not an actual Jewess," confessed Walter Scott.[36] The *Edinburgh Review* groaned at the heavy-handed stupidity of it all: "Nobody likely to read Miss Edgeworth's writings, entertains such an absurd antipathy to Jews as she here aims at exposing," and garden-variety Jew-haters wouldn't be moved by such an extravagant tale.[37] In a sunny mood, *Blackwood's* deplored "the prejudices which are still cherished, we fear, to a great extent against that unhappy race," but worried that the blatant implausibility of Edgeworth's tale militated against its having an impact. "We regret, for the sake of this oppressed and injured people, that her zeal has in this case rather outrun her judgment; and that, by representing all her Jewish characters as too uniformly perfect, she has thrown a degree of suspicion over her whole defence."[38] The *British Critic* pressed a similar charge against Cumberland's *The Jew:* there might well be virtuous Jews, but none of them would so sedulously disguise their virtues in public.[39] Cobbett's Ethnicus detected a different flaw in Cumberland's attempt: "A Jew who gives away his money for the mere pleasure of doing good, without shew or profit, is such a monstrous caricature as no real Jew can see without contempt."[40]

Thomas Love Peacock guffawed at the mechanical formula all these authors followed. "If I were to take all the mean and sordid qualities of a little Jew broker," his Mr. Flosky announces, "and tack on to them, as with a nail, the quality of extreme benevolence, I should have a very decent hero for a modern novel. . . ."[41] Why did all these

[35] Maria Edgeworth to Rachel Mordecai, 21 June 1821, *Education of the Heart,* p. 23.
[36] Walter Scott to Joanna Baillie, 24 July [1817], *The Letters of Sir Walter Scott,* ed. H. J. C. Grierson, 12 vols. (London: Constable & Co., 1932–1937), 4:478.
[37] *Edinburgh Review* (August 1817) 28(56):403.
[38] *Blackwood's Edinburgh Magazine* (August 1817) 1(5):520.
[39] *British Critic* (July 1795) 6:11.
[40] *Political Register* (6 September 1806) 10(10):404.
[41] *Nightmare Abbey* [1818], in *The Works of Thomas Love Peacock,* Halliford edition, ed. H. F. B. Brett-Smith and C. E. Jones, 10 vols. (London: Constable & Co., 1924–1934), 3(1):52, 3(1):148.

authors so diligently stick to the formula? Why could they imagine only Jews with conventionally vicious exteriors masking stunningly virtuous interiors? Sheva, Abednego, Ephraim, Montenero: are these four characters or the same character recycled? (Not that the later authors were plagiarizing from Cumberland or from Charles Dibdin's suggestion; rather that the problem they independently confront, of how to grapple with literary tradition and audience expectations, seems to lend itself to the same line of attack.) Are they even one character, one recognizably human figure, or just a one-dimensional type, as dehumanized in its way as the familiar hateful Jews? (Compare: "They all look alike.") Could any author of this period, however talented and bold, have imagined and realized a genuinely individual Jew? Could the audience have made sense of such a figure? So were the authors stuck in a bind, needing to begin with something like a moneylender with a heavy accent to have the audience recognize a Jew?

In fact, these authors thought they were doing Jews a generous service. They were puzzled, even irritated, by the Jews' churlish responses. Before staging *The Jew,* Cumberland had written an essay sympathetic to the Jews—"These poor people seem the butt, at which all sects and persuasions level their contempt"[42]—and produced another attractive Jew, Abraham Abrahams, who promised a grateful display for a sympathetic play. "The comedy has been written and acted," reported an acerbic Cumberland; "Mr. Abrahams has had his wish: In the matter of the promise he seems to have reckon'd *without his host.*"[43] In his *Memoirs,* Cumberland fulminated against Jewish ingratitude.

> Not a word from the lips, not a line did I ever receive from the pen of any Jew, though I have found myself in company with many of their nation; and in this perhaps the gentlemen are quite right, whilst I had formed expectations, that were quite wrong; for if I have said for them only what they deserve, why should I be thanked for it? But if I have said more, much more, than they deserve, can they do a wiser thing than hold their tongues?[44]

[42] Richard Cumberland, *The Observer: Being a Collection of Moral, Literary and Familiar Essays,* 5th ed., 6 vols. (London, 1798), 2:78.

[43] Cumberland, *Observer,* 2:84–85.

[44] *Memoirs of Richard Cumberland: Written by Himself* (London, 1806), pp. 457–58; also in *Memoirs of Richard Cumberland: Written by Himself,* 2 vols. (London, 1807), 2:203.

Folklore had it that Cumberland went on to jest that he was glad the Jews hadn't offered any compensation, lest he be accused of receiving stolen goods.[45] But the lack of suitable gratitude rankled. Cumberland took his revenge in a novel featuring one David Owen, "that Jew-born miscreant," an impudent braggart who stuffs the pages full of his villainous acts, among them raping and driving crazy a virtuous woman.[46]

Thomas Dibdin himself was drawn up short. In 1802, his *Family Quarrels* featured a comic ballad in which the male singer longed for various "beauties of the Jewish persuasion." The Jews mobilized in the theater and—shades of the O.P. riots—audibly protested. "It vont do! it vont do, I tell you! take it away! take it to Sadler's Vells!" In recalling these tawdry events, Dibdin mustered all the heart-rending tones of wounded innocence. "Heaven knows that I, who had written and even played Abednego in 'the Jew and the Doctor,' and Ephraim in the 'School for Prejudice,' with no trifling applause from the critics . . . never entertained, as Fribble says, 'the minutest atom of an idea' that the harmless joke, as harmlessly suggested, could be taken as the most distant intention of giving offence."[47] Whatever Dibdin's understanding of his ballad, of the impeccable credentials he should have gained from his earlier productions, his protestation misses the systematic interconnections between polite and snarling contempt. In the circumstances, how innocent could such a ballad be? Could its meaning possibly be fixed by Dibdin's mental states? The Jews succeeded in extracting revisions—recall that closing off this kind of speech might well open up otherwise unavailable possibilities, so it's glib to take this as a defeat for free speech—and the play went on to become a great success.[48]

Edgeworth, too, wondered sadly why the Jews didn't lavish grateful affection on her. "I really should be gratified if I could have any testimony even were it ever so slight from those of your persuasion that they were pleased with my attempt to do them justice," she informed

[45] Stanley Thomas Williams, *Richard Cumberland: His Life and Dramatic Works* (New Haven, CT: Yale University Press, 1917), p. 237.

[46] Richard Cumberland, *John de Lancaster*, 2 vols. (New York, 1809), 1:247, 2:80–82. Consider Walter Scott's reactions in *Biographical Memoirs of Eminent Novelists* [1821], in *The Prose Works of Sir Walter Scott, Bart.*, 28 vols. (Edinburgh, 1834–1836), 3:212–13 [1825]; "Cumberland's *John de Lancaster*" [1809], in *Prose Works*, 18:146–47.

[47] *Reminiscences of Thomas Dibdin*, 1:339, 1:341, 1:339.

[48] *Reminiscences of Thomas Dibdin*, 1:345.

Mordecai. "But except for you, my dear Madam, and one or two other individuals in England, I have never heard that any of the Jewish persuasion received Harrington as it was intended. A book or merely a print of any celebrated Jew or Jewess or a *note* expressing their satisfaction with my endeavors or with my intentions would have pleased—I will not say my vanity—but my heart."[49] Happier or luckier than Cumberland or Dibdin, though, she later recorded some appropriate acknowledgments of her novel, among them "a most superb portfolio" embroidered with the name *Harrington* and various flowers.[50]

Surely these writers saw themselves as graciously condescending to the lowly Jews. Then yearning for acknowledgment is desiring that their own status as superior be consecrated. (Here's another riposte to the flattened reading of Hegel: there are certain kinds of weighty recognition that can be offered only by inferiors. No equal can ooze submissively cloying gratitude in response to condescension.) And the annoyance is caused by the Jews' failing to take their part in the appointed ritual, being truculent instead of obsequious. Recall Collier's formulation of the rule when the Duke of Devonshire brought him his lunch: "I should be most ungrateful not to make all the return in my power." Recall too how the duke's "noble nostrils" would dilate if anyone dared to be presumptuous when he condescended. These writers are peeved not at any failure of reciprocity among equals, but at the audacious insubordination of the underlings. So the overdone praise, the exhibition of Jews as saints, is still caught up in contempt.

## IN SEARCH OF THE REAL JEWS

Then again, we might characterize the overdone praise as an attempt to drive a logical wedge and pose a question: are Jews Jews? That is, take these people called Jews; do they share the traits we ascribe to Jews? Are they greedy and smelly? On this reading, *Jew* is ambiguous. It picks out members of a religious group (let's finesse the question of whether they are race, nation, tribe, or whatever else). It also delin-

---

[49] Maria Edgeworth to Rachel Mordecai, 21 June 1821, *Education of the Heart*, p. 23.

[50] Maria Edgeworth to Mrs. Ruxton, 1 December 1824, in Frances Anne Edgeworth, *A Memoir of Maria Edgeworth*, ed. her children, 3 vols. (London: privately printed, 1867), 2:252; Maria Edgeworth to Rachel Lazarus, 15 January 1823, *Education of the Heart*, pp. 33–34.

eates a profile of those people. The ambiguity surfaces in Cobbett's vehement rejection of London, "its inhabitants, indeed, pretty well corrupted by the crapulous crowds which the taxes have drawn together in its environs, and by the swarms of Jews that carry on their usurious traffic in its centre."[51] Are these nominally Christian financiers who become Jewish insofar as they lead lives devoted to the pursuit of ugly lucre? Or are they religious Jews? The ambiguity also allows Cobbett to be coy, maybe unaccountable, in claiming that the newspaper press is under the control of Jews: for again he refers to both stockjobbers and "the sons of Israel," and either locution might or might not refer to religious Jews. Cobbett didn't always flirt with ambiguity. He lambasted the jobbers holding Greek bonds as "Jews in soul though Christians by profession"; one wonders which sort of Jew is more loathsome and why.[52] Ambiguities aside, the question *are Jews Jews?* could be used to suggest that Jews aren't all that bad, that it's unfair to credit the members of the class with the traits of the profile.

Now we can also flip the question: take the people who have these traits, who are sordidly moneygrubbing and whatever else; are they members of the religious group Jews? Or are they other people? Then these other people, not religious Jews, qualify as Jews in one perfectly straightforward sense. (Compare how gender spins away from any straightforward reference to biological men and women, so that we can detect effeminate men or for that matter masculine fugues.) And then Jew-hating and Jew-baiting are sports one can delight in without a single member of the Jewish religion in view. For some time the sport may depend on the background conviction that anyway most religious Jews are contemptible in the ordinary way. But not forever, although such claims still will percolate in the historical background.

Thomas Dibdin didn't just portray Jews and suffer witnessing his drama being assaulted by Jews. He was branded a Jew by one of his fellows in the theater. As requested, Dibdin had penned some songs for him, telling him "I should depend on his honour for some sort of remuneration. . . ." Months later, the performer preening himself on earning over £1,000 from the work, Dibdin nudged him about payment. Offended, the performer told a friend that Dibdin "was a Jew

[51] William Cobbett, *Cobbett's Manchester Lectures, in Support of His Fourteen Reform Propositions* (London, 1832), p. 20. For another instructive case of ambiguity, see Arthur Murphy, *Seventeen Hundred and Ninety-One* (London, 1791), p. 16.

[52] *Political Register* (29 September 1827) 64(1):3.

to ask money from a 'brother performer'. . . ."[53] Not that he had converted, not that he was secretly circumcised, not that he spent time crowing over the crucifixion: just that insinuating the cash nexus in the context of a warm fictive kinship system betrayed precisely the hideous traits associated with (religious) Jews, constitutive of (contemptible) Jews. Mrs. Storace trampled on fictive and real kinship, ruthlessly exacting her allotted share for performing in an opera even though it meant beggaring her brother, the composer. She proceeded "with the severity of a Jew"; "parsimony seems to have eradicated every other passion from her breast."[54] Dibdin and Storace weren't alone. They were surrounded, in a Britain crammed full of Jews, their numbers vastly exceeding the twenty or thirty thousand of demographic lore.

"I will use you as bad as a Jew" became a London proverb. The lexicographer recording it commented, "The horrid exactions and cruelties practised on this people by our forefathers, would justify the idea that they were, themselves, in these instances, but very bad Christians."[55] Here the harsh Christians are Jews. And the intimation may well be that the long-suffering, meek, humble Jews are Christians: for one can drive the same logical wedge through that category, distinguishing members of the religious group from those sharing a set of traits conventionally associated with them.

The day's writers toyed with finding Jews in their midst, even with being Jews themselves. Negotiating with a publisher, Fanny Burney turned to Charles Burney: "I claim your counsel, assistance, & promised *Jewish callousness*."[56] Fabulously wealthy writer and art collector William Beckford reflected on his efforts to procure one celebrated canvas: "The Jewish Abercorn is asking 3,000 pounds for his Parmigiano, but the Jewish Beckford won't give it."[57] Byron didn't mind

[53] *Reminiscences of Thomas Dibdin*, 1:356–57.

[54] Joseph Haslewood, *The Secret History of the Green Room*, 2d ed., 2 vols. (London, 1792), 1:164.

[55] Francis Grose, *A Provincial Glossary; with a Collection of Local Proverbs, and Popular Superstitions*, 2d ed. corrected (London, 1790), sig. G2.

[56] Mme d'Arblay to Charles Burney, 5 July 1795, *The Journals and Letters of Fanny Burney (Madame D'Arblay)*, ed. Joyce Hemlow and others, 12 vols. (Oxford: Clarendon, 1972–1984), 3:126.

[57] William Beckford to Gregorio Franchi, 26 June 1808, *Life at Fonthill 1807–1822 with Interludes in Paris and London: From the Correspondence of William Beckford*, trans. and ed. Boyd Alexander (London: Rupert Hart-Davis, 1957), p. 72.

smearing Jews. But he was impartial enough to smear himself: planning the sale of an estate, the liquidation of his debts, and the purchase of annuities, he sighed, "You see I must turn Jew myself at last."[58] So too Southey was no slouch when it came to lambasting the Jews but assumed Jewish garb himself, promising journalistic retaliation against reviewers panning his poems: "I shall very likely pay them in kind with Jews interest."[59] Joining the club of distinguished literary Jews, Keats professed himself "confident I shall be able to cheat as well as any literary Jew of the Market and shine up an article on any thing without much knowledge of the subject, aye like an orange."[60] (Jews were well known for peddling oranges in the streets.[61])

Leading politicians played the same game—and had it played against them. Thanks to their role in the fateful 1753 effort to relieve the Jews of their disabilities, the Whigs became known as Jews.[62] Decades later, Whig leader Charles James Fox faced the same disturbing bantering. A heavy gambler, he would stagger home, rise late, and trudge into his antechamber to deal with Jewish moneylenders to pay off his debts. Fox designated the room his Jerusalem chamber.[63] In

[58] Byron to John Hanson, 25 June 1809, *Byron's Letters and Journals,* ed. Leslie A. Marchand, 13 vols. (London: John Murray, 1973–1994), 1:207.

[59] Southey to Grosvenor Charles Bedford, 11 December 1807, *New Letters of Robert Southey,* ed. Kenneth Curry, 2 vols. (New York: Columbia University Press, 1965), 1:464. Note too Southey to Bedford, 31 [July] 1793, *New Letters,* 1:30; Southey to Caroline Bowles, 18 March 1828, *The Correspondence of Robert Southey with Caroline Bowles,* ed. Edward Dowden (Dublin, 1881), p. 135.

[60] Keats to C. W. Dilke, 22 September 1819, *The Letters of John Keats,* ed. Hyder Edward Rollins, 2 vols. (Cambridge, MA: Harvard University Press, 1958), 2:179. See too John Constable to William Carpenter, November 1830, *Correspondence,* ed. R. B. Beckett, 6 vols. (Ipswich: Suffolk Records Society, 1962–1968), 4:145.

[61] An Englishman, *Brief Remarks on English Manners, and An Attempt to Account for Some of Our Most Striking Peculiarities* (London, 1816), p. 32; *Real Life in London; or, the Rambles and Adventures of Bob Tallyho, Esq. and His Cousin, the Hon. Tom. Dashall, through the Metropolis; Exhibiting a Living Picture of Fashionable Characters, Manners, and Amusements in High and Low Life,* 2 vols. (London, 1824), 1:478, 2:384; "Shadrack, the Orangeman; or, The Biter Bit," in *The Universal Songster; or, Museum of Mirth,* 3 vols. (London, 1825–1826), 1:27; *Blackwood's Edinburgh Magazine* (November 1827) 22(132):593–95; *Destructive* (16 March 1833), quoted in Joel H. Wiener, *The War of the Unstamped: The Movement to Repeal the British Newspaper Tax, 1830–1836* (Ithaca, NY: Cornell University Press, 1969), p. 227.

[62] Thomas W. Perry, *Public Opinion, Propaganda, and Politics in Eighteenth-Century England: A Study of the Jew Bill of 1753* (Cambridge, MA: Harvard University Press, 1962), p. 74.

[63] *The Last Journals of Horace Walpole: During the Reign of George III from 1771–1783,* ed. A. Francis Steuart, 2 vols. (London: John Lane, The Bodley Head, 1910), 1:7 [6 Febru-

1784, one cartoon offered a Jewish moneylender, submissively bent over to expose his rear end, and Fox inserting an auger. "I'll bore you by — If you don't produce money immediately, you Jewish son of a bitch," snarls Fox. "O Shveet Shir let me up and you shall have the monies," pleads the Jew. The caption explains that the Jew had come to "a certain person" seeking repayment of a large debt, but had been subjected to this treatment and confronted with a demand for £1,000 more "instantly. This is a fact well authenticated."[64] One foreigner thought Fox looked suspiciously like a Jew.[65] "It is I," boasted Cobbett, "who have set all the Jew-politicians at work to talk about exchanges and bars of gold."[66] (By thrusting the parlous state of the national finances onto the political agenda, by making his infamous vow that he'd be broiled on his gridiron if his dire predictions didn't come to pass,[67] wasn't Cobbett himself betraying Jewish proclivities?) Richard Brothers, religious visionary, self-proclaimed prophet and descendant of King David, had a knack for spying Jews in the highest reaches of the British state. William Pitt, Gilbert Elliott, Charles Grey, and even George III himself were Jewish.[68] No wonder Brothers was arrested, decreed insane, and squirrelled away in a madhouse.[69]

Yet others, never threatened with institutionalization, displayed a razor-sharp political rationality in trafficking in the very same charges. (Tricky business, in this paranoid and ugly territory, to sort out the crazy people.) Dismissing Pitt as an unscrupulous wretch, the editor of the *Bee* told Bentham, "As to Pitt, he is a very Jew,—he will say, at this moment, the very reverse of what he intends to do, if he

---

ary 1772]; also with variations in Charles James Fox, *Memorials and Correspondence,* ed. Lord John Russell, 3 vols. (London, 1853–1854), 1:71.

[64] *BMC* no. 6617 [10 June 1784].

[65] Carl Philip Moritz, *Journeys of a German in England in 1782,* trans. and ed. Reginald Nettel (New York: Holt, Rinehart and Winston, 1965), p. 52 [13 June 1782].

[66] *Political Register* (22 December 1827) 64(13):796. See too *John Bull* (23 June 1833) 13(654):197.

[67] A picture of the gridiron graces many issues of the *Political Register;* see George Spater, *William Cobbett: The Poor Man's Friend,* 2 vols. (Cambridge: Cambridge University Press, 1982), 2:368, 2:413, 2:423–25, 2:586–87 n. 85, 2:587 n. 88.

[68] Richard Brothers, *A Revealed Knowledge of the Prophecies and Times . . . Book the Second* (London, 1794), pp. 54–55; Brothers to William Pitt, 20 October 1795, in Brothers, *An Exposition of the Trinity* (London, 1796), p. 53; Brothers, *Exposition,* p. 40.

[69] *A Letter of Richard Brothers, (Prince of the Hebrews) to Philip Stephens, Esq. with the Answer* (London, 1795), p. 21.

think it can effect any little object."[70] In the run-up to Catholic eman-
cipation, one propagandist exploited the nefarious image of Jews and
Catholics in cahoots to overthrow the respectable Protestant establishment. But maybe the barbarians were already inside the gates.
True, he conceded, "Many have been Lords of the Treasury in former
times, who wanted only *circumcision,* to make them PERFECT JEWS."[71]
The gag was good enough to be recycled a dozen pages later: "The
CIRCUMCISED are, in all respects, fit to be *Excisemen,* and . . . the
EXCISEMEN are most of them fit to be *circumcised. . . .*"[72] Venerable
radical John Cartwright ferreted out Jews and their allies lurking everywhere in politics: a "Jew-shielding Lord," "*Tory Jews*" opposing parliamentary reform, "Jew traders in rotten borough patronage" corrupting the country.[73] (The Jewish Sir Manasseh Masseh Lopes was
convicted of corrupting electors in 1819 and served two years in
jail.[74]) Thomas Moore already had pictured Cartwright, with his notorious enthusiasm for annual elections, as a Jewish quack hawking his
fraudulent medicine for the body politic:

> VILL nobodies try my nice *Annual Pill,*
>
> Dat's to purify every ting nashty avay?
>
> Pless ma heart, pless ma heart, let me say vat I vill,
>
> Not a Chrishtian or Shentleman minds vat I say![75]

[70] James Anderson to Bentham, 15 May 1791, in *The Correspondence of Jeremy Bentham,*
ed. Timothy L. S. Sprigge and others, 10 vols. to date (London: Athlone Press; Oxford:
Clarendon, 1968–), 4:297. See too *Anti-Jacobin* (16 April 1798) no. 23, p. 178; *John Bull*
(19 December 1824) 4(51):412; John Belchem, *'Orator' Hunt: Henry Hunt and English
Working-Class Radicalism* (Oxford: Clarendon, 1985), p. 242.

[71] *An Epistle from a High Priest of the Jews, to the Chief Priest of Canterbury, on the Extension
of Catholic Emancipation to the Jews* (London, 1821), p. 3.

[72] *Epistle from a High Priest,* p. 18.

[73] John Cartwright, *The English Constitution Produced and Illustrated* (London, 1823),
pp. xvii, 97, 401.

[74] John Cannon, *Parliamentary Reform 1640–1832* (Cambridge: Cambridge University Press, 1973), p. 177. To the scorn of his opponents, Peel would later rely on Sir
Manasseh's assistance at the polls: Robert Peel, *Memoirs,* ed. Lord Mahon and Edward
Cardwell, 2 vols. (London, 1856–1857), 1:342; *Blackwood's Edinburgh Magazine* (May
1830) 27(166):723.

[75] "The Annual Pill: Supposed to Be Sung by OLD PROSY, the Jew, in the Character
of Major C-RTW — GHT," in *The Poetical Works of Thomas Moore,* ed. A. D. Godley (London: Oxford University Press, 1915), p. 610. *Blackwood's Edinburgh Magazine* (March
1819) 4(24):726 prints the poem and attributes it to Gregson.

The closing line reminds the reader that the likes of Cartwright are to
be dismissed contemptuously. No Jewish quack doctor could enjoy
epistemic authority. When he says that no one minds what he says, he
doesn't mean that no one finds him offensive. He means that he's
ignored as he babbles away.

Joseph Priestley—Burke's nemesis, scientist, Unitarian, radical—
was splattered with this mud. Very much of his day in insisting on the
rational credentials of Christianity, Priestley decided that the same
considerations dictating that one accept the veracity of the Old Testament dictated the veracity of the New.[76] Perhaps the Jews' wretched
treatment, he conjectured, explained their ignoring those beseeching them to accept the true faith.[77] But he decided to attempt the
feat of conversion and so published a series of *Letters to the Jews*. These
are masterpieces of sanctimony:

> Be not, therefore, offended, if, with great sincerity, but with equal affec-
> tion, I must observe, that, according to appearances, there is no other
> cause of God's displeasure against you besides your rejection and per-
> secution of the prophets of your own nation, Christ and the apostles,
> who were sent to *you* in the first place, and who confined their instruc-
> tions to your nation, till, being rejected by you, they were directed to
> preach the gospel to the Gentiles.[78]

Emphasizing the consistency and shared evidence of Judaism and
Christianity, Priestley went as far as holding that the two religions
"are, in reality, but one."[79] The thought encouraged him to become
an early cheerleader for Jews for Jesus: "You ought to declare yourselves Christians, though without ceasing to be Jews," he urged.[80]

Somehow, the Jews were unmoved. David Levi joined print combat

---

[76] See for instance Priestley, *Letters to a Philosophical Unbeliever: Part II: Containing a
State of the Evidence of Revealed Religion, with Animadversions on the Two Last Chapters of the
First Volume of Mr. Gibbon's History of the Decline and Fall of the Roman Empire* (Birmingham,
1787), pp. vi–vii.

[77] Priestley to Rev. T. Lindsey, 5 July 1786, in John Towill Rutt, *Life and Correspondence
of Joseph Priestley*, 2 vols. (London, 1831–1832), 1:392.

[78] Joseph Priestley, *Letters to the Jews; Inviting Them to an Amicable Discussion of the
Evidences of Christianity*, 2d ed. (Birmingham, 1787), pp. 16–17.

[79] Priestley, *Letters to the Jews*, p. 56.

[80] Joseph Priestley, *Discourses on the Evidence of Revealed Religion* (London, 1794),
p. 404.

with Priestley. Agreeing that faith ought to be grounded in reason, Levi demurred, "We are destitute of the most *convincing,* and *persuasive* arguments in favor of Judaism, viz. fat Bishopricks, Deaneries, Rectories, and Vicarages. . . ."[81] The swipe was artless: as a Unitarian, a Dissenter outside the Church of England, Priestley had no such persuasive arguments for his faith, either. In that way, Jews and Unitarians were as one.

Another response to Priestley, published under a pen name, was probably by a bishop, George Horne, posing in the pamphlet as a Jew. Dismissing Priestley's arguments as palpable embarrassments, the sort of thing he could have crafted while asleep, a sneaky Horne exults in Priestley's belief that Judaism and Unitarianism are very close. Leave your "mungrel religion," he taunts Priestley, and become a Jew. Why ever not? Because—here Horne spends several pages graphically imagining poor Priestley writhing and screaming—circumcision is painful. Anyway, Horne concludes, Priestley is such a bad Christian that the Jews wouldn't accept him anyway.[82] Bucking public opinion, Priestley described Jews as "the most conspicuous, and in the eye of reason and religion, the most respectable, nation on the face of the earth."[83] In that way, too, Jews were just like Christians—or even better. Horne's acidulous attack is designed to resist that ridiculous conclusion. He does so by writing off a Unitarian, a sorry excuse for a Christian, as no better than a Jew.

Authors and political figures, then, could be cast as Jews. So could the nations of Britain. A barber in one of the *Waverley Novels* muses, "But the Scots never eat pork—strange that! some folk think they are a sort of Jews." He adds that they like to refer to George III as "the second Solomon, and Solomon you know, was King of the Jews; so the

[81] David Levi, *Letters to Dr. Priestly, in Answer to Those He Addressed to the Jews; Inviting Them to an Amicable Discussion of the Evidences of Christianity,* 2d ed. (London, 1787), pp. 95, 14. For Priestley's response to Levi, see *Letters to the Jews: Part II: Occasioned by Mr. David Levi's Reply to the Former Letters* (Birmingham, 1787). For a temperate follow-up to their exchange, see James Bicheno, *A Friendly Address to the Jews . . . to Which Is Added, a Letter to Mr. D. Levi* (Providence, 1795). Priestley's analysis endured: see Thomas Thrush, *Letters to the Jews: Particularly Addressed to Mr. Levy of Florida* (York, 1829).

[82] Solomon de A. R., *The Reply of the Jews to the Letters Addressed to Them by Doctor Joseph Priestley* (Oxford, 1787), pp. 19–20, 24, 28–31, 32.

[83] Priestley, *Discourses on the Evidence,* p. 154.

thing bears a face, you see."[84] Thomas Moore tinkered ironically with the suggestion that the Irish were Jews, that the lost wandering tribe had settled there.[85] The English themselves could be cast as Jews. In 1779, Walpole took no pleasure in the confirmation of his prediction that the war with America would drag on. "I do not ambition being a Jeremiah, though my countrymen are so like the Jews."[86]

These ubiquitous Jews occupy the most elite positions in literature and politics. They invade the center of the metropolis and people the countryside. This isn't the fabled statistically disproportionate representation of those of the Jewish persuasion or race or nation or tribe. But it is about real Jews, if you like; for the gloss on Jew that points to such abhorrent traits as miserliness is perfectly real. It is one way the category *Jew* is given salience, one way social actors oriented themselves to their world. When that ever charitable Parson Holland reviled one of his Christian neighbors as "a perfect Jew,"[87] when a correspondent attributed "the cheating habits of Jews" to Americans,[88] they still trafficked in contempt.

But this contempt could boomerang. One Jewish writer conceded that "Jews are fond of money; but a fondness for money is so universal a passion amongst all ranks of society, especially in a large commercial nation, that it would at first seem strange that any one class of men should be considered as exclusively governed by it": so wasn't contempt for Jews a displaced anxiety about immersion in commerce?[89] If Jews were contemptible in seeking money in unproductive ways, mused the *Anti-Jacobin Review*, they weren't alone; Christians too

---

[84] *Fortunes of Nigel* [1822], in Walter Scott, *Waverley Novels*, 48 vols. (Edinburgh, 1829–1833), 27:177.

[85] Thomas Moore, *Memoirs of Captain Rock, the Celebrated Irish Chieftain, with Some Account of His Ancestors*, 5th ed. (London, 1824), pp. 7–8.

[86] Walpole to Horace Mann, 16 June 1779, *The Yale Edition of Horace Walpole's Correspondence*, ed. W. S. Lewis, 48 vols. (New Haven, CT: Yale University Press, 1937–1983), 24:484.

[87] *Paupers and Pig Killers: The Diary of William Holland, a Somerset Parson 1799–1818*, ed. Jack Ayres (Gloucester: Alan Sutton, 1984), p. 40 [23 June 1800]; see too *Diary*, p. 180 [25 October 1809], and *The Journal of the Rev. William Bagshaw Stevens*, ed. Georgina Galbraith (Oxford: Clarendon, 1965), p. 158 [22 May 1794].

[88] Thomas MacDonald to Lord Grenville, 24 October 1800, in Historical Manuscripts Commission, *Report on the Manuscripts of J. B. Fortescue, Esq., Preserved at Dropmore*, 10 vols. (London, 1892–1927), 6:359.

[89] Barnard Van Oven, *An Appeal to the British Nation on Behalf of the Jews* (London, 1830), p. 44. See too Basil Montagu, *A Letter to Henry Warburton, Esq. M.P. upon the Emancipation of the Jews*, 2d ed. (London, 1833), p. 16.

would have to plead guilty.[90] Marvelling at the baroque idiocies of the law, Bentham drily noted, "To strain at a gnat, and swallow a camel, is a character not peculiar to the Jewish Lawyers."[91] Now it's not some invidious *they* serving as the object of contempt; it's a group identified as *we*. Well might Gisborne counsel his fellows to relax their savage contempt for Jews: when they looked in the mirror, they all too often found Jews peering back.

## DRAMATIC AND MELODRAMATIC BLACKS

Blacks too were inspected on stage and in fiction and credited with superhuman virtues. Here too a syndrome that begins specifically as racist contempt for blacks spins free, just as gender spins free from biological men and women, just as Jewishness spins free from Jews. So people can direct racist contempt against the whites officially at the top of the racial hierarchy: not by urging that whites have their own characteristic vices, but by urging that the traits associated with blacks actually are found in whites. I suppose this qualifies as democratization or equality of a melancholy sort.

One earnestly uplifting primer offered the history of an "honest negro" sagely inclined to take racism as a parochial affection for the local color. "In some parts of the world I have seen men of a yellow hue, in others of a copper colour, and all have the foolish vanity to despise their fellow-creatures as infinitely inferior to themselves."[92] The Negro's narrative, chock full of valiant struggle against wild animals and a happy life with innocently different customs— "We negroes, whom you treat as savages, have different manners and different opinions"[93]— offered stirring lessons in fraternity to its wide-eyed readers. It was lifted wholesale and reprinted as historical fact in an anti-slavery tract.[94]

Years before she sanitized the Jews in *Harrington*, Maria Edgeworth set out to redeem the African slaves of Jamaica. "The Grateful Negro"

[90] *Anti-Jacobin Review* (February 1811) 38:182.

[91] *A Comment on the Commentaries* [1774–1776?], in Jeremy Bentham, *A Comment on the Commentaries and A Fragment on Government*, ed. J. H. Burns and H. L. A. Hart (London: Athlone Press, 1977), p. 245 n. d.

[92] Thomas Day, *The History of Sandford and Merton, a Work Intended for the Use of Children*, 7th ed., 3 vols. (London, 1795), 3:234–35.

[93] Day, *Sandford and Merton*, 3:238.

[94] *The Negro: A Sketch of the Birth and Education of an African Indian*, 5th ed. (Salop, 1822), pp. 6–48.

of 1802 offers a cursory tour through a familiar terrain. Its cruel Mr.
Jefferies scoffs, "You are partial to negroes; but even you must allow
they are a race of beings naturally inferior to us."[95] Benevolent Mr.
Edwards purchases Caesar and his dearly beloved wife Clara from Jefferies. Awestruck by this bonanza, Caesar is unwilling to cooperate
with a slave uprising. "The principle of gratitude conquered every
other sensation. . . . His heart beat high at the idea of recovering his
liberty: but he was not to be seduced from his duty, not even by this
delightful hope. . . ."[96] Edgeworth tightens the screws by having poor
superstitious Caesar believe that a sorceress has killed his wife but can
bring her back to life—if he cooperates with the uprising. Still, he
won't budge. "The conflict in his mind was violent: but his sense of
gratitude and duty could not be shaken by hope, fear, or ambition;
nor could it be vanquished by love."[97] He pretends to yield to the
sorceress, but zips off to warn his beloved master and save the day. So
Caesar's virtues make him the perfectly submissive, obedient, and
trustworthy slave. An appropriately paternalistic slavery, a plantation
headed up by Edwards instead of Jeffries, is apparently just fine: so
Edgeworth finds it painless to suggest that Caesar is doing his duty in
resisting the uprising.

    In Prince Hoare's *The Prize* of 1793, Juba is suffused with the same
unearthly gratitude:

> You care of money, care no more,
> No tink if you be rich or poor,
>    My mind employ;
> Me stay with you; no sorry, no!
> And where away my Massa go,
>    Go poor black boy.
> You good to me, dat keepy here,
> No, Massa! dat you never fear;
>    Long time destroy:
> You know death kill, but leave one part
> He never kill de loving heart
>    Of poor black boy.[98]

---

[95] "The Grateful Negro" [1802], in Edgeworth, *Tales and Novels,* 2:404.
[96] "Grateful Negro," in *Tales and Novels,* 2:412.
[97] "Grateful Negro," in *Tales and Novels,* 2:417.
[98] Prince Hoare, *The Prize, or, 2, 5, 3, 8* (Dublin, 1793), p. 6.

This inauspicious lyric was deemed good enough to make it into an anthology of popular songs.[99]

Frederick Reynolds's *Laugh When You Can* of 1799 treated its audiences to another heroically grateful slave. Delville has emancipated Sambo, but the latter remains incurably devoted to his former master's interests:

> DELVILLE. Psha!—go where I ordered you, sir; and for the future no impertinence, Sambo:—cease to interfere in matters that don't concern you.
>
> SAMBO. Nay, but this, sir—
>
> DELVILLE. How! do you demur?—recollect who you are.
>
> SAMBO. I do—I am your slave.
>
> DELVILLE. No—not my slave—I gave you liberty.
>
> SAMBO. You did, Sir; and that made me your slave.—Gratitude has bound me faster to you than all the chains of Africa! 'Tis now fifteen years since you brought me to England; during which time you have fostered me, educated me, and treated me more as a brother than a servant!—and now, when I warn you of your danger, you call it impertinence!—Ah, sir!—rather say 'tis selfishness; for my fate is so involved with yours, that if your heart bleeds, Sambo's will break, I'm sure.[100]

This is gratitude melting into a communion of interests and identity: love by any other name. But it's a love requiring no alteration whatever in Delville's identity, total self-abnegation in Sambo's. Enslaved, the blacks are slaves; freed, they remain slaves anyway. It's a perpetual motion machine of deference and subordination.

One last take on this trope, repeated as ploddingly as that of the publicly penny-pinching but privately openhanded Jew, comes from Thomas Morton's 1816 play, *The Slave*. Captain Clifton of the English army winds his way back to Surinam to wed the slave Zelinda, by whom he has fathered a child. The heroically noble Gambia, in love with Zelinda, wants revenge on Clifton, but to serve his beloved Zelinda he saves Clifton from insurrectionary slaves. The governor

---

[99] *Crosby's Modern Songster, Being a Selection of the Most Approved Songs Airs &c. from the Late Operas with Many Favorite Songs, Sung at the Different Places of Public Entertainment* (London, 179–), pp. 54–55.

[100] Frederick Reynolds, *Laugh When You Can* [1799], in *Modern Theatre*, ed. Inchbald, 2:151.

offers Clifton the right to emancipate one slave, and he chooses
Gambia.

> GAMBIA. (*Electrified at his name being pronounced, becomes violently
> agitated.*)—Free! a man! let me control this strong emotion! it will
> not be!—thou open, liberal air!—thou teeming, bounteous
> earth!—thou interminable expanse of heaven!—thou sponta-
> neous wilderness of nature!—thou art mine! all, all are mine! for I
> am nature's free-born child! the tongues of angels, to pour forth
> the gratitude of a heart, swelling with its dignities! bursting with its
> joys! alas! I am unfit for thanks or converse! a few moments, spare
> me—Generous Briton! prophetic be my tongue! when thro' thy
> country's zeal, the all-searching sun shall dart his rays in vain, to
> find a slave in Afric—[101]

But enough of these spastic paroxysms of eloquence. Gambia's day in
the sunshine of freedom is short-lived. Imprisoned for a $500 debt,
Clifton is mysteriously freed, because someone pays the bond. Of
course it is Gambia, who has sold himself back into slavery.

> CLIFTON. Amazed, oppressed, what shall I say—how act? Oh, I were un-
> worthy the name of man, did I suffer this generous sacrifice! And is
> that the being with whom the proud European denies fellowship?
> if we are not brothers, let the white man blush that he is alien to
> the blood that mantles in that noble breast.[102]

Ambitious with his dramatic trowel, lavishly spreading it on thick, Morton isn't through. Gambia proceeds to win over a villain about to rape
Zelinda with further death-defying stunts of acrobatic self-immolation.

Actual black slaves were credited with the same elevated sentiments
of gratitude. George Pinckard, a student of the West Indies, described
the Spendlove estate—its name suggests we are dealing with allegory,
but it's presented as straightforwardly factual—where the master was
so benevolent that his slaves were attached "to his person and his
interest by the secure ties of affection and gratitude." Like Caesar,
they "voluntarily offered to lay down their lives" to defend their beloved master against a slave insurrection.[103] Modulating the point

---

[101] Thomas Morton, *The Slave* (London, 1816), pp. 35–36.
[102] Morton, *Slave*, p. 44.
[103] George Pinckard, *Notes on the West Indies*, 3 vols. (London, 1806), 1:367; see too
2:204–9.

slightly, Coleridge took gratitude to be the rightful stance of slaves. "You are always talking of the *rights* of the Negros," he chided one interlocutor; "as a rhetorical mode of stimulating the people of England *here*, I don't object, but I utterly condemn your frantic practice of declaiming about their Rights to the Blacks." This might sound like the not-in-front-of-the-children motif, the strictures against offering the lower orders toxic nourishment, truths better kept veiled. Officially, though, it's different. "They ought to be forcibly reminded of the state in which their brethren in Africa still are, and taught to be thankful for the Providence which has placed them within means of grace."[104] Capture, the long march, the middle passage, the ordeals of slavery: all are vindicated as the exceedingly mysterious way savages were brought to the true Christian faith. What greater boon? What more suitable reason for gratitude?

How do these hugely grateful blacks compare with the hugely generous Jews? Scratch a Jew's flinty exterior, counsels one string of literary works, and you discover a fetching and utterly opposite interior. But the renditions of these blacks don't depend on any such contrived use of public and private. The slaves hide no virtues under vicious masks. They wear their virtue on their sleeves. Yet that virtue, grateful submission, is precisely the virtue defining a good slave. So these slaves are not the moral cretins paraded for the reader's supercilious delectation in the pages of Burchell's tour of southern Africa, the ones so hopelessly unresponsive to moral considerations that the translator balked at putting questions to them. But their moral sensibilities are contorted, all virtues but one atrophied, that one cancerously expansive. Learn the astonishing hidden facts about Jews and realize that they're not miserly moneylenders at all, but legitimate candidates for warm fellow-feeling, even for self-reproach at Christian stinginess. Learn the transparently open facts about blacks and realize that they're perfect candidates for slavery. All they need is warm if firm treatment from a benevolent paternalist, not nasty whippings.

Not everyone took this view. I suspect that *The Blackamoor Washed White* didn't offer such edifying lessons in deference.[105] Comedy

---

[104] *Table Talk*, in *The Collected Works of Samuel Taylor Coleridge*, ed. Kathleen Coburn, Bart Winer, and others, in progress (Princeton, NJ: Princeton University Press, 1969–), 14(1):386 [8 June 1833].

[105] *Reminiscences of Henry Angelo*, 2 vols. (London, 1830), 2:253.

aside, in 1833, Legion embraced a slave insurrection. "There is not a colonial witness who does not, (when it is convenient) swear to the brutal ignorance of the slave," he admitted; "but now we learn that this poor, humble, degraded outcast from human nature, can be actuated by the same high-minded feeling which associates Hampden and Russell with the proudest recollections of our domestic history," with Washington and Bolivar, with the tenacious pursuit "of disinterested patriotism."[106] This formulation has the same structure as that of the secretly generous Jewish miser: the blacks' real virtues, disguised by colonial cant, equip them for starring roles in the proudest moments of English history. But Legion's voice was drowned out in a din.

So, too, some blacks on stage raise different dilemmas. Consider the plight of one black actor, Ira Aldridge, dubbed the African Roscius after the great classical Roman comic actor. (Garrick and William Henry West Betty earned the name before Aldridge, who confusingly was also called Keene.) *John Bull* was taken with his Gambia.[107] The *Morning Post* embraced his talent as a sign of what educated blacks could accomplish; the *Dramatic Magazine* was pleased with his Othello.[108]

Others were decidedly unimpressed. "Owing to the shape of his lips," pronounced the *Times,* "it is utterly impossible for him to pronounce English in such a manner as to satisfy even the unfastidious ears of the gallery."[109] The shape of his lips: lodging his inadequacies in physiology guaranteed that no political agency could redeem him. Before being taken with the African Roscius's Gambia, *John Bull* reprinted what purported to be a letter from him: "MISSA NUSPAPER BRINTER.—I hab ver glad gif sudh satifac genral for my blaying Jakesbeer and other pards of drammee, and I bow greed many danks particleer Otello."[110] *Figaro in London,* always attentive to the London stage, was irritated by "a stupid looking, thick lipped, ill formed African calling himself the African Roscius," "nothing but an ordinary

[106] *A Second Letter from Legion to His Grace the Duke of Richmond* (London, 1833), p. 101.

[107] *John Bull* (25 February 1827) 7(324):62.

[108] *Morning Post* (December 1825), quoted in Herbert Marshall and Mildred Stock, *Ira Aldridge: The Negro Tragedian* (London: Rockliff, 1958), pp. 67–68; *Dramatic Magazine* (1 July 1829), quoted in Marshall and Stock, *Ira Aldridge,* p. 84.

[109] *Times* (11 October 1825), quoted in Marshall and Stock, *Ira Aldridge,* pp. 61–62.

[110] *John Bull* (3 December 1826) 6(312):390.

*Niger,*" and was incredulous that anyone could think a black skin could qualify him to play Othello.[111] A handbill was posted defending Aldridge and denouncing the "base and unmanly attempts" to chase him from the stage.[112] Weeks later, *Figaro* rejoiced in "having hunted the Nigger from the boards of Covent Garden" and at least consigning him and his disgusting displays to a less reputable theater.[113]

Could the African Roscius do a credible job playing Othello? I take it that's a question about his talent, not the shape of his lips or the color of his skin. Or so it is for us. (We hope.) Yet credibility has a history, too, and others had different concerns. Contemporaries were exercised by the question of Othello's color and race. Just how dark was a Moor? and did he qualify as black?[114] John Byng noted one waiter, "black, a very Othello, a quick intelligent fellow,"[115] and the character of one theatrical romp referred in passing to Othello as "the black devil."[116] Fanny Burney's *Camilla* offers an inadvertently hilarious staging of Shakespeare's play, with Othello's face "begrimed with a smoked cork" and Sir Sedley Clarendel, the fop, addressing Othello as "Poor Blacky!" and "honest Mungo" from the audience.[117] "Othello," opined *Blackwood's,* "beyond all doubt, was a blackamoor."[118] (Beyond all doubt: but what's a blackamoor?) Others too were happy to enlist Othello as a black.[119]

---

[111] *Figaro in London* (22 September 1832) 1(42):168.

[112] Crito, "The African Roscius to the Public" [6 April 1833], quoted in Marshall and Stock, *Ira Aldridge,* p. 118.

[113] *Figaro in London* (27 April 1833) 2(73):68.

[114] For background, see Jack D'Amico, *The Moor in English Renaissance Drama* (Tampa: University of South Florida Press, 1991).

[115] John Byng, *The Torrington Diaries,* ed. C. Bruyn Andrews, 4 vols. (London: Eyre & Spottiswoode, 1934–1938), 2:179 [13 June 1790].

[116] *Poor Covent Garden! or, A Scene Rehearsed* (London, 1792), p. 11.

[117] Fanny Burney, *Camilla, or A Picture of Youth* [1796], ed. Edward A. Bloom and Lillian D. Bloom (Oxford: Oxford University Press, 1983), pp. 318, 323.

[118] *Blackwood's Edinburgh Magazine* 33(203):132. For *moorish* as black, see *Letters of the Late Ignatius Sancho, an African,* 5th ed. (London, 1803; reprint ed. London: Dawsons of Pall Mall, 1968), pp. xvi (of reprint preface), v, 136, 156, 218, 221, 294.

[119] Haslewood, *Secret History,* 2:168; Mary Russell Mitford, *Our Village,* 5 vols. (London, 1824–1832), 4:13–15; Benjamin Disraeli, *Vivian Grey* [1826–1827], ed. Herbert van Thal (London: Cassell, 1968), p. 6; William Hone, *The Table Book,* 2 vols. (London, 1827–1828; reprint ed. Detroit: Gale Research Co., 1966), 1:181; Macaulay to Mrs. Edward Cropper, 3 October 1834, *The Letters of Thomas Babington Macaulay,* ed. Thomas Pinney, 6 vols. (Cambridge: Cambridge University Press, 1974–1981), 3:77; Maria Edgeworth to Rachel Lazarus, 11 July 1837, *Education of the Heart,* p. 298.

Charles Lamb wasn't so sure. In *Tales from Shakespear,* he thought Othello was black.[120] Several years later, he adopted a more complicated position. True, it was inspiring to read the play and imagine Othello as black. But "the Moors are now well enough known to be by many shades less unworthy of a white woman's fancy"; Shakespeare had inadequate knowledge of foreign lands. And it was anything but inspiring to watch a staging of the play with a black Othello, where every viewer must "find something extremely revolting in the courtship and wedded caresses of Othello and Desdemona. . . ."[121] Coleridge, too, assailed dramatic tradition. At one lecture, "Mr. C. ridiculed the idea of making Othello a negro, he was a gallant Moor, of royal blood, combining a high sense of Spanish and Italian feeling" and a "noble nature"; at another, he insisted that Shakespeare couldn't have "so utterly ignorant as to make a barbarous *Negro* plead Royal Birth," when everyone knew Negroes were known only as slaves.[122] Whether swayed by new information about foreign countries, shuddering antipathy to interracial romance, or suspicions about the emotional capacities and ignoble nature of blacks, the distinguished actor Edmund Kean offered a dramatic innovation in these years, portraying Othello in light brown skin.[123]

Had Shakespeare only had the decency and foresight to make Othello another incarnation of gratitude—he might have needed a different plot—these sentiments wouldn't have arisen. It would be rash to claim that this was the only virtue one could get away with attributing to blacks onstage, but it does surface with depressing regularity. Again, it doesn't subvert any hostile preconceptions about blacks, as say crediting Jews with splendid philanthropy does. It only perfects them in their allotted role as underlings.

[120] *Tales from Shakespear* [1807, text of 1809], in *The Works of Charles and Mary Lamb,* ed. E. V. Lucas, 6 vols. (New York: Macmillan, 1913), 3:213–15.

[121] "On the Tragedies of Shakespeare" [1811, text of 1818], in *Works of Charles and Mary Lamb,* 1:125.

[122] *1813 Lectures on Shakespeare and Education,* in *Works of Coleridge,* 5(1):555; *1818–1819 Lectures on Shakespeare,* in *Works of Coleridge,* 5(2):314. See too *Table Talk,* in *Works of Coleridge,* 14(1):25 [6 January 1823]; *Diary, Reminiscences, and Correspondence of Henry Crabb Robinson,* ed. Thomas Sadler, 2 vols. (Boston, 1869), 1:198 [23 December 1810]. Seventeenth-century critic Thomas Rymer, not yet flattened by the burdens of Shakespeare's canonical status, caustically took Othello's being black as a sign of sheer dramatic incompetence: *The Critical Works of Thomas Rymer,* ed. Curt A. Zimansky (New Haven, CT: Yale University Press, 1956), pp. 131–64 [1692].

[123] *Othello,* ed. Julie Hankey (Bristol: Bristol Classical Press, 1987), pp. 57, 222.

Reverse the sexes, though, and Lamb's uneasiness with interracial romance could fuel comedy. Fox didn't just look Jewish and didn't just deal with Jews in his Jerusalem chamber. He was "remarkably black," as Walpole put it—though naturally this dark complexion didn't implicate his race—and suffered the indignity of being the stooge in an arranged marriage that was never in the cards. Anxious as always about his gambling debts, Fox was imposed upon by a woman who persuaded him that she could win him the hand of a newly arrived Jamaican heiress worth £80,000. But she had no such heiress to deliver and eventually put Fox off with the claim that the heiress was of mixed race.[124]

So the story went, anyway: Samuel Foote seized on it in his *Cozeners* of 1778. Toby Aircastle (Fox) won't marry Betsey Blossom, even though he loves her, because he's waiting for a promised woman "as rich as a Jew" from the Indies.[125] Mrs. Fleecem, out to swindle Aircastle's family, suggests that maybe Aircastle's complexion should be darkened a bit so that the fair lady in question will find him familiar. The great moment arrives and Aircastle approaches Marianne, in bed in a dark room.

TOBY. . . . —Miss—Miss.

MARIANNE. Who be dat dere.

TOBY. I—dat dere; one may find out by her tongue she is a foreigner.[126]

Decades later, one woman remembered that "the laugh was universal so soon as the black woman appeared."[127] The laugh is accentuated because Aircastle isn't yet in on the joke. Foote is shrewd enough to heighten the tension, to delay the resolution:

TOBY. . . . may I crave leave to kiss your lily white hand?

MARIANNE. Yes.

TOBY. On my knees let me thank you, fairest creature—her skin is vast soft—they be wonderful pretty things I have brought you—a'n't you mighty curious to see them?

MARIANNE. Yes.

---

[124] I've combined the different accounts in *Last Journals of Walpole,* 1:269–70 [December 1773] and *The Journal of Sir Walter Scott,* ed. W. E. K. Anderson (Oxford: Clarendon, 1972), pp. 471–72 [9 May 1828].

[125] Samuel Foote, *The Cozeners* (London, 1778), p. 50.

[126] Foote, *Cozeners,* p. 66.

[127] *Journal of Scott,* p. 472 [9 May 1828].

TOBY. May I draw the curtain a bit, only just to give you a glimpse?
MARIANNE. Yes.
TOBY. So I will—I should be glad to take a peep at her too; she is mighty
   agreeable body; does not talk much, indeed, but is vast sensible,
   whatever she says—this, I believe, is the string—I wonder if she is
   as handsome as Betsey Blossom—gad, if she is, Miss Blossom must
   look out for somebody else I can tell her. . . .[128]

He fumbles along, awkwardly parading his gifts, until he finally notices what the audience has been tittering at all along:

TOBY. . . . —hey! what is this? Lord have mercy on me, she is turned all
   of a sudden as black as a crow—sure as can be a judgment for
   forsaking poor Betsey.
MARIANNE. Massa, won't you come here?
TOBY. Not I.
MARIANNE. I come to you.
TOBY. The devil you will; you must run pretty fast then—keep off me—
   holloa house; stop the black thing that is hard at my— [Exit[129]

Unlike the lecherous slaveholders, like some of their critics, Aircastle is disgusted at the thought of making love to a black woman. Unlike Lamb's imagined audience, unanimously disgusted at a white woman's caressing a black man, Foote's audience is laughing uproariously. Doubtless both disgust and laughter betray nervous tension. And perhaps *Othello* could have been successfully staged as a comic romp, *The Cozeners* as a sordid tragedy. But again it mattered enormously whether a white man was taking sexual possession of a black woman or a black man was taking sexual possession of a white woman.

### AN OVERABUNDANCE OF BLACKS AND SLAVES

Let's turn to detecting blacks and slaves in the most unlikely places, of seeing their faces, too, in the mirror. Jewish faces could shimmer into black faces at a moment's notice. The Dahomans of Africa practiced circumcision, reported one traveller.[130] Mocking the derisory success of the Society for Conversion of the Jews, atheist Robert Taylor de-

---

[128] Foote, *Cozeners,* p. 67.
[129] Foote, *Cozeners,* p. 68.
[130] Archibald Dalzel, *The History of Dahomy, an Inland Kingdom of Africa; Compiled from Authentic Memoirs* (London, 1793), p. xviii.

nounced those who would feel for "a quintave of tricky, obscene ourang-outangs, who have fingered *de monish*" and claimed to adopt Christianity.[131] Like Jews, blacks and slaves were liberally honeycombed through British society. The status of slavery was tied intimately to the contemporary understanding of race, or anyway the black race, so that "I'll be no man's negro" meant "I will be no man's slave."[132]

Unsurprisingly, one could smear one's opponents as black. Exasperated in one of his running disputes with Henry Hunt—the left was given to bitterly fratricidal divisions—Cobbett branded him a "FOOL-LIAR": "The fellow has as much *low cunning* as any animal that ever existed, and his *disregard of truth* is equal to that of a Negro. . . . Your FOOL-LIAR seems to be, in this respect, upon *a perfect equality with the Negroes*."[133] Here we see a wedge driven between the racial population and the traits associated with them, opening the possibility that others possessing the traits can be described as black. Cobbett drives the wedge to hurl unmitigated contempt at his opponent. He may be playing on Hunt's business selling shoe polish, "matchless blacking," which led to his being called "the Blacking Man."[134]

Others drove the same wedge in more tortured ways, wondering whether their fellows, even they themselves, might qualify as black or as slaves. What point was being pressed by the cartoonist displaying women dressed in the height of fashion as black apes fighting each other?[135] Less obscure, artists and politicians sometimes described themselves as black. "I have worked like a negro," protested Southey, contemplating the huge stack of books he had to review.[136] "I am 'a pitiful-hearted negro' and can't keep resentment," Byron told his publisher in explaining that he could no longer hold a grudge.[137] "All 'worky, worky' as the Negro says," recorded Thomas Moore in his

---

[131] *Lion* (28 August 1829) 4(9):264.

[132] Pierce Egan, *Grose's Classical Dictionary of the Vulgar Tongue, Revised and Corrected* (London, 1823), s.v. *Negroe*.

[133] *Cobbett's Two-Penny Trash; or, Politics for the Poor* (April 1832) 2(9):200–201.

[134] Belchem, *'Orator' Hunt*, pp. 168–71.

[135] *BMC* no. 15609 [1828?].

[136] Southey to Miss Barker, 1804, *Selections from the Letters of Robert Southey*, ed. John Wood Warter, 4 vols. (London, 1856), 1:254.

[137] Byron to John Murray, 24 October 1822, *Letters and Journals*, 10:18. Note too Byron to Murray, 4 September 1817, *Letters and Journals*, 5:262; John Clare to George Darley, 3 September 1827, *The Letters of John Clare*, ed. Mark Storey (Oxford: Clarendon, 1985), p. 398.

journal.[138] All worky, worky, as the Negro says, and as the Negro does: so as the Negro is. Wilberforce referred to Thomas Clarkson, fellow crusader against the slave trade, as "another white negro."[139] The point is not that these opponents of the slave trade sympathize with Negroes, but that their work in the cause is as unflagging, as uncompensated, as reviled as the work of slaves. And though I've uncovered no cases of the Scottish or English nations being cast as black, one of Moore's incisive poems played with Irish colonists turning into blacks.[140]

Prince William, though, did report that the Scottish highlanders "are in a more miserable state than the negroes in the West Indies."[141] Here's an assessment of comparative misery tied to a slightly different use of the mirror. Take the social status of *slave,* ostensively defined by the plight of those Caribbean blacks, and use it as a template in thinking about the plight of others in English society. Then, it turns out, slaves are everywhere. The comforting social distance between white resident of Britain and black resident of Jamaica collapses, with dizzying and dispiriting results.

Children were the slaves of parents, charged radicals. "The condition of a negro-slave in the West Indies, is in many respects preferable to that of the youthful son of a free-born European," held Godwin.[142] Mary Shelley, his daughter, affirmed the same cheerless view of the matter. "In my days," laments one of her characters, "the tender years of aristocratic childhood were yielded up to a capricious, unrelenting, cruel bondage, far beyond the measured despotism of Jamaica."[143] (Recall Godwin's rueful sense that a fearless equality between parent and child was not on offer.)

Lovers were slaves, too. In the curious concluding turn of his poetic defense of slavery, Boswell declared,

[138] *The Journal of Thomas Moore,* ed. Wilfred S. Dowden and others, 6 vols. (Newark: University of Delaware Press, 1983–1991), 4:1609 [10–12 July 1834].

[139] Wilberforce to Zachary Macaulay, 17 December 1804, in Robert Isaac Wilberforce and Samuel Wilberforce, *The Life of William Wilberforce,* 5 vols. (London, 1838), 3:198.

[140] "Paddy's Metamorphosis" [1833], in *Poetical Works of Moore,* pp. 646–47.

[141] Prince William to George III, 4 August 1785, *The Later Correspondence of George III,* ed. A. Aspinall, 5 vols. (Cambridge: Cambridge University Press, 1962–1970), 1:175.

[142] William Godwin, *The Enquirer: Reflections on Education, Manners, and Literature: in a Series of Essays* (London, 1797), p. 67.

[143] "The Mourner" [1829], in Mary Wollstonecraft Shelley, *Collected Tales and Stories,* ed. Charles E. Robinson (Baltimore, MD: Johns Hopkins University Press, 1976), p. 86.

> For Slavery there must ever be,
> While we have Mistresses like thee![144]

Mocking the efforts of one women's antislavery association, *John Bull* leered, "Dear ladies—sweet ladies—converting ladies—ye who are used to have devoted—not degraded—slaves every day at your feet, content your gentle hearts by converting *them* into free labourers as soon as you please, but 'do you leave the niggers alone.' "[145] The passage doesn't simply repeat that boilerplate conservative view, suspiciously reminiscent of Rousseau, that actually domestic women are more powerful than submissive men. In claiming that their male lovers are slaves, it frames power and submission in specific and unsettling terms. This was, after all, the same newspaper offering the extended rant against the prospect of black equality in 1935. No wonder they find themselves automatically suggesting, however weirdly, that lover-slaves be emancipated to serve as free laborers. I dare not pursue the metaphor.

Women too were slaves. "Was not the world a vast prison, and women born slaves?" asked Wollstonecraft in 1798.[146] Feisty Harriet Hawthorne rejects the marriage her father has arranged in a novel of that same year: "Restrained and trammelled by laws and customs, women are already slaves to man; no privilege is left for them, but that of choosing their prison and jailor; and this small indulgence I am not inclined to forego."[147] One correspondent in a radical journal noted an eye-opening parallel: it was legal for masters to whip slaves and husbands to whip wives.[148]

---

[144] James Boswell, *No Abolition of Slavery; or The Universal Empire of Love: A Poem* (London, 1791), p. 24.

[145] *John Bull* (5 February 1832) 12(582):45.

[146] *The Wrongs of Women* [1798], in *The Works of Mary Wollstonecraft*, ed. Janet Todd and Marilyn Butler, assistant ed. Emma Rees-Mogg, 7 vols. (London: William Pickering, 1989), 1:88. See too Mary Hays, *Appeal to the Men of Great Britain in Behalf of Women* (London, 1798; reprint ed. New York: Garland, 1974), p. 277.

[147] Mary Ann Hanway, *Ellinor; or, The World as It Is*, 4 vols. (London, 1798; reprint ed. New York: Garland, 1974), 2:130–31.

[148] *Crisis* (24 August 1834), quoted in Anna Clark, *The Struggle for the Breeches: Gender and the Making of the British Working Class* (Berkeley, CA: University of California Press, 1995), p. 187. See too *Pioneer* (31 May 1834) no. 39, p. 383. On married women as slaves, see William Thompson, *Appeal of One Half the Human Race, Women, against the Pretensions of the Other Half, Men, to Retain Them in Political, and Thence in Civil and Domestic, Slavery; in Reply to a Paragraph of Mr. Mill's Celebrated "Article on Government"* (London, 1825), pp. 66–67.

To be a subject, not a citizen, was to be a slave. Or so radicals repeatedly charged in their boldest assault on the time-honored English constitution. "Some may probably think, and certain politicians assert, that poor men have neither the power, nor the right, to make laws. What is this, but to assert, that the poor man's portion in England is slavery?"[149] "EXCLUSION from suffrage," proclaimed Cartwright, "although not *visible on a man's person,* is as truly a *slave-mark,* as the *brand* on a Negro. . . ."[150]

We can distinguish two claims here. First, those excluded from the franchise are likely to be treated badly. One pamphleteer held that the sight of a crimp turning over his victims to serve in the military was worse than that of a newly arrived slave ship being unloaded.[151] (Jews were infamous for working as crimps: more of their undignified labor.[152]) The *Black Dwarf* held that "the treatment of the *poor,* I have frequently remarked, is in all countries nearly the same; and it matters not whether they are *called Negro Slaves,* or *British Freemen*": either way they were subject to capricious treatment.[153] Second, the putative slave-mark, exclusion from the suffrage, is a badge of inferiority, a public stamp of contempt. Apart from any consequences it gives rise to, it's a bit of pernicious political symbolism. Or that's the reading of the practice proposed by these radicals. These claims are run readily together. During the agitation over parliamentary reform, A Journeyman Whitesmith bewailed "the Boroughmongering tyrants" and their

[149] George Dyer, *The Complaints of the Poor People of England* (London, 1793; reprint ed. Oxford: Woodstock Books, 1990), p. 19. See too *The Trial of Joseph Gerrald, Delegate from the London Corresponding Society, to the British Convention: Before the High Court of Justiciary, at Edinburgh, on the 3d, 10th, 13th, and 14th of March, 1794 for Sedition,* rep. Mr. Ramsey (Edinburgh, 1794), p. 19.

[150] Cartwright, *English Constitution,* p. 124; see too pp. xvi, 405, and Cartwright to J. G. Lambton, 7–18 March 1821, in *Black Dwarf* (21 March 1821) 6(12):419–22. And see William Cobbett, *Advice to Young Men, and (Incidentally) to Young Women, in the Middle and Higher Ranks of Life* (London, 1829), §345; Cobbett, *Eleven Lectures on the French and Belgian Revolutions, and English Boroughmongering* (London, 1830), lec. 1, pp. 6–7; *Two-Penny Trash* (November 1831) 2(5):110–11.

[151] *Reflections on the Pernicious Custom of Recruiting by Crimps; and on Various Other Modes Now Practised in the British Army* (London, 1795), p. 14. See too Thomas Urquhart, *A Letter to W. Wilberforce, Esq. M.P. on the Subject of Impressment,* in *Pamphleteer* (1824) 24(48):390.

[152] *Real Life in London,* 1:177 n; Pierce Egan, *The Finish to the Adventures of Tom, Jerry, and Logic, in Their Pursuits through Life in and out of London* [1828] (London, 1887), p. 150.

[153] *Black Dwarf* (3 July 1822) 9(1):8.

oppressive rule. "Is there a Briton who has not, of late years, seen with regret and dismay, the boroughmongers grasping at every right—monopolizing every privilege—and treating our persons, our sufferings, and our petitions, with ridicule and contempt?"[154] (To which one would have to respond, yes, millions of them didn't see it that way.) But it's appropriate that the two claims are run together. This isn't logical confusion; it's a reminder of the view so powerfully articulated by Henry Granville, son of King Naimbanna, that once a group's social status is degraded, they can be treated abominably.

## Workers, Slaves, and the Dignity of Labor

Children, lovers, women, and subjects: they comprise the overwhelming bulk of Britain's population, worse yet many individuals enslaved in one role after another. In short, social critics discovered an embarrassing wealth of slaves. Not just embarrassing, but mortifying: for workers, too, were routinely described as slaves, raising debilitating challenges to the campaign for the dignity of labor. "It is one of the pernicious effects of slavery," warned Southey, "that wherever it exists, labour is thought degrading to a free man."[155]

That British workers were slaves, even worse off than slaves, was a weighty bit of artillery in the proslavery arsenal. Slaves' work, reported one writer, "however strange it may seem, is not so hard as that of most of the laboring poor in Britain."[156] "Sure I am," harrumphed another, "that the labourer in England, who is the *slave* of *necessity*, serves a harder task-master than the African finds in the West-Indies." No slave faced the toxins of the new industrial workplace; no slave was left to die in the streets.[157] Overwhelmed by a lavish party thrown by one colony's governor for the slaves, just another happy moment in their beatific lives, Pinckard sighed, "I bent a thought to Europe, and

---

[154] *Poor Man's Guardian* (3 September 1831) 1(9):70.

[155] Robert Southey, *History of Brazil*, 3 vols. (London, 1810–1819), 2:637.

[156] Robert Norris, *Memoirs of the Reign of Bossa Ahadee, King of Dahomey, an Inland Country of Guiney* (London, 1789; reprint ed. London: Frank Cass, 1968), p. 177.

[157] Gilbert Francklyn, *Observations Occasioned by the Attempts Made in England to Effect the Abolition of the Slave Trade* (London, 1789), p. 11. See too R. C. Dallas, *The History of the Maroons, from Their Origin to the Establishment of Their Chief Tribe at Sierra Leone*, 2 vols. (London, 1803), 2:407.

wished that the tattered and indigent sons of liberty could feel as
happy."[158] *Fraser's* cautioned its readers against the brigades of petitioners seeking an end to colonial slavery. "Before you lend your aid
to these artful and designing men, it will be wise to pause. An immense population are at present in the enjoyment of far greater tem-
poral comforts than the British peasant. Poverty and crime are
scarcely known amongst them—at least crimes of a deep dye—but
this body are termed slaves!"[159] What's in a word?

Intent on deploring the lot of those same poor workers, radicals
too suggested that workers and slaves were hard to distinguish. An
English servant was "in several intelligible and distinct particulars"
better off than a slave in the West Indies, conceded Godwin. Still, the
servant was essentially a slave.[160] (With a different tone, to different
political ends, the editor of *John Bull* pressed the same point in one of
his novels, where a servant refers to "the niggers in the West Hingies,
who are rather better off than we" in wondering about independence.[161]) Cobbett derided the humanitarians fretting about Jamaican slaves. "If they can busy themselves with compassion for the negroes, while they uphold the system that makes the labourers of
England more wretched, and beyond all measure more wretched,
than any negro slaves are, or ever were, or ever can be, they are unworthy of any thing but our contempt."[162] "Our own poor fellow
countryman is a still greater slave, in reality, than the purchased negro," charged the *Poor Man's Guardian;* if the masters owned the
bodies of their workers, not just their labor, they would take better
care of them.[163]

Conservative paternalists adopted the same line. Southey indicted
"a new sort of slave-trade," that of workhouses and travelling preda-
tors supplying children to work in the factories: "When that system
was at its height, the slave-trade itself was scarcely more systematically
remorseless."[164] He described children chimney sweeps as "the little

---

[158] Pinckard, *Notes,* 2:352.

[159] *Fraser's* (October 1830) 2(9):340–41.

[160] Godwin, *The Enquirer,* p. 211.

[161] Theodore Hook, *Maxwell,* 3 vols. (London, 1830), 2:288–89.

[162] William Cobbett, *Rural Rides* [1830], ed. George Woodcock (Harmondsworth:
Penguin, 1985), p. 262; see too pp. 118, 127, 273, 406.

[163] *Poor Man's Guardian* (8 October 1831) 1(15):118. See too *Hone's Reformist Register*
(4 October 1817) 2(11):347–52; *Black Dwarf* (12 August 1818) 2(32):503.

[164] Robert Southey, *Essays, Moral and Political,* 2 vols. (London, 1832), 1:114–15
[1812].

slaves" and urged "abolishing the present trade."[165] (Soot was the villain, explained one writer contemplating the fate of a boy chimney sweep. "He partakes in some degree of the fate of the negro: we lose, in his sooty complexion, all sympathy with him as a fellow-creature. . . ."[166]) Surveying the industrial workplace, he seethed that England had been stuck with "being the white slaves of the rest of the world, and doing for it all its dirty work."[167] Underpaid workers, lamented one observer, "are by us abandoned to a precarious state of indigence (which an enslaved negro might regard with compassion)," providing further cause to reform the poor laws.[168]

Activists against the slave trade and slavery itself had to reject this analogy. Already written off as lunatic idealists, they couldn't very well shoulder a radical critique of wage labor, too, even if they'd wanted to. In 1788, one rebutted the view that slaves were better off than "English peasants": "Have peasants their eyes beat out, their bones broken, their flesh furrowed by the whip, their wives exposed to a bailiff's lust? Are they, without remedy, confined to any, the most unreasonable oppressive master? Are their wives and children taken from them, and sold to distant parts?"[169] In 1795, Granville Sharp responded to the usual litany by insisting on the equal protection of the laws and the poor's right to support from the parish.[170] Several decades later, responses tended more to outright blustering. "A Briton to compare the state of a West-Indian slave with that of an English freeman, and to give the former the preference!" exclaimed

---

[165] Robert Southey, *Essays*, 1:226 [1816].

[166] J. C. Hudson, *A Letter to the Mistresses of Families, on the Cruelty of Employing Children in the Odious, Dangerous, and Often Fatal Task of Sweeping Chimnies*, in *Pamphleteer* (1823) 22(44):409.

[167] Robert Southey, *Letters from England* [1807], ed. Jack Simmons (London: Cresset Press, 1951), p. 211. See too Southey to J. W. Warter, 23 January 1833, *New Letters of Southey*, 2:391; Southey to C. W. W. Wynn, 9 February 1833, *Letters*, ed. Warter, 4:328; Southey to Mrs. Septimus Hodson, 12 February 1833, *New Letters of Southey*, 2:395; Southey to John May, 1 March 1833, *The Letters of Robert Southey to John May 1797 to 1838* (Austin, TX: Jenkins Publishing Co., The Pemberton Press, 1976), p. 256.

[168] John Hill, *The Means of Reforming the Morals of the Poor, by the Prevention of Poverty; and A Plan for Meliorating the Condition of Parish Paupers, and Diminishing the Enormous Expence of Maintaining Them* (London, 1801), p. 11.

[169] James Ramsay ["Ramsey" on t.p.], *Objections to the Abolition of the Slave Trade, with Answers*, 2d ed. (London, 1788), pp. 47–48.

[170] Granville Sharp to Lord Bishop of London, President of the Society for the Conversion and Religious Instruction and Education of Negro Slaves in the West India Islands, 14 January 1795, in Prince Hoare, *Memoirs of Granville Sharp* (London, 1820), p. 391.

Wilberforce; "it is to imply an utter insensibility of the native feelings and moral dignity of man, no less than of the rights of Englishmen!"[171] He had toured the kingdom, reported one churchman, "and he lamented to see the distress of the English poor. But any attempt to compare the worst-treated of our peasantry with the worst-treated slaves, must be grounded either upon profound ignorance or incurable prejudice."[172]

"The greater part of the population of every country are in fact in some degree slaves in reality, though not in name," asserted the *Westminster Review,* attempting some bleak honesty.[173] This untoward parallel between black slaves and white workers threatened the tidy logic of race. In an article headlined, "TO THE WHITE SLAVES OF ENGLAND," the *Pioneer* addressed its working-class readers as "HELOTS!!" and urged them, feebly, "Hold up your abject heads; be manly and erect."[174] It threatened the masculinity of English workers, too, because dependence was a brand of effeminacy. It threatened the comfortable and comforting somnolence of dutifully loyal subjects. The young Coleridge was blunt: "A Poor Man is necessarily more or less a Slave."[175] Soon he hesitated: "Now I appeal to common sense," railed Coleridge, "whether to affirm that the slaves are as well off as our peasantry, be not the same as to assert that our peasantry are as bad off as negro-slaves? And whether if our peasantry believed it, they would not be inclined to rebel?"[176]

Perhaps they would. Perhaps radicals intended their identification of workers as slaves to rouse the sleepy workers, to incite them to political action. But why doesn't the identification yield a withering contempt for workers? Is there another implicit distinction here between human worth and social status, so that one could hold that

[171] William Wilberforce, *An Appeal to the Religion, Justice, and Humanity of the Inhabitants of the British Empire, in Behalf of the Negro Slaves in the West Indies,* new ed. (London, 1823), p. 34.

[172] Testimony of Rev. Joseph Orton, 24 September 1830, at Ipswich Anti-Slavery Meeting, in S. Strickland, *Negro Slavery Described by a Negro: Being the Narrative of Ashton Warner, a Native of St. Vincent's* (London, 1831), p. 81. See too John Jeremie, *Four Essays on Colonial Slavery* (London, 1831), p. 71; Henry Whiteley, *Three Months in Jamaica, in 1832: Comprising a Residence of Seven Weeks on a Sugar Plantation* (London, 1833), p. 22.

[173] *Westminster Review* (April 1827) 7(14):463.

[174] *Pioneer* (2 November 1833) no. 9, p. 65.

[175] *Lectures on Revealed Religion* [1795], in *Works of Coleridge,* 1:126.

[176] *The Watchman* (25 March 1796) no. 4, in *Works of Coleridge,* 2:140.

"negroes are slaves by nature"[177] but deny that white freeborn Englishmen are? But recall how blissfully plastic the concept of race is, the scathing suggestion from Carlile that cotton manufacturing was producing a new degraded race: at the very least, weren't these radicals playing with dynamite?

Consider the dilemma from the point of view of white male workers, desperately clutching whatever shreds of dignity they could, surrounded by undignified, even unholy, mirror images in another macabre political fun-house. They needed to distance themselves not just from slaves, but also from such effeminate wretches as man-milliners, from lowly apprentices and the like, from the desolate poor on the parish, some of them industriously plugging away in the workhouses. But couldn't they have struggled against the invidious beliefs and practices that defined those others as pariahs? Maybe they could have; doubtless some did; and I suppose only that larger struggle conceivably could be finally and definitively successful. But it also would have been heroically and even irresponsibly ambitious.

We're now in a better position to appreciate, or anyway appraise, Francis Place's startling suggestion that the experience of paying workers "produces an inward hatred of them." It's not merely that the cash nexus is a source of social discomfort, that it dissolves the pleasing illusions of domestic servants that they are beloved members of the family. It's that those workers publicly are likened to slaves. Whatever individual employers and workers happened to make of that assessment, it was a prominent part of the landscape, a bit of social context that helped fix the meaning of their actions and make sense of their emotions. However proud they want to be, these workers are tarred and feathered as slaves. It's a singularly short step to seeing them as black, to ascribing to them all the celebrated vicious qualities of Africans.

We're also in a better position to grasp the poignant stakes of the internal divisions among workers. I mean the sort castigated by Alexander Somerville, the radical who wondered why the artisan with long tails on his coat would look down on the humbler laborer with short tails, the engine-maker on the blacksmith. The recipe for producing self-respect and dignity here is brutally simple: evade cosmopolitan views; fix one's attention on a local comparison; make sure it's

[177] William Beckford [d. 1799], *A Descriptive Account of the Island of Jamaica*, 2 vols. (London, 1790), 2:382.

someone lower than oneself; then hold the underling in contempt and use him as a stepping stone to one's own newly elevated status. (And leave him, charitably, to do the same in turn if he can find someone even lower and get away with it. "Cringing and fawning to his superiors," noticed Bentham, "the same man is stiff and even insolent to his inferiors. Nothing is more frequently observed: nothing more natural. For the suffering to which he subjects himself in the one case, he makes amends by the enjoyment of the same kind which he gives himself in the other."[178]) So traversing the divide that Marx later articulated as the difference between a class in itself and a class for itself could never be a simple matter of articulating an account of shared objective interests. It would always have to be in part a matter of discreetly threading one's way through the emotional, cultural, and political minefield of struggles over dignity and contempt.

[178] *Deontology*, in Jeremy Bentham, *Deontology together with A Table of the Springs of Action and The Article on Utilitarianism*, ed. Amnon Goldworth (Oxford: Clarendon, 1983), p. 228 [1814]. Admirers of Gilbert and Sullivan will recall Dick Deadeye.

# STANDING

W HAT SHALL WE make of this endlessly ugly parade of contempt? We could adduce it as evidence for misanthropy, but misanthropy already enjoys plenty of robust support. Or we could ponder the mutilated individuals—both the recipients and dispensers of contempt—caught up in relations of contempt, their disfiguring psychic scars, their shattered or phony self-esteem. But this is to risk thinking of the emotions as invidiously private, sundered from the social practices and public expressions required to make sense of them. It is to forget their political stakes.

Instead, then, I want to explore the interface between enlightenment and contempt, the byzantine dilemmas created by the drive to transform lowly subjects into dignified citizens when all too many of those subjects were objects of contempt. For women and workers, Jews and blacks to emerge on the public stage as citizens, to win dignity and epistemic authority, to be able to participate in political debate and receive a respectful hearing, required more than obtaining the franchise. Their struggle for public standing, as I shall call it, may have been narrowly directed at the legal statutes defining voting rights.[1] But it was inevitably a much more freewheeling campaign against an ominously amorphous opponent, against the shabby treatment they suffered in one social setting after another and the sneers and jeers and contemptuous dismissals others had emotionally invested in that treatment.

Then again, to have a fighting chance in that struggle, to be struggling in the first place, is already to have won minimal public standing. I commence with a cautionary tale, that of a man brought down by charges of homosexuality decades before the love that dare not speak its name, centuries before Stonewall. Not that the British of this period lived before the "invention" of homosexuality. And they had plenty of contemptuous and disgusted names for it. But those caught in the act—if they weren't hanged—didn't campaign for tolerance or rights, didn't make an explicitly political issue of the visceral con-

---

[1] I have found suggestive Judith N. Shklar, *American Citizenship: The Quest for Inclusion* (Cambridge, MA: Harvard University Press, 1991).

tempt they suffered by publicly attacking the legitimacy of the authority wielded against them. Ashamed or angry, they silently withdrew.

## THE SAGA OF WILLIAM BECKFORD

We've encountered William Beckford twice before. He was the diarist crafting rhapsodies for patriarchal government and grateful subordination, bemoaning atheistical ravings and fearing the explosion of anarchy, rapine, and massacre, a couple of years before the French revolution. And he was the art collector unwilling to spend £3,000 on a canvas by Il Parmigiano, dubbing himself and the seller Jews for their haggling. Inheriting a huge Jamaican estate, he was reputed the single wealthiest man in England.[2] An Englishman who produced a sumptuous Arabian romance written in French, he enjoys a curious niche in the literary canon.[3] Gender, political conviction, and wealth conspired to make him a member of the conservative elite in good standing; for a time it looked as though he might prevail in a bid for noble title. But it was not to be.

Beckford's friends had worried about his sexual inclinations. In 1781, Lady Hamilton urged him on in his "important struggle": "What is it for? No less than *honor, reputation,* and all that an honest and noble Soul holds most dear, while Infamy, eternal infamy (my soul freezes while I write the word) attends the giving way to the soft alluring of a criminal passion."[4] Her soul must have frozen a few years later. In 1784, Beckford was discovered *in flagrante* with a young man—or, as Beckford would recall him, "that cowardly effeminate fool William Courtenay."[5] Or was he? Maybe he had been thrashing

---

[2] C. A. G. Goede, *The Stranger in England; or, Travels in Great Britain,* 3 vols. (London, 1807), 3:73; William Hone, *The Every-Day Book,* 2 vols. (London, 1827; reprint ed. Detroit: Gale Research Co., 1967), 2:1371.

[3] Beckford, *Vathek with The Episodes of Vathek,* ed. Guy Chapman, 2 vols. (Cambridge: Constable & Company; Houghton Mifflin, 1929).

[4] Lady Hamilton to William Beckford, 9 January 1781, in J. W. Oliver, *The Life of William Beckford* (London: Oxford University Press, 1932), p. 55.

[5] *The Journal of William Beckford in Portugal and Spain 1787–1788,* ed. Boyd Alexander (London: Rupert Hart-Davis, 1954), p. 61 [4 June 1787]. The historiography of the charge against Beckford is itself bleakly instructive. Cyrus Redding, *Memoirs of William Beckford of Fonthill,* 2 vols. (London, 1859) is silent on the subject. Lewis Melville, *The Life and Letters of William Beckford of Fonthill* (New York: Duffield & Company, 1910), p. 111, rejects the charge outright. In Beckford, *The Vision and Liber Veritatis,* ed. Guy Chapman (London: Constable & Company, 1930), p. xviii, Chapman offers a more

Courtenay for revealing some private correspondence. Courtenay's family, no friends of Beckford, leaned on young William and eventually extracted a confession. Beckford was plunged into ignominy, nibbled on by salacious gossips. "Is it true that Beckford's wife will not leave him," demanded Lord Pembroke, "& after all what was the exact business, how, when, & by whom, & with whom discovered? Who passive, & who active, & where le pauvre Bougre?"[6]

If convicted of sodomy, a capital crime for centuries, members of the lower orders could be hanged—and sometimes were.[7] The pace of such executions quickened in the early nineteenth century.[8] Those of Beckford's social status didn't stick around for such state-sponsored beneficence. They usually set sail hastily for the continent, as Beckford did. The disparity in legal treatment enraged radicals. When the Duke of Cumberland's valet was found dead, many assumed some homosexual affair had led the duke to murder. But an enquiry led to a verdict of suicide.[9] Discovered in the back room of an alehouse with an army private, Bishop Clogher was marched indig-

---

cautiously worded rejection; see too Guy Chapman, *Beckford*, 2d ed. (London: Rupert Hart-Davis, 1952), pp. 58, 182–89. Boyd Alexander, *England's Wealthiest Son: A Study of William Beckford* (London: Centaur Press, 1962), p. 114, concludes that "Beckford was not guilty of sodomy in 1784 and may never have been, *as far as youths of superior upbringing were concerned*." But see a relatively unruffled Brian Fothergill, *Beckford of Fonthill* (London: Faber and Faber, 1979), chap. 13.

[6] Lord Pembroke to Lord Herbert, 16 March 1785, *Pembroke Papers (1780–1794)*, ed. Lord Herbert (London: Jonathan Cape, 1950), p. 269. Note too *The Diary of Joseph Farington*, ed. Kenneth Garlick, Angus Macintyre, and Kathryn Cave, 16 vols. (New Haven: Published for the Paul Mellon Centre for Studies in British Art by Yale University Press), 8:3166–68 [14 December 1807].

[7] Note 25 Henry VIII, c. 6; 5 Eliz. I, c. 17; John Glyde, Jr., *Suffolk in the Nineteenth Century: Physical, Social, Moral, Religious, and Industrial* (London, n.d.), pp. 150–51; John Howard, *An Account of the Principal Lazarettos in Europe . . . Together with Further Observations on Some Foreign Prisons and Hospitals; and Additional Remarks on the Present State of Those in Great Britain and Ireland*, 2d ed. (London, 1791), including a separate table of capital offenses from 1749 to 1771: 17 sentences for sodomy, 15 executed, 2 transported or died. For a court-martial leading to "condemnation" "for an unnatural crime," see William Henry Dillon, *A Narrative of My Professional Adventures (1790–1839)*, ed. Michael A. Lewis, 2 vols. (London: Navy Records Society, 1953–1956), 2:125–26 [June 1809].

[8] A. D. Harvey, "Prosecutions for Sodomy in England at the Beginning of the Nineteenth Century," *Historical Journal* (1978) 21(4):939, 21(4):947–48.

[9] *The Correspondence of George, Prince of Wales 1780–1812*, ed. A. Aspinall, 8 vols. (London: Cassell, 1963–1971), 7:5–8, 7:373–411; Iain McCalman, *Radical Underworld: Prophets, Revolutionaries and Pornographers in London, 1795–1840* (Cambridge: Cambridge University Press, 1988), p. 34.

nantly through the streets. But he later fled, leaving bail of £1,000 behind.[10] The soldier, lacking such splendid assets, went to jail to await his trial. Then again, radicals didn't mind capitalizing on such episodes to bash the church.[11] One M.P. was charged but acquitted in 1833 after some thirty gentlemen testified to his good character. "It was a lame business," commented Greville dolefully, "and nobody can read the trial without being satisfied of his guilt."[12]

Capital punishment wasn't always in the cards. Cobbett, remember, emphasized the crowd's support for radical Daniel Isaac Eaton, unceremoniously stuck in the pillory for his radical publications but solicitously treated. The crowd, he reminded his readers, wasn't always so benevolent: "When, last year, some of the wretches guilty of *unnatural offences* stood in the pillory, on the same spot where Mr. Eaton was exhibited, their features were almost instantly rendered indistinguishable by the peltings in mud, blood, addled eggs, guts, garbage, dead dogs and cats, and every species of filth, while the air was filled with hootings and execrations."[13] One presumes Beckford wouldn't have been particularly ecstatic at this lesser display of public generosity.

Legal penalties aside, homosexuality long had served as an object of disgust, even horror. In a private letter of 1763, the usually garrulous Walpole drew the line at retailing some of Wilkes's jokes, "too gross, I think, to repeat," jokes probably mocking the homosexual relations of an aristocrat, a churchman, and a colonel.[14] The next year, Churchill's poetic jeremiad against the moral decline of *The Times* singled out homosexuality for biting attention. From "the soft luxurious EAST" had come "Sins of the blackest character," sins so

[10] Rictor Norton, *Mother Clap's Molly House: The Gay Subculture in England 1700–1830* (London: GMP, 1992), pp. 216–21.

[11] See for instance *Political Register* (27 July 1822) 43(4):218–50, (10 August 1822) 43(6):376–84; *Republican* (27 December 1822) 6(31):979, (24 October 1823) 8(16): 500–501.

[12] *The Greville Memoirs 1814–1860,* ed. Lytton Strachey and Roger Fulford, 8 vols. (London: Macmillan, 1938), 2:426 [4 December 1833]. Note *The Journal of Thomas Moore,* ed. Wilfred S. Dowden and others, 6 vols. (Newark: University of Delaware Press, 1983–1991), 4:1540 [29 June 1833].

[13] *Political Register* (13 June 1812) 21(24):750.

[14] Walpole to Lord Hertford, 17 November 1763, *The Yale Edition of Horace Walpole's Correspondence,* ed. W. S. Lewis, 48 vols. (New Haven, CT: Yale University Press, 1937–1983), 38:232. See too *The Trial of Richard Branson, for an Attempt to Commit Sodomy, on the Body of James Fassett* (London, 1760).

grave that they precluded the possibility of divine grace. *"Woman* is out of date," railed the poet:

> Women are kept for nothing but the breed;
> For pleasure we must have a GANYMEDE,
> A fine, fresh HYLAS, a delicious boy
> To serve our purposes of beastly joy.[15]

The year of Beckford's disgrace, Cowper reported on an accusation bubbling around his home town for some months, which threatened to make its target "a most infamous character. It amounts to nothing less than a charge of Paederastia." Two boys had pressed the charge repeatedly, once at a Baptist prayer meeting, once in front of the man's wife. They were ready to swear to it. The charges met strenuous denial.[16]

Nothing suggested even glacial change in this climate of opinion during the years Beckford kept a low profile on the continent or for that matter the ensuing years. George III was briefed on the king of Sweden, a "very cold husband" with a "known addiction to a certain detestable vice." Seeking a child, he had smuggled another man into his marital bed.[17] In 1795, Mrs. Piozzi was incredulous at talk of lesbianism: "'Tis now grown common to suspect Impossibilities—(such I think 'em)—whenever two Ladies live too much together," she marvelled.[18] An 1813 pamphleteer shivered over "this moral-blasting evil," "this wide-spreading contagion," a different sort of poison coursing through the body politic. He endorsed the death penalty and thought it a shame that castration would be ineffective.[19] Pierce Egan suspended his usual casual familiarity with the vices of the lower orders in charting the meteoric rise and fall of Samuel Hayward from

[15] *The Times* [1764], in *The Poetical Works of Charles Churchill*, ed. Douglas Grant (Oxford: Clarendon, 1956), pp 397–99.

[16] Cowper to John Newton, 24 December 1784, *The Letters and Prose Writings of William Cowper*, ed. James King and Charles Ryskamp, 5 vols. (Oxford: Clarendon, 1979–1986), 2:314.

[17] "Observations Regarding the Present Circumstances of Sweden" [1787?], *The Later Correspondence of George III*, ed. A. Aspinall, 5 vols. (Cambridge: Cambridge University Press, 1962–1970), 1:333.

[18] *Thraliana: The Diary of Mrs. Hester Lynch Thrale (Later Mrs. Piozzi) 1776–1809*, ed. Katharine C. Balderston, 2d ed., 2 vols. (Oxford: Clarendon, 1951), 2:949 [9 December 1795].

[19] Robert Holloway, *The Phoenix of Sodom, or The Vere Street Coterie* (London, 1813), pp. 30, 16; reprinted in *Sodomy Trials: Seven Documents* (New York: Garland, 1986).

tailor's apprentice to London high society to execution. Along the way, Egan hesitantly reported, Hayward "became something more than suspected of a crime of disgusting atrocity" when he succeeded in extracting a £50 note from "the notorious Sir — —," these euphemisms and omissions, titillating in their way, unmistakably clear.[20]

So for several years Beckford travelled through Europe in a dreary replay of the exuberant Grand Tour he'd taken several years before. Perhaps he hoped to escape the clouds of scandal that would swirl around him for the rest of his life. "When shall I cease acting the part of the Wandering Jew," he implored, "and being stared and wondered at as if I bore the mark of God's malediction on my countenance."[21] "I have been hunted down and persecuted these many years," he stormed. Worse, the newspapers blamed him for his wife's early death. "I sigh for the pestilential breath of an African serpent to destroy every Englishman who comes in my way."[22]

After the ritual time abroad, Beckford returned to England. He led a cloistered life, hurling himself into various enthusiasms: building on his estate at Fonthill[23] and collecting dwarves, fine art, and books, including Gibbon's library of ten thousand volumes, which he seems not to have gotten around to shipping back to England.[24] (He also kept a scrapbook of newspaper stories on sodomy cases.[25]) The occasional visitor was struck by the opulent decadence of it all.[26] Beckford saw these projects as futile attempts to divert his attention from his sexual frustrations. The building was too expensive, he fretted, even for him. "It would be cheaper to find another distraction, and if the

[20] Pierce Egan, *The Life & Adventures of Samuel Denmore Hayward* (London, 1822), pp. 102–3.

[21] *Journal of William Beckford*, p. 124 [6 July 1787].

[22] Beckford to Lady Craven, *circa* 1790, *Journal of William Beckford*, p. 13.

[23] See H. A. N. Brockman, *The Caliph of Fonthill* (London: Werner Laurie, 1956).

[24] *Extracts from the Journals and Correspondence of Miss Berry from the Year 1783 to 1852,* ed. Lady Theresa Lewis, 2d ed., 3 vols. (London, 1866), 2:260 [6 July 1803].

[25] Howard B. Gotlieb, *William Beckford of Fonthill: Writer, Traveller, Collector, Caliph 1760–1844* (New Haven, CT: Yale University Library, 1960), p. 77; see too Beckford to Gregorio Franchi, 22 September 1816, *Life at Fonthill 1807–1822 with Interludes in Paris and London: From the Correspondence of William Beckford,* trans. and ed. Boyd Alexander (London: Rupert Hart-Davis, 1957), p. 194.

[26] See the account of Samuel Rogers's visit in Lady Bessborough to Lord Granville, 28 October 1817, *Lord Granville Leveson Gower (First Earl Granville): Private Correspondence 1781 to 1821,* ed. Castalia Countess Granville, 2 vols. (London: John Murray, 1916), 2:544–45.

wretched Rottier would only pimp for me a little, I would save a good deal."[27] Or again: "A thousand guineas for variorum and Elzevirs, indeed! I'd rather give that for some 'volumes' (you know quite well the sort I mean) which I so much need that there is almost no price I would not pay to get them."[28]

Beckford's experience didn't radicalize him. True, in 1796 he was willing to take a facetious and fictional swipe at the *British Critic*'s ruthless campaign to squelch the rights of man.[29] And in 1834, when he finally republished the travel diaries he had brought out in 1783 and promptly suppressed because of the love letters in them, he was willing to contrast the sordid institutions of the *ancien régime* with the world enjoyed by "the modern children of light."[30] Ordinarily, though, he showed no sympathy with such causes. In 1787, he sneered at the custom in the Portuguese court "to be surrounded by African implings, the more hideous the better, and to dress them out as fine as you are able," blaming the queen: "The Royal family vie with each other in spoiling and caressing D. Rosa, her Majesty's dark-skinned, blubber-lipped, flat-nosed favourite."[31] (England's ambassador to Portugal tried to block Beckford's introduction at court.[32]) In 1829, he smirked at the "patriotic act of condescension" that led Lady Jane Lennox to marry into the Peel family, another aristocrat slumming it by consorting with vulgar industrialists.[33] He didn't exactly lavish affection on the Reform Bill of 1832.[34] Sounding for all the world like a latter-day Burke, he gazed fondly at a wealthy Portuguese monastery and bemoaned the passage of benevolent paternalism:

[27] Beckford to Gregorio Franchi, 17 August 1812, *Life at Fonthill*, p. 128.

[28] Beckford to Gregorio Franchi, 19 August 1812, *Life at Fonthill*, p. 130. See too Beckford to Franchi, 17 July 1814, *Life at Fonthill*, pp. 153–54.

[29] Lady Harriet Marlow [Beckford], *Modern Novel Writing, or The Elegant Enthusiast*, 2 vols. (London, 1796), 2:231–32. Compare Jacquetta Agneta Mariana Jenks [Beckford], *Azemia: A Descriptive and Sentimental Novel*, 2 vols. (London, 1797), 2:105. Both novels are reprinted in *Modern Novel Writing (1796) and Azemia (1797)* (Gainesville, FL: Scholars' Facsimiles and Reprints, 1970).

[30] *The Travel-Diaries of William Beckford of Fonthill*, ed. Guy Chapman, 2 vols. (Cambridge: Constable & Company; Houghton Mifflin, 1928), 1:325.

[31] *Journal of William Beckford*, p. 222 [11 October 1787].

[32] Chapman, *Beckford*, p. 210.

[33] Beckford, *The Vision and Liber Veritatis*, p. 96 [1829].

[34] Compare Melville, *Life and Letters of Beckford*, p. 188, with Redding, *Memoirs of Beckford*, 2:300–301.

> Since those golden days of reciprocal good-will and confidence between the landlord and the tenant, the master and the servant, what cruel and arbitrary inroads have been made upon individual happiness! What almost obsolete oppressions have been revived under new-fangled, specious names! What a cold and withering change, in short, has been perpetrated by a well-organized system of spoliation, tricked out in the plausible garb of philosophic improvement and general utility![35]

It's tempting to think that Beckford should have junked such commitments in the face of his own grim history. Yet radical gestures would have loosened whatever hold on social respectability Beckford could still command.

How tenuous was that hold? In his role as experimental agriculturist, Cobbett wrote to Beckford in 1811, seeking tree seeds.[36] Disraeli didn't just correspond with Beckford; in 1834 he gained an audience with the great man. Afterwards he raved about Beckford's artistic sensibilities.[37] (Beckford liked Disraeli's novels but couldn't stand his smoking.[38]) So here are more or less reputable characters willing to engage in social intercourse with this marked man. Other more or less reputable characters took a more or less disreputable interest in him. In some 1809 travels, Byron came close to meeting him: "We changed horses at an Inn where the great Apostle of Paederasty Beckford! sojourned for the night, we tried in vain to see the Martyr of prejudice, but we could not. . . ."[39] There may be sympathy here, but there's also a goodly dose of adolescent snickering. Byron's curiosity is like that of someone off to poke the Hottentot Venus.

One man reported that Beckford was distinguished by writing ability, wealth, "and still more so by the imputation of a crime which has been alleged against him, of a nature so horrible, that I wish to draw a

---

[35] William Beckford, *Recollections of an Excursion to the Monasteries of Alcobaça and Batalha* [1835], ed. Boyd Alexander (Fontwell, Sussex: Centaur Press, 1972), pp. 226–27.

[36] Cobbett to Beckford, 24 September 1811, in Brockman, *Caliph of Fonthill*, pp. 161–63.

[37] Benjamin Disraeli to Beckford, 13 June? 1834, *Letters: 1815–1834*, ed. J. A. W. Gunn and others (Toronto: University of Toronto Press, 1982), p. 410; Disraeli to Sarah Disraeli, 16 June 1834, *Letters*, p. 412.

[38] Oliver, *Life of Beckford*, pp. 297–304. But see Gotlieb, *William Beckford of Fonthill*, p. 73.

[39] Byron to Francis Hodgson, 25 June 1809, *Byron's Letters and Journals*, ed. Leslie A. Marchand, 13 vols. (London: John Murray, 1973–1994), 1:210.

veil over it, scarcely believing it possible that a man so amiable in every respect could ever have been so depraved." Gibbon reproved him for visiting Beckford. "Even supposing him innocent," urged the great historian, "still some regard was due to the opinion of the world," and he added that no other Englishman acknowledged Beckford's existence.[40] A financially insecure Thomas Moore learned that Beckford—"*the* Beckford"—much enjoyed his *Lalla Rookh* and hoped that Moore would visit him at Fonthill and help him prepare his travel diaries for publication. Maybe the poet could earn a whopping £1,000 for this work. "If he were to give me a hundred times that sum I would not have my name coupled with his," mused Moore; "to be Beckford's *Sub.*—not very desirable—"[41] When Beckford auctioned off his art collection, *John Bull* vehemently protested his return to public attention. "We are sickened to death with the unnecessary shouts of paragraphs with which some of the Morning Papers are grounded, and of which MR. BECKFORD, of Fonthill, is the subject." Efforts to publicize the obsessively catalogued details of his life "are proofs of bad taste and bad morality, from which Englishmen must turn with disgust." Until the auctioneers' advertisements "undertook to call public attention to MR. BECKFORD, it was not the fashion even to mention his name."[42]

So the leaden pall that descended over Beckford isn't imaginary; its alleged presence doesn't depend on any slippery argument from silence. Contemporaries testified explicitly that pederasts must suffer ostracism, a profound contemptuous dismissal laced with disgust and horror. I want now to examine the plight of those smeared as inferior, their efforts—sometimes poignant, sometimes wry—to gain public standing. But I also want to recall that for others, even one fabulously wealthy white male, such efforts weren't in the realm of serious political possibility. So conservatives anguishing over the irreversibility thesis, fearing the opening of Pandora's box, brooding that the struggle for citizenship itself meant that their game was lost, presumably were tempted to think that Beckford, guarded by the forbidding, forbidden walls of Fonthill, was just where he belonged.

[40] *Buck Whaley's Memoirs,* ed. Edward Sullivan (London: Alexander Moring Ltd, 1906), pp. 294, 298 [1797].

[41] *Journal of Thomas Moore,* 1:67 [18 October 1818].

[42] *John Bull* (21 September 1823) no. 145, p. 300, italics reversed. Note too *John Bull* (10 February 1833) 13(635):44.

# TEN

# WOLLSTONECRAFT'S HAIR

IF YOU ARE of that sex, vulgarly called the fair, but which ought always to be called the divine, let me beseech you, if you value your charms, to proceed no further." So warned William Cobbett in introducing one 1795 pamphlet. This is still officially young conservative Cobbett, but it would be rash to infer that the older radical Cobbett discarded such views. "*Politics* is a mixture of anger and deceit," continued the cranky journalist, "and these are the mortal enemies of beauty. The instant a lady turns politician, farewell the smiles, the dimples, the roses; the graces abandon her, and age sets his seal on her front." Women must be segregated from politics, not because they are low and politics is dignified, but because they are high and politics is sordid. So officially the view is that divine women ought not to be defiled. Is this contempt? or profound respect, even cloying deference? Recall the complications: Cobbett may be distinguishing (great) human worth from (poor) social status, but he may also be thinking that women's social status, their being safely locked away in the sublime purity of domesticity, is elevated. If we adopt that view or if we choose to describe such social seclusion in terms of difference, not dominance, we won't be able to make sense of contempt. If we reject that view, however sincerely intended, we will. And again, adoption and rejection alike are politically controversial.

Regardless, women shouldn't even read a political pamphlet. For Cobbett, this isn't a contingent response to the disorienting developments of the French Revolution, with women marching in the streets of Paris. It's a timeless truth about gender. Classical mythology had pressed the same point. "And have we not a terrible example of recent, very recent date? I mean that of the unfortunate *Mary Wolstoncraft*. It is a well known fact, that, when that political lady began

*The Rights of Women,* she had as fine black hair as you would wish to see, and that, before the second sheet of her work went to the press, it was turned as white, and a great deal whiter than her skin."[1] So politics, even writing about politics, even reading about politics, isn't a properly feminine pursuit. Break the rules of gender, trespass on the sphere of masculinity, and the baneful results will show up in one's face, one's skin, one's hair.

Wollstonecraft's hair was powdered when she wrote the *Vindication;* someone seeing her might have thought it was graying, though not entirely white.[2] Then again, Wollstonecraft, just thirty-eight years old, died two years after Cobbett's veiled premonition. (The cause was an infection from delivering the future Mary Wollstonecraft Shelley, not any accelerated aging brought on by penning the *Vindication.*) In 1798, her widower, William Godwin, published a labored defense of Wollstonecraft's life. There he sought to explain the shock with which many readers greeted the *Vindication of the Rights of Woman.* "Many of the sentiments are undoubtedly of a rather masculine description," he admitted. "There are also, it must be confessed, occasional passages of a stern and rugged feature, incompatible with the true stamina of the writer's character." Proudly, though, Godwin framed a rebuttal to these criticisms. "Yet, along with this rigid, and somewhat amazonian temper, which characterised some parts of the book, it is impossible not to remark a luxuriance of imagination, and a trembling delicacy of sentiment, which would have done honour to a poet, bursting with all the visions of an Armida and a Dido." So Wollstonecraft's prose style was appropriately feminine. He conceded that "those whom curiosity prompted to seek the occasion of beholding her, expected to find a sturdy, muscular, raw-boned virago," a mannish woman whose ugliness would reveal her faulty status as woman. But Godwin smugly repelled the indictment: "They were not a little surprised, when, instead of all this, they found a woman, lovely in her person, and, in the best and most engaging sense, feminine in her manners."[3] So women need not forfeit the proprieties of gender

---

[1] *A Bone to Gnaw for the Democrats,* pt. 1 [1795], in William Cobbett, *Porcupine's Works,* 12 vols. (London, 1801), 2:3–4.

[2] Two 1792 portraits show her with powdered hair; a 1797 portrait shows her with uniformly dark hair. See the reproductions in Emily W. Sunstein, *A Different Face: The Life of Mary Wollstonecraft* (New York: Harper & Row, 1975), between pp. 144–45.

[3] William Godwin, *Memoirs of the Author of a Vindication of the Rights of Woman* (London, 1798), pp. 81–83. Consider the echoed language of Godwin, *Life of Geoffrey*

or the beauties of sex in entering the political fray. One imagines an audible sigh of relief exhaled from the pages of Godwin's *Memoirs*.

Wanting women to become more and more masculine every day, Wollstonecraft wouldn't have been pleased with Godwin's defense. Then again, Godwin seems to find it easy to admit women into the public sphere, into discussion on terms of rough equality, the sort idealized and celebrated in Pierce Egan's sketches of coffeehouse life. Or at least into the realm of print discussion of politics. His stance might seem attractive, but it also might seem naive. Ironically, some modern feminists join Cobbett in his conviction that the public sphere is off limits or at least intransigently resistant to women. They diverge, of course, in taking that as an outrage, not a reassuring practice to be maintained.[4]

Mary Wollstonecraft Shelley shrank from public regard. "As to a Memoir," she instructed one magazine editor, "as my sex has precluded all idea of my fulfilling public employments, I do not see what the public have to do with me—I am a great enemy to the prevailing custom of dragging private life before the world. . . ."[5] She might be "a silly goose," she conceded to an old friend, but all she wanted to do was "wrap night and the obscurity of insignificance around me" because of "a love of that privacy which no woman can emerge from without regret—."[6] A retiring personality endorsing familiar norms: but also, as it happens, a woman under duress. Sir Timothy Shelley, the deceased Percy's father, made it abundantly clear to Mary that his willingness to provide even scanty financial support would evaporate if she thrust herself into the public eye.[7] Still, Shelley's plight would

---

*Chaucer, the Early English Poet,* 2 vols. (London, 1803), 2:394: "There is a stern and rugged character in reformation, particularly religious reformation, which we must deplore, while we love the general result."

[4] See for instance Joan B. Landes, *Women and the Public Sphere in the Age of the French Revolution* (Ithaca, NY: Cornell University Press, 1988), especially pp. 7, 204; Nancy Fraser, *Unruly Practices: Power, Discourse, and Gender in Contemporary Social Theory* (Minneapolis: University of Minnesota Press, 1989), chap. 6; Leonore Davidoff and Catherine Hall, *Family Fortunes: Men and Women of the English Middle Class, 1780–1850* (London: Hutchinson, 1987), chap. 10.

[5] Mary Shelley to James Robins?, 5 January 1828, *The Letters of Mary Wollstonecraft Shelley,* ed. Betty T. Bennett, 3 vols. (Baltimore: Johns Hopkins University Press, 1980–1988), 2:22.

[6] Shelley to Edward John Trelawny, April 1829, *Letters of Mary Shelley,* 2:72.

[7] See Shelley to Edward Moxon, 22 January 1834, *Letters of Mary Shelley,* 2:198; Shelley to John Gregson, *circa* 3–4 August 1838, *Letters of Mary Shelley,* 2:298–99.

have been instantly recognizable to many made resolutely uncomfortable by the very idea of public or political women.

Suppose we were to agree on a crisp account explaining how women are excluded from or disadvantaged in the public sphere. (We won't agree on any such account, not least because many want to deny that that's so.) Then two questions would arise. First: how wide an explanatory net must we cast? Does the account focus narrowly on considerations internal to the public sphere, say norms of debate or the content of pamphlets and newspapers? Or does the account range quite broadly across society, say by suggesting that capitalism and patriarchy and racism and liberalism and other nasty *isms* are structurally interconnected? Second: how contingent or necessary are the links specified in the account? Does it just happen to be the case that the footing of political women is precarious? Or is it also true in actual similar worlds? Or is it necessarily true, holding uniformly across nearby possible worlds?

These two questions are sometimes conflated, but they're independent. That is, there's no reason to believe that a narrower account is more contingent, a broader account more necessary. So consider two possibilities, which I introduce solely to explore the logical structure of this terrain, though as it happens both are plausible, at least as far as such highly stylized accounts might be. One: suppose that norms of debate are gendered. It's masculine to be combative, to imagine a conversation as a battlefield on which one must prevail or an opportunity to demonstrate publicly one's superior intelligence. It's feminine to be cooperative, to imagine a conversation as a joint enterprise for advancing the group's understanding of knotty matters, to disavow any proprietary interest in one's previous utterances and try to ensure that no one is humiliated or mortified. The merits of these competing norms aside, the second set is always vulnerable to invasion by the first. (Compare the notion of an evolutionarily stable strategy.) Once a few people start being too assertive, it's hard to bring them to heel. They talk too much, listen not enough, and interrupt frequently. Others will feel compelled to do the same in order to get a word in edgewise. Finally, suppose that this account is hazarded as an explanation of why democratic politics is necessarily unfriendly to women. Then we have a highly local account purporting to be universal. Two: imagine the converse, a contingent structuralism. Family, market, science, religion, and more interlock in quirky, partly conflictual, but massively overdetermined ways to ensure that women have no proper place in the public sphere. But that interlocking logic seems to hold only in this particular society, indeed only at this particular juncture in time. Other societies possessing the same institutions or reasonably close facsimiles of them don't exhibit the same logic. Strictly speaking, it just happens to be overdetermined that women are excluded.

Contemporaries had a reasonable grasp of these dilemmas worth recovering and considering. We are not confronting a massive case of political oblivion or amnesia; still less are we anachronistically supposing that something resembling our own day's feminism must be hiding somewhere in the musty corners of the historical record.

## Against Public Women

Cobbett's touching concern for Wollstonecraft's hair may have been indebted to a 1711 passage from the much reprinted *Spectator.* Bemoaning the frivolities that comprised too much of too many women's lives, the *Spectator* sought out the readership Cobbett wanted to rebuff: "There are none to whom this Paper will be more useful, than to the female World."[8] Yet the urbane essays ventured a solemn warning: "There is nothing so bad for the Face as Party Zeal. It gives an ill-natured Cast to the Eye, and a disagreeable Sourness to the Look," so that the writer "never knew a Party Woman that kept her Beauty for a Twelve-month."[9] More recently, Johnson's circle had sat snickering over the revelation that republican historian Catherine Macaulay spent hours working on her makeup "and even put on rouge," provoking one of the benevolent doctor's immortal barbs: "She is better employed at her toilet, than using her pen. It is better she should be reddening her own cheeks, than blackening other people's characters."[10] (But maybe if she hadn't been such a violent Whig, Johnson would have embraced her, as he did Charlotte Lennox and Fanny Burney.)

[8] *Spectator* (12 March 1711) no. 10, in *The Spectator,* ed. Donald F. Bond, 5 vols. (Oxford: Clarendon, 1965), 1:46.

[9] *Spectator* (5 May 1711) no. 57, in *Spectator,* ed. Bond, 1:243.

[10] *Boswell's Life of Johnson: Together with Boswell's Journal of a Tour to the Hebrides and Johnson's Diary of a Journey into North Wales,* ed. George Birkbeck Hill, rev. L. F. Powell, 6 vols. (Oxford: Clarendon, 1934–1950), 3:46 [29 April 1776].

A norm is under fire, let's say, if it is breached too frequently or if its legitimacy is disputed. These dismissive claims are evidence that the norms in question are under fire. (Recall the paradox of timing: when conservative wisdom is being dutifully followed, there's no point insisting on it. Or worse, insisting on it is likely to inspire curiosity and disobedience.) "Is the practice of public oratory a fit accomplishment for the ladies?" asked one debating society in 1780, "almost unanimously" voting no.[11] Weeks later, though, a ladies-only meeting at another debating society took up a similar query: "Is the study of Politics and the affairs of state compatible with the station and character of the Fair Sex?"[12] Were these ladies themselves already in public, already arguing about a deeply political question, forcibly committed to an affirmative answer? The setting was relatively public in exposing them to the scrutiny of anonymous strangers, but relatively private in excluding men and so limiting the strangeness of the strangers. And they may well have decided that pursuing politics and being a lady were incompatible; or again, we might wonder about how representative a group would show up in such a setting in the first place. One newspaper charged that one of the speakers was a cross-dressing male who disgusted the audience.[13] The women of La Belle Assemblee framed the problem as a leading question: "Ought not the women of Great Britain to have a voice in the election of Representatives, and be eligible to sit in Parliament as well as the men?"[14]

Early in 1788, the newspapers recorded an apparent novelty. In a debating society examination of slavery, one women spoke "with that dignity, energy, and information, which astonished every one present, and justly merited what she obtained, repeated and uncommon bursts of applause from an intelligent and enraptured auditory."[15] Was her performance astonishingly praiseworthy for a (mere) woman? or praiseworthy on its own terms? "It is a disgrace to the modesty of the sex," sniffed the *Times* later that year, "to see a woman debating a question among a parcel of idle apprentice boys," a dis-

---

[11] *London Debating Societies, 1776–1799,* comp. Donna T. Andrew (Great Britain: London Record Society, 1994), p. 87 [16 April 1780].

[12] *London Debating Societies,* p. 97 [2 May 1780].

[13] *London Debating Societies,* p. 98 [2 May 1780].

[14] *London Debating Societies,* p. 111 [14 October 1780].

[15] *London Debating Societies,* p. 220 [20 February 1788].

grace that the city's mayor would be well advised to investigate. "The debating ladies would be much better employed at their needle and thread, a good sempstress being a more amiable character than a female orator."[16]

Opponents of women in politics had to grapple with more than the occasional polite lady rising in a debating society. Again, there was that noisome spectacle from across the Channel, the bands of women who acted decisively in public. At the time, one aristocrat professed to be amused by "the ludicrous sight of a female army proceeding very clamorously, but in order and determined step towards Versailles." His amusement was checked, though, when he reckoned that there were at least five thousand of them and noticed that they were armed.[17] Decades later, these same women, "half unsexed by the masculine nature of their employments," still preyed on Walter Scott's imagination.[18]

Closer to home was a tradition of electioneering women, one tradition Burke never saluted. "The ladies, throwing off all their formalities, all that renders them amiable and attractive, have not blushed to pollute the simplicity of their minds by canvassing butchers and tailors. If I had the law in my hand I would shut them up for a year and a day in penitentiary houses," vowed one bishop in 1784.[19] The mother of one duchess notorious for her electioneering fretted about her daughter's habit: "I must think a business of so very publick a nature in such a place as London is better carried on by men than women."[20]

Others weren't disturbed. John Thelwall disdained the aristocratic overtones of *lady* and addressed some of his audience as "Female Citi-

---

[16] *Times* (29 October 1788) in *London Debating Societies*, pp. 237–38. Compare *The New Art and Mystery of Gossiping: Being a Genuine Account of All the Women's Club's in and about the City and Suburbs of London, with the Manner of Their Club Orders* (Cirencester, 1770).

[17] Lord Robert Fitzgerald to the Duke of Leeds, 7 October 1789, in *English Witnesses of the French Revolution*, ed. J. M. Thompson (Oxford: Basil Blackwell, 1938), p. 69.

[18] *Life of Napoleon Buonaparte* [1827], in *The Prose Works of Sir Walter Scott, Bart.*, 28 vols. (Edinburgh, 1834–1836), 8:171.

[19] Bishop of Llandaff to Duke of Rutland, 21 April 1784, in E. A. Smith, "The Election Agent in English Politics, 1734–1832," *English Historical Review* (January 1969) 84:15.

[20] Lady Spencer to the Duke of Devonshire, 22 July 1788, in *Georgiana: Extracts from the Correspondence of Georgiana, Duchess of Devonshire*, ed. Earl of Bessborough (London: John Murray, 1955), p. 132. See too *John Bull* (22 June 1823) no. 132, p. 197.

zens."[21] Mrs. Olding was chairing a meeting of the Friends of the Oppressed in 1833 when Mrs. Hutson rose to caution the radical audience against the duplicitous Whigs who talked a good game of supporting freedom until they wormed their way into power. How long would the people be misled by such tactics? Appropriating Brougham's easy confidence in enlightenment, she cracked, "The schoolmaster, however, had gone abroad, and she hoped the schoolmistress too." The audience rewarded her with guffaws and applause.[22]

Women too had starring roles in riots.[23] A tantalizing if obscure tradition of political protests featuring cross-dressing men continued, especially in Wales's Rebecca riots of the late 1830s and early 1840s.[24] It's not enough to say that it was prudent of lawbreakers to disguise themselves; we need to know why they chose this particular sort of disguise. Part of the explanation may hang on a popular but misinformed belief that, since the English state ruled over male heads of families, women were not legally accountable for their actions. Real women offered another kind of cover. At Hunt's trial after Peterloo, one witness testified that the crowd was full of women and children. "Many of the women were decent and respectable, and conducted themselves with propriety. Thought this a guarantee for the good order of the meeting, as he considered the presence of ladies always chastened the conduct of men. They were quite the reverse of what might be called profligate Amazons."[25]

A series of women vouched for their interest in politics. "I am obliged to you for your political intelligence," wrote Mrs. Carter to

[21] *The Diary of Joseph Farington*, ed. Kenneth Garlick, Angus Macintyre, and Kathryn Cave, 16 vols. (New Haven: Published for the Paul Mellon Centre for Studies in British Art by Yale University Press), 2:444 [14 December 1795].

[22] *Poor Man's Guardian* (12 January 1833) 2(84):12.

[23] But see the cautions in John Bohstedt, "Gender, Household, and Community Politics: Women in English Riots 1790–1810," *Past & Present* (August 1988) no. 120, pp. 88–122.

[24] Malcolm I. Thomis and Jennifer Grimmett, *Women in Protest 1800–1850* (London: Croom Helm, 1982), chap. 7; E. Richards, "Patterns of Highland Discontent, 1790–1860," in *Popular Protest and Public Order: Six Studies in English History 1790–1920*, ed. R. Quinault and J. Stevenson (London: George Allen & Unwin, 1974), pp. 90–92.

[25] *An Impartial Report of the Proceedings in the Cause of the King versus Henry Hunt, Joseph Johnson, John Knight, James Moorhouse, Joseph Healey, John Thacker Saxton, Robert Jones, Samuel Bamford, George Swift, and Robert Wilde, for a Conspiracy, Tried before Mr. Justice Bayley, and a Special Jury, at York Spring Assizes, on the 16th, 17th, 18th, 20th, 21st, 22d, 23d, 24th, 25th, and 27th of March, 1820* (Manchester, 1820), p. 110.

Mrs. Montagu in 1766, in the midst of a long-running private correspondence published in 1817.[26] (What do such published collections
of women's letters tell us about the public/private distinction? Are
these women writing with publication in mind, looking over their
shoulders at imaginary onlookers? Is the publication freighted with
reservations about divulging what should remain confidential? Or is
it no big deal?) A French traveller in 1810 recorded that politics
served as the subject for dinner-table conversations even before the
women rose to leave the men to their devices. The women "are still
more violent and extravagant than the men, whenever they meddle at
all with politics," he added, though he also noted that women tended
to be quiet "in numerous and mixed company."[27] "I used to read the
paper every day to my uncle," recalled a woman noteworthy for her
utterly faceless ordinariness, "and felt considerable interest in
politics."[28]

One M.P. found himself floundering in trying to counter Mary
Berry and Mrs. Damer's criticisms of one piece of legislation. "I am
ashamed to own that they were better qualified to attack than I was to
defend." He sought consolation in his journal, speculating that their
opposition was tied to personal affection for the Duke of Richmond,
just squeezed out of power. And he resorted to the wisdom of Cobbett
and the *Spectator:* "Pray, Miss Berry, beware of personal spleen if you
are going into opposition. The winning sweetness of Mrs. Bouverie's
countenance and smiles are not sufficient to correct the virulence of
her discourse on political subjects. Your sterner graces may perhaps
frighten us into forgetfulness of your beauty instead of awing us over
to your opinion."[29] George Eden was flabbergasted when the Duchess
of Richmond lit into him at a dinner party. She was "quite foaming at
the mouth with politics," he wrote; "we disputed for an hour and
more, to the great amusement of the whole company, who, though all

[26] *Letters from Mrs. Elizabeth Carter, to Mrs. Montagu, between the Years 1755 and 1800,* 3
vols. (London, 1817; reprint ed. New York: AMS Press, 1973), 1:313 [14 August 1766].
See too *Letters,* 2:92–94 [30 November 1770], 3:177 [21 September 1782], 3:336 [20
October 1792].

[27] Louis Simond, *Journal of a Tour and Residence in Great Britain, during the Years 1810
and 1811, by a French Traveller,* 2 vols. (Edinburgh, 1815), 1:47–48 [5 March 1810].

[28] *Elizabeth Ham by Herself 1783–1820,* ed. Eric Gillett (London: Faber & Faber,
1945), p. 188 [1813].

[29] *The Diaries of Sylvester Douglas (Lord Glenbervie),* ed. Francis Bickley, 2 vols. (London: Constable & Co., 1928), 1:117–18 [5 January 1797].

favourable to her side of the question, were astounded at her violence." (Would a man performing in the same style have been credited with rabid enthusiasm?) Eden transmitted this news and analysis to his mother, Lady Auckland.[30] More complex ironies lurk here. Belligerent Tory Harriet Arbuthnot noted Lady Bessborough's death. "She had lived in the intimate society of Fox, Burke & Sheridan, had been the confidante of many of their most important secrets & had always turned her mind very much to the Whig politics of that day." And she'd been instrumental, across the aisle, in the political education of Mrs. Arbuthnot herself. "I used to go with her very often to the House of Commons, and her criticism upon the debate & her recollections of former times were generally more worth listening to than the debate itself."[31]

Maybe opponents of political women held all the chips. Whatever fantasies the debating societies entertained, women didn't vote and didn't serve in Parliament. Then again, maybe opponents of political women had good cause to be edgy, even strident. Theirs is another nightmare vision of the future, of Pandora's box emptied out, of women in politics.

I mean biological women, to be delightfully crude about it, not just the effeminate state officials serving left and right alike as unpleasant faces in the mirror. Sarcastically assailing demands for the rights of women and genuine universal suffrage, the *Black Dwarf* paused to decide what to do. "Shall I advocate their cause, and try whether they will act better than the men! There is one comfort, they cannot act much worse; and there is one argument in their favour, that three-fourths of the kings and ministers of Europe, are *real old women.*"[32] Mocking the efforts of one indecisive official, worried about the impending funeral procession for two rioters killed by the state, *John Bull* demanded decisive action. "Elderly gentlewomen are useful persons to make tea, and take snuff, and play low whist; but to enforce the orders of Government, and maintain its authority and respectabil-

---

[30] George Eden to Lady Auckland, 6 September 1813, *The Journal and Correspondence of William Lord Auckland*, ed. Bishop of Bath and Wells, 4 vols. (London, 1861–1862), 4:397.

[31] Harriet Arbuthnot, *The Journal of Mrs. Arbuthnot 1820–1832*, ed. Francis Bamford and the Duke of Wellington, 2 vols. (London: Macmillan, 1950), 1:129 [1 December 1821].

[32] *Black Dwarf* (9 September 1818) 2(36):574. See too *Age* (5 August 1832), p. 253.

ity, we would prefer persons of masculine—*minds at least.*"[33] I presume that those intent on dissolving the distinction between sex and gender in the name of social construction or performativity wouldn't be happy to accept these old women as evidence that women were enfranchised and serving in high office more than a century earlier than we previously believed.

Norms under fire are still norms; transgressions still count as transgressions. If we can single out a dominant strand in this thicket of controversy, it's that women are disqualified from any public or political role. Not only is it horribly inappropriate for them; they're no good at it anyway. Unamused by Boswell's witnessing a woman preaching at a Quaker meeting, Johnson let fly another immortal barb: "Sir, a woman's preaching is like a dog's walking on his hinder legs. It is not done well; but you are surprized to find it done at all."[34] Women in politics promoted the reign of petty interests or worse yet personal favoritism, charged John Bennett. Not that the charge should upset them: "I have left them the seeds of every thing, that pleases and captivates in woman. *Their* brows were not intended to be ploughed with wrinkles, nor their innocent gaiety damped by abstraction. They were perpetually to please, and perpetually to enliven." Bennett didn't leave the passive voice—who's doing this intending, anyway?— ominously vague. This scheme was scriptural.[35] One Congregationalist church permitted men to discuss any matters of policy that came up; "the sisters have the liberty of silently expressing their consent or dissent" (no mean feat), "but it seems plain from scripture they have no right of deliberation and reasoning."[36] And again the consequences for women themselves of entering the political fray were momentous, even for those not obsessed with the color of their hair or the desirability of their bodies. "When a woman turns a political crusader," warned the *Quarterly Review*, "she voluntarily divests herself of

[33] *John Bull* (26 August 1821) no. 37, p. 289.

[34] *Life of Johnson*, 1:463 [31 July 1763]. For the story of one woman preacher, see *Some Account of the Life and Religious Labours of Sarah Grubb* (Dublin, 1792).

[35] John Bennett, *Strictures on Female Education* (London, 1787), pp. 120–24.

[36] *The Constitution and Order of the Congregational Church, John-Street, Glasgow, under the Pastoral Charge of the Rev. James Ramsay* (Glasgow, 1801), p. 17. Note the difficulties arising from Ramsay's preaching to women in *State of the Process Commenced by the Very Reverend the Associate Presbytery of Glasgow, against the Rev. James Ramsay* (Glasgow, 1801), pp. 14–16.

that otherwise inviolable respect to which her sex is entitled. . . ."[37]
How did those unhappy with this conventional wisdom fight it?

## UP FROM DOMESTICITY?

In a subversive flank attack, some suggested that precisely because
women were specially dedicated to the domestic sphere, they could
speak out and act in public. Consider the plight of writing women,
sometimes taken as ludicrous and offensive. M. G. Lewis greeted with
dismay the news that Susan Ferrier was writing novels. "As a rule, I
have an aversion, a pity and contempt, for all female scribblers. The
needle, not the pen, is the instrument they should handle, and the
only one they ever use dexterously." Lewis offered one deliberately
demeaning exception, "their love-letters, which are sometimes full of
pleasing conceits; but this is the only subject they should ever attempt
to write about."[38] *Blackwood's* sometimes rejected all women writers:
"A' the leddies o' my acquaintance that write byucks hae gotten a
touch o' the elephanteasis in their legs."[39]

Yet even sullen John Bowles, consumed with the newly dissolute
manners of women, was willing to permit them literary pursuits as
long as they complied with their domestic duties.[40] Walter Scott apologized for varying the formula of his preposterously successful historical novels and attempting a fictional portrait of his own day. He denied any "hope of rivalling the formidable competitors who have
already won deserved honours in this department," chief among
them "ladies . . . gifted by nature with keen powers of observation
and light satire" superbly equipping them to scale literary heights.[41]
(On another occasion, he forlornly compared his own "Big Bow wow

[37] *Quarterly Review* (July 1833) 49:484. Compare *Edinburgh Review* (July 1830)
51(102):582 n.

[38] M. G. Lewis to Charlotte Bury?, n.d., in Charlotte Bury, *Diary Illustrative of the
Times of George the Fourth*, new ed., 4 vols. (London, 1838–1839), 4:117.

[39] *Blackwood's Edinburgh Magazine* (January 1827) 21(121):108. In this dialogue, one
of the Noctes Ambrosianae, the Ettrick Shepherd (James Hogg) immediately meets
the adamant disagreement of Christopher North.

[40] John Bowles, *Remarks on Modern Female Manners, as Distinguished by Indifference to
Character, and Indecency of Dress* (London, 1802), p. 24.

[41] *St. Ronan's Well*, intro. [1832], in Walter Scott, *Waverley Novels*, 48 vols. (Edinburgh, 1829–1833), 33:iii–iv.

strain" to "the exquisite touch" of Austen's *Pride and Prejudice*.[42]) Writing novels was "a task for which women appear to be particularly well qualified," in the assessment of the *Quarterly Review*. They credited women with the same natural talents Scott did, but buttressed that view with a story about their social experience. "They are, generally speaking, gifted with a nice perception of the various shades of character and manners. This faculty is cultivated by constant habit. Private life is every thing to them. The laws of society confine them within its sphere, and they are therefore likely to observe it with care and to describe it with precision."[43] Their counterparts at the *Edinburgh Review* echoed the point the following year.[44] Here again, bonds of political matrimony unite apparent adversaries in unholy community. In 1830, the *Edinburgh Review* renewed the point. Women excelled in novel-writing. Seclusion in the bowels of the family wasn't debilitating. It enabled a finely discriminating moral sensibility and sociological imagination.[45] Here again, women are more fully socialized than rough-hewn men; women play culture to men's nature.

Writing novels brought a constricted publicity. Contrast the reception of Harriet Martineau. Her fiction was a clumsy vehicle for educating the lower orders in the rudiments of political economy. *Fraser's* devoted one of its monthly profiles of leading authors to her. As usual, they printed a full-page portrait with a facing page of prose description. Unusually, their tone was sharp. "It is no great wonder that the lady should be pro-Malthusian," they jeered, since no one would ever attempt to seduce her. Some of their derision was aimed at the absurdities of utilitarian radicalism. But some of it depended on an austere conception of the rightful role of the woman writer. The mind, or at least the ultra-Tory mind, boggled at the spectacle of a woman calmly discussing overpopulation in print: "It was indeed a wonder that such themes should occupy the pen of any lady, old or young, without exciting a disgust nearly approaching to horror." Martineau was unlucky enough to remind the journal of another woman author.

Mother Woolstonecroft, in some of her shameless books—books which we seriously consider to be in their tendency (a tendency only marred by

[42] *The Journal of Sir Walter Scott*, ed. W. E. K. Anderson (Oxford: Clarendon, 1972), p. 114 [14 March 1826].

[43] *Quarterly Review* (January 1814) 10:303.

[44] *Edinburgh Review* (October 1815) 25(50):486.

[45] *Edinburgh Review* (July 1830) 51(102):445–46.

their stupidity) more mischievous and degrading than the professedly obscene works which are smuggled into clandestine circulation, under the terrors of outraged law—boasts that she spoke of the anatomical secrets of nature among anatomists "as man speaks to man." Disgusting this,

but not so disgusting as the ready circulation of discussions of repro-duction, once "veiled with the decent covering of silence" or at least "with philosophical abstraction." Burke's veils and illusions en-chanted the political world. The veils over sexuality at least prevented the world from being manifest in its full nauseating splendor.

> We wish that Miss Martineau would sit down in her study, and calmly endeavour to depict to herself what is the precise and physical meaning of the words used by her school—what is preventive check—what is moral check—what it is they are intended to check—and then ask her-self, if she is or is not properly qualified to write a commentary on the most celebrated numbers of Mr. Carlile's *Republican*. . . .

Bad enough that that scurrilous radical had offered unflinchingly frank counsel on vaginal sponges; worse for a woman writer to join in. Martineau's untoward prose had landed the reluctant writer of *Fraser's* in a dismal predicament, though one still inviting impish aspersions.

> We are sorry, for many reasons, to write this—sorry that we should have to speak in censure of a lady for any thing—sorry that the cause of our censure should be of such a kind—sorry that our pages should be soiled by any allusions to such subjects at all; and we shall therefore escape, as soon as possible, to the refuge of the picture before us. Here is Miss Harriet in the full enjoyment of economical philosophy; her tea-things, her ink-bottle, her skillet, her scuttle, her chair, are all of the Utilitarian model; and the cat, on whom she bestows her kindest ca-resses, is a cat who has been trained to the utmost propriety of manners by that process of instructions which we should think the most efficient on all such occasions. There she sits cooking—
>
> —"rows<br>Of chubby duodecimos;"

certain of applause from those whose praise is ruin, and of the regret of all who feel respect for the female sex, and sorrow for perverted talent, or, at least, industry; doomed to wither in the cold approbation of the political economists. . . .[46]

More unholy community: the snippet of poetry is from Thomas Moore's sarcastic missive to Martineau, whose narrator goes into tightly controlled ecstasies imagining himself coupling off with the prolific author and reproducing—new books.[47]

Several months later, *Figaro in London* pulled the same stunt, cheerfully attributing their inspiration to *Fraser's*. A caricatured Martineau posed glaring at a Malthusian Table of Increase. "This is not, however, the only sour old woman who pores over preventive checks, and proves the truth of the maxim that we have a *surplus* population by being herself an illustration of the fact, that there may be *one too many*." The other old woman in question was another face in the mirror, Brougham himself, to whom the paper attributed a sly insult: "I can assure you, my dear Madam," he allegedly had told Martineau, "so fully convinced am I by our arguments of the expediency of celibacy, that I believe if all women were like yourself, no man would ever think of marrying."[48] (I don't know if Brougham ever made such comments. Several years later, Martineau was bent on refusing an offer of a government pension so she could retain her independence and not be accused of being a hireling. A miffed Brougham blew up: "I hate a woman who has opinions."[49]) One month later, Cobbett published a letter from a correspondent wishing "to have a switching at the shouters of the hussey Martineau" and echoing the same old gibe: "At all events she (if we must use the feminine pronoun) will not trouble the world with any addition to its population."[50]

So the women novelists tread lightly on the public stage. They offer their incisive observations about domestic life and so hesitantly vindicate their presence in public. Martineau and Wollstonecraft, writing

[46] *Fraser's* (November 1833) 8(47):576. For Martineau's Malthusianism, see especially *Weal and Woe in Garveloch* in her *Illustrations of Political Economy*, 9 vols. (London, 1832–1834), vol. 3, pt. 2.

[47] "A Blue Love-Song," in *The Poetical Works of Thomas Moore*, ed. A. D. Godley (London: Oxford University Press, 1915), p. 624.

[48] *Figaro in London* (29 March 1834) 3(121):47.

[49] *Harriet Martineau's Autobiography: with Memorials by Maria Weston Chapman*, 2d ed., 3 vols. (London, 1877), 2:177. But see too Martineau to William Tait, 10 November 1832, in Harriet Martineau, *Selected Letters*, ed. Valerie Sanders (Oxford: Clarendon, 1990), p. 38.

[50] *Political Register* (19 April 1834) 84(3):185.

on hotly contested political questions, have no such vindication to offer. They have strayed too far from the domestic sphere and are punished by forfeiting their sexual desirability. For the gibe against Martineau merely brings into nastier focus what already is looming in Cobbett's report that Wollstonecraft's hair went gray when she wrote the *Vindication:* no man could imagine sleeping with such a woman.

Not just writing, but more overt political action too was defended as flowing from a proper regard to domesticity. If women were charged with maintaining the family, they had to worry about poverty and wages. In 1791, one observer noted a "very singular" and "extraordinary" group of women that met once a year in Litchfield to collect money and distribute it to the poor.[51] In 1793, Fanny Burney pleaded for women to support the emigrant French clergy: "In the cause of tenderness and humanity, they may come forth, without charge of presumption, or forfeiture of delicacy."[52] In 1804, the Ladies' Committee for Promoting the Education and Employment of the Female Poor appealed to women's "natural tenderness of disposition, and their exemption from laborious occupations," suggesting that at least women of a certain social class gained the right to this sort of political activity.[53] In 1832, Henry Hunt received an address from the Female Radical Reformers of Manchester: "We, the female reformers, being mothers, daughters, sisters, and relatives to those who have been for a long time struggling for liberty, feel it our duty to render them a helping hand at this momentous crisis; seeing, as we do daily, our children on the brink of starvation, owing to profligate government."[54] One woman rejoiced in the imminent publication of a list of shopkeepers belonging to "the Unions" (she meant, I think, the National Union of the Working Classes, not ordinary trade unions). "This is what women can do," she said to herself, "this is a part in the drama we can take, without a moment's neglect of our ordinary occupations. The spending of money (especially in domestic concerns) is the province of women, in it we can act without the risk of being called politicians." She cleverly tweaked the biblical mandate into a

[51] Thomas Newte, *Prospects and Observations; on a Tour in England and Scotland: Natural, Oeconomical, and Literary* (London, 1791), p. 16.

[52] Fanny Burney, *Brief Reflections Relative to the Emigrant French Clergy: Earnestly Submitted to the Humane Consideration of the Ladies of Great Britain* (London, 1793), pp. iii–iv.

[53] *The Reports of the Society for Bettering the Condition and Increasing the Comforts of the Poor,* 5 vols. (London, 1798–1808), 4:122.

[54] *Poor Man's Guardian* (21 January 1832) 1(32):254.

call for political action: "Woman was created an helpmate for man, to lessen his cares, to share his troubles . . . therefore, mothers, sisters, wives, join all in assisting those brave patriots, who are using their most strenuous exertions to obtain for the many a restitution of those rights of which the few have so impiously robbed them."[55] These writers underscored the language of kinship to flaunt the domestic obligations that dragged them into politics.

Similarly, evangelical Zachary Macaulay called for women to act against slavery. Any Jamaican overseer, he thundered, was at liberty to expose "in the most shameless manner, in the presence of the whole gang, the person of every female, young or old, who is placed under his authority, and of inflicting on those very parts which it would be deemed in this country an intolerable outrage to expose at all, and which it is indecent even to name, thirty-nine lacerations of the tremendous cart-whip. . . ." Slavery had disrupted gender dynamics central to the logic and practice of English privacy: these audacious overseers made the unspeakably intimate unspeakably public. Women had no choice but to rise up—in the name of defending that privacy—and act: "Let the women of Great Britain hear this, and let them unite their efforts in rescuing their miserable fellow-subjects, the Negro women of Jamaica, and our other colonies, from this horrid and cruel profanation."[56] Official reports of the Sheffield Female Anti-Slavery Society and some joint Ladies' Anti-Slavery Associations, though, didn't credit women with any special obligations to the great cause. But those groups too organized as women, if only to escape badgering about sexual intrigues at their meetings.[57] (So too the Reverend Leigh Richmond's call for women to organize to combat "the deplorable state of the female Israelites . . . your Jewish sisters" was followed by the organization of the Leicester Ladies' Auxiliary Society.[58])

Yet these women against slavery didn't escape hostility. *John Bull* branded their enterprise a hoax: "At one glance the reader will be

[55] *Poor Man's Guardian* (26 May 1832) 1(50):403.

[56] Zachary Macaulay, *Negro Slavery* (London, 1823), pp. 104–5. See too *The Second Report of the Ladies' Association for Calne, Melksham, Devizes, and Their Respective Neighbourhoods, in Aid of the Cause of Negro Emancipation* (Calne, 1827), p. 4.

[57] *Report of the Sheffield Female Anti-Slavery Society* (Sheffield, 1827); *Ladies' Anti-Slavery Associations* (Liverpool, 1827).

[58] *Jewish Repository* (March 1813) 1:113, (September 1813) 1:427–32.

convinced, for whatever purpose females are dragged from the decent privacy of domestic life into an arena for discussion, and a committee for debate, that no female wrote, or could have written, the papers put forth under the alluring assurance that the whole affair is feminine." As if, the paper snorted, mere women understood the economics of duties and bounties. What is more, the paper fretted—these sound perilously like crocodile tears, if only because the newspaper itself was fond of racist diatribes and defenses of slavery—this risible fraud "will sicken the real philanthropist, and make the whole question one of derision, and bring the cause itself into perfect contempt." Summing up, crocodile tears yielding to patently insincere flattery, the paper counselled, "Let these dear, good-natured, kindhearted ladies—for after all, their errors are founded in kindness and the best of feelings—let them be satisfied to act the meritorious part in society for which our well-bred Englishwomen are so admirably qualified," a part having nothing to do with debates on government policy.[59] "Anxious at all times, to keep ladies out of popular discussions, or political controversies," the paper grimly decided that since "the amazons of Clapham and Battersea have taken the field," they would have to publish a refutation of all these ignorant claims about slavery. Ironically, the refutation was "furnished by a lady in the West Indies," about whose political efforts the paper expressed no reservations.[60] Antislavery politics, even justified as Macaulay suggested, didn't creatively or subversively stretch the bounds of a proper regard for domestic life. It simply transgressed them. But even this spirited Tory outlet was willing to accept women's crusade against poverty. At least it published a letter from a man proposing that these misguided Clapham ladies save themselves from "ridicule," "disgrace," and "contempt" by suspending their battle for the slaves and plunging themselves into a new and more suitable cause, erecting a home for poor adults.[61] Not any poor would do, however: the paper's fury was redoubled the next year when it learned that these ridiculous Clapham ladies were out to relieve poor Jews.[62]

[59] *John Bull* (31 August 1828) 8(403):277. See too *John Bull* (2 November 1828) 8(412):348–49, (19 July 1829) 9(449):229–30.

[60] *John Bull* (9 November 1828) 8(413):357.

[61] *John Bull* (9 November 1828) 8(413):358.

[62] *John Bull* (1 March 1829) 9(429):69–70; see too *John Bull* (13 June 1830) 10(496):188–89.

Even conservatives, then, were willing to grant that women's domestic duties could give them political license. But it was limited license: to write novels, not political economy; to act against English poverty, not Jamaican exploitation. If it's at all surprising that women could write a recipe for political involvement, it's relentlessly unsurprising that that involvement had to remain constrained.

## COLLIDING NORMS OF DEBATE

We can detect a similar pattern of limited license in the way contemporaries negotiated a forbidding impasse. On the one hand, women weren't to take up public or political roles. On the other, there was that seductive rough first pass on the basic norm of democratic debate: pay attention to the merits of the argument, not the status of the speaker. What difference could it make if some position was voiced by a woman? Lady Bessborough, consumed with politics for years on end, glided easily between the two norms: "It is the glory and safeguard of England that every one, from the highest to the lowest, has a right to give his opinion free and uncontroll'd. . . . But as nothing can be much more ridiculous than a female Politician, I will have done with this subject. . . ."[63]

From one vantage point, the conflict is only apparent, created by anachronistic misreading or wishful thinking. Perhaps that basic norm of democratic debate, for all its facial equality, was understood to apply only to men. (Or white men. Or Christian white men. Or Christian white men of a certain social status.) When Egan writes, "There is no distinction of persons, it is all 'hail fellow, well met,'" maybe the fellows are, well, fellows, persons otherwise undistinguished but all of the male persuasion. Recall Cumberland's maxim: "The advantages of rank or fortune are no advantages in argumentation; neither is an inferior to offer, or a superior to extort the submission of the understanding on such occasions; for every man's reason has the same pedigree; it begins and ends with himself." Maybe *every man* doesn't include every woman: "The delicacy of sex . . . should never be so overlooked, as to alarm the feelings of any person present, inter-

---

[63] Lady Bessborough to Granville Leveson Gower, November? 1794, *Lord Granville Leveson Gower (First Earl Granville): Private Correspondence 1781 to 1821*, ed. Castalia Countess Granville, 2 vols. (London: John Murray, 1916), 1:102. Note too Lady Bessborough to Gower, 1798, *Granville Correspondence*, 1:218; *Black Dwarf* (19 July 1820) 5(3):105.

ested for their preservation," warned Cumberland in the same collection of essays. "When the softer sex entrust themselves to our society, we should never forget the tender respect due to them," the innocent *our* making it abundantly clear that the society of conversationalists is a social space to which men claim property rights.[64] So too, Cumberland guarded his enthusiastic support for educating women: "The object of my anxiety is the preservation of the female character," not just dedication to domestic duties, but an emphatic reticence in debate. "They are not born to awe and terrify us into subjection by the slashes of their wit or the triumphs of their understanding," lest they be convicted of "loquacity and impertinence."[65] Impertinence or impudence is the vice of the saucy underling who doesn't defer. So now Cumberland's position is this: neither is an inferior to offer submission of understanding, unless the dimension of inferiority being considered is sex. Maybe Egan and Cumberland were blatantly contradicting themselves. Maybe they knew perfectly well what they were up to. Maybe they never thought through the implications of these apparently contradictory commitments.

Their mental states aside, not a few other men found it easy to brush aside the possibility of admitting women to participation as equals in democratic debate. "Tell the little woman she need not be afraid of us," wrote Thomas Grenville in planning a dinner full of leading figures of state, "because she may go up to coffee whenever she is bored with the politicians."[66] The chortling tone betrays no anxiety that the woman in question, not short but demeaned, might want to join the company. Or take a self-deprecating comment—or is it a joke? or a tired nod toward unmeaning propriety?—in an 1808 letter from a woman to a man: "I am no Politician or should be telling you a multitude of News—of the Spaniards drubbing the French &c. &c. but I leave these Matters to wiser heads than mine."[67] Maybe this woman takes her lack of political intelligence as a purely individual

[64] Richard Cumberland, *The Observer: Being a Collection of Moral, Literary and Familiar Essays*, 5th ed., 6 vols. (London, 1798), 3:284–85.

[65] Cumberland, *The Observer*, 4:297–98.

[66] Thomas Grenville to Lord Grenville, 9 January 1805, Historical Manuscripts Commission, *Report on the Manuscripts of J. B. Fortescue, Esq., Preserved at Dropmore*, 10 vols. (London, 1892–1927), 7:251.

[67] Charlotte Reynolds to John Freeman Milward Dovaston, 24 August 1808, *Letters from Lambeth: The Correspondence of the Reynolds Family with John Freeman Milward Dovaston 1800–1815*, ed. Joanna Richardson (Suffolk: Published for the Royal Society of Literature by the Boydell Press, 1981), pp. 21–22.

trait not structured by gender. Maybe not. "Indeed, I believe a great many men appear more foolish to women than amongst themselves," protested Lady Bessborough. "They so often think it necessary to use a sort of jargon *adapted* to the level of our capacities, and a little condescending way of talking of trifles and making little compliments, that it quite provokes me; and if the superiority they assume is not perfectly well grounded, makes them appear ridiculous, as well as much more foolish than they are."[68]

Sometimes, even easy dismissiveness demonstrated awareness that there might be a conflict. Take the preface to one pamphlet: "IT is necessary previously to remark, that the female sex is entirely exempted from every part in this subsequent controversy."[69] *Entirely exempted:* no stammering hesitation there, just brusque finality. Still, *it is necessary previously to remark* this exemption. So the author suspects that some members of his audience may have other expectations, just as Cobbett suspects that a woman might have made the mistake of picking up his pamphlet. Or take an inadvertently ironic confession from *Fraser's.* Congratulating themselves on their strict critical impartiality, the monthly offered one complex exception for women. "There is not an authoress in all England, Scotland, and Ireland, with the adjacent islets, whom we do not take under our especial protection. Let them write what they please, except politics—for that unsexes a woman—and they may be sure of the loudest applause from us."[70] No norms of democratic equality for novelists or poets, but can women join the masquerade with no masks? The point is not that women's political writing will be considered fairly on the merits, but that it will be rejected instantly.

Or take Byron, perched in Italy but eagerly surveying English letters and politics. John Murray, his publisher, also ran the *Quarterly.* Byron airily scolded him for running a harsh review: "What cruel work you make with Lady Morgan—you should recollect that she is a woman—though to be sure they are now & then very provoking—still as authoresses they can do no great harm—and I think it a pity so much good invective should have been laid out upon her. . . ."[71] A

[68] Lady Bessborough to Granville Leveson Gower, 1802, *Granville Correspondence,* 1:318.

[69] James Pimlot, *A Succinct and Benevolent Address, to All the Disaffected Parties in Our Nation, of Every Name and Species* (Birmingham, 1793), p. iii.

[70] *Fraser's* (August 1831) 4(19):2.

[71] Byron to John Murray, 20 February 1818, *Byron's Letters and Journals,* ed. Leslie A. Marchand, 13 vols. (London: John Murray, 1973–1994), 6:12–13.

few years later, Byron was appalled by the suggestion in an anonymous book on Italy that the author had refused to meet him. "You will please to publish the enclosed *note without* altering a word," he barked at Murray; "and to inform the author—that I will answer personally any offence to him.—He is a cursed impudent liar." Remembering Murray's dilatory habits of correspondence and penchant for sloppiness in seeing his work through press, he added, "and answer this. . . . You sometimes take the liberty of *omitting* what I send for publication: if you do so in this instance I will never speak to you again as long as I breathe."[72] A few weeks later, Byron recovered his equanimity. Continuing through the book, he'd noticed "that it is written by a WOMAN!!!" No room for insults and challenges here; not even room for a response. "In that case you must suppress my note and answer—and all I have said about the book and the writer.—I never dreamed of it till now—in extreme wrath at that precious note——I can only say that I am sorry that a Lady should say anything of the kind.—What I would have said to a person with testicles—you know already.—Her book too (as a *She* book) is not a bad one. . . ."[73] There was no sovereign in the republic of letters, Byron would say a few years later. Authors met on terms of equality, so much so that he would brave a duel with an anonymous author. But not when author was authoress: then she earned silent and patronizing dismissal.

Or take George Canning, poised at the onset of a brilliant political career that would propel him all the way to prime minister shortly before his death in 1827. He hoped to find a place to live near some of his family—his uncle Stratford, aunt Hetty, "little Bessy," and more—so that he could enjoy an occasional respite "from the fatigues of publick employment." But this fond dream was rudely shattered.

> I really thought Hetty had come to her senses, and seen that a woman has no business at all with politicks, or that if she thinks at all about them, it should be at least in a *feminine* manner, as wishing for the peace

---

[72] Byron to Murray, 8 September 1820, *Letters and Journals,* 7:173. For Byron's note, see *Marino Faliero* [1820], in Byron, *The Complete Poetical Works,* ed. Jerome J. McGann and Barry Weller, 7 vols. (Oxford: Clarendon, 1980–1993), 4:543–44. For the passage that incensed Byron, see *Sketches Descriptive of Italy in the Years 1816 and 1817,* 4 vols. (London, 1820), 4:159–60 n. Someone must have brought this passage to Byron's attention; it is clear from the outset that these anonymous volumes are by a woman (by name Jane Waldie).

[73] Byron to Murray, 29 September 1820, *Letters and Journals,* 7:183.

and prosperity of her country—and for the success and credit of those of her family (if she has any) who are engaged in the practical part of politicks. . . . But alas! these pretty schemes were all routed and put to flight by a violent altercation which arose, I scarcely know how, between me and Hetty on the very last day of my stay at Wanstead, in which it appeared that her political prejudices and personal hatred of all those with whom I am connected and partiallity to all who hate me, were not done away but had been smothered only with great difficulty and much secret struggle till now, and were ready to blaze out with redoubled vehemence on any accidental occasion. I am grieved at it. But I will not live where I can have no confidence. I should feel very little relief from the fatigues of business and of Parliament, in going among a society where I could not unbosom my thoughts with pleasure or with safety, where I must either sit wrapped up in my own contemplations, force the conversation upon indifferent subjects, or run the risque of having to dispute upon every proposition that I might happen to throw out relative that what had been passing in the world—where anything that happened to have gone amiss would be received with triumph, and anything successful, however deeply even my personal interest might be involved in it, heard with distrust and grudging and despondency.

Canning's emotional heat makes him stumble and lose his usually sure grammatical footing, though the passage is eloquent in its way.

I am truly grieved for Bessy's sake, whom I love and admire exceedingly, and who has a heart and an understanding and above all a sweetness of temper that cannot fail to be loved and admired by all who know her. It vexes me that I can have so little of her society. It vexes me for her sake that she should be breeding up in a school where it does not seem to be understood that a female politician is at best like "a dog walking on his hind legs", as Dr. Johnson very wisely says—a thing out of place and nature, and if a bitter partizan as well as a politician—becomes a plague to herself and to all about her, forfeits the happiness which she might enjoy in the society of her natural friends and connections for a foolish ambition of being admired by men who are too wise to have any sort of respect for them in reality, and who, if they do pretend to admire, do so only the more effectually to conceal their contempt.[74]

[74] *The Letter-Journal of George Canning, 1793–1795*, ed. Peter Jupp, Camden 4th ser., vol. 41 (London: Offices of the Royal Historical Society, 1991), pp. 284–85 [30 June 1795].

For Canning, blissful relaxation in the bosom of his family requires a suspension of political debate. Best for Hetty not to entertain any political pretensions; better for her to adopt a sweetly vacuous patriotism and support his partisan career. (This joint requirement entails that she never dare ask herself the question whether Canning's brand of Tory politics is good for England. Years later, I should note, Canning would confide in his wife on political matters and even seek to justify himself.[75]) But all this passionate blustering, complete with the appeal to Dr. Johnson's now misquoted wisdom, testifies to his sense that these norms are under fire. It isn't Hetty's idiosyncratic confusion, which would have to inspire bewilderment or concern about fledgling psychopathology. So too, if and when little Bessy grows up to be like her mother, obstreperous enough to articulate and defend political convictions, she will be an instantly recognizable social type, taking her allotted place in a preappointed pageant besides allies— and confronting enemies. There are sprawling social stakes to this little incident of domestic disharmony.

Tip the balance further and consider an author committed to the egalitarian norm of discussion but willing or eager to color it when it came to women. On the first page of its first issue, *The Pioneer; or, Grand National Consolidated Trades' Union Magazine* announced it would pay heed to women's interests. Soon the *Pioneer* boasted A Page for the Ladies, publishing letters from women readers along with the editor's cogitations. (Eventually the title was changed to Woman's Page: "Woman is an endearing, social name; but lady has something shockingly aristocratic about it," the journal demurred.[76]) Holding that women's nature was different,[77] that political women ought to segregate themselves—"Neither do we advise them to go and spout at meetings, or make themselves public in any way"[78]—and retain an appropriately feminine style,[79] the *Pioneer* posed as a devout feminist. A flirtatious feminist, too, serving up an insouciant mixture of stand-

---

[75] See for instance George Canning to Joan Canning, 27 January 1810, *The Later Correspondence of George III*, ed. A. Aspinall, 5 vols. (Cambridge: Cambridge University Press, 1962–1970), 5:500–501 n. 2; and note *A Regency Visitor: The English Tour of Prince Pückler-Muskau Described in His Letters 1826–1828*, trans. Sarah Austin, ed. E. M. Butler (London: Collins, 1957), p. 196 [22 April 1827].

[76] *Pioneer* (26 April 1834) no. 34, p. 322.

[77] *Pioneer* (29 March 1834) no. 30, p. 273; (12 April 1834) no. 32, p. 293.

[78] *Pioneer* (22 March 1834) no. 29, p. 262.

[79] *Pioneer* (8 March 1834) no. 27, p. 238; (29 March 1834) no. 30, p. 273.

point epistemology and breathlessly enraptured tones in imagining the payoffs of giving women a voice of their own:

> In the fulness of our heart we invite them to write to us; their tender epistles will give a zest to our magazine, which doubtless our readers would relish. There is poetry in a woman's pen;—their veriest prose is poetry to us. We hope then to hear from the sisterhood: but now ladies, mind and write it yourselves, and indite it yourselves; for if you employ a scribbler it will be sure to lose its pathos; we do not know how to write like you; our thoughts are not your thoughts, nor our ways your ways.— A man cannot feign a woman's feelings;—he does not know her wrongs;—he wrongs her most himself.—He is the tyrant,—she the slave. How can *he* pourtray *her* smothered thought, or write *her* anxious wish? Write yourselves, then, write yourselves. The Pioneer is far away; he cannot see your modest blush, nor know your doubting mind and nervous fear. He cannot tell from whose fair hand the little treasure cometh. Hail, then, the first "brave wench" who sends the Pioneer a valentine. Hail! pretty *Pioneera!*[80]

Hail indeed: but a steady stream of women accepted the invitation and used the pages of the *Pioneer* to advance unflinchingly radical views.

Feminine reserve and democratic equality: there is a real conflict here, not to be bought off by the facile assertion that no one ever seriously meant that egalitarian norm to apply to women. Some people did mean it to and some didn't: the norm, in all its bewitching ambiguity, was the site of bitter political conflict. Already in 1750, Euphelia defended herself in the *Rambler* for daring to sneer at a series of authors. "You are likely enough," Johnson's fictional mouthpiece instructed him, "for I have seen many instances of the sauciness of scholars, to tell me, that I am more properly employed in playing with my kittens, than in giving myself airs of criticism, and censuring the learned." But she wouldn't budge: "You are mistaken if you imagine that I am to be intimidated by your contempt, or silenced by your reproofs. As I read, I have a right to judge. . . ."[81] Johnson perceives a

---

[80] *Pioneer* (26 October 1833) no. 8, pp. 57–58.

[81] *Rambler* (25 August 1750) no. 46, in *The Yale Edition of the Works of Samuel Johnson,* ed. Herman W. Liebert and others, in progress (New Haven, CT: Yale University Press, 1958–), 3:249. See too *Rambler* (1 June 1751) no. 126, in *Works,* 4:310–11; *Rambler* (12 November 1751) no. 173, in *Works,* 5:152–53.

conflict between the traditional cant about women and the crusading egalitarianism of the republic of letters. Euphelia is a not unsympathetic figure in the *Rambler;* despite his cracks about Macaulay's cheeks and preaching women, indictments of Johnson's scant regard for women would be premature.

Or again: Maria Edgeworth's father Richard wrote prefaces to her earlier works. Though he earned his reputation as a dullard, he testified to the same conflict. "MY daughter asks me for a Preface to the following volumes; from a pardonable weakness she calls upon me for parental protection: but, in fact, the public judges of every work, not from the sex, but from the merit of the author."[82] Yet again: in pursuing those historical labors savaged by Johnson, Catherine Macaulay bulldozed her way straight through some opposition. In the British Museum, she wished to read the letters between James I and his favorite lover, the Duke of Buckingham. The archivist tried to screen her access to the steamy letters, "observing that many of them were wholly unfit for the inspection of any one of her sex. 'Phoo,' said she, 'a historian is of no sex,' and then deliberately read through all."[83]

Boswell's friend Temple agreed that one would expect Macaulay, a woman historian, to provide "a panegyric on royalty and the effeminate pleasures of a court," but was "most agreeably disappointed" to discover the opposite in her work.[84] Usually, there was intense pressure on men and women alike to play to gender type. As a woman writer, was Macaulay rewarded for literary cross-dressing? Consider the *Edinburgh Review,* which attributed its ongoing affection for Maria Edgeworth not to any "overweening politeness which might be thought due to her sex," but to "her *manly* understanding" and zeal for improving society.[85] Or consider the *British Critic's* applause for Wollstonecraft's *Letters from Sweden:* "THAT Mrs. Wollstonecraft possesses extensive information and considerable powers of reasoning, the public has been already apprized. It remained for her to show that she is capable of joining to a *masculine* understanding, the finer sensibilities of a female. An heart exquisitely alive to the beauties of nature, and keenly susceptible of every soft impression, every tender

---

[82] Richard Lovell Edgeworth's preface to *Tales of Fashionable Life* [1809], in Maria Edgeworth, *Tales and Novels,* 10 vols. (London, 1848), 4:211.

[83] John Taylor, *Records of My Life,* 2 vols. (London, 1832), 1:209.

[84] W. J. Temple to James Boswell, 7 February 1764, in *Boswell in Holland 1763–1764,* ed. Frederick A. Pottle (London: William Heinemann, 1952), pp. 146–47.

[85] *Edinburgh Review* (January 1814) 22(44):417.

emotion."[86] Here Godwin's memoir is vindicated—more unholy community—by a doughty conservative review.

Conflicts can always be evaded, and I suspect that the desire to evade this one motivated the desire to find some arena besides democratic debate in which women might be good subjects or even good citizens. Priscilla Wakefield proposed that the female nobility set inspiring examples against the dissipation of the day and help shape healthier manners.[87] "I am not sounding an alarm to female warriors, or exciting female politicians: I hardly know which of the two is the more disgusting and unnatural character," insisted Hannah More, no stranger to the press herself. Still, women needed to promote devotion to the common good.[88] Irritated by the smug tone of the *Black Dwarf*'s forays into the rights of women, one woman dashed off a letter explaining that women had no interest in public speaking or voting. They wished only to be instructed in how "to rear patriot sons."[89] All these women are groping for a public role for women that falls short of participating as equals in political debate.

Then there's always the fatuous attempt to split the difference, as if compromise were always fair, never impotent; always sage statesmanship, never the art of making everyone unhappy. In 1828, Carlile endorsed political action for women with a nod to the familiar extension of domestic virtues and obligations. "All public reforms are moral proceedings." All of them: no limited license here, but a blank check. But then, perhaps recalling the norms about feminine reserve, Carlile whipsaws back. "In all such proceedings, women, while their manners are mild and becoming, can never be wrong. The propriety of the thing will rest upon the mode of doing it. Noisy, brawling, ignorant and bad-mannered women are disgraceful every where, in public or in private."[90] Any more disgraceful than brawling men? This

[86] *British Critic* (June 1796) 7:602.

[87] Priscilla Wakefield, *Reflections on the Present Condition of the Female Sex; with Suggestions for Its Improvement* (London, 1798; reprint ed. New York: Garland, 1974), pp. 95–97.

[88] *Strictures on the Modern System of Female Education* [1799], in *The Works of Hannah More,* 9 vols. (London, 1840–1843), 3:14. See too Jane West, *Letters to a Young Lady,* 3d ed., 3 vols. (London, 1806), 2:503, 2:471–75.

[89] *Black Dwarf* (7 October 1818) 2(40):635. Note too Mary Berry, *Social Life in England and France, from the French Revolution in 1789, to That of July 1830* (London, 1831), pp. 9–10.

[90] *Lion* (4 April 1828) 1(14):425.

attempt to serve two masters by magically rolling together robust debate and dainty restraint isn't helpful. For one thing, it wouldn't satisfy those swearing a more unconditional allegiance to either norm. For another, it would cripple women in their pursuit of political projects.

## PRIVATE REFLECTIONS, PUBLIC PREFACES

Evasion and glib compromise aside, consider the analyses offered by women writers, battle scarred and mordantly well informed on the shape of this predicament. Anna Seward found herself chagrined in a 1794 literary exchange with Boswell. "As to Boswell," she told her friend Mrs. Stokes—this letter was published in 1811, part of six volumes of Seward's letters, more private femininity bared for public inspection—"all my friends unite in thinking it utterly beneath me to pursue a controversy with an ungrateful and impudent man, whom I once believed incapable of such conduct as his late letters about me demonstrate." Assertively, Seward assigns herself the high ground in their exchange. She will not lower herself to Boswell's pathetic level. But why not? His letters, she went on, "prove him capable of insulting any person who cannot inflict the punishment of corporal correction. Defenceless against such a being is every woman, who has neither father nor brother to awe the assailant."[91] We saw earlier that sometimes overheated interlocutors didn't content themselves with patiently constructing reasonable arguments and submitting them to the press. Sometimes they dueled or went off to cane or whip newspaper editors. It's tempting to think of such incidents as occasional excesses, the failure of hot-headed rogues to grow up. Seward's bleak suggestion is that these incidents are instead an integral part of the practice of democratic debate. Absent the threat of bodily injury, such writers as Boswell will gaily trample on any and every norm of civility one might wish to embrace. (So Boswell seems to share Byron's principle of testicular standing. Compared to Boswell's impudence, does Byron's decision to stay silent look any less dastardly?) Once

---

[91] Anna Seward to Mrs. Stokes, 20 March 1794, *Letters of Anna Seward*, 6 vols. (Edinburgh, 1811), 3:353. Consider Chesterfield to his son, 1742, *The Letters of Philip Dormer Stanhope, 4th Earl of Chesterfield,* ed. Bonamy Dobrée, 6 vols. (London: Eyre and Spottiswoode, 1932), 2:525.

again, women are at a structural disadvantage in democratic debate, thanks this time to bodily, not mental, weakness.

After reading Mary Berry's comparative social history of England and France, Joanna Baillie wrote to offer a gentle reproval. Berry's treatment of Voltaire's mistress "rather offends as to that delicacy which is expected in the writings of a woman." Most readers might not see it that way, but "others whose judgment and feelings I respect" had reported similar reactions.[92] Berry was unmoved. Or was she? "I have only to say that, if women treat of *human* nature and *human* life in *history* and not in *fiction* (which perhaps they had better not do), human nature and human life are often indelicate; and if such passages in them are treated *always* with the gravity and the reprobation they deserve, it is all a sensible woman can do, and (not writing for children) all she can think necessary."[93] Even a suitably grave woman maybe shouldn't have been caught writing history in the first place, but should have stuck with those safe novels.[94] Yet Baillie concedes that most readers don't seem to be bothered by what bothers her and her sensitive friends. Why doesn't Baillie conclude that their taste is too finicky? Isn't it perverse to cling to such refined sensibilities when they leave women writers at a loss? But such extraordinary refinement is the stamp of excellence marking the woman writer. If that's buried in the subtext of Baillie's letter, the deepest thrust of her reproval is that Berry is forgetting the woman in the writer. Perhaps that's why Berry repeatedly emphasizes her concern with *human* affairs. Yet it isn't obvious what answers to this bid for a gender-free point of view, what conceptual and social space Berry could mean to occupy. I don't mean that "in principle" we can't imagine any such space. I mean to make a stubbornly empirical claim about Berry's world.

Some fifty years before, Fanny Burney had just published her fantastically successful *Evelina.* She was hellbent on keeping her identity as author secret even from her own family. "I would a thousand Times rather forfeit my character as a *Writer,* than risk ridicule or censure as a *Female.*"[95] Seventeen years later, a more poised and accomplished

---

[92] Joanna Baillie to Mary Berry, 9 June 1828, *Extracts from the Journals and Correspondence of Miss Berry from the Year 1783 to 1852,* 2d ed., ed. Lady Theresa Lewis, 3 vols. (London, 1866), 3:371.

[93] Mary Berry to Joanna Baillie, 19 June 1828, *Extracts,* 3:372.

[94] Consider *Helen* [1834], in Edgeworth, *Tales and Novels,* 10:253.

[95] *The Early Journals and Letters of Fanny Burney,* ed. Lars E. Troide and Stewart J. Cooke, 3 vols. to date (Oxford: Clarendon, 1988– ), 3:212 [*circa* 7 January 1779]. So too Sydney Owenson to Mrs. Lefanu, 12 January 1803, in *Lady Morgan's Memoirs: Autobiogra-*

Burney found a softened way of putting the same dilemma. She explained to the princesses of the royal household that in her new *Camilla*, *"Politics* were, *all ways,* left out: that once I had had an idea of bringing in such as suited *me,*—but that, upon second thoughts, I returned to my more native opinion they were not a *feminine* subject for discussion. . . ." Not even in the pages of a novel. Besides, she opined, "it would be a better office to general Readers to carry them wide of all politics, to their domestic fire sides, than to open new matter of endless debate."[96] Maybe the invocation of domestic firesides is best taken as a self-abnegating claim that all novels are good for is relaxation. Then again, maybe the invocation is best taken as a mischievous suggestion that the novel makes its reader feminine: passive, private, silent, gaining a bit of schooling in the subtleties of domestic life.

These private reflections, sly or anguished, are helpful. I want to introduce a series of excerpts from prefaces to published works by women writers, helpful in a different way: not as putatively sincere revelations of inner conviction, but as strategic bids for public attention and respect, attempts to deflect the shopworn criticisms of public women.

Mariana Starke published her 1792 play, *The Sword of Peace,* anonymously. The preface features an imagined gossipy conversation, wondering who the author is. The conversation breaks off:

> Ladies and Gentlemen,
>
> You must excuse my passing you by with the contempt such insignificant individuals deserve, whilst I address a
>
> > GENEROUS PUBLIC.
>
> A woman, however possessed of genius, wit, vivacity, or knowledge of the world, unless she continues to veil them under the modest, delicate reserve, which should ever characterise her sex, destroys their effects, and renders herself a being pitied by men of sense, envied, yet ridiculed, by every woman of her acquaintance.[97]

---

*phy, Diaries and Correspondence,* 2 vols. (London, 1862), 1:229–30. On the dilemmas of a woman writing comedy, see Sophia Gast to Fanny Burney, 19 January 1779, *Early Journals,* 3:238.

[96] Mme d'Arblay to Doctor Burney, 6 July 1796, *The Journals and Letters of Fanny Burney (Madame D'Arblay),* ed. Joyce Hemlow and others, 12 vols. (Oxford: Clarendon, 1972–1984), 3:186.

[97] Mariana Starke, *The Sword of Peace: or, A Voyage of Love,* new ed. (London, 1792), p. vi.

The reader is didactically instructed that only a contemptible gossip worms away at the mystery of the author's hidden sex. The generous public, above such base enquiries, is implicitly taken into the author's confidence. She is a woman, after all; but her bid for trust is a promise of good behavior, fidelity to the traditional norms of gender.

That same year, Hannah Cowley launched her own play with a more deliberate pledge of allegiance to feminine submissiveness.

> HINTS have been thrown out, and the idea industriously circulated, that the following comedy is tainted with POLITICS. I protest I know nothing about politics;—will Miss Wollstonecraft forgive me—whose book contains such a body of mind as I hardly ever met with—if I say that politics are *unfeminine*? I never in my life could attend to their discussion.[98]

Maybe a woman as forbiddingly brainy as Wollstonecraft is entitled to talk politics. Cowley amiably recoils from the subject—and casually adds that nonetheless one of her characters is an emigrant Frenchman and dramatic verisimilitude will require that he talk about what is going on there. Earlier, I suggested that the construction of an authorial persona partly separate from the actual author is tied up with democratic accountability. I'm not sure what to make of a sharp distinction between playwright, play, and character's utterances within the play. But maybe Cowley got away with denying the intrusion of politics, admitting it, and blaming it on her own fictional creation.

More aggressively, Charlotte Smith that same year announced that her novel would indeed contain political debates. "But women it is said have no business with politics—Why not?—Have they no interest in the scenes that are acting around them, in which they have fathers, brothers, husbands, sons, or friends engaged?" Here again is the familiar move, underlined by the repetitive emphasis on kin: the pursuit of domestic obligations requires attention to politics.

> Knowledge, which qualifies women to speak or to write on any other than the most common and trivial subjects, is supposed to be of so difficult attainment, that it cannot be acquired but by the sacrifice of domestic virtues, or the neglect of domestic duties.—*I* however may safely say, that it was in the *observance*, not in the *breach* of duty, *I* became an Author; and it has happened, that the circumstances which have com-

---

[98] Hannah Cowley, *A Day in Turkey; or, The Russian Slaves* (London, 1792), advt.

pelled me to write, have introduced me to those scenes of life, and those varieties of character which I should otherwise never have seen. . . .

Smith is alluding to a fact she does not include in her preface: she left her husband because his temper was "so capricious and often so cruel that my life was not safe."[99] The poet Cowper felt for her. "Chain'd to her desk like a slave to his oar, with no other means of subsistence for herself and her numerous children, with a broken constitution, un- equal to the severe labour enjoin'd her by necessity, she is indeed to be pitied."[100] Before discounting this rote sketch of female frailty, we should consider that Smith's children numbered twelve. Cowper also suspected that she wasn't being paid for her work. One landlord took possession of her goods; another locked her out of his premises.[101] But back to the preface, which wraps up with a calculated defiance of the conventional distinction between public and private.

> If I may be indulged a moment longer in my egotism, it shall be only while I apologize for the typographical errors of the work, which may have been in some measure occasioned by the detached and hurried way, in which the sheets were sometimes sent to the press when I was at a distance from it; and when my attention was distracted by the troubles, which it seems to be the peculiar delight of the persons who are con- cerned in the management of my childrens affairs, to inflict upon me. With all this the Public have nothing to do: but were it proper to relate all the disadvantages from anxiety of mind and local circumstances, un- der which these volumes have been composed, such a detail might be admitted as an excuse for more material errors.[102]

Her unreliable childcare may not be the public's business, but Smith is publishing a reference to it anyway. So she's not neglecting her domestic affairs to be an author. Other people are neglecting her domestic affairs, and that's why she can't acquit herself as compe- tently as she might otherwise. So the public is tauntingly invited to ponder the view that women are specially obligated to care for their

---

[99] Charlotte Smith to Revd. Joseph Cooper Walker, 9 October 1793, in Smith, *The Old Manor House,* ed. Anne Henry Ehrenpreis (Oxford: Oxford University Press, 1989), p. viii.

[100] William Cowper to William Hayley, 29 January 1793, *The Letters and Prose Writings of William Cowper,* ed. James King and Charles Ryskamp, 5 vols. (Oxford: Clarendon, 1979–1986), 4:281.

[101] Cowper to Lady Hesketh, 8–21 May 1793, *Letters,* 4:336.

[102] Charlotte Smith, *Desmond,* 3 vols. (London, 1792), 1:iii–vii.

families. They're not invited to ponder the culpability of her abusive husband, invisible in the preface. Whether from shame or fear of scandal and reprisals, Smith's playful public stance conceals private pathos.

In 1806, Christian conservative Elizabeth Hamilton took a stern view of such playful transgressions. "It must be confessed, that whatever consideration may be given to the circumstances under which a book is written, by those who take a peculiar interest in the writer, it is only to the friends of the individual that they can with propriety be offered as an apology for any apparent defect." Authors' personal problems were one thing, their books another. "With the public, an author has, or ought to have, no other existence than as an author. On the present occasion, no other circumstances than those that are connected with such existence, shall therefore be brought forward."[103] Shortly after, though, Hamilton blithely comments that she will say nothing about theological controversies. "Let those who have power for the contest, arm themselves for the combat; she has been taught to consider her sex as precluded from the field of strife."[104] So the public has no interest in peering behind the curtain of authorship, in unmasking the literary persona. Yet unless we want to convict her of patent confusion, Hamilton's sex isn't one of those invidiously private facts behind the curtain. It's partly constitutive of what sort of author she is.

Nor is this simply a matter of Hamilton's being a steadfast conservative. Vouching for her own "veneration for the scriptures," feminist Mary Hays averred "that if any object can be more disgusting than a man professing a contempt for all religion, it is a woman of the same description."[105] It's one thing to sidestep the routine accusation that political radicalism was inextricably tied up with atheism. It's another to hold that authorship is inextricably tied up with sex and gender. Not that *author* is necessarily male; neither Hamilton nor Hays seems to be saying that. (Though perhaps *author* is presumptively male,

---

[103] Elizabeth Hamilton, *Letters, Addressed to the Daughter of a Nobleman, on the Formation of Religious and Moral Principle*, 2d ed., 2 vols. (London, 1806; reprint ed. New York: Garland, 1974), 1:viii.

[104] Hamilton, *Letters*, 1:xxi.

[105] Mary Hays, *Appeal to the Men of Great Britain in Behalf of Women* (London, 1798; reprint ed. New York: Garland, 1974), pp. 1–2.

women authors freakish departures from the ordinary and unremarkable case.) Rather that authors come in two kinds, male and female; that the public may rightly heed the distinction; and that they're bound by different moralities of discussion.

One could thread one's way through the parallel labyrinth, exploring how readers come in two kinds, male and female, and not just what but how each kind ought to read. Briefly, consider two more prefaces, the first from the youthful Mary Russell Mitford. "The Author is well aware that age and sex have no right to be urged at the critical bar in extenuation of literary errors; yet there may be some gentle readers, who will not refuse to a young and timid female the indulgence, which they would withhold from an older and more practised offender; to their mercy she appeals."[106] Whether male or female, these gentle readers are feminine. Remember that the refrain that women could and should write the best novels was met by the refrain that it was dangerous for women to read novels.

The second is from Mrs. John Sandford, to use the name she chose on her title page. "THE title of the following pages"—*Woman, in Her Social and Domestic Character*—"is, perhaps, their best plea to the indulgence of the reader. It at least embraces a subject which will be regarded as strictly appropriate to a female pen; and it is hoped that this circumstance may be admitted as at once an apology and a recommendation." Perhaps this seems a tad more special pleading than other woman authors were permitting themselves, but Sandford relentlessly forged ahead. "Of course the authoress has written exclusively for her own sex; and to them would she respectfully commit her little book." Sandford bolsters her case by choosing an archaism to emphasize her own sex, by designating her readers as fellow women, and by offering a diminutive description of her book, which is not all that short.[107]

No distinction of persons, a masquerade without masks: these gutsy slogans of democratic equality might seem to depend on a massive and unchallenged exclusion of women. Adopting this view, I've been arguing, would be a mistake. What sort of mistake? If I may invoke some distinctions I distrust, an empirical or sociological or historical

---

[106] Mary Russell Mitford, *Christina, the Maid of the South Seas* (London, 1811), p. ix.
[107] Mrs. John Sandford, *Woman, in Her Social and Domestic Character* (London, 1831), advt.

mistake, not a conceptual or theoretical or philosophical mistake. More important, a mistake that would prevent our gaining a more fine-grained understanding of how contemporaries wrestled with a particularly important normative conflict.

Again: the norm dictating that women cling deferentially to a private existence isn't an attitude held by misogynists. It is bound up with social practices, with who holds the franchise and who doesn't, who holds property in his own name and who doesn't hold it in hers, who rises in the debating society and who doesn't, and so on. So too with the norm of democratic equality. It makes concrete social reference to what goes on in the debating society, the alehouse, the coffeehouse, and so on. Both norms have their aspirational dimensions. Norms are never just innocently read off the behavioral facts of existing practice, which are always shot full of gaffes and outright violations. But neither norm is a freewheeling invention, either.

Mrs. Jameson launched her 1833 volume on women with a preface featuring a lengthy fictional dialogue. Alda, standing in for the author, tries to dodge the criticism she anticipates from her male interlocutor, Medon. "As to maintaining the superiority, or speculating on the rights of women—nonsense! why should you suspect me of such folly?—it is quite out of date."[108] Wollstonecraft's *Vindication of the Rights of Woman* was over forty years old. Yet the two of them instantly fall into the familiar pirouettes. "How I hate political women!" exclaims Medon. "The number of political intriguing women of this time, whose boudoirs and drawing-rooms are the *foyers* of party spirit, is another trait of resemblance between the state of society now, and that which existed at Paris before the revolution."[109] Alda insists on women's lofty patriotic sentiments, on the faulty educations that have crippled their judgment. But she falters: "A time is coming perhaps when the education of women will be considered with a view to their future destination as the mothers and nurses of legislators and statesmen. . . ."[110] Nothing here that Hannah More couldn't readily endorse; no reason to think the landscape was undergoing even glacial change.

---

[108] Mrs. Jameson, *Characteristics of Women, Moral, Poetical, and Historical,* 2 vols. (London, 1833), 1:v–vi.

[109] Jameson, *Characteristics,* 1:xlv.

[110] Jameson, *Characteristics,* 1:xlix.

## POLITICAL CONFLICT TERMINABLE
### AND INTERMINABLE

"In all the theories and projects of the most absurd speculation, it has never been suggested that it would be advisable to extend the elective suffrage to the female sex," Fox instructed the House of Commons in 1797. Like workers, he explained, women were dependents; classical political wisdom thus dictated that they not be placed in the absurd position of having to venture ostensibly independent judgment.[111] Four years before, in fact, while conceding that their claims to the franchise were less secure than those of men, John Cartwright had urged that nonetheless women ought to vote, that "female citizenship would greatly strengthen" freedom.[112] Cartwright would later wobble away from this position.[113] The year after Fox's injunction, radical Thomas Spence would insert a pregnant clause into his draft constitution for a utopian society: "Female Citizens have the same right of suffrage in their respective parishes as the Men: because they have equal property in the country, and are equally subject to the laws, and, indeed, they are in every respect, as well on their own account as on account of their children, as deeply interested in every public transaction." Even he would add a demurrer: "But in consideration of the delicacy of their sex, they are exempted from, and are ineligible to, all public employments."[114] In a typically misanthropic exercise in rational choice analysis, James Mill argued that the central danger of political life is that those with power will pursue their own interests and exploit others. So everyone ought to be admitted to a share of power, except "those individuals whose interests are indisputably in

---

[111] *The Speeches of the Right Honourable Charles James Fox, in the House of Commons*, 6 vols. (London, 1815), 6:363 [26 May 1797].

[112] *A Letter from John Cartwright, Esq. to a Friend at Boston* (London, 1793), pp. 65–66. But see H. T. Dickinson, *Liberty and Property: Political Ideology in Eighteenth-Century Britain* (New York: Holmes and Meier, 1977), p. 253. Contrast the *reductio* in *Association Papers* (London, 1793), pt. 2, no. 9, p. 8.

[113] J. R. Dinwiddy, *Radicalism and Reform in Britain, 1780–1850* (London: Hambledon Press, 1992), p. 288; *Black Dwarf* (14 November 1821) 7(20):682.

[114] *Trial of Thomas Spence in 1801 together with his Description of Spensonia, Constitution of Spensonia, End of Oppression, Recantation of the End of Oppression, Newcastle on Tyne Lecture Delivered in 1775, also, A Brief Life of Spence and a Description of His Political Token Dies*, ed. Arthur W. Waters (Leamington Spa: privately printed at the Courier Press, 1917), p. 98.

cluded in those of other individuals," such as women, "the interest of almost all of whom is involved either in that of their fathers or in that of their husbands."[115] William Thompson pounced on Mill for this slip in his political logic.[116] But Mill's claim, like Fox's apparent historical howler, isn't merely a mistake. It might better be taken as symptomatic, a sign of powerfully ideological currents at work.

But not, again, currents working their will behind the backs of witless actors, not a monolithically structured discourse exerting itself through its passive mouthpieces. For contemporaries knew that there were deep problems here. Women found some room, however limited, to maneuver, just as their conservative opponents understood all too well that they didn't hold all the justificatory cards. "At the present day, indeed," grumbled Richard Polwhele in his jeremiad, *The Unsex'd Females,* "our literary women are so numerous, that their judges, waving all complimentary civilities, decide upon their merits with the same rigid impartiality as it seems right to exercise towards the men. The tribunal of criticism is no longer charmed into complacence by the blushes of modest apprehension." This claim, too, has the same structure and significance as the putative mistakes of Fox and Mill. On its face, it's false; but it captures in stark outline one motif in a blurred picture. And it provokes Polwhele to the same kind of riposte offered by Cobbett: "Alas! the crimsoning blush of modesty, will be always more attractive, than the sparkle of confident intel-

---

[115] James Mill, *Essay on Government* [1820], in *Utilitarian Logic and Politics: James Mill's 'Essay on Government', Macaulay's Critique and the Ensuing Debate,* ed. Jack Lively and John Rees (Oxford: Clarendon, 1978), p. 79. The Benthamite *Gorgon* (22 August 1818) no. 14, pp. 109–10 already had staked out this position. The master himself vacillated on the issue: see *Plan of Parliamentary Reform* [1817], in *The Works of Jeremy Bentham,* ed. John Bowring, 11 vols. (Edinburgh, 1843), 3:463; *Radical Reform Bill,* in *Works of Bentham,* 3:564; *First Principles Preparatory to Constitutional Code* [1822], ed. Philip Schofield (Oxford: Clarendon, 1989), pp. 96–100; "Constitutional Code: Matter Occasioned by Greece" [1823], in *Securities against Misrule and Other Constitutional Writings for Tripoli and Greece,* ed. Philip Schofield (Oxford: Clarendon, 1990), p. 260; *Constitutional Code,* vol. 1 [1830], ed. F. Rosen and J. H. Burns (Oxford: Clarendon, 1983), p. 29. Bowring reports that Bentham held Mill's views on the abilities of women "abominable": *Works of Bentham,* 10:450.

[116] William Thompson, *Appeal of One Half the Human Race, Women, against the Pretensions of the Other Half, Men, to Retain Them in Political, and Thence in Civil and Domestic, Slavery; in Reply to a Paragraph of Mr. Mill's Celebrated "Article on Government"* (London, 1825), especially pp. 9, 14.

ligence."[117] This riposte expresses not just exasperation but also anxiety that equality is running amok.

So, too, contemporaries toyed with exploring the gendered aspects of democracy itself. That project is already gestured toward in Burke's protestations of love for "a manly, moral, regulated liberty," presumably contrasted to the effeminate liberty constructed by the French revolutionaries. Or in his contrast between publicity and diplomatic reserve: "I admit that reason of state will not, in many circumstances, permit the disclosure of the true ground of a public proceeding. In that case silence is manly, and it is wise."[118] More savagely, Walter Scott commented that "a woman's brain is sometimes as inconstant as a popular assembly," the endless cycles of legislation, amendment, and repeal standing for feminine indecisiveness.[119] Talkativeness itself was a sign of femininity, and weren't legislatures and alehouses stuffed with chatterboxes? "Every man thinks and says that every woman talks more than he," drily commented Mitford; "it is the creed of the whole sex,—the debates and law reports notwithstanding."[120]

Or one could pick out the masculine aspects of democracy. Disdaining the Burkean appeal to prejudice, Wollstonecraft wrote, "This mode of arguing, if arguing it may be called, reminds me of what is vulgarly termed a woman's reason. For women sometimes declare that they love, or believe, certain things, *because* they love, or believe them."[121] At least those in democratic debate were called on to give reasons, respond to criticisms, pursue justifications. The learned William Drummond detected the same gender dynamic. The bold pursuit of philosophic argument, he pleaded, "was the proud distinction of Englishmen, and the luminous source of all their glory. Shall we

[117] Richard Polwhele, *The Unsex'd Females: A Poem, Addressed to the Author of The Pursuits of Literature* (London, 1798; reprint ed. New York: Garland, 1974), p. 16 n. †.

[118] *Letters on a Regicide Peace* [1796–1797], in *The Works of the Right Honorable Edmund Burke*, 9th ed., 12 vols. (Boston: Little, Brown, 1889), 5:336.

[119] *Peveril of the Peak* [1822], in *Waverley Novels*, 28:67. See too Anthony Stokes, *Desultory Observations, on . . . Great Britain* (London, 1792), p. 50 n.

[120] Mary Russell Mitford, *Our Village*, 5 vols. (London, 1824–1832), 1:222.

[121] *Vindication of the Rights of Woman* [1792], in *The Works of Mary Wollstonecraft*, ed. Janet Todd and Marilyn Butler, assistant ed. Emma Rees-Mogg, 7 vols. (London: William Pickering, 1989), 5:182–83. See too Benjamin Flower, *The French Constitution; with Remarks on Some of Its Principal Articles; in Which Their Importance in a Political, Moral and Religious Point of View, Is Illustrated; and the Necessity of a Reformation in Church and State in Great Britain, Enforced* (London, 1792), pp. 105–7.

then forget the manly and dignified sentiments of our ancestors, to prate in the language of the mother, or the nurse, about our good old prejudices?"[122] Taking much the same line against Burke, Paine condemned prejudice and applauded reason. Republics, by which Paine meant governments that replaced the hereditary succession of monarchy and aristocracy with elections and representation, rested on reason. (Or so he liked to say.) In a whimsical flourish, Paine proclaimed that in republics, "the human faculties act with boldness, and acquire, under this form of government, a gigantic manliness."[123]

Gigantic manliness indeed: here political invective became awfully gruff. William Hone's *Political House that Jack Built,* stuffing dangerously radical sentiments into the lilting rhythms of the children's ditty, featured a Cruikshank engraving of a printing press. "THIS IS **THE THING**," Hone explained, that would poison the verminous placemen plundering Britain and destroying her constitution.[124] In the day's vernacular, *thing* referred to the male genitals, *thingumbobs* to testicles.[125] Hone surely wanted the heavy-handed humor. "Under the Boroughmongering system," he already had explained in his attack on electoral corruption, "the nation cannot hope for a body of wise and enlightened legislators. A *thing* with a hat and two boots on, one of which it spats now and then with a switch, walks into the house, sticks itself upright, or reclines on one of the benches, and when the division comes, remains, or goes forth into the lobby, as needs be:— this is a *Borough-Monger's Member!*"[126] Here it is old corruption screwing the long-suffering people. Other radicals chimed in, their use of *thing* sometimes summoning up the genitals, sometimes a frightful monster.[127] The printing press, its lever cocked defiantly, would pene-

---

[122] William Drummond, *Academical Questions* (London, 1805; reprint ed. Delmar, NY: Scholars' Facsimiles & Reprints, 1984), p. xiv.

[123] *Rights of Man* [1791], in *The Life and Works of Thomas Paine,* 10 vols. (New Rochelle, NY: Thomas Paine National Historical Association, 1925), 6:200.

[124] William Hone, *The Political House that Jack Built,* 30th ed. (London, 1819), as paginated in *Radical Squibs & Loyal Ripostes: Satirical Pamphlets of the Regency Period, 1819–1821,* ed. Edgell Rickword (New York: Barnes & Noble, 1971), p. 41. See the response in M. Adams, *A Parody on the Political House that Jack Built: or The Real House that Jack Built* (London, 1820), n.p.

[125] Pierce Egan, *Grose's Classical Dictionary of the Vulgar Tongue, Revised and Corrected* (London, 1823), s.v. *thingumbob.*

[126] *Hone's Reformist Register* (20 September 1817) 2(9):277.

[127] See for instance *Black Dwarf* (27 February 1822) 8(9):297–303, (10 April 1822)

trate the dark recesses of secrecy and prejudice. We may see in that beautifully engraved printing press presented to Caroline a phallus with which she could gird herself for battle. Perhaps radicals here took their lead from Burke himself. In a moment of mawkish melodrama, the *Reflections* present Marie Antoinette, "almost naked," flying out of her chamber as "a band of cruel ruffians and assassins . . . pierced with a hundred strokes of bayonets and poniards" her bed.[128] It would be discreet to withhold comment.

In short, contemporaries noticed a pointed conflict between femininity and democracy. It's tempting to think that such conflicts can't forever be evaded, that eventually people will have to resolve them. But wallowing in these conflicts has seductions of its own.

"Till of late," held Maria Edgeworth in one of her narrative voices in 1795, "women were kept in Turkish ignorance; every means of acquiring knowledge was discountenanced by fashion, and impracticable even to those who despised fashion. Our books of science were full of unintelligible jargon, and mystery veiled pompous ignorance from public contempt. . . ." But now enlightenment was on the march. The public demanded clarity of exposition; "the art of teaching has been carried to great perfection" by the thirst for learning. The refrain is every bit as smug as it would be in Brougham's hands thirty years later. But here the march of intellect wasn't simply beneficial to the lower orders. It was revolutionizing gender relations. "All this," concluded Edgeworth ambitiously, "is in favour of women."[129] Yet again, hyperbole emphasizes one aspect of a richly contradictory reality. The farmer's wife of a story Edgeworth published six years later is aware that the real story is more complex. Her husband says all kinds of news is of interest to him. "And to me," she chimes in, "not excepting politics, which you gentlemen always think so polite to keep to yourselves; but, you recollect, I was used to politics when I lived with my uncle at Cardiffe. . . ."[130]

---

8(15):483–84, (10 July 1822) 9(2):59; William Cobbett, *Rural Rides* [1830], ed. George Woodcock (Harmondsworth: Penguin, 1985), p. 90.

[128] *Reflections on the Revolution in France* [1790], in *Works*, 3:325.

[129] Maria Edgeworth, *Letters for Literary Ladies: to Which Is Added, An Essay on the Noble Science of Self-Justification* (London, 1795), pt. 1, pp. 64–65, reprinted with variations in Edgeworth, *Tales and Novels*, 8:445.

[130] "Angelina; or, L'amie inconnue" [1801], in Edgeworth, *Tales and Novels*, 1:238.

By 1831, Edgeworth was interrupting herself in the middle of a letter to her fast friend, the American Jewess who once had chided her for her literary Jew-hating. "I am surprised to find I have written so much of what I scarcely ever write—*Politics.* But though I feel it is not a woman's department and that as she can do nothing, she had better say nothing; yet all is so out of its place now that I have got out of mine."[131] She had indeed written on politics, not just in this private letter to her female friend, but in public, to a huge audience of male and female strangers, for years on end. If she was out of place, she had been there an awfully long time. But maybe she wasn't out of place at all. Maybe she had problems making sense of the place she was occupying, making it more capacious, finding a vocabulary and a set of political strategies that promised to make it an entirely comfortable place in which she could feel at home. And maybe her problems are still with us, even if we do not routinely impeach the femininity of women writers, even if we no longer entertain the view that their writing disfigures their womanly good looks. Should women write on "politics, or political economy, or pugilism, or punch?" demanded *Fraser's,* the temptations of alliteration capsizing the point at hand. "Certainly not. We feel a determined dislike of women who wander into these unfeminine paths; they should immediately hoist a mustache—and, to do them justice, they in general do exhibit no inconsiderable specimen of the hair-lip."[132]

[131] Maria Edgeworth to Rachel Lazarus, 4 November 1831, *The Education of the Heart: The Correspondence of Rachel Mordecai Lazarus and Maria Edgeworth,* ed. Edgar E. MacDonald (Chapel Hill, NC: University of North Carolina Press, 1977), p. 215.

[132] *Fraser's* (October 1833) 8(46):433.

# ELEVEN

# THE TROUBLE WITH
# HAIRDRESSERS

⸻ ⚬⚬⚬ ⸻

IT IS A FACT not to be denied, however much to be deplored, that
the art and mystery of barbery has, without any assignable reason,
sunk exceedingly from that high estimation in which it was anciently
held; and that though all the world continues still as much obliged to
it as ever, it has become the object of nearly all the world's contu-
mely."[1] Or so claimed one breezy 1824 guide to London. But just
what was contemptible about barbers?

In one novel, also from 1824, cranky but endearing Mr. Ramsay
spurns the strawberries brought by a niece he loathes and recom-
mends that she deliver them to "a barber's bairn two doors aff." " 'Pon
my word, uncle,' said Miss Bell in great indignation, 'I have something else to do than to pick strawberries for barber's brats, indeed.' "[2] It might seem that, Scottish accent and vocabulary aside, the
exchange could be placed anywhere, any time. But the guide to London does not claim that hairdressers are always lowly and therefore
contemptible. It notices a change in their status. Nor is the London
guide idiosyncratic. In Walter Scott's *Antiquary,* set in the 1790s, old
Caxon the barber "sighed over the disrespect into which his art had
so universally fallen."[3] We can also canvass earlier examples of affection and esteem for barbers, hairdressers, shavers, peruquiers, *les*

---

[1] Sholto and Reuben Percy [ Joseph Clinton Robertson and Thomas Byerley], *London: or Interesting Memorials of Its Rise, Progress & Present State,* 3 vols. (London, 1824),
1:353.

[2] *The Inheritance* [1824], in *The Works of Susan Ferrier,* Holyrood edition, 4 vols. (London: Eveleigh Nash & Grayson Limited, 1929), 2:154.

[3] *The Antiquary* [1816], in Walter Scott, *Waverley Novels,* 48 vols. (Edinburgh, 1829–
1833), 5:147; for the setting, 5:i; note too 6:111–14 for bantering about Caxon's stupidity. A *caxon* is a kind of wig. For a dramatic adaptation of this novel, see Isaac Pocock
and Daniel Terry, *The Antiquary* (London, 1820).

*friseurs,* and other practitioners of the tonsorial arts. By the 1760s, "that's the barber" had emerged as a slang term of all-purpose commendation.[4] Then again, in 1709 the *Tatler* already was trying to figure out "whence it should proceed, that of all the lower Order, Barbers should go further in hitting the Ridiculous, than any other Set of Men."[5] Picking up another of his many whores in London, clutching instinctively at a low-status disguise, Boswell "called myself a barber."[6] To some extent, anxieties about longstanding developments are masquerading as claims about change.

Figaro, to clutch one promising straw, was well known on the English stage. The operas by Mozart and Rossini as well as dramatic adaptations of the Beaumarchais plays were popular. "Who is there," demanded *Blackwood's* in 1823, "whose heart does not beat joyously to the very sound of the Barber of Seville?"[7] But Flaubert's crack, that Figaro was one of the causes of the French Revolution, isn't immediately on point. As far as I know, the English Figaro, unlike his French progenitor, launches into no denunciations of the aristocracy. He doesn't instruct them that they've merely taken the trouble to be born; he doesn't make any pointed jests about public opinion; nor does he even applaud freedom of the press. Even in the hands of a translator as radical as Holcroft, he is just another cunning rogue.[8] No wonder that the radical *Poor Man's Guardian* contemptuously dismissed Figaro as politically innocuous.[9] So Figaro isn't our man.

At the risk of rounding up a usual historiographical suspect, though, I do want to suggest that the French Revolution is central to explaining the newly degraded status of hairdressers—or at least how

[4] Boswell to John Johnston, 9 July 1763, *The Correspondence of James Boswell and John Johnston of Grange,* ed. Ralph S. Walker (New York: McGraw-Hill, 1966), pp. 86–87; *Boswell in Search of a Wife 1766–1769,* ed. Frank Brady and Frederick A. Pottle (New York: McGraw-Hill, 1956), p. 160. Sixty years later it was still recognizable: John Fawcett, *The Barber of Seville: A Comic Opera, in Two Acts; as Performed at the Theatre Royal, Covent Garden* (London, 1818), p. 6; Pierce Egan, *Grose's Classical Dictionary of the Vulgar Tongue, Revised and Corrected* (London, 1823), s.v. *dandy.*

[5] *Tatler* (25–28 June 1709) no. 34. See too A Barber, *An Address to the Worshipful Company of Barbers in Oxford,* 2d ed. (Oxford, 1749).

[6] *Boswell's London Journal 1762–1763,* ed. Frederick A. Pottle (New York: McGraw-Hill, 1950), p. 272 [2 June 1763].

[7] *Blackwood's Edinburgh Magazine* (October 1823) 34(214):672–73.

[8] *The Barber of Seville, or the Useless Precaution; a Comedy in Four Acts* (London, 1776); Thomas Holcroft, *The Follies of a Day* (London, 1811); Fawcett, *Barber of Seville;* Henry R. Bishop, *The Marriage of Figaro,* 2d. ed. (London, 1823).

[9] *Poor Man's Guardian* (23 July 1831) 1(3):21.

they executed their triumphant procession from being ridiculous in the *Tatler* to being contemptible in the guide to London. British hairdressers embodied some classic anxieties about equality, anxieties sharpened by those dastardly events across the Channel. Quirky though they seem, hairdressers can help us figure out what egalitarians are demanding and what their conservative opponents are unhappy about. Why should hairdressers, of all unlikely candidates, have come to exemplify equality, even to be a cultural obsession? The question raises knotty issues about contingency and explanation which I shan't explore. Suffice it to say that hairdressers happened to occupy a social position that made it possible to demonize them. Others could have occupied such a position (and perhaps some did); even given the facts of the matter, hairdressers needn't have been demonized. But it happens that they were and that we can learn from their daffy appearance on the sordid stage of cultural politics. Once again, apparently bizarre and trivial historical flotsam are tossed up with the most august matters of political theory.

## FRIZ, FRIZ, FRIZ

In 1766 and 1820, we find French hairdressers advertising that they could make one look young again.[10] The vain old general of Charlotte Smith's *Old Manor House* attempts to look young by "putting on toupees and curls," making himself ridiculous instead of attractive to the young woman he's smitten with.[11] One onlooker, struck by the elderly Cobbett's vibrant health, was tempted to attribute his "very white hair" to the use of powder.[12] And in Sheridan's *Trip to Scarborough,* Young Fashion sighs that women fall in love on the basis of mere appearance, and Lory responds, "Sir, Taylors and Hair-dressers are now become the bawds of the nation—'tis they that debauch all the women."[13]

[10] *The Yale Edition of Horace Walpole's Correspondence,* ed. W. S. Lewis, 48 vols. (New Haven, CT: Yale University Press, 1937–1983), 7:357 [1766]; *Journals of Dorothy Wordsworth,* ed. E. de Selincourt, 2 vols. (New York: Macmillan, 1941), 2:328 [1820].

[11] Charlotte Smith, *The Old Manor House* [1793], ed. Anne Henry Ehrenpreis (Oxford: Oxford University Press, 1989), p. 142. See too Benjamin Disraeli, *Vivian Grey* [1826–1827], ed. Herbert van Thal (London: Cassell, 1968), pp. 1–3.

[12] *The Diaries of Absalom Watkin: A Manchester Man 1787–1861,* ed. Magdalen Goffin (Phoenix Mill: Alan Sutton, 1993), p. 112 [3 and 10 January 1830].

[13] *A Trip to Scarborough* [1781], in *The Dramatic Works of Richard Brinsley Sheridan,* ed. Cecil Price, 2 vols. (Oxford: Clarendon, 1973), 2:577.

Think of how easy it is to become invested in one's hair, to think of it as crucial to maintaining youth, good looks, or one's very identity. Harriet Martineau has one family worry that if they force their elderly servant to stop wearing hair powder, he will die.[14] Think too of how easy it is to become invested in others' hair, to see it as betraying distasteful facts. One antislavery writer denied that the woolly hair of Negroes was a badge of inferiority.[15] "False curls" and powdered head, revealed one poet, aided in the outrageous deception practiced by the fine lady of London, "A modern Venus, who, if stript of dress, / Is age, deformity, and ugliness."[16] Babbling Miss Larolles, a figure of cheap laughs and stern moral reproval of the frivolities of the upper classes in Fanny Burney's *Cecilia,* is in agony at her inability to find her hairdresser before a masquerade. "I was forced to have my hair dressed by my own maid, quite in a common way; was not it cruelly mortifying?"[17] In the same novel, Mr. Briggs instructs Cecilia that wearing a simple bob wig is a sure sign of a good man. This absurd miser wears a wig, even though he frets about economizing on shaving rags and about combing out his wig so aggressively that it loses some hairs.[18] Jane Austen's Robert Watson thanks the ladies for their condescension in admitting him and apologizes for his disorderly appearance: "We got here so late, that I had not time even to put a little fresh powder in my hair."[19] Here, even dehumanization reached its limit: the men of Shrewsbury's workhouse were entitled to be shaved at least once a week.[20] Fussy attention to facial hair became a defining mark of British manhood. *John Bull* vaunted in the absurdities of the hopelessly uninformed liberal benevolence that ordered that slaves

[14] Harriet Martineau, *Illustrations of Taxation,* 5 vols. (London, 1834), 1:113.

[15] William Dickson, *Letters on Slavery . . . to Which Are Added, Addresses to the Whites, and to the Free Negroes of Barbadoes; and Accounts of Some Negroes Eminent for Their Virtues and Abilities* (London, 1789), pp. 71–72.

[16] "A London Receipt to Make a Modern Fine Lady," in Lady Sophia Burrell, *Poems,* 2 vols. (London, 1793), 2:35. The image goes back at least as far as Swift: see "The Progress of Beauty" [1719], "The Lady's Dressing Room" [1732], and "A Beautiful Young Nymph Going to Bed" [1734] in Jonathan Swift, *Poetical Works,* ed. Herbert Davis (London: Oxford University Press, 1967), pp. 172–75, 476–80, 517–19.

[17] Fanny Burney, *Cecilia, or Memoirs of an Heiress* [1782], ed. Peter Sabor and Margaret Anne Doody (Oxford: Oxford University Press, 1988), p. 25.

[18] Burney, *Cecilia,* pp. 452–53, 745, 94.

[19] *The Watsons* [1804–1805], in *The Novels of Jane Austen,* ed. R. W. Chapman, 3d ed., 6 vols. (Oxford: Oxford University Press, 1987), 6:357.

[20] Frederic Morton Eden, *The State of the Poor,* 3 vols. (London, 1797; reprint ed. Bristol: Thoemmes Press, 1994), 2:629.

be provided with two razors a year: "*Negroes have no beards—and never shave.*"[21] *Blackwood's* offered some wry bantering on the weighty question of why a Rabbi Moses Edrehi never shaved.[22]

Care of the self, it turns out, demands a surprising amount of care of the hair. Concern with hair threads its way through Boswell's papers. Arriving in London, he budgeted £6 a year to have his hair dressed pretty much daily.[23] In 1763, he was moved to poetry in reflecting on how rapidly hair styles changed.[24] "To keep nerves firm," he counselled himself the next year, "shave fine."[25] In 1772, he dashed off a letter to Garrick to thank him for "a handsom wig made by your own Operatour" and wondered why his wife so disliked wigs.[26] Several years later, he tried growing his hair longer again to please her, but the wig he was obliged to wear during legal proceedings made him too hot; at his wife's advice, he had his hair cut off again.[27] (Another doting husband haughtily refused such complaisant submission to his wife's desires: "He was not the sort of person who let his hair grow *under his wig* to please his wife."[28] But this was the least of Caroline's problems with the refractory Prince of Wales.) In 1789, Boswell was so distraught over the disappearance of his wig—"I could not long remain an object of laughter"—that he promptly travelled twenty-five miles to get a new one.[29] So, too, Boswell recorded a parade of hairdressers: the one who butchered a reading of Hume's

---

[21] *John Bull* (1 April 1832) 12(590):109. The same misconception shows up in *BMC* no. 17158 [28 June 1832].

[22] *Blackwood's Edinburgh Magazine* (June 1829) 25(153):788–89.

[23] *Boswell's London Journal 1762–1763*, ed. Frederick A. Pottle (New York: McGraw-Hill, 1950), p. 336 [1762].

[24] *Boswell in Holland 1763–1764*, ed. Frederick A. Pottle (London: William Heinemann, 1952), pp. 98–99 [21 December 1763].

[25] *Boswell in Holland*, p. 189 [22 March 1764].

[26] Boswell to Garrick, 10 September 1772, *The Correspondence of James Boswell with David Garrick, Edmund Burke, and Edmond Malone*, ed. Frank Brady and others (New York: McGraw-Hill, 1987), pp. 43–44.

[27] *Boswell: The Ominous Years 1774–1776*, ed. Charles Ryskamp and Frederick A. Pottle (New York: McGraw-Hill, 1963), pp. 262–63 [17 March 1776].

[28] *Diaries and Correspondence of James Harris, First Earl of Malmesbury*, ed. his grandson, 4 vols. (London, 1844), 4:223 [2 March 1803].

[29] *Boswell: The English Experiment 1785–1789*, ed. Irma S. Lustig and Frederick A. Pottle (New York: McGraw-Hill, 1986), p. 11 [23 August 1789]. See too the distraught Mme Duval in Fanny Burney, *Evelina, or The History of a Young Lady's Entrance into the World* [1778], ed. Edward A. Bloom and Lillian D. Bloom (Oxford: Oxford University Press, 1982), pp. 149, 151.

*History of England* Boswell requested to help him fall asleep,[30] the San Remo barber who dared to flaunt the fleurs-de-lis of royal France,[31] the "perfidious Gaul" (punning on his name, Gall) who didn't show up on time,[32] a gossip retailing stories of somber Dr. Young's mistress,[33] the barber who procured him a cheap messenger,[34] and more.[35] Boswell was loquacious, peculiar too, but I see no reason to believe his obsession with hair and hairdressers was idiosyncratic.

But hair does far more elaborate symbolic work than serving as a marker of youthful vitality and good looks. In 1795, Pitt's government passed a tax on hair powder.[36] For a while, those who continued to wear powder were ridiculed as guinea pigs.[37] In 1796, Coleridge, then a young radical, bemoaned those who continued to squander powder, largely composed of flour, while poor men went hungry.[38] (In 1810, a conservative Coleridge was powdering his own hair.[39]) Yet George Rose, an M.P., worried about the decline of the use of hair powder, not just because of government revenues, but "to avoid other mischief which I am very sure is not enough attended to, the distinction of dress and external appearance. The inattention to that has been a

---

[30] *Boswell's London Journal,* p. 252 [3 May 1763].

[31] *Boswell on the Grand Tour: Italy, Corsica, and France 1765–1766,* ed. Frank Brady and Frederick A. Pottle (London: William Heinemann, 1955), p. 248 [14 December 1765].

[32] *Boswell in Search of a Wife,* p. 272 [3 September 1769].

[33] *Boswell for the Defence 1769–1774,* ed. William K. Wimsatt, Jr. and Frederick A. Pottle (New York: McGraw-Hill, 1959), p. 32 [19 March 1772].

[34] *Boswell: The Ominous Years,* p. 110 [31 March 1775].

[35] *Boswell: The Ominous Years,* p. 308 [2 April 1776]; *Boswell: The Applause of the Jury 1782–1785,* ed. Irma S. Lustig and Frederick A. Pottle (New York: McGraw-Hill, 1981), p. 142 [17 May 1783]; *Boswell: The Great Biographer 1789–1795,* ed. Marlies K. Danziger and Frank Brady (New York: McGraw-Hill, 1989), p. 151 [12 August 1791].

[36] 35 Geo. III, c. 49. For the debate on the tax, see especially *Parliamentary Register* 41:68–72 [23 March 1795], 41:155–56 [30 March 1795, third reading and passage of the bill].

[37] *Times* (14 December 1795) in John Ashton, *Old Times: A Picture of Social Life at the End of the Eighteenth Century* (London, 1885), p. 62; *BMC* no. 8628 [6 March 1795]. See too *BMC* no. 8629 [10 March 1795], reproduced in *The Works of James Gillray: 582 Plates and a Supplement Containing the 45 So-Called "Suppressed Plates"* (London, 1850–1851; reprint ed. New York: Benjamin Blom, 1968), pl. 117.

[38] *The Watchman* (9 March 1796), in *The Collected Works of Samuel Taylor Coleridge,* ed. Kathleen Coburn, Bart Winer, and others, in progress (Princeton, NJ: Princeton University Press, 1969–), 2:80. See too *The Reign of the English Robespierre* (London, 1795), p. 7.

[39] Charles Lamb to Dorothy Wordsworth, 13 November 1810, *The Letters of Charles and Mary Anne Lamb,* ed. Edwin W. Marrs, Jr., 3 vols. to date (Ithaca, NY: Cornell University Press, 1975–), 3:62.

great support of Jacobinism."[40] If social status isn't going to be evanescent, it has to be displayed: Rose didn't need to read Marx to
understand the daily reproduction of social life. So decisions about
what to wear and how to do one's hair aren't innocent matters of
mere personal preference. They are politically charged. Similarly, it
spoke volumes when Lord Bathurst cut off his pigtail after the passage
of the Reform Bill of 1832.[41] "By God," exclaimed one doughty conservative,"when a man cuts off his queue, the head should go with it."[42]

For those of the higher orders, hairdressing was elaborate business.
Hair was plastered, powdered (up to two pounds of powder per
head[43]), curled, lubricated with pomatum or bear grease or Macassar
oil. This mass of stuff had to be combed out and reapplied daily: it
must have gotten horribly messy overnight, and anyway it must have
supported an imposing population of flora and fauna. One manual
for hairdressers reports that in 1745 hairstyles became newly elaborate:[44] I suppose the final defeat of bonnie Prince Charlie and the
Jacobites encouraged a new round of devotion to the pageantries of
legitimate monarchy. And what better advertisement of one's identity
and convictions than a careening tower of powdered curls on top of
one's head? In 1777, Samuel Johnson teased his dear friend Hester
Thrale by rejoicing in her decision to discard her wig. But he warned
her, "Do not take too much time in combing, and twisting, and paper-
ing, and unpapering, and curling, and frizzing, and powdering, and
getting out the powder, with all the other operations required in the
cultivation of a head of hair."[45] In 1786, Fanny Burney's hairdresser

---

[40] George Rose to William Wilberforce, circa 1802, Private Papers of William Wilberforce, ed. A. M. Wilberforce (London, 1897), pp. 87–88. Before the tax, Fox was similarly worried about casual dress: The Diaries of Sylvester Douglas (Lord Glenbervie), ed.
Francis Bickley, 2 vols. (London: Constable & Co., 1928), 1:39 [15 January 1794].

[41] Note "Lament for the Loss of Lord B-th—st's Tail," in The Poetical Works of Thomas
Moore, ed. A. D. Godley (London: Oxford University Press, 1915), p. 607. Compare the
story of Naples in 1799, The Penny Magazine of the Society for the Diffusion of Useful Knowledge (25 August 1832) 1(25):206–7.

[42] Mary Somerville, Personal Recollections, from Early Life to Old Age (London, 1874),
p. 45.

[43] The Journal of Mary Frampton, from the Year 1779, until the Year 1846, ed. Harriot
Georgiana Mundy (London, 1885), p. 36 [1791]. Another observer recalled "a solid
pound of hair powder" being used in the 1780s: Reminiscences of Henry Angelo, 2 vols.
(London, 1830), 1:423.

[44] James Stewart, Plocacosmos: or the Whole Art of Hair Dressing (London, 1782), p. 242.

[45] Johnson to Hester Thrale, 10 October 1777, The Letters of Samuel Johnson, ed.
Bruce Redford, 5 vols. (Princeton, NJ: Princeton University Press, 1992–1994), 3:95.

spent two hours one evening working on her hair; he still wasn't finished when she had to jump up and serve the Queen.[46] This might seem extraordinary, but Charles Knight, reminiscing on the early 1800s, reported that "Those who had to preserve a genteel appearance spent an hour each day under the hands of the hair-dresser."[47] Wide-eyed disbelief must have greeted the *Morning Post*'s 1789 report that the Earl of Scarborough kept "six French frizeurs, who have nothing else to do than dress his hair."[48] Outsiders were struck by the time-consuming complexity of it all. "I have to stay longer under the hands of my English hairdresser than I ever did under a German one," reported one German traveller.[49] Asked by George III how she liked London, one newly arrived duchess replied, "Not at all, your majesty, for it is knock, knock, knock, all day; and friz, friz, friz, all night."[50]

By around 1830, hairstyles were simpler: the *Bristol Job Nott* reported, "Nor is the hair-dresser any longer the important personage he used to be, when ladies and gentlemen thought it necessary to sit under his hands for an hour at a time, to have their hair frizzled, and made a sort of dust-bag of powder and pomatum."[51] And one student of the poor laws took hairstyles to be emblematic of civilization's artifices: "The extravagance of our hair-dressers and tailors, in deforming our persons, affords a favourable opportunity for chastising the vanity and regulating the taste of the public."[52] But the move to simplicity isn't the replacement of a symbolic or expressive language with some-

[46] Fanny Burney, *Diary & Letters of Madame D'Arblay,* ed. Charlotte Barrett, 6 vols. (London: Macmillan, 1904), 2:457–58 [13 August 1786].

[47] Charles Knight, *Passages of a Working Life during Half a Century,* 3 vols. (London, 1864–1865), 1:49.

[48] Quoted in Ashton, *Old Times,* p. 45. So too Lady Stanhope recalled that her mother, when in London, thought only two French hairdressers good enough: *Memoirs of the Lady Hester Stanhope, as Related by Herself in Conversations with Her Physician,* 3 vols. (London, 1845), 2:15.

[49] Carl Philip Moritz, *Journeys of a German in England in 1782,* trans. and ed. Reginald Nettel (New York: Holt, Rinehart and Winston, 1965), p. 68 [17 June 1782].

[50] Lady Charlotte Bury, *Diary Illustrative of the Times of George the Fourth,* new ed., 4 vols. (London, 1838–1839), 3:118–19 [15 December 1815].

[51] *Bristol Job Nott* (5 April 1832) no. 17, p. 68; see too Frida Knight, *University Rebel: The Life of William Frend (1757–1841)* (London: Victor Gollancz, 1971), p. 31; Thomas Erskine, "The Barber: Parody upon Gray's Celebrated Ode of 'The Bard,'" in *The Poetical Register and Repository of Fugitive Poetry, for 1810–1811* (London, 1814), pp. 327–31.

[52] C. D. Brereton, *An Inquiry into the Workhouse System and the Law of Maintenance* (Norwich, 1826), p. 4.

thing purely functional or instrumental; rather it's just a change in the reigning codes. That is, someone whose hairstyle is simple doesn't escape making any symbolic claims, even if he wants to. Instead, he claims—depending on the local code—to be classically austere, athletically disciplined, vigorously masculine, hardnosed, efficiency-minded, or whatever else. And he will effortlessly be read as pressing those claims, even if he doesn't intend to, even if he is oblivious to the code.

So the day's "crops," with their short hair, stood for a fierce devotion to republican virtue. The association of short hair with that stern politics stretched back a long way. In 1746, "The Modern Fine Gentleman," "quite a Frenchman in his garb and air," sports "cropt greasy hair" and "loudly bellows out his patriot speeches" against the corrupt administration.[53] The Puritan roundheads of the seventeenth century earned their name by adopting much the same hairstyle. So Dibdin's popular song, "Miss Muz, the Milliner, and Bob, the Barber" inveighed against the introduction of effete high fashion to a respectable small town, with mannered haircuts standing in for corruption, "ringlets careless flowing" for virtue.[54] So the young Gladstone fretted that his contemporaries' haircuts did "not betoken a manly age or character."[55] The language of hair can be manipulated crassly, too. In 1829, the Glasgow police began shaving the heads of drunks found unconscious in the streets, using nakedness as a badge of dishonor— and perhaps creating problems for the bald.[56] Cataloguing types of criminal punishment, Bentham lit on mandatory shaving of head or (for Jews, say) beard as an instance of "complex afflictive punishments" that would render their victims ugly and contemptible.[57] So hair, every bit as much as clothes, made the man—and the woman.

---

[53] "The Modern Fine Gentleman" [1746], in *The Works of Soame Jenyns, Esq.*, 4 vols. (London, 1790), 1:66.

[54] *The Universal Songster; or, Museum of Mirth*, 3 vols. (London, 1825–1826), 2:229–30. Compare Whimsibrain's plight in Archibald MacLaren, *Fashion; or, The World as It Goes* (London, 1802), pp. 8–9; see too *Ayrshire Legatees* [1821], in *The Works of John Galt*, ed. D. S. Meldrum and William Roughead, 10 vols. (Edinburgh: John Grant, 1936), 2:277. Unpowdered hair is a badge of sage virtue in Robert Bage, *The Fair Syrian*, 2 vols. (London, 1787; reprint ed. New York: Garland, 1979), 1:177, 1:234.

[55] William Ewart Gladstone, *The Gladstone Diaries*, ed. M. R. D. Foot and H. C. G. Matthew, 11 vols. (Oxford: Clarendon, 1968–1990), 1:482 [25 April 1832].

[56] *John Bull* (11 October 1829) 9(461):322.

[57] *Principles of Penal Law*, in *The Works of Jeremy Bentham*, ed. John Bowring, 11 vols. (Edinburgh, 1843), 1:417, 1:418.

Here's Bentham, the innocent abroad, intent on visiting a Polish court in 1787: "My respect for Justice determined me to call in the assistance of a hairdresser." But he had trouble finding someone properly equipped and knowledgeable, and ended up with a man ready to use a tallow candle for pomatum and to apply the powder with "a pair of dirty hands."[58]

Travelling in France in 1769, Horace Walpole was amused by the appearance of neatly manicured trees picking up dust from the chalky roads: "I assure you it is very difficult, powdered as both are all over, to distinguish a tree from a hairdresser."[59] A couple of decades later, things French and hirsute became less amusing. English observers paid fretful attention to rapidly changing French hairstyles, to shaggy sans-culotte hair and well-pomaded muscadin hair, trying desperately to discern the deep meaning and vicissitudes of the Revolution by deciphering the language of hair. In 1790, an aristocrat dourly reported to Grenville that *petits maîtres* in Paris "have sacrificed their curls, *toupées,* and *queues;* some of them go about with cropped locks like English farmers without any powder, and others wear little black scratch wigs, both these fashions are called *Têtes a la Romaine,* which is a comical name for such folly": a nice attempt, this, at snubbing a studied piece of republican symbolism.[60] Less cool was Henry Fuseli's 1802 condemnation of the new appearance of French soldiers, exemplary of the frightful decadence of revolutionary politics: "The disuse of powder,—the cropped heads,—the *Chin shaved & the throat unshaved,* which is a beastly custom making a Man like an Animal . . . makes up all the alteration that the French have undergone."[61] All the alteration: not that only hairstyles had changed in France (for who could be exercised by that alone?), but that the French destruction of civilization was manifest not just in the eradication of monarchy and aristocracy, not just in the swarms of angry women out in

[58] *The Correspondence of Jeremy Bentham,* ed. Timothy L. S. Sprigge and others, 10 vols. to date (London: Athlone Press; Oxford: Clarendon, 1968–), 3:604–5 [diary, 9 December 1787].

[59] Walpole to Earl of Strafford, 8 September 1769, *Walpole's Correspondence,* 35:336.

[60] Earl of Mornington to W. W. Grenville, 27 September 1790, in Historical Manuscripts Commission, *Report on the Manuscripts of J. B. Fortescue, Esq., Preserved at Dropmore,* 10 vols. (London, 1892–1927), 1:608.

[61] *The Diary of Joseph Farington,* ed. Kenneth Garlick, Angus Macintyre, and Kathryn Cave, 16 vols. (New Haven, CT: Published for the Paul Mellon Centre for Studies in British Art by Yale University Press, 1978), 5:1849 [12 September 1802].

the streets, not just in the public campaigns against Christianity, but in the hairstyles adopted by the French.

Who performed these hairdressing services? Once London, and still in the early nineteenth century small towns, had flying barbers, armed with shaving cream and a basin of boiling hot water, going door to door to shave their clients.[62] Boasting in 1805 about his pristine Botley, "the most delightful village in the world," Cobbett was proud to report that it still had no barber of its own: "The barber comes three miles once a week to shave and cut hair!"[63] Professionals also opened up storefronts. Even large households might have no one specifically denominated a hairdresser,[64] but servants were expected to master such arts. Patrick, the servant accompanying whimsical Dr. Syntax on tour, knows how to shave and how to tend to wigs.[65] Similarly, John Cam Hobhouse fired one servant in less than two years: "He cannot shave well & is too expensive," Hobhouse noted in his diary.[66] One woman shaved her husband and their dinner guest.[67] Then again, some households valued hairdressers enough to retain someone specializing in the art. When Cumberland took his family to Spain in 1780 to pursue secret diplomatic negotiations for the British government, he had only three English servants, one "a London hairdresser . . . whom I took for the convenience of my wife and daughters."[68]

[62] John Thomas Smith, *Ancient Topography of London* (London, 1815), p. 38. Compare the description of Chinese barbers, essentially flying barbers who do their work right in the street, in *The Penny Magazine of the Society for the Diffusion of Useful Knowledge* (3 May 1834) 3(134):172.

[63] William Cobbett to John Wright, August 1805, in Lewis Melville, *The Life and Letters of William Cobbett in England & America*, 2 vols. (London: John Lane, The Bodley Head, 1913), 1:242.

[64] Samuel and Sarah Adams, *The Complete Servant, Being a Practical Guide to the Peculiar Duties and Business of All Descriptions of Servants* (London, 1825), pp. 5–7 has rosters of servants for even lavish estates; none includes a hairdresser. But various recipes they offer (pp. 162–64, 168, 170–71, 247) make it clear that servants are tending to hair, and they attribute some of the responsibilities involved to the valet (pp. 362–65).

[65] William Combe, *The Second Tour of Doctor Syntax, in Search of Consolation* (London, 1820), pp. 46, 128; Combe, *The Third Tour of Doctor Syntax, in Search of a Wife* (London, 1821), pp. 123, 253.

[66] *Byron's Bulldog: The Letters of John Cam Hobhouse to Lord Byron*, ed. Peter W. Graham (Columbus, OH: Ohio State University Press, 1984), p. 149 n. 2.

[67] *The Journal of the Rev. William Bagshaw Stevens*, ed. Georgina Galbraith (Oxford: Clarendon, 1965), p. 90 [28 June 1793].

[68] *Memoirs of Richard Cumberland: Written by Himself*, 2 vols. (London, 1807), 2:28; also in *Memoirs of Richard Cumberland: Written by Himself* (London, 1806), p. 336.

Hairdressers were overwhelmingly male.[69] This fact gave rise to some uneasiness about gender that I want briefly to note. In 1789, crusty traditionalist John Bennett complained, "Ladies are certainly injudicious in employing so many *male* friseurs about their persons. The custom is indelicate. . . ."[70] In 1798, avant-garde feminist Mary Hays wondered why "women of the inferior classes" didn't serve as hairdressers and why upper-class women "admit without scruple— men hair-dressers."[71] That Bennett and Hays echo one another is a reminder of the scope of the day's feminism, its deliberate regard for the purity of women of a certain status. The concern is for the tense economies of anonymity, body space, and sexuality, a recurrent re-frain in the sources: so we learn from one colloquial dictionary that a prostitute might be labelled "as common as a barber's chair, in which a whole parish sit to be trimmed"; so the male genitals might be re-ferred to as a barber's sign, defined not quite innocently enough as "a standing pole and two wash-balls."[72] Other sexualities were in play, too: in 1739, the barber of Oxford's Wadham College testified against the warden for harassing him. The warden had tried to shove his hand into the barber's breeches on one occasion. "How dost do, my dear Barber?" said the warden affectionately on another. "It's fine Weather, my dear Barber. How does thy Cock do, my dear Barber? Let me feel it."[73]

So hair mattered, and not just that of political women going gray and sprouting mustaches. Peter Pindar's droll epic, *The Lousiad*, me-morializes George III's aghast discovery of a louse on his plate and his ensuing order that the kitchen staff receive haircuts and wear wigs. But the staff, sturdy freeborn Englishmen, will have none of it and

---

[69] Smith, *Topography*, p. 38 mentions (and so finds noteworthy) three women hairdressers.

[70] John Bennett, *Letters to a Young Lady, on a Variety of Useful and Interesting Subjects*, 2 vols. (Warrington, 1789), 1:240 (and note 1:241–42).

[71] Mary Hays, *Appeal to the Men of Great Britain in Behalf of Women* (London, 1798; reprint ed. New York: Garland, 1974), p. 200. See too Society for Bettering the Condi-tion of the Poor, *Extract from an Account of the Ladies Society, for the Education and Employ-ment of the Female Poor* (London, 1804), p. 8.

[72] Pierce Egan, *Grose's Classical Dictionary of the Vulgar Tongue, Revised and Corrected* (London, 1823), s.v. *barber's chair, barber's sign.*

[73] *A Faithful Narrative of the Proceedings in a Late Affair between the Rev. Mr. John Swinton, and Mr. George Baker, Both of Wadham College, Oxford* (London, 1739), pp. 17–18.

assert that only "In France, where men like spaniels lick the Throne," could such an order be issued or followed.[74] In 1779, the actual soldiers of Captain Fuller balked at an order from the Duke of Richmond that they cut off their hair. "Some said they would sooner be run through the body, & others that the Duke should as soon have their Heads." But they complied when the captain himself decided to perform the work.[75]

All this frizzing also implicates social order. Whether conceived of as body politic or patriarchal family or great chain of being, society depended on hierarchy and subordination, place and degree, rank and station. Overmighty subjects were a threat, but dutiful aristocrats were entitled to respect. So too lowly hairdressers were absurd or pernicious if they swaggered with pretensions, but amiable if they minded their manners or knew their place. With a studiously nostalgic glow, Mary Russell Mitford summoned up the view in the 1820s, recalling "William Skinner, wig-maker, hair-dresser, and barber" from "the little primitive town of Cranley, where I spent the first few years of my life": "Although, doubtless, the he-people find it more convenient to shave themselves, and to dispense with wigs and powder, yet I cannot help regretting, the more for his sake, the decline and extinction of a race which . . . formed so genial a link between the higher and lower orders of society."[76] (Less piously, Cartwright subverted the traditional body politic: "The COMMONS, constituting the very soul and body of our political existence; to which the king is the mere *hand,* and the lords the *powdered hair.* . . ."[77]) There were black hair-

---

[74] *The Lousiad* [1785–1795], in John Wolcot, *The Works of Peter Pindar, Esq.*, 4 vols. (London, 1797–1806), vols. 1 and 3; the quotation is at 1:171.

[75] Fanny Burney to Susanna Elizabeth Burney, 30 May–1 June 1779, *The Early Journals and Letters of Fanny Burney,* ed. Lars E. Troide and Stewart J. Cooke, 3 vols. to date (Oxford: Clarendon, 1988–), 3:291. Note the narrator's dismay at his new military haircut in Thomas Hamilton, *The Youth and Manhood of Cyril Thornton,* 3 vols. (Edinburgh, 1827), 2:44–46. So too 1830 orders that the cavalry remove their mustaches kicked up a fuss: see *BMC* nos. 16180 [*circa* July 1830], 16181 [*circa* July 1830], 16226 [21 August 1830], 16513 [August 1830].

[76] Mary Russell Mitford, *Our Village,* 5 vols. (London, 1824–1832), 3:164–65. For another affectionate sketch of the "Amiable, contented, respected race!" of hairdressers, see William Hone, *The Table Book,* 2 vols. (London, 1826–1827; reprint ed. Detroit: Gale Research Co., 1966), 1:242–47.

[77] *A Letter from John Cartwright, Esq. to a Friend at Boston* (London, 1793), p. 25.

dressers,[78] but that isn't why Mitford says *race*. Hers is an amiable contempt for an order of inferior beings who, like Bentham's lawyers, share distinctive traits, even if they don't inherit them.

That means the hairdresser's job is a paradoxical one. He gives the higher orders the kind of hair that identifies them as high. So his job is, in part, the reproduction of social status. But that system of social status assigns him a lowly position. Perhaps hairdressers consoled themselves—or gnashed their teeth—in reflecting that their august customers were helpless without them. Perhaps they took illicit pleasure in tinkering with their own hair or making their customers' hair just a bit too extravagant. Like any other social actors, they had some room for maneuvering within the confines of their role. But if they stepped too far outside it, if they were not in the end dutiful certifiers of status, there would be trouble.

If overweening lords and saucy subjects are a threat to social order, much worse is freewheeling talk of equality. On its face, equality threatens hierarchy and subordination: but that just means that it threatens the very possibility of social order, if the patriarchal family or body politic or great chain of being is the most cogent account we can muster. Conservatives, clinging to this older model of social order, are then appropriately indignant at the demand for equality. It's not fundamentally a matter of maintaining the power and privileges of the better off, the triumph of sinister interests, though that helps. It's a matter of safeguarding order, of preventing the crazed and bloody chaos that had erupted in France from penetrating Britain, and there is no reason to doubt the sincerity of conservative anguish in this realm. Again, my claim is that hairdressers became exemplary of the meanings of equality in this period, that in following their dubious careers and public images, we can securely grasp the slippery concept of equality, or at least the political roles it played in this fateful interlude.

## DIGNITY OF LABOR

"The occupation of a hair-dresser, or of a working tallow-chandler, cannot be a matter of honor to any person,—to say nothing of a

[78] *The World* (27 July 1789), quoted in Folarin Shyllon, *Black People in Britain 1555–1833* (London: Oxford University Press for the Institute of Race Relations, 1977), p. 96; Smith, *Topography*, p. 38.

number of other more servile employments."[79] So decreed Edmund
Burke in the *Reflections on the Revolution in France*. Characteristically
blunt, Burke echoed *ancien régime* wisdom: there is no dignity in labor.
Honor or dignity here is a positional good: some (aristocrats, M.P.s,
maybe lawyers) can have it only if others (hairdressers, tallow-
chandlers, maybe farmers) don't. Harriet Arbuthnot sneered at the
keeper of the privy purse under George IV by referring to him not
just as "the greatest rogue in England" but also as a barber.[80] A pamphleteer censured the pretensions of hairdressers who dared to call
themselves gentlemen: "The word gentlemen re-echoes from one end
of the kingdom to the other. We have gentlemen of the whip, gentlemen of the quill, gentlemen of the scissars, gentlemen of the razor,
gentlemen of the comb."[81] But this linguistic excess makes nonsense
of being a gentleman, which requires that others be not so genteel.
Or, in one observer's scathing words, it requires that we recognize
"bawds, milliners, hair-dressers, tallywomen, and many other reptiles
of the same class."[82] Even an earnest moralist was willing to stoop to
the same vitriolic parade of horribles. Little Harry Sandford's morals
are deep and authentic, not the superficial kind gained by associating
with "barbers, taylors, actors, opera-dancers, milliners, fidlers, and
French servants of both sexes."[83]

Still, some remained committed to the dignity of labor. One of
Burke's critics chided him. "More is said," protested Capel Lofft,

[79] *Reflections on the Revolution in France* [1790], in *The Works of the Right Honourable
Edmund Burke*, 9th ed., 12 vols. (Boston, 1889), 3:296.

[80] *The Journal of Mrs. Arbuthnot 1820–1832*, ed. Francis Bamford and the Duke of
Wellington, 2 vols. (London: Macmillan, 1950), 1:153–54 [24 March 1822], 2:101–2 [3
April 1827]; note too Charles Arbuthnot to Lord Liverpool, *circa* 7 October 1823, in
*The Correspondence of Charles Arbuthnot*, Camden Third Series, vol. 65, ed. A. Aspinall
(London: Offices of the Royal Historical Society, 1941), pp. 54–55. For a similar use of
*washerwoman* as an epithet, Benjamin Disraeli to Ralph Disraeli, 17? September 1830,
in Benjamin Disraeli, *Letters: 1815–1834*, ed. J. A. W. Gunn and others (Toronto: University of Toronto Press, 1982), p. 162.

[81] James Lawrence, *On the Nobility of the British Gentry, or the Political Ranks and Dignities of the British Empire, Compared with Those on the Continent*, in *The Pamphleteer* (1824)
23(45):200. Lawrence, *On the Nobility*, p. 202 reports "a similar abuse in Germany, that
every barber there receives his letters addressed to him, to the noble-born."

[82] *Real Life in London; or, The Rambles and Adventures of Bob Tallyho, Esq. and His
Cousin, the Hon. Tom Dashall, through the Metropolis; Exhibiting a Living Picture of Fashionable Characters, Manners, and Amusements in High and Low Life*, 2 vols. (London, 1824),
2:404 n.

[83] Thomas Day, *The History of Sandford and Merton, a Work Intended for the Use of Children*, 7th ed., 3 vols. (London, 1795), 1:26–27; note too 3:149.

"than, in this age, an ingenuous and enlightened mind might have been expected to utter, on the degrading ignorance attendant on certain occupations"; Lofft thought it better "to expand the gates and enlarge the avenues to the Temple of Honour."[84] Wordsworth was quite the dandy in his student days at Cambridge, with his hair powdered.[85] In the *Prelude*, he looked back sardonically at his affectations:

> Behold me rich in monies: and attired
> In splendid garb, with hose of silk, and hair
> Powdered like rimy trees, when frost is keen.
> My lordly dressing-gown, I pass it by.
> With other signs of manhood that supplied
> The lack of beard.—[86]

With the dawning of revolutionary bliss, Wordsworth complained that nobility "has a necessary tendency to dishonour labour."[87]

Like man-milliners, hairdressers were loathsome in part because they were caught on the wrong side of some gender boundaries. The widow of *Fashionable Levities* grimaces that she has no interest in "a coxcomb,—a fluttering summer insect,—a talkative creature, full of insipid gesture, laughter, and noise, who pays more attention to his hair than to his intellects"; but Welford warns her that there are all too many such repulsive dandies. "The ladies are grown so enamoured of delicate limbs, and effeminate faces, one would imagine they wished to have their lovers women in every thing."[88] Those effeminate faces were neatly framed by effeminate hairdressers. The process, shot through with primping and preening, sensuality and decadence, invited mockingly breathless rhapsodies:

[84] Capel Lofft, *Remarks on the Letter of the Rt. Hon. Edmund Burke, Concerning the Revolution in France, and on the Proceedings in Certain Societies in London, Relative to That Event* (London, 1790), pp. 35–36.

[85] "The Lake Poets: William Wordsworth" [1839], in *The Collected Writings of Thomas de Quincey*, ed. David Masson, 14 vols. (Edinburgh, 1889–1890), 2:266.

[86] William Wordsworth, *The Fourteen-Book Prelude* [1850], ed. W. J. B. Owen (Ithaca, NY: Cornell University Press, 1985), p. 62.

[87] *A Letter to the Bishop of Llandaff* [1793], in *The Prose Works of William Wordsworth*, ed. W. J. B. Owen and Jane Worthington Smyser, 3 vols. (Oxford: Clarendon, 1974), 1:45.

[88] Leonard MacNally, *Fashionable Levities* [1785], in *The Modern Theatre; a Collection of Successful Modern Plays*, ed. Elizabeth Inchbald, 10 vols. (London, 1811), 10:71.

> BELLA tells me FRISÈ's here;
> Who with FRISÈ can compare?
> Sweetest man!—for dressing hair!
> O, I would, if I had time,
> Praise his skill in flowing rhyme!
> How he twists and how he twirls,
> How he shapes the bending curls,
> How he spreads the smooth pomatum,
> Sweet as Lord EFFEMINATUM;
> The downy puff his hand he takes in,
> *Poudre de mille fleurs* he shakes in.[89]

The jubilant barber of one popular song had no illusions about his masculinity:

> A tailor being but the ninth part of a man,
> Has long been recorded, deny it who can:
> Tho' that is less manhood than tongue can express,
> Yet I'll make it appear that a barber has less.[90]

The same link to effeminacy afforded one radical an opportunity to blast magistrates languishing on the job: "I have known some of these powdered monkeys spend as much time under the hands of a *frizeur* as might be necessary to remove public grievances, and lavish away more hours at their toilet than one of the feminine gender. . . ."[91]

In *The Box-Lobby Challenge,* Cumberland permitted his audience some nasty chuckles—and maybe some nagging apprehensions—by exploring what would be at stake in conceiving hairdressers and others as dignified workers, not menial servants. Provincial Sir Toby and his manservant Joe have arrived in London, and Joe salutes a waiter:

---

[89] Miss Kitty R. to Miss Harriet F., 1780, "Modern Manners," in Samuel Hoole, *Poems,* 2 vols. (London, 1790), 1:42. Note too Mr. Ralph Rusty to John C. Esq., "Modern Manners," in Hoole, *Poems,* 1:116–17, on "the soft Earl of DEWDROP" and his confusion on losing three curls.

[90] "Shave Well, and Shave All," in *Richardson's New Songster, Containing All the Most Favourite and Popular Songs for the Present Year* (Derby, 1833), p. 7.

[91] John Butler, *Brief Reflections upon the Liberty of the British Subject* (Canterbury, *circa* 1792), in *Political Writings of the 1790s,* ed. Gregory Claeys, 8 vols. (London: William Pickering, 1995), 3:387.

JOE. Harkye, you boy! skip-jack! tapster!

WAITER. What do you want, Clodpole? is that your way of speaking to a
waiter? I fancy you have been more accustomed to alehouses than
hotels.

JOE. Oho! you call your house an hotel, and yourself a waiter—very
well! then pray Mr. Waiter of an hotel, send me hither one of your
barbers to comb out Sir Toby Grampus's perriwig.—Do you understand that?

WAITER. I'll send you a hair-dresser, we don't call 'em barbers, unless we
mean to affront 'em. Where the plague have you lived. [*exit*

JOE. So, ho! here's a new language to learn; a man's mother-tongue I
perceive is of no use in this place.[92]

The long-suffering mother tongue is, as always, a political battlefield.
If *barber* has too much obloquy built into it, choose a new name. Anyway, the passage is unstable, maybe deliberately so. The waiter and his
still invisible ally, the hairdresser, want to upgrade their own status.
But the waiter moves to do so by berating Joe. As the travelling servant of a provincial squire, is Joe irreprievably low? Or does his rude
behavior, failing to address the waiter with due respect, mean that he
deserves his riposte?

The hairdresser's arrival doesn't produce any celebrations of fraternity. He and Joe don't treat one another as comrades in arms against
some oppressive upper crust. Indeed, the hairdresser is supremely
confident that he is Joe's superior, Sir Toby's too. He scorns Sir Toby's
wig as hopelessly antique, presumably not up to chic London stan-
dards: "Dam'mee! if I woudn't as soon comb out the tower lyons, as
this rum gig of a caxen." While he's at it, he manages to insult Sir
Toby's coat:

HAIR-DRESSER. . . . which now is of the longest standing in the family,
you, or that damn'd old quiz of a coat you are dusting?

JOE. Damn'd old quiz of a coat! what a graceless reprobate you are!
Damme, how you barbers swear! where do you expect to go?

We jaded secular humanists might miss the force of this question:
swearing, the thought is, sends one to hell. That Joe himself swears in

---

[92] Cumberland, *The Box-Lobby Challenge* (London, 1794), pp. 8–9; the play is reprinted in *The Plays of Richard Cumberland*, ed. Roberta F. S. Borkat, 6 vols. (New York:
Garland, 1982), vol. 4.

the very act of denouncing swearing is surely another bit of heavy-handed humor. The hairdresser plays dumb:

> HAIR-DRESSER. Half the town over before night, then to my girl and my
> bottle. As for your wig, comb it those that like, I'll not touch a
> bristle of it. [*exit*[93]

When Sir Toby learns what has happened, he exclaims, "Oh, that I had the knave in Monmouthshire, I'd make him sing another tune!"[94] Country bumpkin meets city slicker; affable gentry confronts impudent underling; pious Christian is rebuffed by worldly cynic; country virtue is foiled by courtly corruption.

It's clear that Cumberland invites his audience to sympathize with Sir Toby and Joe, but not entirely clear why. Suppose that waiter and hairdresser had been furnished another script, one making them genial and self-deprecating, like Walter Scott's Caxon. Caxon's master tells him, "You are a goose"; "'It's very like it may be sae,' replied the acquiescent barber,—'I am sure your honour kens best.'"[95] Then, surely, Sir Toby and Joe would have kept their footing, would have restrained any growls about newfangled London, would have found their mother tongue and social repertoires under control. But how would their audience have reacted? and how would Cumberland have wanted them to react? Would they have seen the entire exchange as unremarkable? Or would some of them—artisans in the pit, say— have been hissing, complaining about Toby's easy arrogance, wondering that Joe has the stupidity to believe that Toby's higher status casts its glow on him, or just condemning Cumberland for being hopelessly out of touch with the ways of actual workers? Would they have thought that waiter and hairdresser were commendably acting in character? or would they have reviled them as inauthentic? or would they have heard the entire exchange as dripping with arch irony, assuming that no self-respecting waiter or hairdresser could actually be so deferential? Would they have noticed the possibility that the underlings gain their self-respect precisely by being deft in the laborious arts of deference, in identifying with their allotted role and impeccably performing its duties? that, not at all paradoxically, they take pride in being inferior?

[93] *Challenge,* p. 9.
[94] *Challenge,* p. 11.
[95] *Antiquary,* in *Waverley Novels,* 6:203.

More intractable yet: suppose waiter and hairdresser were genuinely self-deprecating, pleased to have the opportunity to be a bit
craven in assisting Sir Toby, but Joe and Sir Toby themselves prized
the dignity of labor and tried to impart to waiter and hairdresser a
more dignified sense of self. Imagine how agonizing the ensuing conversation would be for all parties. Joe and Sir Toby might wonder if
their own commitments to the dignity of labor were just another way
of being patronizing, something like the leftist version of *noblesse
oblige*. Or they might be so complacently fond of their position that
they would fail to notice that waiter and hairdresser were baffled—or
held them in cheerfully seething contempt for failing to acquit themselves competently in their own higher social position.

The iterations are endless, increasingly misanthropic too, and I
leave them aside. Instead, consider celebrated comic actor David Garrick dropping by to visit Dr. Burney, in the midst of submitting to the
attentions of his hairdresser. Garrick, "wonder-struck at his amazing
skill in decorating the Doctor's *tête*," sat studiously observing the proceedings. "The man, highly gratified by such notice from the celebrated Garrick, briskly worked on, frizzing, curling, powdering, and
pasting, according to the mode of the day, with assiduous, though
flurried importance, and with marked self-complacency." Garrick let
his famously plastic face grow ever more fascinated, ever more vacuous, and so flustered the hairdresser, who began to realize he was
being ridiculed. "Scared and confounded, the perruquier now
turned away his eyes, and hastily rolled up two curls, with all the speed
in his power, to make his retreat." But not before Garrick, "dolorously,
in a whining voice, squeaked out" a request for the man to tend to his
own wretched bob wig, a request sending the man hurtling out of the
room and erupting into frantically nervous laughter.[96]

Or consider this 1778 conversation among Samuel Johnson, Fanny
Burney, Hester Thrale, and Lady Ladd. "The *subject* was given by Lady
Ladd; it was *The Respect due from the lower Class of the people*." She complains that Mrs. Thrale doesn't bother with the niggling rituals of
deference: "I remember, when you were at my House, how the Hair
Dresser flung down the Comb, as soon as you were dressed, & went
out of the room without making a Bow." Mrs. Thrale responds, "All
the better, for if he *had* made me one, Ten thousand to one if I had

[96] Fanny Burney, *Memoirs of Doctor Burney*, 3 vols. (London, 1832), 1:346–49.

seen it! I was in as great haste to have done with *him,* as he could be to have done with *me.* I was glad enough to get him out of the Room; I did not want him to stay Bowing & Cringing."

"If any man had behaved so insolently to *me,*" answers Lady Ladd, "I would never again have suffered him in my House." "Well," scoffs Mrs. Thrale, "your Ladyship has a great deal more dignity than I have!" Dr. Johnson chimes in with his trademark maxim: "Subordination is always necessary to the preservation of order & decorum." Lady Ladd adds, "I have no notion of submitting to any kind of impertinence: & I never will bear to have any person *Nod* to me, or enter a Room where I am, without Bowing." Then Dr. Johnson is wry: "But, Madam, what if they *will* Nod; & what if they *won't* Bow?—how then?" "Why I always tell them of it."

Mrs. Thrale's rejoinder: "O, commend me to that! I'd sooner never see another Bow in my life, than turn Dancing master to Hair Dressers."[97] I haven't the space (or ample enough evidence) to pursue the story here, but in the earlier eighteenth century the dancing master was as much an exemplary figure of contempt as is the hairdresser after the French Revolution. So Mrs. Thrale is not just witty and brash, but subtle, even brilliant. It is the province of a lowly dancing master to teach people how to bow gracefully. She won't dream of lowering herself by playing dancing master to her own servant. As long as the man combs her hair competently, let him flounce out of the room without the appointed ceremonies. Who cares?

Well, Lady Ladd and Dr. Johnson do; and so did thousands of others. In a properly functioning household, they would insist, Mrs. Thrale never would have been subjected to such impudence in the first place. Only her own prior derogation of duty has made her servants so pert that they dare omit the bows and curtsies that certify their lowly status. (Not the mere fact of bowing and curtseying, but the asymmetric routines built up around them. They are to bow to her; she of course need not bow back. She may address them by first or last name, as she pleases; they must always address her with an honorific.) Nor, they would insist, are the stakes trivial, and we must reprove Mrs. Thrale's breezy dismissal of the matter. Mrs. Thrale's retort to Lady Ladd—"Your Ladyship has a great deal more dignity than I have!"—is biting, even acidulous: she means that Lady Ladd is

[97] *Early Journals and Letters of Fanny Burney,* 3:130–31 [1778].

too stiff and surly about her status, that she should loosen up. But, they would insist, the higher orders must resist such unbecoming temptations, for the domestic household is a microcosm of society. Mrs. Thrale does her servants no favors in omitting the delicate, almost invisible, marks of formality and distance that must regulate their relationship. Not only does she leave them at sea, unsure how to execute their role; she also forfeits the consecration of hierarchy so essential to order. For Mrs. Thrale to be negligent of her duties is to license disorder in her house and at large.

Lofft's proposal, that the avenues to public honor be enlarged, can't furnish a fully democratic conception of the dignity of labor. For honor must remain positional, so some occupations must remain low. That is why one pamphleteer's 1791 complaints aren't what one might expect. The government, he declares, "have reduced us to the hard condition of daily labourers. . . . They have made us a people of pedlars, of taylors, of weavers, of barbers, of brokers, of lackeys, of gamblers, of man-milliners, and if ought can derogate still more from the dignity of man."[98] Other workers may have dignity or honor, but not barbers or man-milliners. Once again, we find workers themselves divided. Cruikshank's take on the scriptural question, "Is the labourer worthy of his hire?" was to juxtapose a Mr. Frizem, solemnly instructing the lady of the household that his rate as hairdresser was a guinea an hour, with her stunned maidservant, blankly repeating the colossal wage.[99] Francis Place, himself a tailor, reported, "I can imagine nothing except being a footman or a common soldier as more degrading than being either a barber or a tailor."[100]

Critics seized on the thought that equality is not pernicious but impossible, that the demand for equality is always in vain. *Blackwood's,* which once identified its readership as "polished Tories,"[101] gives us a *reductio* of the campaign for the dignity of labor, "The Confessions of a Footman" by Thomas Ticklepitcher. Ticklepitcher is a stupid oaf seeking sympathy, perhaps redress, for "the grievances of footmen; a set of

---

[98] A Friend to the People, *A Review of the Constitution of Great Britain* (London, 1791), pp. 22–23. See too *Memoirs of Henry Hunt, Esq. Written by Himself, in His Majesty's Jail at Ilchester,* 3 vols. (London, 1820–1822), 3:238.

[99] John Wardroper, *The Caricatures of George Cruikshank* (London: Gordon Fraser, 1977), p. 129 [1 November 1829].

[100] *The Autobiography of Francis Place (1771–1854),* ed. Mary Thale (Cambridge: Cambridge University Press, 1972), p. 216.

[101] *Blackwood's Edinburgh Magazine* (January 1831) 29(175):61.

men, I do believe, more universally persecuted than any other body of artists within his Majesty's dominions." Ticklepitcher proudly launches into a narrative that doesn't begin to vindicate his complaints; instead it caustically exposes the nonsensical, even hilarious, nature of his brief. He had been a magnificently incompetent barber's apprentice. At the implausible climax of his labors, he managed to cut off three quarters of a prestigious client's hair.[102] Thus the need for a new line of work; thus too a pointed challenge as to whether such buffoons and their asinine work could ever warrant dignity. Not for the first time, puffy Jacobin abstractions are supposed to be skewered by piercing conservative examples.

The dignity of labor also impinges on public standing, as I've called the admittedly amorphous matter of full membership in society, including the right to participate in political discussion on terms of equality, not to be dismissed out of hand with contempt. English observers remarked on a story from America about a black hairdresser who dutifully served white clients but threw blacks out of his shop.[103] Or consider the bold radical cornered. William Godwin, furious over the rejection of his tragedy, fired off a harsh letter to John Kemble. Kemble assured him that his play had received due attention and that its rejection was in the interests of both theater and author. Not, he assured him a bit disdainfully, that it "resembled the Production of those unfortunate 'Sempstresses, Hairdressers and Taylors' you condescend to waste your Contempt on. . . ."[104] Poor Kemble wasn't edgy just because theatrical types were traditionally disreputable. Godwin might have forgotten, might never have known, that Kemble was the son of a hairdresser.[105] Whatever the dignity of hairdressers, presumably they couldn't write passable tragedies. Godwin's contempt meshes all too easily with that of young Cobbett for an unfortunate hair-

[102] *Blackwood's Edinburgh Magazine* (November 1823) 14(82):590–94. So too "The Barber" of the popular song is a hopeless failure at his job: *Universal Songster,* 1:349.

[103] *Quarterly Review* (January 1819) 21:129; Zachary Macaulay, *Negro Slavery* (London, 1823), pp. 25–26.

[104] Kemble to Godwin, 20 September 1801, Abinger Mss., reel 2. Kemble is clearly quoting from Godwin's letter, but I haven't located that letter in the sadly disorganized Abinger Mss. Godwin's diary, 29 August 1801, Abinger Mss., reel 1, refers to what I assume is the same play as "Mirza"; Godwin to Kemble, 10 September 1801, Abinger Mss., reel 3 refers to it as "Abbas, King of Persia." Abinger Mss., reel 5 has a rough draft of Godwin dated 11 January 1806 saying that they have had a play of his since 20 October 1804 and complaining about delays in staging it.

[105] *BMC* nos. 11426–11428 [November 1809].

dresser "who (poor man!) dreamt, in evil hour, that he was born a poet. Of his play it may be truly said, that it is the most abominable nonsense that ever issued from the skull of a coxcomb, a *republican* coxcomb, who is always ten degrees more foolish than coxcombs of any other species."[106]

## PUTTING ON AIRS

So, too, a seemingly dignified hairdresser could always be exposed as a buffoon putting on airs. *Blackwood's* also gives us a soliloquy by Frizzle:

> So! This is a most delicate piece of workmanship! Confoundedly clever. The hairs are woven better by half than they grow in the skin—more regular like—and the curl it takes! and the fine oily gloss! and the colour!—It's a pleasure to put such a wig out of hand—a wig, as the poet says, "beating nature." Zounds! I wonder people are such fools as to wear their own hair! That curl a little more to the left, to give a sort of carelessness—so. To be sure, though I say it that should not say it, there is not an artist of more genius in my line in the whole West End. It must be confessed, though, that few men have had my advantages. 'Prenticed in Piccadilly—placed for improvement in Regent Street—a foreign tour—two days at Calais—hang this straggling lock! It won't sit becoming! I've a great mind to clip it. No; that'll do. That's quite *comy fo,* as the French say.[107]

The pretensions are hopeless. It isn't hairdressers as such who are dignified, but Frizzle is especially admirable because of his distinctive advantages. But his advantages amount to working in fashionable neighborhoods and taking a paltry version of a young gentleman's Grand Tour. Yet aristocracy on the cheap isn't dignity, and any complacent Tory reading *Blackwood's* is permitted a patronizing grin at Frizzle's gross mispronunciation of *comme il faut.*

Market competition could give rise to ludicrous affectation. *John Bull* reported that "Within one hundred miles of Drury-lane the passengers can find 'the original shaving shop;' 'the old original shaving

---

[106] *Political Censor* (May 1796) no. 4, in William Cobbett, *Porcupine's Works,* 12 vols. (London, 1801), 3:432.

[107] *Blackwood's Edinburgh Magazine* (July 1826) 20(114):42.

shop' and 'the real original shaving shop.' "[108] They also found an 1828 advertisement worth reproducing at length:

> J. LEAVER, ARTIST IN DECORATIVE HAIR,—In *disseminating his Gratitude* for experienced favours, *assumes the honour* of announcing to the Ladies, Gentlemen, and adjacent residents of Chelsea, that he has *removed from Bond-street, to those eligible premises,* No. 13, ADAM'S PLACE, NEAR THE SIX BELLS, KING'S ROAD, a commodious Shop, elegantly adapted for a characteristic display of all the various modernized devices of ornamental hair. *And desires to insinuate that providing acknowledged ability, enthusiastic regard, accompanied with commodities which are both vilis et bonum, be the superinducements or avenues leading to Business.*—J. L. unhesitatingly asserts that he possesses all these even to perfection. . . .
>
> As HAIR CUTTER, J.L. is incontestibly declared by amateurs of his profession *to be the ne plus ultra of the present Erea.*
>
> As HAIR DRESSER, *he soars lofty* in the estimation of some of the first circles of courtiers at the west end.
>
> As PERUKE AND SCALP MAKER, *his name has become proverbial, both in the Metropolis, and on the Continent,* he will deceive the sapient connoisseur, *he is the best sembler of nature extant.* . . .[109]

Once again, inadvertently hilarious mistakes; once again, a putative bid for dignity still caught up in the logic of positional goods: Leaver's standing is purchased at the price of his competitors' ignominy. Then again, he can't buy this kind of standing anyway. *John Bull* clearly expects their readers to react with disdain and we can make our own conjectures about the reactions of Leaver's potential clients. Perhaps *John Bull* embellished the advertisement, the stuff of slapstick; it's hard to imagine Leaver proudly writing the text (or hiring a consultant to do it for him?), harder still to imagine it attracting new customers. But they almost surely didn't invent it from whole cloth and I suspect any embellishments were negligible: the *Age* ran a strikingly similar advertisement in 1825 in the midst of the regular advertisements,[110] and I don't think the day's papers were playing games with the boundaries of fact and fiction.

---

[108] *John Bull* (5 November 1827) 7(360):350.

[109] *John Bull* (23 March 1828) 8(380):94; italics here are added by the newspaper to single out passages for particular scorn.

[110] *Age* (27 November 1825) no. 29, p. 232. For more examples of pretentious advertising by hairdressers, T. Bowman's advertisement in the *Times* (22 June 1795), in John Ashton, *Old Times: A Picture of Social Life at the End of the Eighteenth Century* (London,

The *Bull* ran Leaver's advertisement in an ongoing series snottily entitled "The March of Intellect" and designed to show that no such march was in progress. Several years later, Rusticus contributed a nasty bit of doggerel to the same series.

> "There's barber Snip, in yonder town, it's marvellous I'm sure,
> How well he understands the laws, and all about the poor;
> But as for poor, there'd soon be none, if he could but be sent,
> To talk about them sort of things before the Parliament.

> For he can tell about the tithes, and 'nopolies and that;
> And all the ministers and lords, he's got their names so pat;
> And talks about 'em just as free as if they were his kin;
> And then, for squires and gentry-folk he does not care a pin."

> "But Grout," says I, "now don't you think he'd better stick to trade:
> I'm sure that's what my good old father would have said;
> 'My son,' said he, 'be diligent, and labor in your station,
> But leave to wiser heads than thine to manage for the nation.' "

> "Your father was a worthy man, and, for his time, correct,"
> Says Grout, "but then, he never knew the March-of-Intellect;
> And that's the very thing that now makes many folks so wise;
> And soon will teach the blind to see as well as if they'd eyes."[111]

A hairdresser in Parliament, full of visionary schemes of social improvement: as effective a *reductio* of enlightenment as giving sight to the blind. Whatever miracles Brougham intended to pull off, he wasn't Christ.

## INTRIGUES OF DECEPTION

Market competition and mobility are familiar as threats to status hierarchy: recall all those impoverished noble families holding their

---

1885), p. 74; and Bowman's advertisement in the *Morning Post* (18 March 1800), in Ashton, *The Dawn of the XIXth Century in England: A Social Sketch of the Times,* 2 vols. (London, 1886), 2:45–50; *Real Life in London,* 1:79 n; the whimsically pretentious razor-grinder's handbill in *The Memoirs of J. Decastro, Comedian,* ed. R. Humphreys (London, 1824), pp. 233–34; *John Bull* (13 July 1828) 8(396):223; William Hone, *The Year Book* (London, 1832; reprint ed. Detroit: Gale Research Co., 1967), cols. 1508–1509. For mockery of similar scenes from France, Isaac D'Israeli, *Domestic Anecdotes of the French Nation, during the Last Thirty Years* (London, 1794), pp. 273–74.

[111] *John Bull* (11 May 1834) 14(670):149.

noses and marrying off their scions to the daughters of vulgar merchants. We find some of the same dynamics at the bottom of the
status hierarchy. Identity here is always fluid and negotiable, not for
fancy postmodern reasons but because ambitious inferiors were social
climbers on the move, unscrupulous rascals willing to pass themselves
off as that which they were not. Here too, hairdressers are exemplary.
Stung by his failure to win noble title, William Beckford revealed that
"the late imperious Marquess of Abercorn's mother was the *illegitimate*
offspring of Mrs. Bracegirdle an actress and Mr. Secretary Craggs,
who was himself the *legitimate* son of a village Barber."[112] (Whose lineage here is most dishonorable? and why?) For Beckford, the issue is
one of tainted blood. No one with such obscure and disreputable
ancestors ought to be able to amount to anything.

But some did. Edward Sugden, son of a hairdresser, became Baron
St. Leonards and lord chancellor.[113] The breathless London journal,
*Figaro in London,* mocked him on the opening page of its opening
issue and turned his ignoble descent into a running gag.[114] If one
deliciously flighty source is to be believed, the Prince of Wales displayed his stingy gratitude for dinner by offering a used wig: "There,
as you are getting bald, is a very superior wig, made by—I forget the
man's name, but it was not Sugden."[115] Sugden got in his licks, too.
Teased on entering Parliament, he allegedly shot back, "I am come
into the House to give a dressing to the Whigs."[116] Charles Abbott,
son of a hairdresser, became lord chief justice and so a baron, Lord
Tenterden.[117] His unseemly descent tainted his aristocratic status, so
that years later another great man, "complaining that he was to be
put on the footing of Abbott," insisted on becoming an earl.[118]

But the problem wasn't merely that the progeny of hairdressers
were climbing the status hierarchy. Brazenly, hairdressers themselves
were. In 1792, Anthony Stokes surveyed the cultural scene with bleak,

[112] William Beckford, *The Vision and Liber Veritatis,* ed. Guy Chapman (London: Constable & Company, 1930), p. 111 [1829].

[113] *DNB* s.v. *Sugden, Edward Burtenshaw.*

[114] *Figaro in London* (10 December 1831) 1(1):1, (7 April 1832) 1(18):71, (21 July
1832) 1(33):130. See too *BMC* no. 15151 [19 April 1826].

[115] *Memoirs of Lady Stanhope,* 2:101.

[116] *Autobiography of Miss Cornelia Knight, Lady Companion to the Princess Charlotte of
Wales,* 2 vols. (London, 1861), 2:203.

[117] *DNB* s.v. *Abbott, Charles, first Lord Tenterden.*

[118] *The Life and Times of Henry Lord Brougham Written by Himself,* 3 vols. (Edinburgh,
1871), 3:504.

maybe jaundiced, eyes. He found the British credulous to a fault. For example, he reported, he had hired a barber who spoke a corrupt version of Welsh and tried to turn him into a proper footman to no avail; then into a proper law clerk, but again to no avail. So he fired the man—who promptly "set up an academy to teach the learned languages," hiring a clergyman not in orders to do the actual work and succeeding splendidly.[119] Instructively, that same year Jacobin novelist Charlotte Smith produced a "very intelligent" and "honest" barber. A bit character in her novel, he's nonetheless a pointed reminder of the political stakes of sneering at these ambitious men.[120]

No such honest intelligence for Dr. Grigsby, butt of ferocious humor in John O'Keeffe's *World in a Village.* Grigsby is on his way up in the world: once a hairdresser, he's now an apothecary, eager to be a wine merchant, too. "That fellow was a good barber till money spoiled him," complains Jollyboy. Grigsby is in fact a pompous ass. His mask slips now and again: "I'll bring you the change in a frizzling of a *toopee,*" he politely tells one character. "Bring my razor—hem—my amputating knife!" he orders another. He's mercilessly attentive to the perquisites and obligations of his newfound status: "As I'm now bemuff'd and bewig'd, I must support the condign dignity of a physician.—hum! ha!" His shabbiness is revealed on the return of noble Charles, a shipwrecked sailor in a tattered coat who happens now to be worth £200,000. "Isn't this Grigsby the barber, dress'd very odd for a friseur!" he muses. "A worthy fellow he is—" but Grigsby snubs him decisively. You can guess how this lamentable affair unfolds.[121]

In her *Memoirs of Modern Philosophers,* Elizabeth Hamilton turned to this theme, too. Alphonso Vallaton, a stylish rogue passing himself off as man of quality, seduces Julia Dermond with Godwinian babble: marriage, he explains cunningly, is the opposite of love, which must be free. He then abandons her; mortified, she and her father die. And who is this Vallaton? "No better than a shabby hair-dresser." "Mr.

---

[119] Anthony Stokes, *Desultory Observations, on . . . Great Britain* (London, 1792), pp. 29–30.

[120] Charlotte Smith, *Desmond,* 3 vols. (London, 1792), 2:237–38. See too Thomas Jarrold, *A Letter to Samuel Whitbread, Esq. M.P. on the Subject of the Poor Laws* (London, 1807), pp. 21–22; Thomas Moore, *Memoirs of Captain Rock, the Celebrated Irish Chieftain, with Some Account of His Ancestors,* 5th ed. (London, 1824), pp. 143–45; Hone, *Year Book,* cols. 1505–1508.

[121] John O'Keeffe, *The World in a Village* (London, 1793), pp. 2, 8, 67, 31, 17, 19–20.

Vallaton," explodes one character, "is a London hair-dresser, a common friseur, a fellow who—good heavens! that such a fellow should ever have the impudence to sit at my table! He richly deserves that my servants should kick him down stairs."[122] No doubt tending to the hair of the higher orders, observing at close range their clothing, their accents, their physical postures, had enabled Vallaton to assume his counterfeit identity.

In 1831, *Fraser's* gasped at the ludicrous explosion of popular education, with incompetents at the helm. "It is the reading public who have the greatest reason to be astonished. The schoolmaster has been so thoroughly abroad, that now there are as many masters as scholars; all are in the act of teaching. The barber teaches the smith the noble art of elocution. . . ."[123] In 1833, the Duke of Wellington sniffed at the haphazard education of the youth of elite Russian families. "A French, English or German tutor is introduced into the family; generally a Frenchman. He may be equal to the task which he undertakes. But he is generally a hairdresser or a dancing master or an adventurer of some kind or other, and the scholar turns out accordingly."[124] (Weirdly, some clients were mostly interested in appearances. Showing up for an interview as tutor to a young nobleman, William Paley was anxious about the questions he might face; "but when he came he was only desir'd to go directly to a Barber, get his hair cut, his beard shav'd, then to a tailor for a coat and waistcoat of more modern shape, and then come again to be look'd at the next day."[125]) These hairdressers are frauds, prevailing with a gutsy mixture of luck and pluck, also with a blithe disregard for the niceties of integrity.

We are up against another disturbing facet of equality. In categories like equal opportunity, individual mobility, and the career open to talents, we are used to seeing hardworking and talented individuals of humble origins clawing their way to fame and fortune. However frequent such cases may be, though, that's an excessively moralized or

---

[122] Hamilton, *Memoirs,* 3:164, 1:292.

[123] *Fraser's* (August 1831) 4(19):33.

[124] Wellington to Lord Francis Egerton, 25 December 1833, Historical Manuscripts Commission, *The Prime Ministers' Papers: Wellington Political Corrrespondence I: 1833–November 1834,* ed. John Brooke and Julia Gandy (London: Her Majesty's Stationery Office, 1975), p. 400.

[125] Lady Bessborough to Granville Leveson Gower, December 1807, *Lord Granville Leveson Gower (First Earl Granville): Private Correspondence 1781 to 1821,* ed. Castalia Countess Granville, 2 vols. (London: John Murray, 1916), 2:314.

congratulatory portrait. We should learn to submerge those meritorious victors in a swirling ocean of upward and downward mobility, some of it well earned and deserved, some haphazard and incongruous, some downright cruel. The market, after all, is no theodicy. The virtuous make money; the vicious lose money; the virtuous lose money; the vicious make money. Not just money, but social status, the respect and contempt of others, and more. The inventor Arkwright "began life as a Barber, invented some machinery, got a patent, and made a fortune."[126]

That hoary wisdom on social order taught contemporaries to expect a firmly enduring hierarchy. Individual mobility, even family mobility over the generations, is a threat. True, some noble families petered out for lack of an heir; true, the Crown created new ones. However common, though, such events were ordinarily lamentable. The quintessential noble families had been around for centuries, eldest sons dutifully taking up their titles and estates in turn, younger sons disappearing into the church or the military or some other vaguely respectable institution, daughters making their prudently arranged marriages. And the quintessential commoners remained commoners, often taking up the same occupations as their parents. From this point of view, the world of equal opportunity is precarious, a world where no one can be sure of his identity or status, a demonic world of flitting shadows and shapeshifters—in short, a disorderly world. In 1830, *Fraser's* reported with considerable dismay that "every ambitious hair-dresser, butcher, or enlightened green-grocer" was scrimping and saving to send his sons off to mechanics' institutes and London University.[127]

The barber who managed to march to fame and fortune could always be lampooned as hopelessly vulgar, putting on airs, forever besmirched by his base history. Drawing on French vaudeville, Thomas James Thackeray gives us a rollicking 1830 farce, *The Barber Baron.* A mere Strasbourg barber, Alexander Hannibal Frissac, enters the Frankfurt lottery and wins the Barony of Ormsberg. "The barber,"

---

[126] *The Greville Memoirs 1814–1860,* ed. Lytton Strachey and Roger Fulford, 8 vols. (London: Macmillan, 1938), 3:5 [26 January 1834].

[127] *Fraser's* (September 1830) 2(8):165. Contrast Henry Wansey, *The Journal of an Excursion to the United States of North America, in the Summer of 1794* (Salisbury, 1796), p. 81 [24 May 1794].

warns one character, "is lord of this principality, and it matters little to me or to you, whether the blood in his veins flows from the great white kind, or from a bason of soap suds." But it matters enormously. Frissac can't carry off the role. "You'll find your prince a fine fellow too," he assures his new vassals; "I have no doubt we shall get on together as smooth as a razor-strop." He complains that he hasn't handled a chin in a week and is eager to keep shaving others. Appallingly, a company of barbers marches solemnly toward him: "Deign to accept this double cauliflower periwig, my lord, as a tribute of respect to your professional talents and a pledge of our allegiance." But in the moralized world of a staged farce, this inversion cannot last. Frissac is successfully scared off the estate by a ghost story and sells out cheap. A good-natured clown, he doesn't mind discovering the hoax. "From a poor prince I return a wealthy barber—so success, say I, to the Frankfort lottery!"[128] Even a lottery showering one with money, the audience is assured, can't disturb the verities of status. You can take the hairdresser out of the shop, but you can't take the shop out of the hairdresser.

More disturbing is Narcissus Fitzfrizzle, the "would-be Gentleman" of an 1838 farce. Spirited into a ball under false pretenses, he surveys the glittering room and sighs,

> I must have a good deal of the essence of impudence about me to enter into such a first-rate shop—ahem—house I mean. (*Looking off,* R.) Ah! there they are. Oh dear, what a ravishing sight! what beauty! what elegance! what splendid heads of hair! and what dresses! I never have seen anything to equal this; not even at the Crown and Anchor, or the Gordon Arms. Oh, why was I not born a gentleman! Cruel fate, why did you make me a hair-dresser! Why havn't I the right to dance and flirt with these beautiful creatures? Why—oh, why havn't I a title and twenty thousand a-year?[129]

The plaintive tones might seem impotent, but they might also underline the arbitrariness of birth. Justifying Fitzfrizzle's lowly status would

---

[128] T. J. Thackeray, *The Barber Baron; or, the Frankfort Lottery: A Farce, in Two Acts* (London, 1830), pp. 11, 16, 17, 36. I take the admittedly obscure mention of the "great white kind" to refer to the "great white throne" of *Revelations* 20:11 and so serve as a symbol of forbidding purity.

[129] Charles Selby, *The Dancing Barber: A Farce, in One Act* (London, 1838), pp. 3, 13.

be an unenviable task: so contemporaries often rushed to assure each other that hierarchy was in the interests of everyone, rich and poor, and that it was divinely mandated to boot.

Perhaps drawing on the work of his second cousin, William Makepeace Thackeray revisited these themes in *The Comic Almanack* for 1840.[130] Barber Cox's wife unexpectedly becomes an heiress, so he hands over his shop to his assistant, Crump. But his life in high society is a roiling cascade of absurd embarrassments. He can't hunt. He's ripped off to the tune of £1,000 betting at billiards. He has no grasp of opera or ballet. He plunges into the water while boarding a boat for France. He learns in France that the apparent aristocrat he'd proudly socialized with is actually a horse trainer in Paris. He loses a dispute in court about title to his land and finds himself in debtors' prison, where none of the vultures who'd been greedily consuming his wealth deigns to visit him. But poor old Crump, previously snubbed in no uncertain terms by his wife, does visit, and when he gets out of jail Cox sets up shop again as a hairdresser. Like Frissac, he's relieved to regain his place. "And if we are not happy, who is? . . . I can't flourish out of my native *hair*."[131] Here again, the audience is invited to snicker, to remember that even in a world of topsy-turvy mobility, hairdressers remain lowly hairdressers no matter where they find themselves. Thackeray's tale already had been told in 1796 by that enterprising seller of fine razors and razor strops, George Packwood. In one of his slapstick advertisements, he portrayed himself as "a knight of the comb, or more vulgarly speaking a hair dresser," stumbling from one disaster to another at a baronet's dinner. Yet this version of the tale is merely a diverting dream: "After two or three hours nap in my easy chair, I awoke from the vision of a dream, and found myself in the midst of my warehouse, famed for Razor Strops, &c. at No. 16, Gracechurch-Street, London."[132]

[130] For the family tree, *The Letters and Private Papers of William Makepeace Thackeray*, ed. Gordon N. Ray, 4 vols. (Cambridge, MA: Harvard University Press, 1946), 4:461–67.

[131] William Makepeace Thackeray and others, *The Comic Almanack* (London, 1882), installations from 1:210 to 1:246 [1840]. For another farce with an ambitious hairdresser and intrigues of deception, J. M. Morton, *The Barbers of Bassora: A Comic Opera, in Two Acts* (London, 1838).

[132] George Packwood, *Packwood's Whim: The Goldfinch's Nest; or, The Way to Get Money and Be Happy* (London, 1796), pp. 4–7. On Packwood, see Neil McKendrick, John Brewer, and J. H. Plumb, *The Birth of a Consumer Society: The Commercialization of Eighteenth-Century England* (Bloomington, IN: Indiana University Press, 1982), chap. 4.

Then again, Frissac and Cox are fictional characters, and the belly laughs elicited by these farces betray some anxiety, too. Real life was less consoling: those insidious hairdressers detected by Stokes and Wellington were apparently splendidly successful in their social climbing. Others capitalized on the symbolic language of hair for some illicit social climbing of their own. In 1795, the *Times* reported that "Even the beardless apprentice willingly pays his sixpence on a Sunday, and issues forth from the polite regions of Shoreditch and Whitechapel, with his head decorated as fine as a peer on a birth night."[133] One celebrated criminal escaped the clutches of the English Navy by having his landlady douse his head with flour (she had no powder on hand). "She complimented me upon my genteel appearance, and added, that she was sure if I was met by any of my own officers, they would not know me in this garb." He regretted on another occasion failing to have his whiskers shaved and his hair cut in time to avoid being identified at the police station.[134] Dibdin's popular song, "The Wisdom's in the Wig," makes the argument that the young Marx would later make on money: owning the right wig overwhelms one's actual personal qualities.[135] So too the *Black Dwarf* would wryly explore just how fragile the imposing pageantries of office were: without the right sort of wig, a judge couldn't be respected.[136] In fact, judges were expected to keep on their wigs even when they were off the bench.[137] Morosely contemplating that abbey in ruins, jotting down his poetic celebration of mystification, John Byng had noticed that judges relied on their wigs. Now the point was no longer safely buried in a private journal. It was out in public and pressed with gleeful vengeance. Franchise apart, I've argued, such developments were turning sleepy subjects into alert citizens.

[133] *Times* (7 January 1795), quoted in Clive Emsley, *British Society and the French Wars 1793–1815* (London: Macmillan, 1979), p. 50.

[134] James Hardy Vaux, *The Memoirs of James Hardy Vaux, Including His Vocabulary of the Flash Language,* ed. Noel McLachlan (London: Heinemann, 1964), pp. 137, 186 [1816]. See too Alexander Somerville, *The Autobiography of a Working Man* (London, 1848), p. 354.

[135] "The Wisdom's in the Wig," in *Universal Songster,* 2:231–32. For Marx's argument on money, see Thomas Holcroft, *The Man of Ten Thousand* (London, 1796), p. 66, and Holcroft, *He's Much to Blame* (London, 1798), p. 48, both reprinted in *The Plays of Thomas Holcroft,* ed. Joseph Rosenblum, 2 vols. (New York: Garland, 1980).

[136] *Black Dwarf* (29 September 1819) 3(39):636–37.

[137] Horace Twiss, *The Public and Private Life of Lord Chancellor Eldon, with Selections from His Correspondence,* 3 vols. (London, 1844), 1:339–40.

## SUBJECTS AND CITIZENS

Let's return to the hairdresser's shop: someone in the chair, the hairdresser busily tending to him, maybe a few clients waiting. They didn't sit silently. The "chattering dexterity of a friseur"[138] was notorious. In 1774, Richard Graves furnished a barber who, "with a voluble tongue, as he was preparing his razor, ran over the heat of the weather, dustiness of the rods, and other general topics, which those artists have ready at hand, for the entertainment of their customers, and to divert their attention from the pain which often attends the operation under the most skilful performer."[139] In 1818, Charles Lamb saluted his barber: "I can truly say, that I never spent a quarter of an hour under his hands without deriving some profit from the agreeable discussions, which are always going on there."[140] When Scott's Lord Nigel Glenvarloch finally rises from the chair and staggers away from the barber, his "ears, so long tormented with his continued babble, tingled when it had ceased, as if a bell had been rung close to them for the same space of time."[141] Souffrance, the barber of Prince Hoare's *My Grandmother,* drones on for so long that hapless Vapour has to leave before he ever gets shaved.[142] In Robert Bage's *Hermsprong,* one character importunately warns another not to make his son a barber: "Barbers' shops, you know, are receptacles of scandal."[143]

[138] *The Diary of Benjamin Robert Haydon,* ed. Willard Bissell Pope, 5 vols. (Cambridge, MA: Harvard University Press, 1960–1963), 2:282 [21 September 1820].

[139] Richard Graves, *The Spiritual Quixote: or, The Summer's Ramble of Mr. Geoffry Wildgoose,* 2d ed., 3 vols. (London, 1774), 1:122.

[140] *The Works of Charles and Mary Lamb,* ed. E. V. Lucas, 6 vols. (New York: Macmillan, 1913), 1:202 n. 1 [1818]. For instantly recognizable banter, sometimes on politics, see *The Barber's Chair* [1846] in Douglas Jerrold, *The Barber's Chair, and The Hedgehog Letters,* ed. Blanchard Jerrold (London, 1874). See too a sulky Francis, Lord Gardenstone, *Travelling Memorandums, Made in a Tour upon the Continent of Europe, in the Years 1786, 87 & 88* (Edinburgh, 1791), pp. 81–82 [17 October 1786].

[141] *Fortunes of Nigel* [1822], in *Waverley Novels,* 27:178.

[142] Prince Hoare, *My Grandmother* (London, 1794), pp. 9–12. In Isaac Pocock, *Any Thing New?* (London, 1811), hairdresser Jeremiah Babble is a gossipy ninny: note for instance pp. 18–19. Harriet Martineau, *Illustrations of Political Economy,* 9 vols. (London, 1832–1834), 2(1):10 appreciatively gives us the industriously talkative Carey the barber: "Happy would it be for society if every office were filled with equal zeal and industry!" See too Archibald MacLaren, *The Lottery Chance; or, The Drunkard Reclaim'd* (London, 1803), p. 4.

[143] Robert Bage, *Hermsprong; or, Man as He Is Not,* 2d ed., 3 vols. (London, 1799), 1:11. Note too how the malicious gossip of a "prattling hairdresser" backfires in Maria

Scandal and malicious gossip aside, this small talk might seem unexceptional and unexceptionable. As Graves notes, it helps distract one's attention from the pain of shaving. Or, as we might suspect, it helps relieve social discomfort: the hairdresser is a stranger whose job requires him to violate all the norms of body space. But on that list of general topics ready at hand was politics. In 1773, Walpole lamented, "What is England now?—A sink of Indian wealth, filled by nabobs and emptied Maccaronis! A senate sold and despised! A country overrun by horse-races! A gaming, robbing, wrangling, railing nation, without principles, genius, character or allies; the overgrown shadow of what it was!—Lord bless me, I run on like a political barber—"[144] In 1783, Cowper thought that the barber at Olney was one of the best sources of political news in town.[145] Travelling in 1794, John Byng was pleased to encounter "a good inn, where there was good cream and a political barber—as barbers should be—"[146]

By the late eighteenth century, recall, coffeehouses perhaps had fallen rather silent, but there were plenty of other social settings available for democratic discussion: debating societies, alehouses, mechanics' institutes, and the like. Think of the hairdresser's shop as an exemplary site of political discussion and recall the estimate that genteel contemporaries spent as much as an hour a day with a hairdresser. A 1791 Liverpool newspaper affirmed that "without Newspapers, our coffee-houses, ale-houses and barbers' shops would undergo a change next to depopulation."[147] The 1797 *Encyclopedia Britannica* mentioned "a newspaper, with which at this day those who wait for their turn at the barber's amuse themselves."[148] One 1799 etching portrays a man in the barber's chair, reading the *London Gazette*. Hungry for political news, the barber leans over and reads aloud,

---

Edgeworth's "Manoeuvring" [1809], in her *Tales and Novels,* 10 vols. (London, 1848), 5:80.

[144] Walpole to Horace Mann, 13 July 1773, *Walpole's Correspondence,* 23:499.

[145] Cowper to Rev. John Newton, 26 January 1783, *The Letters and Prose Writings of William Cowper,* ed. James King and Charles Ryskamp, 5 vols. (Oxford: Clarendon, 1979–1986), 2:100.

[146] John Byng, *The Torrington Diaries,* ed. C. Bruyn Andrews, 4 vols. (London: Eyre & Spottiswoode, 1934–1938), 4:13 [7 May 1794].

[147] *Liverpool General Advertiser* (9 June 1791), quoted in Frank O'Gorman, *Voters, Patrons, and Parties: The Unreformed Electoral System of Hanoverian England 1734–1832* (Oxford: Clarendon, 1989), p. 286.

[148] *Encyclopedia Britannica,* 3d ed., 18 vols. (Edinburgh, 1797), 3:6 s.v. *barber.*

obliviously driving his straight razor into the nose of the hapless man, who screams in protest.[149]

Two skeptical worries arise. Perhaps newspapers were vanishing from hairdressers' premises. Here's one 1815 observer of London: "About eighty years back, when the newspapers were only a penny a-piece, they were taken in by the Barbers for their customers to read during their waiting time."[150] And here's one 1824 observer of rural life: "Be it known to my London readers, that the shoemaker's in a country village is now what (according to tradition, and the old novels) the barber's used to be, the resort of all the male news-mongers, especially the young."[151] Yet in 1833, Charles Lamb was exercised by people reading newspaper paragraphs aloud "in barbers' shops and public-houses."[152] A radical placard of 1835 urged a boycott of shops, including hairdressers', subscribing to stamped papers.[153] Or maybe all that these newspapers show is that hairdressers' shops were like the more silent coffeehouses, sites of thoughtful reading, not political discussion. But around 1817 one Glasgow hairdresser's shop was "the arena of all local discussion."[154] "Barbers are not more celebrated by a desire to become the most busy citizens of the state," reported one of Hone's correspondents in 1826, "than by the expert habit in which they convey news."[155] In 1828, *Blackwood's* offered a shaving shop with a newspaper on the premises—and a hairdresser confessing that he's "just a little bit of" a politician.[156] Ebenezer Elliott testified to the ongoing tradition in the 1830s:

> MACLATHER, the radical barber of Perth,
> Was the saddest of all politicians on earth;
> But his business increased, while his thoughts darker grew
> For his shop was a news-shop, and barber's shop too.[157]

[149] *BMC* no. 9483 [1799].

[150] Smith, *Topography*, p. 38.

[151] Mitford, *Our Village*, 1:282.

[152] *Last Essays of Elia* [1833], in *Works of Charles and Mary Lamb*, 2:198–99.

[153] Joel H. Wiener, *The War of the Unstamped: The Movement to Repeal the British Newspaper Tax, 1830–1836* (Ithaca, NY: Cornell University Press, 1969), p. 240.

[154] William Hone, *The Every-Day Book*, 2 vols. (London, 1827; reprint ed. Detroit: Gale Research Co., 1967), 1:1272.

[155] William Hone, *Table Book*, 1:405.

[156] *Blackwood's Edinburgh Magazine* (November 1828) 24(145):615.

[157] "Burns, from the Dead," in Ebenezer Elliott, *The Splendid Village: Corn Law Rhymes; and Other Poems* (London, 1833), p. 66.

After the French Revolution, political discussion had unsavory ties to atheism: so did hairdressing. Bad enough that some hairdressers chose to stay open on Sunday, to the dismay of upright Christians. In 1782 in Tideswell, our German traveller found plenty of people lolling about one Sunday at the local barbershop.[158] Hannah More denounced the practice of putting hairdressers to work on Sunday, as if they didn't have souls to be saved.[159] Moved by More's plea, Queen Charlotte dismissed her own Sunday hairdresser.[160] Dr. Johnson avoided being shaved on the Sabbath; so did Boswell's father.[161] Boswell himself, more devoted to the niceties of presentation of self, missed church one Sunday because his barber didn't show up in time to shave him.[162] A facetious 1809 poem recounted the purportedly true story of the titanic combat between a barber and a preacher about such Sunday openings: the barber tried to shave the preacher's rear end, the preacher bashed him on the head with Foxe's *Book of Martyrs*, and finally the barber prevailed by ramming his shaving brush into the preacher's mouth and slamming him on the head with his pewter basin.[163] (Then again, some Leeds hairdressers organized to prevent anyone from doing Sabbath business.[164] And Methodist hairdressers suffered financially for refusing to do business on the Sabbath.[165]) Worse, some hairdressers sold Sunday newspapers, a recent innovation.[166] Young Miss Ann of one popular song from the early 1800s is so bent on having her hair curled that when her mother cries that she has no paper left, she shoots back, "come do not be idle / But tear a few leaves from the family bible."[167] Thomas Hood's wily

[158] Moritz, *Journeys of a German in England,* p. 158 [30 June 1782].

[159] *Thoughts on the Importance of the Manners of the Great to General Society* [1798], in *The Works of Hannah More,* 9 vols. (London, 1840–1843), 2:249–50.

[160] M. G. Jones, *Hannah More* (Cambridge: Cambridge University Press, 1952), p. 109.

[161] *Boswell for the Defence,* p. 109 [11 April 1772]; *Boswell in Extremes 1776–1778,* ed. Charles McC. Weis and Frederick A. Pottle (New York: McGraw-Hill, 1970), p. 117 [26 April 1777].

[162] *Boswell: The Great Biographer,* p. 91 [11 July 1790].

[163] J.M.L., "The Barber, the Preacher, and the Beards: Founded on Fact," *Poetical Magazine* (August 1809) 1(4):189–91.

[164] *John Bull* (29 October 1826) 6(307):351.

[165] James Lackington, *Memoirs of the First Forty-Five Years of the Life of James Lackington,* new ed. (London, 1792), pp. 259–60.

[166] John Bowles, *A Dispassionate Inquiry into the Best Means of National Safety* (London, 1806), pp. 114–15.

[167] "The Curly Hair," in *Later English Broadside Ballads,* ed. John Holloway and Joan Black, 2 vols. (London: Routledge & Kegan Paul, 1975–1979), 2:288.

1825 etching, "The Progress of Cant," an exhaustive catalogue of the
day's worries and inanities, noticed this one, too: a banner hangs
from the barber's shop saying, "NOBODY IS TO BE SHAVED DURING
DIVINE SERVICE BY COMMAND OF THE MAGISTRACY"; but the banner is
ripped, so the H in SHAVED is missing.[168]

This connection too precedes the Revolution. In 1752, Fielding directed a crushing salvo at the imagined speech of James Skotchum,
barber, who held forth in broken dialect: "Sir, I ham of Upinion, that
Relidgin can be of no youse to any mortal Sole. . . ."[169] Yet all this
political chatter seemed newly ominous after the French Revolution,
for it endangered the crucial distinction between subjects and citizens.
Imagine Benjamin Robert Haydon, forced to wonder what his political
commitments finally amounted to when confronted with a republican
barber who commented, while cutting his children's hair in 1831, "Sir,
*we* don't want a King. We want a cheap government like America, & we
will have it."[170] This demand is cool and outrageously radical.

Edmund Burke had an incisive retort to abstract talk of the rights
of man. Lingering in viciously loving detail over particular invidious
characters who could become citizens, Burke hissed,

> I can never be convinced that the scheme of placing the highest powers
> of the state in church-wardens and constables and other such officers,
> guided by the prudence of litigious attorneys and Jew brokers, and set in
> action by shameless women of the lowest condition, by keepers of hotels,
> taverns, and brothels, by pert apprentices, by clerks, shop-boys, hair-
> dressers, fiddlers, and dancers on the stage . . . can never be put into any
> shape that must not be both disgraceful and destructive.[171]

[168] *BMC* no. 14815 [1825]. The etching is reproduced in John Clubbe, *Victorian
Forerunner: The Later Career of Thomas Hood* (Durham, NC: Duke University Press, 1968),
facing p. 18. Pierce Egan, *The Show Folks!* (London, 1831), p. 40 mentions a plate by
Theodore Lane entitled "Sunday Morning—The Barber's Shop." The plate seems not
to be listed in *BMC*. Nor is it in Egan, *The Life of an Actor* (London, 1825), which has
twenty-seven plates by Lane.

[169] *Covent-Garden Journal* (28 January 1752) no. 8, in Henry Fielding, *The Covent-
Garden Journal and A Plan of the Universal Register Office*, ed. Bertrand A. Goldgar (Middletown, CT: Wesleyan University Press, 1988), p. 61.

[170] *Diary of Haydon*, 3:573 [30 October 1831]. The barber's language is evidence that
Paine's arguments from the 1790s still lingered in popular culture. Contrast the solic-
itous tones of a hairdresser seeking political information from Lord Eldon in Twiss, *Life
of Eldon*, 1:162–63.

[171] *Letter to a Member of the National Assembly* [1791], in Burke, *Works*, 4:4–5. *A Letter
from Mr. Burke, to a Member of the National Assembly; in Answer to Some Objections to His Book*

Merely naming these contemptible characters, puncturing the Jacobins' glittering generalities and unmasking the concrete realities of democracy, is enough to show that citizenship is a noisome, even noxious, ideal.

But Joseph Gerrald, hoping to convene a popular constitutional convention, indignantly demanded, "*What have I to do with politics? Nothing.* From this important question, my countrymen, so weakly and wickedly answered, have arisen all the evils which have afflicted England through a long succession of ages."[172] Like other radicals, he steadfastly addressed his readers as "Fellow Citizens."[173] So the hairdresser, still prattling away about politics after the French Revolution, could no longer be so innocent a figure. He looked too much like a bold citizen, voicing independent views and ready to act on them. One 1792 allegory on the French National Assembly emphasized that citizenship meant that "not a day passed without petitions from *Schoolmasters, Journalists, Artists, Barbers, Fishwomen, &c. &c.*"[174] And again, France was making perilously clear how sanguinary the world of citizenship might be.

Not that other subjects were all that inclined to defer to hairdressers. Remember that Birmingham church-and-king mob that burned down Joseph Priestley's house: as they set off for Joseph Ryland's house, Ryland directed his hairdresser to intercede on his behalf. But the hairdresser would testify—defensively? indignantly? proudly?—that he didn't know the mob and that even Ryland didn't believe he had "any influence" with them.[175] Dramatists must have chuckled as they exploited the interface between intrigues of deception and bold claims of citizenship. In *The Mermaid*, Proteus loses his job "for attempting, as we say at our debating society, to emancipate

---

on *French Affairs*, 5th ed. (London, 1791), pp. 3–4 has trifling variations but the same curious triple negative, which I take to be for emphasis.

[172] Joseph Gerrald, *A Convention the Only Means of Saving Us from Ruin* (London, 1793), pp. 2–3.

[173] Maurice Margarot in *The Trial of Maurice Margarot, Before the High Court of Justiciary, at Edinburgh, On the 13th and 14th of January, 1794, on an Indictment for Seditious Practices*, rep. Mr. Ramsey (New York, 1794), p. 20; contrast Cobbett's *Gazette* (January 1800), *Porcupine's Works*, 11:140.

[174] *Memoirs of Hildebrand Freeman, Esq. or A Sketch of "The Rights of Man"* (London, 1792), p. 35.

[175] *A Full and Accurate Report of the Trials of the Birmingham Rioters* (London, 1791), pp. 76–78.

or liquidate poor *Lord Crop.*" He promptly disguises himself as a hair-dresser to make his way.[176] In a farce, *Figaro in London,* only tenden-tiously connected to the renowned Figaro of France, the hairdresser is accused of making commercial headway out of fraudulent puffs, such as his boast that he has a live bear on the premises to supply his bear grease. But he's even more versatile. Adam marvels, "Then he can talk politics, and give news about the minister chaps; he can say what they're going to do." "He must be an impostor if he talks in that way," snaps back Crop, "for it's more than ministers can say them-selves, I'll warrant me."[177] Then again, the *Black Dwarf* rejoiced in the government's defeat in the Queen Caroline affair and the ensuing pathetic status of the ministers. "The saintly Sidmouth is the jest of every village-barber," crowed the journal. "Anger relaxes its muscles in contempt. . . ."[178] But the *Bristol Job Nott* reveled in the tale of a radical hairdresser put decisively in his place. Clipping away at a navy officer's locks, the hairdresser explained that he would redistribute the wealth, taking half of everyone's assets. The officer responded by paying him half what he asked for.[179]

Consider a story making the rounds in London clubs in the 1820s. The story is apocryphal at best: it's about Henry Dundas's service as Home Secretary, an office he held from 1791 to 1794, so it was being told decades after the putative event; but for my purposes it doesn't matter if it's true. Anyway, the story: Dundas had to return to Edin-burgh after being hassled by a mob there unhappy with his repressive policies. Waking up in his hotel, he sent for a barber. "The Tonsor, who happened to be a wag," greeted Dundas and prepared to shave him. "At length, flourishing his razor, he said in a sharp and stern voice,—'We are much *obliged* to you, Mr. Dundas, for the part you lately took in London.' 'What!' replied the Secretary, 'you are a politi-cian, I find?—I sent for a *barber.*'" (And what might this contrast amount to?) After shaving half of Dundas's face, "the knight of the pewter basin" drew his razor across Dundas's throat and rushed off into the street. Convinced he was being murdered, Dundas clutched

---

[176] Andrew Franklin, *The Mermaid* (London, 1792), p. 24. I've corrected the punctuation.

[177] Gilbert Abbot à Beckett, *Figaro in London: A Farce, in Two Acts* (London, 18--), p. 22.

[178] *Black Dwarf* (15 November 1820) 5(20):687.

[179] *Bristol Job Nott* (13 December 1832) no. 53, p. 210.

his apron to his throat and made "a loud guggling noise." The doctors came, hovered around, and finally persuaded him to remove the apron so they could tend to him. But his throat was intact: the hairdresser had used the back end of the razor.[180]

The Reform Bill of 1832 only made matters worse, further jeopardizing time-honored wisdom about faceless subjects by promoting what conservatives saw as democratic frenzies. Now, conservatives thought, the infectious plague from across the Channel finally had erupted. Warned *Fraser's,* "In these perilous times, when you submit your chin to a barber never talk about politics till you ascertain his principles on these matters. It is dangerous to put one's throat in the mercy of a man armed with a razor, especially if he be a red-hot politician; which all shavers are, without exception."[181] Think about the conditions in which it never occurs to one to worry that the hairdresser, maybe a complete stranger, is holding a lethal weapon to one's throat, and how one might learn instead to notice and fret about such matters. (Think too about why we might not applaud those who notice as paragons of prudence.) Lord Eldon recalled cross-examining one barber "rather too severely." Wishing to make amends, he promised to give him some business next time he passed through his town. "He said with great indignation, I would not advise you, Lawyer, to think of that, or to risque it."[182] One presumes this wasn't precisely threatened homicide: so perhaps *Fraser's* warning was hyperbole. Perhaps it's not that one might literally have one's throat slit, not even in the phony way Dundas did; it's rather that a world in which a lowly hairdresser presumes to offer political views is lethal. Working on the Westminster election of 1807, Francis Place and others were taunted as "nobody, common tailors, and

[180] Charles Marsh, *The Clubs of London,* 2 vols. (London, 1828), 1:292–95. I found no account of this story in Holden Furber, *Henry Dundas: First Viscount Melville 1742–1811* (London: Oxford University Press, 1931) or Michael Fry, *The Dundas Despotism* (Edinburgh: Edinburgh University Press, 1992). John Oswald, *Review of the Constitution of Great-Britain,* 3d ed. (London, 1792), p. 34 tells a suspiciously similar story about the Roman emperor Julian. See Edward Gibbon, *The History of the Decline and Fall of the Roman Empire* [1776–1788], ed. J. B. Bury, 7 vols. (London: Methuen, 1909; reprint ed. New York: AMS Press, 1974), 2:444.

[181] *Fraser's* (December 1832) 6(36):715.

[182] *Lord Eldon's Anecdote Book,* ed. Anthony L. J. Lincoln and Robert Lindley McEwen (London: Stevens & Sons, 1960), p. 87 [1824–1827]. For an instance of Eldon being splendidly generous to a hairdresser, see Twiss, *Life of Eldon,* 1:135–36.

Barbers. . . . We were laughed at for our folly, and condemned for our impudence."[183]

In *Quentin Durward*, Scott exhibited Louis XI with a "wily tonsor" doubling as a political adviser. Not the type to cringe before royalty, the man glared at Louis "with an expression of sarcastic contempt, which he scarce attempted to disguise."[184] Scott was faithful, as ever, to the historical record: Olivier le Daim in fact rose under Louis XI from barber to minister; Parlement would later duly reward his audacious success by executing him. (Claire Clairmont recorded the story, also one about a drunken slave of a hairdresser who abandoned the Russian emperor in a public parade when he saw his mistress glaring at him.[185]) Anyway, here history would repeat itself, first as farce, then as tragedy: Lord Althorp, Chancellor of the Exchequer, reported *John Bull* "in serious sober sadness," "actually writes letters—confidential letters—to a barber at Northampton, one SHARP—which confidential letters are read as publicly in Northampton as the confidential communications of a barber's shop usually are." Worse, moaned the paper, Althorp had written, "PRAY, WATCH MY CONDUCT, AND LET ME KNOW WHEN I AM WRONG."[186] For *John Bull*, this isn't an ordinary contact between elected official and citizen. It isn't even a commendable act of condescension. It's a grotesque travesty, with Althorp stupidly abasing himself by stooping to conversation on equal terms, if not to subservient pleading, with a lowly barber who ought to be a submissive subject. Not for subjects to admonish ministers; at most, the subjects can report a perceived grievance; but it must remain up to the ministers to decide what, if anything, to do about it.

Again, we shouldn't restrict our understanding of democracy to the soporific technical requirements of the franchise, the various schedules of the Reform Bill, the mathematical intricacies of voting schemes, and other legal rules, important though they are. The social and cultural transformations enabling a barber to advise a minister (not to mention the continuities making that noteworthy, even abhorrent) are every bit as crucial. At stake here are public standing and

---

[183] Quoted in E. P. Thompson, *The Making of the English Working Class* (New York: Vintage Books, 1966), p. 465.

[184] *Quentin Durward* [1823], in *Waverley Novels* 31:227, 31:240.

[185] *The Journals of Claire Clairmont*, ed. Marion Kingston Stocking with David Mackenzie Stocking (Cambridge, MA: Harvard University Press, 1968), pp. 346–47 [7 August 1825], 393 [18 December 1825].

[186] *John Bull* (9 September 1832) 12(613):292; see too *John Bull* (30 December 1832) 12(629):421. Compare *Black Dwarf* (6 March 1822) 8(10):355.

epistemic authority: who counts as a participant in public dialogue? or, more generally, whom ought we listen to—and believe—and why? Take Sir Brooke Boothby's condemnation of Paine's *Rights of Man,* "written with the logic of shoemakers and the metaphysics of barbers."[187] The sneer is supposed to be devastating, to dramatize not just Paine's idiocies but his obvious lack of standing and credibility. Or again: disgusted by Anna Barbauld's failure to appreciate Sir Philip Sidney, Robert Southey sputtered, "The remark of Mrs. Barbauld upon the works of such a man can be compared to nothing but the blasphemies of a Jew dealer in old clothes, or the criticisms of a French barber upon Shakspeare."[188] Precisely because such characters are contemptible, we need not listen to what they have to say.

Returning the compliment, Thomas Love Peacock has the virtuous Mr. Forrester reprove Mr. Feathernest (Southey, so dubbed for the money he pocketed as poet laureate) by urging the merits of the life of a barber. Feathernest is appalled: "A barber, Sir!—a man of genius turn barber!" But Forrester is adamant: "The poorest barber in the poorest borough in England, who will not sell his vote, is a much more honourable character in the estimate of moral comparison than the most self-satisfied dealer in courtly poetry, whose well-paid eulogiums of licentiousness and corruption were ever re-echoed by the 'most sweet voices' of hireling gazetteers and pensioned reviewers."[189] Typically the poorest barber wouldn't have had the vote anyway; still, if the world of periodical reviews was as deeply corrupt as Forrester claims, the barber's views are more trustworthy.

All that political talk was easily enlisted as evidence that political talk was every bit as intoxicating for the lower orders as conservatives feared. "In politics I took delight, / But now I'm quite in desperation," confessed the barber of one radical song.[190] Desperate or not, other hairdressers took action. The lists of leading radicals of the day are peppered liberally with their names; but so are the lists of spies employed by the Home Office; here again hairdressers are alarmingly unpredictable shapeshifters. One of those ubiquitous spies attending

[187] Sir Brooke Boothby, *Observations on the Appeal from the New to the Old Whigs, and on Mr Paine's Rights of Man* (London, 1792), p. 98.

[188] Southey to Miss Barker, 26 January 1805, *Selections from the Letters of Robert Southey,* ed. John Wood Warter, 4 vols. (London, 1856), 1:314–15.

[189] *Melincourt* [1817], in *The Works of Thomas Love Peacock,* Halliford edition, ed. H. F. B. Brett-Smith and C. E. Jones, 10 vols. (London: Constable & Co., 1924–1934), 2:188, 2:189.

[190] "Spence and the Barber," in *Spence's Songs* (London, 1802), pt. 2, n.p.

meetings of the London Corresponding Society (LCS) and other radical groups told the government in 1794 that one Stiff, a hairdresser,
claimed to be capable of teaching a "manual and platoon exercise" for
revolutionary arming clubs.[191] Another hairdresser, George Widdison,
testified at the trial of Thomas Hardy that he made pikes for the
Constitutional Society of Sheffield.[192] Edward Gosling testified at the
same trial, turning out to be not just a hairdresser but also a spy.[193] John
Lovett, a London hairdresser, chaired the infamous Chalk Farm meeting of 14 April 1794.[194] Robert Robinson, a social climber who began
as a hairdresser's apprentice and finished a Baptist minister, founded
the Cambridge Society for Constitutional Information.[195] John
Tunbridge, a hairdresser, joined three different radical groups and
filed a steady stream of weekly reports to the government in 1798 and
1799.[196] Robert Lodge, part-time hairdresser, was implicated in membership in the United Britons.[197] E. J. Blandford, a Spencean revolutionary, was another part-time hairdresser.[198] One Lomax, a Manchester barber, was taken into custody after the insurrectionary blanket
march of 1817, but was immediately released: journalist and Jacobin
sympathizer Archibald Prentice was sure that he too was a spy.[199]

[191] *Selections from the Papers of the London Corresponding Society 1792–1799*, ed. Mary
Thale (Cambridge: Cambridge University Press, 1983), p. 149.

[192] *The Trial of Thomas Hardy for High Treason*, rep. Joseph Gurney, 4 vols. (London,
1794–1795), 2:249–50; for more of Widdison, *Trial of Hardy*, 1:325–38, 2:245–62.

[193] *Trial of Hardy*, 2:352–70. Gosling was charged with entrapment in James Parkinson, *A Vindication of the London Corresponding Society* (London, 1794), in *Political Writings*,
ed. Claeys, 4:377–78.

[194] Albert Goodwin, *The Friends of Liberty: The English Democratic Movement in the Age of
the French Revolution* (Cambridge, MA: Harvard University Press, 1979), p. 328. For the
proceedings from that LCS meeting, *The First Report of the Committee of Secrecy of the House
of Commons, on the Papers Belonging to the Society for Constitutional Information, and the
London Corresponding Society, Seized by Order of Government, and Presented to the House by Mr.
Secretary Dundas, on the 12th and 13th of May 1794* (London, 1794), pp. 28–32; *Selections
from the Papers*, ed. Thale, pp. 133–40.

[195] Nicholas Roe, *Wordsworth and Coleridge: The Radical Years* (Oxford: Clarendon,
1988), pp. 88–89.

[196] J. Ann Hone, *For the Cause of Truth: Radicalism in London 1796–1821* (Oxford:
Clarendon, 1982), p. 63.

[197] Roger Wells, *Insurrection: The British Experience 1795–1803* (Gloucester: Alan Sutton, 1983), p. 233.

[198] David Worrall, *Radical Culture: Discourse, Resistance and Surveillance, 1790–1820*
(New York: Harvester Wheatsheaf, 1992), pp. 146–63.

[199] Archibald Prentice, *Historic Sketches and Personal Recollections of Manchester: In-
tended to Illustrate the Progress of Public Opinion from 1792 to 1832* (London, 1851), p. 97.
Lady Stanhope claimed that Napoleon employed two London hairdressers as spies:
*Memoirs of Lady Stanhope*, 2:289.

## A Tale of Three Pamphlets

So far, much ado about hairdressers, and many mocking and abusive words put into their mouths by leering and hostile opponents. But what did hairdressers themselves think and say? I've located three pamphlets written by hairdressers—or, more accurately, purporting to be written by hairdressers; authenticity is hard to obtain in these matters.[200] The author of the first, published in 1793 in Edinburgh, defiantly identifies himself on the title page as A. Scott, Citizen and Hairdresser. It might seem shrewd to brandish this apparently oxymoronic identity. But actually, Scott is no hairdresser. He wants to make transparent the travesty of calls for democracy while pretending to endorse the politics of Tom Paine. The agenda is clear right from the start in Scott's soothing tones:

> You have been harrassed, citizens, with various publications of late, many of them of so grave a cast, that you have not had patience to read them, and others so abstruse and philosophical, that you have not been able to understand them. Allow me then, who am but an uneducated man like yourselves, and have had no means of improvement, but what I have received in conversation with my customers, who are many of them of the first rank for learning, as my business lies much in the neighbourhood of the university; but though uneducated, I am fully conscious of an equality of rights with all other men, and particularly of my own share of common sense, not the least important of those rights. Allow me, then, to lay before you, in the plainest manner, those reasons, that have convinced me, (for till very lately I was a loyal subject) that the plan of our present reformers is rational, sound, and fraught with the greatest blessings to this country, and therefore ought to be adopted.[201]

But maybe political argument is too complex for mere hairdressers to follow. Maybe the problem is that Paine's sophistries really can dissolve the loyalty of subjects in an instant. Maybe the pursuit of citizenship is just another deplorable kind of social climbing. The reasons Scott adduces for adopting Paine's politics are manifestly laughable:

[200] Patricia Hollis, *The Pauper Press: A Study in Working-Class Radicalism of the 1830s* (London: Oxford University Press, 1970), pp. 319–27 lists well over one hundred London and provincial radical unstamped papers from 1830–1836, including (p. 319) the humorous *Barber's Journal* from April 1835, which I have not seen.

[201] A. Scott, *Plain Reasons for Adopting the Plan of the Societies Calling Themselves the Friends of the People, and Their Convention of Delegates, As Copied from the Works of Mr. Tho$^s$ Paine: in a Serious Address to the Citizens of Edinburgh* (Edinburgh, 1793), p. 2.

he insists the constitution must be destroyed because of "the great prosperity of the nation."[202] Like a practiced vaudeville artist, though, Scott ignores his own blunders—until, in the midst of his cheery exposition, he falters:

> But, on considering the matter a little deeper, and diving into the designs of our worthy President of the society of the friends of the people, and his sage Vice, I now am convinced that their design is to put an end to all commerce and to all the arts, and to bring us back to the primitive state of simplicity and virtue, in which our predecessors were in this island some thousands of years ago, when every man was his own taylor and shoemaker, and weaver and butcher, and carpenter and mason, and baker and brewer, not to say barber and hair-dresser also. For, though they must always have had beards and hair, (though not periwigs), yet I suppose that in the times I allude to, they gave themselves very little trouble about them.[203]

Scott methodically hammers the point home: the demand for democracy is quite literally the demand for the end of civilization. One can't be a citizen and hairdresser, whatever a title page claims, because a world of democratic citizenship will put an end to hairdressers along with all the other civilized occupations, driving the British back to a state of nature.[204]

The second pamphlet, published in 1795 in London, is by Pasquin Shaveblock, Shaver Extraordinary. Shaveblock (whoever he was[205]), out to mock the clergy of England and the war with France, offers a sermon and commentary on *Ezekiel* 5:1, which he mischievously abridges: "Son of man, take unto thee—a Barber's Razor." A diligent reader of his Bible, Shaveblock also notices the perennially interesting *Isaiah* 7:20, prophesying the day when the Lord shall shave with a razor.[206] (In 1782, an Oxford freethinker made merry with the same passages.[207]) A sustained barrage of sarcastic inversions undercuts any commitment like Burke's to the view that hairdressers aren't dignified. They're just as dignified as anyone else. In fact, more or less

---

[202] Scott, *Plain Reasons*, p. 5.

[203] Scott, *Plain Reasons*, p. 8.

[204] See too *Edinburgh Review* (January 1804) 3(6):358.

[205] There is no reference to this pamphlet in Halkett and Laing.

[206] Pasquin Shaveblock, *The Shaver's New Sermon for the Fast Day,* 3d ed. (London, 1795), pp. 7, 7 n.

[207] Moritz, *Journeys of a German in England,* p. 136 [25 June 1782].

everyone turns out to be a hairdresser, or a shaver, in a series of riotous carnival inversions. There are legal shavers, political shavers, and military shavers. (The usage isn't eccentric: over the years, cartoonists had produced Fox as a political shaver, Napoleon as a political shaver, and Brougham as a political shaver.[208]) And there are clerical shavers:

> Do they not lather us with encomiums on the constitution of the established church—on the divine excellency of her hierarchy—on the exactness of her discipline—on the sublimity of her services—the orthodoxy of her creeds—and the ability and piety of her priests?—And verily, my brethren, do they not also shave us? Do they not shave us by tythes and first fruits?—by Rectors' rates, and Lecturers' rates?—by briefs and collections? Ah! my brethren, who can deny them equal praise for plentiful lathering and close shaving?[209]

Shaveblock refuses to concede that lowly hairdressers aren't entitled to political views. "As for politics, that science is almost peculiar to us."[210] Returning to the dignity of labor, Shaveblock jauntily adds, "Permit me to add a word, as to the *dignity* of our profession, which can not only boast of prelates and prime-ministers among its practitioners, but even of popes and princes."[211] Biblical, ancient, and English history produce their rosters of illustrious shavers. Finally, in one last glorious inversion Shaveblock mocks the thought that hairdressers are too humble to criticize and argue, but must always defer to authority:

> There is one other class of people I must just mention—those who, though not able to shave themselves, have yet the temerity to find fault with their shavers. Alas! sirs, how should you be able to criticize our conduct? How should you know how to raise a lather, or to strop a razor—much less to direct us in the very act of shaving? But you complain we shave too close, too rough, or the like—but do you know better than we, whose business and study it is?—for shame, my brethren! no more complaining, but submission—unconditional, unlimited submission. "It is the great misfortune of the present day, that every subject is

---

[208] *BMC* nos. 6577 [10 May 1784], 10601 [September 1806], 14772 [May 1825].
[209] Shaveblock, *Shaver's New Sermon*, p. 9.
[210] Shaveblock, *Shaver's New Sermon*, p. 30.
[211] Shaveblock, *Shaver's New Sermon*, pp. 30–31.

open to vulgar investigation," not excepting the sublime mystery of shaving.[212]

The quotation is a paraphrase of an angry charge Burke presses against the champions of enlightenment: "It has been the misfortune (not as these gentlemen think it, the glory) of this age, that everything is to be discussed, as if the Constitution of our country were to be always a subject rather of altercation than enjoyment."[213] I don't know if Burke suffered the indignity of seeing his abstruse sentiments lampooned by vulgar Shaveblock. But Boswell, amused by the bragging of an ambitious jack-of-all-trades hairdresser, had the effrontery to tease Burke about being a political barber, shaving the ministry and grinding razors of state.[214]

The third pamphlet is far less polished. In literary terms, it's abrupt and disjointed, jerking erratically from one theme to another, with no sustained focus or momentum; and one would need finer eyesight than I have to detect any genuine working-class eloquence in its pages. It's by the radical hairdresser we've already encountered, John Lovett, who chaired the Chalk Farm meeting. Publishing in 1793 in London, Lovett astutely adds "H.D." to his name on the title page. This semi-private joke is a way of thumbing his nose at the conventions that led scholars to festoon their title pages with all their degrees, a move democrats saw as an illicit bid for epistemic authority.[215] Readers might defer to John Lovett, H.D., in ignorance that his apparent degree was that of hairdresser. They'd do better to ignore all those obscure abbreviations.

Like Shaveblock, Lovett is a prophet of enlightenment, but his inversions are less sly, more biting, approaching a jeremiad:

> The people have been long in ignorance, but that is beginning to disappear . . . learning is become more general than in former times, and the people assemble more into large towns, and by conversation diffuse knowledge through each other: by this means the rich, if they do

[212] Shaveblock, *Shaver's New Sermon*, p. 32.

[213] *Reflections on the Revolution in France*, in *Works*, 3:352.

[214] *Boswell: The Applause of the Jury 1782–1785*, ed. Irma S. Lustig and Frederick A. Pottle (New York: McGraw-Hill, 1981), p. 115 [21 April 1783].

[215] Note the riposte of John Harrison, *A Letter to the Right Hon. Henry Dundas, M.P. Secretary of State, &c. &c. or, An Appeal to the People of Great-Britain* (London, 1794), pp. 18–19 to the claim that as "only a Razor-maker of Sheffield, a poor man of no consequence," he is "not very fitly calculated to reform a state."

not mend their manners, morals, and behaviour towards mankind, will be looked on at some future period with as much contempt as they now look on those in a lower sphere of life.[216]

Lovett had to leave the countryside, much as he loved farming, because like many others, he was becoming desperately poor.[217] Heading to the big city, he became a hairdresser. (An economist would note that the occupation has low entry costs.) Ironically, hairdressing itself invites his condemnation:

> What can be said in favour of hair-dressing? which is one of the most destructive fashions that ever was invented. By it a vast number of people are rendered useless to society, a great deal of the necessaries of life are destroyed, and cloathes in abundance.
>
> There is many poor men that absolutely rob their families of the supports of nature through this mistaken and ridiculous pride. They will go and pay sixpence to have their head filled with flour and lard, to make it ten times more uncomfortable than it would be combed through like a farmer's, when at the same time their children are at home crying for bread.
>
> The utility of hair-dressing is completely done away: it was invented to shew a distinction in rank, and was in use only by the higher orders of people, but now it is so far degenerated, that by taking a walk in the Park, you would not be enabled to distinguish the apprentice boy from his grace.[218]

No dignity in hairdressing here: the point of the enterprise is to make pernicious status distinctions, and thanks to those apprentices, like the beardless ones noticed by the *Times,* the currency of hair has become counterfeit anyway. So hairdressers labor in vain toward a bad end.

Perhaps there was no dignity for Lovett, either, whose life affords one last ironic twist. He, too, was probably a government spy, lurking on the shadowy payroll of the Home Office under Dundas's administration. (It's tempting to surmise that Dundas himself knew of Lovett, even that he remembered him when confronting that straight-edge razor in Edinburgh; but this is hoping for too much.) Though he was

---

[216] John Lovett, *The Citizen of the World* (London, 1793), pp. 15–16; and note pp. 34–35.

[217] Lovett, *Citizen,* p. 5.

[218] Lovett, *Citizen,* pp. 29–30.

arrested along with other LCS leaders after the Chalk Farm meeting, unlike them he wasn't indicted. Cecil Thelwall, wife of the LCS leader, had her suspicions. Surprising, she mused, that a man so frequently making irresponsibly violent proposals—the insinuation is that he was a spy attempting entrapment—was allowed to walk away scot-free.[219] He quickly disappeared, apparently moving to New York with enough money first to set up shop as a grocer and then to purchase two hotels.[220] Undignified, even inglorious: but another case of successful social climbing, more testimony to the corrosive power of equality, courtesy of the Home Office.

[219] Cecil Thelwall, *The Life of John Thelwall* (London, 1837), pp. 214–15.

[220] *Biographical Dictionary of Modern British Radicals,* ed. Joseph O. Baylen and Norbert J. Gossman, 3 vols. (Sussex: Harvester Press, 1979–1988), 1:303–4.

# TWELVE

# THE FATE OF A TROPE

IT HAS EMERGED as the best-known passage of Burke's *Reflections on the Revolution in France*. Burke must have been amazed, even appalled, by its fate. For the passage is stuck inconspicuously into yet another prolix lament on the dizzying innovations introduced by the French revolutionaries. "When ancient opinions and rules of life are taken away," sighs Burke, "the loss cannot possibly be estimated. From that moment we have no compass to govern us, nor can we know distinctly to what port we steer." The revolutionaries, bold, ambitious, and dreadfully irresponsible, have shredded one crucial rule of life. European civilization, Burke explains, has long depended on "the spirit of a gentleman, and the spirit of religion," aristocracy and the church interlocking to uphold social order, intellectuals patiently serving both. But now those intellectuals have decided that they want to rule. This rash decision will topple a politically felicitous balance. It won't be too good for the intellectuals, either. These melancholy thoughts inspire elegiac regret: "Happy, if learning, not debauched by ambition, had been satisfied to continue the instructor, and not aspired to be the master!" Then comes the infamous punchline: "Along with its natural protectors and guardians, learning will be cast into the mire and trodden down under the hoofs of a swinish multitude."[1]

*A swinish multitude:* with dizzying speed, it emerges as one of the day's cant phrases, right alongside *the march of intellect* and *poisoning the minds of the lower orders*, as well as others I'm not focusing on, such as *the church is in danger*. Its reception and transformation are ironic ripostes to the argument Burke is making in introducing the image.

---

[1] *Reflections on the Revolution in France* [1790], in *The Works of the Right Honorable Edmund Burke*, 9th ed., 12 vols. (Boston: Little, Brown, 1889), 3:334–35.

Clever writer though he was, he didn't invent this image or the background commitments it so vividly embodies. Foot firmly planted in his forefathers' tracks, he confidently placed himself in a distinguished, even hoary, ancient tradition. Yet in the abruptly new world of his day, the phrase came to take on new and repellent meanings.

In exploring Burke's antecedents, pride of place goes to Scripture. Recall the Gospels' injunction: "Give not that which is holy unto the dogs, neither cast ye your pearls before swine, lest they trample them under their feet, and turn again and rend you."[2] Recall too the episode where Jesus casts out devils by sending them into the bodies of some swine, which hurl themselves into the water and drown.[3] As always, the haunting cadences of the King James Bible were readily available to the English. The question was just what use to put them to.

At his 1794 trial, radical Joseph Gerrald must have taken smarmy pleasure in eruditely exposing one of Burke's predecessors. It was "a monkish writer, who was an enemy to the Reformation," he charged, who had appropriated the image to mock popular literacy. Deploring the translation and publication of the holy Scriptures, this monk had written, "Pity it is, that this evangelical pearl should be trodden down under the foot of *swine*."[4] Gerrald here urges that Burke, this eloquent mouthpiece so eagerly adopted by the regime, reveals the cloven foot of Catholicism, that his contempt for popular literacy and enlightenment is at one with Catholics' illicit desire to keep the Gospels out of the hands of popular readers. The same point, recall, had been pressed by Eaton. But it didn't save Gerrald from a criminal sentence and it didn't diminish the regime's regard for Burke.

I don't know if Burke knew the manuscript of this monk, one Henry Knighton, and his complaint about Wycliffe.[5] He must have known the works of Martin Marprelate, a diabolically acute Elizabethan polemicist, and Marprelate's glancing blow at an "antichris-

[2] *Matthew* 7:6.

[3] *Matthew* 8:30–32; *Mark* 5:11–16; *Luke* 8:32–33.

[4] *The Trial of Joseph Gerrald, Delegate from the London Corresponding Society, to the British Convention: Before the High Court of Justiciary, at Edinburgh, on the 3d, 10th, 13th, and 14th of March, 1794 for Sedition*, rep. Mr. Ramsey (Edinburgh, 1794), p. 202. The same bit of erudition is displayed in Thomas Cooper, *A Reply to Mr. Burke's Invective against Mr. Cooper, and Mr. Watt, in the House of Commons, on the 30th of April, 1792*, 2d ed. (London, 1792), p. 36.

[5] See *Chronicon Henrici Knighton, vel Cnitthon, Monachi Leycestrensis*, ed. Joseph Rawson Lumby, 2 vols. (London, 1889–1895), 2:152.

tian swinish rabble."[6] But we can leave the question of Burke's knowledge aside, for the meaning and resonances of his language aren't defined or exhausted by his understanding of them. There is a widely available stock of categories here, another venerable tradition of describing the lower orders as the mob, the multitude, the many-headed monster.[7] The *Bristol Job Nott*'s decree that "the mob is an animal with many heads, but no brains" was anything but original.[8] John Wade's echo of the decree—"The mob has many heads, but no brains"— isn't any more original.[9] But it is more baffling because Wade boasted militantly radical credentials. So we need to ask why radicals would indulge in such lofty dismissals. Were they revealing a hidden elitism and contempt for those they officially championed? Were they wholly in the clutches of a hegemonic discourse? Or what?

The many-headed monster swirls together with the equally distinguished pursuit of animal imagery to dehumanize one's opponents, a pursuit which sometimes turned in porcine directions.[10] Launching another salvo against the idiocies of popular politics, Dr. Johnson charged that the masses were always dependent on the views of their superiors. When they weren't dutifully deferring, they were mechanically rejecting: "The peers have but to *oppose* a candidate, to ensure him success. It is said, the only way to make a pig go forward, is to pull him back by the tail. These people must be treated like pigs."[11] Zany Lord George Gordon, leader of the militantly Protestant London riots of 1780 that bear his name, confirmed his insanity in the eyes of his contemporaries by converting to Judaism. In a rapturous letter, he

[6] *The Marprelate Tracts 1588, 1589,* ed. William Pierce (London: James Clarke, 1911), p. 56.

[7] For that earlier tradition, see for instance Christopher Hill, *Change and Continuity in Seventeenth-Century England* (Cambridge, MA: Harvard University Press, 1975), chap. 8.

[8] *Bristol Job Nott* (20 December 1832) no. 54, p. 214.

[9] John Wade, *History of the Middle and Working Classes; with a Popular Exposition of the Economical and Political Principles Which Have Influenced the Past and Present Condition of the Industrious Orders* (London, 1833), p. 590.

[10] See Keith Thomas, *Man and the Natural World: Changing Attitudes in England 1500– 1800* (London: Allen Lane, 1983), chap. 1. For an audaciously broad contextualization of porcine imagery, see Peter Stallybrass and Allon White, *The Politics and Poetics of Transgression* (Ithaca, NY: Cornell University Press, 1986), chap. 1.

[11] James Boswell, *The Journal of a Tour to the Hebrides, with Samuel Johnson, Ll.D.* [1786], in *Boswell's Life of Johnson: Together with Boswell's Journal of a Tour to the Hebrides and Johnson's Diary of a Journey into North Wales,* ed. George Birkbeck Hill, rev. L. F. Powell, 6 vols. (Oxford: Clarendon, 1934–1950), 5:354–55 [24 October 1773].

indicted the American Congress: "They suck the Sow of Corruption. They return to wallow in the mire."[12]

Brainless, medusa mob and filthy, stupid pigs, married by one of the great masters of English prose in a ceremony of political necromancy, emerged as a swinish multitude. Or, more often than not, as *the* swinish multitude. From his day to ours, Burke has been misquoted routinely.[13] Ever the meticulous critic, Hazlitt noticed the mistake.[14] Some of Burke's apologists plunked down their chips on the political significance of that indefinite article. "The expression of *swinish multitude* has been most cruelly misinterpreted," complained one anonymous writer, "and made a by-word to incense the populace against him. But it is clear that he only speaks of a supposed particular multitude . . . for had he spoken of the common people in a general sense, *the multitude* would have been the proper grammatical ex-

---

[12] Lord George Gordon to Elias Lindo and the Portuguese, and Nathan Salomon and the German, Jews, 26 August 1783, *Anglo-Jewish Letters (1158–1917)*, ed. Cecil Roth (London: Soncino Press, 1938), p. 188.

[13] See for instance, explicitly attributing the phrase with the definite article to Burke: A Friend to the People, *A Review of the Constitution of Great Britain* (London, 1791), p. 45; Cooper, *Reply to Mr. Burke's Invective*, pp. 10, 13, 36; *Pig's Meat* 1:263; *Persecution: The Case of Charles Pigott: Contained in the Defence He Had Prepared, and Which Would Have Been Delivered by Him on His Trial, if the Grand Jury Had Not Thrown Out the Bill Preferred Against Him* (London, 1793), p. 33; Hugh, Lord Sempill, *A Short Address to the Public, on the Practice of Cashiering Military Officers without a Trial; and a Vindication of the Conduct and Political Opinions of the Author* (London, 1793), p. 30 n; Thomas Walker, *A Review of Some of the Political Events Which Have Occurred in Manchester, during the Last Five Years: Being a Sequel to the Trial of Thomas Walker, and Others* (London, 1794), p. 127; *The Trial of Wm. Winterbotham, Assistant Preacher at How's Lane Meeting, Plymouth before the Hon. Baron Perryn, and a Special Jury, at Exeter; on the 25th of July, 1793: for Seditious Words Charged to Have Been Uttered in Two Sermons Preached on the 5th and 18th of November, 1792,* 2d ed. (London, 1794), p. 68 n. †; John Butler, *The Political Fugitive: Being a Brief Disquisition into the Modern System of British Politics; and the Unparalleled Rigor of Political Persecution: Together with General Miscellaneous Observations on the Abuses and Corruptions of the English Government* (New York, 1794), p. 89; *Trial of Gerrald*, p. 202; Pigott, *A Political Dictionary: Explaining the True Meaning of Words* (London, 1795), p. 109 s.v. *rabble;* E. P. Thompson, *The Making of the English Working Class* (New York: Vintage Books, 1966), pp. 89, 90; Iain McCalman, *Radical Underworld: Prophets, Revolutionaries and Pornographers in London, 1795–1840* (Cambridge: Cambridge University Press, 1988), p. 122.

[14] "Butts of Different Sorts" [1829], in *The Complete Works of William Hazlitt*, ed. P. P. Howe, 21 vols. (London: J. M. Dent and Sons, 1930–1934), 20:198. Note too *The Plain Speaker* [1826], in *Works of Hazlitt*, 12:271. For another scrupulously correct attribution, see The Political Societies of Norwich to the Secretary of the London Corresponding Society, 25 June 1793, in *The Trial of Thomas Hardy for High Treason*, rep. Joseph Gurney, 4 vols. (London, 1794–1795), 1:249.

pression."[15] William Windham, Burke's parliamentary acolyte, bitterly assailed the nefarious subversion of the master's words.[16] So
Burke harbored no sweepingly general contempt for the lower orders. He only ventured a narrow reflection on the contingent actions
of one particular mob.

I wonder. It would be difficult to name the particular mob Burke
might have had in mind in this passage. Besides, the *Reflections* are
forever poised on the edge of allegory, each idiosyncratic episode of
the distressing history he steels himself to explore coruscating with
universal political significance. Slippery arguments about literary
form aside, though, consider the fruits of a desultory search through
the rest of Burke's works. Burke shrinks with horror from the revolutionaries' decision to commemorate Bastille Day by exposing Louis
and Marie Antoinette "to the derision of an unthinking and unprincipled multitude": a concrete mob, but is Burke privy to concrete
knowledge of its character? or is he making a reflex judgment, that is
no judgment at all, about the character of the multitude?[17] Burke
marvels at the dubious spectacle of "a great genius like Mr. Fox" embracing the downfall of France's absolute monarchy. After all, what
replaced it was "the tyranny of a licentious, ferocious, and savage multitude," revelling in its newfound authority by "insolently" smashing
inherited traditions: surely nothing to celebrate.[18] Or again: "an
hired, frantic, drunken multitude" had the chilling audacity to applaud as Louis was decapitated.[19] Once again, we might wonder: a
particular mob or a mob revealing the very essence of the scum
uppermost?

A decade before the *Reflections,* Burke was strutting in the House of
Commons, boasting that were the "the smallest rights of the poorest
people in the kingdom" threatened, he would take their side in a civil
war. Already too, though, Burke was fearing popular licentiousness.
Should such exploited wretches seek to excuse themselves from the
constraints of "morality and virtuous discipline, then I would join my
hand to make them feel the force which a few united in a good cause

[15] *An Historical Essay on the Ambition and Conquests of France, with Some Remarks on the
French Revolution* (London, 1797), p. 172.
[16] William Windham, *Speeches in Parliament*, 3 vols. (London, 1812), 1:259 [5 January
1795].
[17] *A Letter to a Member of the National Assembly* [1791], in *Works*, 4:23.
[18] *An Appeal from the New to the Old Whigs*, 2d ed. [1791], in *Works*, 4:78.
[19] *Remarks on the Policy of the Allies with Respect to France* [1793], in *Works*, 4:415.

have over a multitude of the profligate and ferocious."[20] The passage invokes another indefinite article and a mob contrasted with the poverty-stricken, deserving for their mute humility in the face of exploitation. But surely it refers not to one particular mob but to a ubiquitous possibility. Several months after penning the *Reflections,* Burke was waxing lyrical—and explicitly universal. "A system of French conspiracy is gaining ground in every country," he warns. "This system, happening to be founded on principles the most delusive indeed, but the most flattering to the natural propensities of the unthinking multitude, and to the speculations of all those who think, without thinking very profoundly, must daily extend its influence."[21] Privately he already had referred to "the blind fury of the Multitude."[22] Privately too he already had insisted that "the tyranny of a multitude is a multiplied tyranny," that in societies such as France and England it was surely better to submit to the despotism of one than that of the many.[23] It might be invidiously partisan to cry that the jig is up, that here Burke stumbles and reveals just that sweepingly general contempt for the lower orders that the anonymous writer wished to rescue him from. But it might be, to invoke an arcane term of art which has fallen on hard times in the academy, true.

Consider one last letter, where Burke himself forgets the allegedly critical distinction between articles definite and indefinite—and places himself in the ranks of hoggish indignity:

> I trust, that the Royal Oak will long flourish; and shed its Acorns, in plenteous Showers, on us the quiet swinish Multitude below; whilst the barren bloody pole of Liberty set up by Revolutionary Societies, is burnt, to singe the Bristles, and to smooth the heads and Hams, of the wild Boars of the Gallick Forests, who would come hither to root up and to trample down the British harvests.[24]

Was Burke feeling contrite about the language he'd adopted in the *Reflections* or sardonically thumbing his nose at those who took offense? The letter is unequivocally scornful. Burke is writing to the

[20] "Speech on Repeal of the Marriage Act" [15 June 1781], in *Works,* 7:134.

[21] *Thoughts on French Affairs* [1791], in *Works,* 4:355.

[22] Burke to Dr. John Erskine, 12 June 1779, *The Correspondence of Edmund Burke,* ed. Thomas W. Copeland, 10 vols. (Chicago: University of Chicago Press, 1958–1978), 4:85.

[23] Burke to Captain Thomas Mercer, 26 February 1790, *Correspondence,* 6:96.

[24] Burke to Sir John Scott, 11 January 1796, *Correspondence,* 8:369–70.

attorney general, who was facing instructions to prosecute John Reeves, head of the Association for Preserving Liberty and Property against Republicans and Levellers, for his allegedly unconstitutional suggestion that the houses of Parliament could be "lopped off" from the tree of monarchy. And Burke adds a scorching postscript, wondering if this paragraph qualifies him too for prosecution. Immediate context aside, the letter's contempt for the lower orders seems general indeed. English subjects are quiet, tame, domesticated; French subjects are dangerous, wild, rampaging; but they're all pigs in the end. The letter also admits bemused responses to this frenzied flourish of Burke's literary powers: what's so consoling in the image of pigs being bombarded by acorns?

Burke is caught helplessly in the predicament that many urged made a sham of his defense of illusion. Burke, I've suggested, sought to maintain a schism between deferential subjects, instinctively loyal, and argumentative citizens, inquisitively skeptical. Only the tiny political nation needed to—could be permitted to—shoulder the daunting demands of citizenship. Subjects needed tradition, an unthinking allegiance to a history scripted out of veils and illusions. Citizens needed criticism, a willingness to knock down the stage machinery that obscured the transgressions of Hastings in India. Starry-eyed subjects should gaze on the nobility as the Corinthian capital of polished society. Coolly rational citizens should confront the news that many nobles were perfectly ready to play parasites, pimps, and buffoons. The same schism, remember, explains the attorney general's failure to prosecute the first part of Paine's *Rights of Man,* which he thought would fall into the hands of elite readers capable of seeing through its lethal stupidities, and his spirited prosecution of the second part on learning that the lower orders were greedily ingesting the poison. The same schism motivates Coleridge's apparent attempt to bifurcate the morality of discussion, to insist that authors not address a popular audience as they would a learned and politically responsible one. It also motivates his peremptory dismissal of the very idea of a reading public or a philosophic populace. Finally, the schism is at the heart of the notion of poisoning the minds of the lower orders, the heartfelt conviction that they are unsuited to reading and political debate.

With this schism in mind, suppose we ask: who was the audience for Burke's *Reflections?* Whom did he intend to read it? Who actually did

read it? Such questions reveal that Burke's rhetoric is unstable.[25]
Sometimes Burke imagines himself writing for a broader audience
and even obligingly includes himself in their ranks, just as he joins the
swinish multitude in his letter. Take for instance his skirting his way
around the trial and execution of Charles I: regicide is inflammatory
stuff for a popular audience. Or take his staunch embrace of a stolid,
even stubborn, political psychology: "Thanks to our sullen resistance
to innovation, thanks to the cold sluggishness of our national character, we still bear the stamp of our forefathers."[26] The first person re-
doubles the solidarity assumed between Burke and his broad audience. But Burke fought heroically in Parliament for innovations,
defended the rebellious American colonists, and drew up plans for a
sweeping reorganization of the finances of the royal household. So
the staunch embrace of cold sluggishness is deceptive—or worse. The
mention of a swinish multitude is different. Here Burke arrogantly
distances himself from the vulgar lower orders. Elsewhere too, he
clearly imagines himself as writing for genteel readers. Recall for instance that unflinchingly harsh assessment of the undignified plight
of the laboring classes: "Let there be no lamentation of their condition. It is no relief to their miserable circumstances; it is only an insult
to their miserable understandings." The third person underlines the
obvious: one wouldn't talk this way to the workers themselves.

Whether or not Burke realized in publishing his *Reflections* that the
reading public was bigger and socially more diverse than he might
wish, too many popular readers stumbled across *a swinish multitude*.
They didn't relish the language, which they took as insolent and insulting. Or, better, some of them did relish the language, which they
must have exulted over as an invaluable gift. As radicals saw it, Burke
had blundered. He had exposed the nub of the contempt that the
reigning establishment had for the people of England. Gleefully, radicals promptly seized on Burke's language and ran it into the ground.
Daniel Isaac Eaton's rakishly radical periodical, *Politics for the People*,
sometimes subtitled *A Salmagundy for Swine*, sometimes *Hog's Wash*,
published a "Remonstrance of the Swinish Multitude, to the Chief
and Deputy Swineherds of Europe."[27] The inference is barbed: if the

---

[25] I'm indebted here to Hanna Pitkin.
[26] *Reflections,* in *Works,* 3:344.
[27] *Politics for the People* 1(5):54–62 [1793]. The former subtitle is on the title pages of

people are swinish, what does that make their rulers? The journal also produced an "Address to the Numerous Herd of Tradesmen, Mechanics, and Labourers, and Others, Comprized under the Appellation of the Swinish Multitude."[28] Lest any readers even momentarily forget the matter, its pages were peppered heavily with contributions from A Ci-Devant Pig, Brother Grunter, Gregory Grunter, Porkulus, Gruntum Snorum, Old Bristle-Back, A Young Pig, A Liberty Pig, A Pig with One Ear, The Learned Pig, and more. (Learned pigs, trained to perform dauntingly cerebral stunts, were carnival attractions of the day.[29] In America, Cobbett singled out one for scorn and linked it to the swinish multitude.[30]) Another radical journal frequently lapsing into burlesque, *Pig's Meat,* published two saucy ditties, each labelled "Edmund Burke's Address to the Swinish Multitude." A typical stanza:

> YE Swinish Multitude who prate,
> What know ye 'bout the matter?
> Misterious are the ways of state,
> Of which you should not chatter.[31]

Some forty years after Burke's *Reflections,* thirty-five years after his death, the language in all its infamy endured. The *Poor Man's Guardian* published a letter from "ONE OF THE 'SWINISH' MULTITUDE."[32] "The swinish multitude have had their tails soaped," taunted the *Pioneer.* "Ye cannot hold them in your grasp."[33]

So the *ancien régime* stood for shameless contempt: that was the shocking implication of Burke's language. One collection of radical

---

vols. 1 and 2, the latter on 1(10):147 [1793], announcing no. 11. Compare *Anti-Jacobin* (4 December 1797) no. 4, p. 30.

[28] *Politics for the People* 1(6):70–72 [1793].

[29] For learned pigs in England, see for instance Richard D. Altick, *The Shows of London* (Cambridge, MA: Belknap Press, Harvard University Press, 1978), pp. 40–42; Henry Morley, *Memoirs of Bartholomew Fair* (London, 1859), pp. 480–81. Altick, *Shows,* p. 307 notices a learned cat and a learned goose.

[30] *Porcupine's Gazette* (8 June 1797), in William Cobbett, *Porcupine's Works,* 12 vols. (London, 1801), 6:20; *Gazette* (29 June 1797), in *Porcupine's Works,* 6:68; *Gazette* (17 July 1797), in *Porcupine's Works,* 6:288–89.

[31] *Pig's Meat* 2:39; see too *Pig's Meat* 1:250–51; *Politics for the People,* vol. 1, pt. 2(2):15–16 [1794].

[32] *Poor Man's Guardian* (8 October 1831) 1(15):114.

[33] *Pioneer* (9 November 1833) no. 10, p. 73.

humor was, "notwithstanding the contempt in which you are held by Mr. Burke," dedicated "to the swinish multitude," addressed as "Friends and Fellow Citizens."[34] One radical who beat a hasty retreat to America barely controlled his fury at the "peers, princes, pimps, and bishops . . . debauched with the intoxicating fumes of claret drops and harlot smiles" who casually voted to kill a hundred thousand men in combat. "These are they who look with scornful contempt upon the rustic, weather-beaten peasant, and the half-starved mechanic, whom poverty has stripped of flesh and raiment, and who labour under the opprobrious epithet of *the swinish multitude*."[35] The sophisticated radicals of Norwich's Society of Gentlemen sneered at "the sublime and matchless masters of modern refinement and elegance" who dared to term a sadly degraded people a swinish multitude.[36] John Thelwall assailed "the virulent and unprincipled malignancy of stigmatising the oppressed, laborious and most valuable classes of society as a 'swinish multitude' "; note that he scrupulously respected Burke's indefinite article but still took him to be pressing a general claim.[37]

Indignantly rejecting Burke's language, the radicals tried to show that democracy stood not for blood in the streets, not for outrageous levelling and the end of civilization, but for human dignity. Neither Reformation monk nor Elizabethan polemicist, their language strikingly like Burke's, had had to worry much about such apocalyptic inferences and enthusiastic projects. Burke was embarrassed because he kept clinging to ancestral wisdom and ignored social change: the rise of political debate in alehouses, the increased thirst for newspapers and political pamphlets. Several years after publishing the *Reflections,* Burke took acerbic pleasure in noting that he was being toasted in the radical clubs: "Mr. Burke, and thanks to him for the discussion he has provoked."[38] Grimly contemplating

---

[34] *Tom Paine's Jests, Being an Entirely New and Select Collection of Patriotick Bon Mots, Repartees, Anecdotes, Epigrams, Observations, &c.* (London, 1793), p. iii, italics and small capitals removed.

[35] Butler, *Political Fugitive,* p. 89.

[36] A Society of Gentlemen, *The Cabinet,* 3 vols. (Norwich, 1795), 2:255.

[37] John Thelwall, *Sober Reflections on the Seditious and Inflammatory Letter of the Right Hon. Edmund Burke, to a Noble Lord,* 3d ed. (London, 1796), p. 62.

[38] *A Letter to William Elliot, Esq.* [26 May 1795], in *Works,* 5:109.

the giddy gyrations and noxious novelties of the last few years of English politics, he urged, as we've seen, "New things in a new world! I see no hopes in the common tracks." Here again is the Burke fully aware of historicist rebuttals to ancestral wisdom. But then here too is the Burke who should have been ruefully aware that he couldn't prudently have counted on getting away with his crack about a swinish multitude. Yet again, whether Burke was remorseful or unrepentant, his phrase became infamous.

## In Search of the People

If Burke had in mind a particular multitude, he found it hard to keep only them in mind. No wonder that *Blackwood's* gulped, embraced the definite article, and defiantly insisted that Burke "had only proclaimed a truth acknowledged by every rational understanding" in branding the multitude swinish.[39] No doubt, held the journal during the agitation for parliamentary reform, many people in and around England's cities wanted reform, even revolution.

> But what honest and humane reformer would wish such allies? Heaven forbid that we should ever apply any insulting epithet to the People. But look there—behold the swinish multitude. Look at their tails contorted in desperate obstinacy, that will neither be led nor driven—and telling as plainly as tails can tell, that it is an equal chance whether the bestial herd will make a charge upon women and children, or higglety-pigglety go headlong, in demoniac suicide, into the sea. Look, we beseech you, at their eyes—their small red eyes so fiery with greed and lust! Their snouts scenting all the airts for garbage, and their tusks stone-whetted and sharp as the mower's scythe—their hoofs—say rather their cloots— "oh, call them pale, not fair"—raking the mire fore and aft! And their hides horrid from nape to rump with angry bristles, at once the terror and delight of cobblers;—and if you still have your doubts whether or no these be indeed such reformers as you would choose either to send you to, or represent you in Parliament, why you have only to solicit their voices—their most sweet voices—and your wavering mind will be settled by one unanimous grunt from the old boars and sows, and by a multifarious and multitudinous bubble-and-squeak from all the infant schools

[39] *Blackwood's Edinburgh Magazine* (January 1834) 35(217):34.

of piggies, on recovering from which, if you are a Christian, you will exclaim in soliloquy, "The voice of the swine is the voice of the devil."[40]

The Christian sentiments extorted from the reader aren't charity and compassion, but a righteous wrath and indomitable devotion to resisting Satan. So the lower orders aren't endearing figures of meek humility. Their lower status doesn't enable any patronizing affection. They are fiends to be loathed.

If the voice of the swine is the voice of the devil (a point already suggested by replacing *hoofs* with *cloots,* traditionally associated with Satan), the swinish multitude invites a magically potent, even sublime, form of contempt. One of Blake's manuscripts casts Satan's minions as grunting hogs, another bit of God's majestic handiwork inviting some bantering, even sniping:

> He turnd the Devils into Swine
> That he might tempt the Jews to Dine
> Since which a Pig has got a look
> That for a Jew may be mistook.[41]

Here contempt and dehumanization register themselves in Jewish faces. I suspect that Blake was capitalizing on the well-known dietary law, itself a stamp of foreign weirdness, that proscribed Jews from eating pork. Surely others capitalized on it. One wag referred to the Jewish boxers enlisted by Mendoza in the O.P. riots as "his *anti-swinish multitude.*"[42] Jews were exhibited in cartoons as longing for pork and even casually referred to as *porkers.*[43] Jews, devils, and swine, ranged against upright Christian conservatives: we can locate the associations here in Burke's work. Burke's politics are never far removed from his theology. In a high-minded moment, remember, he underwrites a sprawling social contract with a divine teleology. Yet his politics also are never far removed from pungent condemnations of the Jews. In a scurrilous moment, remember, he opines that England is infested with too many shabby Jews to hang and would be happy to ship them

---

[40] *Blackwood's Edinburgh Magazine* (May 1831) 29(180):728–29. *Airts* are points of the compass.

[41] "Everlasting Gospel" [1818?], in *William Blake's Writings,* ed. G. E. Bentley, Jr., 2 vols. (Oxford: Clarendon, 1978), 2:1057.

[42] *The Rebellion; or, All in the Wrong,* 2d ed. (London, 1809), p. 37 [9 October 1809].

[43] *BMC* nos. 8536 [1794?], 12146 [20 September 1813]; Pierce Egan, *Grose's Classical Dictionary of the Vulgar Tongue, Revised and Corrected* (London, 1823), s.v. *porker.*

off to France. Even his despairing cry, at the center of his anguished portrait of contemporary politics, that his is an age of "sophisters, economists, and calculators" would summon up stockjobbers and moneylenders—that is, Jews—for many readers.[44] These apparently disparate sentiments merge in another promiscuous commingling of high and low, not just for Burke but for anyone flirting with talk of the swinish multitude.

So too this terrain features the explosion of competing status hierarchies, of background debates about who is genuinely high, who low, who elegant, who swinish. Ironically, Burke's trope, apparently the beating heart of contemptuous hierarchy, could be democratized: that is, one could open an equal-opportunity contest to identify the real swinish multitude. Or at least the real mobs. (Soon, though, we'll see some ghastly cases of high-born pigs.) Reeves's Association circulated a pamphlet arguing that properly dutiful workers weren't part of the mob, but that "low manners, rioting, drunkenness, dishonesty, and a defiance of the laws" qualified those of higher rank for inclusion in the mob.[45] "I call any assembly of people a mob," reported Hazlitt, as though he were recording his idiosyncratic linguistic habits and not pressing a charged political judgment, "(be it the House of Lords or House of Commons) where each person's opinion on any question is governed by what others say of it, and by what he can get by it."[46] Here, those falling short of a resolutely independent and disinterested judgment, the sort featured in much democratic theory, forfeit social status and dignity.

Setting Jews and mobs aside, let's contemplate another central thrust of *Blackwood's* assault. "Heaven forbid that we should ever apply any insulting epithet to the People": an odd introduction, it might seem, to the ensuing riot of colorful epithets it would be hard to describe as complimentary. One might surmise that the journal was winking piously before launching its earnest vitriol. But I'm inclined to read the passage more innocently. No insulting epithets for the people, but this swinish multitude doesn't qualify as the people. Perhaps they forfeit their claim to that inspiring title by their crude behavior; in revealing themselves as sordid animals, they disqualify

[44] *Reflections*, in *Works*, 3:331.

[45] *Association Papers* (London, 1793), pt. 2, no. 10, pp. 4–5.

[46] *Political Essays, with Sketches of Public Characters* [1819], in *Works of Hazlitt*, 7:13. See too Gerrald's speech of 21 November 1793, quoted in *Trial of Joseph Gerrald*, p. 20.

themselves as people. "When you separate the common sort of men from their proper chieftains," urged Burke, "I no longer know that venerable object called the people in such a disbanded race of deserters and vagabonds. For a while they may be terrible, indeed,—but in such a manner as wild beasts are terrible."[47] Or perhaps the lower orders never could have qualified as the people. Perhaps that honorific, that badge of public standing, can't be applied to anyone beneath the middle classes. These constructions of *Blackwood's* language aren't arbitrary. Their hatred of reform also drove them to explode that freedom was "in danger of being beaten down by bestial feet. That many-mouthed Monster, the Swinish Multitude, erects its bristles, and grunts fiercely in the sky, pretending to be the People. The People indeed!"[48]

Nor is *Blackwood's* idiosyncratic. "Mobs are *the devil in his worst shape*," warned young Cobbett.[49] Yet cowardly humanitarians debased themselves by submitting to the mob: "It is, now-a-days, so much the fashion to humour and to flatter this swinish beast, that very few people *speak out*," a reluctance Cobbett never seems to have been inhibited by.[50] Prudence demanded not capitulating to the irrationalities of public opinion, but manfully resisting them. "It is our object, as it should be the object of every subject, to defend the *people* of Britain against the *populace*."[51] Years later, Cobbett changed his tune. Workers provided England's wealth and glory. "With this correct idea of your own worth in your minds, with what indignation must you hear yourselves called the Populace, the Rabble, the Mob, the Swinish Multitude; and, with what greater indignation, if possible, must you hear the projects of those cool and cruel and insolent men" who were plotting to limit parish relief, to curtail marriages, to promote emigration and colonization.[52] Before and after his political somersault, Cobbett treats *swinish multitude* and the like as contemptuous indications that the target group has no standing. The change

[47] *Appeal from the New to the Old Whigs,* in *Works,* 4:176.

[48] *Blackwood's Edinburgh Magazine* (January 1831) 29(175):141.

[49] *A Summary View of the Politics of the United States* [1794], in *Porcupine's Works,* 1:63.

[50] Cobbett to William Windham, 20 October 1801, *The Windham Papers,* 2 vols. (London: Herbert Jenkins, 1913), 2:177; with variations in Lewis Melville, *The Life and Letters of William Cobbett in England & America,* 2 vols. (London: John Lane, The Bodley Head, 1913), 1:137.

[51] William Cobbett, *A Collection of Facts and Observations, Relative to the Peace with Bonaparte, Chiefly Extracted from the Porcupine* (London, 1801), pp. 72–73, 95–96.

[52] *Political Register* (2 November 1816) 31(18):545–46.

is just that the mature radical disavows contempt for workers. His motto becomes, "No society ought to exist, where the labourers live in a hog-like sort of way."[53]

Men of property, warned one writer, shouldn't pretend that their happiness and prosperity mean that the people are well-off. "Do these men comprise the whole people? No. Not a tenth, perhaps not a fiftieth part of the people." True, their bustling activity attracts a lot of attention. "My unfashionable idea of *the people,* however, comprises the Swinish Multitude, as well as the men of some property."[54] Byron rose in the House of Lords to caution his fellow peers not to permit their hatred of the Luddites bashing machinery to obscure their dependence on the lower orders. "It is the Mob, that labour in your fields & serve in your houses, that man your navy & recruit your army, that have enabled you to defy all the world, & can also defy you, when Neglect & Calamity have driven them to despair." Haughty contempt, then, wouldn't do. Nor would cavalierly dismissing the Luddites as extremists. "You may call the people a Mob, but do not forget, that a Mob too often speaks the sentiments of the People."[55]

These comments suggest that the lower orders, even the swinish multitude, be recognized as the people. Then again, they also recognize that doing so is a matter of political controversy, by no means to be settled by consulting a dictionary. So conservatives refused to bestow such recognition, such dignity, on the lower orders. The political force of Coleridge's unpublished note, "Of the Profanation of the Sacred Word 'The People,'" is indisputable. "Every brutal mob, assembled on some drunken St. Monday of faction, is '*the People*' forsooth, and now each leprous ragamuffin, like a circle in geometry, is at once one and all, and calls his own brutal self 'us the People.'" Worse, to be a friend of the people was taken to mean flattering the mob, not trying to "elevate" them, to endow them with enough discipline and rationality to be entitled to freedom.[56] For Coleridge, this

[53] William Cobbett, *Rural Rides* [1830], ed. George Woodcock (Harmondsworth: Penguin, 1985), p. 126.

[54] Daniel Stuart, *Peace and Reform, against War and Corruption* (London, 1794), p. 104.

[55] Byron, *The Complete Miscellaneous Prose,* ed. Andrew Nicholson (Oxford: Clarendon, 1991), p. 25 [27 February 1812].

[56] "Of the Profanation of the Sacred Word 'The People'" [*circa* 1816–1820], in *The Collected Works of Samuel Taylor Coleridge,* ed. Kathleen Coburn, Bart Winer, and others, in progress (Princeton, NJ: Princeton University Press, 1969–), 3(3):247–48.

abuse of language was every bit as shameless as the radicals thought Burke's mention of a swinish multitude.

In 1831, *Fraser's* offered some "Rumbling Murmurs of an Old Tory over the Fate of His Quondam Friends." Said Tory professed hatred for "the rabble great" because they were powerful, contempt for "the rabble small" because they weren't. Neither was entitled to govern. Amusingly, the Tory confessed he was "intimately acquainted with . . . that bulk of men who compose the labouring classes of the country; and, when they are fed with bacon and beans, as they ought to be, they are a most honourable, honest, truth-speaking, and hardfisted generation." He disavowed all contempt for these "lowest orders," uneducated as they were. This fetching concession set the stage for pelting his real adversaries with the filthiest mud he could lay his hands on.

> The lower orders I despise. The whey-faced shopman, who takes his tea at a coffee-shop in Clerkenwell, and reads the *Times* 'noose peeper'—the horator at westries—the intellectual bagman travelling in brown paper or green vitriol, and deeply imbued with the march of mind—the satisfied hearer of the lecturer at the Hinstitutions, and the still more satisfied lecturer himself—the smug apprentice, who defies his master—the Templar spark, who finds out that common law is unphilosophical, and reads a hessay to prove it at the academies—the gentlemen of the press—the crack-writers of liberal magazines—these and all the rest of the *mendici, mimi, balatrones*—these are the lower orders, these the true and ever-to-be despised mob.[57]

These are the familiar denizens of the coffeehouses and mechanics' institutes, tricked out with Cockney accents to emphasize their magnificent unfitness for such elevated pursuits, just as the author laces his impeccable prose with Italian to emphasize his own secure standing in the world (not republic) of letters.

*Fraser's* vengefully returned to the battlefield a couple of months later to lambaste the £10 franchise, a prospect more dreadful than universally enfranchising men, women, "the halt, blind, and maimed," and even "lunatics and idiots":

> The unwashed artisan, the pale-faced pipe-smoker at the Pig and Whistle, belching forth in base English the baser cockney of the *Times*,—the

[57] *Fraser's* (June 1831) 3(17):649–50.

operative taught to know his rights, and, knowing, to maintain them, by
Taylor of the Rotunda and Horsemonger Lane Gaol, and other offcasts
of Mechanics' Institutes and Universal Knowledge Societies,—in a word,
the foetid rabble of towns are the very worst part of the population, who
sympathise with all that may insult their superiors, may drag down every
thing respectable to be trampled on by a multitude, to call which swinish
would be an atrocious insult to the progeny of pigs, if in their stupidity
they fancy it may enable them to flavour the politics of the pot-house
with beer at a penny a pot less than the existing prices.[58]

*Fraser's* employs a shrewdly contorted status hierarchy. The lower orders are higher than the lowest, but more contemptible: they earn
their contempt by flouting the basic rules defining their status, by
putting on airs in ways the lowest don't. (Compare: "My countrymen
must be degenerated into a *swinish multitude* indeed, to find any nutri-
ment in such a mess of pigs-meat, as these wretched caterers" such as
Paine have dished out.[59]) They are so contemptible that pigs are
more elevated: though the closing jab reveals that they are quintessentially piggish, their fascination with alehouse politics really driven
by a desire to get soused a bit more cheaply.

It's hard to distinguish people from pigs in Edgeworth's *Belinda* of
1801, too. An unruly mob about to assault the protagonists are suddenly distracted by "a person who was driving up the lane a large herd
of squeaking, grunting pigs. The person was clad in splendid regi-
mentals," not the usual pig-driver. The mob, delighted to learn that
such a distinguished fellow had a bet that he and his pigs could out-
race some turkeys close behind, instantly forgot their wrath and
marched along with him. When he vaunted "in triumph over the
heads of 'the swinish multitude,' " it is obvious neither whose heads
are being referred to nor what political point, if any, is being
pressed.[60] (In 1828, Edgeworth would assure a correspondent, "I feel
as keenly as you do the monstrous, the disgusting absurdity of letting
the many-headed, the greasy many-headed monster rule. The French

[58] *Fraser's* (August 1831) 4(19):5.

[59] Gilbert Wakefield, *An Examination of the Age of Reason, or An Investigation of True
and Fabulous Theology, by Thomas Paine* (London, 1794), p. 47. See too E. P. Thompson,
*Witness against the Beast: William Blake and the Moral Law* (New York: New Press, 1993),
p. 172.

[60] *Belinda* [1801], in Maria Edgeworth, *Tales and Novels*, 10 vols. (London, 1848),
3:52–53.

Revolution gave us enough of the majesty of the people."[61]) Nor were such startling inversions and identities confined to the world of prose. Workers around Oxford griped that farmers supplied milk to their pigs instead of selling it to the poor.[62] One observer reviled the sour oat cakes fed to workhouse denizens as "scarcely food for a PIG."[63] Pigs, disclosed a horrified anatomist of Manchester exploitation eager to notice the revolting smell, lived in yards shared by the poor, even in their houses.[64] Cobbett was unnerved by newspaper reports on the lives of the poor. "It is related of them, that they eat horse-flesh, grains, and have been detected in eating out of pig-troughs. In short, they are represented as being far worse fed and worse lodged than the greater part of the pigs."[65]

In 1818, Hazlitt published an essay entitled, "What Is the People?" "—And who are you that ask the question?" was its opening challenge.[66] The brilliance here isn't best understood as that of an elaborate argument. Hazlitt's challenge is a deliberate attempt to transform the rhetorical lay of the land, to make it politically preposterous to strike the pose adopted by Coleridge and *Fraser's*, to insinuate a vocabulary in which Burke's *swinish multitude* has to count as at best a horribly unfortunate indiscretion. Just where did Coleridge, *Fraser's*, and the rest of these haughty conservatives imagine they stood? Or, as we might say, who the hell did they think they were, anyway?

## SUBJECTS, CITIZENS, AND PUBLIC OPINION: A RECAPITULATION

They thought they were brave and perceptive observers, resolutely bucking the tide of madness to challenge the very views Hazlitt wished to promote. If the lower orders had to remain loyal subjects, to

---

61 Maria Edgeworth to Captain Basil Hall, 12 October 1828, in Frances Anne Edgeworth, *A Memoir of Maria Edgeworth*, ed. her children, 3 vols. (London: privately printed, 1867), 3:19.

62 Frederic Eden Morton, *The State of the Poor,* 3 vols. (London, 1797; reprint ed. Bristol: Thoemmes Press, 1994), 2:587.

63 G. B. Hindle, *Provision for the Relief of the Poor in Manchester 1754–1826* (Manchester: Manchester University Press for the Chetham Society, 1975), p. 49.

64 James Phillips Kay, *The Moral and Physical Condition of the Working Classes Employed in the Cotton Manufacture in Manchester,* 2d ed. (London, 1832; reprint ed. London: Frank Cass, 1970), pp. 32, 41.

65 *Cobbett's Poor Man's Friend: or, A Defence of Those Who Do the Work and Fight the Battles* (London, 1826), p. 4.

66 *Political Essays, with Sketches of Public Characters* [1819], in *Works of Hazlitt,* 7:259.

eschew enchanting visions of citizenship, better to side with *Fraser's* and cast at least the patrons of coffeehouses and mechanics' institutes as swinish. If the world of feverish political debate was shot through with pathologies, if its rational credentials were bankrupt, then the people's claims to agency were bankrupt, too. It's an alluringly short step to the further Kantian inference that if they are not acting rationally, they are not free, not even human, but to the extent of their irrationality parts of mechanical nature. Animals, one might say. Pigs. Here again, I want to urge that we not think of such ugly, contemptuous, even contemptible language as *a swinish multitude* as stuff that it's better to pass over in silence, indicating nothing more significant than a prejudice or attitude of Burke's. I'd urge that stricture even for Dr. Parr's disgust at the "huge form" and putrid smell of a vulgar woman and her husband: "I could not help congratulating myself that I had been breathing fresh air instead of being crammed with these swinish citizens, within the filthy sty of the inside."[67] Instead we should dwell on the deep internal connections between such language and officially weighty political matters. We can reconstruct what background premises make the language attractive, what political work it does.

Burke framed the stakes differently from the Kantian gloss I've sketched. "All direction of publick humour and opinion must originate in a few."[68] "The people are not answerable for their present supine acquiescence. Indeed they are not. God and nature never made them to think or to Act without Guidance and direction," he held. Were they to refuse to submit to their natural betters, though, they would become blameworthy. Here irrationality, in the shape of wilful defiance, creates agency or at least responsibility; duly mandated deference leaves the people unaccountable for their actions, even if they act wrongly.[69] Yet this variant framing still leads inexorably to the conclusions that citizenship is a sanguinary ideal and public opinion isn't properly autonomous.

This lofty disdain for subjects could only be confirmed by some radicals' impatient explosions. John Reeves received a letter, ominously signed "Ghost," addressed to "Bastards of Liberty":

---

[67] Samuel Parr to Rev. Dr. Routh, 22 July 1794, *The Works of Samuel Parr, LL.D.*, ed. John Johnstone, 8 vols. (London, 1828), 7:658.

[68] Burke to the Marquess of Rockingham, 22–23 August 1775, *Correspondence*, 3:190.

[69] Burke to the Duke of Richmond, 26 September 1775, *Correspondence*, 3:218.

As you have advertized for Constitutional Information I would contribute my mite towards the illumination of your asinine noddles by informing you that one of the greatest faults in the British Constitution is that it suffers such boobies as you to disgrace the national Character in the eyes of the rest of Europe by such Jackassical-proceedings as your Blackguardshits have lately adopted. As there are some among you who may have the grace to get yourselves hanged I would recommend you to make Interest to engage some Vacant lamp post of Gallic manufacture in order that you may swing like nobles of nature and Champions of Liberty. . . . Once more Be firm Be consistent Be uniformly ridiculous Be undeviatingly absurd. Get your names scratched out of the list of Men of Common Sense and Common Honesty & then Go to the Devil. . . .

An unruffled Reeves patiently filed the letter, endorsing it "Scurrilous & Insolent."[70] Here's another version of the structural impasse: conservative disdain and radical fury can only reinforce one another.

But again, other democrats insisted on civility. At the massive 14 April 1794 outdoor rally at Chalk Farm, John Thelwall needled the inevitable spies in the audience. He told them to report that they had had "an opportunity of learning good manners, order, and decorum from the Swinish Multitude."[71] The sarcasm protests the familiar mapping that suggested the lower one's status, the more meager one's deliberative abilities. *Tait's Edinburgh Magazine* was aghast at the colossal ignorance of the House of Lords. "They treat the nation like a herd of brutes who would be unable to conduct themselves with common propriety did not their betters think and act for them."[72] So too Hazlitt contemplated the dismal juxtaposition between reverence for inherited monarchy and disdain for democracy. "Any one above the rank of an ideot is supposed capable of exercising the highest functions of royal state. Yet these are the persons who talk of the people as a swinish multitude, and taunt them with their want of refinement and philosophy."[73]

[70] Ghost to John Reeves, 10 December 1792, British Library, Add. Mss. 16921, ff. 119–20. The crack about the lamp posts summons up the dread slogan of the Parisian mobs who hanged bishops: *Toutes les évêques aux lanternes.*

[71] Frida Knight, *The Strange Case of Thomas Walker: Ten Years in the Life of a Manchester Radical* (London: Lawrence & Wishart, 1957), p. 170.

[72] *Tait's Edinburgh Magazine* (May 1832) 1(2):141.

[73] "What Is the People?" in *Political Essays* [1819], in *Works of Hazlitt,* 7:274–75.

It's not necessarily a matter of native stupidity. If reason stands for critical debate, tradition for unthinking deference, the worry is that an educated populace will dare to question authority. In 1799, the still radical Robert Southey penned a poetic address to a pig daring to resist having his nose bored, an address dripping irony at those who imagined that social order required dutiful submission.

> Pig! 'tis your master's pleasure—then be still,
> And hold your nose to let the iron thro'—
> Dare you resist your lawful Sov'reign's will?
> Rebellious swine! you know not what you do![74]

Never one to relinquish a good joke or a bad one, Southey also produced a poem addressed to one Jacob, whom I take to be the eponymous Jew, proudly rebutting his claim that pigs are obstinate, ugly, and filthy.

> Is he obstinate?
> We must not, Jacob, be deceived by words,
> By sophist sounds. A democratic beast
> He knows that his unmerciful drivers seek
> Their profit and not his.[75]

This poem plays on the vicissitudes of comparative contempt, inviting the reader to identify with the narrator's voice and rally to the pig's defense against the accusations of a mere Jew. But the defense is troubling, perhaps even troubled.

> The Pig is a philosopher, who knows
> No prejudice.[76]

So he doesn't mind being dirty: but maybe that's a characteristic piece of absurd philosophical enthusiasm, evidence of the transparent absurdities following the decision to junk history in the name of

[74] "Ode, to a Pig, while His Nose Was Boring," *Morning Post* (8 July 1799), in *The Contributions of Robert Southey to the Morning Post,* ed. Kenneth Curry (University, AL: University of Alabama Press, 1984), p. 160.

[75] "The Pig: A Colloquial Poem," in Southey, *Metrical Tales and Other Poems* (London, 1805), p. 132. Compare "The Sow of Feeling," in *The Works of Robert Fergusson* (London, 1807), pp. 181–84.

[76] "The Pig," in *Metrical Tales,* p. 134.

reason.[77] The Jew's agreement with this contrived defense of the piggish life is secured, finally, by the smell of beans wafting along on a breeze and summoning up the delicious prospect of bacon. It's a cheap shot, maybe, at Jews' taking forbidden pleasures. It surely reminds the reader what these pigs are finally good for: slaughter.

One 1795 popular song, "Wholsome Advice to the Swinish Multitude," hammered away at the suggestion that what Burke and the rest really resented was that subjects had become less docile. (One impecunious hairdresser was dragged into court that same year for posting a sign over his shop reading, "CITIZEN SHAVER TO THE SWINISH MULTITUDE."[78]) Here's the opening stanza:

> You lower class of human race, you working part I mean,
> How dare you so audacious be to read the works of Pain,
> The Rights of Man—that cursed book—which such confusion brings,
> You'd better learn the art of war, and fight for George our King.

And here's the first chorus:

> But you must delve in politics, how dare you thus intrude,
> Full well you do deserve the name of swinish multitude.[79]

This suggestion that the real fear is that subjects won't dutifully march off to battle has reasonable grounds. After all, one leading conservative fretted that "the minds of the people become sore and ulcerated" in times of political trouble. He warned against "the pernicious consequence of destroying all docility in the minds of those who are not formed for finding their own way in the labyrinths of political theory, and are made to reject the clew and to disdain the guide."[80] That same conservative cautioned that "if you once teach poor laborers and mechanics to defy their prejudices," they might discover an unsettling solidarity with the French revolutionaries and decide "that this war is, and that the other wars have been, the wars of

---

[77] See generally Charles Hawtrey, *Various Opinions of the Philosophical Reformers Considered; Particularly Pain's Rights of Man* (London, 1792).

[78] *BMC* no. 8696 [25 November 1795].

[79] "Wholsome Advice to the Swinish Multitude: A New Song" [1795], in *Later English Broadside Ballads*, ed. John Holloway and Joan Black, 2 vols. (London: Routledge & Kegan Paul, 1975–1979), 1:278.

[80] *Appeal from the New to the Old Whigs*, in *Works*, 4:201, 4:202.

kings": "All the props of society would be drawn from us by these doctrines, and the very foundations of the public defence would give way in an instant."[81]

Not to be coy, this conservative was Burke himself, and he is vanishingly close to defending political docility as the virtue of farm animals being led to the knife. Before the French Revolution, the Society for Constitutional Information (SCI) had asserted that, deprived of the franchise, Englishmen were "degraded to a Level with the very *Cattle in the Field,* or *the Sheep in the Fold,* which have *no Voice* to say, '*Why are we bought and sold! Why are we yoked and laden with heavy Burthens! Why are we fleeced and led to the Slaughter!*' "[82] In 1793, Charles Pigott assaulted the arrangements with Hanover to supply mercenaries, which offered dreadful confirmation of Burke's language: "If the PEOPLE are SWINE, he who sells them, who receives so much money for the slaughter of each, is, to all intents and purposes, a SWINE, or HOG-BUTCHER."[83] Other radicals unearthed decidedly interesting possibilities here. Why, wondered Bentham, did Britain maintain an army of fifty thousand? Was it to deal with the threat of "the ten millions of two-legged swine, with the illegitimacy and the unincumbered and undisturbed prosperity in which they wallow" in far-off America? No, it was for the threat posed by France. Oh, and for one other use:

> Exists there that reader, who has not already told it to himself? Yes, it is to return to all plans of reform, to all petitions for reform—to all groans—to all complaints—to all cries for mercy—the proper, and properly, and already proposed answer, the bayonet. The bayonet? Yes: by the blessing of God, the bayonet. But is it altogether so sure, that, should matters come to the push, the direction that will be prescribed by legitimacy is exactly the direction in which the bayonets will move? The men by whom they will be pushed, of what class are they? Are they of the

[81] *Observations on the Conduct of the Minority* [1793], in *Works,* 5:40, 5:41.

[82] "Declaration of Rights, without Which No Englishman Can Be a Free Man, nor the English Nation a Free People," *Collection of Materials Promoting the Political Views of the Society for Constitutional Information* (London, 1780–1782), pp. 16–17. See too Byron, "Ode on Venice" [1819], in *The Complete Poetical Works,* ed. Jerome J. McGann and Barry Weller, 7 vols. (Oxford: Clarendon, 1980–1993), 4:202–4.

[83] *Persecution: The Case of Charles Pigott,* p. 33. See too Birmingham Society for Constitutional Information, *Address* (Birmingham, 1792), p. 7.

blood royal?—are they of the peerage? Are they not of the swinish multitude?—are they not as perfect swine as we are? Is it possible they should ever forget it? And when, in a direction that is not pleasing to him, the swine is driven, is he not apt to retrograde?[84]

Dr. Johnson could wryly dismiss the porcine people who marched in the reverse of the direction one prodded them: but he didn't imagine them thrusting bayonets. And Southey, remember, had worried that England was in such a sorry state that only the soldiers could safeguard social order: but how reliable were the soldiers, anyway?

Better, thought conservatives, to squelch such unsavory reflections. In 1809, Coleridge jotted in his notebook, "Christianity too . . . has its esoteric philosophy or why are we forbidden to cast pearls before Swine? But who are these Swine? Are they the Poor, and Despised? the Unalphabeted in worldly Learning?—O no!—the Rich, whose hearts are steeled by Ignorance of Misery & Habits of receiving slavish obeisance."[85] He played a different tune in public when he rallied to the defense of his old friend, Southey.

Southey had scrapped the youthful radicalism that saw him planning a utopian socialist commune with Coleridge in the name of redoubtable loyalty to the regime, not to mention the status—and cash—flowing from his 1813 appointment as poet laureate. Embarrassingly, several years later radicals discovered and published the manuscript of *Wat Tyler,* a play celebrating a legendary moment in the history of English radicalism which Southey had dashed off in three mornings in 1794.[86] The play, not worth a moment's hesitation as literature, was politically momentous: it made Southey seem a base hireling and unctuous hypocrite who betrayed his political convictions and succumbed to the sweet seductions of royal corruption. In the midst of the fracas surrounding its publication, with journals, pamphleteers, and parliamentary speakers weighing in, Coleridge took to the newspapers. It was courageous, he doggedly maintained, for Southey to hold the office of poet laureate. His opponents rev-

---

[84] *Plan of Parliamentary Reform* [1817], in *The Works of Jeremy Bentham,* ed. John Bowring, 11 vols. (Edinburgh, 1843), 3:437. I've omitted two words that bollix up the sixth sentence.

[85] *The Notebooks of Samuel Taylor Coleridge,* ed. Kathleen Coburn, in progress (New York: Pantheon Books, 1957–), 3(1):3617 24.29 [1809].

[86] *Diary, Reminiscences, and Correspondence of Henry Crabb Robinson,* ed. Thomas Sadler, 2 vols. (Boston, 1869), 1:357 [2 May 1817].

ealed nothing but their base resentment: "Galled they are to the quick, by seeing men of great talents, extensive information, experience in the world, by the world esteemed, proud of the trappings of Royalty." Southey's pride in his office had nothing to do with base lucre, everything to do with sanctifying monarchy. Radicals had to be furious at such potently expressive acts. "They spread a grace around the Throne, they inspire a reverence for it; they contributed to preserve that sacred awe which was the other day in St. James's Park, trodden down by the hoofs of the Swinish multitude."[87]

Some six weeks before Coleridge's defense, that is, an angry crowd had hurled projectiles and broken the window of the Regent's coach. The proceeding weeks were anxious times for the regime, exhilarating times for radicals. The *Black Dwarf* published a bravura display of bleakly comic genius, mocking the authorities' endless disrespect for the good people of London, their inability to recognize popular agency, by envisioning them choosing to press charges against the stones and potatoes seized by the crowd.[88] Less amused and less amusing, the privy council granted warrants for the arrest of the Spencean Philanthropists; the government suspended habeas corpus; Manchester radicals orchestrated a rally with marchers clad in blankets to flaunt and protest their poverty. Just after Coleridge's salvo, Cobbett high-tailed it to America rather than stick around and face more politically motivated prosecution. ("Mr. Cobbett carries with him the contempt and scorn of every manly mind in England," scoffed the *Black Dwarf*.[89] English diplomats were informed—marvel at the man's diabolic powers—that from Long Island Cobbett was "a principal agent" in a plot to spring Napoleon from St. Helena.[90])

Coleridge must have worried fitfully about what I've styled the irreversibility thesis, must have wondered whether those swinish hoofs had shattered the spell of royalty once and for all. He should have worried, too, about whether his inept decision to brandish Burke's language was well calculated to calm agitated radicals or make their audience any less sympathetic. Two years later, the *Black Dwarf* rev-

[87] *Courier* (17 March 1817), in *Works of Coleridge*, 3(2):452.

[88] *Black Dwarf* (19 February 1817) 1(4):60–62.

[89] *Black Dwarf* (9 April 1817) 1(11):170; see generally *Black Dwarf* (2 April 1817) 1(10):155–58, (9 April 1817) 1(11):161–70.

[90] Charles Bagot to Lord Castlereagh, 6 October 1817, *Memoirs and Correspondence of Viscount Castlereagh, Second Marquess of Londonderry*, ed. Charles Vane, 12 vols. (London, 1848–1853), 11:381.

elled in the conviction that political illusions were defunct. Could a
resurrected Burke "see the multitude whom he designated and
treated as swine, mixing with men, and acting like men, reasoning,
deliberating," he would react with consternation. "The last of his dis-
ciples are gathering round the fire of delusion, and mixing up a fresh
charm to destroy the effects of the *magic,* which has placed the multitude erect as men. But I fear now, it will avail them little, to attempt to
restore the swinish doctrines."[91] Whether it was temperate argument
or riotous assaults on the royal family, something seemed to be shat-
tering venerable habits of deference and loyalty, working its magic on
the subjects of England. Was it black magic or white? Was it transforming the swinish multitude into dignified citizens? or transforming trusty subjects into a swinish multitude with the effrontery to demand a political voice? Those questions were at the center of the
day's political controversies.

## CONTINGENCY AND NECESSITY: ANOTHER RECAPITULATION

So too was the vexing matter of just what inimitable features earned
the people their endearing sobriquet. Were they swinish by nature? or
by education? Was it a matter of mob psychology, a social dynamic
afflicting any large group? or of inborn stupidity? And if the people
were currently swinish, did they have to be? Would they remain so
forever? Or could they be transmuted into something more recognizably human?

The multitude, decreed Arthur Young, "are never governed by reason, but by trifles and ceremonies. . . ."[92] Southey—no youthful radical sympathies bubbling up here—charted the rise of "the maddened
and misguided rabble" in Spain.[93] They rapidly lose any claim to particularity as he rattles off a string of boilerplate claims about mob
psychology.[94] So too he decried England's "hordes of savages of its
own breeding, ready to rise and commit any excesses."[95] The lan-

[91] *Black Dwarf* (7 July 1819) 3(27):439.
[92] Arthur Young, *Travels in France during the Years 1787, 1788 & 1789,* ed. Constantia
Maxwell (Cambridge: Cambridge University Press, 1950), p. 221 [23 August 1789].
[93] Robert Southey, *History of the Peninsular War,* 3 vols. (London, 1823–1832), 1:272.
[94] Southey, *History of the Peninsular War,* 1:278, 1:286, 1:515, 1:518, 1:743.
[95] Southey to Mrs. Bray, 24 November 1831, *Selections from the Letters of Robert Southey,*
ed. John Wood Warter, 4 vols. (London, 1856), 4:249.

guage insinuates that these subjects are like Africans. Southey didn't take the masses to be ineducable. But the education they sorely needed would reinforce their moral and religious inclinations "so as to secure ourselves from a mob-revolution," not equip them for citizenship.[96]

As Wordsworth wrestled with the *Prelude*, his language registered a vacillation on these matters. Consider just a few lines from the thirteen-book *Prelude*, lines already present in the 1805–1806 version and unchanged in 1818–1820. Preparing to return to England after gaining more world-weary wisdom than he'd bargained for in France, Wordsworth pauses to wonder what might have been "in despite / Of what the People were through ignorance / And immaturity. . . ."[97] This language leaves studiously open the question of contingency. Could the ignorance be remedied? Does immaturity point to a later maturity? Not necessarily: when the king is father of his people, no one expects them to take their allotted place as adults. Juxtapose the language of the fourteen-book *Prelude* of 1850: "in despite / Of what the People long had been and were / Through ignorance and false teaching. . . ."[98] Here the mention of false teaching tilts the passage toward blaming the state of the people on a specific contingency. The introduction of the past perfect reinforces that reading. *Long had been:* not so far back as one might imagine, so perhaps not so far in the future, either.

Others were more aggressive, more explicit, with a program for political education and reform very different from Southey's. The Holborn Society of the Friends of the People complained that governments, "France excepted," seemed to think that people were formed for their benefit. So Burke, "a vile apostate, has had the audacity to substitute for the bulk of human kind, the epithet of *Swinish multitude:* and according to the present order of things, it must be admitted that Mr. B. chose a very proper term—but we dare anticipate a few revolving suns will revert his elegant appellation, and ren-

---

[96] Southey to Sharon Turner, 24 February 1817, *The Life and Correspondence of Robert Southey*, ed. Charles Cuthbert Southey, 6 vols. (London, 1849–1850), 4:247. Note too Southey, *Essays, Moral and Political*, 2 vols. (London, 1832), 2:25–26 [1817]; Southey, *The Life of Wesley; and The Rise and Progress of Methodism*, 2 vols. (London, 1820), 2:460.

[97] William Wordsworth, *The Thirteen-Book Prelude*, ed. Mark L. Reed, 2 vols. (Ithaca, NY: Cornell University Press, 1991), 1:272 [1805–1806], 2:177 [1818–1820].

[98] Wordsworth, *The Fourteen-Book Prelude*, ed. W. J. B. Owen (Ithaca, NY: Cornell University Press, 1985), p. 202 [1850].

der his memory as contemptible as his political creed."[99] Burke's audacity here seems to consist in sober honesty, in refusing to delude
himself with democratic vistas. Exactly who stands for illusion?

But democrats refused to conflate social status and human worth,
refused to agree that the dismal lot of the people was what they deserved or all they could attain. Or even if they deserved their shabby
treatment, they didn't deserve to be kept in the predicament that
made them so undeserving. "While we agree with you that the People
are treated like Swine," the London Corresponding Society (LCS)
advised the Political Societies at Norwich, "we are forced to acknowledge that some among them, from their *Sloth* and *Ignorance,* scarcely
deserve better Usage. . . ." Still, "unceasingly labouring to meliorate
their Condition," the LCS struggled gamely on for parliamentary
reform.[100]

So too Vicesimus Knox: "If the poor are really of the description of
swine, the spell of the enchantress, Circe . . . consists only of ignorance and vice; and the sole mode of removing their bestiality" would
be educating them.[101] The poor were dazed victims of priestcraft and
statecraft. "Why," demanded Thomas Walker, "are the mass of people,
the poorer class, the swinish multitude, as Mr. Burke contumeliously
terms them, so generally adverse to their friends, and so blindly the
dupes of their oppressors?" The framing of the question invites a
crude theory of false consciousness, which Walker obligingly supplies:
"Because they are ignorant."[102] Once again, could it be rational for
workers to spurn the lead of these radical "friends"? Even if we don't
stipulate that rationality just means adopting the radical agenda, even
that is if we want a procedural account of rationality, that must be a
politically controversial question. For, again, conservatives and democrats disagree on what sorts of epistemic norms ought to enjoy the
stamp of communal authority.

So too Henry Hunt, famed orator of infamous Peterloo. In 1820,
stuck in jail, he looked back at the 1790s, when the people of England

---

[99] *Holborn Society, of the Friends of the People; Instituted 22d November, 1792, for the Purpose
of Political Investigation* (London, 1792), p. 1.

[100] LCS to Secretary of the Political Societies at Norwich, draft, 25 July 1793, in *The
Second Report from the Committee of Secrecy to the House of Commons,* 4th ed. (London,
1794), app. E.

[101] Vicesimus Knox, *The Essence of the Calm Observer* (London, 1793), p. 51.

[102] Walker, *Review,* p. 127. See too *The Rights of Swine: An Address to the Poor* (London,
1795?).

"were made drunk with their own ignorance and folly." "The nation was drunk with the clamour" of war hysteria, he added, "particularly the *lower orders* (for they then truly merited the degrading appellation)." The state lurched into action to prevent Tom Paine from lifting the conjurors' spell and liberating these benighted subjects. Apparently the ministers succeeded, at least for a time: "They had so contrived to addle the brains of the multitude that their heads had been wool-gathering ever since; their vision had been then so mystified, and their brains had been so confused by the mountebank tricks of Pitt and his associates, that nothing but the pen of a Cobbett could bring them to their right senses again." No wonder Hunt mischievously amended the traditional John Bull to John Gull: what better name for a fellow so readily deceived by duplicitous politicians?[103]

An 1831 letter from A Labourer in Cobbett's *Political Register* noticed another resonance in Burke's language. "THOSE who have been in the habit of calling us (the poor people) the '*swinish multitude,*' take it for granted that our propensities to procreation are precisely the same sort as those of pigs": images of working-class fecundity scared up Malthusian nightmares. Happily, reported the Labourer, Cobbett had "shown us how we became a 'swinish multitude'" in his *History of the Protestant Reformation,* with its biting account of legal changes in property and the poor laws drastically reducing the poor's security. And now, as the Labourer saw it, he triumphantly had demolished the phony statistics backing the Malthusian case.[104] We might not share the Labourer's glowing assessment of Cobbett's arguments, but we can still grasp the point of his trying to expose contingent facts about social practices where conservatives were prone to find timeless truths about the innate qualities of the lower orders.

The appeal to contingency explains how radicals could themselves adopt contemptuous language, how Wade could echo the *Bristol Job Nott* and tranquilly report that the many-headed monster had no brains, how the LCS could hold that the people deserved to be treated as swine. Still, these radicals are in a sticky position, needing to exude savage indignation on behalf of those whose lives they are deriding. They're vulnerable to accusations that they are cowardly dreamers, fond of their own illusions about the authentic desires of

[103] *Memoirs of Henry Hunt, Esq. Written by Himself, in His Majesty's Jail at Ilchester, in the County of Somerset,* 3 vols. (London, 1820–1822), 1:133, 1:140–41, 2:177–78, 2:383.

[104] *Political Register* (11 June 1831) 72(11):650.

the lower orders, the desires they surely would have if only they were properly educated. They're sitting ducks—recall Malthus's rejoinder to Godwin—for a stern slap of bracing reason, the injunction that they face facts, however unpleasant.

At least one radical was willing to bite the bullet. During its run from 1817 to 1824, Thomas Wooler's *Black Dwarf* was acclaimed—and denounced—as a tireless and pugnacious voice of radicalism. Yet he too harbored fear and loathing of the people. Take this parody of Shakespeare, written during a jail sentence that didn't even begin to deter Wooler from his crusade:

> What a piece of work is man!
> How contemptible in reason;
> How ridiculous in faculties!
> In form and movement, how like a monkey!
> In apprehension, how like an ape![105]

Eventually, he ran out of steam. "Into such a torpid state have the people of this wise country sunk," he moaned in one of the last issues, "that I am not quite certain whether I shall be long able to find . . . matter enough to apologize for a monthly epistle. They are all dull as the tortoise in winter; and nothing can rouse them out of their trance."[106] He'd even surrender the lingering hope that the people were dazed. Penning a "Final Address" to his trusty readership, Wooler declared, "In ceasing his political labors, the Black Dwarf has to regret one mistake, and that a serious one. He commenced writing under the idea that there was a PUBLIC in Britain, and that public devotedly attached to the cause of parliamentary reform." But he'd been mistaken. Any apparent agitation was driven by the exigencies of poverty, by mere animal hunger—Wooler doesn't quite mention pigs—not invigorating dreams of citizenship. So he closed up shop, without even a glimpse in the direction of vanguard politics. No talk of unyielding stupor here: "The majority has decided, in its cooler moments, for 'things as they are.' The minority must abide the result of its decision."[107]

Not that every case of radical contempt for the lower orders can be understood as depending on background claims about how contin-

---

[105] *Black Dwarf* (6 June 1821) 6(23):802.
[106] *Black Dwarf* (1 June 1824) 12(15):433.
[107] *Black Dwarf* (1824) 12:v–vi.

gent their current contemptibility is. Sometimes, after all—recall Shelley's willingness to be "a worshipper of equality" one month and sting his father's lawyer with a haughty snub another—would-be radicals and democrats are merely posing in a parlor game. Sometimes their respect for the lower orders is superficial. That might be right about Byron. He shrank from "the fickle reek of popular breath"[108] and wondered at the indifferent reception of some of his later work. "You see what it is to throw pearls to Swine—as long as I wrote the exaggerated nonsense which has corrupted the public taste—they applauded to the very echo—and now that I have really composed within these three or four years some things which should 'not willingly be let die'—the whole herd snort and grumble and return to wallow in their mire."[109] And it might be right about Sheridan, who allegedly consoled himself at newspaper attacks after his 1812 electoral defeat with these generous reflections: "These unlettered assassins of the press season their bubble-and-squeak messes according to the taste of the swinish multitude; and when they have hashed up the victim of their ruffianism, they throw in a little sauce *piquante,* in order to tickle their palates, and make the maw-wallop go down pleasantly. Thus they please the pigs."[110] Perhaps Byron and Sheridan were only momentarily disaffected. Perhaps Byron entertained the possibility of refining the swinish popular taste. Perhaps Sheridan thought journalists responsible for corrupting the reading public and held out hopes for a more high-minded press. Perhaps not.

## ARTLESS OR CRAFTY SUBVERSIONS?

Maybe these radicals, plagiarizing from their conservative opponents, were unwittingly complicit in the degradation of the lower orders. Maybe their audience missed the subtle structure of their appeals to contingency. Or maybe the reproduction of the discourse surrounding *swinish multitude* had nasty political consequences not intended or foreseen by any individual speakers. Then again, maybe it was politi-

---

[108] *Childe Harold's Pilgrimage* [1814], in *Complete Poetical Works,* 2:181.

[109] Byron to Percy Shelley, 20 May 1822, *Byron's Letters and Journals,* ed. Leslie A. Marchand, 13 vols. (London: John Murray, 1973–1994), 9:161. Shelley anticipated "the bigoted contempt and rage of the multitude" in *Laon and Cythna* [1817], *The Complete Poetical Works of Percy Bysshe Shelley,* ed. Neville Rogers, 2 vols. to date (Oxford: Clarendon, 1972–), 2:106.

[110] Charles Marsh, *The Clubs of London,* 2 vols. (London, 1828), 1:274.

cally bracing to ingest this poisonous vocabulary and vomit it back
defiantly at the smug Tories so fond of it.[111] Maybe once it became a
commonplace, it was ineluctably tempting to cast it as an ensign revealing the central role of contempt in the struggle against
democracy.

Surely there were plenty of artless attempts at subversion, ineffec-
tual at best, clumsily vindicating conservative scorn at worst. "Did not
Edmund Burke," asked *Pig's Meat* solemnly, "then very improperly
term his starving fellow-creatures the Swinish Multitude?" Indeed he
did: "He therein blundered most egregiously. For on very slight observation, he would find real Swine to be more noble animals, and far
from being so obsequeous." Real swine would never patiently endure
hunger and exploitation, would never dutifully march off to war.[112]
Or take a radical toast from 1817: "May the Spencean Hogs never
cease their grunting till they have got their rights."[113] I suppose the
attempt here is to motivate the reader by triggering his self-loathing,
by making him realize that indeed he is contemptible. I suppose too
there are more incisive strategies.

Worse still are wooden inversions. In 1792, the SCI resolved "that
the people of this Country are not, as Mr. Burke terms them, SWINE;
but rational beings, better qualified to separate truth from error than
himself, possessing more honesty, and less craft."[114] One can imagine
the supporting story which might be told, starring an unscrupulous
Burke allowing his ambition to overrun his integrity and a people
lifted from the pages of Rousseau, whose very simplicity, even stupidity, vouchsafes their political decency. Still, the resolution looks
like a bit of mindless bluster, a cursory effort to rally the troops when
their courage is flagging. Then, too, there are complex ironies hard
to pin down. Quoting the actual sentences from Burke's *Reflections,*
not just the telltale phrase, David Williams sneered, "This will offend
his countrymen, the common Irish, who resent any sarcastic refer-

---

[111] On these matters, compare the perspectives of Olivia Smith, *The Politics of Language 1791–1819* (Oxford: Clarendon, 1984), esp. pp. 82–83, and Marcus Wood, *Radical Satire and Print Culture 1790–1822* (Oxford: Clarendon, 1994).

[112] *Pig's Meat* 1:263.

[113] McCalman, *Radical Underworld,* p. 122.

[114] SCI resolution, 23 March 1792, in *The Trial of John Horne Tooke, for High Treason,*
rep. Joseph Gurney, 2 vols. (London, 1795), 1:178. See too *Black Dwarf* (17 September
1817) 1(34):566.

ence to their fellow-creatures."[115] Williams was industriously cataloguing the vices of Burke's work. But how did he want his readers—the work was also published in Dublin[116]—to react? And how might they reasonably—or unreasonably but predictably—have reacted? These instances provide plausible evidence for the claim that it was unhelpful for radicals to tinker with this explosive language.

Still, I tend to think that Burke's language cried out for subversion—and that no one is so wholly confined within a discourse that creativity, agency, fighting back becomes impossible. A friend of Southey fretted about the parliamentary investigation into the Duke of York, who had bestowed military promotions in accordance with the dictates of his former lover, thus establishing a brisk trade in money, sex, and power: "This investigation stirs up the Swinish Multitude to Blasphemy." Here Southey, "swinishly inclined" himself, as he put it, didn't mind a bit of unmasking.[117] Or consider the opening of the sizzling 1793 *Address, to the Hon. Edmund Burke: From the Swinish Multitude.*

> OVERFLOWING with gratitude, we can no longer refrain from offering, with that humility with which the *common people* ought to approach so respectable and so consistent a character, our acknowledgements for the extremely elegant and respectful epithet which your meekness, your gentleness, and above all your fondness for the people have induced you to bestow on them. Deign, thou tried friend of the people, to accept our thanks: and, should we, in any part of this grateful address, unfortunately blunder upon a reproach where you might have hoped for a compliment, condescend to pardon the error, and impute it to the *swinishness* of our nature.[118]

The *Address* goes on to nail Burke—"thou flower of chivalry and spirit of civility"—for the embarrassments he faces once that vulgar reading public is eavesdropping on publications meant for the tiny political

[115] David Williams, *Lessons to a Young Prince, by an Old Statesman, on the Present Disposition in Europe to a General Revolution,* 5th ed. (Dublin, 1791), p. 172.

[116] For the complete publishing history, see *Political Writings of the 1790s,* ed. Gregory Claeys, 8 vols. (London: William Pickering, 1995), 3:23 n. 1.

[117] John Rickman to Southey, 15 February 1809, and Southey to Rickman, 18 February 1809, quoted in Geoffrey Carnall, *Robert Southey and His Age: The Development of a Conservative Mind* (Oxford: Clarendon, 1960), p. 90.

[118] James Parkinson, *An Address, to the Hon. Edmund Burke: From the Swinish Multitude* (London, 1793), pp. 5–6.

nation: readers might be confused, it suggests with some asperity, about just whom Burke meant to label a swinish multitude. Perhaps "the compliment was really intended for the sordid herd which help to fill up a court," the ones Burke himself had referred to—the *Address* here exults in published evidence and the joys of quoting, themselves palpable evidence of Burke's dilemma—as parasites, pimps, and buffoons.[119]

Imagining an insurrection of the swine, the *Black Dwarf* let his imagination run riot and furnish a political bestiary.

> Some little grunter may creep into a royal cradle in the midst of the confusion; and the stalls of the bishops, deans, and prebends, be metamorphosed into genuine pig-sties, and be polluted by popular swine. The "HIGHER ORDERS" of animals are quite alarmed. The watch-dogs of the state, Dr. Slop and the Courier, "bay the moon with hideous howl!" The younger puppies of the pack startle as if the wolf were at their heels; and the wise old hounds are preparing to avoid the scent. The *asses* of the system are throwing off their usual patience, and by their plunging, threaten their riders, the bonzes, and other great men with the mire. The statesman and judge-like owls begin to suspect the effects of their gravity, and to look about for *royal oaks* and *hollow*-trees, wherein to hide themselves from the effects of the *blaze of day*, which begins to dawn in the horizon of reason. The jays, starlings, and magpies of the system are quite offended that the swinish multitude should encroach upon their peculiar privileges of speech. In short, all the forest is in arms, against the insolent pretensions of the lower orders.[120]

No schematic inversions here, but a furious onrush of disturbing associations which suggest how utterly partial and opportunistic Burke's language was. Two can play that game, suggests the *Dwarf*, and I can play it better than he can.

Another dedication, this one from an acerbic history of England recounted as if it were the Old Testament, saluted the "SOVEREIGN SWINE!" and drily promised a review stretching from "the first mighty hog of Normandy to the present great and glorious hog of Hanover."

[119] Parkinson, *Address,* pp. 9–10.

[120] *Black Dwarf* (7 July 1819) 3(27):437. See too *Black Dwarf* (13 December 1820) 5(24):835–36. Dr. Slop, a name borrowed from *Tristram Shandy,* was bestowed on John Stoddart of the *New Times:* see William Hone, *Buonapartephobia: The Origin of Dr. Slop's Name,* 10th ed. (London, 1820), in Hone, *Facetiae and Miscellanies* (London, 1827). For a forlorn response, see John Stoddart, *Slop's Shave at a Broken Hone* (London, 1820).

The title vouchsafed unto you by your sublime, beautiful, and pensioned godfather, EDMUND BURKE, you have long borne without the inheritance. To you it has been a barren sceptre, a title of great honour, but no emolument: instead of the comforts of swine, instead of your days being spent in eating, and drinking, and sleeping, they have been spent in watching, and toiling, and fasting. You have carried burdens like asses; you have laboured like horses; you have been kicked, cuffed, and beaten, like spaniels; you have been insulted and derided like monkeys; you have been kept as hungry as ravens, and you are now as lean as hounds.

In truth, you have not been the real swine of the land, only the *feeders* of swine; whom you have fed in courts, and churches, and palaces, where they wallow in ease, and luxury, and ignorance; where they feed, not on the husks, but the kernels, not on the crumbs of the rich, but on the inheritance of the poor.[121]

Like any other trope, Burke's *swinish multitude* calls into play associations and meanings that don't do the political work he wants. Some may run skew to his agenda; some may subvert it. And pigs, like nobles, weren't famous for being hard working. "The Negroes have an observation, that among the white men, every living thing is made to work: 'The dog workee; the ox workee; the ass workee; the horse workee; the men and the women workee; every thing workee but the hog: he be a Gentleman.'"[122]

So pigs—bloated, luxuriating in the mud, sunning themselves—lead decidedly idle lives. This cheery thought suggests further subversive possibilities. Take "The Hog of Pall Mall," an affectionate salute to the future George IV, nearing the end of his tenure as Prince of Wales, already corpulent, one might even say succulent:

[121] Nathan Ben Saddi, *The Chronicle of the Kings of England, from William the Norman to the Death of George III: Written after the Manner of the Jewish Historians* (London, 1821), p. 1. Note the heated review of a 1799 edition of Ben Saddi's work in *The Guardian of Education* (May 1802) 1(1):68–76. The original is Nathan Ben Saddi [Robert Dodsley], *The Chronicle of the Kings of England: Written in the Manner of the Ancient Jewish Historians* (London, 1740).

[122] Thomas Newte, *Prospects and Observations; on a Tour in England and Scotland: Natural, Oeconomical, and Literary* (London, 1791), p. 192. See too *The Diary of the Rev^d. William Jones 1777–1821,* ed. O. F. Christie (London: Brentano's, 1929), p. 258 [1 October 1816].

Tis in Pall Mall there lives a Pig,
That doth this Mall adorn,
So fat, so plump, so monstrous Big,
A finer ne'er was born.

This Pig so sweet, so full of Meat,
He's one I wish to kill.
I'll fowls resign on thee to dine,
Sweet Pig of fine Pall Mall.[123]

The menacing humor depends in part on the prevalence of Burke's phrase, once crisp and jubilant, now bedraggled and morose. It's one thing to expose the rulers as swineherds, another to turn the tables and brand them as swine.

Burke himself suffered the same fate: another contingency, not the inexorable dictates of some objective structure or unfolding process; still, at least for democrats with some relish for intemperate rhetoric in a good cause, something he richly deserved. That 1793 *Address*, intimating that Burke was just another corrupt hireling who betrayed his allegiance to the American revolutionaries for a pension, made him look faintly ridiculous: "You are blest with a snug corner, in the warmest part of the stye, for grunting libels against THE SWINISH MULTITUDE."[124] More decorously and so more nastily, Cartwright refers to Burke's "snorting scorn of every thing built on human RIGHTS."[125] Another popular song from around 1800, "The Swinish Prophet: or, The Pig Turned Conjuror," seems to take aim at Burke. It credits this prophesying pig with a noble descent from Lord Bacon: not, I take it, because of a mistake about Burke's family tree, but for delight in the irresistible pun. That aside, surely Burke is implicated by the pig's wary, even jaundiced, stance on popular reform:

Like pigs some should be rung i'th'nose, to keep them in their
    station,
As pigs turn up the turnip fields, they'd fain turn up the nation.
But all their tricks and artful ways are now well understood, sir,
So piggy gave a grunt, and said, march off, you mean no good, sir.

[123] McCalman, *Radical Underworld*, p. 119 [1817/1820].
[124] Parkinson, *Address*, p. 28.
[125] John Cartwright, *The Comparison: In Which Mock Reform, Half Reform, and Constitutional Reform, Are Considered* (London, 1810), p. 42.

So ye grunters and grumblers of this happy nation,
Like little piggy wiggy be contented in your station,
Since some must be high, sir, and some must be low, sir,
And piggy has relations, who on two legs now do go, sir.[126]

Pigs everywhere, high and low, nobles and statesmen parading the ensigns of porcine grandeur right alongside the swinish multitude: another pristine scheme of social status collapses in confusion as Burke himself is unmasked as a pig.

Other distinguished politicians suffered the same fate. Gillray specialized in the genre. In 1798, he exhibited Pitt and Dundas driving swine with the faces of their political opponents.[127] In 1807, he cast a furious George III—"O you cursed ungrateful Grunters!"—in his endearing role as simple farmer, driving parliamentary humanoid pigs into the sea of perdition.[128] In 1806, with too many politicians seeking too few places under the regent, Gillray produced "More Pigs than Teats," with tiny pigs with human faces scrambling for their place at the sow.[129] In 1810, with Perceval finding it difficult to form a ministry, another cartoonist produced "More Teats than Pigs."[130] Cobbett, indefatigable champion of agricultural improvement, was called "the Hampshire hog."[131] One cartoonist exhibited the guinea pigs, those vain souls willing to pay Pitt's tax on hair powder to preserve their dainty appearance, as a swinish multitude.[132] But the accu-

---

[126] "The Swinish Prophet: or, The Pig Turned Conjuror" [*circa* 1800], in *Later English Broadside Ballads*, 2:214–15. See too John Aitken, *The Swinish Multitude's Push for Reform: A Poem, in Three Cantos* (Glasgow, 1816).

[127] *BMC* no. 9230 [22 June 1798], reproduced in *The Works of James Gillray: 582 Plates and a Supplement Containing the 45 So-Called "Suppressed Plates"* (London, 1850–1851; reprint ed. New York: Benjamin Blom, 1968), pl. 200.

[128] *BMC* no. 10719 [18 April 1807], in *Works of Gillray*, pl. 337.

[129] *BMC* no. 10540 [5 March 1806], in *Works of Gillray*, pl. 311.

[130] *BMC* no. 11527 [January 1810?].

[131] Ian Dyck, *William Cobbett and Rural Popular Culture* (Cambridge: Cambridge University Press, 1992), p. 118; *The Real or Constitutional House that Jack Built*, 8th ed. (London, 1819), as paginated in *Radical Squibs & Loyal Ripostes: Satirical Pamphlets of the Regency Period, 1819–1821*, ed. Edgell Rickword (New York: Barnes & Noble, 1971), p. 73.

[132] *BMC* no. 8628 [6 March 1795]. See too *A Political Dictionary for the Guinea-Less Pigs, or, A Glossary of Emphatical Words Made Use of by That Jewel of a Man, Deep Will, in His Administration, and His Plans for Yoking and Putting Rings in the Snouts of Those Grumbling Swine, Who Raise Such Horrid Grunting, When Tyrannical Winds Blow High* (London, 1795).

sation that a person is a pig has special salience when pressed against Burke.

## Coda: Christian Charity and a Jovial Toast

In closing, I want one last time to haul out poor irascible John Skinner, whose travails among his insubordinate parishioners might remind us of what Burke's lofty images of a political community built around Christian communion amounted to on the ground. "I am heartily sick of the flock over which I am nominated and placed," fumed the good rector; "instead of being a shepherd, as I told the methodistical beldame when she twitted me with the name, I am in fact a pig driver; I despise myself most thoroughly for suffering irritation from such vermin."[133]

This heady brew of contempt and self-contempt is, once again, not simply a matter of Skinner's quirky and tortured sensibility. It's also wrapped up in a set of understandings and practices that define Skinner as the representative of the Anglican church, entrusted with care of the faithful—and the faithless; and that also embody less than flattering judgments about the status and worth of the parishioners. Every person has an immortal soul: there, again, is the nub of Christian egalitarianism. But thinking of the parishioners as a flock, Christ—or his local humble servant and representative, Skinner—as their shepherd, summons up the now familiar benevolent paternalism. Skinner is their superior, they his subordinates. That's already a kind of contempt, but it enables genuine care and affection. Yet Skinner finds it all too easy to work himself into a lather when he contemplates the saucy underlings not as wayward children or stray sheep but as a swinish multitude.

So choice of animal can make a colossal difference. Sheep are one thing, pigs another. And monkeys a third: in another sly inversion, contemporaries wondered if a chimpanzee or orangutan could be elected to Parliament.[134] Worse, radicals in Sheffield and Manches-

---

[133] John Skinner, *Journal of a Somerset Rector 1803–1834*, ed. Howard and Peter Coombs (Bath: Kingsmead, 1971), p. 192 [11 June 1822].

[134] Walpole to George Montagu, 9 January 1752, *The Yale Edition of Horace Walpole's Correspondence*, ed. W. S. Lewis, 48 vols. (New Haven, CT: Yale University Press, 1937–1983), 9:127; *Black Dwarf* (14 February 1821) 6(7):225. This is the central gag of *Melincourt* [1817] in *The Works of Thomas Love Peacock*, Halliford edition, ed. H. F. B. Brett-Smith and C. E. Jones, 10 vols. (London: Constable & Co., 1924–1934), vol. 2.

ter held parades with a "crowned jack-ass" to proclaim their devotion to monarchy.[135] And the ordinary ritual of chairing the successful parliamentary candidate was spoofed in Westmoreland, with some wits "parading a calf's head, decked in yellow ribands," the color of the conservative Lowther faction running successfully against Brougham.[136] It's rash to say that animal imagery is necessarily insulting: one can be brave as a lion or clever as a fox, say. Nor does choice of animal guarantee anything about whether contempt is prowling in the margins. We might counter the benign Christian shepherd and his flock with a charming comment from that great friend of the people, Charles James Fox, radiating his own disdain for the idiocy of rural life: "The husbandmen and labourers thought so little of public matters that he should as soon think of consulting the sheep on the propriety of impropriety of Peace as the people who had the care of them, or in general the lower order Peasantry." (Urban life, thought Fox, bestowed the dignity of citizenship on the people: "In towns, from their ale-houses, clubs, &c., they turned their thoughts more to political subjects."[137]) Nor does the mere mention of a pig guarantee that the speaker is emotionally invested in any salacious contempt: contemporaries' offhand saying, *an't please the pigs*, was tacked on casually to mean something like *if circumstances permit*.[138] But *swinish multitude* is pointedly dehumanizing. It has its home in a web of commitments comprising a combative conservatism, one threatening the lowly subjects with visceral contempt if they dare to step out of line and entertain dangerous presumptions about their status, perhaps one marking them as contemptible even when they dutifully defer. It dramatizes the political force of thinking that humanity itself is a di-

[135] Marquis of Buckingham to Lord Grenville, 8 November 1792, Historical Manuscripts Commission, *Report on the Manuscripts of J. B. Fortescue, Esq., Preserved at Dropmore*, 10 vols. (London, 1892–1927), 2:327–28.

[136] *Westmorland Election, 1818: An Account of the Proceedings at Appleby, from Saturday, the 27th of June, to the Final Close of the Poll* (Kendal, 1818), p. 42. For angry comments about the support offered Lowther by Wordsworth and Southey, see Thomas Love Peacock to Percy Shelley, 5 July 1818, *Works of Peacock*, 8:199; Peacock to Shelley, 19 July 1818, *Works of Peacock*, 8:201.

[137] *The Political Memoranda of Francis Fifth Duke of Leeds*, ed. Oscar Browning (London, 1884), p. 213 [29 December 1794].

[138] See *Gentleman's Magazine* (September 1790), in *The Letters and Prose Writings of William Cowper*, ed. James King and Charles Ryskamp, 5 vols. (Oxford: Clarendon, 1979–1986), 5:47.

mensional concept, so that those of higher social status are more fully human than others.

We instinctively shrink from these views only because of our own formally democratic pieties. Burke and his imagery have gone down to crashing defeat. Some of his contemporaries, sympathetic to his views, thought it unfortunate for him to talk that way. One woman whose family suffered in the Birmingham riots declared, "I am so far a Democrat that I am a friend of the people while they are under due subjection, and I take offence at hearing them called the swinish multitude; but God preserve me from being under the government of the people. Of all tyrants, that many-headed monster is the worst."[139] Couple this prudently diplomatic concern with veils and secrecy with the alarming new developments—the rise of alehouse discussion, political clubs, mechanics' institutes, and the rest—that made it easy for base workers to eavesdrop on the polite conversation of their betters. The mortifying inference is that it's increasingly hard for conservatives to state and defend their view on the merits.

Later norms of debate made it publicly unacceptable to castigate the swinish multitude, even to seem to tiptoe in that direction. Recall the antinomy: ruling such speech out-of-bounds closes off some possibilities in the realm of speech, not least spirited defenses of the Burkean position; but it also enables other possibilities that otherwise would be unavailable. The proscription on *swinish multitude* and its scurrilous cousins serves as a guarantee to members of the community that their public standing will not be assaulted, at least not so blatantly. So it is simultaneously a proscription on speech and a fundamentally democratic rule. It leaves Burkean contempt without a publicly reputable foothold, a sentiment that has to go underground or be avowed only surreptitiously. That's precisely its point.

In his *Rights of Man,* Paine declared that the emotional tables were being turned on Burke: "He has taken up a contemptible opinion of mankind, who in their turn, are taking up the same of him."[140] (We would say *contemptuous,* not *contemptible,* in the opening clause; but Paine's point, telescoped unhappily, is that it's contemptible to be so

---

[139] Catherine Hutton to Mrs. André, 27 February 1794, *Reminiscences of a Gentlewoman of the Last Century: Letters of Catherine Hutton,* ed. Catherine Hutton Beale (Birmingham, 1891), p. 115.

[140] *Rights of Man* [1792], in *The Life and Works of Paine,* 10 vols. (New Rochelle, NY: Thomas Paine National Historical Association, 1925), 6:261.

contemptuous.[141]) So they were. In November 1792, the people of Sheffield took to the streets to celebrate France's military victories. Burke was displayed in effigy, riding a swine.[142] In January 1793, Burke was burned in effigy south of Sheffield. The judicious crowd offered a suitably loving toast: "The Swinish Multitude. May they hold in contempt the man who first gave that appelation to free Britons."[143] It's a telling irony: Burke himself became contemptible by shamelessly flouting democratic norms of debate, by advertising his contempt for ordinary men and women, where they were demanding to be treated as conversational equals. No sleepy and compliant subjects here. And no repose for poor Edmund Burke.

A splendid cartoon, published during the repressive campaigns of the 1790s and the war with France, portrayed a crazed William Pitt, wearing only a diadem stamped DESTRUCTION, riding a majestic white stallion, brandishing a serpent in one hand and a flaming sword in the other. Burke, a winged fiend with pitchfork in hand, is in the horse's flowing tail, egging on Pitt. The horse is overrunning members of the parliamentary opposition: a rotund Fox, clutching a paper marked PEACE, staggers back in dismay. And the horse is trampling left and right on pigs, identified in the caption as the multitude, some fleeing, some already dead.[144] The cartoonist was playing with the millenial fantasies of Richard Brothers, the ecstatic religious writer who identified Pitt and the King as Jews and landed in an asylum for his troubles. Yet these pigs would be resurrected, not at the end of time but over the next couple of centuries, as dignified citizens, forever trailed by grunts of derision.

[141] *Contemptible* then could still bear the meaning of *contemptuous:* see *OED* s.v. *contemptible,* adj., sense 2.

[142] Eugene Charlton Black, *The Association: British Extraparliamentary Political Organization 1769–1793* (Cambridge, MA: Harvard University Press, 1963), p. 257.

[143] *Correspondence of Burke,* 7:340.

[144] *BMC* no. 8655 [4 June 1795]. The print is reproduced in Paul J. Korshin, *Typologies in England 1650–1820* (Princeton, NJ: Princeton University Press, 1982), pl. 22, between pp. 110–11.

# INDEX

ABOUT THE AUTHOR

Don Herzog teaches law and political theory at the
University of Michigan. He is the author of
*Without Foundations* and *Happy Slaves*.